AIR
TRANSPORTATION

The 747 Superjet

AIR TRANSPORTATION

Fifth Edition

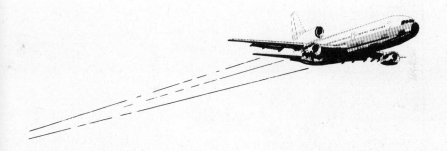

Robert M. Kane, B.B.A., M.B.A.

Allan D. Vose, B.B.A.

KENDALL/HUNT PUBLISHING COMPANY
DUBUQUE, IOWA

Dedicated to the pioneers of aviation--

Past

Present and

Future

Contents

Preface

The purpose of this text, when it was first published in 1967, was to be a basic introduction to the air transportation industry. Since the first printing, the authors have received repeated requests to add the subject of business aspects of air transportation.

Accordingly, in the third edition four new chapters were added to accomplish this extended purpose. They deal with the subjects of air carrier management and organization, economics, accounting and financial analysis, and legal aspects.

In this fourth edition the material throughout the text has been updated to reflect the many changes that have taken place in the air transport industry in recent years. For ease of comprehension the chapters have been separated into three parts. Each part and chapter is intended to be complete within itself. This provides for any individual order of study desired and also for easy reference material purposes.

It is recommended and hoped that the use of this book will encourage the reader to make a more complete study into any of the subjects covered using the text as a take-off point to further learning.

Grateful acknowledgments are hereby made to the personnel of the Civil Aeronautics Board, Federal Aviation Administration, Department of Transportation and the Air Transport Association for resource material they have graciously supplied.

Acknowledgment is extended to the students, who it is hoped, will find the subject of air transportation as fascinating as watching a jumbo jet lift its huge massive bulk gracefully from the airport runway to airborne flight. Both events never cease to cause continuing amazement in that they would appear unbelievable and impossible, yet it can and does occur.

R.M.K.
A.D.V.

Development of
Air Transportation

FAA 10-YEAR FORECAST

FAA predicts continued growth in aircraft movements and passengers boarded. System activity growth rates projected in the 10 year plan covering 1973-1982, show these increases:

	1972	1982	Increase
Air carrier aircraft handled by FAA ARTCC	12.4 Million	16.5 Million	33%
General aviation aircraft handled by FAA ARTCC	4.8 Million	15.9 Million	231%
Military aircraft handled by FAA ARTCC	5.0 Million	5.2 Million	4%
Aircraft operations logged by FAA towers	53.6 Million	103.9 Million	94%
Instrument operations logged by FAA towers	19.4 Million	31.7 Million	63%
Flight services logged by FSS	50.4 Million	125.6 Million	149%
Passenger enplanements total domestic and international	182.9 Million	442.0 Million	142%
Passenger enplanements international only	18.4 Million	52.4 Million	185%

GENERAL AVIATION OPERATIONS

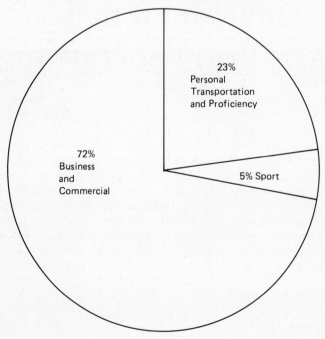

23% Personal Transportation and Proficiency

72% Business and Commercial

5% Sport

CHAPTER
I
ⱱⱱⱱ

Importance of Air Transportation

The airplane, and therefore the beginning of aviation, is not yet more than the span of a normal lifetime. It was on December 17, 1903, that Orville Wright left the ground from the sand dunes of Kitty Hawk, North Carolina, in what was to become the world's first controllable powered flight. At that moment of take-off he ushered in what has proved to be the greatest period in the history of mankind.

The history of man, as much as we know of it, goes back about two million years. Walking was his only means of transportation during the first one and three-quarter million years; and as transportation has developed, so has man. In those prehistoric and ancient times a man's knowledge of the world was limited to approximately a ten mile radius from where he lived, because that was all the distance which he was able to travel. The only means of transportation was by foot. This early man had the customs and language of his tribe, the only people with whom he lived and worked. The knowledge of that group of people was all the knowledge that existed in the world as far as they were concerned.

Civilization did not begin to develop to any extent for thousands of years. The various groups or clans of people who then lived on the various parts of the earth had no way to communicate with each other. In fact, they did not realize that any people other than themselves even existed.

When man finally domesticated animals, he used them to ride on their backs, and his limits and knowledge of the world expanded.

Civilization began to develop and flourish along the inland waterways and the coastal areas of the oceans, because man had invented and learned the use of the boat for water transportation. This made it possible for him to find and visit with other groups of people. He took his knowledge to these people, and at the same time carried back their culture to his own people. For about 4,000 years, civilization developed along the waterways because of water transportation. The various groups of humans were then able to begin to communicate with each other. Culture and knowledge, which are the basis of society, were beginning to spread, all because of travel being possible due to available transportation.

Along came the wheel, which is considered one of the most important inventions mankind has ever known. It was first introduced into the Mediterranean area indirectly by the Chinese, according to history. The Romans then carried it into Europe during their years of conquest. The wheel, and the many mechanical refinements which it produced, greatly speeded up man's ability to travel. Invention followed invention over the centuries, until finally just after the turn of the twentieth century the air age came into being as a result of the Wright Brothers' flight in 1903. Their first airplane, which was nothing more than an oversized glider upon which an engine had been placed, developed about 16 horsepower. The first sustained flight lasted only 12 seconds. The modern jet engine on today's airliners, which now streak through the skies, develop many thousands of pounds of thrust horsepower.

The Wright Brothers flew in their first airplane at a speed of 31 miles per hour. Some military airplanes fly in excess of 2,000 miles per hour and with the introduction of the supersonic transport commercial aircraft will also be able to attain this speed.

In 1974 the certificated airlines of the United States carried over 208 million passengers, a total of about 164 billion passenger miles. (One passenger mile is equal to one passenger carried a distance of one mile.) The airlines today hold the position as the number one common carrier in the interstate passenger business.

Airline traffic will increase to 524 million passengers in 1984, according to new Federal Aviation Administration projections. This is an annual 10-year forecast.

Federal Aviation Administration said domestic passengers will climb to 461.2 million in fiscal year 1984 with international passengers increasing to 62.8 million. Revenue passenger miles are expected to grow even faster because of longer trip lengths. Federal Aviation Administration said revenue passenger miles will reach 500.5 billion in fiscal year 1984.

The air carrier fleet is expected to grow from the current level of about 2,500 aircraft to nearly 3,600 aircraft. Although 60% of the fleet is expected to be

AIR TRANSPORT FORECAST 1970-80

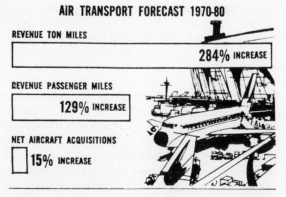

REVENUE TON MILES

284% INCREASE

REVENUE PASSENGER MILES

129% INCREASE

NET AIRCRAFT ACQUISITIONS

15% INCREASE

The Air Transport Association forecasts increases in revenue ton miles (RTM) of air cargo, revenue passenger miles (RPM) and in the U.S. aircraft fleet operated by scheduled and certificated airlines between 1970 and 1980. The increases, in terms of percentages, are based on 1970 statistics.

widebody aircraft in fiscal year 1984, Federal Aviation Administration predicted that load factors on United States carriers will rise to nearly 60% compared to the current 50% mark.

Actually, commercial air transportation has barely passed its youth. In these relatively few short years the airlines have developed in a remarkable fashion. This tremendous growth was accelerated by the jet age, which signaled a complete change for the airline industry; one which was marked by a phenomenal change.

A survey conducted by the Gallup Organization for the United States scheduled airlines found that only 55 percent of all adult Americans have taken a trip on a scheduled airline.

Some highlights of the survey are:

Sixty-one percent of all adult men have flown, while 50 percent of women have flown.

Twenty-four percent of all adult Americans took a trip by a scheduled airline in the past 12 months.

Those who did fly within the past 12 months took an average of 5.5 trips each.

By purpose of trip, the 24 percent taking trips last year were: 6 percent business, 14 percent personal or pleasure and 4 percent included business and pleasure.

A great, untapped market of future potential air travelers is therefore available. Many of these new air travelers will take to the skies in high speed jets. Surface methods of transportation are rapidly becoming obsolete due to the relatively higher expense to the passenger. Many examples exist today where a dollar for dollar comparison will show that it is cheaper for a traveler to fly or a shipper to send cargo by airline than to use conventional surface means of transportation, to say nothing of the many intangible benefits, such as greater comfort and greatly reduced savings in time.

The hopes and promises for future civilization are in the air. The jet age in the United States promises to make available more jobs with greater security for aviation-minded people. It also means a better way of living tomorrow for all citizens. Through its ever continuing progress the airline industry of the United States has become one of the most vital economic forces in our capitalistic system of free enterprise. Commercial air transportation will continue to increase. Aviation in itself is progress and a sound commercial air transportation industry is essential.

Probably the most astounding thing about aviation is that it has become so important in such a short time. It is easy to understand the rapid growth of aviation's influence if it is remembered that aviation means the air age—the age of the wing—a period of time characterized by air travel and transportation. It is these two facts, that air travel knows few physical obstacles and that it decreases the time of transportation so greatly, which have caused dramatic changes in the course of human events.

PERCENT OF U.S. POPULATION THAT HAVE TRAVELED
ON CERTIFICATED AIR CARRIERS

	*1962	*1965	*1970	1971	1972	1973	1974
All Adults	33	38	47	49	54	54	55
Sex							
Men	37	42	51	53	58	58	61
Women	30	34	44	46	51	51	50
Age							
18-24 years	—	—	—	52	54	50	50
25-34 years	—	—	—	60	62	66	63
35-49 years	33	37	50	46	58	55	59
50 years and older	30	33	40	44	48	49	51
Occupation							
Professional and Business	57	63	72	70	75	75	78
Clerical and Sales	45	43	60	66	64	67	66
Manual Workers	26	29	37	41	45	45	49
Farmers	16	14	24	18	37	33	26
Non-Labor Force	31	34	40	43	45	45	46
Income							
$15,000 and over	57	65	80	74	78	77	75
$10,000-$14,999	—	—	59	60	62	58	56
$ 7,000-$ 9,999	—	46	42	45	52	47	48
$ 5,000-$ 6,999	32	34	39	42	40	48	48
$ 3,000-$ 4,999	24	28	30	34	39	36	37
Under $3,000	17	20	27	28	36	34	32
Size of Community							
1,000,000 and over	—	—	59	63	65	64	68
500,000-999,999	42	47	61	61	67	71	70
50,000-499,999	41	45	52	55	58	59	55
2,500-49,999	32	39	46	39	43	50	57
Under 2,500	—	—	30	35	44	38	40
Region of the Country							
East	39	41	52	51	57	59	59
Midwest	29	33	42	45	51	51	50
South	22	30	37	39	45	43	45
West	50	55	67	68	70	70	73

*Data based on population 21 years of age and older, all other data based on those 18 and older.

It is now possible to travel from coast to coast in less than six hours by commercial aircraft. Military aircraft fly this distance in much less time. It took the pioneers, who expanded our country westward, six months to travel from Independence, Missouri, to San Francisco, a distance only half as great. In the days of horse and buggy travel, one who lived on a farm or in a village may have journeyed all day to reach the county seat. Today, by airplane, anyone can reach the nation's capital in a small part of a day, no matter where he lives in the continental United States. As a matter of fact, one can reach by air any capital of any nation from any airport anywhere in the world more readily than George Washington could reach Philadelphia from Mt. Vernon by stagecoach.

Until the present century, people lived very much as did those who founded our country. These early pioneers and all others before them to the dawn of civilization lived in the age of the wheel. Today we live in the age of the wing: the air age.

The invention of the airplane wing made it possible for man to travel through the air and over obstacles, such as mountains, deserts, swamps, and ice caps which make surface travel slow and costly, if not impossible. Moreover, air transportation is swift beyond the most fanciful imagination of a generation ago.

Aviation is of importance in the ways in which it influences everyday living. It will affect everyday life because it affects social, economic, and political surroundings. It affects modern man because it affects the way all people live and work and because it has influenced greatly the nature of relationships with other nations. It enables people the world over to travel with greater ease and to cover the globe with unique and beneficial contributions of their cultural systems. World leaders can readily assemble in conference.

The importance of commercial air transportation can be summed up in three ways: (1) Economic, (2) Social, and (3) Political.

ECONOMIC

It is through their continuous efforts in the public interest that the airlines of the United States have moved forward. This is the prevailing attitude of the airlines. The jet equipment program was revolutionary, not only in terms of airline effort, but also in terms of the benefits for the nation. The progress of the airlines in the past two decades has been brought about by constant endeavor in such areas as safety, operational techniques, and in services designed to make flight more pleasant and convenient for the passenger.

A look at the early airline industry and the same industry today will readily indicate the growth of air transportation. As a result of governmental legislation in 1938, the airlines became an organized industry. At that time there were 23 airlines. Today there are about 31 certificated airlines, although the number fluctuates slightly due to mergers and other corporate action.

In 1938 less than 300 cities and towns were served by airlines. The number of cities today which receive direct air service approaches a thousand, of which 116 are jet service. In 1938, the newly certificated airlines had little more than 300 airplanes, and these were of the small, twin-engine type, in comparison with

AIRLINE SERVICE IN 1973
(In Thousands)

Available Seat Miles

1.	United	49,383,884
2.	American	39,005,759
3.	Trans World	38,611,925
4.	Pan American	36,234,006
5.	Eastern	30,532,145
6.	Delta	29,311,469
7.	Northwest	19,593,377
8.	National	11,886,451
9.	Continental	11,692,700
10.	Western	11,043,425
11.	Braniff	10,937,994
12.	Allegheny	6,798,775
13.	Frontier	2,471,584
14.	Hughes Airwest	2,456,954
15.	North Central	2,039,284
16.	Piedmont	1,987,611
17.	Southern	1,643,569
18.	Texas International	1,484,784
19.	Ozark	1,295,944
20.	Alaska	690,488
21.	Hawaiian	551,785
22.	Aloha	413,791
23.	Wien Air Alaska	279,971
24.	Caribbean-Atlantic	111,434
25.	Reeve Aleutian	77,207
26.	Aspen	18,976
27.	New York Helicopter	15,031
28.	Wright	14,296
29.	San Francisco & Oakland Helicopter	9,662
30.	Kodiak-Western Alaska	2,217
31.	Chicago Helicopter	420
32.	Western Alaska	189

Revenue Passenger Miles

1.	United	27,029,304
2.	American	20,654,338
3.	Trans World	20,440,696
4.	Pan American	19,518,614
5.	Eastern	16,875,804
6.	Delta	15,022,048
7.	Northwest	8,007,850
8.	Western	6,357,481
9.	National	5,900,240
10.	Continental	5,661,379
11.	Braniff	5,488,661
12.	Allegheny	3,290,862
13.	Frontier	1,308,123
14.	Hughes Airwest	1,259,908
15.	Piedmont	994,351
16.	North Central	955,840
17.	Southern	721,135
18.	Texas International	681,904
19.	Ozark	617,480
20.	Hawaiian	354,908
21.	Alaska	353,970
22.	Aloha	255,891
23.	Wien Air Alaska	106,689
24.	Reeve Aleutian	36,362
25.	Caribbean-Atlantic	35,738
26.	Aspen	10,221
27.	New York Helicopter	7,057
28.	Wright	5,493
29.	San Francisco & Oakland Helicopter	3,591
30.	Kodiak-Western Alaska	1,007
31.	Chicago Helicopter	288
32.	Western Alaska	74

Note: Caribbean-Atlantic merged with Eastern Air Lines on May 15, 1973 and Western Alaska with Kodiak Airways on April 1, 1973.

Passengers Enplaned

1.	United	30,250
2.	Eastern	26,201
3.	Delta	24,604
4.	American	21,163
5.	Trans World	14,148
6.	Allegheny	10,822
7.	Pan American	10,409
8.	Northwest	7,987
9.	Western	7,908
10.	Braniff	7,553
11.	National	6,862
12.	Continental	6,449
13.	North Central	4,194
14.	Hughes Airwest	3,625
15.	Piedmont	3,526
16.	Frontier	3,375
17.	Hawaiian	2,554
18.	Southern	2,494
19.	Ozark	2,264
20.	Texas International	2,150
21.	Aloha	1,819
22.	Alaska	534
23.	New York Helicopter	371
24.	Wien Air Alaska	333
25.	San Francisco & Oakland Helicopter	226
26.	Caribbean-Atlantic	155
27.	Aspen	90
28.	Wright	60
29.	Reeve Aleutian	43
30.	Kodiak-Western Alaska	21
31.	Chicago Helicopter	16
32.	Western Alaska	2

Source: Air Transport Association of America

Employment and Payroll

U.S. Scheduled Airlines

	1973	1972	1971	1970*	1969	1968	1967	1966	1965	1964	1963
Pilots and Copilots	27,192	26,880	26,242	25,807	26,262	24,554	23,425	21,019	16,881	15,136	14,262
Other Flight Personnel	7,567	6,820	6,658	7,029	8,387	7,953	7,531	6,788	5,091	4,415	4,048
Pursers, Stewards and Stewardesses	42,819	39,408	35,682	34,274	33,621	29,970	25,100	20,925	17,322	14,470	13,109
Communications Personnel	1,948	2,080	2,275	2,777	3,264	3,403	3,316	3,174	3,123	3,195	3,716
Mechanics	47,049	45,570	45,759	48,177	52,886	52,046	50,016	45,327	41,667	39,360	34,453
Aircraft and Traffic Servicing Personnel	90,193	88,098	84,931	83,637	86,462	82,950	74,943	66,641	57,532	51,944	49,056
Office Employees	59,891	58,974	58,114	59,992	63,743	63,158	59,257	50,961	44,162	40,325	37,867
All Others	34,840	33,297	32,524	35,681	37,297	36,417	32,435	29,193	25,017	22,973	22,376
Total Employment	311,499	301,127	292,185	297,374	311,922	300,451	276,023	244,028	210,795	191,818	178,887
Total Payroll ($000)	4,640,370	4,192,081	3,843,872	3,659,716	3,322,719	2,921,120	2,491,330	2,097,588	1,755,401	1,536,603	1,320,400

* Figures for 1970 are understated due to the effects of a Brotherhood of Railway and Airline Clerks strike against Northwest Airlines and an Air Line Pilots Association strike against Mohawk Airlines.

Intercity Passenger Travel in the United States

(Passenger Miles in Millions)

	1973	1972	1971	1970	1969	1968	1967	1966	1965	1964	1963
Common Carriers											
Airlines	126,317	118,138	106,438	104,146	102,717	87,508	75,487	60,591	51,888	44,141	38,457
Railroads	9,299	8,561	9,908	6,179	7,622	8,737	10,920	12,903	13,260	14,048	14,396
Motor Buses	26,400	25,600	25,500	25,300	24,900	24,500	24,900	24,600	23,800	23,300	21,800
Total	162,016	152,299	141,846	135,335	135,239	120,693	111,306	98,094	88,948	81,489	74,653
Air Share (%)	78.0	77.6	75.0	77.0	76.0	72.5	67.8	61.8	58.3	54.2	51.5

Source: Air Transport Association of America.

today's aircraft, which number almost 2,500. Of these airliners of today, most of them are jet aircraft. In the early days of the airlines' passenger carrying business, 5,000 daily seats were available in the United States. Today, almost 200,000 seats are available, each and every day.

In the early 1930's the beginning airlines had airplanes that flew little more than 100 miles an hour. By 1950, their airplanes were capable of 300 miles per hour. Today, the jet transport is capable of 600 miles per hour. The commercial airliner of the 1980's is well into the development stage and will carry passengers at almost three times the speed of sound or in excess of 1800 miles per hour.

In the year 1939, twenty-four million dollars was the amount of money paid to a total of 13,000 airline employees. The amount of money the 297,374 airline employees received in 1970 was over 3 1/2 billion dollars.

One outstanding feature of all this increase in growth and better service to the public is that the average fare an airline passenger paid in 1939 was 5.6 cents per mile, while today the average fare is only 6.4 cents per passenger mile; an infinitesimal increase bearing in mind the increased cost of doing business, as well as the increased level of prices, has been rising consistently since 1939.

Airlines of the United States carry the majority of the world's air commerce. The industry has grown to a point where transoceanic flights are merely a matter of every day occurrence.

With regard to the number of passenger miles traveled by common carriers between the cities of the United States, the airlines' share is over 78% of the total of intercity travel.

Commercial air transportation is a young industry that has made rapid progress; more progress than any other means of transportation has ever done before.

This unprecedented growth in air transportation has not been brought about without obstacles and problems presenting themselves. Air transportation can develop only as far as facilities permit. Aircraft have developed faster than the facilities upon which they must depend. This is especially true of airports.

The government has recognized the fact that the airlines are like a public utility, and as such the service they offer is said to be in the public interest for the need of the United States citizen. This public interest concept includes three basic areas. First is commerce: By this is meant the everyday business of the country. It includes transportation of passengers as well as air cargo. Second, the airlines' public interest includes the postal service. Tons upon tons of letters travel by air, and since 1953 much of the First Class mail, which normally went by railroad, goes by airline. The third aspect of public concern includes National Defense which is discussed later in the chapter.

The aerospace industry can be classified into three groups:

I. Aerospace Manufacturing Industry
   1. Aircraft
   2. Aircraft Engines
   3. Aircraft Parts and Accessories
   4. Missiles
   5. Spacecraft

II. Air Transport Industry (Air Carriers)
   1. Domestic Trunk
   2. International and Territorial
   3. Local Service
   4. Intra-Hawaiian
   5. Intra-Alaskan
   6. All Cargo
   7. Helicopter
   8. Supplemental
   9. Commuter
   10. Non-Certificated

III. General Aviation
   1. Business Flying
   2. Commercial Flying
   3. Instructional Flying
   4. Personal Flying

The Aerospace Manufacturing Industry includes all research, development, fabrication, assembly, and sales operations relating to airplanes, missiles, parts, accessories, and equipment. This industry also includes maintenance, modification facilities, and major overhaul.

The Air Transport Industry contains the activities of the commercial airlines. The routes flown, the rates charged, and safety are carefully regulated by the federal government.

General aviation consists of all other aviation activities except those of the military services.

The United States Aircraft Manufacturing Industry became capable of producing 100,000 units per year during World War II. Employment climbed to over 1.3 million people. After the war ended, production dropped to a rate of 6 percent of its wartime capacity, because enough civilian aircraft had been produced to satisfy the needs. The industry began to expand at the start of the Korean War and has since grown into one of the most important industries in the United States.

In recent years, over half of the federal government's budget had been allocated to national defense, and a large portion of this has been directed to the Aerospace Manufacturing Industry. During the period from 1947 to 1961, 89 percent of the total sales of 51 of the largest aerospace companies was to the federal government.

The number of jobs created by this industry is tremendous, as is the wide variety of skills necessary to produce the product. In 1956, the amount of money spent for research and development in the industry exceeded that of all other industries.

October, 1958, brought into being a new era, the era of commercial jet transportation in the United States. Pan American World Airways inaugurated regular scheduled service from New York City to Paris and later National Airlines inaugurated the first domestic jet service with leased Pan American jets.

The jet era entered a second generation in February of 1970 when Pan American World Airways introduced Boeing 747 service between New York and London. The 747 is capable of carrying 362 passengers in comparison to the Boeing 707 which Pan American flew in 1958 which carried 150 passengers.

Since 1949, the number of revenue passengers carried by both domestic and international airlines has more than quadrupled. In the same period revenue passenger miles flown by the trunks quintupled and the sales revenue has reached over 6.2 billion dollars. The international carriers expect that the free world demand for international transportation by air will be an estimated 90 billion revenue passenger miles in 1975. United States flag carriers will take about 27 billion of the 90 billion revenue passenger miles. The United States flag carriers will haul freight and mail totaling about 2 billion ton miles by 1980.

The economic effects of the present air transport industry are a sharp shrinkage of distance in terms of time, a greatly expanded transport capacity of the jet in comparison to propeller driven aircraft, a tremendous increase in the number of people using air transportation for business and pleasure, and a major shifting of traffic volume from surface to air.

General Aviation is flying for business including agricultural, charter, instructional, as well as personal. The use of business aircraft permits a company to expand its sales volume by increasing its market coverage. Agricultural flying has found value in the aerial application of chemicals to land, crops, and forests; control of insects has been of great value. General aviation activities in part also include pipeline control, forestry patrol, mapping, aerial photography, mineral prospecting, advertising and stocking lakes with fish.

Instructional flying accounts for about 28 percent of general aviation flying and tends to fluctuate, however, due to the demand for airline pilots.

Personal flying tends to remain fairly constant at about 23 percent of the total hours flown in general aviation. The current value of the general aviation fleet exceeds 700 million dollars and numbers over 100 thousand aircraft of all types and speeds. This segment of aviation is expected to experience remarkable growth in the future years.

The federal government's role is significant. Legislation must be strong but flexible enough to create the conditions that encourage healthy competition and growth in civil aviation. These conditions, which are essential to a strong national economy, result from domestic and international trade and commerce, travel and transportation. The federal government also plays a leading part in safety and economic regulations and in the support given to all aviation interests through research services, air traffic control, airport construction, airmail, weather information, and many other services.

SOCIAL

The effects of the automobile on our daily habits of living will provide a clue to what even far greater changes will be brought about by air transportation.

A philosopher once said, "Transportation is civilization." He saw many years ago that the civilizations of the world depend upon transportation for their existence. Air transportation has produced significant changes in population trends. The airplane has helped to redistribute populations. Through the use of air transportation heretofore untouched resources have been developed. This is especially true in South and Central America where the mode of transportation progressed from the ox cart stage directly to the air age. Many internal areas which were virtually inaccessible due to the lack of roads have been developed as a direct result of the use of the airplane.

In the early history of the United States mass movements of people traveled from the East across the Western Plains using the covered wagon as their means of transportation. The railroad followed the wagon train trails and finally stretched its iron tentacles to the Pacific Coast. Today's air traveler covers this route in a matter of hours and does so in complete comfort.

Air transportation has altered educational concepts; our understanding of geography has changed. No longer is the shortest distance between Chicago and London in a northeasterly direction. By flying over the top of the world, for instance, the distance between these two cities is greatly reduced. Likewise, a direct non-stop flight from San Francisco to Tokyo would not be southwestward across the Pacific by way of the Hawaiian Islands. Rather, the shortest distance in miles and time would be a great circle route north from San Francisco over Alaska, and down the northern Japanese Islands. The measurement is no longer in miles, but in the hours and minutes of time.

It took George Washington half a day to travel between Philadelphia and New York. Today this same half-day travel by commercial jet aircraft would allow a passenger to leave New York, fly to California, and return.

Air transportation in the United States has reached its present state of development within a relatively short period of time. In recent years, aeronautical technological improvements have taken place at an unprecedented rate. The people of the world have finally realized the advantages of air travel and are using this means of transportation in large numbers. Due to the time saving element of speed alone, air transportation has become invaluable from the standpoint of business and commerce, the postal service, and national defense.

Aviation has become an influence in the life of every individual citizen of our nation. The magnitude of its effects has increased as new developments in aircraft have progressed. These effects stem from the fact that aircraft surmount obstacles to surface transportation. To a pilot and his passengers, the hazardous reef, the frozen waste, the precipitous mountain, the jungle, and the desert become merely features of a changing scene lying beneath an aerial pathway.

The impact of aviation has been felt in all the fields of mankind's endeavors.

POLITICAL

The third aspect of the importance of air transportation and vital to public concern includes National Defense.

Aviation has helped to make our country one of the most powerful nations of the world and to place it in a position of world leadership.

Before aircraft reached their present stage of development, the countries of the Western Hemisphere were protected from outside attack by surface obstacles such as the ice cap over the Arctic area and by the oceans, east and west. Today attack, if it comes, will be from the skies. Defense today rests upon air power and diplomacy rather than upon physical barriers.

It is essential that people grasp the concept of air power as not belonging solely to an arsenal of military weapons. On the contrary, there can be no air power without the civil elements of aerospace manufacturing, air transportation, airports, industrial and scientific research. However, the strength of the civil element of air power is to a large extent nourished today by the needs of military aviation. The result is that they are inseparable; both make the entity of American air power. They both have common objectives, that of the well being of the nation.

George Washington once said, "To be prepared for war is one of the most effectual means of preserving the peace." These words are as alive today as they were when he spoke them. The concept they illustrate lies at the source of our National Defense program. The principle the words express is old; the means we have adopted to preserve the peace is new. Air power is our modern method. Air power is peace power. Until a better way for achieving a lasting peace is discovered, the American people must use, as its principal instrument of defense, air power, the most powerful instrument of peace known today.

The Air Transport Command and the Naval Air Transport Service of World War II helped establish the pattern of world aviation. They proved air transportation as a vital arm of war. Its remarkable postwar achievement in the Berlin airlift established it also as an instrument of national policy in peacetime. Considerable credit for helping to get this force off the ground in time of crisis goes to the airlines. Their equipment, crews, personnel, and organizational experience provided a necessary foundation upon which was built a military air transport organization.

After the war, this military operation repaid the airlines with interest. It gave them a complete network of intercontinental airways, ready for long-range air transport operation. It gave them technological knowledge that ordinarily would have taken decades to acquire. Hundreds of C-46 and C-47 aircraft, both twin-engine airplanes, were used to lift tons of cargo over the treacherous Himalaya Mountains. Each operation of these airplanes brought new information. Each flight over the Hump and across an ocean was, in a sense, an experiment, and each flight contributed to a mass of data on airlift performance and efficiency which in peacetime would have taken several years to accumulate.

On February 26, 1963, President Kennedy signed Executive Order No. 11090, which redefined the emergency preparedness functions of the Civil Aeronautics Board. In preparing this national emergency plan, there are two organizations which play a large role. The first of these is the War Air Service Program (WASP), which is a program designed to provide for the maintenance of essential civil air routes and services, and to provide for the distribution and redistribution of air carrier aircraft among civil air transport carriers after the withdrawal of aircraft allocated to the Civil Reserve Air Fleet. The second is the Civil Reserve Air Fleet (CRAF), which are those air carrier aircraft allocated by the Secretary of Transportation to the Department of Defense to meet essential military needs in the event of an emergency. The Director of the Office of Emergency Planning shall advise and assist the President in determining policy for the performance of this order.

As air transportation profited from the wartime activities of military air transportation, so today's military forces profit from airline activity. One of the lessons learned for national defense was the importance of commercial air transportation as an essential part of our national security. As a potential military auxilliary of the United States, the airlines are closely tied to military aviation through a plan known as the Civil Reserve Air Fleet (CRAF). This fleet is subject to call by the Defense Department on twenty-four hours' notice. The United States airline fleets stand by to serve the country in a national emergency. Through the Civil Reserve Air Fleet plan, long-range turbine powered air carrier aircraft stand ready to go into military service. This tremendous fleet would afford an immediate airlift to supply troops and supplies to any point in the world. The maintenance of this stand-by fleet does not cost the government one cent. It would require millions upon millions of dollars to build a fleet of this size for government use and would stand idle until a national emergency would arise. To keep this fleet in ready service would cost the government many more millions of dollars annually.

The Civil Reserve Air Fleet is currently made up of modern jet aircraft modified for military purposes. All are in commercial operation, but earmarked for military use when needed. Their value has been placed at exceeding $400,000,000. Added to the airlines' annual cost of training its crews and of maintenance, the value of the Civil Reserve Air Fleet approaches three-quarters of a billion dollars.

Military movements are arranged through the military bureau of the ATA, and the air transport system can handle large numbers of personnel on short notice. For one particular movement, 2,596 men from 10 different installations were accommodated on one day, 701 men on regular flights and the rest on 16 charters. During one month of 1967, over 62,000 troops were moved.

All requests for military lift have been handled under contract charter, or on regular passenger flights. When fully activated in a national emergency, the scheduled airline portion of the Civil Reserve Air Fleet can provide the military with three billion ton-miles of lift.

The CRAF airlift capability continues to expand as new airplanes are added to the fleet.

Air transportation has come a long way in terms of importance to the National Defense and contribution to the nation's economy, yet its potential has barely been tapped.

CHAPTER
II
vvv

The Beginning of
Commercial Air Transportation

Since the Wright Brothers' first successful flight on December 17, 1903, it has taken the airplane more than six decades to attain its present proportions of recognition and utility in the role of a commercial vehicle. Its first practical use in this respect was as a mail carrier. The airmail story has been one of healthy growth in which determination made possible the final acceptance of airmail into the United States transportation and economic system. The story is an interesting one of the not too distant past that can be recalled by some pilots still actively flying today.

Airmail was born during the week of September 23rd to the 30th in 1911, at Long Island. There an airplane took off and delivered mail to the Mineola Post Office, about ten miles distance.

The pilot, Earl Ovington, flying a Bleriot Monoplane carried about fifteen pounds of letters daily during the week long air meet. He flew the short distance to the Mineola Post Office where he dropped the mail pouches to the ground. The postal employees picked them up, and the mail continued on its way in the usual surface manner. Although the mail did go by air, there was no practical value to it other than an attraction for the air show. These letters marked "Aeromail" have become valuable as a collector's item. This experiment in airmail had the cooperation of the postal officials.

The following year saw 31 additional such experimental airmail flights. In every flight, the Post Office cooperated by giving permission and supplying the mail, but did not assist with the expense.

The authorization for these experiments came from a law introduced by Morris Sheppard, a Representative from Texas, in June 1910, "To definitely determine whether aerial navigation may be utilized for the safe and rapid transmission of the mails."

In 1912, the Post Office Department, encouraged by the success of these experimental airmail flights, urged Congress to appropriate money to launch an airmail service. However, the Congress was far from convinced and preferred to keep the mail on the ground; they did not appropriate any money.

It was not until 1916 that Congress made available for airmail service the lavish sum of $50,000 out of its "steamboat or other powerboat service" appropriation. World War I interrupted development; but before the war ended

The first airmail flight in the U.S., September 23, 1911.

Earl Ovington—Long Island, New York, September 1911.

in 1918, Congress appropriated $100,000 for the establishment of an experimental airmail route as well as the purchase, operation, and maintenance of airplanes. Sheppard again was responsible for this appropriation.

Captain Benjamin B. Lipsner, an army engineer who had helped perfect an improved aircraft engine oil during the war was put in charge and made responsible for this operation.

The War Department furnished the planes and the pilots from the Army Signal Corps. The pilots were to be engaged in cross-country flight training and the transporting of the mail was secondary.

Lipsner had earlier convinced Otto Praeger, the Second Assistant Postmaster General that the airmail service was feasible and that he could develop a system showing the cost of operation. Lipsner, after establishing the service was discharged from the army and became the first "Superintendent of the Aerial Mail Service," on July 15,1918. He resigned some months later due to a disagreement over the expenditure of funds.

Much credit for the initial impetus in the inauguration for airmail service goes to Otto Praeger, often called "The Father of Airmail." As Second Assistant Postmaster General from 1915 to 1921, he possessed a long range vision, that during the early years of national air policy, contributed immensely to the establishment of commercial aviation. Otto Praeger's goal was not only to foster air commerce, by the support of an airmail service so that private capital could be attracted to create a new industry, but also to make the airplane a carrier of mail so that it would be made to measure up to requirements of dependability and regularity which would develop its potential. He could not have been more correct. The development of commercial aviation almost exactly paralleled his early thinking.

The first experimental airmail route was between Washington, D.C., and New York City, with a stop at Philadelphia to change pilot and airplanes. The total distance of the first route was 218 miles.

Four Curtiss Jenny (JN-4H) army training airplanes were used having a 150 horsepower Hispano Suiza engine and a capacity of 150 pounds of mail. The first Jenny, Aircraft number 38262, was delivered from Philadelphia to Washington, D.C. by Major Reuben Fleet and turned over to Captain Lipsner on the morning of May 15, 1918. Fleet later left the army and eventually became head of the Consolidated Aircraft Corporation.

The inauguration of the first official airmail route took place that same morning when President Wilson autographed the first letter addressed to the Postmaster of New York City. This letter, along with the three pouches of mail, was placed in the front cockpit of the Jenny. The load amounted to 140 pounds of about 6,600 letters, 300 of which were addressed to Philadelphia. The gross revenue for this mail was about $1,584.

The President's party included Mrs. Wilson, Postmaster General Burleson, Otto Praeger, the Postmaster of Japan, and the Assistant Secretary of the Navy, Franklin D. Roosevelt. The press and many spectators were also present to view the memorable occasion. The location chosen was the Polo Grounds; although it had not been built for a flying field, it had ample level ground.

The Curtiss "Jenny."

May 15, 1918, the beginning of the first official U.S. airmail route. Shown are: Otto Praeger, Assistant Post Master; Merit Chance, Washington Post Master; Albert Burleson, Post Master General; President Woodrow Wilson.

Lt. George Boyle was selected to make the first flight. At 10:30 a.m., May 15, 1918, with the mail on board and everything ready, the order was given to start the engine of the Jenny. The mechanic called "contact," the ignition switch was turned on and five mechanics forming a chain pulled the propeller. The engine coughed once but failed to start. Four more times they tried with the same result. After much confusion and embarrassment it was discovered that someone had neglected to fill the gas tank. Only after three cans of gas had been siphoned from a nearby dismantled airplane and poured into the empty tank did Lt. Boyle get his engine started.

With order restored and the crowd cheering, the airplane took off. Lt. Boyle, for some unexplained reason, turned south instead of north and became lost. It was not long before he had to make a landing in an open field near Waldorf, Maryland. The mail was sent back to Washington by truck, where it went on by train to Philadelphia and New York.

The day was not lost, however, because the plans for the first day called for Lt. Torrey Webb (who later became an executive of the Texas Oil Co.) to take-off from Belmont Park, New York, at 11:30 a.m. with the first southbound airmail. He arrived at Philadelphia without incident and turned the mail over to Lt. James Edgerton, who flew it on to Washington, D.C., where he delivered it safely and made the inauguration of airmail a success.

The airmail schedule soon settled down to a routine with Edgerton, Webb, and four other army pilots alternating between Washington, D.C., Philadelphia and New York.

Two months later, 88 flights had been completed out of 100 that had been scheduled. During the first year, 1,263 flights had been scheduled, but only 55 had to be cancelled. Another 53 were forced down due to bad weather, and 37 others because of engine trouble. The record was nearly 90 per cent and 128,000 miles flown carrying 193,000 pounds of mail.

The Post Office for the first year, spent $138,000, while the total revenue from airmail postage was $160,000. The success of this effort made the United States the first country to have daily scheduled airmail service.

A special stamp was quickly made up for the beginning of the airmail service. It had a rose-colored background with a picture of a Jenny in blue. The stamp sold for 24 cents. On May 14, 1918, the day before the first Post Office flight, it was discovered that the Jenny on the stamp had been printed in an inverted position. The upside down stamps had been sold at the Washington, D.C. Post Office. Only one sheet had not been recovered, the rest had been found in time and destroyed. The one sheet had been sold to a stamp collector who did not notice the error immediately. The Post Office tried to buy back the 100 stamps for the purchase price of $24.00, but the buyer refused to sell, realizing their value. The sheet was eventually broken up and if one were to be sold today, its value to collectors would be enormous. A center line block of four once sold for nearly $50,000. The entire sheet would be priceless if it were still intact.

The experimental airmail service between New York-Philadelphia-Washington launched on May 15, 1918, continued until August 10, 1918.

The special stamp issued for the inauguration of the airmail service in
which the "Jenny" was printed upside down.

Since it was the intention of the Post Office Department to operate the
service with the Postal Service's own equipment, an order for six custom built
mail planes was placed with the Standard Aircraft Company of Elizabeth, New
Jersey. These planes, advanced for their day, were powered with 150 horsepower
Hisso engines and had special mail pits located underneath the center sections of
the upper wings. The acceptance of these airplanes marked the real beginning of
commercial aviation. Six civilian pilots were hired at a salary of $3,600 to
$5,000 a year and replaced the army pilots.

On Monday, August 12, 1918, the Post Office Department began the world's
first regular permanent civilian airmail service. Pilot Max Miller was at the
controls of the first airplane taking off that day with airmail from Washington,
D. C. Miller was an experienced pilot for those days, since he had accumulated
over 1,000 flying hours and had been an army flight instructor at San Diego,
California. He was the first civilian pilot hired. He met and later married Otto
Praeger's stenographer who was actually the first airmail employee. Max Miller
burned to death over New Jersey two years later while carrying the mail.

Edward Radel was hired as the chief mechanic. He was also a musician and
later played the saxophone for many years with the Fred Waring band.

The base of operations was moved from the Polo Grounds to the flying field
at College Park, Maryland.

The airplane left Washington, D.C., August 12, at 11:35 a.m. carrying 222 pounds of mail and arrived at Philadelphia at 1:00 p.m. where Maurice Newton took over and landed at Belmont Park race track, New York, at 2:15 p.m. Two other pilots flew the southbound trip from New York to Washington in three and one-half hours starting at noon.

On May 15, 1919, service was established between Cleveland and Chicago, with a stop at Bryan, Ohio; the first step in what later became the first transcontinental route linking New York and San Francisco.

On July 1, 1919, operations were extended from Cleveland to New York with a stop at Bellefonte, Pennsylvania, thus opening the New York to Chicago route. The service performance during that period was remarkable, considering that there were no radio facilities, no marked airways or other navigational aids. Airmail was flown on those routes in connection with the railroad service. The airplane would carry the mail during the day and at night the mail would be turned over to the train to carry it, since aircraft did not fly in the night-time hours. During 1919, over the three routes in operation, eight planes flew 1,900 route miles daily with a performance record showing more than 95 per cent of scheduled miles completed.

On May 15, 1920, service was extended westward from Chicago to Omaha, Nebraska, and on August 16, the St. Louis to Chicago route was opened. This is the route that Charles Lindbergh later flew as an airmail pilot. On September 8, 1920, the last leg of the transcontinental route was opened from Omaha, Nebraska to San Francisco. The dream of transcontinental airmail service became a reality. Even though airplanes flew only during the daylight hours, airmail bettered coast-to-coast train time by 22 hours.

On February 22, 1921, the first through transcontinental airmail airplane took to the air, a truly great moment, for it meant flying the mails through long, black, beaconless nights. It took 33 hours and 21 minutes to complete the flight from the West Coast to Long Island.

The heroics of this flight are an epic in the annals of aviation history. The first airplane to leave New York westbound was forced down shortly after take-off. The second airplane made it to Chicago but could go no further due to bad weather. The first eastbound airplane which left San Francisco crashed in Nevada and the pilot was killed. The second eastbound plane got to Reno, Nevada. There another pilot took it on to Cheyenne, Wyoming, where he arrived 12 hours after the mail left San Francisco. Another pilot carried it on to North Platt, Nebraska. The hero of the flight, Jack Knight, took off late in the evening in a DeHaviland; and while enroute, some people on the ground lighted fires for him to follow. He landed at Omaha at 1:00 a.m. only to find that the airplane that was planned to meet him and had been grounded in Chicago. In cold, ice and snow and being unfamiliar with the route, Knight continued on with only an automobile road map to guide him. He could not land at Des Moines, Iowa, his intended stop, because of snow on the airport; he went on to Iowa City. There the ground crew which was supposed to light the guiding bonfires had gone home thinking the flight had been cancelled. A night watchman at the airfield heard the engine of the airplane and lighted a flare. As Knight landed, he ran out of gas. The watchman helped refuel the airplane; and in snow and sleet, Knight again took off and encountered fog. By some miracle he found Chicago and landed safely at 8:40 in the morning. The airmail was then uneventfully carried on to New York to complete the first through transcontinental delivery.

Jack Knight demonstrated that the old Motto of mail carriers, "neither rain, nor snow, nor heat, nor gloom of night can stay these couriers from the swift completion of their appointed rounds," could now be applied to airmail pilots.

In the first half of 1923, the Post Office built a lighted airway between Cheyenne and Chicago; and in August, for a four day period, a regular schedule was flown from New York to San Francisco using this lighted airway during the night-time hours. Another test period of thirty days in July, 1924, so thoroughly demonstrated the feasibility of transcontinental airmail that it continued on as regular operation.

From this beginning grew our present system of navigable airways. It was the Post Office who gave aviation not only this beginning, but also the first practical night flying.

In 1927, not only the lighted airways, but also radio communication, was transferred to the Department of Commerce.

By July, 1924, regular 24-hour transcontinental airmail service was in operation. In those days it cost 24 cents to send a letter across the country, while today the domestic rate is eleven cents an ounce, with a large quantity of first class mail being carried between major cities by air for the only first class rates.

Aircraft equipment was quite a problem for the fledging airmail service. In November, 1918, DeHaviland DH-4 military observation planes were placed in service flying the airmail. They had to be withdrawn because of weak spots in their design and modified by strengthening the landing gear and moving the gasoline tank to the center section immediately behind the engine. Before the modification, the tank had been located behind the pilot's cockpit, making a crash landing practically guaranteed a flaming death when the pilot found himself pinned between a ruptured fuel tank and a red-hot Liberty engine. For this reason, the DH-4's were nicknamed "Flying Coffins." With modifications, the DH-4B, as it was then known, became the standard work-horse of the airmail and held that place until1926, although many other types were used.

The instrument panel on the DH-4 contained an ignition switch, an air speed indicator, a tachometer, a water temperature gauge, and an altimeter which registered 1,000 feet of altitude for each half inch around the periphery of its scale. Since the latter was more sensitive to changes in temperature than it was to altitude, the pilot almost had to be a mathematician, a statistician, and a magician to interpret what the altimeter readings meant. There was a magnetic compass which, on an easterly or westerly heading oscillated all the way from north to south when the air was rough.

With no navigational aids, no aerial sign posts, no radio, the pilots still carried the mail in weather that stopped all surface traffic. The pilots strapped a road map to their thigh; and if there were no clouds, fog, rain, sleet, or snow to obstruct the view, they could look over the side of the open cockpit, locate a river, a railroad track, a distinctive barn, or some other landmark, and thus determine their course. Flying the "iron beam" literally meant following a railroad track. During bad weather and low ceilings, more than one pilot had to climb suddenly to avoid a head-on collision with a railroad locomotive.

It was the requirement of airmail which fostered the development of night flying, instrument flying, meteorological service, Federal Airways, hard surface runways, radio communications, and multi-engined airplanes. When the airplane was forced to produce the exacting performance necessary to keep the system of American business flowing smoothly, it either had to literally show up or quit. It conformed, but it wasn't easy. Those persons working against great handicaps made it work; they were of the United States Airmail Service. Thus the commercial value of air transportation became a reality.

These pages and many more could not do justice to the historic achievements in the lives of all those pioneers who contributed so greatly to make air transportation the great and vital operation it is today.

The next time you receive an airmail letter, remember the airmail pioneers—those people whose tireless efforts and confidence in the future provided the foundation upon which commercial air transportation was built.

CHAPTER
III
⋁⋁⋁
Establishment
of the Airline Industry

It is a knowledgeable fact that the Post Office, through the development of airmail, was directly responsible for the beginning of commercial air transportation and of the airline industry; therefore, the Post Office can be credited with being the father of United States commercial air transportation.

Benjamin Franklin, who established the Postal Service at the birth of the United States, recognized the importance of such a service. He said that a progressive nation requires a good communication system. His policy for the Post Office was that it should assist and help develop all new forms of transportation which would in turn, provide a better mail delivery. Examples of this fact were the mail subsidies paid to the early stage coach lines who depended upon mail pay to stay in operation; only then were they able to provide passenger service. Their real income was from the transportation of mail. The historically famous Pony Express was established solely because of the lucrative mail payment offered to the contractors.

The government assistance in the growth of the early railroads is further evidence of the federal policy to encourage new forms of transportation. In this case the government granted land to the railroads for rights of way on which to lay their tracks and then loaned or gave them money for equipment.

By 1925 the Post Office had conducted the airmail service long enough to prove the practicability of such a commercial, non-military, use of the airplane. It was generally understood that the Post Office operation would only be temporary and that as soon as it was feasible, the carrying of the mail by air would be turned over to private industry.

In 1918 it was estimated that it would take at least five years before this transfer could take place. By the time the mid 1920's were approaching, the Post Office was ready to ask private industry to take over the airmail operation.

The story of private companies beginning to carry airmail is also the history of the inception and growth of the commercial airline industry.

The last flight of the Post Office operation took place on September 9, 1927. Beginning in June of 1927, the Post Office pilots were released as the newly formed airlines took over the airmail routes. There were 43 pilots at the time in the Postal Service, and an additional 600 employees in ground jobs. All of these had contributed to more than 12 million airmail miles having been flown.

The entire cost to the United States government for the airmail service, from its beginning in 1918 until the last flight in 1927, was 17 1/2 million dollars. During these nine years about five million dollars in airmail postage sold to the public constituted the gross income. The difference of 12 1/2 million dollars cannot be counted as a loss since it was a very small price to pay for the establishment of commercial air transportation and the United States airline industry; an industry which has repaid this debt many times over, not only in taxes, but in valuable service to both the government and to the public.

AIRMAIL ACT OF 1925

Civil air transportation got its start in the United States when on February 2nd, Congress passed the Airmail Act of 1925; also known as the Kelly Act because it was Representative Clyde Kelly of Pennsylvania who sponsored and led the congressional fight for its passage.

This Act made possible the awarding of contracts, to private contractors, for the transportation of airmail. Therefore, the purpose of the law was to provide for private airmail contractors, as clearly indicated in the title of the Kelly Act; "An Act to Encourage Commercial Aviation and to Authorize the Postmaster General to Contract for the Mail Service."

One important feature of the Kelly Act was that the amount of compensation paid to an air carrier could not be more than four-fifths, or 80 per cent, of the revenue derived from the sale of airmail postage from such mail. This feature was a compromise with those in Congress who were opposed to the federal government paying for the development of the airline industry. The remaining 20 per cent was for the ground handling expense of the airmail. In essence, the operation of the airmail under the Kelly Act would not cost the government. This feature proved to be the main weakness in the Kelly Act.

By the middle of 1925, Postmaster General Harry S. New advertised for bids on eight airmail routes. These routes were to be short feeder routes in order to allow the airlines time to gain experience, and then after they had proved themselves, the transcontinental routes would be awarded. Only those companies with proper experience and equipment were eligible to bid.

On September 15, 1925, bids for the eight routes were filed with the Postmaster General and opened on October 7. There were ten companies who submitted seventeen bids. Three were dispensed with due to lacking proof of financial responsibility; and as a result, only five routes were immediately awarded. By the beginning of 1926, twelve Contract Airmail Routes had been awarded. These are listed on the following page.

These routes awarded under the Kelly Act were for feeder lines branching off into the main transcontinental route. Because of economic conditions and a desire to reduce costs in the department, it was then decided that bids would be given on main routes. On January 15, 1927, the bid for the San Francisco to Chicago portion of the route was awarded to the Boeing Airplane Company and

Route No.	Company	Route	Began Operating
CAM 1	Colonial Air Lines	New York to Boston	June 18, 1926
CAM 2	Robertson Aircraft Corp.	Chicago to St. Louis	April 15, 1926
CAM 3	National Air Transport	Chicago to Dallas	May 12, 1926
CAM 4	Western Air Express	Los Angeles to Salt Lake City	April 17, 1926
CAM 5	Varney Speed Lines	Elko, Nevada, to Pasco, Washington	April 6, 1926
CAM 6	Ford Air Transport	Detroit to Cleveland	February 16, 1926
CAM 7	Ford Air Transport	Detroit to Chicago	February 15, 1926
CAM 8	Pacific Air Transport	Los Angeles to Seattle	September 15, 1926
CAM 9	Charles Dickenson	Chicago to Minneapolis	June 7, 1926
CAM 10	Florida Airways Corp.	Atlanta to Jacksonville	September, 1926
CAM 11	Clifford Ball	Cleveland to Pittsburgh	April 21, 1927
CAM 12	Western Air Express	Pueblo, Colorado, to Cheyenne, Wyoming	December, 1926

Edward Hubbard. Several months later, the joint contract was turned over to Boeing Air Transport. At the time the western sector was awarded, no acceptable bid was received for the route east of Chicago. This was determined later by awarding a contract to National Air Transport on March 8, 1927.

Although Colonial Air Lines received the first airmail contract, the honor for being the first in operation goes to Henry Ford, who owned Ford Air Transport.

In the early days of commercial aviation, the name Ford was equally known in aviation as well as the automobile industry. As early as 1923, Ford became interested in an all metal, internally-braced wing, monoplane designed by William B. Stout. Ford bought Stout's factory, put three engines on the aircraft instead of one, and the result became known as the Ford Tri-Motor, or more affectionately, the "Tin Goose." It was such a strong and dependable aircraft that it became the leading passenger aircraft for many years.

This type aircraft was later used to found air transportation in South America. In fact, some of them are still in operation today, a record unequalled by any other type of airplane.

In April, 1925, Ford, using his single engine airplanes, began flying a scheduled route from Detroit to Chicago to Cleveland, for the exclusive use of the Ford Company. Thus Ford not only operated the first airmail route by a private contractor, but also is credited with one of, if not the first, air freight operations as well as one of the first airlines to carry passengers.

Under the Kelly Act, a Contract airmail carrier was paid up to eighty per cent of the postal revenue of the airmail he carried. In trying to avoid subsidy, the Congress created a problem in computing payment to the carrier. Because the airmail was handled both by the Post Office and by the airline, each letter had to be counted before it was loaded aboard the airplane so that the postage could be apportioned between the Post Office and the air carrier. Under this system, an irrational distribution of airmail payments occurred.

The Postmaster solved these inequalities by the first amendment to the Kelly Act, approved June 3, 1926. New contracts were provided for at rates not to exceed $3.00 per pound for the first 1,000 miles and thirty cents a pound for each additional 100 miles. Again compensation was based upon nonsubsidy; this was still a weakness.

In February, 1927, an airmail postage rate of ten cents per half ounce between any two points in the United States became effective and provided a great impetus to the public in the use of airmail.

The first amendment to the Kelly Act did away with the difficult method of counting each letter carried, and the second amendment passed in May, 1928, did away with assuring the government against losses. Thus subsidy quietly came into the airline industry. The second amendment also reduced the airmail postage to five cents an ounce and a 95 per cent increase in airmail traffic resulted. The airlines could actually receive more money for carrying the airmail than the cost of the postage on the mail carried. To the young profit starved airlines, this presented a golden opportunity. Now that they were being paid by the pound to carry the airmail, several of the airline companies began sending large quantities of airmail, as private citizens, destined to go over their routes. They sent thousands of letters stuffed with paper, even telephone directories and spare parts. One airline contractor mailed two tons of lithograph material from New York to Los Angeles. It cost him over $6,000 in postage; but he was paid $25,000 by the Post Office to carry it, a neat profit in anyone's business sense.

Obviously the opportunity for these inequalities had to be corrected; and so the third amendment to the Kelly Act so completely changed it that it was in reality the second major law passed by Congress having to do with airmail carried by the Private contractors. This piece of legislation was called the Airmail Act of 1930, the McNary-Watres Act.

AIR COMMERCE ACT OF 1926

When the Kelly Act provided that the airlines would carry the airmail, it was apparent that they were neither financially able, nor large enough to provide from the maintenance and operation of the airway system that was organized for the Post Office operation.

Therefore, on the heels of the Kelly Act, Congress passed another major piece of legislation known as the Air Commerce Act of 1926; the purpose of which was to promote air commerce. This law charged the federal government with the operation and maintenance of the airway system, as well as all aids to air navigation, and to provide safety in air commerce generally through a system of regulation.

It was unlike the other Acts which had to do with airmail legislation. It left no doubt that the federal government was strongly in the picture of the growth and development of aviation by way of aiding and encouraging air transportation.

The function of safety regulation was to be carried out by the Department of Commerce; therefore, the Bureau of Air Commerce was established.

Among the safety regulations provided were the requirements of registration and licensing of aircraft and the certification and medical examination for pilots.

THREE-ENGINED AIRPLANE OF THE THIRTIES MEETS
THE THREE-ENGINED AIRPLANE OF THE SIXTIES

Civil penalties were allowed to enforce these requirements. This was the start of what later became the Civil Aeronautics Administration and today the Federal Aviation Administration.

The Kelly Act and the Air Commerce Act, beyond any doubt, provided the foundation of civil air transportation in the United States.

AIRMAIL ACT OF 1930

The Airmail Act of 1930, also known as the McNary-Watres Act, was passed April 29, 1930, and was an attempt to unify the industry.

Up until this time, the newly organized airlines were not interested in carrying passengers. Even during the 1930's the airline airplanes were referred to as mail planes while today, when an airliner passes overhead it is thought of as a passenger airplane, even though airmail is aboard.

An important event which was to have a vast effect upon the development of the airline industry, took place in November, 1928, when Herbert Hoover was elected President and shortly thereafter appointed Walter Brown as the new Postmaster General. It was Brown who initiated the passage of the McNary-Watres Airmail Act of 1930.

It was under Brown's administration that the second phase of the airline industry's development took place. Brown became a most controversial figure and even today is both violently criticized or praised for the part he played in the development of civil air transportation and airline history.

Upon taking the office of Postmaster General, given to him for being partly responsible for Hoover's nomination, he began a thorough study of the problems of aviation. He felt that the airlines should be able to develop profitably without the help of airmail payments; he further believed that competition was necessary in the airline industry to stimulate growth. In a meeting with the airline leaders, Brown encouraged them to develop a profitable passenger business and in this manner became independent of the subsidy of airmail contracts. Postmaster Brown's goal was a system of three self-supporting transcontinental airline systems, he therefore urged the airlines to form three large transcontinental companies. He was perhaps 20 to 30 years ahead of time in his thinking.

The Airmail Act of 1930 gave Brown, as Postmaster General, dictatorial power over the airline industry; therefore, commercial air transportation took on the characteristics of a federally regulated industry. Brown had power to grant an airmail contract without competitive biding. The law placed extensive power in the hands of one man. He stated at the time that if the airlines were ever to become self-supporting they had to carry passengers and compete with each other. He felt that the airline industry needed leadership and he was the one to give it. Postmaster Brown arranged that his office be able to extend or consolidate routes in public interest. This resulted in several smaller companies joining together in order to qualify for an airmail contract.

The new law brought about a change in the method of computing mail pay rates which paid the airlines for space instead of weight. This encouraged the airlines to purchase larger aircraft, which in turn gave rise to passenger traffic. In addition to computing the new airmail rates on space, the McNary-Watres Act also provided for variables such as bad terrain, bad weather, night flying, radio equipment, and multi-engine aircraft.

Brown met with the contracting airlines to discuss the new airmail contracts and plan for passenger service. It became clear that the airlines were not willing as yet to move in this direction. This further forced Brown into assuming the responsibility of leadership of the airline industry and to use the far reaching powers granted to him under the McNary-Watres Airmail Act of 1930. He made it apparent that he believed an airline should be a large, sufficiently financed company and that the transcontinental airmail routes must be conducted by one company. Since there was no large single airline, mergers of several smaller companies then resulted. This action contributed to the beginning of the corporate entities of airlines that we know today, such as United Air Lines, American Airlines, and Trans World Airlines. Many smaller companies were left out. To them it meant no mail contract and no contract meant going out of business. Brown therefore got the large transcontinental airline companies that he wanted.

The four years Brown was Postmaster General resulted in a consolidated airline route pattern emerging and the great air carrier companies of today being formed.

Brown has been called both good and evil since he acted in a direct fashion; but in looking back, it becomes obvious that the airline industry development would have been much slower were it not for his accomplishments.

The complaints of the small airlines left out of the picture were heard in Washington, and with a Presidential election coming up, it made a good basis for political discussion.

As we know from history, the Republican Party lost to the Democratic Presidential candidate, Franklin D. Roosevelt, who upon taking office, placed in the office of Postmaster the figure of James A. Farley of New York.

When Brown left office he left behind 34 established airmail routes. The per mile cost of airmail was 54 cents, whereas it had been $1.10 when Brown entered office. The result was good if no attention was paid to those who had been trampled upon.

Since 1932 the word had gone out through the halls of Congress for the cancellation of the airmail contracts awarded in 1930. In early 1933 a House committee expressed its feelings that certain interlocking relationships had prevented the development of aviation and resulted in wasteful expenditures of public funds. It was the committee's recommendation that the powers of the Postmaster be restrained.

With Roosevelt in office, a special committee headed by Senator Hugo Black (later to become a Supreme Court Justice) was convened to investigate the airmail situation. They seized the airline files and soon became of national notice. The main outcome was to crucify Walter Brown by saying he had favorites among the airlines and even charged him with collusion between him and the larger airlines. His methods drew the attention of the Black Committee who made much to do about it. Brown's defense was that he acted in the manner according to his beliefs for the public interest.

The new Postmaster General, James Farley, maintained that the routes had been awarded at a series of secret meetings held in May and June of 1930, which were called the Spoils Conferences.

The main point was that all but two of twenty contracts went to United Aircraft and Transport Corporation, Aviation Corporation of Delaware, and the North American Aviation Group of General Motors.

Brown subsequently retired to his home in Ohio and became the dean of Toledo politics and the head of the Republican Party there. He died at the age of 91 in 1961.

On February 9, 1934, as a result of the Black Committee investigation, James Farley issued an order which cancelled all domestic airmail contracts on charges of collusion. The army, he said, carried the airmail originally in 1918 and they could do it again. General Benjamin Foulois, an aviation pioneer and Chief of the Air Corps, was called upon to do the job.

In taking over the airmail on February 19, 1934, the route mileage was greatly reduced. The ill equipped army was given ten days to get the schedules in operation. The air corps itself was struggling for recognition and had not been given adequate funds to even accomplish their growth.

The day before the army took over, the airlines demonstrated their progress and ability to carry the mail, as well as to show the ridiculousness of the Postmaster's order. A new Douglas type airliner, the DC-2, with two famous pilots at the controls, Jack Frye of Trans World Airlines and Eddie Rickenbacker of Eastern, flew the last load of mail from Los Angeles, California, to Newark, New Jersey, for a new transcontinental flying record of 13 hours.

The ill prepared and poorly equipped Air Corps had tragic results in its effort to carry out Farley's order. Three days before they were to take over the airmail routes, three pilots were killed on their way to begin their assignment and another crashed but escaped serious injury.

The record for the first week's operations was equally tragic; five army pilots were killed and six more seriously injured, eight airplanes ruined and $300,000 property damage. A few days later, two more pilots were killed and one critically injured.

The needless slaughter went on into March of 1934. Finally after 66 crashes, 12 deaths, and a cost to the government of nearly four million dollars, President Roosevelt ordered the army to cease flying the airmail on June 1, 1934, after nearly six months' operation.

At the time of the cancellation of airmail contracts, the airlines were receiving from 42 1/2 cents to 54 cents per mile; it cost the army $2.21 during its operation. It was obvious that for economy, and service as well as safety, the airlines could do a much better job.

As a result, all the former airmail contractors were given a three month contract to transport airmail. Before the time expired it was apparent that airmail legislation had to be completely revamped.

It was not until 1941 that Brown was vindicated when the United States Court said that the charges of collusion against him were untrue. Therefore, the cancellation of the airmail contracts, the pilots killed, the property damage and the high expense were all unnecessary except as a period in the historical development of United States air transportation.

This action of the court made it possible for the airlines, whose airmail contracts had been cancelled by Farley, to claim and receive about two and one-half million dollars in damage.

AIRMAIL ACT OF 1934

The remedial act to prevent the happenings which existed during Brown's administration was passed in June, 1934, and was known as the Airmail Act of 1934 or the Black-McKellar Act.

Under the provisions of this act, airmail contracts were to be granted upon competitive bidding, as was the case before 1930. However, that no contract would be awarded to any company who had been involved in the supposed collusion. The three air carriers involved in the alleged collusion did show up at a meeting on April 20, 1934, called by Farley to issue new contracts. The three airlines had disguised themselves by changing their names slightly; American Airways became American Airlines, Eastern Air Transport became Eastern Airlines, and Transcontinental & Western Air just added the suffix "Inc." Furthermore, the control of the industry was placed in the hands of three agencies of the federal government. This joint administration was divided between the Post Office, the Interstate Commerce Commission and the Department of Commerce.

The Post Office awarded all airmail contracts and enforced the regulations governing airmail. The Interstate Commerce Commission was to set the rates of mail pay to the contracting airlines as well as to review all rates periodically. The Department of Commerce had established the Bureau of Air Commerce (the ancestor of the present Federal Aviation Administration) whose function it was to provide safety in air transportation and also to maintain, operate, and develop the airway system.

The Act of 1934 also created a Federal Aviation Commission to study aviation policy and was headed by Clark Howell of Atlanta. The commission submitted its report on February 1, 1935 and recommended a separate organization be created to control the airline industry. Senator Pat McCarran, during debate on the Black-McKellar Act suggested this same course of action.

A minor provision of the act, seemingly unimportant at the time, required the separation of airline companies and aircraft manufacturers. It was considered a matter of safety that airplane users not be controlled by those who controlled the airplane builders. Had this been allowed, an airline might be required to buy an airplane of a manufacturer which was also owned by the same holding company. This action further resulted in the final organization of the present day airline corporate names.

An indirect but most important result of the 1934 trouble was the growth of passenger service. The airlines realized that their future lay not upon dependence on airmail contracts, but upon the development of passenger traffic; therefore, the major airlines began forming Traffic and Sales Departments for the purpose of promoting and selling passenger travel. By the end of 1936 the income from passengers exceeded the income from airmail transportation.

Both the air transport industry and the federal government learned many valuable lessons during the early months of 1934. Among these was the conviction that a healthy air transport service was essential to the nation's economic and political strength and the time was at hand to revise the existing air legislation. It took four years of discussion before satisfactory legislation was finally enacted.

In order to do a good job for both the airlines and public, the federal government decided it must have regulatory power over the airline industry and that it must regulate air commerce in the same way that it regulated interstate and foreign commerce. The authority by which it conducted these functions stemmed from the United States Constitution.

By 1938 the airline industry was an established and recognized segment of the American way of life. The airlines had airmail contracts, and they were developing passenger service. Also, the economic and business condition of the entire United States was improving after the disastrous years of the depression. Aircraft manufacturers had begun providing aircraft to the airlines for passenger service.

All seemed well with the industry, in fact it was going too well. There began situations which resulted in uneconomic passenger route duplication and rate cutting.

CIVIL AERONAUTICS ACT - 1938

The airlines approached the government and suggested working out a basic set of guiding principles. The three agencies under the Airmail Act of 1934 were overlapping in authority which worked a further hardship upon the airlines.

After several months of study by the industry leaders and government officials, a completely new all encompassing law was passed affecting civil aviation in the United States. The new law found its constitutional basis in Article I, Section 8, of the United States Constitution, known as the Commerce Clause. The progression of authority was the Interstate Commerce Commission Act of 1887 and the essentials of the new law from the then recently passed Motor Carrier Act of 1935.

The Civil Aeronautics Act, which was introduced by Senator Pat McCarran and Representative Clarence Lea, passed the Congress on June 23, 1938. The McCarran-Lea Act amended or repealed all major existing and previous legislation having to do with aviation in any way.

The mechanics of the Civil Aeronautics Act were simple. All air transportation regulation, both economic and safety, was administered by three separate agencies.

These original three agencies consisted of:

1. The Civil Aeronautics Authority, composed of five members who were to establish aviation policies by legislation of safety and economics of air transportation.

2. An Administrator of Aviation was appointed in order to carry out the safety policies of the Authority while the Authority provided for the execution of the economic regulations concerning the air transport industry.

3. An Air Safety Board was formed as an independent group of three men responsible for the investigation of aircraft accidents.

For the first time the airline industry could look upon a firm regulatory system, making it possible to plan for future development.

After the functioning of the Authority, the Administrator, and the Air Safety Board began, it became obvious that some duplication of authority existed and that an adjustment was necessary. Therefore, President Roosevelt in April and June of 1940 proposed changes that became effective on June 30, 1940, and became known as the 1940 amendment to the Civil Aeronautics Act.

The results of the organizational changes were the reshuffling of functions into two agencies instead of three. The first was the Civil Aeronautics Board, which was to be an independent group of five men reporting to the President of the United States, whose function it was to exercise legislative and judicial authority over civil aviation, as well as executive control in the area of air carrier economic regulation. The investigation of aircraft accidents also became a responsibility of the Civil Aeronautics Board.

The second agency created by the Amendment of 1940 to the Civil Aeronautics Act of 1938, was the Civil Aeronautics Administration headed by an Administrator whose function was to be solely the execution of safety regulation, including enforcement and promotion of aviation safety as well as the entire operation of the airway system. The Civil Aeronautics Administration was placed under the Department of Commerce.

Included in Title IV of the economic regulation of the Civil Aeronautics Act of 1938 was section 401e, which stated that the carriers who had provided adequate and continuous airmail service from May 14 to August 22, 1938, the effective date of the act, would receive a permanent Certificate of Convenience and Necessity for those routes. This clause was called the Grandfather Clause, and the first airline to receive this award was Delta Air Corporation. Only a violation of the Act can cause an airline to lose its Grandfather rights. These airlines, receiving their permanent certification in this manner, were the following:

American Airlines	Eastern Airlines
Braniff Airways	Inland Airlines
Chicago and Southern Airlines	Mid-Continent Airlines
Continental Airlines	National Airlines
Delta Air Corporation	Northeast Airlines
Northwest Airlines	United Airlines
Pennsylvania-Central Airlines	Western Air Express
Transcontinental & Western Air	Wilmington-Catalina Airlines

Of these 16 carriers, six have faded away through mergers or reorganization. Chicago and Southern and Northeast merged with Delta; Inland merged with Western; Mid-Continent merged with Braniff; Pennsylvania-Central became Capital, which later merged with United; Transcontinental and Western changed their corporate name to Trans World Airlines. Additional carriers will fade away through mergers.

Civil air transportation continued under the Civil Aeronautics Act for a period of twenty years, and the Act provided the practical machinery for the development of civil air transportation. It formulated continuing public service objectives and provided the means whereby these objectives could be established. The purpose of the Act was not only to regulate civil air transportation, but also to develop and encourage its growth.

Because of the growing importance of the air transport industry to the economy and the national defense of the United States in the later 1930's, the writers of the Civil Aeronautics Act agreed that air transportation must be kept a strong and dynamic force.

Time alone proved the truth of their wisdom.

FEDERAL AIRPORT ACT OF 1946

Prior to 1946, the airports of this country were financed and operated by state, county, or municipal governments. The cost of building and maintaining these airports was very high and because of this factor, the development of airports was slow. It was the purpose of the Federal Airport Act to give the United States a comprehensive system of airports, administered by the Civil Aeronautics Administration. Small communities which needed airports to help develop their social and economic structure, theoretically were supposed to benefit from this program.

The Congress appropriated $520,000,000 for a seven year period to aid in the development of this airport system; however, the money had to be spent on operational facilities (runways, etc.). This federal aid program was organized so that the federal government would pay as much as 50% of the cost and that the airport (sponsor) would pay the balance, or at least 50% of the cost. As far as the large cities were concerned, this was excellent because they could issue and sell bonds to pay for their share of the cost; however, for the small cities, even 50% of the cost of development was too much of a burden. The purpose of the legislation was failing since the small cities did not benefit.

In 1953, President Dwight D. Eisenhower suggested that the Act be amended so that it would include a provision that the money could be spent on public buildings (terminals) as well as operational facilities.

In 1958, Congress passed a bill which would continue the Act until 1963 with an increase in appropriations. However, the Eisenhower administration disagreed and the Undersecretary of Commerce for transportation said that the construction, maintenance, and operation of civil airports was primarily a matter of local responsibility. The President vetoed the bill by saying, "I am convinced that the time has come for the federal government to begin an orderly withdrawal from the airport grant program."

The Senate Committee on Interstate and Foreign Commerce then stated that: "The committee is convinced that the capital investment required to bring airport facilities up to the present and future needs of this Nation is far beyond the financial capacity and capabilities of local communities with continued effective assistance and encouragement from the federal government."

Congress later passed and the President approved a bill which extended the Act through 1961.

For an airport or governmental unit to be available for such money, it is necessary that the airport be in the National Airport Plan. Under the Federal Airport Act, the Administrator of the Federal Aviation Administration is directed to prepare such a plan. In formulating the plan, the Administrator shall take into account the needs of both air commerce and private flying, technological developments, probable growth, and any other considerations he may find appropriate.

The money which is appropriated for use is divided into two areas: 75% is distributed for projects among the several states and 25% is placed in a discretionary fund for the Administrator to use as he sees fit for airport construction. One half of the 75% is apportioned to the States, based on population, and the other half is based on land areas. The discretionary fund allows the Administrator to choose the projects regardless of their location.

As a condition to his approval of a project, the Administrator shall receive in writing a guarantee that the following provisions will be adhered to:

1. The airport will be available for public use without unjust discrimination.
2. The airport will be suitably operated and maintained.
3. The aerial approaches will be cleared and protected and future hazards will be prevented.
4. Proper zoning will be provided to restrict the use of land adjacent to the airport.
5. All facilities developed from federal aid shall be made available to the military.
6. All project accounts will be kept in accordance with a standard system.
7. All airport records will be available for inspection by an agent of the Administrator upon reasonable request.

On May 17, 1966, the Senate Commerce Committee gave approval to a bill to continue for an additional three years a program authorizing 75 million dollars annually in federal matching funds for airport construction. This extended the Federal Airport Act to June 30, 1970.

The airlines and the air industry can develop only as rapidly as the facilities they use; the Federal Airport Act has aided this development.

AIRPORT AND AIRWAY DEVELOPMENT ACT OF 1970

The Second Session of the 91st Congress passed an act to provide for the expansion and improvement of the airports and airway systems of the United States. In order to do this the Congress also provided for the imposition of an airport and airway user charge. In declaring the policy of this law they stated that the Nation's airport and airway system is inadequate to meet the current and projected growth in aviation. In order to meet the demands of interstate commerce, the postal service, and the national defense, substantial expansion and improvement are necessary to meet the proper requirements of the 1970's.

The Secretary of Transportation is directed by this Act to prepare and publish a national airport system plan for the development of public airports. The plan shall show, for at least a ten year period, the type and estimated cost of airport development necessary to provide a system of public airports adequate for the needs of civil aeronautics. In developing this plan, the Secretary is directed to consider the relationship of each airport to the rest of the transportation system including all modes of intercity transportation.

One section of this act provides for the Secretary to make available grants of funds to planning agencies to develop airport master plans.

In order to develop a proper airway system and adequate airports, the Secretary may authorize the following grants: For the purpose of acquiring, establishing, and improving air navigation facilities he may authorize for expenditure not less than $250 million for each fiscal year from 1971 through 1975. For airports served by air carriers certificated by the Civil Aeronautics Board, the Secretary may authorize grants of $250 million for each fiscal year from 1971 through 1975. Also included in this group of airports are those general aviation airports which serve to relieve congestion at airports having high density traffic serving other segments of aviation. Thirty million dollars has been made available for the fiscal years 1971 through 1975 for airports serving segments of aviation other than air carriers. The Secretary is authorized to apportion the funds in the following manner for air carrier airports:

A. One third of the funds will be distributed to the various states. One half of this amount distributed according to the geographic size of the state and the other half according to the size of the population.

B. One third of the funds will be distributed to the sponsors of airports served by certificated air carriers in the same ratio as the number of passengers enplaned at each airport of the sponsor bears to the total number of passengers enplaned at all such airports.

C. One third to be distributed at the discretion of the Secretary.

The Secretary is authorized to apportion the funds for general aviation airports in the following manner:

A. 73 1/2 per cent to the states based on the distribution related for air carrier airports.

B. 1 1/2 per cent for Hawaii, Puerto Rico, Guam, and the Virgin Islands.

C. 25 per cent to be used at the discretion of the Secretary.

The most controversial section of this act appears to be a section which amends the Federal Aviation Act of 1958 by adding Section 612. This section is titled "Airport Operating Certificates." The Administrator is empowered to issue airport operating certificates to airports serving air carriers certificated by the Civil Aeronautics Board and to establish minimum safety standards for the operation of these airports.

Any person desiring to operate an airport serving certificated air carriers must file with the Administrator an application for an airport operating certificate. If after an investigation, the Administrator finds the applicant properly equipped and able to conduct a safe operation, he shall issue an airport operating certificate. The details for this procedure of airport certification may be found in the Federal Aviation Regulation Part 139.

It shall be unlawful for any person to operate an airport, serving air carriers certificated by the Civil Aeronautics Board, without an airport operating certificate, or in violation of the terms of that certificate.

Title II of the Airport and Airway Revenue Act of 1970 amends the original Act of 1950 to establish new and increased taxes which are imposed on the users of the airport and airway system. These taxes include the following:

1. An 8 per cent tax on airline tickets for most domestic flights.
2. A $3.00 charge on airline tickets for most international flights beginning in the United States.
3. A 5 per cent tax on air freight waybills.
4. A 7 cent tax on fuels used in non-commercial aviation.
5. A basic annual registration tax of $25.00, plus an added charge (2 cents per pound for piston aircraft, and 3 1/2 cents per pound for jets) applicable to aircraft over 2,500 pounds.

As a result of the Airport and Airway Development Act of 1970, the Federal Aviation Administration has adopted a new Federal Aviation Regulation, titled Airport Aid Program. The new regulation prescribes the policies and procedures for administering the Airport Development Aid Program and the Planning Grant Program. Both of these programs were established by the Airport and Airway Development Act of 1970. The new regulation, Part 152, incorporates the general requirements of Part 151 which governed the old Federal Aid Airport Program and will remain in effect for that program until all of its projects are completed.

PART
TWO

VVVVV

Regulation of
Air Transportation

CHAPTER
IV
VVV

The Federal Aviation Act - 1958

The Civil Aeronautics Act of 1938 was basically a constitution of aviation upon which the aviation industry could expand and develop. It was general in character and left the interpretation of the specific nature to the Civil Aeronautics Board, in the matter of economic regulation, and the Civil Aeronautics Administration, in the area of adherence to air safety.

As the years progressed from 1938 and the air industry developed, particularly after World War II, it became apparent that some changes had to be made. Amendments and revisions were passed to take care of minor current adjustments; however, the main points of contention were becoming more severe. Many plans were forthcoming which ranged from overhauling and modernizing the Civil Aeronautics Act, to a completely new method of aviation regulation. Some of those men proposing changes had been responsible for the writing and enactment of the Civil Aeronautics Act in 1938; a few felt that aviation regulation had not been carried out according to their intended meaning. Some of their arguments, no doubt, had just foundation. It is sufficient to state that no major change came about and the Civil Aeronautics Act remained in effect for twenty years until the passage of the Federal Aviation Act in 1958. This act, however, is not entirely new; it is largely a reenactment, in amendment form, of the prior Civil Aeronautics Act. The economic regulatory provisions set forth therein are unchanged, therefore, pre-1959 judicial and administrative decisions interpreting and applying predecessor provisions of the Civil Aeronautics Act are of precedential value with respect to the Federal Aviation Act. The Federal Aviation Act is the old Civil Aeronautics Act in practically every respect except one; and that is the expanding of power in the area of air safety. The Civil Aeronautics Administration became the Federal Aviation Agency. Whereas, the Civil Aeronautics Administration was under the Department of Commerce, the Federal Aviation Agency was organized at an independent level answerable only to the Congress and the President of the United States. With the enactment of the Department of Transportation in 1966, the Federal Aviation Agency became the Federal Aviation Administration and was placed under the Secretary of Transportation.

The circumstances which led to the Federal Aviation Act of 1958 were the obvious need of improved air traffic control after a series of mid-air collisions, some of which involved military aircraft.

The first of these accidents occurred on June 30, 1956 over the Grand Canyon. The aircraft involved were a Trans World Airlines' Constellation and a United Airlines' DC-7. Both aircraft fell into the Canyon.

TWA Flight 2 left Los Angeles International Airport at 9:00 a.m. bound for Kansas City; and three minutes later, bound for Chicago, UAL Flight 718 took off from the same runway. At 10:31 a.m. Flight 2 and Flight 718 collided over the Grand Canyon.

The probable cause, according to the official Civil Aeronautics Board Accident Report, was that the pilots did not see each other in time to avoid the collision. It is not possible to determine why the pilots did not see each other, but the evidence suggests that it resulted from any one, or a combination of the factors concerned with intervening clouds, visual limitations, preoccupation with normal cockpit duties, attempting to provide passengers with a more scenic view, physiological limits to human vision, or insufficiency of enroute air traffic advisory information due to inadequacy of facilities and lack of personnel in air traffic control.

The second accident involved a DC-7B owned by Douglas Aircraft Company and a USAF F-89J near Sunland, California on January 31, 1957. The DC-7B crashed into a junior high school playground killing 3 students and injuring 70 others. The F-89J crashed in the Verdugo Mountains.

The probable cause was the high rate of near head-on closure at high altitude, which together with physiological limitations, resulted in a minimum avoidance opportunity during which the pilots did not see the other's aircraft.

The third accident was between a United Airlines DC-7 and a USAF F-100F near Las Vegas, Nevada, on April 21, 1958.

The probable cause of this mishap, according to Civil Aeronautics Board investigation, was a high rate of near head-on closure at high altitude; human and cockpit limitations; and the failure of the Nellis Air Force Base and the Civil Aeronautics Administration to take every measure to reduce a known collision exposure.

These accidents and other occurrences caused Congressional action. The Federal Aviation Agency was granted expanded authority in air safety. It would not be hampered organizationally or budgetwise as had been the case of the Civil Aeronautics Administration. The Federal Aviation Agency was able to make long range plans and to implement these plans without interference.

The Federal Aviation Act of 1958 worked virtually no changes of substance in the economic regulatory provisions but made several revisions in the safety program. While the Board retained its duties in the fields of air carrier economic regulation and aircraft accident investigation, the Board's safety rule-making powers were transferred to the Administrator of the Federal Aviation Agency, with the result that the latter official then promulgated the very regulations and standards which he administers and enforces. The Board's role in safety rule making is presently limited to participation as an interested party in FAA proceedings.

A second important revision of prior law concerns procedure in certificate suspension and revocation cases (Section 609). Whereas under the former law, only the Board could suspend or revoke in the first instance; the new act contemplated initial action by the Administrator, subject to the certificate holder's privilege of appeal to the Board. Apart from these matters, the Federal Aviation Administrator has, in addition, substantially all the powers and duties of his predecessor under the 1938 Act, plus a clearer authority to allocate the navigable airspace as between military and civilian users.

Whereas the Civil Aeronautics Board had been responsible for the enactment of air safety legislation, and such regulations carried out by the Civil Aeronautics Administration in their executive capacity, the power of air safety legislation was transferred to the Federal Aviation Agency. The Civil Aeronautics Board retained the responsibility of aircraft accident investigation and, of course, economic regulation of the air carriers.

All research and development concerning air safety which had been going on was consolidated and placed in the care of the Federal Aviation Agency. Therefore, the work of such agencies as the Airways Modernization Board, the Air Coordinating Committee, and the National Advisory Committee for Aeronautics could be coordinated at one location and under one agency; namely, the Federal Aviation Agency.

The area of economic regulation of the air transportation industry was not altered in any way. The Federal Aviation Act was passed hurriedly in the closing days of Congress in 1958. No attempt was made to change or modify any economic regulation of the air transport industry. Many aviation interests today feel that this should be done.

In the study of present federal regulation of air transportation, it must be borne in mind that such regulation is now much as it was in 1938 except in the area of air safety, including air traffic control.

It must be understood that although the Federal Aviation Act is the law of the land in aviation matters, it is very broad and in many cases loose in definition. This fact is not a weakness, for the Civil Aeronautics Board and the Federal Aviation Administration are to interpret and apply the law within the framework of the Act. Therefore, the Civil Aeronautics Board prepares and keeps current various economic regulations for the general routine of specific items, whereas the Federal Aviation Act is the basis for this specific regulation.

The Federal Aviation Act was passed by Congress on August 23, 1958. That part of the law dealing with the creation and the organizational structure of the Federal Aviation Agency became effective on that date. The main body of the law was placed in effect on the last day of the year, 1958.

Officially the Federal Aviation Act is known as Public Law 85-726, 85th Congress, S.3880.

The introductory paragraph very clearly states the purposes of the new law as to:

1. Continuing the Civil Aeronautics Board.
2. Creating a Federal Aviation Agency (Administration).
3. Providing for the regulation and promotion of Civil Aviation.
4. Providing for the safe and efficient use of the airspace.

Structurally, the Act is divided into fifteen main divisions called "Titles." Each title is divided into various sections which in turn have several sub-sections. Reference is made to any part of the Act by stating the Title number and section combined; thusly 411 means the eleventh part of the fourth Title.

In viewing the Titles it will be seen that Title II deals with the organization, functions, and general powers of the Civil Aeronautics Board; Title IV, Air Carrier Economic Regulation is the direct responsibility of the Civil Aeronautics Board and indicates the majority of the work which they perform. Title VII, Aircraft Accident Investigation, was a function of the Civil Aeronautics Board but transferred to the National Transportation Safety Board under the Department of Transportation.

The organization, powers, and duties of the Federal Aviation Administration, headed by the Administrator, are outlined in Title III. The main responsibilities of the Administrator, and therefore the Federal Aviation Administration, are stated in Title V, Nationality and Ownership of Aircraft, as well as Title VI, Safety Regulations of Civil Aeronautics.

The remaining Titles of the Act, although none-the-less important, deal with miscellaneous aviation matters. Refer to Appendix 1.

Title I is introduction and contains four sections.

Section 101. Definitions.
Section 102. Declaration of Policy for the Civil Aeronautics Board.
Section 103. Declaration of Policy for the Federal Aviation Administrator.
Section 104. Public Right of Transit.

Each of these sections are discussed below.

Section 101 -- Definitions

Except for the minor changing of words to a more modern connotation, the definitions, of which there are thirty-six, have not been altered. In 1938, the writers of the Civil Aeronautics Act wanted to be sure the terms and words they used within the act were generally understood by all; therefore, the definitions represent an effort at standardization.

The statutory definitions are of great importance, since application of the substantive regulatory provisions of the Act depend upon them to a large extent, and since the definitions also include certain substantive grants of power. Thus, the definition of "air commerce" largely fixes the scope of the Federal Aviation Administrator's jurisdiction in the safety field because the substantive provisions of Title VI, Safety Regulations of Civil Aeronautics, are couched in terms of "air commerce." It should be observed that the definition of "air commerce" is exceedingly broad, as it includes not only what is traditionally regarded as interstate and foreign commerce (physical movement of aircraft across state and international boundaries and the transportation within a single state of persons or property moving to or from another state), but also all transportation of mail, operations or navigation within the limits of any Federal airway, and any operation or navigation which may endanger safety in air commerce. This definition is generally regarded as conferring Federal jurisdiction in safety matters with respect to all flights of aircraft, since all flights, whether commercial or private, and irrespective of whether they cross state lines or operate within a Federal airway, represent a potential danger to interstate commerce. Moreover, counsel for the Board and the Administrator, and thus far some courts, have considered the definition to be so broad as to vest in the federal government exclusive jurisdiction in safety matters, thus preempting the states from enacting air safety regulations under their general police powers.

On the other hand, the definition of "air transportation" which fixes the scope of the Board's regulation under Title IV, Air Carrier Economic Regulation, is considerably narrower than the definition of "air commerce." "Air transportation" includes only common carriage by aircraft "in commerce between" the states, etc., and the carriage of mail by aircraft. This definition is believed to confer jurisdiction over the common carriage of persons and property only in those areas traditionally regarded as constituting interstate and foreign commerce. Unlike in the safety field, the definition does not preempt the entire economic field to the exclusion of the states, and the courts have in certain context so held. Thus, while the Board's economic jurisdiction is believed to extend to all common carrier movements of aircraft across state lines and within the territories, and to movements of aircraft within a state but engaged in interstate transportation of more than a minimum amount, there is no direct economic jurisdiction over purely intrastate transportation. However, there may be jurisdiction in the Board to control intrastate operations of interstate carriers on proper findings of necessity therefore to preserve or benefit the interstate operations. On the other hand, air transportation of mail, whether interstate or purely intrastate, falls within the definition of air transportation, except for certain special transportation defined elsewhere as beyond the Board's jurisdiction.

Another important term is "air carrier" defined as any United States citizen "who undertakes, whether directly or indirectly or by a lease or any other arrangement, to engage in air transportation." This definition serves to fix the Board's jurisdiction over "indirect air carriers" and the definition provides further that the Board "may by order relieve air carriers who are not directly engaged in the operation of aircraft" from the various regulatory provisions of the statute. This provision has been used to establish the classification of Air Freight Forwarder and to exempt both them and other indirect air carriers such as Railway Express (an "air carrier' as to air express) from the Certificate of Convenience and Necessity and other provisions of the Act.

Mention should also be made of the term "aeronautics" defined as "the science and art of flight." Since the control provisions of the statute (Sections 408 and 409) confer jurisdiction over relationships between air carriers and persons engaged in a "phase of aeronautics," this definition permits considerable breadth in the application of the statute. It has been held to include manufacturing companies, leasing companies, and a host of other persons engaging in activities closely related to air carrier operations.

The examples listed are for the purpose of illustration, and only those which bear special attention will be discussed.

Administrator means the Administrator of the Federal Aviation Administration.

Board means the Civil Aeronautics Board.

Aircraft means any contrivance now known or hereafter invented, used, or designed for navigation of or flight in the air.

Civil aircraft means any aircraft other than public aircraft.

Civil aircraft of the United States means any aircraft registered as provided in this Act.

Public aircraft means an aircraft used exclusively in the service of any government or of any political subdivision but not including any government owned aircraft engaged in carrying persons or property for commercial purposes.

Citizen is anyone, a partnership or corporation, who is a citizen of the United States or its possessions.

Persons means any individual, firm, co-partnership, corporation, company, association, joint-stock association, or body politic; and includes any trustee, receiver, assignee, or other similar representative thereof.

Foreign air carrier means any person, not a citizen of the United States, who undertakes, whether directly or indirectly or by lease or any other arrangement, to engage in foreign air transportation.

Supplemental air carrier means an air carrier holding a Certificate of Convenience and Necessity authorizing it to engage in supplemental air transportation.

Supplemental air transportation means charter trips in air transportation, other than the transportation of mail by aircraft, rendered pursuant to a Certificate of Convenience and Necessity issued pursuant to Section 401 (d) (3) of this Act to supplement the scheduled service authorized by Certificates of Convenience and Necessity issued pursuant to Sections 401 (d) (1) and (2) of this act.

Interstate air commerce, overseas air commerce, and *foreign air commerce,* respectively, mean the carriage by aircraft of persons or property for compensation or hire, or the carriage of mail by aircraft, or the operation of aircraft in the conduct of a business or vocation.

Interstate air transportation, overseas air transportation, and *foreign air transportation,* respectively, mean the carriage by aircraft of persons or property as a common carrier for compensation or hire or the carriage of mail by aircraft.

Air man means any individual who engages, as the person in command or as pilot, mechanic, or member of the crew, in the navigation of aircraft while under way; and any individual who is directly in charge of the inspection, maintenance, overhauling, or repair of aircraft, engines or propellors, and any individual who serves in the capacity of aircraft dispatcher or air traffic control tower operator.

Ticket agent means any person, not an air carrier and not a bona fide employee of an air carrier who, as principal or agent, sells or offers for sale any air transportation, or negotiates for, or holds himself out by solicitation, advertisement, or otherwise as one who sells such transportation.

Airport means a landing area used regularly by aircraft for receiving or discharging passengers or cargo.

Landing area means any locality, either land or water, including airports, which is used, or intended to be used, for the landing and take-off of aircraft, whether or not facilities are provided for the shelter, servicing, or repair of aircraft, or for receiving or discharging passengers and cargo.

Federal airway means a portion of the navigable airspace of the United States designated by the Administrator as a Federal airway.

Appliances means instruments, equipment, parts, and accessories which are used in the navigation, operation, or control of aircraft in flight, and which are not parts of the aircraft, aircraft engines, or propellers.

Spare parts means parts, appurtenances, and accessories of aircraft (other than aircraft engines and propellers), of aircraft engines (other than propellers), of propellers and of appliances, maintained for installation or use in an aircraft, aircraft engine, propeller, or appliance, but which at the time are not installed or attached.

Propeller includes all parts, appurtenances, and accessories thereof.

Mail means United States mail and foreign-transit mail.

Navigable airspace means airspace above the minimum altitudes of flight prescribed by regulations issued under this Act, and shall include airspace needed to insure safety in take-off and landing of aircraft.

Navigation of aircraft or navigate aircraft includes the piloting of aircraft.

Operation of Aircraft or operate aircraft means the use of aircraft, for the purpose of air navigation. Any person who authorizes the operation of aircraft, whether with or without the right of legal control (in the capacity of owners, lessee, or otherwise) of the aircraft, shall be deemed to be engaged in the operation of aircraft within the meaning of this Act.

Possessions of the United States means (a) the Canal Zone, but nothing herein shall impair or affect the jurisdiction which has heretofore been, or may hereafter be, granted to the President in respect of air navigation in the Canal Zone; and (b) all other possessions of the United States. Where not otherwise distinctly expressed or mainfestly incompatible with intent thereof, references in this Act to possessions of the United States shall be treated as also referring to the Commonwealth of Puerto Rico.

United States means the several States, the District of Columbia, and the several Territories and possessions of the United States, including the territorial waters and the overlying airspace thereof.

Section 102 -- Declaration of Policy for the Civil Aeronautics Board.

This section, originally a part of the Civil Aeronautics Act of 1938, is analogous to the National Transportation Policy contained in the Interstate Commerce Act and provides that the Board shall consider, among other things, the specific factors there set forth "as being in the public interest, and in accordance with the public convenience and necessity." Since throughout the substantive provisions of the Act, the Board is required as a prerequisite to various actions to find either "public interest" or "public convenience and necessity," Section 102 serves in part as a statutory definition of these terms. It speaks, however, only in terms of air carriers and air transportation, and counsel for the Board have contended that this section, among others, permits the Board to award operating authority to air carriers and to take other regulatory action with respect to air transportation without regard to the possible adverse competitive impact that such action might have upon surface carriers.

In performing its responsibilities under the Act the Civil Aeronautics Board shall consider the following as being in the public interest in accordance with the public convenience and necessity:

a. Encourage and develop an air transport system for the present and future needs of the Commerce, Postal Service, and National Defense of the United States.

b. The regulation of air transportation to assure safety, foster sound economic conditions, and to improve the relations between air carriers.

c. Promote adequate, economical, and efficient air service at reasonable charges in the public interest.

d. Promote competition necessary to assure development of air transportation for the Commerce, Postal Service, and National Defense of the United States.

e. Promote Safety.

f. Promote, encourage, and develop civil aeronautics.

Section 103 -- Declaration of Policy for the Administrator.

This section was written in 1958 at the time the Federal Aviation Agency was created by the legislation of the Federal Aviation Act. It parallels the previous section concerning the Civil Aeronautics Board in that it specifies several factors which the Administrator shall consider as being in the public interest.

As previously stated, the Federal Aviation Act created the Federal Aviation Agency to replace the Civil Aeronautics Administration. The Administrator is charged with encouraging civil aviation and air commerce in the United States. In exercising his authority, he must consider the needs of the national defense and of commercial and general aviation, as well as the public right to use the navigable airspace of the United States.

Specifically, the Administrator is authorized to prescribe rules governing the safe and efficient use of the navigable airspace; to provide for necessary air navigation facilities; to promulgate air traffic rules; to grant exemptions from his own regulations when the public interest requires it; to veto federal non-military expenditures for airports and air navigation facilities if such are deemed by him as being not reasonably necessary for use in air commerce or not in the interest of national defense; to make recommendations to the Secretary of Transportation concerning weather services for air commerce; to disseminate and exchange information relative to civil aviation; to engage in long-range planning, research and development with respect to the utilization of the navigable airspace; and to provide for improved control of air traffic.

In the performance of his duties under the Act, the Administrator of the Federal Aviation Administration shall consider the following as being in the public interest:

a. The regulation of air commerce to promote and develop safety.

b. Promote, encourage, and develop civil aeronautics.

c. Control the use of the navigable airspace of the United States and the regulation of both civil and military operations therein.

d. Consolidate research and development of air navigation facilities.

e. Develop and operate an air traffic control system for both civil and military aircraft.

Section 104 – Public Right of Transit.

This section of the Act recognizes the rights enjoyed by free people; a precious right that is not abundant in many countries on earth. To a person born in the United States, Section 104 is taken for granted because it recognizes the public right of freedom of the United States citizen to use the navigable air space of the United States.

The declaration of a public right of freedom of transit through the navigable airspace of the United States has been the subject of considerable controversy in law suits involving low-flying aircraft. "Navigable airspace" is defined as airspace above the minimum altitudes of flight prescribed by regulations issued under this Act, and shall include airspace needed to insure safety in take-off and landing of aircraft. The Administrator prescribes such altitudes in the exercise of his safety rule-making powers. Prior to the passage of the Federal Aviation Act, when the Board was the body which promulgated the minimum altitude regulation, the Board's position in the courts was that the freedom of transit provision relieved aircraft operators from technical claims of trespass but that it did not serve to extinguish a landowner's rights in the case of an actual "taking" of property occasioned by low-flying aircraft. In such latter circumstances, contended the Board, the landowner would have his state law remedies against the person causing the damage.

CHAPTER

V

ⱽⱽⱽ

Department of Transportation

President Lyndon B. Johnson in March of 1966 sent a special message to Congress requesting that they create a twelfth cabinet department to cope with the country's transportation problems. One of the main reasons for creating such a department was to centralize, under one department, the many federal agencies regulating the transportation systems.

In signing the Bill creating the new department, President Johnson said, "the old system was inadequate even though transportation is the nation's biggest industry which involves one dollar of every five dollars in the United States economy."

It is anticipated that during the next twenty years transportation in the United States will double its present size.

The Civil Aeronautics Board Chairman told the House Government Operations Committee that the President's recommendations will provide the necessary improvements. He stated that the new department would not make any radical changes in air transportation. Also speaking before the Committee was the Federal Aviation Administrator who felt that transferring the Federal Aviation Administration to the Department of Transportation would not hurt commercial aviation. He stated that any Secretary of Transportation, working for the President in looking at the tremendous importance of commercial aviation today, is not going to wade in and throw this operation into chaos, because nobody can be that stupid.

Senator A. S. Monroney (D-Okla.) said that transferring the Civil Aeronautic Board's safety responsibilities would be unwise. He suggested that aviation safety problems have little relationship to safety problems of other modes of transportation.

General William McKee, the Federal Aviation Administrator, disagreed that aviation safety practices are unique to the aviation industry. He said, "Many of the fundamental principles of safety are applicable in any mode of transportation." McKee also regarded the creation of the Department of Transportation as a promotion of transportation and not as a demotion of aviation.

It is important to note that in passing the law, Congress provided that it would not give up its say on transportation. The Secretary's recommendations will have to be approved by the President and by Congress before they can take effect. Refer to the Department of Transportation Act 1966, Section 4 (a).

The airlines recommended the Civil Aeronautics Board retain its present powers over accident investigation and safety appeals. This recommendation was not accepted, however. The airlines felt that there was no pressing problem in this area.

The Department of Transportation Act was passed on October 15, 1966, creating a department consisting of parts of 31 agencies, employing approximately 100,000 persons. Its first budget exceeded 6 1/2 billion dollars. This Bill is known as Public Law 89-670, 89th Congress, H.R. 15963.

The purposes of the Act are stated in Section 2; that Congress established a Department of Transportation in the public interest to:

1. Assure the coordinated, effective administration of the transportation programs of the federal government.

2. Facilitate the development and improvement of transportation service.

3. Encourage government, carrier, labor, and others to cooperate in achieving transportation objectives.

4. Stimulate technological advances.

5. Provide general leadership.

6. Recommend policies and programs to the President and the Congress.

The Department of Transportation is headed by the Secretary of Transportation, who is appointed by the President with the advice and consent of the Senate.

The Secretary is responsible for exercising leadership, under the direction of the President, in transportation matters including those involving National Defense. He is also directed to provide leadership in the development of national transportation policies and programs and to make recommendations to the President and the Congress. He is to promote and undertake development, collection, and dissemination of technological, statistical, economic and other information pertaining to domestic and international transportation. The Secretary consults with the Secretary of Labor involving labor-management relations, contracts, problems and in promoting stable employment conditions.

The Secretary of Transportation is directed to undertake research and development relating to transportation, with particular attention to aircraft noise. He is also directed to consult with other Federal departments and agencies on the transportation requirements of the government, including the procurement of transportation or the operation of their own transport services. The Secretary must also consult with state and local governments.

Any orders and actions of the Secretary or the National Transportation Safety Board in the Exercise of their functions, powers, and duties shall be subject to judicial review.

The President with the advice and consent of the Senate appoints the Under Secretary of Transportation. The Under Secretary is to perform such powers, functions, and duties as the Secretary shall prescribe and during the absence or disability of the Secretary he shall exercise the duties of the Secretary.

DEPARTMENT OF TRANSPORTATION ORGANIZATION

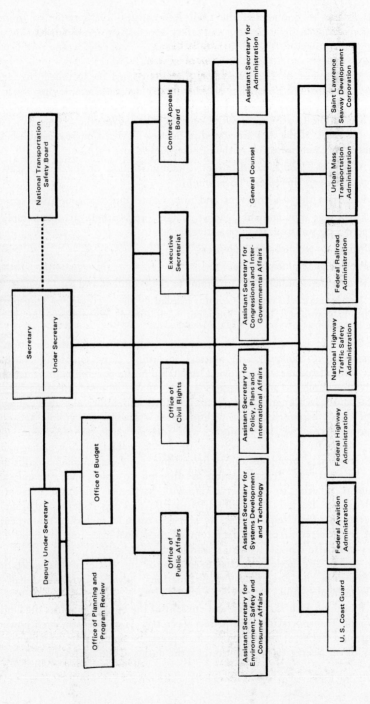

The Secretary of Transportation is assisted by four Assistant Secretaries and a General Counsel who are appointed by the President with the advice and consent of the senate. Their duties will be prescribed by the Secretary.

In addition there is in the Department an Assistant Secretary for Administration who is appointed by the Secretary under civil service classification with the approval of the President.

The Department of Transportation consists of the normal intra-agency operating departments, such as: Office of Planning and Program Review, Office of Budget, Office of Public Affairs, Office of Civil Rights, Executive Secretariat and Contract Appeals Board.

The staff assignments are carried out by the Assistant Secretaries and the General Counsel. The Assistant Secretary for Policy and International Affairs is responsible for the analysis of all DOT systems and internal information. He handles the development of policy and plans as well as the review of these policies and plans. The international programs of the Department are coordinated by the Assistant Secretary. Also included under his authority is the Office of Facilitation.

The Assistant Secretary for Environment, Safety and Consumer Affairs is responsible for the coordination of programs within this area involving himself in the necessary research to advance the Nation's transportation system. This Assistant Secretary is given the obligation to carry out the special projects of the Department of Transportation. He is also responsible for the relations between the DOT and local communities.

The Assistant Secretary for Systems Development and Technology is responsible for systems engineering, noise abatement, telecommunications, and research and development policy, plans, and resources.

The Assistant Secretary for Congressional and Inter-Governmental Affairs is responsible for the relationship of the DOT to other governmental units.

The General Counsel provides each Office and Assistant Secretary with the proper legal counsel.

The Assistant Secretary for Administration is responsible for the business like management of the Department of Transportation involving personnel, systems, administrative operations, security, investigations, logistics, and audits. He is also responsible for the operation of the Office of Emergency Transportation.

The main function of the Department is the promotion of current and future transportation which includes protecting the public's interest. The Department has a mandate to reflect in every program, safety in all areas. Equally important is the goal of achieving the most efficient, coordinated transportation system possible with a fair return to the corporation at the lowest cost to the user.

Specific areas of responsibility that the Department has, involve oil spillage, Uniform Time Act, emergency transportation, noise abatement, highway beautification, resource conservation, and the interstate highway program. In carrying out these responsibilities the DOT must work closely with independent regulatory bodies such as; the Interstate Commerce Commission, the Civil Aeronautics Board, the Federal Maritime Commission, and the Federal Power Commission.

In the Department of Transportation there are seven operating agencies:

1. Coast Guard.
2. Federal Aviation Administration.
3. Federal Highway Administration.
4. Federal Railroad Administration.
5. St. Lawrence Seaway Development Corporation.
6. National Highway Traffic Safety Administration.
7. Urban Mass Transportation Administration.

In this text we will be concerned only with the Federal Aviation Administration.

The Department of Transportation Act of 1966 transferred to the Secretary all the functions, powers, and duties of the Civil Aeronautics Board and of the Chairman, members, and offices under Title VI, (Safety Regulation of Civil Aeronautics), Title VII, (Aircraft Accident Investigation), of the Federal Aviation Act of 1958. Provided, however, that these functions shall be exercised by the National Transportation Safety Board (NTSB). Decisions of the NTSB shall be administratively final. Appeals as authorized by law shall be taken directly to the courts.

NATIONAL TRANSPORTATION SAFETY BOARD

The NTSB's duties include determining the cause or probable cause of transportation accidents and reporting facts, conditions, and circumstances relating to accidents. The NTSB is also responsible for reviewing on appeal the suspension, amendment, modification, revocation or denial of any certificate or license issued by the Secretary or by an Administrator.

The NTSB exercises the functions, powers, and duties relating to aircraft accident investigation transferred to the Secretary.

In the exercise of its functions, the NTSB shall be independent of the Secretary and the other officers of the Department. The NTSB shall report to the Congress annually on the conduct of its functions under thisAct and the effectiveness of accident investigation in the Department, together with such recommendations for legislation.

The NTSB consists of five members appointed by the President with the advice and consent of the Senate. No more than three members of the NTSB can be of the same political party. The members may be removed by the President for inefficiency, neglect, or malfeasance of office. The members of the NTSB shall be appointed for a term of five years and at the expiration of the term will continue to serve until a successor has qualified. Three members shall constitute a quorum.

The President designates, from time to time, one of the members of the NTSB to serve as Chairman and one as Vice Chairman. The Vice Chairman acts as Chairman in the event of the absence or incapacity of the Chairman, or in the event of a vacancy in the office of Chairman. The Chairman is the chief executive and administrative officer of the NTSB, who is responsible for the appointment and supervision of personnel employed by the NTSB. He is

ORGANIZATION CHART

NATIONAL TRANSPORTATION SAFETY BOARD

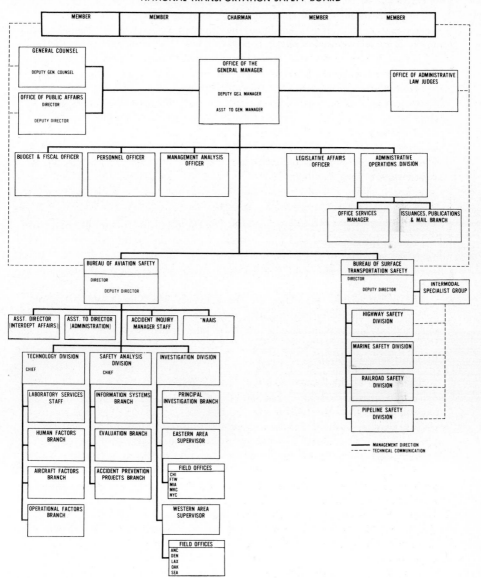

*National Aircraft Accident Investigation School

responsible for the distribution of business among the NTSB's personnel and the use and expenditure of funds. The Chairman shall be governed by the policy of the Board and by its decisions, findings, and determinations.

The Board is authorized to establish any rules or procedures as are necessary to carry out its functions. The Board has the same power as the Secretary in holding hearings, issuing subpenas, examining witnesses and receiving evidence. The Board is also authorized, on a reimbursable basis, to use the available services of other agencies.

The provisions of the Act state that all safety functions are transferred to the Department of Transportation. In connection with this provision, the Bureau of Safety under the Civil Aeronautics Board, was transferred to the Secretary of Transportation.

Serving under the Board Members are four Offices and two Bureaus that carry out the specific operating functions included in the Board's mission and in accordance with Board policy.

Office of the General Manager

The office of the General Manager assists the Chairman in the discharge of his duties as the executive and administrative head of the Board; coordinates and directs the activities of the staff; is responsible for day-to-day operations of the Board; and develops plans and procedures to achieve the Board's programs and objectives.

The duties within this office are the activities which deal with personnel, fiscal matters; administrative support services, docket material, processing formal board actions, and authenticating records for any official purposes.

Office of General Counsel

The Office of the General Counsel has the responsibility for providing legal advice and assistance to the Board and its Bureaus. They also perform the function of Congressional liaison.

The General Counsel prepares opinions for Board approval on matters of appeal. This involves a detailed analysis of the record, briefs of the parties, and a draft proposal of the Board's opinion. The General Counsel represents the Board in the U.S. Courts in matters dealing with appeals, enforcement of Board orders, and in the collection of civil penalities. They also prepare briefs in matters involving certiorari pleadings filed in the U.S. Supreme Court.

The Office of the General Counsel prepares Board comments on proposed legislation, drafts legistative proposals of the Board, and prepares both proposed rules and amendments to existing rules. He renders legal assistance to both the Bureau of Aviation Safety and the Bureau of Surface Transportation Safety during investigations, preparation of reports, and processing of requests for taking of depositions in private litigation arising out of accidents.

60,118 FATALITIES
IN TRANSPORTATION ACCIDENTS
1973

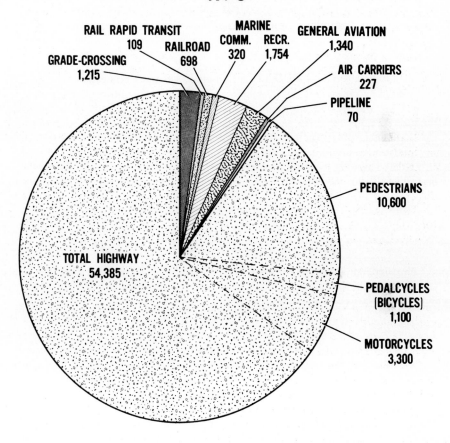

RAIL RAPID TRANSIT
109

RAILROAD
698

MARINE
COMM. RECR.
320   1,754

GENERAL AVIATION
1,340

GRADE-CROSSING
1,215

AIR CARRIERS
227

PIPELINE
70

PEDESTRIANS
10,600

TOTAL HIGHWAY
54,385

PEDALCYCLES
(BICYCLES)
1,100

MOTORCYCLES
3,300

NATIONAL TRANSPORTATION SAFETY BOARD

Office of Public Affairs

The Office is responsible for the Board's public affairs programs and for policies relating to maintaining communications between the Board and all news media, the industry, and the public. The Board members use this Office to Guide them in matters pertaining to public or press relations.

The Office of Public Affairs serves as the official spokesman for the Board on public announcements relating to the Board's actions and decisions. It carries out these functions both in Washington and at the scene of any accident. All press releases, accident reports, statistical reviews, technical studies, appeals, and safety recommendations are announced and distributed from this Office.

Office of Administrative Law Judges

This Office has the responsibility for conducting formal proceedings that may be required by the Board. These include safety enforcement proceedings, appeals from FAA orders, and petitions for review. The Administrative Law Judges function as trial judges issuing subpoenas, administering oaths, holding prehearing conferences, ruling on procedural requests, and receiving evidence.

Upon completion of a proceeding the Judge will review the evidence and issue an initial decision. If no appeal is filed by any party in the case this initial decision becomes the Board's final decision. If an appeal is taken the Board will then further investigate the case and issue their own opinion. A further discussion of the NTSB and its function is found in Chapter 7.

BUREAU OF AVIATION SAFETY

The Federal Aviation Act, Title VII, Aircraft Accident Investigation, as amended by the Department of Transportation Act, states that it shall be the duty of the National Transportation Safety Board to:

A. Make rules and regulations governing notification and reporting of accidents involving civil aircraft.

B. Investigate such accidents and report the facts, conditions and circumstances relating to each accident and the probable cause.

C. Make such recommendations to the Federal Aviation Administrator as, in its opinion, will tend to prevent similar accidents in the future.

D. Make such reports public in such form and manner as may be deemed by it to be in the public interest.

E. Ascertain what will best tend to reduce or eliminate the possibility of, or recurrence of accidents by conducting special studies and investigations on matters pertaining to safety in air navigation and the prevention of accidents.

The Bureau of Aviation Safety serves as the focal point for the NTSB in assuring that these responsibilities are adequately and fully carried out.

The Office of the Director develops and manages a program for investigation, analysis and prevention of aircraft accidents and promotion of air safety. He recommends the Bureau's goals and program objectives, formulates policy and procedure and directs the work of the Bureau.

There are four staff offices. Three of these offices assist the Director in the everyday management of the Bureau. This staff support consists of providing program planning, coordination and evaluation; resource forecasting and budgeting; organization, personnel and training; and general administrative support. The fourth staff office is the National Aircraft Accident Investigation School (NAAIS). This school develops the curriculum and conducts formal training in the procedures and techniques of aircraft accident investigation. NAAIS manages and operates the school in conjunction with the Federal Aviation Administration with whom a formal inter-agency agreement has been made.

The Bureau of Aviation Safety is composed of three operating Divisions; (1) Technology, (2) Safety Analysis, and (3) Investigation.

Technology Division

The chief of this division plans and supervises the engineering and technical staff assistance in the areas of aerodynamics, structures, powerplants, propellers, instruments, systems, radio, and other electronic aids to navigation and traffic control; flight testing, flight recorders, maintenance, and human engineering, which includes environmental and medical aspects of accident investigation. He reviews proposed Federal Aviation Regulations to develop NTSB comments.

Within the group there are areas that specialize in providing engineering support to major accident teams and plans and conduct special safety studies in engineering areas to ascertain trends, areas which need attention to improve air safety, and develop and propose air safety recommendations.

The Field Offices are assisted by assigning human factors specialists to participate in field investigations when needed. They conduct special human factors studies as related to particular accidents under investigation. They will conduct special safety studies in the human factors area to develop trends to propose recommendations for air safety.

In addition, employees will be provided for special assistance on team conducted accident investigations which present unusual technical problems. They initiate Safety Recommendations in the aircraft airworthiness area and provide technical support in review of proposed safety rule making and International Civil Aviation Organization matters falling in the airworthiness area.

Safety Analysis Division

It is the duty of this division to plan and supervise the Bureau's accident analysis program which includes developing and directing a system for the analysis of all investigative findings to determine the probable cause and prepares and publishes public reports. The division analyzes statistics for the discernment of trends and identifies areas of predictability in aviation safety for publication in the form of Safety Alert Warnings and Bulletins. They compile and maintain comprehensive statistics covering all phases of aircraft accidents and related matters in United States Civil Aviation. Located in this division is a special branch that is solely responsible for establishing projects for accident prevention.

Investigation Division

The division supervises the Bureau's accident investigation activities and co-ordinates the formation of major accident investigation activities and coordinates the formation of major accident teams as accidents occur. This assures the right composition of skills and availability of personnel. The Investigation Division provides overall direction to special studies pertaining to safety in air navigation and the prevention of accidents. The members of this division recommend participation or observation in aircraft accidents that may occur in foreign countries. It develops safety recommendations for transmittal to other government agencies and reviews proposed Federal Aviation Regulations to develop NTSB comments.

One area within this division provides overall supervision to the investigation of all major, catastrophic aircraft accidents through the deployment of centralized teams headed by an Investigator-in-Charge and assisted by Senior Technicians and a Hearing Officer who coordinates and directs the efforts of various personnel and groups assigned to the investigation. The employees maintain liaison with public information officials during the course of accident investigations to assure that appropriate factual information is provided to news media. They provide technical briefings to NTSB members, other government agencies, and various interested groups as a specific investigation may warrant.

Another area develops and monitors accident prevention and safety promotion for designated geographic areas throughout the United States, with emphasis on general aviation. They investigate aircraft accidents and submit reports for all fatal general aviation accidents, air carrier non-fatal accidents or other occurrences falling within an office's geographic jurisdiction. These offices maintain liaison with local Federal Aviation Administration officials regarding accident information and aviation safety and assist in the investigation of aircraft accidents that are investigated by centralized teams by providing additional team members, logistic and administrative support. They promote air safety and accident prevention through discussion with officials of local and state government, other federal agencies, the aviation industry, trade and labor associations, civil groups, and airports. They conduct special air safety studies and initiate safety recommendations based upon investigations of accidents and incidents. The Field Office responds to, or forwards to Bureau headquarters, local public requests for information on air safety matters.

BUREAU OF SURFACE TRANSPORTATION SAFETY

The Bureau is the focal point in the Board's investigation of surface accidents and for advising the Board of probable causes of accidents relating to railroad, marine, highway, and pipeline transportation. It is responsible for developing safety recommendations in these areas.

In the conduct of its work it also assists the Board in conducting public hearings of such accidents and undertakes special studies in surface transportation safety and accident prevention.

CHAPTER
VI
VVV

The Federal
Aviation Administration

Historically the Federal Aviation Administration dates from the Air Commerce Act of 1926 which created the Bureau of Air Commerce in the Department of Commerce. This was the first legislation by the federal government in aviation safety.

The prime reason for the enactment of the Federal Aviation Act in 1958 was to expand upon and improve aviation safety. Under this law the Federal Aviation Agency was created as an independent agency and superseded the Civil Aeronautics Administration and the Airways Modernization Board. In addition to the functions previously performed by these bodies, the Federal Aviation Agency assumed the safety regulatory functions transferred from the Civil Aeronautics Board along with the latter's related personnel and property.

Certain military personnel of the Army, Navy, Air Force, Marines, and Coast Guard are assigned to the Federal Aviation Administration to insure that the interests of national defense are properly safeguarded and that the Federal Aviation Administrator is adequately advised of the needs and individual problems of the armed forces. Thus the maximum practicable correlation of needs and objectives common to not only civil, but also military aviation, is assured. This was further effected by the provision for unified control of all air traffic and for common air navigation facilities adapted to the needs of both civil and military aviation.

Not only are military personnel augmenting the Federal Aviation Administration but also several hundred Federal Aviation Administration employees are serving at military bases to aid the common system. The final objective is the complete operation by the Federal Aviation Administration of all air traffic control facilities.

Another fundamental purpose in establishing the Federal Aviation Agency (Administration) was to reduce the diffusion of federal authority in United States aviation; therefore to strengthen and unify control of the national airspace and the administration of matters relating to safety in flight.

The structure of the Federal Aviation Administration is based upon a clear-cut concept of sound management.

A discussion of the various departments of the Administration are given on the following pages; reference is made to the organizational chart.

THE ADMINISTRATOR

The Administrator of the Federal Aviation Administration is appointed by the President and confirmed by the Senate. He also serves as principal aviation advisor to the Secretary of Transportation.

The Administrator is responsible for the exercise of all powers and the discharge of all duties of the Administration. In so doing, he does not have to submit his decisions for the approval of any individual or group.

The Administrator must be a United States citizen and a civilian and have experience in aviation. He cannot have any pecuniary interest in, or own any stock or bonds in any aeronautical enterprise, nor shall he engage in any other business, vocation, or employment.

The responsibilities of the Administrator as outlined in the Federal Aviation Act of 1958 are:

1. The regulation of air commerce in such manner as to best promote its development and safety and fulfill the requirements of national defense.

2. The promotion, encouragement, and development of civil aeronautics.

3. The control of the use of the navigable airspace of the United States and the regulation of both civil and military operations in such airspace in the interest of the safety and efficiency of both.

4. The consolidation of research and development with respect to air navigation facilities as well as the installation and operation thereof.

5. The development and operation of a common system of air traffic control and navigation for both military and civil aircraft.

The Administrator, the Secretary of Defense, the Administrator of the National Aeronautics and Space Administration and the Secretary of Transportation are directed to exchange information pertaining to their own programs and policies. The Federal Aviation Administrator with the Department of Defense, furthermore, develop plans in the event of war; this being, of course, for emergency conditions.

The selection, employing, and appointing employees subject to Civil Service laws necessary to carry out his responsibilities as well as the conducting of studies of personnel problems inherent to the provisions of the Act are also related duties of the Administrator. He is directed to use the facilities of other civil or military agencies.

The President of the United States may transfer to the Administrator any functions for safe and efficient air traffic control.

The Administration is authorized by the Federal Aviation Act to acquire, establish, and improve air navigation facilities wherever necessary and to operate and maintain these facilities; to publish aviation maps and charts necessary for the safe flight of aircraft and to provide facilities and personnel for the regulation and protection of air traffic. As such, the Federal Aviation Administration issues air traffic rules.

The Administrator may grant exemptions from the requirements of any rule or regulation if he finds it necessary in the public interest.

When it is essential to the defense of the United States, prior notice will be given to the Administrator as soon as practicable, and every effort is so made to consult with him.

In order to conform to policies, no airport construction can be undertaken unless notice is given to the Administrator so that he may advise aviation activities as to the effects upon the use of the airspace.

With regard to developmental planning, the Administrator makes plans and formulates policies with respect to the orderly development and use of the navigable airspace, he supervises developmental work on aircraft as well as testing and evaluating systems, facilities, and devices to meet the needs for safe and efficient air traffic control.

The Administrator publishes written reports on all proceedings and investigations in which formal hearings were held and states his conclusions and decisions. The compilation of these reports constitutes in part the annual report submitted to the President and the Congress.

In the exercise of his duties, the Administrator may delegate to any properly qualified person the functions of the examining, inspecting, and testing necessary to the issuing of airmen, aircraft, and other certificates.

In describing the mission of the Administrator, the Federal Aviation Act states that the Administrator determines and establishes the Administration objectives and priorities and guides the development of and approves long-range plans for achieving Administration objectives. He establishes policy and issues Administration rules and regulations. He approves broad legislative, budgetary, and fiscal proposals and represents the Administration with the President, the Congress, other agencies, the aviation community, and the general public, in addition to taking individual action of major significance. The Administrator exercises control over, evaluates, and takes steps to ensure the adequacy and continued improvement of overall Administration performance.

THE DEPUTY ADMINISTRATOR

The Deputy Administrator is also appointed by the President and confirmed by the Senate. The Deputy Administrator is responsible for the direction and execution of Administration operations and for coordinating the activities of the regions and various technical staff services and offices, as well as the operations of the Bureau of National Capital airports. During the absence of the Administrator, the Deputy serves as Acting Administrator.

The Deputy Administrator must also be a citizen of the United States and is appointed with due regard for his fitness to carry out the duties vested in him. As stated for the Administrator, the Deputy shall be experienced in aviation, have no financial interest in any aeronautical enterprise nor engage in any other business or employment.

The Deputy Administrator participates with and assists the Administrator in the overall planning, direction coordination, and control of Administration programs.

DEPARTMENT OF TRANSPORTATION
FEDERAL AVIATION ADMINISTRATION

OFFICE OF AVIATION MEDICINE

It is the mission of this office to apply aviation medicine knowledge to the safety and promotion of civil aviation. The office is concerned with the solution of medical problems peculiar to civil aviation. It is headed by the Federal Air Surgeon, who develops and recommends to the Administrator the standards, rules and regulations governing the mental and physical fitness of airmen and other persons who support flight activity. In addition to medical certificates of civil airmen and maintenance and processing of their medical records, they designate and train Aviation Medical Examiners. Any licensed physician may apply for this designation and, if qualified, receive Federal Aviation Administration courses in civil aviation medicine and related fields.

In two of its most important medical research projects, the Federal Aviation Administration is exploring the aging processes of the human body, and the physical and psychological environments of air traffic control personnel. In a broad, five-point medical program, the Administration is working in the fields of biophysics, aviation psychology, environmental physiology, clinical examination, and employee health. Furthermore, Federal Aviation Administration is studying the relation of human reaction to jet aircraft characteristics. The effects of ventilation, temperature and humidity on aircrews and passengers at high altitudes are also being studied.

The Federal Aviation Administration's medical staff participates in the investigation of certain fatal air carrier accidents. Their approach involves examination of the operating personnel of the aircraft and conditions aloft. Some of the country's leading forensic pathologists—physicians who specialize in analyzing death from violence—are on the Federal Aviation Administration's consulting staff to assist with the work of accident investigation.

The Office of Aviation Medicine is composed of four divisions, each charged with a specific function for which the Federal Air Surgeon is responsible:

1. The establishment of medical standards for mental and physical fitness of airmen, air traffic controllers, and others whose health affects flight safety.
2. The administration of examination and certification programs which relate to the above mentioned medical standards.
3. The administration of occupational health and industrial hygiene engineering programs.
4. The administration of medical research and educational programs.

OFFICE OF GENERAL AVIATION

This office advises and assists the Administrator in the exercise and performance of his statutory responsibilities in the promotion, encouragement, and development of civil aeronautics as these relate to general aviation. The department fosters understanding of the activities at the Administration by state and local government officials, and by organizations, educational institutions, and associations concerned with aviation. He advises the Administrator, headquarters elements, and regional officials of views of these groups toward Administration policies and programs and of general aviation problems.

This department also serves as a focal point for the development of materials and programs of aviation education for use by school and college administrators, teachers, and students. They also advise Administration officials as to appropriate programs of cooperation with all elements of the educational system.

OFFICE OF CIVIL RIGHTS

This is a relatively new office and provides the Administrator with staff assistance in all areas of civil rights. The director of this office is charged with the responsibility of maintaining equal opportunities for all groups of people seeking FAA employment. He is also responsible for equal opportunity employment by FAA contractors and by recipients of Federal Assistance.

The Office of Civil Rights will investigate any charge of discriminary practice and will create an affirmative civil rights action program.

OFFICE OF PUBLIC AFFAIRS

The members of this office promote, participate in, and conduct coordinated information programs to insure that major programs and policies of the Administration are effectively and consistently presented and that the public, the aviation community, and Federal Aviation Administration employees are kept informed of Administration activities.

OFFICE OF THE GENERAL COUNSEL

The General Counsel has overall responsibility for the legal activities of the Administration and provides legal counsel to all offices and services. The office also conducts the Administration litigation, ruledrafting and interpretation, tort claims, enforcement, legislative, codification, and contract appeals programs.

In cooperation with legal staffs in the Regions, the General Counsel's Office oversees all legal activities of the Administration. These include providing necessary legal advice and services in support of all Federal Aviation Administration functions, as well as responsibility for the legislative program, protection of Administration legal interests in litigation and accident investigations, the legal aspects of rulemaking and the interpretation and enforcement of rules and regulations. This office also deals with other departments and agencies in the formal negotiation of international aviation agreements.

ASSOCIATE ADMINISTRATORS

In addition to the seven staff offices just described, the Federal Aviation Administration is organized into five associate Administrators. They are responsible for the following departments: Plans, Manpower, Operations, Administration, and Engineering and Development.

POLICY DEVELOPMENT AND REVIEW

The Associate Administrator for Policy Development and Review is responsible for the direction of programs for agency planning efforts and policy development within the Federal Aviation Administration. He develops broad policy, objectives, and plans to achieve the Administration's basic missions; prepares long-range forecasts; conducts environmental studies and international aviation affairs.

An office under this Associate Administrator conducts various economic analysis relating to the function of the FAA. They are responsible for preparing investment analysis and in turn recommending amounts of aviation charges, such as the recent international transportation tax for all passengers departing the United States. The forecast division of this office conducts national, regional, and terminal forecasts for other departments relating to offices such as; Airport Services, Air Traffic Services, and Flight Standards.

Other employees are responsible for advising on the goals, policies, and objectives of our national aviation system. They create the National Aviation System Plan and integrate this system into planning for airports, airspace, and regulations.

An important feature is to develop policy for the evaluation and control of aircraft noise, exhaust emission and sonic boom. They also seek to develop standards for human response and structural response to sonic boom and noise, combined with this they forward to the proper agency for research and development those standards that are developed. The office is also charged with measuring those factors which play upon the environment.

Another area of vital concern to the Federal Aviation Administration is in international aviation affairs. The Administrator is assisted in achieving U.S. and Administration objectives in international aviation affairs through:

1. The formulation and coordination of policy plans, programs, and related matters affecting the international activities of the Administration.

2. The provision of guidance and support to all Administration elements having international responsibilities.

3. The overall evaluation of Administration programs and activities in meeting such objectives.

4. The administration of aviation assistance programs conducted by the Administration.

One main activity carried on in cooperation with the State Department's International Cooperation Administration (ICA), is the formation of Civil Aviation Technical Assistance Groups to provide technical assistance to other countries. There are usually about 33 of these groups operating worldwide at the invitation of the governments concerned. They act as consultants on safety matters, supervise construction and modernization of airports and the installation of airways and navigation facilities, and provide legal and organizational assistance.

Another joint project carried out by the Federal Aviation Administration and International Cooperation Administration is the training of foreign nationals. Every year hundreds of men from many of the nations in the free world come to the United States for training in all phases of civil aviation. Courses ranging from six weeks to eighteen months are given these students in subjects such as advanced flying techniques, air traffic control, maintenance and repair of air navigation facilities, airways communications, airplane and engine mechanics, aviation law and airport management. These foreign technicians are also given practical experience working with the Federal Aviation Administration, the commercial airlines, manufacturers, engineering firms and factory service schools before returning to their homelands.

In the field of international aviation relations, this office is the focal point of contact with the International Civil Aviation Organization (ICAO) of which the United States is one of 86 member countries. Through ICAO, international practices and safety procedures are standardized so that pilots everywhere in the world operate under the same set of rules. The Federal Aviation Administration, on behalf of the State Department, provides the full-time services of the United States Member of the ICAO Air Navigation Commission in Montreal, and the United States Civil Representative on the NATO Committee for European Airspace Coordination (CEAC) in Paris.

The office also furnishes technical advice in the negotiation of agreements involving intergovernmental exchange of commercial air rights, and the recognition of airworthiness of aircraft manufactured abroad. Additionally, this office is the center for the exchange of civil aeronautical information with foreign governments.

MANPOWER

The Associate Administrator for Manpower directs a program for personnel management, manpower requirements, training, career development, and labor relations.

The members of this office ensure that the Administration has a modern, progressive personnel management program, which meets effectively and efficiently the needs of management and employees. The main function of this office is to develop and coordinate personnel programs and develop policy in this area. They are responsible for wage and salary administration as well as position classification, work weeks, hours on duty, and special allowances. Another division works out various employee benefits such as; awards, employee performance, insurance, counseling, recreation, and leave administration.

The highly specialized nature of the Federal Aviation Administration's work requires a program of continuous training at established Federal Aviation Administration schools and by correspondence for both management and technical personnel.

In the technical areas, training falls into three major categories: air traffic control, facilities, and flight standards.

Although considerable training is conducted in the Regions, in Washington and at the National Aviation Facilities Experimental Center, the principal activity is centered at the Federal Aviation Administration school at the Aeronautical Center located at Oklahoma City, Oklahoma. More than 100 courses of study, both beginning and advanced, are offered with some on a continuous schedule and others periodically, these courses range from introductory studies in air traffic control to the training of experienced pilots and technicians to meet the Federal Aviation Administration requirements.

As in any large company a good relationship is necessary between the employees and the corporation. A government agency is no exception to that basic management principle. Therefore the Federal Aviation Administration has a department whose responsibility is to create various employee benefits such as awards for outstanding service, employee performance, personal insurance of all types, counseling, leave administration and different types of recreational activities.

AIR TRAFFIC MANAGEMENT AND AIRWAY FACILITIES

The Associate Administrator for Air Traffic Management and Airway Facilities coordinates the direction of programs for flight safety, air traffic control, airspace utilization, airport development, and the installation, operation, and maintenance of Air Traffic Control and Air Navigation facilities.

The members of this office provide for the management of civil and military air traffic in the navigable airspace by developing and recommending national policies and establishing national programs, regulations, standards, and procedures for management of the airspace, operation of air navigation and communications systems and facilities; separation and control of, and flight assistance to, air traffic; provides for the security control of air traffic to meet the national defense requirements; operates the Administration national and international flight information and cartographic program.

They assist the Administrator in developing the plans, standards, and systems for control of air traffic.

Air traffic control is concerned with (1) keeping aircraft safely separated while operating in controlled space: on the ground, during take-off and ascent, enroute, and during approach and landing; and (2) providing pre-flight and in-flight assistance services to all pilots.

The first is accomplished under a highly specialized system of control procedures from two types of facilities: Air Route Traffic Control Centers and Airport Traffic Control Towers. Centers supervise the operation of aircraft flying under Instrument Flight Rules (IFR) in controlled air space; Towers supervise the operation of aircraft on and in the vicinity of airports. This separation is achieved by an extensive system of radar and radio communications. Short-range radar is used by Towers to control arriving and departing aircraft. Long-range radar, which extends outward to 200 miles and upward to 60,000 feet, is used by Centers to control enroute traffic. As an economy measure, many of the radars used by air traffic controllers serve a dual purpose in as much as they are used by the military in the air defense radar warning network. Radar control requires direct, instant voice—radio communication between control personnel and pilots.

The second major function is carried out by a third air traffic facility; namely, the Flight Service Station. Although these Stations have no control functions of their own, they are of paramount importance in air traffic service. They provide pre-flight weather briefings and in-flight following service to any pilot who requests them; they broadcast local and area weather reports, changes in radio frequencies, operating conditions at certain airports, temporary airport restrictions and similar notices of interest to airmen. One of the Stations' most important duties is the search and rescue operation put into effect when an aircraft is overdue at its reporting Station or destination; another is the assistance they give to aircraft in difficulty, orienting the pilot and directing him to an emergency airport.

The three facilities—Centers, Towers, and Stations—are linked by thousands of miles of teletype and interphone lines. Their personnel are in constant touch with one another, with aircraft aloft and with the operations offices of the military services and the scheduled airlines. Federal Aviation Administration employees are assigned to various units of the Air Defense Command, Strategic Air Command and Tactical Air Command to assure continuous liaison between the Federal Aviation Administration and the Department of Defense.

Electronic computers have been installed in the busier Air Route Traffic Control Centers in the Eastern States and comprise the world's only computer-to-computer air traffic control network. The essential facts of a pilot's flight plan are fed into these machines, which automatically calculate his estimated time of arrival over designated check points within the Center's area of responsibility. The machines also print this information on flight progress strips, which are placed in front of controllers who use them for separating traffic in their individual sectors.

Efficient use of the navigable airspace by the various types of users is a principal concern of the Air Traffic Service. Since January, 1959, many areas previously restricted to military use only have been abolished, others reduced in size, and still others placed at the disposal of civil aircraft when military maneuvers are not in progress. These actions have resulted in the return to the public of some 25,000 square miles of airspace.

A related activity is the issuing of rules and regulations governing air traffic and noise reduction in the immediate vicinity of terminal areas.

While progress has been made recently in installing new equipment, the problem of designing and engineering a comprehensive, modern system for optimum airspace utilization is far from solved. An intensive review by a distinguished panel of systems engineers called Project Beacon, has concluded that many essential improvements can be made. New programs are being set in motion to modernize the present network into an up-to-date system.

There is a group responsible for promoting safety of flight of civil aircraft in air commerce by assuring: airworthiness of aircraft, competence of airmen, adequacy of flight procedures and air operations, evaluation of in-flight facility performance for compliance with prescribed standards, effective development, utilization and maintenance of the Administration's aircraft fleet.

The Flight Standards Service is responsible for one of the major program areas of the Federal Aviation Administration. To promote aviation safety, they develop rules and establish standards governing the flight safety program activities carried out in the geographic regions.

Their functions can be separated into the following six areas.

AIRMEN. A key objective of the FAA is the development of safety minded airmen. An airman must have a certificate and an appropriate FAA rating to work in any capacity in an aircraft engaged in air commerce. Certificated airmen must meet required minimum physical requirements, possess aeronautical knowledge, and demonstrate certain skills pertaining to the certificate and rating. In 1965, the Flight Standards program activities included certificating some 9,400 student pilots; 38,000 private pilots; 23,000 commercial pilots; and 5,200 airline transport pilots. As for aviation mechanics, some 3,450 presently hold inspection authorizations enabling them to perform aircraft airworthiness inspections. The Federal Aviation Regulations provide for the original issuance and annual renewal of these authorizations, most important to overall maintenance and continued airworthiness.

AIRCRAFT. The safety minded airman program is complemented by a safe aircraft program. To be used in air commerce, new models of aircraft, aircraft powerplants, and propellers must meet minimum standards of design, workmanship, construction, and performance prescribed by the Flight Standards Service.

SAFETY RULES. As part of its mission to promote aviation safety, Flight Standards Service continually reviews its rules, regulations, and standards in view of changing conditions created by the dynamic growth of aviation. The types of rulemaking for which this office is responsible includes safety rules prescribing the certification standards that airmen and aircraft must meet, airworthiness directives to correct material deficiencies encountered in service, and technical standards.

ENFORCEMENT. In addition to establishing aviation safety rules and standards, the Flight Standards program also involves responsibility for enforcing these rules and standards. In an average year, in excess of 4,000 alleged violations of the Federal Aviation Regulations are investigated and reported upon by the field inspectors.

FLIGHT INSPECTION. The Flight Standards Service is responsible for the program of systematic inspection of air navigation and traffic control facilities. The facilities inspected include visual aids such as runway identification lights, visual glide slopes, and approach lights. The aircraft maintained by the Administration for this purpose carry aloft special equipment to measure the accuracy of signals emitted by the ground radio facilities. The air navigation facilities utilized by both civilian and military aircraft are flight inspected from just above the ground surface to an altitude of 45,000 feet. Development and certification of instrument flight procedures, instrument approach procedures, and holding and departure routes are continuing demands of a dynamic and rapidly growing industry.

ACCIDENTS. Flight Standards field inspectors participate in the investigation of aircraft accidents. When an accident occurs, responsibility for determining the probable cause rests with the National Transportation Safety Board. The FAA must participate with the National Transportation Safety Board in the investigation of accidents because of the Administration's responsibilities; however, the NTSB alone determines the probable cause of an accident.

This service establishes standards for certifying the safety of the entire air transportation system, including the airworthiness of aircraft and parts, the flight competence of airmen, the accuracy of navigation aids and the licensing of flight schools, ground schools, and repair stations.

Flight safety inspectors ride in the cockpits of airline airplanes on a spot check basis to observe routine flight operations. They also supervise the maintenance and operations policies and activities of all air carriers; periodically check the competence of pilots and mechanics; and inspect navigation aids to assure their constant operating reliability.

This Regional and systemwide surveillance involves the establishment, revision and enforcement of the Federal Aviation Regulations which the Federal Aviation Administration originates. These regulations affect the design, manufacture, and certification of aircraft and engines, and establish qualifications for pilot, navigator, flight engineer, mechanic and airplane dispatcher, all of whom must be certificated. A program for recodification and simplification of these rules of the air (some originated in 1938) is being undertaken.

An important tool in the Flight Standards program is the Federal Aviation Administration's fleet of airplanes. Among these are the aircraft that check navigation aids along the Federal airways at three levels; low, under 14,500 feet; intermediate, from 14,500 to 24,000; and high, above 24,000; to insure accuracy and adequacy of these services to airmen. These check airplanes are airborne electronic laboratories equipped with devices for fast, frequent, and economical checking of radio ranges, instrument landing systems, communications systems, and other aids to flight.

One office assures the appropriate acquisition, construction, and installation of air navigation, air traffic control, and aeronautical communication facilities of the National Airspace System; and to provide for the procurement of real and personal property, transportation and services in support of all Administration programs; and the management of real and personal property and transportation.

This office fosters and promotes the development of a national system of airports as an element of the overall Federal Aviation Administration National Airspace System.

It is the staff function of this department for establishing standards, specifications, and guides for planning, designing, constructing, maintaining, protecting, and providing for ground safety at civil airports. This Airport Service is the principal staff element of the Administration with respect to National airports system planning, as an integral part of the Administration's National Airspace System. It also serves a staff function in dealing with the Federal Aid Airport Program, conveyance of land for public airport purposes, records on the Nation's airports, and compliance with terms of grant agreements.

They provide for technical representation at meetings of organizations concerned with national standards and recommended practices relating to airports. The department cooperates with and operates within policy guidelines established by the Office of International Aviation Affairs in representing the Administration's interests in international airports matters.

The Airport Service provides guidance to regions for promoting defense and emergency readiness and damage control at civil airports. They develop national plans for emergency management of civil airports and for the direction of Federal activities for their restoration after attack, including determining need for equipment, material, and supplies.

ADMINISTRATION

The Associate Administrator for Administration directs programs for administrative management, security, procurement, supply system management, and property management. He serves as the office manager for the entire Federal Aviation Administration.

The work of this office is to promote operational effectiveness throughout the Administration by developing, implementing, and evaluating the Admistration management methods, internal controls, administrative systems and organizational structure.

The major function of this office is the efficient utilization of the Federal Aviation Administration's money and men. The office maintains fiscal accounts and directs the audit program, conducts studies of organization, methods of work and standards of performance and recommends or institutes improvements in these fields. It is concerned with the procurement of services and their utilization, as well as with the development of reports and statistics on program accomplishments and deficiencies. Other administrative functions include records management, historical and library services, publications planning, duplicating, mail and aeronautical information services.

Another office ensures that the Administration budgetary needs are accurately identified and defined and that they are effectively presented to the Bureau of the Budget and Congressional Committees. The members of this office see that funds appropriated to the Administration are effectively utilized. A principal element of this office is an independent analysis of program requirements, and the furnishing of advice and assistance to the Administrator, Budget Review Board, and other Administration officials on budgetary matters. This office develops and recommends the overall Administration policies, standards, systems, and procedures pertaining to the Administration's five year budget programs, budget estimates and justifications, fiscal programs, allotments and apportionments, and staffing authorizations.

The main function of one department is to advise the Administrator on the best possible methods of procurement and the accountability of the material. This office is responsible for developing a comprehensive logistics and procurement policy. A division within the office governs the use of real and personal property owned by the FAA as well as telecommunications services. They are responsible for all motor vehicles of the department and for the allocation of space within FAA buildings. Another division deals strictly with all contracts entered into by the FAA.

Employees also respond to requests for studies of internal programs and how well they satisfy the Federal Aviation Administration's goals. The study would be for the purpose of determining how well the Administration's programs are organized and operated. Recommendations are made directly to the Administrator for changes in program emphasis or resources. Examples of typical assignments would be for them to study the Office of Aviation Medicine, the Flight Standards Service, or an FAA Regional Office. The nature of the studies make it a very flexible arm to the Administrator for use at his discretion to work in areas where he would like to become better informed.

The Director of this office assures the highest possible standards of ethical, trustworthy and nondiscriminatory conduct among employees and representatives; nondiscriminatory practices by contractors and sponsors' contractors and related organizations; personnel security; security of information and property; and the conduct of investigations to meet the needs of the Federal Aviation Administration.

This office also investigates criminal violations of statutes under FAA jurisdiction and assures that the Administration has a professional fact finding investigative program which effectively and economically meets the needs of management, excluding investigations of aviation accidents.

One division located within this office is the Air Operations Security division. They are responsible for the protection of air transportation against criminal acts such as bombings and hijackings. They have the authority to implement preventive methods to deter criminal acts.

An office reporting to the Associate Administrator for Administration provides independent advisory services to the administrator and other top management and operating officials to assure prudent use and proper protection of resources, confirms the reliability of financial data for integrity of business transactions, identifies opportunities for improvement in operational economy and efficiency and appraises conformity with applicable laws, regulations, and policy.

The members of this group provide for audits of projects sponsored by public agencies under the Federal Aid Airport Program and examine financial records and advise regarding the financial capability of air carriers.

The Office of Headquarters Operations provides under a single managerial responsibility the personnel, accounting, plant operation, and other support services for Administration headquarters elements, and as assigned or agreed upon, support services for other Administration elements in the Washington area.

This office was established on July 1, 1963, to provide administrative support to the Washington headquarters of the Federal Aviation Administration. The administrative service assumed included building management, supply, publishing and graphics, printing, and data processing.

ENGINEERING AND DEVELOPMENT

The Associate Administrator for Engineering and Development is directed to coordinate research programs for the development of the National Airspace System. He directs the research into aircraft and associated environment. He is responsible for the management of installation of designated NAS and ATC subsystem elements.

This office sees to it that the air navigation, air traffic control, and aeronautical communications system, facilities, and equipment of the National Airspace System function continuously at acceptable levels of performance, and the maintenance of the system and associated environmental facilities is efficient, economical, and responsive to operational needs, the requirements of aviation safety, and national defense.

The members of this office perform or arrange for research, development and engineering required to analyze, formulate, and design the improvement and modernization of the National Airspace System. They provide criteria for implementation of NAS systems, procedures, and equipment for use in Administration or Administration-approved activities.

This Office has been assigned the duty of developing programs for aircraft and systems research, as well as developing technical information for improved safety rules and regulations.

The National Airspace System Program is designed to improve and develop the airspace system. Based generally on recommendations of Project Beacon, presidentially requested in 1961 and elaborated by FAA's System Design Team, the NAS plan is progressively updated to keep with technological advances and national needs.

There are two areas of aviation which are causing considerable research and experimentation. They are at the very ends of the air transport spectrum; short-haul air transport and supersonic air transport.

The Federal Aviation Administration has very strong feelings regarding the importance of short-haul air transportation. They are undertaking a project to research practical ways to move large numbers of people over short geographical distances. The Northeast Corridor of the United States is a prime example. The traffic flow between Boston, New York, Philadelphia, and Washington has already resulted in the Civil Aeronautics Board holding hearings regarding the economics of short-haul movements. The project includes determining the capabilities of Vertical and Short Take-off and Land (V/STOL) aircraft.

The second area of research involves the highly controversial supersonic transport. Research is being conducted for the development of a supersonic transport and to coordinate the entry of foreign SST's into the United States aviation system. The origin of the SST program started in August of 1961 when Congress provided for 11 million dollars for the first year of a two year study. In the late 1960's, as a result of protests by those concerned with preserving the environment, the Congress of the United States refused to provide further funding. The FAA is continuing studies and plans in the area of commercial supersonic flight for the purpose of eliminating areas of concern regarding supersonic flight over populated areas and concerns that this type of flight will affect the environmental balance.

The National Aviation Facilities Experimental Center provides, operates, and administers a national test center comprised of experimental standard operating facilities and environment for the use and benefit of Administration research and development programs; to perform technical and operational test and evaluation of aviation concepts, procedures, facilities, and equipment; and to perform other program and support functions as assigned by the Administrator.

The Center has the task of modernizing the country's air transportation system to keep pace with the increasing air traffic volume. To accomplish this, four major technical systems are under development. Operations in each of the four major systems are designed to produce safer, more efficient air transportation. These systems are: air traffic control and navigation; aviation weather; aircraft safety research; and airports.

Testing and evaluation operations in these systems are carried out at the National Aviation Facilities Experimental Center located at the site of the former Naval Air Station near Atlantic City, New Jersey.

Research projects now under way cut across the four major technical program areas. Several are directed toward analysis of enroute air traffic flow and delay, and terminal traffic flow and delay. Special studies are being made of conditions in high density air traffic areas to determine what additional or revised traffic control procedures may be needed to expedite traffic movement and reduce the potential for mid-air collision. Other projects concern effects of aircraft operational characteristics on air traffic control, design of traffic control facilities, and human factor analysis related to air traffic control facilities. Several research projects deal with air traffic measurement and forecasts, and procedures for identification of aircraft.

The Federal Aviation Administration research and development effort grows continuously as engineers and scientists pioneer in known and new fields of technology and science to keep pace with the needs of aviation in this new but fast growing jet age. The Federal Aviation Administration's Systems Research and Development Service, while most pressed to resolve the critical immediate problems of congested airways and overworked manual facilities, is ever mindful of tomorrow's total aviation needs. Research and development activities are planned and conducted accordingly.

One of the most important installations at NAFEC is the simulation laboratory, where the techniques of graphic and dynamic simulation, machine computation, and data reduction are applied to air traffic control and air navigation problems. Each new system or device is thoroughly tested under simulated conditions. All Federal Aviation Administration testing under actual flight conditions is conducted at NAFEC.

The airfield has three runways; the longest extends 10,000 feet and is 200 feet wide. Two smaller runways measure 6,000 by 150 feet, and 5,000 by 150 feet. In addition to the control tower, there are two large hangars and over 100 other structures. NAFEC's buildings enclose more than 750,000 square feet of floor space.

The field activities and Regions of the FAA are located and function as follows:

Aeronautical Center

The Aeronautical Center is located at Will Rogers World Airport in Oklahoma City.

The Center has been located in Oklahoma City since 1946, and is the FAA's major logistical and service center. It serves as the base for maintenance and modification of FAA aircraft, training of agency personnel, supply of material, keeping of records for airmen and aircraft, and medical research in civil aviation. Today, the Center represents an investment of more than 45 million dollars in buildings, additional millions of dollars in equipment, employs 4100 people and brings nearly 50 million dollars into Oklahoma annually in payroll.

Among the various divisions within the Aeronautical Center are:

1. The FAA Academy, which is the agency's principal source of aviation technical knowledge. The Academy offers directed study as well as resident courses for specialists who man airport control towers, air route traffic control centers, and flight service stations. It also trains the engineers and technicians who install and maintain the nation's aerial navigation, traffic control, and communications equipment.

   Through its Flight Standards Training Branch, the Academy provides initial and recurrent training for their air carrier, general operations and maintenance inspectors.

2. The Civil Aeromedical Institute conducts research to identify human factor causes of aircraft accidents, prevent future accidents, and to make those accidents which do occur, more survivable.

   CAMI also operates the program for medical certification of all civil airmen. This involves reviewing about 500,000 reports of physical examinations each year.

   Aeromedical Research and Education programs study such problems as fire protection, hypoxia, stress analysis, sonic boom effects, noise, vision, disorientation, drug and alcohol effects, fatigue, time zone effects, and cockpit design.

3. The Flight Standards Technical Division handles a broad range of civil aviation operational and safety support activities. The span of effort extends from writing airmen examinations and developing airworthiness standards, through the keeping of airmen and aircraft records, to identification of problems affecting aviation safety.

4. Flight inspection of the National Airspace System is conducted by the National Flight Inspection Division. Utilizing a fleet of both low altitude piston and high altitude jet and jet-prop aircraft equipped with special

electronic gear, NFID continually checks the ground-based electronic navigation, approach and landing equipment throughout the nation.

5. Additional division at the Aeronautical Center include the Procurement Division, the Aircraft Services Base, the Data Services Division, the FAA Management Training School, the Transportation Safety Institute, and the FAA Supply Depot.

Regional Offices

The Federal Aviation Administration Regional Offices serve as an extension of the national headquarters and solve the day to day problems that arise in the regions. The Regional Offices plan the functions that will occur in the region such as; statistics, navigational aids, regional man power, and the administering of examinations and inspections. They are responsible for the standardization of maintenance and engineering practices of the airlines within the region.

The regions have offices in major cities who conduct operations dealing with Air Carriers and General Aviation.

There are nine domestic continental Regional Officers.

1. New England Region located at Boston, Massachusetts.

2. Eastern Region located at New York, New York.

3. Southern Region located at Atlanta, Georgia.

4. Great Lakes Region located at Chicago, Illinois.

5. Central Region located at Kansas City, Missouri.

6. Southwest Region located at Fort Worth, Texas.

7. Rocky Mountain Region located at Denver, Colorado.

8. Western Region located at Los Angeles, California.

9. Northwestern Region located at Seattle, Washington.

In addition to the above nine Regional Offices, there are three international Regional Offices.

1. Alaskan Region located at Anchorage, Alaska.

2. Pacific-Asia Region located at Honolulu, Hawaii.

3. Europe, Africa and Middle East Region located at Brussels, Belgium.

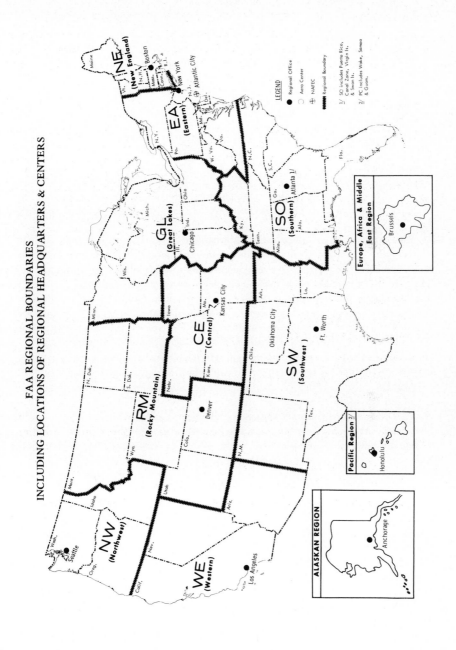

FAA REGIONAL BOUNDARIES
INCLUDING LOCATIONS OF REGIONAL HEADQUARTERS & CENTERS

NE (New England) — Boston

EA (Eastern) — New York, Atlantic City

GL (Great Lakes) — Chicago

SO (Southern) — Atlanta 1/

CE (Central) — Kansas City

SW (Southwest) — Oklahoma City, Ft. Worth

RM (Rocky Mountain) — Denver

NW (Northwest) — Seattle

WE (Western) — Los Angeles

LEGEND
● Regional Office
○ Aero Center
✛ NAFEC
▬ Regional Boundary

1/ SO includes Puerto Rico, Canal Zone, Virgin Is. & Swan Is.
2/ PC includes Wake, Samoa & Guam.

Europe, Africa & Middle East Region — Brussels

Pacific Region 2/ — Honolulu

ALASKAN REGION — Anchorage

VII

vvv

Safety in Air Transportation

The regulation of aviation safety rests primarily in the hands of the Federal Aviation Administration of the United States Federal Government. It is complete and encompasses all aspects of aviation safety from the proper registration of aircraft, the regulatory functions of air traffic control, and the certification of aircraft and airmen, to the investigation of aircraft accidents. The basis of these rules are found in Titles V, VI, and VII of the Federal Aviation Act.

The registration of all aircraft nationally is required and it is unlawful for any person to operate, in air navigation, any aircraft that is not properly registered by its owner; or to even operate any aircraft within the United States which is not eligible for registration. The registration requirements of aircraft are not too unlike the registration requirements for automobiles. However, whereby automobiles are registered in various individual states, aircraft are registered nationally with the federal government by the Federal Aviation Administration. This makes for greater standardization and easier control. An aircraft in the United States may be eligible for registration if it is owned by a citizen of the United States and if it is not registered under the laws of any other country.

Certain public aircraft of the Local, State, and Federal government are also registered but military aircraft are not included.

It is the responsibility of the aircraft owner to see that the aircraft is legally registered. After making the necessary application to the Federal Aviation Administration the aircraft owner is issued a certificate of registration. Therefore, any registration certificate may be suspended or revoked by the Federal Aviation Administration for any cause which may render the aircraft ineligible for registration.

The issued certificate is conclusive evidence of nationality for international purposes, but not in any proceeding under the laws of the United States. Registration shall not be evidence of ownership of an aircraft in any proceedings in which the ownership is in issue.

It is the responsibility of the Federal Aviation Administration to establish reasonable rules and regulations for the registration and identification, of not only aircraft, but also aircraft engines, propellers and appliances in the interest of safety; these items must not be used in violation of any rule or regulation of the Federal Aviation Administration.

The Federal Aviation Administration maintains a system for recording any conveyance which affects title to any civil aircraft in the United States as well as any lease, mortgage, equipment trust or contract of conditional sale.

All conveyances or instruments of ownership must be valid and properly recorded in the office of the Federal Aviation Administration.

The regulations state clearly the limitation of security owners liability in that no person having an interest in, or title to, any civil aircraft shall be liable by reason of his interest or ownership for any injury or death of persons as well as damage or loss of property on the surface of the earth caused by such aircraft, unless the aircraft was in the actual control of the owner at the time of the injury, damage, or death that was caused.

In the public interest the Federal Aviation Administration provides for the issuance of dealer's aircraft registration certificates and for their use in the connection with aircraft eligible for registration by persons engaged in the business of manufacturing, distributing or the selling of aircraft.

This system of recording aircraft ownership is very much like that of the system of recording deeds.

The major change in the safety regulation of aviation was brought about with the passage of the Federal Aviation Act of 1958 in which the Federal Aviation Administration was created to supersede the Civil Aeronautics Administration. Unlike the Civil Aeronautics Administration which was in the Department of Commerce, the Federal Aviation Agency was organized with independent status responsible only to the President of the United States. With the passage of the Department of Transportation Act in 1966, the organization was transferred to that department.

Title VI of the Federal Aviation Act contains the principle substantive provisions relating to safety regulation in effect presently.

Prior to the passage of the Federal Aviation Act, in 1958, the Civil Aeronautics Act divided the authority for aviation safety between the Civil Aeronautics Board and the Civil Aeronautics Administration; the Board legislated safety rules and the executive responsibilities rested upon the Civil Aeronautics Administration.

The Federal Aviation Act divested the Civil Aeronautics Board of its former safety rule--making powers and transferred these to the Federal Aviation Administration where all aviation safety is administered by the Federal Aviation Administration. The National Transportation Safety Board possesses jurisdiction to review certain actions taken by the Federal Aviation Administration.

The Administrator of the Federal Aviation Administration has the power, as well as the duty, to promote safety of flight of civil aircraft in air commerce by prescribing and constantly revising, to keep us up to date, the various safety regulations governing the standard for aviation safety.

These regulations of the Federal Aviation Administration include the following:

A. The minimum standards governing the design, materials, workmanship, construction, performance, inspection, servicing and overhaul of aircraft, engines, propellers and appliances as well as the equipment and facilities for such inspection and production of aircraft to determine safety and the periods of time for inspection and overhaul.

B. The rules and regulations affecting the reserve supply of fuel to be carried in flight.

C. The rules in the interest of aviation safety which cover the maximum number of hours or periods of service which airmen may perform in a given period of time; such as daily, weekly and monthly.

The regulation of safety includes all other practices and procedures connected with the national security and safety of aircraft that the Federal Aviation Administration may find to be necessary.

Exemptions may be granted from the requirements of any safety regulation if the Federal Aviation Administration may find it to be in the public interest to do so.

In prescribing the many rules and regulations, the Federal Aviation Administration must give full consideration to the duty resting upon the air carriers to perform their services with the highest possible degree of safety in the interest of flying public.

This, in a manner of speaking, has placed the burden of responsibility upon the air carriers in that as a public service industry it is their obligation to maintain the highest degree of aviation safety in airline operation.

The regulation of aviation safety is controlled through the issuance of various safety certificates by the Federal Aviation Administration. There are five major types of these certificates:

1. Airman.
2. Aircraft.
3. Air Carrier Operating.
4. Air Navigation Facility.
5. Air Agency.

The first are *Airman Certificates.* The Federal Aviation Administration requires the certification of all persons engaged as an airman in connection with aircraft. Airmen are pilots, mechanics, traffic controllers and the like. The Federal Aviation Administration establishes the requirements, both mental and physical, in the testing of airmen to determine their qualifications before the necessary Airman Certificate is issued. Any person is eligible to hold an Airman Certificate if he properly qualifies, however, the Federal Aviation Administration may prohibit or restrict the issuance of an Airman Certificate to aliens or may make such issuance dependent on the terms of the reciprocal agreements entered into with the foreign home government of the person involved.

For a more detailed description of the Airman Certificate, the reader is directed to the current Federal Aviation Regulations governing Airman Certificates.

Aircraft Certificates include those for Type, Production, and Airworthiness. Any interested person may file with the Federal Aviation Administration an application and subsequently be granted a Type certificate for an aircraft,

aircraft engine, propeller or appliance after the proper investigation and inspection has been made.

The Federal Aviation Administration may, and usually does, require the applicant to conduct tests in the interest of aviation safety, including flight tests as well as tests of materials. If the Federal Aviation Administration finds that the aircraft, or other part, meets the minimum standards for safety, then the Type Certificate will be issued. In the process of obtaining this certificate, the applicant must submit all technical drawings and any other data as well as a workable model to demonstrate the safety of the design. This inspection on the part of the Federal Aviation Administration is very costly and time consuming and is as complete technically as is humanly possible. The expense for this is borne by the designer or applicant for the Type Certificate and this process usually takes a long period of time. In the case of the first commercial jet transport it was a matter of several years.

No aircraft, aircraft engine, propeller or aircraft appliance can be produced and sold to the public if there has not been a Type Certificate issued. This certificate is granted to the separate and exacting design and as such may be transferable or sold from any individual or corporation to another.

If at any time during production the design is altered or improved in any way, then the Federal Aviation Administration must approve and either amend the original Type Certificate, or in the case of a major change, issue a new Type Certificate. This is what occurs when a new model aircraft of the same basic design is produced.

An aircraft or aircraft part cannot simply be produced. In order to do so the manufacturers must hold a valid Production Certificate issued by the Federal Aviation Administration. The Federal Aviation Administration will inspect the facilities and other equipment to determine if the producer can satisfactorily produce exact duplicates of the aircraft or part for which a Type Certificate is in effect. The Federal Aviation Administration makes various inspections and tests of the manufacturer holding a Production Certificate to assure that the products being made continues to conform with the Type Certificate. This is being continually done in the interest of aviation safety to protect the public and is a complex system in the case of a large complicated structure such as a jet transport aircraft or its major component parts.

The certification of the type design and of the producer would appear sufficient to insure safety. It is complete, that is, until the aircraft is sold to the public. From then on it becomes the responsibility of the registered owner of the aircraft to see that it is maintained in an airworthy condition. Therefore, all aircraft being flown for any reason must have been issued, and currently hold, a valid Airworthiness Certificate issued by the Federal Aviation Administration. If the aircraft is found to be in a safe condition for operation, the Airworthiness Certificate will be granted.

This certificate must be in the aircraft and displayed in plain view at all times of operation. Furthermore, the Federal Aviation Administration may prescribe the type of service in which the aircraft may be used, as well as such other conditions in the interest of safety.

The Airworthiness Certificate is valid for a period of twelve months; before the expiration of this time it is the responsibility of the owner to have the aircraft properly inspected and the certificate renewed. This is generally known as "relicensing" of aircraft and insures that the necessary maintenance and repair, as are necessary, will be performed before the Airworthiness Certificate is reissued.

In some respects, although to a much greater detail, the Airworthiness Certificate of civil aircraft is equal to the inspection sticker on automobiles that is required by most municipalities and states in the country.

No fee is charged for the issuance of the Airworthiness Certificate, however, it will cost the owner to have the aircraft serviced, prepared and made ready for the inspection.

Many non-Federal Aviation Administration persons, who have the adequate experience and qualifications, are designated by the Federal Aviation Administration to conduct this inspection. They are persons who own, operate or are employed by an aircraft service company that is itself approved by the Federal Aviation Administration. The persons designated will also be certificated airmen holding an Airframe and Powerplant Mechanic Certificate.

The third significant aviation safety certificate, issued by the Federal Aviation Administration, is the *Air Carrier Operating Certificate* which is issued to all air carriers transporting the public for hire. This includes the Non-certificated and Supplemental air carriers as well as the certificated air carriers.

The Air Carrier Operating Certificate is granted in the interest of safety by the Federal Aviation Administration and is not to be in any way confused with the economic authority of the Certificate of Convenience and Necessity issued by the Civil Aeronautics Board.

A certificated air carrier may possess a valid Certificate of Convenience and Necessity but it cannot operate its aircraft until it has a current valid Air Carrier Operating Certificate.

Each such certificate will prescribe the terms, conditions and the limitations as are reasonably necessary to assure safety in air transportation; furthermore, it will specify the points to and from which, as well as the airways over which, the air carrier is permitted to operate.

At any time that the air carrier enlarges its route system and serves new airport cities or introduces a new type of aircraft, its Air Carrier Operating Certificate must be amended after proper inspection and approval by the Federal Aviation Administration.

Safety regulation concerning air carriers recognizes the duty and responsibility of the individual air carrier and charges them with conducting their aviation activities in the highest degree consistent with safety in the public interest.

It is a function of the Federal Aviation Administration to make inspections of airline aircraft not only for the purpose of determining that a proper level of safety is being maintained but also the purpose of advising and cooperating with the air carriers in the inspection and maintainance of their equipment.

With regard to the fourth aviation safety certificate the Federal Aviation Administration has power to inspect, classify and rate any facility of air navigation available for the use of civil aircraft as to its suitability for such use. If found to be adequate for the needs of safety, a certificate is issued as an *Air Navigation Facility*. Landing areas, lights, radio-directional apparatus and like equipment used in the navigation of aircraft, are air navigation facilities.

The fifth and final type of aviation safety certificate issued by the Federal Aviation Administration, in control of aviation safety, is the *Air Agency Rating certificate*. Representative of air agencies are flight and ground training schools as well as aircraft maintenance and repair facilities.

Before a flight school, for example, can be awarded an Air Agency Certificate it must possess, in good safe condition, the necessary flight equipment, the proper maintenance facilities and personnel as well as certificated instructors. Not only must they have adequate facilities including classrooms and teaching equipment but also their curriculum for flight and ground courses must be approved by the Federal Aviation Administration.

A certificated aircraft repair agency must demonstrate that it has the proper tools, shops, equipment and personnel to adequately repair an aircraft or engine commensurate with the best practices of safety.

Regardless of the type of certificate issued, the Federal Aviation Administration has the power to reinspect any aircraft, airman, or any holder of a safety certificate at any time. If upon reinspection the Federal Aviation Administration determines that safety is not being adhered to in the utmost standard, the Federal Aviation Administration may order the amending, modifying, suspending, or revoking, in whole or in part, any certificate that has been issued. This can only take place after notification to the offender and a hearing held in which he may defend himself.

Any person whose certificate is so affected may appeal the Federal Aviation Administration order to the National Transportation Safety Board who may, after due notice and hearing, uphold, amend, modify or even reverse the Federal Aviation Administrator's order. The filing of such an appeal with the National Transportation Safety Board can stay the effectiveness of the Administrator's order pending the final disposition of the case, unless the Administrator advises the National Transportation Safety Board that an emergency exists and aviation safety requires the order to become effective immediately. If this occurs the National Transportation Safety Board must dispense with the appeal within sixty days.

The review proceeding by the National Transportation Safety Board actually takes the form of a new hearing in which the National Transportation Safety Board is not bound by the findings which led the Administrator to decide adversely to the defending applicant.

After the hearing the National Transportation Safety Board issues its own decision and the Administrator is bound by it.

Anyone who is then unsuccessful in their appeal to the National Transportation Safety Board has the privilege of going to the courts for review. In any court action the Administrator shall be made a party to the proceedings and is joined with the National Transportation Safety Board as party-respondent.

The various regulations concerning aviation safety are most complete, definite and positive. It is contrary to the laws to operate any civil aircraft that does not have current effective Registration and Airworthiness Certificates; to perform in the capacity of an airman without having been issued the necessary Airman Certificate, or even to employ such a person. No air carrier may conduct public air transportation without holding an Air Carrier Operating Certificate and no one possessing an Air Agency or Production Certificate may violate any term, condition or limitation of the certificate.

Any violators of safety regulations are subject to civil penalties; moreover, in appropriate cases the courts may enjoin such violators or direct compliances with the safety regulations. Criminal penalties do not exist for safety violations, however.

Foreign aircraft and airmen may be exempted from any safety regulatory provision if the Federal Aviation Administrator finds it to be in the public interest.

Together with the Federal Aviation Administrator's powers and duties as stated in Title III of the Federal Aviation Act, and aviation safety rule-making under Title VI, there exists a well rounded comprehensive system of safety regulation extending in its coverage from the designer's drawing board to all aspects of aviation functions.

AIRCRAFT ACCIDENT INVESTIGATION

When the Civil Aeronautics Act was formulated in 1938, there was created an Air Safety Board whose duties and responsibilities included that of aircraft accident investigation.

Under President Roosevelt's reorganization plan in 1940 this Air Safety Board was eliminated and its responsibilities of aircraft accident investigation became that of the Civil Aeronautics Board where it remained under the Federal Aviation Act of 1958. Under the Department of Transportation Act of 1966, accident investigation was transferred to the National Transportation Safety Board.

In general, it is the duty of the NTSB to make rules and regulations governing the notification and the reporting of aircraft accidents. The NTSB makes recommendations to the Federal Aviation Administration that will tend to prevent or eliminate similar accidents in the future. All reports of investigations and findings are made public in the public interest.

The NTSB may conduct special investigations pertaining to air safety and accident prevention, and ascertain that which will reduce or eliminate the causes of aircraft accidents in the future.

In discharging its duties the NTSB has the power to hold hearings and to compel testimony.

The authority for removal of aircraft wreckage remains solely with the NTSB; therefore no wreckage can be moved or disturbed until officially released by the NTSB. There are immediate exceptions to this, however, as in the case of aiding and removing any persons which may be in the wreckage, or moving the wreckage if it is a public hazard such as being located on an active airport runway or on a public highway; all wreckage must be preserved for the Board's investigation.

Temporary specialized personnel may be employed by the NTSB to further its investigations.

When requested by the NTSB, the Federal Aviation Administration is authorized to conduct aircraft accident investigations in behalf of the NTSB; and, furthermore, the Federal Aviation Administration may participate in the accident investigations conducted by the NTSB to the extent under which the circumstances may warrant. The reports of the Federal Aviation Administration may be used by the NTSB in determining the probable cause of the accident, but basically the Federal Aviation Administration is prohibited from taking any part in the final determination of the cause of the accident.

All aircraft accidents involving injury or damage must be reported to the NTSB; however, not all accidents are necessarily investigated.

Due to the volume of its work, and therefore the inability of the NTSB to investigate every aircraft accident, the NTSB has delegated to the Federal Aviation Administration the authority to investigate in behalf of the NTSB, all accidents involving those occurring to aircraft weighing less than 12,500 pounds maximum certificated gross take-off weight. For practical purposes this includes all light aircraft and small twin-engine aircraft. The NTSB itself investigate all accidents occurring to airline aircraft and to all aircraft, regardless of ownership, weighing in excess of 12,500 pounds gross weight.

The reasoning here is that when an aircraft accident occurs the Federal Aviation Administration makes an investigation to determine if any safety regulations had been violated. Therefore, in the matter of accidents involving small aircraft, the findings of the Federal Aviation Administration will be reported to the NTSB, thereby eliminating duplication of effort.

The authority for aircraft accident investigation of the NTSB is found in Section 5 of the Department of Transportation Act.

It is interesting to note that one aspect of accident investigation concerns the availability of the information obtained in such accident investigations to private litigation for use in aircraft accident damage suits. No part of any report made by the NTSB relating to any accident, or the investigation thereof, shall be admitted as evidence or used in any suit or action for damages growing out of any matter mentioned in the accident report issued by the NTSB.

The courts have held that this provision renders inadmissable only the NTSB's formal reports and does not require exclusion of testimony of the NTSB investigators and private persons having firsthand factual knowledge concerning an accident. The NTSB has promulgated rules setting forth the circumstances under which it will permit its investigators to give testimony in damage suits.

In the case of aircraft accidents involving both civil and military aircraft, the NTSB shall provide for the necessary participation in the investigation by the appropriate military authorities involved. In accidents involving only military aircraft and in which a function of the Federal Aviation Administration may be involved, the military authorities will provide for participation in the investigation by the Federal Aviation Administration. Such might be the case when air traffic control rules were violated.

With respect to other accidents involving solely military aircraft, the military authorities may provide the Federal Aviation Administration and the NTSB with any information which in the judgment of the military would contribute to the promotion of aviation safety.

In any accident which involves substantial questions of public safety in air transportation, the NTSB may establish a Special Board of Inquiry consisting of three members. One member shall be from the NTSB and he will act as the Chairman of the Special Board of Inquiry; the remaining two members will represent the public and they are appointed by the President of the United States. The public members of the Special Board of Inquiry must be qualified by virtue of their knowledge and experience in aviation.

When such a Special Board of Inquiry convenes to investigate, it has all of the authority equal to that of the NTSB.

As long as there are aircraft flying there will always, no doubt, be accidents. It is most improbable that the day will arrive when air travel will be one hundred per cent safe. Risk is the price paid for motion; this has been true since man first began to transport himself from place to place. However, the risk in commercial air transportation is a calculated one and can be reduced by doing all that is humanly possible through research and technological advancement.

Unlimited amounts of funds can be spent in the pursuit of greater safety but it is none-the-less true that the closer one comes to gaining perfection the more difficult and elusive it becomes. A point can be reached in aviation safety where the law of diminishing returns sets in. This is when a vast expenditure will provide only a meager improvement. There is, therefore, an economic limit to safety in commercial air transportation, but this point is indefinite. While the air carriers have a moral obligation to the flying public they must recognize and contend with the economic limitations.

Through the efforts of the air carrier industry and the government agencies, the percentage of accidents and fatalities, to the total miles flown and passengers carried in commercial air transportation, have been constantly decreasing. For instance, in the year 1972 there were only 0.10% fatalities for each 100,000,000 passenger miles flown by the United States certificated air carriers. The Domestic Trunk air carrier's passenger fatality rate for 1972 was 0.13.

An excellent reflection of this continuing improvement in aviation safety is the attitude in the position taken by the major life insurance companies. Not

Comparative Transport Safety Record

Passenger Fatalities per 100 Million Passenger Miles

	1973	1972	1971	1970	1969	1968	1967	1966	1965	1964	1963
U.S. Scheduled Airlines											
Domestic											
Fatalities	128	160	174	0	132	258	226	59	205	65	48
Rate	0.10	0.13	0.16	0.00	0.14	0.30	0.30	0.09	0.38	0.14	0.12
International and Territorial											
Fatalities	69	0	0	2	0	47	0	0	21	94	73
Rate	0.19	0.00	0.00	0.007	0.00	0.18	0.00	0.00	0.12	0.63	0.59
Total											
Fatalities	197	160	174	2	132	305	226	59	226	159	121
Rate	0.12	0.10	0.12	0.001	0.11	0.27	0.22	0.07	0.31	0.26	0.23
Motor Buses											
Fatalities	n.a.	29	14	2	8	31	23	13	44	19	38
Rate	n.a.	0.17	0.08	0.02	0.05	0.16	0.11	0.06	0.23	0.10	0.21
Railroads											
Fatalities	6	47	17	10	9	13	13	27	12	9	13
Rate	0.07	0.56	0.23	0.09	0.07	0.10	0.09	0.16	0.07	0.05	0.07
Autos											
Fatalities	35,000 E	35,200	34,200	34,800	37,200	36,500	34,800	34,800	32,500	31,500	28,900
Rate	n.a.	1.9	1.9	2.1	2.3	2.4	2.4	2.5	2.4	2.4	2.3

E Estimated

Five-Year Averages of Airline Safety Statistics

	Passenger Fatalities per 100 Million Passenger Miles	Passenger Fatalities per One Million Aircraft Miles	Revenue Plane Miles per Fatal Accident (000)	Fatal Accidents per 100,000 Flights
1939-1943	2.39	0.29	34,151	n.a.
1944-1948	2.01	0.37	46,422	n.a.
1949-1953	0.95	0.25	75,623	0.28
1954-1958	0.37	0.12	131,112	0.19
1959-1963	0.43	0.19	162,389	0.16
1964-1968	0.22	0.12	233,263	0.15
1969-1973	0.09	0.06	571,660	0.08

Source: Air Transport Association of America

many years ago any person who flew as a passenger was not covered for the duration of the flight. Today, due to improved safety, these provisions seldom exist and usually such clauses now do not include flight on certificated air carriers. Likewise airline piloting was considered a hazardous occupation and required the payment of higher premiums for life insurance coverage. Presently the insurance companies, because of the safe level of airline flying, do not require airline pilots to pay more for life insurance than the average person.

No less expensive life insurance can be obtained anywhere than from the insurance vending machines located at airport terminal buildings for passenger trip coverage. A few nickels and dimes will purchase thousands of dollars worth of life insurance. The insurance companies are betting at the odds of 2,500 to 1 that the passenger will not become a fatality.

In time past, particularly before and after World War II, passenger traffic decreased perceptible immediately following a major airline crash. It would then take thirty days to six months before normal traffic flow could be regained. Currently, however, the flying public better understands aviation and when major accidents occur, although some passengers may cancel their reservations, there are many others who are willing to take their place and no total decrease in passenger traffic occurs.

It is a statistical fact that the most dangerous part of making an airline flight is the drive by automobile to and from the airport. The experienced airline passenger breaths a sigh of relief when he becomes airborne because the average airline passenger realizes that he is many times safer in an airline seat than in the seat of a moving automobile.

A recent study of all major airline accidents over a ten year period indicated that 60.3% of the persons involved survived and 39.7% were fatalities. The average number of survivors per accident was 14.7% and the average fatality rate per accident was 9.7 persons.

Weather conditions were found to be a contributing factor in 57.5% of the accidents occuring in the ten year period surveyed.

The most hazardous portion of a flight appears to be in the vicinity of the airport. There were 43.3% of the accidents on the approach or in the process of landing while 18.9% took place on take-off; the remaining 37.8% happened to the aircraft while in normal flight.

The Civil Aeronautics Board accident reports were used in the study and it was found that in less than six per cent of all accidents the Board was unable to determine the probable cause.

As Robert Serling points out in the concluding paragraph of his book "The Probable Cause," if a passenger was born on an airliner and flew continuously during his entire lifetime, he could not expect to be involved in a fatal crash until he reached the age of seventy six years. Serling also noted that a passenger on a certificated United States air carrier has a 99.99978 per cent chance of completing any given flight safely.

The ignorance of how safe air transportation is, has been the traditional foe of the industry. There are many figures available to prove that air transportation has become a very safe business. The Civil Aeronautics Board points out that a passenger who boards a United States jetliner can expect to fly 16,000 revolutions of the earth before the probabilities will involve him in a fatal accident. Also, the Civil Aeronautics Board states that it is statistically seven times safer to ride a mile in a certificated United States airline than to drive one mile in an automobile.

In working to make flight safer, the National Transportation Safety Board has budgeted over 3 million dollars to investigate accidents. In the crash of a Boeing 720 near Miami the Board invested more than $100,000 in finding the probable cause. This does not include vast sums of money spent by the manufacturer of the airplane, the airline, the Federal Aviation Agency, the Air Line Pilots Association, the Air Traffic Control Association, the Flight Engineers International Association, and the Air Line Dispatches Association, as well as many others.

As a result of a major accident many law suits are instituted. On December 16, 1960 a mid-air collision occurred over Staten Island and from that accident came more than 100 separate law suits. Plaintiffs sought close to 80 million dollars in damages from the two airlines and the Federal Aviation Agency. Some air carriers fail to earn that much in an entire year.

In conclusion, the time honored saying is true: "Aviation is not inherently dangerous but to a far greater extent than the sea, it is unremittingly unforgiving of carelessness."

ACCIDENTS, FATALITIES, FATALITY RATES U.S. CERTIFICATED ROUTE AIR CARRIERS SCHEDULED DOMESTIC AND INTERNATIONAL PASSENGER SERVICE 1964-1974

Year	Accidents Tot	Accidents Fatal	Fatalities Pasg	Fatalities Crew	Fatalities Oth	Fatalities Tot	Passengers Carried**	Passenger— Miles Flown (000)	Pasg Fatality Rate Per 100 Million Passenger— Miles Flown
1964	53	9	200	26	1	227	81,762,273	61,022,488	0.261
1965	63	7	226	27	0	253	94,662,314	71,796,399	0.315
1966	53	4	59	13	0	72	109,390,556	83,142,197	0.071
1967	51	8	226	24	5	255	132,088,038	103,381,996	0.219
1968	53	13*	305	34	6	345	150,162,701	119,612,578	0.255
1969	48	7	132	17	3	152	159,213,414	132,161,593	0.100
1970	39	2	2	0	1	3	171,697,097	139,157,806	0.001
1971	41	6*	174	14	6	194	173,664,737	145,678,876	0.119
1972	43	7	160	13	13	186	188,938,932	159,722,015	0.100
1973	32	6	197	20	0	217	202,207,000	171,436,549	0.115
1974P	41	7	420	40	0	460	204,600,000	163,900,000	0.256

P Preliminary

*Includes midair collisions nonfatal to air carrier occupants.

**Beginning in 1970, carriers were required to report revenue passenger enplanements, whereas prior to 1970 revenue passenger orginations were reported.

Note—Passenger deaths occurring in sabotage accidents are included in the passenger fatality column but excluded in the computation of passenger fatality rates (1964-74).

National Transportation Safety Board
Washington, D.C.
January 6, 1975

CHAPTER
VIII
ᐯᐯᐯ

The Civil Aeronautics Board

The Civil Aeronautics Board derives its authority from, and is organized in accordance with, the Federal Aviation Act of 1958, as amended by the Department of Transportation Act of 1966. It is an independent federal agency comprised of five members appointed for a six-year term by the President with the advice and consent of the Senate, with no more than three members appointed from the same political party. Each year the President designates one member as Chairman and another as vice chairman.

Each member of the Board must be a citizen of the United States and no member shall have any pecuniary interest or own any stock or bonds in any civil aeronautics enterprise. Also, no member of the Board shall engage in any other business, vocation, or employment. Three members of the Board shall constitute a quorum.

The Board exercises its power independently. Its decisions are not subject to review by any executive department or agency, except for the approval of the President required in Board decisions granting or affecting certificates for overseas and foreign air transportation, and foreign air carrier permits.

In general, the Board performs two major functions:

1. Regulation of the economic aspects of domestic and international United States air carrier operations and of the operations of foreign air carriers to and from the United States.

2. Participation in the establishment and development of international air transportation.

The Board's function dealing with aviation safety was transferred to the Department of Transportation.

The functions of the Board are described briefly in the following paragraphs.

Economic Regulation. The Board is responsible for granting authorizations to air carriers to engage in interstate and foreign air transportation. It issues permits to foreign air carriers authorizing them to engage in air transportation between the United States and foreign countries, and also authorizes the navigation of foreign civil aircraft in the United States for other purposes.

The Board has jurisdiction over tariffs and the rates and fares charged the public for air transportation; it establishes rates for the carriage of mail by air carriers; and it authorizes and pays public service revenue (subsidy) to certain air carriers where required for the development of an adequate air transportation system.

In the interest of maintaining regulated competition, the Board passes on mergers, acquisitions of control and interlocking relationships involving air carriers; and passes on contracts for cooperative working arrangements between air carriers. The Board also has jurisdiction over unfair competitive practices of air carriers and ticket agents selling air transportation.

The Board regulates the accounting practices of air carriers and requires them to file regular financial and operating reports with the Board. Much of the information from these reports is published by the Board and thereby made available to other government agencies and to the general public.

International Civil Aviation. The Board consults with and assists the Department of State in the negotiation of agreements with foreign governments for the establishment or development of air routes and services between the United States and foreign countries.

FUNCTIONS OF THE BOARD MEMBERS

The Board members are charged with carrying out the duties and responsibilities of the Board under the Act and the statutes. Action initiated pursuant to the Board's own initiative or by any document authorized or required to be filed with the Board originates in or is referred to the appropriate organizational unit for study and recommendation to the Board. The Board has the authority to delegate any of its functions to a division of the Board, an individual Board member, a hearing examiner or an employee or employees of the Board.

In addition to his duties as a member of the Board, the Chairman serves as presiding officer at meetings of the Board, determines the order in which day-to-day matters will receive attention of the Board, and by virtue of his role as Chairman, acts as Spokesman for the Board before committees of Congress. The Chairman is responsible for the executive and administrative functions of the Board.

THE MANAGING DIRECTOR

The Managing Director assists the Chairman in discharging his function as executive and administrative head of the Board. He coordinates and directs the activities of the staff and recommends plans to achieve the Board's program objectives in most efficient manner.

It is the duty of the Managing Director to appoint and supervise the personnel employed by the Board and distribute the business of the Board among the offices and personnel. He is also responsible for the use and expenditure of funds subject to the limitations and qualifications set forth.

OFFICE OF COMMUNITY
AND CONGRESSIONAL RELATIONS

The members of this office serve as the Board's representatives to local communities, state governments, consumer and civic groups and perform liaison for the Board with various aviation organizations and interests. They also serve as a primary communications link between the Board and individual members of Congress and between the Board and the various Congressional committees interested in the Board's policies and activities.

This office acts for the Board as its spokesman and develops proposed solutions in areas of relationships between the Board and individual communities or states and the air carriers and maintains and discusses Board relations and policies with members of Congress and their committees. He serves as a representative of the Board to civic groups in furthering the understanding of problems.

The members of this office interpret Board policy and regulations as they affect local communities and act as a liaison with different aviation groups. They also originate responses to all Congressional mail.

OFFICE OF INFORMATION

This office is responsible for originating, developing and carrying out the Board's information and public relations programs, policies and actions. It plans, directs and coordinates the informational activities of the Board's Bureaus and Offices in order to keep the public thoroughly informed of the Board's activities.

The Office of Information prepares or reviews, with the other offices, proposed press releases and other information materials. The members of this office identify the type of material to be covered by a press release, serve as the primary channel through which inquiries from the public and press are handled, and review articles and speeches by Board officials in advance of the release. They arrange for press conferences, radio and television appearances and advise Board Members of the general public reaction.

OFFICE OF THE SECRETARY

This office, directed by the Secretary, who also serves as Deputy Managing Director, has the important function of performing as a clearing house and repository for official Board documents. It receives, records, files, distributes and serves copies of official docket material and records and files financial and operational statistical reports. It also performs the highly essential functions

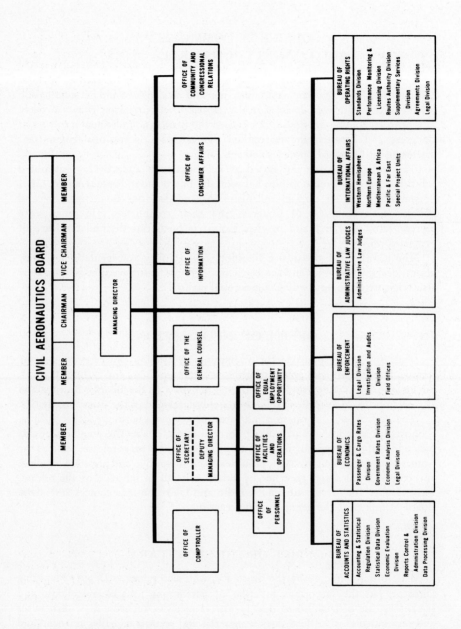

CIVIL AERONAUTICS BOARD

MEMBER | MEMBER | CHAIRMAN | VICE CHAIRMAN | MEMBER

MANAGING DIRECTOR

OFFICE OF COMMUNITY AND CONGRESSIONAL RELATIONS

OFFICE OF CONSUMER AFFAIRS

OFFICE OF INFORMATION

OFFICE OF THE GENERAL COUNSEL

OFFICE OF COMPTROLLER

OFFICE OF SECRETARY
DEPUTY MANAGING DIRECTOR

OFFICE OF PERSONNEL

OFFICE OF FACILITIES AND OPERATIONS

OFFICE OF EQUAL EMPLOYMENT OPPORTUNITY

BUREAU OF ACCOUNTS AND STATISTICS
Accounting & Statistical Regulation Division
Statistical Data Division
Economic Evaluation Division
Reports Control & Administration Division
Data Processing Division

BUREAU OF ECONOMICS
Passenger & Cargo Rates Division
Government Rates Division
Economic Analysis Division
Legal Division

BUREAU OF ENFORCEMENT
Legal Division
Investigation and Audits Division
Field Offices

BUREAU OF ADMINISTRATIVE LAW JUDGES
Administrative Law Judges

BUREAU OF INTERNATIONAL AFFAIRS
Western Hemisphere
Northern Europe
Mediterranean & Africa
Pacific & Far East
Special Project Units

BUREAU OF OPERATING RIGHTS
Standards Division
Performance Monitoring & Licensing Division
Routes Authority Division
Supplementary Services Division
Agreements Division
Legal Division

involving processing material from the staff requiring action by the Board, records Board actions and issues, digests and indexes official documents evidencing such action.

The Secretary reports directly to the Managing Director and is responsible for recording all formal actions of the Board; for processing, including review as to accuracy, form, and content, of all documents evidencing such action; and for authenticating Board records for any official purpose. He has legal custody of all the records and documents of the Board, and passes on the eligibility of persons to have access to the Board's minutes. The Secretary also certifies transcripts of records to the Appellate Courts to which Board proceedings have been appealed.

In the capacity of Assistant Managing Director, he carries out such duties and activities as may be assigned by the Chairman of the Managing Director.

Reporting directly to the Office of Secretary are the Offices of Personnel, Facilities and Operations and Equal Employment Opportunity.

Personnel

The Office of Personnel administers a comprehensive, progressive and vigorous personnel program designed to meet the needs of the Civil Aeronautics Board and its employees and administers the security programs within the agency. This office recommends personnel policies, standards and procedures compatible with laws and regulations adapted to the CAB's particular needs. The members of this office participate with other offices in special projects having overall management interest, such as organizational and methods studies, operations surveys and program evaluations.

It maintains liaison with the Civil Service Commission and other agencies concerned with personnel administration, and administers an employee relations and services program designed to increase employees' morale and job satisfaction. The Director administers an employee development and evaluation program designed to improve employee productivity and utilization, and position classification and wage administration programs designed to achieve the objective of equal pay for equal work.

The Director administers a personnel staffing program designed to obtain and retain the services of the best qualified employees.

Facilities and Operations

This Office of Facilities and Operations is responsible for development of a continuing program for acquiring, maintaining, and disposing of all Board furniture, equipment and items of supply, acquiring and distributing building space, operating the central files program and providing central printing, reproduction, and distribution services to the Board.

This office is divided into three sections: (1) communications and records, (2) general services, and (3) printing and publications.

The Director administers a program to provide adequate and efficient administrative services for the entire Board and advises the Managing Director and the Assistant Managing Director for Operations and other staff on administrative services.

Equal Employment Opportunity

The Office of Equal Employment Opportunity is designated as the Board's coordinator of civil rights and equal employment opportunity.

OFFICE OF CONSUMER ADVOCATE

They perform the necessary research and conduct correspondence to assure that each complaint receives appropriate attention.

The employees of this office receive and process the consumer complaints regarding the problems which arise in the use of air service.

Through correspondence and meetings with the carriers and ticket agents, they call attention to general deficiencies and improved services needed so that complaints are reduced and public service improved.

OFFICE OF THE GENERAL COUNSEL

The General Counsel has primary responsibility for advising the Board on the legal aspects of policy matters, including the preparation of Board rules, opinions and orders; advises all Offices and Bureaus of the Board on matters of important legal significance or unusual complexity, and on other legal matters on request.

This office represents the Board in litigation (except enforcement matters); provides counsel as required at negotiations, testimony at CongressionalHearings, depositions, and conferences involving significant legal considerations.

The General Counsel advises and represents the Board on legal matters relating to defense mobilization and internal administration.

The Office of the General Counsel consists of the following organizational components: Rules and Rates Division, Routes Division, and Litigation and Legislation Division.

Rules and Rates Division

This Division reviews the legal aspects of recommendations for action submitted to the Board by operating Offices and Bureaus, involving novel or difficult legal question relating particularly to mail rates, commercial rates, subsidy payments, inter-carrier agreements, and anti-trust and labor matters as they pertain to the Board's functions.

Routes Division

With respect to formal route proceedings, the members of this Division review the legal aspects of recommendations for action submitted to the Board by the operating Bureaus, involving novel or difficult legal question relating to air carrier routes, route structure, and operating authorizations. They also review the legal aspects of international law and international civil aviation matters as they pertain to the Board's functions.

Litigation and Legislation Division

This Division represents the Board, in collaboration with the Department of Justice, in court actions (except enforcement) to which the Board is a party, or is interested, in order to sustain action previously taken by the Board including preparation of the record, the drafting of all necessary briefs, motions, and other documents, and arguments of the case before the court.

The members of this Division undertake legal research, and renders legal opinions based thereon, on legal problems of general or fundamental significance. With respect to economic enforcement proceedings, they provide assistance to the Board and individual members in connection with the preparation of opinions and orders. The members of this Division make recommendations to the Board as to (1) the disposition of petitions of discretionary review of initial decisions; (2) the disposition of petitions for reconsideration of final decisions; (3) the appropriate action to be taken on other motions or petitions filed subsequent to the issuance of the examiner's decision; (4) the disposition of the merits where review of the examiner's decision is granted and no oral argument is held; and (5) the action to be taken upon appeals from the refusal of the Director of the Bureau of Enforcement to docket a complaint. The Legislative Section within the Division examines legislative proposals of interest to the Board and prepares recommended Board comments, drafts proposed bills, and prepares official written statements for use in hearings before Congressional committees.

OFFICE OF COMPTROLLER

This office is responsible for administration of the Board's financial management system, including participation in the fundamental aspects of program development, executive review and evaluation; performs fiscal and administrative accounting activities; and administers subsidy payment functions.

The Office of the Budget develops both broad and specific financial policies that will facilitate achievement of the Board's future and annual budget goals and objectives. The members of this office evaluate proposed programs and program requirements and recommend priorities for the allocation of resources to each program.

It prepares the budget justifications and attends hearings before the Bureau of the Budget and Congressional committees. The Director exercises an effective control system over the financial resources of the Board and compares actual performance with planned objectives in the operating budget and provides reports to the various levels of management. These reports include cost of operations and program accomplishments. He provides advice to the responsible program managers on the financial aspects of utilizing the Board's resources most effectively in attaining the program objectives.

The line functions of the CAB are conducted by Bureaus, as follows:

BUREAU OF ACCOUNTS AND STATISTICS

Recommending establishments of, and administering a uniform system of carrier accounts and reports, and auditing carrier records to assure conformance is the work of this Bureau. They administer a data processing program to meet the overall needs of the Board, and participate in the development of automatic data processing systems.

They prepare recurrent and special accounting, cost and statistical reports showing current and historical data and operating results of the air transport industry.

The Director of this Bureau advises the Board on policies and programs with respect to carrier accounting and reporting, carrier audits, electronic data processing, and statistical and cost reporting. This Bureau is divided into three divisions; (1) Accounting, Costs and Statistics, (2) Information Validation and (3) Automated Information Systems.

Accounting, Costs and Statistics Division

The members of this Division direct the development of the cost and statistics program of the Board, including the provision of basic statistics and the planning of a centralized cost finding program. This Division is divided into three Sections; (1) Cost Finding Section, (2) Statistical Projects Section, and (3) Statistical Reports Section.

Information Validation Division

The Chief administers a program to formulate and recommend a uniform system of accounting and reports for air carriers, and to supervise the receipt, validation and interpretation of such reports. Within this Division there are two Sections, the first is the Accounting Regulation Section which develops and recommends the Uniform System of Accounts and periodic financial and operational reports and revisions, and recommends modifications and waivers of the Uniform System. The second section, Carrier Reports, prepares procedures for and examines the financial and operational reports of carriers for completeness of data and substantive conformance with statutes and the uniform accounting and reporting requirements; prepares letters of exception to carriers, where necessary; and corrects reports as authorized.

The Chief of this Division develops and supervises a program to audit carrier books to establish that they accurately reflect operating results and conform to prescribed regulations and statutes. He also schedules audits and reviews audit reports and recommendations, and otherwise directs the work of the several regional audit offices.

Automated Information Systems Division

This Division administers an overall data processing program for the Board, including assistance in planning and developing management and program operational systems.

BUREAU OF ECONOMICS

This Bureau serves as the primary Economic Advisor to the Board on all economic policies and programs, including the over-all development, review, coordination and formulation of economic plans and objectives.

It carries out the service mail rate, commercial rate, tariff, and subsidy programs of the Board.

The Bureau of Economics is headed by a director and is comprised of the following divisions: (1) Passenger and Cargo Rates Division, (2) Government Rates Division, (3) Planning, Programming and Research Division. The Director advises the Board on all significant economic policies and programs, and administers a program to review, develop and recommend economic policies. He provides leadership and guidance to all the Bureau's program, especially with respect to policy matters, with the view to assuring the economic soundness of recommendations and decisions.

Passenger and Cargo Rates Division

It is the duty of this department to administer matters dealing with the determination of service mail rates pursuant to Section 406 (Rates for Transportation of Mail) of the FAA Act and the regulation of commercial rates and tariffs pursuant to Sections 403 (Tariffs of Air Carriers), 404 (Rates for the Carriage of Persons and Property) and 1002 (Complaints to and Investigations by the Administrator and the Board) of the Act. The Chief of this division is also responsible for rates for the military under Section 416 (Classification and Exemption of Carriers) of the Act, and commercial rate aspects of resolutions of the International Air Transport Association.

He participates in planning, formulating, and recommending passenger fare and cargo rate policy with a view toward guiding the air carriers and assisting in the development of a rate structure conducive to the economic soundness of the air transport industry and the public interest. The Chief of the Passenger and Cargo Rates Division takes action with respect to rate matters and practices affecting rates which are pending before the Board.

Under the Passenger and Cargo Rates Division there are three sections: (1) Rates and Practices, (2) Tariffs, and (3) Legal. The following functions are common to both the Tariffs Section and the Rates and Practices Section.

A. Participates in planning and developing policy statements and statements setting forth program objectives.

B. Recommends action, or takes action where authority has been delegated, with respect to specific cases.

C. Recommends the initiation of investigation and suspension, or the investigation of tariff filings.

D. Recommends changes in Economic and Procedural Regulations and the Board's legislative program, and assists, as requested, in formulating them.

E. Prepares studies designed to provide background material on current problems.

F. Refers to the Bureau of Enforcement for appropriate action information of apparent violations of the Act or of Board regulations.

Rates and Practices Section

In addition to the responsibilities listed above the Rates and Practices Section performs the following functions.

A. Conducts informal service mail rate conferences pursuant to the Procedural Regulations.

B. Prepares statements of provisional findings and conclusions, show cause orders, orders of investigation, orders of investigation and suspension, exemption orders, and orders disposing of International Air Transport Association and other rate agreements.

C. Recommends whether fares, rates, charges, and related rules which are the subject of formal complaints should be investigated and suspended.

D. Prepares relevant exhibits, analyzes exhibits and other data, and provides expert witnesses in formal and informal proceedings.

E. Maintain Board liaison with the International Air Transport Association (IATA) and, in coordination with the Tariffs Section, recommends appropriate action with respect to IATA agreements concerning rates, fares, charges and related practices.

Tariffs Section

In addition to the responsibilities listed above, the Tariffs Section performs the following functions.

A. Maintains a file of currently effective and proposed tariffs for public inspection.

B. Reviews all tariff filing for conformity with filing requirements.

C. Recommends appropriate action on applications for permission to effect tariff changes on less than statutory notice, involving new or substantial questions of policy.

D. Recommends appropriate action on applications for free or reduced rate transportation filed pursuant to Sections 403 (b) and 416 (b) of the Federal Aviation Act.

Legal Section

The third section in the Rates Division is the Legal Section which prepares statements, orders and recommendations involving considerations primarily legal in nature and drafts and reviews all orders in informal or non-hearing matters.

Government Rates Division

The Chief of this division administers the subsidy provisions of Section 406 (b) of the Act, and of the Government Guaranty of Equipment Loans Act of 1957. He participates in planning, formulating and recommending programs and policies for the disposition of all matters affecting subsidy; processes specific subsidy rate determinations for all subsidized carriers; provides economic assistance for the disposition of cases with subsidy implications; prepares recommendations from the Board to the Secretary of Transportation as to the Government Guaranty of private loans to air carriers for the purchase of more modern aircraft. This Division recommends changes in the Economic and Procedural Regulations and items for the Board's legislative program, and assists, as requested, in formulating them.

Planning, Programming and Research Division

The Chief of this Division develops and recommends over-all economic plans and programs for the Board in cooperation with the Bureau of Operating Rights, Bureau of International Affairs and Bureau of Accounts and Statistics; and advises the Board on all Economic policy formulation. This Division is divided into three sections: (1) Economic Planning and Programming, (2) Economic Research and (3) Economic Performance Evaluation.

Economic Planning and Programming Section

The members of this Section prepare and recommend economic policies and objectives of the Board, and translates these into specific plans and programs for the Board consideration and adoption. They recommend changes in Economic and Procedural Regulations and items for the Board's legislative program and, as needed, participates in preparing such changes and items.

Economic Research Section

This Section makes studies in depth in support of economic programs of the Board (except bilateral negotiations). These studies are to help shape the economic policies of the Board, to help evaluate these policies and their effect on the air carrier industry, and to help the Board and staff in the decisional process.

Economic Performance Evaluation Section

They make evaluations of individual carrier, group, and industry economic performance to determine whether, and to what extent, the Board's explicitly enunciated plans and programs were achieved, as well as the reasons and justifications for performance deviation from original goals. The members of this Section relate airline trends to concurrent developments in other transport modes, as well as to developments in the general economy itself that can have significant impacts on the airline and/or its chief competitors. They perform case-by-case reviews as directed by the Board on regulatory cases handled by other departments of the Board.

BUREAU OF ENFORCEMENT

The Bureau of Enforcement is responsible for the development and execution of a program to obtain observance of the economic provisions of the Federal Aviation Act of 1958, as amended, of the relevant provisions of the Clayton Antitrust Act and the Railway Labor Act, and of all economic orders, regulations and other requirements promulgated by the Board.

The Director of this Bureau plans, develops and directs programs for the enforcement of the economic provisions of the Act and all orders, rules, regulations and other requirements issued by the Board. He advises the Board and its staff in the establishment of policies and regulations which will facilitate observance of the Act and other requirements directed by the Board. The Director also maintains liaison with other Government agencies in connection with enforcement of the economic regulations.

The Director is authorized to institute and prosecute in the proper court, as an agent of the Board, all necessary proceedings for the enforcement of the provisions of the Act or any rule, regulation, requirement, or order, or any term, condition or limitation of any certificate or permit, and for the punishment of all violations. He is authorized to determine, in accordance with the Board policy, in each case where a relationship has been established illegally prior to the Board approval required under Section 408 and 409 of the Act, whether "exceptional circumstances" exist which would justify processing an application for approval of such relationship notwithstanding the existence of the violation. If the Director finds the existence of "exceptional circumstances" he will submit a memorandum to the Director, Bureau of Operating Rights, with a copy to the Office of the General Counsel, setting forth the basis for his findings and advising the Bureau that because of the existence of "exceptional circumstances" there is no impediment of the processing of an application for approval of the relationship on its merits.

This Bureau is comprised of two Divisions.

Legal Division

This Division negotiates with air carriers, Air Freight Forwarders, travel agents, and other entities subject to Board jurisdiction in cases of informal complaints filed with the Board by a passenger, a shipper, or a carrier, to obtain voluntary compliance with the Act or Board regulations, or agreement to formal stipulations or other consent agreements to cease and desist violative practices.

The members of this Division institute and prosecute in formal proceedings before the Board, actions against air carriers, Air Freight Forwarders, travel agents, and other entities subject to Board jurisdiction alleging violations of the Act or Board orders and regulations and seeking revocation or suspension of operating authority or entry of orders to cease and desist. They institute and prosecute on behalf of the Board, through the Department of Justice and appropriate United States Attorneys, civil and criminal actions looking toward compliance with the provisions of the Act or regulations of the Board including appeals.

It represents the Board as intervenor in litigation between private parties involving possible violations of the Act.

Investigation Division

The members of this Division initiate and conduct investigations of alleged or suspected violations of the economic provisions of the Act and of the Board's

Economic Regulations on its own initiative, or by request of the Board, the Bureau of Enforcement or any other department. They conduct investigations into suspected violations on the basis of complaints received from outside individuals, organizations, air carriers, or other governmental agencies. The members then make reports on the investigation for use by the Bureau in considering enforcement action.

This Division performs investigations of complaints involving alleged misconduct of Board personnel except the personnel of the Bureau of Enforcement.

BUREAU OF ADMINISTRATIVE LAW JUDGES

The Bureau of Administrative Law Judges is responsible for the conduct and disposition of all formal proceedings arising under the Federal Aviation Act. This Bureau is comprised of the Chief Administrative Law Judge and the Administrative Law Judges.

The Chief Administrative Law Judge administers and supervises the activities of the Bureau and supervises the assignment of cases for hearing and assigns and schedules cases to oral argument before the Board. He performs liaison work with the examiners to prevent delays, insure uniformity, and consults on precedents, policies and practices of the Board.

The Chief Administrative Law Judge establishes or recommends policies and procedures in the conduct of formal proceeding and at times conducts proceedings as an examiner. He approves or disapproves requests for changes in procedural requirements in connection with economic cases for good cause shown, provided that an extension of time for filing documents shall not be granted within three days of the date originally set for filing except in cases involving unusual hardships on the requesting party.

The Administrative Law Judges conduct proceedings involving the economic regulatory powers of the Board under Titles IV and X of the Act, including issuance of Certificates of Public Convenience and Necessity concerning both domestic and foreign operations, issuance of Foreign Air Carrier Permits, mail, passenger and property rate cases, mergers, acquisitions of control, interlocking relationships, and enforcement cases.

In carrying out these proceedings, Administrative Law Judges hold hearings, make initial decision, and carry out the other requirements of the Administrative Procedures Act and the Board's procedural regulations, in accordance with the duties, powers and the delegations of authority to Administrative Law Judges stated in the Board's Rules of Practice (Parts 301 and 302) and Organization Regulations (Part 385).

By delegation of authority from the Board each Administrative Law Judge is authorized to:

A. Give notice concerning and hold hearings.

B. Administer oaths.

C. Examine witnesses.

D. Issue subpena and take or cause depositions to be taken.

E. Rule upon offers of proof and receive relevant evidence.

F. Regulate the course and conduct of the hearing.

G. Hold conferences, before or during the hearing, for the settlement or simplification of issues.

H. Rule on motions and dispose of procedural request or similar matters.

I. Within his discretion, or upon the direction of the Board, certify a question to the Board for its consideration and disposition.

J. Render an initial decision orally on the record or in writing if, before the close of the hearing, any party so requests in cases relating to rates, fares or charges, classification rules or regulations or practices affecting such matters or value of service, or mail compensation.

K. Renders a recommended decision orally on the record or in writing in cases where the action of the Board is subject to the approval of the President pursuant to Section 801 of the Federal Aviation Act of 1958.

BUREAU OF INTERNATIONAL AFFAIRS

The Bureau of International Affairs advises the Board on the formulation of positions to be taken by the United States on international civil aviation matters; provides representation for international conferences affecting aviation policy and for bilateral negotiations and consultations with foreign governments concerning air rights; represents the Board with the Department of State and with other agencies on international matters; and prepares general and special studies in the field of international aviation to advise and assist the Board to carry out its responsibilities in the economic development of international aviation.

The Office of the Director advises the Board on the formulation of positions to be taken by the United States on international aviation matters. He directs the participation of the Bureau's staff, in negotiation of bilateral agreements with foreign countries and in consultations under such agreements, and the working out of day-to-day problems arising from the operation of both United States and foreign airlines in international air transportation, both under and outside of bilateral agreements. He directs staff analyses of route requests of foreign governments and of competitive effects on United States airlines. The

Director represents the Board before Congressional committees, interdepartmental committees, government and industry groups and international conferences.

Geographic Areas Division

This Division performs the daily operating work of the Bureau and plans and prepares recommended Board positions for international air transport negotiations. The Bureau's personnel assigned generally act as the Bureau's representatives on the United States negotiating team to assist the Board Members assigned to specific negotiations.

In connection with bilateral aviation activities, the Bureau participates in:

A. Drafting and negotiating new agreements or amendments to existing agreements.

B. Consulting with foreign governments with respect to divergent views concerning the interpretation and application of such agreements.

C. Conducting informal discussions with foreign governments and foreign airlines and with United States international airlines to resolve problems arising under or in the absence of air transport agreements.

D. Formulating United States positions in the above situations based on economic analysis of the traffic experience of the airlines concerned. Close cooperation and coordination with the Board, with the other operating Bureaus and Offices within the Board, with the Department of State and with industry are exercised.

Project Development Division

The Chief of this Division makes recommendations concerning policies and objectives with respect to United States international aviation relations; monitors on a continuing basis established international policy and, where necessary, suggests modifications to meet changing conditions, effecting close coordination with the Department of State and other agencies and industry. He performs studies in depth concerning anticipated negotiations with specific countries where (1) a unique situation exists lacking established guidelines or (2) continued efforts to resolve outstanding problems over a long period of time having been unproductive; develops recommended negotiating positions on both route and policy issues; and participates in negotiations related thereto.

BUREAU OF OPERATING RIGHTS

This Bureau administers matters arising under economic regulations Sections 401, 402, 404, 405 (b), 407 (a), through (c), 408, 409, 411, 412, 415, 416, 417, 1002, 1104, and 1108 (b) of the Federal Aviation Act, as amended, relating to all carrier relationship matters. It participates in developing objectives with respect to operating rights for consideration of the Board. The Director of this Bureau advises the Board on policies and programs with respect to the economic regulation of the air transport industry involving routes and agreements matters. This Bureau is comprised of five Divisions; (1) Licensing Units, (2) Standards Division, (3) Supplimentary Services Division, (4) Agreements Division, and (5) Legal Division.

The responsibilities of these Divisions are described briefly.

Licensing Units Division

This Division is responsible for the grant or denial of applications for authority involving Domestic Trunk, International, and Local Service Air Carriers holding or applying for Certificates of Convenience and Necessity for scheduled air transportation issued under Section 401 of the Act. This includes consolidation, merger and acquisition of control and additions, suspensions, deletions or other modifications of existing route authority, and grants of new route authority. The division of Trunkline Carriers is accountable for granting or denying applications by air carriers holding or applying for Foreign Air Carrier Permits, involving direct foreign air transportation, and also for applications for interchange operations between air carriers.

Standards Division

This Division is responsible for the standardization of all economic regulations relating to routes and agreements.

Supplementary Services Division

The members of this Division rule on the operating authority for supplemental, charter, air taxi and indirect air carrier service, including air freight forwarders. It is necessary for any of these carriers to seek the approval of this division before changing their business name or adopting a trade name.

Agreements Division

The members of this Division approve or disapprove agreements filed pursuant to Section 412 of the Act, except those resolutions of the International Air Transport Association which set forth agreements on rates, fares, or tariffs rules. They grant or deny applications for approval of interlocking relationships, and act to determine if there is in existence any unauthorized interlocking relationships. Another important function of this Division is to rule on the application for consolidation, merger or acquisition of control other than between certificated air carriers.

Legal Division

This Division administers the legal aspects of all the functions performed by this Bureau and provides legal advice to the Director of the Bureau.

In addition to these services each Division, except the Legal Division, provide some common function such as; preparing exhibits, supplying expert witnesses, drafting orders, and recommending changes in the Economic and Procedural Regulations.

CHAPTER

IX

∨∨∨

Air Carrier
Economic Regulations

The Air transportation industry of the United States is regulated federally to a far greater extent than many other industries. In fact, as time progressed since 1938 when the Civil Aeronautics Act was passed, this federal regulatory control has increased. Unlike any other segment of American business enterprise, the air carriers have found themselves wholly or in part under government control since their inception during the decade of the 1920's. As has been seen in previous chapters, it was the action of the federal government, through the Post Office promotion of airmail, that led to the creation of the commercial air transport industry. Since the degree of control is so positive, hardly any act of consequence can be undertaken without federal knowledge or approval. This is true in the area of economics as well as safety.

The purpose of this chapter is to present and interpret the basic law from which all economic regulation of air transportation is derived. It must be remembered that although Title IV of the Federal Aviation Act is the foundation of air carrier economic regulation, the Civil Aeronautics Board, who is the agency responsible for carrying out economic regulatory activities, issues economic regulations which govern the daily economic business affairs of the air carriers. It therefore behooves every student of air transportation and every employee of an air carrier, as well as all those either directly or indirectly involved in or associated with air transportation, to have a knowledge of the substance of air carrier economic regulation.

The various sections of Title IV, of which there are seventeen will be discussed separately.

Section 401 – Certificate of Public Convenience and Necessity

No air carrier shall engage in certificated air transportation unless it has in force and has been granted a Certificate of Convenience and Necessity issued by the Civil Aeronautics Board.

Application for such certificates shall be made in writing to the Board. Upon the filing of an application, the Board shall give due notice to the general public and to any other persons as they may determine. Any interested person, therefore, may file with the Board a protest, of opposition to, or in support of, the issuance of a certificate. The application will then be set for public hearing and the Board is instructed to process the application as speedily as possible; this provision is not regarded as requiring them to prefer applications for certificates over other types of proceedings.

The Board may issue a certificate only if it finds that the public convenience and necessity require a particular service and that the applicant is fit, willing, and able to perform such service and will abide by the requirements of the Act and regulations thereunder. Certificates may be granted as to any part of the transportation applied for, in terms of either routes or classes of traffic (persons, property, or mail, or subdivisions of these classes), and on either a temporary or permanent basis. Certain public conveniences and necessity standards are set forth in the Declaration of Policy. Other appropriate factors to be considered are the overall policies of the Act as reflected by the various substantive provisions, policies of related statutes, etc. The fitness tests are not defined in the statute. However, the Board requires a showing of ability to finance, inaugurate, and operate a given service, and may deny authority on ground of the applicant's unwillingness to abide by lawful requirements as evidence by past unlawful conduct. Additionally, United States citizenship must be shown. The issuance, denial, amendment, or withdrawal of a certificate authorizing foreign or overseas air transportation is subject to the approval of the President.

The certificate shall specify the terminal points and the intermediate points, if any, between which air transportation is authorized, and the service to be rendered; the various rights conferred by a certificate, and the imposition of reasonable terms and conditions. Among the rights conferred is the right to engage in charter trips or perform any special service without regard to the points named in its certificate, under regulations prescribed by the Board. The Board has prescribed such regulations in Part 207 of the Economic Regulations. Additionally, it may be stated that the charter authority conferred extends only to the class of traffic for which the carrier is certificated.

The Board is prohibited from imposing conditions which restrict the right of an air carrier to add to or change schedules, equipment, accommodations, and facilities for performing the authorized transportation and service as the development of the business and the demands of the service shall require.

The Board makes extensive use of the power to impose conditions on certificates. Standard provisions applicable to all certificated air carriers and relating to nonstop service, service patterns, use of airports and change in airports, etc., are contained in Board regulations (Parts 202 and 203 of the Economic Regulations), and these provide that they are part of the conditions imposed upon certificates. The Board also imposes, from time to time, specific conditions upon individual certificates at the time of their issuance.

Sections 401 (f) and 401 (g) deal primarily with the duration, termination, amendment, suspension, and revocation of certificates. Each certificate shall be effective from the date specified and will continue in effect until suspended or revoked as in the case of a permanent certificate. A certificate may also be issued for a limited period of time; this is a temporary certificate. If service is not inaugurated within a period to be fixed by the Board (not less than 90 days), the Board may, after notice and hearing, cancel the certificate. The Board may revoke certificates, in contrast to exemption authority, for violations of the Act or regulations only after it has formally found the violation and given the carrier a reasonable time thereafter in which to comply. The Board may alter, amend, modify, or suspend a certificate in whole or in part if it finds that the public convenience and necessity so require. The Board has used this provision to suspend points served by one carrier and to substitute the services of another carrier on appropriate findings of need thereof. The power is also believed to permit the ordering of a carrier to serve additional points. The Board has taken the general position, however, that it cannot use its power in such fashion as would work a basic alteration in the character of a particular operation.

A certificate cannot be transferred unless Board approval is given as being consistent with the public interest; a certificate shall not confer any proprietary or exclusive rights in the use of the airspace or air navigation facilities. Abandonment of a route requires prior Board approval, whether it be permanent or temporary. Certificated air carriers must comply with certain provisions of the Railway Labor Act and certain minimum wages and hours of employment for pilots.

Whenever authorized by its certificate, an air carrier is required to transport airmail and to provide transportation for airmail when requested to do so by the Postmaster General. For transporting airmail the air carrier shall be entitled to receive reasonable compensation. A method is further provided whereby the Postmaster General may request new certifications to provide airmail service.

Section 402 — Permits to Foreign Air Carriers

This section prohibits unauthorized foreign air transportation between foreign points and the United States by foreign air carriers, and specifies the method by which such carriers may seek and obtain permits to engage in such transportation. It is generally comparable to Section 401 in relation to United States air carriers requiring notice and hearing on applications; prohibiting transfers except upon Board approval; authorizing the imposition of conditions; etc. As in the case of certificates authorizing international operation by the United States air carriers, Board action on foreign air carrier permits is subject to approval by the President. It may be stated that foreign air routes are generally established through bilateral agreements calling for reciprocal rights between the nations involved. The Board must, however, pass upon an application in the light of the standards of this section even though the matter may be the subject of a bilateral agreement.

Section 403 — Tariffs of Air Carriers

No discounting or rebating is allowed, and every air carrier is required to file its tariffs with the Board, to keep them open to public inspection, and to observe them so long as they are in effect. The Board is empowered to prescribe the form and manner of publishing tariffs and to specify their content with reference to certain classification, rules, and practices in relation to the service. Tariffs may be changed only on 30 days' notice unless sooner permitted to become effective by the Board.

Any air carrier, under conditions as the Board may prescribe, may grant reduced rate air transportation to ministers of religion on a space available basis.

Section 404 – Rates for Carriage of Persons and Property

It shall be the duty of every air carrier to provide the transportation authorized by its certificates; to provide safe and adequate service; to establish just and reasonable rates. Unjust discriminations and undue or unreasonable preferences in air transportation are prohibited. This is in conjunction with the provisions of Section 1002 relating to the fixing of rates and divisions of rates, establishing through service, and otherwise prescribing methods of enforcing the statutory responsibilities of air carriers.

Section 405 -- Transportation of Mail

The various powers and duties of the Postmaster General, and the responsibilities of air carriers with respect to the transportation of mail is specified here. The Postmaster General is authorized to make rules and regulations, not inconsistent with the Act or the Board's rules, for the safe and expeditious carriage of mail by aircraft; requires air carriers to file schedules with the Board and the Postmaster General, and directs the latter to designate the schedules on which mail is to be carried; empowers the Postmaster General to require carriers to establish additional mail schedules, subject to a right of appeal to the Board; and directs him to tender mail to certificate holders to the extent required by the Postal Service. The Board is empowered to fix maximum mail loads; the air carriers are required to transport the mail tendered and submit evidence of the performance of such mail service.

The section also provides that the Postmaster General shall have authority to fix rates to be charged foreign countries for the transportation of their airmail by United States carriers; that he may contract for certain emergency and experimental mail service; and that postal employees, while traveling on official business relating to transportation of mail by aircraft, shall be entitled to free transportation pursuant to regulations prescribed by the Board.

Section 406 -- Rates for Transportation of Mail

The Board is empowered and directed to fix and determine the fair and reasonable rates of compensation for the transportation of mail by aircraft as well as to prescribe the method of compensation as by the aircraft mile, pound mile, weight or space.

In fixing and determining fair and reasonable rates, the Board may fix different rates for different classes of air carriers and services. Paragraph "b" of this section states: "In determining the rate in each case the Board must take into consideration, among other factors, the *need of each such air carrier* for compensation for the transportation of mail sufficient to insure the performance of such service, and together with *all other revenue* of the air carrier, to enable such air carrier under *honest, economical and efficient management,* to maintain and continue the development of air transportation to the extent and of the character and quality required for the *Commerce, the Postal Service and the National Defense of the United States.*"

The most important parts of this statement are: need of each such air carrier; all other revenue; honest, economical, and efficient management. The courts have held that the Board must consider the need of an entire air carrier in fixing rates and that such rates cannot be fixed on a divisional basis without regard to profits from other operating divisions of the air carrier. This is known as the Offset Principle.

In determining other revenue, the Board cannot include capital gains derived from the sale of flight equipment if the air carrier submits written evidence to the Board that an amount equal to the gains has been reinvested for the purchase of other flight equipment or deposited in a fund for the purpose. Furthermore, the Board cannot take into account any losses sustained from the sale or disposition of flight equipment.

The standard of honest, economical, and efficient management requires a screening of actual operating results for past periods and a projection for future rates of the types and levels of expenditures which the Board will support with mail pay. Not all expenses, even through perhaps legitimate from a practical business standpoint, will be recognized for mail pay purposes. Generally speaking, the Board, after determining the level of operations and type of expenditures which it will support, provides subsidy mail pay at a level which will meet the carrier's expenses, including taxes, and provide a fair return on the investment. Again, this amount relates to the entire system and may include subsidy pay for a route on which mail is not in fact transported. In determining investment and expenses, the Board is generally governed by recognized principles of public utility law, including the principle that rates shall not be fixed retroactively after the date of the institution of a new rate proceeding.

There are two types of mail rates. The first is "service" which is payment for the act or service of transporting airmail. The service rate is designed to cover the actual cost to the air carriers for carrying the mail plus a fair return on their investment. Service rates are usually fixed on a ton-mile basis for the mail actually carried.

The second type of mail rate is "need" pay, or Public Service Revenue, commonly referred to as subsidy. This rate is over and above the service rate pay and is a rate of pay greater than just compensation which is designed to sustain the airline's operation. Need pay rates are usually fixed on a plane-mile basis without regard to mail actually transported.

The Board disburses the subsidy portion of mail pay, and the Postmaster General pays the service rate for mail actually transported. The Board has established a multi-element uniform service rate formula to determine the rates which the Postmaster General will pay for most domestic transportation, which consists of a rate for miles of carriage plus a uniform station or handling cost according to the class of city involved. This assures a uniform price to the Post Office and places all carriers on an equal basis in competing for mail. In the case of a subsidized carrier, the Board pays the subsidy at a rate generally fixed on a plane-mile basis without regard to mail transported, as contrasted to service rates which are fixed on poundage basis, less the amount of service pay received by the carrier from the Post Office Department.

It may be observed that, except in emergency and experimental situations, mail may be transported only by carriers authorized by the Board and at rates fixed by the Board. Moreover, an authorization to transport mail generally includes all mail irrespective of the postage thereon; hence, so-called surface mail (mail not bearing airmail postage), if it is tendered for transportation by the Postmaster General, may lawfully be transported, at rates fixed by the Board, by an air carrier otherwise authorized to transport mail.

The Board may also authorize a carrier to transport mail by exemption and fix rates for such exempted transportation. However, the Board's policy has been not to subsidize a carrier transporting mail only by exemption. The Board has on occasion issued certificates for mail transportation which contain a condition that subsidy will not be paid.

Section 407 -- Accounts, Records, and Reports

The Board requires annual, monthly, periodic, and special reports from air carriers, as well as specific answers to all questions upon which the Board may deem information to be necessary. Also, a copy of any contract that an air carrier may enter into must be filed with the Board.

Each air carrier shall submit a list showing the names of each of its stockholders holding more than five per cent of the entire capital stock. Furthermore, each officer and director shall transmit to the Board a report describing the shares of stock or other interests held by him in any air carrier, common carrier, or any company which has to do with any phase of aviation activity.

The Board prescribes the form of all accounts and records kept by air carriers including the movement of traffic, as well as the receipts and expenditures of money; and the length of time such accounts and records are to be preserved. It is unlawful for air carriers to keep any accounts or records other than those prescribed and in any other form except upon Board approval and if such additional accounts and records do not impair the integrity as required by the Board. In any case the additional accounts and records cannot constitute an undue financial burden on the air carrier.

This regulation has led to a complex detailed system known as the Uniform System of Accounts and Reports. The purpose of such a system is that all air carriers report their financial and other statistical data to the Board in the same standardized manner. This obviously is necessary if the Board is to know what is taking place throughout the airline industry and regulate the economics of the industry accordingly.

The Board has access to inspect all accounts and records as well as all equipment, lands and buildings of air carriers; also, all documents, papers and even correspondence. They employ special agents and auditors who carry out this function.

Section 408 -- Consolidation, Merger, and Acquisition of Control

This section governs certain interrelationships between air carriers, between air carriers and surface carriers, and between air carriers and persons engaged in any other phase of aeronautics. It prohibits, without prior Board approval, mergers of and common control between such persons, and precludes purchases, leases, etc., of a substantial part of an air carrier's properties. Despite the fact that many of the specific prohibitions in the section in terms run only against the acquisition of control of an air carrier by some other person, the Board has construed the section as being applicable to all common control situations between the classes of persons enumerated therein.

A person seeking approval of an acquisition of control is required to file an application with the Board, and the Board, after hearing, may approve upon certain findings. It must find that such acquisition will not be adverse to the public interest and that it will not result in a monopoly. Further, if the applicant is a surface carrier, the Board cannot approve the application unless it finds that the transaction in question will promote the public interest by enabling such carrier other than an air carrier to use aircraft to public advantage in its operation and will not restrain competition. This prohibition not only serves to preclude the acquisition of air carriers by surface carriers, but also represents a standard to be considered by the Board when a surface carrier or its affiliate makes application for a Certificate of Public Convenience and Necessity.

Interests in certain ground facilities such as ticket offices, hangars, and the like are expressly excluded from the coverage of this section.

Section 409 -- Prohibited Interests

This section is directed against management of an air carrier through participation therein of persons holding positions in or control over other air carriers, surface carriers, or persons engaged in other phases of aeronautics. Board approval of such interlocking relationships is required. The section also makes it unlawful for any officers or directors to profit from the sale of securities issued by an air carrier.

Section 410 -- Loans and Financial Aid

No government loan or financial aid shall be awarded to any air carrier without prior approval of the Secretary of Transportation.

Section 411 -- Methods of Competition

The law prohibits unfair or deceptive practices or unfair methods of competition in air transportation, and the Board is authorized, after notice and hearing, to compel air carriers and ticket agents to cease and desist from any such practice found to exist. Generally speaking, the section is to the air carrier field what Section 5 of the Federal Trade Commission Act is to other fields. False or misleading advertising, or the use of a name confusingly similar to that of another air carrier, are examples of the type of activity which the section is designed to reach.

Section 412 -- Pooling and other Agreements

This section requires the filing with the Board of all agreements between carriers relating to the pooling or apportioning of earnings, losses, traffic, equipment, and all other cooperative working arrangements. The Board is empowered to approve or disapprove any such agreement, except that it may not approve a compensation agreement between an Air Freight Forwarder and a common carrier subject to the Interstate Commerce Act. Agreements filed under this section range from contracts relating to the sharing of airport public address facilities to major agreements of the type for which approval is required under Section 408.

Section 413 -- Form of Control

Whenever reference is made to control, it is immaterial whether such control is direct or indirect. This section is an aid of Sections 408 and 409 and is believed to demonstrate a Congressional intent to reach all actual control situations irrespective of their form.

Section 414 -- Legal Restraints

This section provides that persons affected by Board orders entered under Sections 408, 409, and 412 shall be relieved from the antitrust laws and all other legal restraints to the extent necessary to enable such persons to do anything authorized, approved, or required by the Board's orders. The section, in effect, immunizes Board approved transactions from the antitrust laws and other laws which might otherwise prohibit them. In this connection, it should be noted that the Board is also responsible for enforcing the Clayton Act as against air carriers.

Section 415 -- Inquiry into Air Carrier Management

The Board is authorized to inquire into the management of the business of any air carrier and to require full and complete reports from air carriers and from any person controlling or controlled by such air carrier.

Section 416 -- Classification and Exemption of Carriers

This is the exemption provision previously referred to as being the source of operating authority of the non-certificated air carriers. It enables the Board to classify carriers and to exempt them by class or individually from the requirements of Title IV of the Act (other than certain labor provisions), provided that the Board finds that enforcement of such requirements would be an undue burden on such air carrier or class of air carriers by reason of the limited extent of, or unusual circumstances affecting, the operations of such air carrier or class of air carriers and is not in the public interest.

As noted, the statute permits exemption from practically all of the requirements of Title IV, including but not limited to the certificate provisions. Further, with respect to most provisions, there is no requirement for formal proceedings prior to granting exemptions. The Board has made extensive use of the section and has promulgated special rules of practice governing exemption applications. The Board's use of the exemption has ranged from permitting the carriage of a particular person on a particular flight or exempting minor transactions from reporting of Section 408 requirements, to such major matters as establishing classes of non-certificated air carriers.

In recent years, the courts have indicated that the Board should use the exemption power more sparingly and that more explicit findings should be made prior to granting an exemption. The tests of limited extent, unusual circumstance, and undue burden warranting exemption are not defined in the statute; and the courts appear to be increasingly insistent that the Board spell out in detail the basis for its grants.

Section 417 -- Special Operating Authorizations

This section, added to Title IV during recent years, provides that the Board may grant authority to Supplemental Air Carriers to conduct air transportation on a temporary basis if it is required in the public interest.

The Board may initiate an investigation on it's own or upon the request of an air carrier.

The Board will permit authority to serve a given route temporarily, if the regular certificated air carrier's capacity is insufficient to meet the public need.

The Board may permit service on a route which is not being regularly served.

The temporary authority for the Supplemental Air Carriers' operation will contain limitations affecting the frequency of service, type and size of aircraft used. The temporary permission is good for only 30 days, but may be extended for a total of 60 days.

CHAPTER

X

vvv

Air Carriers

Although it was not until after 1925 that the airline industry began to emerge and develop, there were two notable early attempts at purely commercial passenger operation in the United States.

The first so called air carrier, called "The St. Petersburg-Tampa Airboat Line," started carrying passengers on January 1, 1914. Three seaplanes, powered by a six cylinder aluminum engine which gave a top speed of sixty miles per hour, were used. They had an open cockpit for the one or two passengers. The pilot, Tony Jannus, was a well established aviator for the time.

The company flew seasonally for only a three month period and established the remarkable record of 1,274 passengers carried at $10 a round trip across Tampa Bay between St. Petersburg and Tampa, Florida, with no injuries or fatalities. The entire route was a distance of 21 miles. A surprisingly accurate schedule was maintained with but a few days of foul weather preventing some flights.

By the end of March, 1914, the company closed down after not having made sufficient money to warrant continuing; but indicated the future success of the airplane as a commercial transport carrier.

The next notable early venture in passenger air transportation took place on the route between Key West, Florida and Havana, Cuba by the "Aeromarine Airlines." From 1921 to 1924, they operated seasonally over this route and they began operating between Miami and Nassau as well as Detroit to Cleveland. Eleven flying boats were used to carry 6,814 passengers but the company ceased operating because of the lack of sufficient profit.

By the passage of the Civil Aeronautics Act in 1938, the air carrier industry began to mature. A section of this Act stated that the Civil Aeronautics Authority (later to become the Civil Aeronautics Board) could classify airlines for the purpose of regulatory control. Since that time new classes have been added and several changes have occurred. It is necessary, therefore, to review them in the knowledge of the further development of the United States commercial air transport industry. In the discussion of the several classes of air carriers a brief background and the characteristics of each are given.

At the outset it must be recognized that an air carrier is a Common Carrier. A Common Carrier is one who transports the public for hire and operates on a fixed schedule. There are two other types of carriers; Contract and Private. A

Aeromarine Airlines, 1921-24.

Contract Carrier is one who transports the public for hire but not on a fixed schedule. A Private Carrier is a privately owned and operated vehicle such as an automobile.

In addition to air carriers, there are four other transportation systems of common carriers. They are: Road, Rail, Water, and Pipe. All forms of public transportation fall within these five types of common carriers.

Practically all air carriers in the United States today, transporting the majority of the air traveling public, are Certificated Air Carriers. To be certificated, an air carrier must have been granted, by the Civil Aeronautics Board, a Certificate of Convenience and Necessity. This certificate states the regular defined routes and the cities to be served by fixed schedules transporting the public (including passengers and property).

A Certificate of Convenience and Necessity can be of either permanent or temporary duration; permanent for an indefinite period, or temporary for a stated number of years, usually one to five.

The Civil Aeronautics Act required the possession of a Certificate of Convenience and Necessity by a certificated airline and made the Civil Aeronautics Board the responsible authority for granting the certificate in the public interest. Public interest, or being in the public need, means for the Commerce, Postal Service and/or the National Defense of the United States.

The Civil Aeronautics Act further provided for the automatic granting of a Certificate of Convenience and Necessity, in 1938, to those air carriers who had been in continuous operation, and in possession of an airmail contract, for a period of ninety days prior to the passage of the Act. This was known as the Grandfather Clause and was Section 401e of the Civil Aeronautics Act of 1938.

DOMESTIC TRUNK AIR CARRIERS

As a result of the Grandfather Clause, sixteen major domestic airlines were granted Certificates of Convenience and Necessity. Thus, the first classification of air carriers, is known as Domestic Trunks and became the nucleous of the airline industry. The Domestic Trunks can trace their beginnings from the early days of the airmail private contractors after the passage of the Airmail Act in 1925.

The main characteristics of a Domestic Trunk are the operation of medium and long stage length routes serving the large metropolitan areas as well as the medium size cities. These routes have relatively high density traffic volume and in order to perform this type of operation, large equipment (aircraft) are used. The characteristics of the Trunks are starting to take on a new look. They are trying to drop many of the medium stage routes to medium size cities and concentrate on the long stage routes to metropolitan areas. Domestic service is limited to the continental limits of the United States, although most of the Domestic Trunk airlines now go outside of the country which places them in the next classification.

The Trunks have a permanent Certificate of Convenience and Necessity. In fact, at the time that this class was established as a result of the Civil Aeronautics

Act in 1938, there was no thought as yet of a temporary Certificate of Convenience and Necessity.

Of the original sixteen airlines granted permanent Certificates of Convenience and Necessity under the Grandfather Clause, there are now eleven as a result of mergers during the years.

As a result of overcompetition on many routes and skyrocketing operational costs, the Domestic Trunks entered the 1970's looking for merger partners. As the 1980's approach there may be fewer Domestic Trunks in the United States. In the late 1920's, Walter Brown was attempting to form the fledgling airline industry and he suggested three major airline systems. Fifty years later his suggestion may prove to be accurate.

The current eleven Domestic Trunk Air Carriers, along with the location of their headquarters office, are given below.

American Airlines	New York, New York
Braniff International	Dallas, Texas
Continental Air Lines	Los Angeles, California
Delta Air Lines	Atlanta, Georgia
Eastern Airlines	New York, New York
National Airlines	Miami, Florida
Northwest Airlines	St. Paul, Minnestoa
Pan American World Airways	New York, New York
Trans World Airlines	New York, New York
United Air Lines	Chicago, Illinois
Western Airlines	Los Angeles, California

Redefinition of Domestic Traffic

Effective January, 1970, the Civil Aeronautics Board (CAB) revised its definition of Domestic Traffic to include all traffic between the United States mainland and Hawaii and Alaska. This traffic had, in the past, been considered as International and Territorial.

Because of this redefinition, the Domestic and International and Territorial traffic and financial data for 1969-1972 are not strictly comparable to 1968 and previous years.

INTERNATIONAL AND TERRITORIAL AIR CARRIERS

The second classification that was established in 1938 was International Air Carriers which were United States Flag airlines that operated between the United States and a foreign country. Later, the class was expanded to International and Overseas which included routes defined as being between the continental United States and one of its territories or possessions.

Another classification that was established in 1938 was Territorial Air Carriers, which meant those air carriers that were conducting certificated flight operations within a territory of the United States. However, with the airline industry continuing to expand the original classes had to be realigned and new classes formed.

Today's classification, International and Territorial Air Carriers includes those United States airlines operating between the United States and foreign countries as well as those airlines which operate over international waters to territories and possessions of the United States. Examples of the latter are flights to the Caribbean.

In the International and Territorial class will be found those air carriers that are strictly international in the true sense in that they do not operate within the United States but entirely outside the country.

Another group within this class are the Domestic Trunk Air Carriers who have been granted international routes by the extension of their domestic routes into Mexico, South and Central America, and the Caribbean as well as to other foreign countries.

The characteristics of an International and Territorial Air Carrier are the flying of routes outside the continental limits of the United States. This includes from the United States to foreign countries, between foreign countries and over international waters. This requires the use of large equipment over long stage length routes. Permanent Certificates of Convenience and Necessity are possessed by those air carriers in this group.

The major International and Territorial Air Carriers currently operating, and their headquarters office location are the following:

American Airlines	New York, New York
Braniff International	Dallas, Texas
Delta Air Lines	Atlanta, Georgia
Eastern Airlines	New York, New York
National Airlines	Miami, Florida
Northwest Airlines	St. Paul, Minnestoa
Pan American World Airways	New York, New York
Trans World Airlines	New York, New York
Western Airlines	Los Angeles, California

INTRA-HAWAIIAN AIR CARRIERS

The present third classification to be discussed is the Intra-Hawaiian Air Carriers who fly between the many islands of the State of Hawaii.

Their unique characteristic is inter-island which dictates the use of medium size aircraft, usually twin engine, and short stage length routes.

The only two air carriers in this class are:

Aloha Airlines	Honolulu, Hawaii
Hawaiian Airlines	Honolulu, Hawaii

727-100
93-131 passengers

BAC-111
65-89 passengers

DC-9
80-125 passengers

B-747
320-490 passengers

707
121-219 passengers

727-200
120-189 passengers

737
103-115 passengers

CV-880
88-110 passengers

DC-10
270-380 passengers

DC-8
105-259 passengers

INTRA-ALASKAN AIR CARRIERS

The fourth classification of air carriers is the Intra-Alaskan Air Carriers, who operate solely within the State of Alaska. For the most part they are characterized by seasonal operation due to the trend of business and weather. They use small and medium equipment on short to medium stage length routes.

The list of these airlines confining their flying service within the boundaries of Alaska that are in current operation are:

Alaska Airlines
Kodiak Airlines
Reeve Aleutian Airlines
Wien Air Alaska Airlines

Upon reviewing the first four classifications of air carriers it will be noted that some companies appear in more than one class. This, of course, has been approved by the Civil Aeronautics Board and represents an extension of the air carrier's original routes.

DOMESTIC LOCAL SERVICE AIR CARRIERS

The fifth major air carrier classification, Domestic Local Service Air Carriers, (also unofficially called Feeders), did not come about until 1945, when the establishment of their particular type of air service was permitted by the Civil Aeronautics Board. They have had a difficult development but have now shown indications of stabilization and profit.

During World War II about fifty per cent of the airlines' aircraft were engaged in military contracts, leaving a severe shortage for civilian use, particularly at a time when the demand for air travel increased.

One notable lack of air service was between the small communities and the major trunk airline cities. As early as August, 1943, the Civil Aeronautics Board began an investigation into the feasibility of such local air service. The investigation showed that there was no immediate prospect of profitable passenger traffic; since the route distance would be so short, there was no indication that the airmail service could be improved upon over the existing surface facilities; as far as air cargo was concerned there simply was not any.

In spite of the bleak picture in regard to local service profitability, the Civil Aeronautics Board allowed the certification, in 1945, of twenty companies in 46 States on the basis of the Board's power to experiment in air transportation. Since it was to be an experiment the Certificates of Convenience and Necessity were granted for a three year period. This was the first time that temporary certificates came into being.

The Trunk airlines opposed the certification of the Local Service Air Carriers because they no doubt were afraid that they would grow larger in time and create undue competition. In issuing the order for certification for Civil Aeronautics Board made it quite clear that this was not be the case. It was the Civil Aeronautics Board's intention to restrict the Feeders to small cities of approximately 25,000 population and less. They were also to confine their route operation within a small geographic area and were not allowed to give non-stop through service between any one small city and the terminus Trunk airline stop. Once this policy was established the Trunks were satisfied and favored the Local Service air carriers because it meant they would bring added traffic to them from the smaller cities and communities.

The Local Service Air Carriers' costs were high due to short length routes, low traffic density and the use of small aircraft. This condition has improved with the expansion of their routes and the purchase of jet aircraft.

Due to the obvious lack of sufficient profit the Local Service airlines required a large subsidy payment in the form of mail pay.

Several of these new airlines never started flying while others did not have their Certificates of Convenience and Necessity renewed at the expiration of their three year certificate.

In 1948, while still receiving the major portion of their income from mail pay, the remaining existing Local Service Airlines had their Certificates of Convenience and Necessity renewed for a five year period. About the time these certificates expired in 1953, the Local Service Air Carriers were requesting that their certificates be made permanent. Their valid argument was that since they only had a temporary life they could not attract invested capital, make long range bank loans or enter into funded debt. Without new money they could not hope to acquire better facilities and more economical aircraft to lower unit cost and thus lessen their dependence on subsidy.

The Civil Aeronautics Board denied their plea on the grounds that the experimental period was to continue and in 1953 the Certificates of Convenience and Necessity were again renewed for another five year period. Before they expired an investigation was started resulting in a Civil Aeronautics Board case. By 1958, the outcome of this case was that the Civil Aeronautics Board reluctantly granted permanent certification but in a unique manner. A review of all the routes was made and those that proved profitable were permanently certificated; the cities that were not supporting enough traffic, for at least a break even condition, were continued on the temporary basis. This policy by the Civil Aeronautics Board is known as "Use It or Lose It." A minimum standard was set of five passengers boarded daily to be reached after a year and a half. If this did not occur then the route was to be ordered abandoned or continued for a longer temporary period. The responsibility for supporting and continuing air service to these below profit cities was placed upon the cities themselves, hence the term "Use It or Lose It." In regard to this policy Senator A. S. Monroney said in a speech before the Association of Local Transport Airlines:

"I recognize the need to re-evaluate the cities which should be served, and, in this connection, I do not believe we have adequate standards or accurate measurements to decide the difficult question as to which cities can justify continued service.

These small communities cannot generate enough traffic to support service by F-27's, Convairs or the new short-haul jets. But there are new, small, twin-engine aircraft available today, capable of carrying six to ten passengers, which are being used for this very purpose in scheduled service with this type of aircraft, either through actual operation by local service carriers, or through contractual agreements with the many taxi operators in the country which already own these small aircraft."

The turning point for the Local Service Air Carriers occurred when the Civil Aeronautics Board adopted the Class Mail Rate. This is the formula which determines the subsidy to the Local Service Air Carriers for providing service to cities which do not produce sufficient revenue to cover the cost. This action gave these carriers a future to look forward to and an impact on the financial community.

As a result of permanent certification the Local Service Air Carriers could and did acquire much needed capital to purchase new F-27 and F-227 turbo-prop aircraft and twin-engine jet aircraft. Their plight was also aided by Congress providing a guaranteed loan for the purchase of new aircraft. Therefore, their condition has improved greatly.

The Local Service Air Carriers are now giving better service and have become less dependent on subsidy (public service revenue).

As in the case of the Trunks, increasing costs have slowed the profit picture for the Local Service Air Carriers and they too are looking for merger partners. By the 1980's they should be reduced in number. As the Trunks try to reduce medium stage routes the Locals are picking them up and the classification, Local Service Air Carrier, becomes a misleading name. For example, Southern Airways which started in Georgia, Alabama, and Mississippi as a Local Service Air Carrier now has routes extending to New York and Chicago in the North and to Miami in the South. Ozark, the Local Service Air Carrier of Arkansas and Missouri, extends eastward to New York. The three "Feeders" on the West Coast have merged creating a "Feeder" airline from Calgary, Alberta, Canada, in the North to points in Mexico in the South. Their eastern most point is Salt Lake City. The Local Service Air Carrier concept of "Feeder" is gone; it has become "Regional" air carrier.

The Local Service Air Carriers and their headquarters location are currently as follows:

Air New England	Boston, Mass.
Allegheny Airlines	Washington, D.C.
Frontier Airlines	Denver, Colorado
Hughes Air West	San Francisco, California
North Central Airlines	Minneapolis, Minnesota
Ozark Air Lines	St. Louis, Missouri
Piedmont Airlines	Winston-Salem, North Carolina
Southern Airways	Atlanta, Georgia
Texas International Airlines	Houston, Texas

ALL CARGO AIR CARRIERS

The next classification of air carriers to appear chronologically are the All Cargo Air Carriers.

Shortly after the close of World War II several individuals and small, independent companies entered into charter, non-scheduled activities. This was a result of available surplus military cargo aircraft and discharged servicemen who had gained experience during the war in the various services, such as the Air Transport Command and the Naval Air Transport Service.

They conducted their civilian post war flights under the exemption of certain economic regulations of the Civil Aeronautics Acts which permitted charter flights by non-certificated air carriers. Predominately they were one or two airplane operations that carried air freight wherever the business opportunity appeared and for whatever rates the traffic and competition would allow. When the competition became too great, as a result of the appearance of literally hundreds of them, many began carrying passengers in the same manner. This created choas in the air industry, not only within their own ranks, but also with the certificated air carriers.

Eventually the Civil Aeronautics Board legislated economic regulatory control. The laws were mainly directed towards these passenger carrying non-certificated air carriers. This caused a hardship upon the truly air cargo companies since they were not carrying passengers but transporting air freight only. The Civil Aeronautics Board recognized their situation and after an investigation and a case, concluded that they should have a valued position in air transportation. This was the Air Freight Case of July, 1949, which allowed for the awarding of Certificates of Convenience and Necessity to All Cargo Air Carriers. For the second time, since the requirement of Certificates of Convenience and Necessity in 1938, the certificates were granted for a temporary period which was to be five years.

The original four All Cargo Air Carriers were Slick Airways, United States Airlines, The Flying Tiger Line, and Air News.

Of the original group certificated in 1949, Air News was not successful and never really got underway; United States Airlines, after a somewhat successful time but a difficult financial and organizational period, also ceased operations. Both companies' certificates were not renewed after a time of inactivity.

The newly certificated All Cargo Air Carriers enjoyed the same rights and privileges as did other certificated airlines, however, certain limitations were placed upon them at first, due to the nature of their business activities. Such limitations were that they could not transport passengers and would not be permitted to engage in conducting air mail services, simply because they did not have definite routes.

It has only been recently that the Civil Aeronautics Board has allowed all Cargo Air Carriers to enter into contracts with the Post Office and also to transport passengers on a charter only basis.

Due to the growth of their air cargo activities, the All Cargo Air Carriers now conduct scheduled service between designated areas in the United States which serve major cities along the route. It is even now possible, due to necessity, to reserve space on board a given flight for an amount of air freight.

The potential of the all cargo industry is still immense when it is understood that less than one tenth of one per cent of the Intercity freight in the United States today travels by air, and most of this upon the passenger carrying Domestic Trunk Airlines.

The All Cargo Air Carriers have had to sustain themselves with military contracts; also the lack of a truly, economically operating air cargo aircraft has been one of the major problems. Only now, since the introduction of the wide body aircraft such as the Boeing 747 does the future hold a glimmer of brightness.

The Certificates of Convenience and Necessity were renewed at each expiration date, however they are now permanent.

The list of the present All Cargo Air Carriers include:

Airlift International	Miami, Florida
The Flying Tiger Line	Los Angeles, California
Seaboard World Airlines	New York, New York

HELICOPTER AIR CARRIERS

Although Leonardo Da Vinci first presented the idea of the rotary wing, it took over two hundred years until it was further developed. Spiral wing is the literal meaning of the word helicopter.

The first successful helicopter in the United States was built by Igor Sikorsky in 1939, after having started experimenting in Russia as early as 1908.

Helicopters were produced for the military by the end of the World War II but saw no real practical use. It was not until 1946 that the first helicopter was certificated for commercial purposes. Using the helicopter for local air mail service was experimented by the Post Office shortly thereafter and received enthusiastic support of the Postmaster General in his 1947 fiscal report.

The vertical take-off and landing ability and unnecessary requiring of conventional runways, made the helicopter ideal for intra-city service. Due to the size of the metropolitan areas and traffic congestion delaying air mail delivery, the helicopter was tried as a mail carrier in Los Angeles. The service so speeded up the delivery of mail from the airport, central Post Office and outlying districts that the first air carrier company to use helicopters was formed and started flying in October 1947. Los Angeles Airways using helicopters exclusively, became the first air carrier of its kind to be granted a temporary Certificate of Convenience and Necessity. In so doing the Civil Aeronautics Board recognized the unusual serviceable advantages of the helicopter and created the classification Helicopter Airmail Lines. Originally they were restricted to a fifty mile radius of the main Post Office and could carry only air mail. However, with the advent of larger and better models of helicopters they have become certificated by the Civil Aeronautics Board to carry not only air mail but also passengers and air cargo. The classification is now known as Helicopter Air Carriers.

Two other air carriers utilizing helicopters in the same manner were certificated to operate in Chicago and New York. Later, another Helicopter Air Carrier started service in the San Francisco-Oakland area.

The characteristics of the Helicopter Air Carrier is, of course, extremely short stage length; intra-city or metropolitan area. The expenses of operating helicopters are extremely high in comparison to conventional aircraft. As a result of this high operational cost, along with extreme short stage, the Helicopter Air Carriers have had to rely heavily upon government subsidy in the form of air mail payments. Although the major portion of their gross revenues has been from mail pay the helicopter companies have proved the value of this type of service. In 1965, the policy of the government was changed to that of eliminating subsidy to the Helicopter Air Carriers.

The Certificate of Convenience and Necessity held by the three Helicopter Air Carriers are temporary. These carriers are:

Chicago Helicopter Airways
New York Airways
San Francisco & Oakland Helicopter Airlines

SUPPLEMENTAL AIR CARRIERS

For an understanding of this classification of air carriers it is necessary to recall the events already discussed in the history leading to the establishment of the All Cargo Air Carriers which pertain to the passenger carrying activities of the non-certificated airlines, many of which were only interested in passenger traffic and not air cargo. They equipped their aircraft to carry passengers and did so in charter flights.

Their facilities were inadequate and their maintenance generally poor. This led to a relatively high accident rate and subsequent enforcement, by the Civil Aeronautics Administration, of safety regulations.

Economic regulations were also soon forthcoming, but in some cases the companies or individuals acted in flagrant and direct violation of such controls. Only after years of litigation was a place in air transportation recognized for the honest, well meaning and equipped, non-certificated air carrier. This, of course, is the present classification of Supplemental Air Carriers.

The reason for their being was to relieve pressure on high density Domestic Trunk routes, when this occurred seasonally.

On such routes as New York -- Miami, during the height of the winter season, if the Trunk Air Carriers did not have sufficient seats available, it was the intention of the Civil Aeronautics Board that this overload of traffic could be carried by a Supplemental Air Carrier. Therefore, their flight operations each month are limited between any two domestic cities. They may, however, conduct unlimited charter flights. There are approximately 13 such companies currently in existence, although their numbers fluctuate from year to year.

Since the advent of the jet transport, which brought about a sufficient number of passenger seats available, the purpose of the Supplemental Air Carrier is becoming less necessary. In recent cases they have been denied operations by the Civil Aeronautics Board because the existing Trunk Air Carriers have the capacity to serve even an abnormally high seasonal demand. This situation does not bother them too greatly because practically all of the Supplemental Air Carriers are under contract with the military to transport both troops and supplies. They have found this to be a more lucrative and dependable source of income.

The Supplementals have found another extremely lucrative, but less dependable, source of income in charter work throughout the United States and foreign countries. This type of service is being strongly opposed by the Trunks, Internationals, "Regionals," and Foreign Air Carriers.

Although the Supplemental Air Carriers are certificated, they are so only to the extent of the meaning and scope of their services as defined by the Civil Aeronautics Board. (Refer to Page 48 for CAB definition.) Their certificate is a Certificate of Convenience and Necessity that does not contain the same requirements and authorizations granted to the other classes of air carriers previously discussed. Their operations are conducted by exempting them from requirements for scheduled passenger and airmail service.

INTRA-STATE AIR CARRIERS

In some states there may be found a classification of air carrier that has developed in recent years known as Intra-state Air Carriers. Their operations are limited to an area within the borders of one state. Their right to operate is granted by an agency of that state.

They are not subject to the economic regulations of the Civil Aeronautics Board since the nature of their operations do not cross state lines.

Characteristically they resemble the Local Service Air Carriers when they began operation in 1945. The Intra-state Air Carriers serve the small and medium populated communities whose traffic density is low. Their routes are designed to originate and terminate at the larger airport cities. This group has not developed as rapidly as first expected.

COMMUTER AIR CARRIERS

As the Local Service Air Carriers started to expand by seeking longer stage routes, larger metropolitan areas, and larger aircraft, a new group of airlines started to appear. The Local Service Air Carriers were plagued with outdated equipment and low density routes. The new aircraft being developed at this time were capable of carrying 90 to 120 passengers while the Local's outdated equipment handled 44 to 50 passengers. In order to fill these new aircraft, higher density routes were sought and approved by the Civil Aeronautics Board. The result was that many communities on low density routes felt a reduction in air service.

Out of this came a new breed of air carrier; the Commuter Air Carrier. Many Commuters developed from air taxis while others were totally new corporations. Commuter Air Carriers differ from air taxis in that they fly a published schedule on specific routes whereas the air taxi flies on demand anywhere the passenger wants to go. The Commuters have two basic controls placed upon them in a ddition to safety requirements. These are: (1) meeting prescribed liability insurance, and (2) operating aircraft with a gross takeoff weight of less than 12,500 most popular commuter aircraft. The Civil Aeronautics Board determined a new limitation, rather than the 12,500 pound limit it is now a 30 seat/7,500 pound revenue payload. The Bureau of Operating Rights have stated that Commuter Air Carriers must be encouraged to continue, "but Commuter operations shouldn't be allowed to enter long haul high density markets except possibly to provide specialized service with non-competitive equipment."

Commuter Air Carriers are not issued a Certificate of Convenience and Necessity by the Civil Aeronautics Board and therefore are not controlled as far as the routes they serve or the fares they charge, however the Federal Aviation Administration does regulate their safety programs. Some of these new carriers are providing substitute service into cities where Trunks and Locals have suspended service, however the major carrier is responsible for service to these cities if a Commuter fails to provide adequate service. Commuter Air Carriers are now serving as designated mail carriers in many markets. The next step for the Commuters is to seek to obtain route protection from some governmental agency. Today, commuter routes have the same characteristics that the Local Service Air Carriers had prior to the expansion in the 1960's, that is, short haul and low density. New Commuter Air Carriers are constantly emerging, however, their failure rate is very high. The Commuter Air Carriers transported nearly five million passengers during the fiscal year 1972. The number of Commuters involved was 162. The number of flights increased 12.4% over the previous year while the amount of passengers increased 14%. Of the 1,325 pairs of cities receiving commuter passenger service, 236 averaged 10 or more passengers per day. The average length of passenger trip was 100 miles.

For a Commuter Air Carrier to be successful, it must start with the proper financial backing and have a management team that controls the flow of cash adhering to sound principles. Careful selection of equipment and routes tied to a service that is highly passenger oriented are other features necessary for a viable carrier. Commuter Air Carriers must accept the responsibility that they are airlines and not air taxis, if they adopt the philosophy that they are large air taxis they are doomed to failure.

This segment of the industry and government must watch the potential impact of lack of economic regulations and over competition. The Commuter Air Carriers are the most dynamic part of the air transportation industry at the present time.

NON-CERTIFICATED AIR CARRIERS

In what might be termed a diversified group of miscellaneous air transportation operators, is the classification Non-Certificated Air Carriers.

It is not the intention or nature of business of those in this class to give scheduled flight activities. In lieu of a Certificate of Convenience and Necessity they are required to possess a Letter of Registration issued by the Civil Aeronautics Board.

This class is composed of two unlike divisions.

The first are called Air Taxi, and as the name implies, they offer air transportation when and to wherever the passenger may desire. The rates for this special service are much higher than for a certificated air carrier. Air Taxi operations are allowed by the Civil Aeronautics Board under authorization through the exemption process and they may operate aircraft that have a certificated gross take-off weight of 12,500 pounds or less. For the most part this means single engine or light twin engine airplanes. Many helicopters may also be found in this group.

Air Taxi companies may be found throughout the United States at many airports of all sizes. Presently there are about 2,700 listed with the Civil Aeronautics Board, although the numbers constantly are changing; 937 use multi-engine aircraft and 102 others operate helicopters.

The second division of Non-Certificated Air Carriers are known as Air Freight Forwarders who also conduct business under the exemption authority by the Civil Aeronautics Board.

Surface freight forwarding has been in existence since man has been engaged in business. With the advent of the airplane it was natural that freight forwarding should take to the air.

An Air Freight Forwarder is a consolidator or middleman between the shipper and the airline company. His nature of business is to collect individual shipments, consolidate them into a large load destined to a given city, and have the airline carry them. He is in reality a customer of the airline.

The rates charged by the Air Freight Forwarder cannot be more to the public than those of the airline. He earns a profit only by the spread between what he receives from the individual shipper and the price he pays to the airline company for quantity shipments. A further source of income is by giving extra services, such as packing and special handling, to the shipper.

The Air Freight Forwarder does not own or operate aircraft, but since he receives the public property for transportation by air, he is in reality engaged indirectly in air transportation and as such is subject to economic regulations of the Civil Aeronautics Board.

Currently there are approximately 150 Air Freight Forwarders in operation both in domestic and international services.

FOREIGN AIR CARRIERS

Those airline companies that are registered in a foreign country, but none-the-less conduct air transport services to and from the United States, are termed Foreign Air Carriers. In order to conduct such scheduled flights they must be granted a Foreign Air Carrier Permit issued by the Civil Aeronautics Board.

Foreign Air Carriers are allowed to discharge and enplane traffic at gateway or international airports of entry, they are not allowed to carry traffic between any two domestic points in the United States.

A more detailed discussion concerning this subject will be found in Chapter XI dealing with Foreign and International Air Transportation.

The CAB now has power over rates set by foreign carriers when flying to the United States.

THE AIR TRANSPORT ASSOCIATION

The trade association of the certificated air carriers of the United States, which acts as a service group to the airline industry, is the Air Transport Association of America. Their headquarters are located at Washington, D. C.

The purposes of the association are three-fold.

1. To advance the common interests of the certificated airline industry.

2. To develop better services for the public.

3. To share in national defense.

The Air Transport Association pools the talents of the air industry to tackle a wide range of common interests, from design standards for new aircraft to the cutting of red tape of international travel. They have a common motive; that of maintaining the best system of air transportation that is possible for the benefit, not only of the individual airline, but also for the national economy and the general public.

The Association is financially supported by the member airlines; the amount they pay is based upon their gross income. Currently there are approximately 42 members.

When the airline industry was in its adolescent stage, the young companies gathered together at a meeting in Chicago in 1936; this was the beginning of the Air Transport Association. Representatives of 17 airlines established the prime objective to promote the airline business in general and to serve the welfare and interest not only of the Association members but also the public at large.

The Air Transport Association accomplishes its task through a system of conferences and committees. The conferences are composed of representatives from the airlines who are appointed by the airlines and work with each other and the association staff on broad areas of interest. Decisions made by either of the two main conferences, namely Operations and Traffic, must be unanimous. All member airlines have an equal voice in major decisions affecting the entire industry.

The conferences appoint committees, which are made up of specialists in their given field, to pursue specific tasks. The committees are strengthened by the addition of special staff technicians of the Air Transport Association.

The department description is as follows:

The Operations and Engineering Department acts to develop safety by continually working toward the improvement of air transportation through more efficient airline operations. The Operations and Engineering Department serves the Operations Conference and the Engineering and Maintenance Committees who are composed of various airline representatives. One of the major functions of the department is the continuous consultation and cooperation with various governmental agencies such as the Federal Aviation Administration, the Federal Communications Commission, and the Civil Aeronautics Board. Such cooperation extends over a wide range of subjects including safety regulations for airline operations, air traffic control, navigation, and landing aids, as well as improved airport lighting.

The Operations Section is concerned with a wide variety of government regulations, procedures, facilities, and services which have an effect on the safety and the efficiency of the conduct of airline flights. Some of the facilities and services which they deal with include airports, weather reporting, aeronautical charting, the designation of airways and restricted and warning areas. Such other matters concern accident investigation procedures, air navigation hazards and noise abatement procedures.

The Air Navigation and Traffic Control Section is concerned with the national system of controlling aircraft in flight and with the development of all types of aids to air navigation. This section has the job of keeping the airlines informed of the latest steps which are taken by the government to improve air traffic control.

The Engineering Division has broad responsibility of maintaining close coordination between the airlines in dealing with engineering and maintenance.

The function of the Finance and Accounting Department, although less spectacular than the flying end of the business, is none the less one of the most critical in airline operations. This department serves the Airline Finance and Accounting Conference composed of the various financial officers of the certificated air carriers. One of the department's most important services in operating the Clearing House which has been established by the Conferences and handles more than 80 million dollars a month in interline settlements. The Department further promotes uniformity in airline accounting procedures.

The Personnel Relations Department serves the Personnel Relations Conference and conducts an advisory, research and statistical program concerned with personnel and industrial relations matters. Their responsibilities range from day to day problems of personnel to the broad programs affecting the entire industry. Special studies are undertaken on all phases of personnel and industrial relations.

The Traffic Department serves the Air Traffic Conference of America by working continually toward the improvement of passenger service by finding better ways of ticketing and baggage handling.

The interline concept, which allows passengers to use a number of airlines on a single trip without re-ticketing or rechecking baggage, could not function without the closest cooperation between the airlines. The job of welding this cooperation into one unified system is the responsibility of the Traffic Department.

This department publishes a manual consisting of 140 pages of details which cover reservations, ticketing, baggage and cargo handling. They also consolidate, publish, and keep current with the Civil Aeronautics Board, all joint rules, passenger fares and cargo rates on behalf of the certificated airlines. This enables the Civil Aeronautics Board and the public to deal with one source concerning tariffs.

A Research and Economics Department gathers, analyzes, and interprets data regarding the traffic, finances and operations of the airline industry, other

lbs. The 15 passenger Beech-99 and 19 passenger DeHaviland Twin Otter are the
forms of transportation and the economy in general. This information is used by
the airlines to help determine industry policies.

The Legal Department is another service group which furnishes counsel to
the Air Transport Association management as well as its various departments,
conferences and committees. The Legal Department prepares legal opinion,
contracts, resolutions and other documents, and represents the Air Transport
Association in all legal matters.

The Public Affairs Department deals with all air transport matters at the
state and local level. This is done through a public affairs committee which
maintains liaison with other civil aviation associations to keep all advised of the
airline industry's need to cooperate in joint matters.

Since the air transport industry is closely regulated by the federal
government, it logically has a direct interest in the enactment of sound aviation
legislation. The Federal Affairs Department serves as a channel between the
industry and the Government. It is a source of factual information about the
airlines for Congressional committees and for individual congressmen; and it
provides a means whereby the view of the airlines may be conveyed to Congress.

The Public Relations Department fills the need of informing the public
about the airline industry. It provides information on the industry to
educational groups and also distributes material for educational purposes. Press
releases come from this department. An annual statistical report covering various
aspects of the airline industry is published by the Public Relations Department
and they also act in an advisory capacity to all officers of the Air Transport
Association as well as the member airlines.

The following are members of the Air Transport Association of America.

Member Airlines

*Air Canada	Hughes Air West
Alaska Airlines	National Airlines
Allegheny Airlines	North Central Airlines
Aloha Airlines	Northwest Airlines
American Airlines	Ozark Air Lines
Braniff International	Pan American World Airways
*C.P. Air	Piedmont Airlines
Continental Airlines	Southern Airways
Delta Air Lines	Texas International Airlines
Eastern Airlines	Trans World Airlines
The Flying Tiger Line	United Air Lines
Frontier Airlines	Western Air Lines
Hawaiian Airlines	Wien Air Alaska Airlines

*Associate Member

CHAPTER
XI
∨∨∨

International and Foreign
Air Transportation

The growth and development of International and Foreign Air Transportation has not paralleled that of domestic air transportation in the United States.

It is necessary to understand exactly what is included in the terms International and Foreign as used in air transportation. As is generally used, International Air Transportation is the conducting of air transportation, by an air carrier of the United States, outside of the nation to another country. The class of United States air carrier known as International and Territorial represents this definition and was discussed in the previous chapter.

Foreign Air Transportation, on the other hand, is the operation of air carriers of nations other than the United States. In some cases Foreign Air Carriers perform air service to and from the United States.

"Overseas" refers to a type of air route and is geographic in nature; it is not a classification of air carrier. It is a type of operation conducted by United States air carriers flying from the continental United States to a point outside the continental limits but still a state, territory or possession of the United States. This type of operation can be performed by an International and Territorial Air Carrier. An example would be a flight from Miami, Florida, to San Juan, Puerto Rico, or from San Francisco, California to Honolulu, Hawaii.

One point to be noted in the study of International and Foreign Air Transportation is that while the United States International Air Carriers are privately owned corporations, Foreign Air Carriers for the most part are either wholly or partially owned by their governments.

The progression of international conferences and conventions which resulted in the evolution of the present legal framework under which international and foreign aviation operates is reviewed briefly below.

Paris Convention -- 1919

In 1919 at Paris the International Convention for Air Navigation recognized that each nation has complete and exclusive control of the air space above its territory, thus preventing the airlines of a country from flying over another without permission.

For the purpose of the convention the territory of a state shall be understood as including the national territory, both that of the mother country and of the colonies, and the territorial waters adjacent therein.

This convention was ratified by twenty-six countries and served as the legal document for international air transportation outside the Western Hemisphere. The United States did sign the convention papers. However, it was not ratified by this country because the convention was associated with the League of Nations to which the United States did not belong.

The main fact of this convention was the establishment of Sovereignty of Air Space theory.

Pan American Convention on Commercial Aviation -- 1928

This conference, also known as the Havana Conference, was modeled after the Paris Conference and recognized that every country has complete and exclusive sovereignty over the air space above its territory and territorial waters. This convention was signed by twenty-one countries which also included the United States.

Warsaw Convention -- 1929

This was the first international convention pertaining to liability and has been ratified by more than sixty countries including the United States.

The Warsaw Convention was signed in October, 1929 and went into effect on February 13, 1933. This Convention was recognized almost immediately as the most important document in international and foreign commercial air transportation. In 1934, the United States Senate gave its consent to the Convention.

The Warsaw Convention provided the rules of air carrier accident liability in international air transportation. It prescribes that the airline is liable for damages for death or injury to passengers, destruction, loss, or damage to baggage and goods, and loss resulting from delay in transporting passengers, baggage, and merchandise. It also sets standards for passenger tickets, cargo waybills and other air travel documents.

After World War II ended, many people suggested, especially in Great Britain, a revision of the Warsaw Convention. In the United States, those who urged for a revision wanted an increase in the liability limits which at that time were only $8,300 per person.

These discussions continued until September, 1955, when the Convention was amended. The diplomatic conference called for this event met at Hague, at which the United States was represented, and there was signed the so-called Hague Protocol to the Warsaw Convention. This Protocol made two major changes in the Convention. First it doubles the monetary limit to $16,600 as the maximum recovery for death, and second, it extended to agents of the carrier the limitation of liability now provided to the carrier. The Protocol has been signed and ratified by some 45 countries. The United States signed the Protocol on December 1, 1964. The subject of ratification of this document by the United States has been most controversial.

The Interagency Group on International Aviation, in August of 1962, made two recommendations to the Secretary of State. These were:

1. That the United States ratify the Hague Protocol, which, upon ratification by a sufficient number of states, would raise the liability of carriers in international aviation from the present limit of $8,300 to a new limit of $16,600.

2. That the United States enact legislation which would require United States flag carriers operating in international air transportation to provide all passengers with automatic accident insurance for each passenger insured in an accident, in addition to the recovery provided for in the Hague Protocol.

In August, 1964, Secretary of State, Dean Rusk recommended that the Senate of the United States give its advice and consent to the ratification of the Protocol.

Chicago Conference -- 1944

In September of 1944 the United States government invited the allied and neutral powers to attend an international conference to be held in Chicago. This conference came about after discussions between the United States and Great Britain in 1943. Fifty-four allied and neutral nations attended only Saudi Arabia and the Soviet Union did not attend.

This conference had three major objectives: (1) the establishment of an International Air Interim Council, (2) the establishment of provisional world air route arrangements, and (3) an agreement on principles for a permanent aeronautical body and a multilateral aviation convention.

Four different proposals for the organization of civil aviation were presented by the United States, Great Britain, Canada, and a joint Australia-New Zealand plan, however it finally resulted in secret talks between the United States, Great Britain, and Canada to resolve the issue.

After thirty-seven days of continuous meetings the Chicago Conference resulted in five documents being established.

1. Bilateral Agreement Rules
2. Provisional International Civil Aviation Organization
3. Permanent International Civil Aviation Organization
4. International Air Transit Agreement (Two Freedoms)
5. International Air Transport Agreement (Five Freedoms)

1 -- Bilateral Agreement Rules

One of the three major objectives of the Conference concerned air routes. At first it was the desire of the leaders of the conference to develop a multilateral air transport agreement, which many countries would enter into an agreement regarding air routes. However, the Multilateral Transport Agreement was rejected by a majority of the States and all that was left to work out commercial freedoms, were bilateral negotiations. The first of these bilateral agreements was called the Bermuda Agreement which will be discussed later in this chapter.

2 -- Provisional International Civil Aviation Organization

An interim organization was established by an agreement on June 6, 1945. Most of its structure patterned along the lines of what the permanent organization was to be: provisional Assembly, provisional Council and a provisional Secretariat. This provisional organization was replaced by the permanent organization when the Chicago Conference was ratified by the necessary 26 States on April 4, 1947.

3 -- Permanent International Civil Aviation Organization (ICAO)

Membership in the ICAO comes under three classes of States: (1) signatory states which include all those States who were first to ratify the Conference; (2) members of the United Nations other than original members; and (3) other states which were those who were at war with the Allies (Italy, Austria, Finland, Japan, and Germany). The ICAO has obtained the status of a United Nations specialized agency.

The organization of ICAO is divided into three main bodies which are the Assembly, the Council, and the Secretariat.

The Assembly of the Organization is much like the General Assembly of the United Nations. Each of the States has one vote and decisions in most cases are taken by a simple majority vote. The Assembly has three statutory committees and has the power to establish special committees. It holds a full scale meeting every three years and holds limited meetings annually.

The Council is the governing body of the ICAO and consists of 21 member States elected by the Assembly for a three year period. The President of the Council is elected and is eligible for re-election. Two subordinate bodies of the Council were provided. These are the Air Navigation Commission and the Air Transport Committee. The Council also provided for the Committee on Joint Support of Air Navigation Services and the Finance Committee.

The Secretariat consist of a Secretary General who is appointed by the Council and has five main divisions: Bureau of Administration and Services; Legal Bureau, the Technical Assistance Bureau; Air Transport Bureau; and the Air Navigation Bureau. The ICAO is headquartered in Montreal, Quebec, Canada.

The functions of the ICAO are three fold; regulatory, judicial, and executive. The regulatory functions pertain only to adopting and amending the Technical Annexes. ICAO judicial role is in exercising mandatory arbitration in disputes between States relating to the interpretation of the Conference. The Rules of Procedure are very similar to that of the International Court of Justice and the Council's decisions may also be appealed to this body. The Council will give advisory opinions to member States when they ask for it. The ICAO executive functions are divided into economic, administrative, and technical matters. They collect and publish all economic data of interest to the member States and register the bilateral agreements. An example of the technical functions would be the technical assistance provided for underdeveloped nations and joint navigation meetings.

To date the most effective accomplishments of the ICAO has been the standardization of technical matters.

4 -- International Air Transit Agreement

This is the Two Freedoms agreement which is referred to as the technical freedoms. The first of these Freedoms is the right of an aircraft to fly over the territory of another country who has agreed to it. This would allow an airline to fly from New York to Rome, passing over such other countries as Great Britain, France, and Switzerland. The second of these Freedoms conveys the right of an airplane to land for technical reasons such as refueling or repairs but not for commercial purposes such as picking up or discharging passengers. For example the flight enroute to Rome from New York could land at London to refuel.

5 -- International Air Transport Agreement (Five Freedoms Agreement)

This agreement was signed by 16 States and consisted of the two technical freedoms plus three more commercial freedoms.

The first of these commercial freedoms is the right to carry traffic from the plane's country of origin to another country. For example an airline carrying passengers from New York to Paris. The second commercial freedom refers to the right to pick up traffic in other countries and return to the home country of the airline. Such as a flight originating in Rome and carrying passengers to New York. The third commercial freedom is the right for an airline to carry traffic between countries outside of its own country.

The two technical freedoms and the three commercial freedoms are referred to as the "Five Freedoms." Today, because of the fact that only a few countries have accepted this doctrine, it is virtually non-existing.

Bermuda Agreement -- 1946

The Bermuda Agreement was the first bilateral agreement entered into by two countries involving civil aviation. The Representatives of the United States and Great Britain met in Bermuda to work out this agreement. It became the pattern agreement for all United States bilateral aviation treaties. The Bermuda Agreement also serves as a model, because of its flexibility, for all other nations who desire to enter into such agreements.

For the United States and Great Britain the Bermuda Agreement was a compromise. The two nations granted to each other the "Five Freedoms" in accordance with certain general provisions which were: government approval of rates, adequate traffic capacity, and a review of the carriers' operation in compliance with the principles.

The United States made one major concession in that it agreed that the international rates and fares would be subject to agreements that would be made through the International Air Transport Association. The British agreed to the United States' proposal that no predetermination of capacity be offered by either party and that an arbitration procedure be provided. Also, either party was free to end the agreement on one year's notice. This is the most complicated bilateral air agreement in existence, last amended in 1966 in which there are 15,275 potential route segments every year subject to negotiation.

THE UNITED STATES POLICY ON INTERNATIONAL AND FOREIGN AIR TRANSPORTATION

Prior to World War II the United States had no policy on International and Foreign air transportation except to develop flag carriers through airmail payments. Almost all of these operations were conducted by Pan American World Airways. Pan American's position as the only carrier in international competition resulted in achieving a dominant position and in always seeming to be in the position of the best qualified carrier to receive the air mail contracts. Since the close of World War II, the Board has taken the position that it is in the public interest to have more than one carrier, whenever possible, of the United States operating on international routes. As a result, many Trunk Air Carriers were awarded international routes as extensions of their domestic routes.

After World War II the United States adopted a policy which was that there should be adequate incentives to stimulate efficiency in operations. Also, that by reducing costs and rates the full economic potentials of the industry would be realized. Our policy was that the United States should continue to develop and place in service the newest equipment and best procedures; also, to ensure that the United States flag carriers would carry passengers proportional with the importance of the United States as a transportation market and that healthy financial conditions would ensure an influx of adequate capital.

The importance of international air transportation parallels the social, economic, and political factors discussed in Chapter One.

During the 1950's, United States Flag Carriers, carried the largest percentage of passengers in international flights. Today, the percentage is dwindling steadily and it appears that it will continue. United States maritime shipping has declined until only a fraction of the shipping is done by United States shipping interests. This must not be allowed to happen to United States International Air Carriers.

A great deal of international problems has come from smaller countries who feel that their air carriers cannot compete directly with United States air carriers. All too often these countries may try to restrict United States air carriers by influencing their schedules and service. The members of our government are usually unwilling to protest or request arbitration. These smaller countries, also, are reluctant to furnish statistical data regarding fifth-freedom traffic.

The United States, if it is going to regain some of its losses, must engage in more realistic negotiations for route exchanges.

The United States government had no stated policy regarding international air transportation before World War II because Pan American World Airways and Pan American-Grace Airways (Panagra) carried almost all of the international air operations at that time. The Congress of the United States encouraged the concentration of one airline effort, since our laws made no such provision. Pan American's monopoly policy was a result of its own initiative.

After World War II, our policy changed to one of the maximum development of international air transportation. This policy was decided that no foreign flag airline seeking part of the industry would be excluded.

PASSENGER TRAVEL BETWEEN THE U.S. AND FOREIGN COUNTRIES*

(Thousands of Passengers)

	1973	1972	1971	1970	1969	1968	1967	1966	1965	1964	1963
Passengers via Air	26,659	25,020	20,784	18,960	16,605	14,160	12,456	10,589	8,996	7,657	6,356
Passengers via Sea	1,964	1,863	1,758	1,711	1,714	1,378	1,397	1,570	1,608	1,651	1,727
Total via Air and Sea	28,624	26,883	22,542	20,671	18,319	15,538	13,853	12,159	10,604	9,308	8,083
Air Share (%)	93.1	93.1	92.2	91.7	90.6	91.1	89.9	87.1	84.8	82.3	78.6
Passengers via Foreign-Flag Airlines	12,038	11,380	9,033	8,490	7,481	6,259	5,792	5,109	4,509	3,897	3,155
Passengers via U.S.-Flag Airlines	14,621	13,640	11,751	10,470	9,124	7,901	6,664	5,480	4,487	3,760	3,201
U.S. Flag Airlines' Share (%)	54.8	54.5	56.5	55.2	54.9	55.8	53.5	51.8	49.9	49.1	50.4

*Figures are exclusive of travel over land borders (except Mexican air travel), crewmen, military personnel and travelers between continental United States and its possessions.

Source: U.S. Department of Justice, Immigration and Naturalization Service.

The United States' policy was described in the "International Air Transport Policy" of the 79th Congress (1945-1946). This policy was fivefold:

1. United States aviation would continue to be progressive in the development of new equipment and operating procedures.
2. Adequate incentives would compel efficiency in operation.
3. Full economic potentialities of air transport would be realized by widening the market.
4. Healthy financial condition would assure the inflow of adequate capital.
5. United States airlines would carry a volume of world traffic proportional with the importance of the United States as a market for air transport services.

There are four major problems which the United States' airlines face in competing with international carriers.

1. Rate cutting: Practically all bilateral agreements, which the United States becomes a party to, provides that the rates charged by the foreign airlines on routes to the United States be subject to approval of the Civil Aeronautics Board. However, not withstanding the acceptance of the powers of the CAB, the United States permits certain foreign airlines to transport the public at a rate lower than that charged by United States airlines.

This practice in certain sections of the world is costing the United States airlines millions of dollars a year.

2. Foreign government support of their airlines: Many foreign airlines flying into the United States are either owned or financially controlled by their respective governments and therefore, are not affected by the profit motive.

There are other examples of foreign government support such as the use of administrative power to influence the flow of traffic to their airline, requiring government employees to use the facilities offered by their airline, and foreign governments require that nationals of third countries having contractual relations with them, use their airline.

3. Route inequalities: Over many of the routes flown between the United States and foreign countries, the foreign airlines have more favorable routes than the United States carriers. Most of these inequalities can be adjusted within the framework of the existing bilateral agreements.
4. Restrictions on United States airlines: In order to protect the level of traffic carried by the foreign government's airline, these governments frequently restrict the schedules, type of equipment and capacity of the United States carriers.

On April 24, 1963, an Interagency Steering Committee presented to President Kennedy a statement on international air transport policy. The United States policy for air transport includes the following nine principles:

1. Basic Framework: The United States government will maintain the present framework of bilateral agreements by which air routes are

exchanged among nations and the right to carry traffic on them are determined according to certain broad principles.

2. Air Route and Service: Our policy is to provide air service where a substantial need develops. The present network of international air routes is rather fully developed. Consequently, an expansion of the present route structures must be approached with caution.

The problem is the number of carriers on a particular route or market, such as the North Atlantic which is served by approximately nineteen carriers.

On the other hand, in regions of the world where air service is still inadequate, our policy is to encourage nations to develop adequate local and regional service.

3. Capacity Principles: The United States supports the Bermuda capacity principles which flexibly govern the amount of service individual carriers may offer to the world traveling and shipping public.

Our policy, then, will be to oppose both arbitrary capacity restrictions and the stretching of those principles to the point of abuse.

4. Air Carrier Pooling: There has been a common practice among foreign air carriers to form combinations or pools which divide revenues, traffic, equipment and spare parts on a particular route or market. We must not encourage pools which will be a detriment to our competitive system, however; our dealing with foreign pools must be on a case-by-case basis. United States carriers will be permitted to participate in them only when the national interest requires.

5. Rates: International air transport rates are recommended by the air carriers acting through their organization, known as the International Air Transport Association (IATA), and approved by the governments concerned.

Our acceptance of the IATA mechanism is predicated upon strict adherence by the air carrier to their IATA agreements. If the agreements are violated we will have to reconsider our relationship to IATA and our authority over violations. We cannot abdicate our responsibility to protect the traveler and the shipper.

6. Competition among United States carriers: The Congress of the United States has examined the question and decided that the United States flag international service shall continue to be provided by more than one carrier. This policy is sound and deserves to be reaffirmed.

The principles governing the nature and extent of competition among United States air carriers will continue to require considerable study and evaluation in the light of changing factors.

7. Development of Air Cargo: The United States will press for lower cargo rates of a kind best calculated to stimulate the growth of the air freight industry and benefit the shipping public. Among other things, the United States will explore the feasibility of obtaining an experimental short-term agreement with European countries and Canada which would

provide for the reciprocal exchange of all-cargo aircraft rights allowing substantially greater flexibility.

8. Supporting Facilities: The United States will cooperate in the development of international air traffic control and navigation systems, tele-communications, meteorological and other technical services.

The United States must develop an equitable system of user charges for its air navigation and other airway services, to apply to all international air carriers.

9. Aviation assistance to less developed countries: More intensive consideration shall be given in the foreign aid program to the contributions that internal and regional aviation programs can make to economic development in less developed countries.

In 1971, President Richard M. Nixon announced a new policy on international aviation to supersede the policy adopted in 1963. The new policy contains the following items:

1. The United States will continue the system of exchanging air transportation rights through bilateral agreements. However, attempts to restrict U.S. flag carrier operations will be opposed. The United States will not pay excessive prices for rights where there is little need.

2. Impairment to scheduled service by charter operations should be prevented although charter services are a valuable component to air transportation. Both scheduled and supplemental operators should be given a fair opportunity to compete for the bulk transportation market. Agreements with other nations should be reached regarding charter rights of foreign carriers.

3. The United States will continue to abide by the provisions of IATA governing the economic regulations. Within this machinery the United States will continue to promote the broadest range of potentially profitable services which will appeal to the broadest consumer market based on the lowest cost of operating an efficient system.

4. In view of the numerous benefits derived from competition the United States will maintain a flexible policy on certificating U.S. carriers on competing international routes. A special effort should be made to improve the competitive position of U.S. carriers in relation to foreign carriers.

5. The present system for exchanging bilateral agreements covering all cargo services should be continued because of the important national defense needs as well as the commercial needs.

6. Certainty, speed, and sufficiency of recovery by the injured party will be the primary objective of the policy of the United States regarding carrier liability.

7. Foreign air carriers having marginal financial backing must be required to hold minimum amounts of liability insurance.

8. All practical measures to facilitate international air movements should be developed.

9. Our current policy regarding user charges, fees, and taxes are essentially sound.
10. The United States and their regulatory agencies must consider the potential effects that international air transportation has on the balance of payments.

PRESIDENTIAL AUTHORITY OVER INTERNATIONAL AVIATION

The Federal Aviation Act of 1958 gives to the President of the United States the power to choose the routes which United States International Air Carriers may operate, also, the President has the power to select the air carrier to operate the route.

The Civil Aeronautics Board, as the economic regulator of United States air transportation, first holds a hearing as in any other route case and receives testimony from the parties involved in the proceedings. The next step taken by the Board is to review the record and make its recommendations to the President.

The President then has the responsibility of correlating the Board's recommendations with the data he has regarding foreign affairs which may have a bearing on the case and applicant.

There have been several cases where the President, in exercising his power, has not followed the Board's recommendations, such as: American Airline's Mexico City Operation, Latin American Service Case and the West Coast-Hawaii Case.

INTERNATIONAL AIR TRANSPORT ASSOCIATION (IATA)

The International Air Traffic Association was the forerunner of today's IATA. It was established in 1919 at the Hague by six European airlines. This group made substantial progress by standardizing tickets and waybills. Later, they worked on items involving technical and operational matters. World War II ended the Association's usefullness.

In 1945, air carriers from 31 nations met in Havana to establish an international association because of the failure of the governments at the Chicago Convention to resolve the economic question of commercial rights and rates. They set up their headquarters in Montreal, Canada.

IATA's declared purpose is:

1. To promote safe, regular, and economic air transportation for the benefit of the peoples of the world.
2. To foster air commerce and to study the problems which are related.
3. To provide means for discussion among the airlines engaged directly or indirectly in international air transportation.
4. To cooperate with the International Civil Aviation Organization and other international organizations.

The main function of the IATA is the economic regulation of international air transportation. In regard to rates, three Regional Traffic Conferences set international rates by unanimous resolutions. The rates become binding on the airlines providing the countries do not object. Those who violate the law are subject to heavy fines and, because of this strict regulation, IATA was involved in an antitrust hearing in the United States.

The majority of airlines of the world are either active or associate members of IATA. It is a voluntary association open to any airline company whose country is a member (or eligible to be a member) of the ICAO.

The main organization of IATA consists of the Annual General Meeting which is the policy making body.

The Executive Committee is comprised of senior airlines executives elected by the Annual General Meeting for three years. This committee provides the policy direction of the organization.

The Association's secretariat is headed by a Director General who handles a staff of over 200 employees. They have two main offices, one in Montreal, and the second in Geneva. Regional Technical Representatives are based in Geneva, Nairobi, Bangkok, and Rio de Janerio. The IATA Traffic Services Offices are based in New York and Singapore.

There are five standing committees: Finance, Legal, Technical, Traffic Advisory, and Medical. Serving on these committees are individuals nominated by the airlines to serve as experts on behalf of the industry.

Finance: The principal duty of this committee is the operation of a Clearing House. This clearing house is responsible for settling airline monthly accounts for interline revenue transactions. They deal also with other financial aspects of the carriers' operations which are of common interest.

Legal: The Legal Committee is responsible for all legal matters relating to the formulation of policy. These legal items include; conventions, liability, and security. They review agreements relating to the organization, technical and traffic documents, procedures and practices.

Technical: This committee is to achieve safety and technical efficiency in international air transportation. To do this, technical workshops are held to exchange operational and technical information and experience. Consultation is held with ICAO to develop standards for ground facilities, air traffic control, navigation aids, communications, weather services, runways, and terminal buildings.

Traffic Advisory: The Regional Traffic Conferences are the most publicized activity of IATA because they directly affect the consumer in that they result in the negotiated fares and rates. All decisions are in the form of resolutions and require unanimous airline support and are subject to review by their governments before becoming effective. This committee has a Compliance Office to enforce IATA violations.

Medical: They deal with the physiological, psychological, hygenic and general medical aspects of all matters relating to the safety and efficiency of flight crews and passengers in flight and at airports, and of all ground personnel.

IATA assists in cooperation between scheduled international airlines to find solutions to problems that would be beyond the resources of a single carrier. It serves as the spokesman for the industry relating to government organizations, manufactures, research organizations, and other trade associations.

HIJACKING CONVENTION

Due to the increased incidents of seizure of aircraft for various purposes, which have occurred in recent years, many nations of the world met at The Hague in 1970.

As a result, the Convention for the Suppression of Unlawful Seizure of Aircraft was completed on December 16, 1970. The terms of the Convention were to become effective thirty days after the ratification by the tenth country.

With the acceptance by the United States Senate and the President, ratification of the United States was completed on September 14, 1971 and proclaimed by the President of the United States on October 18, 1971.

The Convention entered into force on October 14, 1971, and to date has been ratified by 26 countries.

MONTREAL CONVENTION

The Convention for the Suppression of Unlawful Acts Against the Safety of Civil Aviation entered into force on January 26, 1973. The law gives effect to the Hijacking Convention by providing the President of the United States with authority to suspend air service to any country which he determines is encouraging hijacking in opposition to the Hijacking Convention.

The law orders the Federal Aviation Administration to provide regulations requiring that all air carrier passengers and their carry-on baggage be screened by detection devices. Also, it requires a federal air transportation security force to be stationed at major airports under the auspices of the Federal Aviation Administration.

The full text of these Conventions can be found in the Appendix.

PART
THREE

vvvvv

Administration of
Air Transportation

CHAPTER
XII
ᵥᵥᵥ
Air Carrier
Management and Organization

Although charged with the responsibility of functioning in the public interest, and to a great extent having its business activities regulated by the federal government, a certificated air carrier is, nonetheless, organized to be a profit making enterprise. However, some air carrier administrators may facetiously doubt this to be true.

Notwithstanding government action, the success of an air carrier directly depends upon the ability and degree of good management. Any company should be able to show good profits when the economic cycle is up and passenger loads are high. At such times managers can show profits in spite of less-than-acceptable management policies and control.

The true test of good management comes when the economic cycle drops, when competition becomes intensified (either normally or induced) or when the general level of costs increase without a proportionate income increase by way of increased fares permitted by the Civil Aeronautics Board.

A major air carrier president said recently "that there does not have to be an air carrier in the country that isn't making a profit, but that some have simply lost sight of the goals of free enterprise. The air industry's problem is in management. The companies that control costs can earn a profit and conversly, managements that do not concentrate on cost control effectively are the money losers."

An air carrier produces a product the same as a company manufacturing consumer goods for household use. The difference, of course, is that the manufacturing company produces a tangible product that the purchaser can see and touch and keep for future use.

An air carrier produces an intangible product which is a service. This service, like the services of a doctor, lawyer, or teacher is not a physical inanimate object. The product of service of an air carrier is air transportation. Once the passenger has used the service that he purchased, it is gone and all that he can show for it is a receipted ticket and the fact that he is in a different city than before he received the product of the air carrier service. This change of location was the reason for his purchase. This fact has to do with the economic theory of time and place utility.

Specifically, the production of an air carrier is an Available Seat Mile (or Ton Mile). This is one seat, flown one mile, in scheduled air transportation service.

The sole purpose of all the air carrier equipment, facilities and personnel is directed toward that end.

The sales or income of the air carrier occurs when this seat is filled with a fare paying passenger. It then becomes a Revenue Passenger Mile.

The relationship of what the air carrier produces, Available Seat Miles (ASM) to what it sells, Revenue Passenger Miles (RPM), is expressed in a percentage known as Load Factor. A measure of air carrier success can be taken by its load factors, including planned, actual and break-even. Load factor is a most important guide for air carrier management. Unless it can keep its production (ASM) in balance with its sales (RPM), earnings will suffer.

Since good, efficient management is an absolute to air carrier achievement, it is necessary to understand what is meant by management and what it does or is supposed to do.

Philosophically, management is defined as the art and science of controlling resources and human effort to attain a desired objective. Management is not only the collective group of those who conduct the affairs of an organization but also the activities which that group performs.

An air carrier, by definition in the Federal Aviation Act, Title I, Section 101-3, means any citizen of the U.S. who undertakes, — — — — — — — — — — — — — — — — — — —, to engage in air transportation.

By combining the definition of management with that of an air carrier, the definition of Air Carrier Management is then [that group involved in] the art and science of planning, organizing and controlling a company engaged in transporting the public by air, for profit.

The traditional functions of management are to plan, organize and control. The fundamental element in management is decision making. Decisions are made by gathering the facts relating to the subject at hand, then studying these facts and finally using this knowledge gained to reach a logical conclusion—the decision.

In the process of managing, established rules, laws, truths or facts are used as guides, or tools of the trade. These are reliable and irrefutable and have been discovered throughout man's experience in business activity. They are known as Principles of Management. These principles are to be used in much the same way that the scientist uses reliable principle laws of physics and mathematics.

Many principles of management have been established since the industrial revolution and the rise of big business. One of the earliest modern day contributors was Frederick W. Taylor, known as the "father of scientific management."

Not all principles of management are equally applicable to all commercial enterprises. Their use and degree of importance depend upon the nature of the particular product of the company.

PRINCIPLES OF AIR CARRIER MANAGEMENT

There are certain basic principles of management that are of particular importance to air carriers because of their producing an air transportation service. Some of these are discussed below.

Fixed Responsibility   Organizational Structure
Lines of Authority   Functionalization
Lines of Communication   Flexibility
Span of Control

Fixed Responsibility

Responsibility is the obligation to do a job; this principle fact includes being held accountable for the day to day successful operation of the company. Adequate maintenance and safety is not only a moral obligation to the flying public but also an economic fact. Preventive maintenance is the air carrier policy rather than "replace when worn out."

All levels of management personnel, whether at the line or staff level, must possess a high degree of reliability. One illustration is clear when the on time departure of flights is considered. Late departures play havoc with the entire scheduled operation of an air carrier. No doubt there are delays which occur that are beyond the control of the management, but with proper planning and assumption of responsibility, these may well be the only cause for a delayed flight departure.

Fixed responsibility means that each person must perform his job properly and at the necessary time. If the job is not completed adequately, the cause should be readily determined and steps taken to correct that cause and prevent it from reoccurring. Air carriers have traditionally had a high level of fixed responsibility due to the very nature of their operation. Any pilot will attest to this, their lives and those of their crew and passengers depend upon not only their ability to accept an obligation to do their job properly, but also the entire airline work force who back them up.

Lines of Authority

If responsibility is the obligation to do a job, then the right to get that job done is known as authority, which implies the right to command. Responsibility must always be coupled with corresponding authority. Fixed responsibility and authority must be assigned for each activity and job if a successful operation of the air carrier is to be achieved.

The exact extent of responsibiltiy and authority must be clearly defined and understood by all personnel. Confusion results when this principle is violated. Certainly no one can be held accountable if he does not know exactly what is expected of him. A company handbook or organizational manual should be prepared showing an organization chart and a detailed explanation of lines of responsibility and authority at all levels. Job descriptions should also be included.

Authority and responsibility fall into two general categories, formal and informal. Formal is depicted on the organization chart and refers to the positions in the plan of the company. Informal refers to the individuals assigned to the positions as a result of their experience, knowledge of the tasks involved and their ability to lead.

Lines of Communication

This principle is extremely important to air carriers simply because of the very nature of their business activities. A manufacturing plant with all of its activities and personnel under one roof, or in one location, will not have difficulty with this principle. The degree of complextiy comes into focus when the extent of the air carrier's activities are considered. Of necessity the air carrier business is spread over its entire route structure which may extend worldwide. The movement of aircraft requires an efficient communication system. To keep pace with the increased demand for information, most major air carriers use Electronic Data Processing systems to aid in scheduling maintenance on aircraft. Also, electronic reservation systems are in wide use to speed and control the multitude of reservations that take place system wide. This allows a passenger to be given immediate confirmation for a seat on a flight rather than have to wait as much as twenty-four hours, as was the case not too many years ago when reservations were practically hand done.

A successful air carrier must build and maintain a communication network that will supply information to all levels of authority. When decisions and policies are made, all personnel affected must be notified. Likewise, all levels must receive communication from those levels responsible to them. In this way they are receiving information to provide for better control and coordination. Communication works two ways; from the top of the company down through all levels to the work force, and upward in reverse order. Only in this manner can all levels be properly informed. The flow of communication must be kept simple and direct to be effective.

Economic losses can occur as a result of communication system breakdowns. For example; an error in the reservations on a flight that is reported full when in reality it is not. Much embarassment, to say nothing of loss of revenue, takes place when the flight is ready for boarding and few passengers show up. This example is hypothetical but it has been known to happen. Or perhaps when an aircraft has not been prepared for a flight due to a breakdown in communications. This results in the passengers being ready and no aircraft available to carry them.

Management control is closely dependent upon communication procedures and information systems.

Span of Control

This principle refers to limiting the number of subordinates that any one individual in the organization is required to supervise. There is a definite limit to the number of people an individual can supervise effectively. Although there is no fixed rule, five to seven subordinates reporting to a major supervisor is sufficient. Circumstances and the individual executive's abilities vary extensively.

Supervision of too many persons will lead to trouble, if not confusion, since the supervisor will not have time or capacity, or both, to devote to any one subordinate to do an adequate job of supervising. He will become distracted by the large number of contacts that he is required to make, and therefore neglect more important matters. As the number of subordinates increases arithmetically the number of relationships increase geometrically until a point is reached which is beyond the control of the supervisor. When this happens some subordinates tend to make their own decisions, sometimes out of necessity, and a total breakdown in the structure may soon result.

As the organization level decreases from the president of the company to the supervisor level, the number of persons to be supervised can increase to ten to fourteen.

The senior executives control the activities of personnel having charge of more complicated and diverse functions. The supervisor or crew chief can handle more subordinates because they are all usually in his immediate area within his sight. For example, a maintenance crew chief in charge of a turn-around inspection of an aircraft between flights, or the reservation supervisor whose telephone reservationists are located in one room. In both examples all workers are doing the same relative job.

Organizational Structure

Organization is the structural framework, depending upon the work to be done, of grouping the activities of the company according to their purposes, for administration and control. It is a process of combining the work that groups and individuals have to perform to achieve maximum results. Organization is the formation of an efficient machine to operate effectively and attain the required objectives of the enterprise.

The traditional and oldest type of organizational structure is the Line organization. This is characterized by chain of command, direct lines of responsibility, authority and communication. It best exists in very small firms.

The Staff organization is an extension to the Line by making available specialized, advisory personnel. Their job is to advise the Line on matters of decision but not to command. The Line may or may not use the Staff advise accordingly as they see fit to do so. The Staff advises and the Line commands.

The responsibility of the air carrier management is to keep the Line and Staff departments and functions in proper balance.

All large enterprises are of the Line and Staff type of organization.

Functionalization

Air carriers, due to their complex nature of business activity, have developed into the highest, or Functional, type of organization structure.

The Functional type of organization provides for the Staff to have authority over lower Line personnel. However, this authority is only in the Staff's area of speciality of function.

Examples of air carrier Functionalization follow:

Maintenance, inspection and repair of aircraft is a detailed function. Before an air carrier can place a new type of aircraft into service, it must submit and have approved by the Federal Aviation Administration, a complete maintenance manual. All maintenance on every part of the aircraft must be performed according to this manual of standard operating procedures. It is the responsibility of the engineering and maintenance Staff members to prescribe, in detail, the exact manner that any aircraft component will be inspected and maintained as well as the criteria for its period of use and replacement. No matter where or when throughout the air carrier geographic system the job takes place, it will be done according to the procedure outlined by the Staff. If difficulties arise or unusual questions are to be answered, it is the Staff who are to be contacted for direction. Who does the job and at what physical time is the responsibility of the immediate Line organization. What and how the worker does his job is established by the Staff. When and where he does it is the responsibility of the Line.

Another example of air carrier functionalization appears in the accounting and reporting of financial and traffic statistical data.

The Civil Aeronautics Board has established a detailed uniform system of accounting and reporting. The financial and traffic recording throughout the entire air carrier system is the responsibility of the finance department Staff as to what and how the books are kept and the reports made. Seeing to it that the job is done and information transmitted to the Civil Aeronautics Board is a Line responsibility.

Flexibility

The ability to change is the broad definition of flexibility. It applies to management and provides for adjustment to varying levels of production.

The air carrier industry, in part due to its ever changing dynamic nature, must operate with a great degree of flexibility to provide for the ever occuring uncertainties. It is truly said that the only sure fact one can depend on, while employed by an air carrier, is that conditions will change constantly. It is this fact that makes the industry so attractive to people.

Technological flexibility is the change to ever newer types of aircraft to produce a better service to the air traveling public.

Marketing flexibility exists when management policies of air carriers constantly change the service offered to the public, such as new types of promotional flights including, vacation plans, tours, delayed and round trips. Air carrier management proves its worth when it can adjust to seasonal changes and business cycle changes without serious losses to its economy or efficiency.

Although flexibility means change, it does not mean change simply for the sake of changing. A balance between liberalism and conservatism is essential. There are those who, once they have found a good workable method, will not depart from it. Changing methods, policies, etc., are always occuring. The key to good management is in knowing when to change in order to keep up with or to exceed the competing air carriers.

Examples exist where an air carrier converted its entire fleet to a new untried type of aircraft. The aircraft, although sound in the safety sense, proved too costly to operate on the company's route structure; serious losses resulted. Another air carrier used the same type aircraft to its advantage because it had a route structure to which the aircraft proved to be best adapted.

Some air carrier managements have taken the "wait and see" attitude by letting their competition break in a new type aircraft, a new electronic reservation system or a new approach to management labor relations. If the "new" proves successful then they adopt it. The cost for this delay is relinquishing the advantage.

Some managements rush to the new equipment, techniques or policies without adequate fact gathering to substantiate their decision. This borders on speculation and although profits may result, the odds are against this type of management success. However, the pressure of competition may force management.

Air carrier management is continuously faced with the question "to change or not to change"; and, if so, when?

CHARACTERISTICS OF AIR CARRIERS

All things have certain physical characteristics, additionally, human beings have certain mental characteristics that result in individual behavior patterns. Industries, like people, as well as different companies within an industry, have their own characteristics. To truly appreciate the service that this industry performs is to understand the Characteristics which influence its development, performance and success. Some of the more important characteristics of air transportation are:

Government Regulation

Perhaps no other industry in the United States is more closely regulated than Air Transportation. Although the air carriers are privately owned financial corporations with public stockholders, they are not free to manage as they please.

The Air Transportation industry, very much like a public utility, exists in the public interest, to serve the public. In order to do so effectively the Federal Aviation Act, the aviation law of the land, provides for controls. The Civil Aeronautics Board and the F.A.A. are the federal agencies who exercise these controls.

The F.A.A. controls all aspects of the safety of aircraft, their operation, maintenance and flight crew.

The C.A.B. controls all aspects of economics pertaining to the routes that the air carriers fly and the rates that are charged the public for being carried on those routes.

To a lesser degree, other federal agencies, State and local governments regulate less obvious aspects of air carrier operations. The President of the United States has direct power over international routes.

It is interesting to note that while air carrier rates are regulated, air carrier costs are not, nor could they be. This usually results in costs rising faster than rates, resulting in a profit squeeze.

A Service Industry

Air Transportation is a service industry. The product of the air carrier is intangible, it is a service providing time and place utility. After receiving the service the passenger has no evidence of it other than being in a different location than where he started.

The air carrier produces for sale an available seat mile (one seat flown one mile). When the seat is occupied by a fare paying passenger it then becomes a revenue passenger mile (one passenger flown one mile).

The Airline product of an "available seat mile" is a highly perishable product because once the flight has ended and the seat was not occupied by a paying passenger, it is lost forever. It cannot be put on a shelf or placed back in inventory to be used at a later time.

Highly Sensitive Demand

Until recently, business reasons accounted for the greatest demand for air travel. A recent survey indicated that business travelers continue to make the most number of repeat trips. However, among all air passengers, 61% now travel for pleasure or other personal reasons, while 26% travel for business and 13% travel for both pleasure and business.

Like many industries Air Transportation has high and low seasons of demand for their services. Some months of the year have higher passenger demand than others. For instance, summer vacation months and the East coast route to Florida following the Christmas/New Year season. One major air carrier does one third of its yearly passenger volumn business during the three summer months. An uneven demand exists certain weeks of the month as well as days of the week, with the weekend being the peak travel days. Hours throughout the day are also uneven in demand. The highest daily demand for air travel is in the early morning before 10:00 A.M. and in the late afternoon after 4:00 P.M.

Uneven demand creates cost problems. It is too costly to equip for high demand periods, then have personnel and aircraft idle during slack times.

Air Transportation is a highly elastic demand. The quantity of passengers is greatly affected by any moderate change in price or any service where price is involved. Lower fares will generate more traffic, while higher fares will discourage air travel. For this reason changes in fares are usually very slight. The advantages of air travel are greater than any small increase in price to the average air traveler.

Highly Competitive Industry

The policy of the C.A.B. is to provide competition between air carriers to produce improved air service to the public. An unprofitable condition will result when there are not enough passengers to support the air carriers serving a route. Competition will result with new route awards, mergers of companies, interchange agreements and even the creation of new companies or new classes of air carriers.

Of the top 400 domestic passenger markets, 365 now have competition by at least two air carriers.

Since air fares are regulated, any change will affect all air carriers on the same route. Competition therefore is mainly in services to the passengers.

When an air carrier is granted a route award to serve a route that is already being served by another air carrier, it must offer competitive schedules. An excessive capacity of available seats results, that is, more seats than passengers to fill them.

A Growth Industry

Because of the population and industrial expansion of the United States, the Gross National Product, the yearly total of all goods and services produced, averages about three and one-half percent increase annually. The yearly growth rate for the air transport industry averaged about twelve percent. The growth of Air Transportation has been phenomenal in about fifty years since the industry had its beginning in 1925, with Ford Tri-Motor aircraft, to today and "Jumbo" Jets. During these years, especially since World War II, the assets of the industry have repeatedly doubled. A share of air carrier common stock, although not a noted yearly dividend earner, grows considerably in value. The air transport industry is a growth industry in that its total investment has rapidly increased and will no doubt continue to do so.

Sensitive to Fluctuation in National Economy

Air Transportation is not a vital consumer commodity such as food and shelter. As mentioned above the majority of air travelers today fly for pleasure reasons. Therefore, the Air Transportation industry is very susceptible to the ups and downs of the national economy. Both business and pleasure travel are reduced during periods of sustained downward trends in the general economy of the United States. In an economic recession people tend to not travel for pleasure and only for business when necessary. During periods of national prosperity the airlines experience a high rate of traffic growth, in some cases as much as 18% or more a year.

The time between ordering a new aircraft and when it is delivered ranges from three to five years. Air carriers place their orders for aircraft based upon their future planned capacity to handle the normal increase. If an economic recession should occur and these aircraft are delivered, then the companies find themselves with a substantial excess seating capacity. The delivery of new aircraft requires much lead time to allow the air carrier time to hire and train additional pilots, mechanics, flight attendants, ramp personnel and many other specialists required in their operation. The overall expansion of the economy of the nation will no doubt increase at an average rate not withstanding the highs and lows experienced. The total result will be a continued average growth in airline expansion. The problem arises when average growth is not constant each year. In a period of a sluggish economy the growth rate of the air industry is decidedly cut back. A problem can also result in a period of unusually high national economy. When the growth rate is too great and the airline capacity therefore cannot keep up with this overly rapid expansion. Either condition will cause a higher than normal cost of operation resulting in lower profits or in some cases no profits at all and even losses.

Forecasting the future economic condition of the country is a very difficult task; it approaches the impossible in Air Transportation. The C.A.B. forecasts the traffic growth and its estimates differ from those made by the F.A.A. These in turn differ from the forecast of the Department of Transportation, the Air Transport Association and even the individual air carriers. It is the hope of the industry that the highs and the lows will be more evened out.

Interdependence of Functions

Perhaps the most unique characteristic of an air carrier is that all departments and every function is interrelated and dependent upon each other in much the same way that each link in a chain depends upon all the others. Each department, like each link, must carry its own responsibility or contribute its strength for the success of the entire operation. Every activity in an air carrier, from reservations to aircraft maintenance, is so interrelated that when one event occurs it has effect upon all other activities. This fact is one reason for the necessity of the high degree of coordination and control required and the functionalized organization structure. In few large industries is teamwork and "esprit de corps" so essential or in evidence.

Geographic Distribution

This characteristic is associated with the subject of "centralization-decentralization." Centralization is practical when activities are located in one location or under one executive having responsibility for all activities of a specific type, therefore all decisions, plans, policies and orders emit from a central point. Centralization is used to advantage in purchasing materials and supplies which results in savings and better prices by buying in quantities.

Reservations is an example of centralized control. All stations selling seats on a given flight must coordinate through one central point.

Flight operations is another activity that must be centralized for successful results.

Certain air carrier activities must be centralized for planning, control and general administration purposes. The system established may be generated centrally but the accomplishment of the system is done wherever necessary.

Decentralization is somewhat a division of labor whereby decisions and functions are the responsibility of all levels where they occur. This reduces the amount of communication necessary with the headquarters. Decentralization prevents costly delays and stimulates initiative. It permits freedom for those in the field to concentrate on things where their greater "on the spot" knowledge can achieve faster action, better service and lower costs. Decentralization aids in eliminating frustration of those in the field from having to go through headquarters for decisions that they can best make locally. Good management will delegate responsibility to the field levels where they can make significant contributions.

Obsolescence and Technological Change

Because of the dynamic nature of air carriers, resulting from their rapid growth, their equipment and policies are in a constant state of going out of use. This applies to methods and techniques as well as systems. A new model aircraft is hardly placed into operation when its successor is in the final stages of development. Too rapid a change is costly. Some turbo-prop aircraft were hardly introduced when jet aircraft were being delivered. Aircraft, from an operational standpoint, never wear out because their parts are constantly being replaced. What does wear out is their usefulness in an economic sense.

The introduction of the jet age, was a technological revolutionary change. The methods of flying, servicing and maintaining were radically new. So too were the new management systems which the air carriers had to adopt. Those companies with less flexible managements were slower in adjusting to the changes and suffered higher costs and diminishing profits as a result. Many air carrier managements were replaced and many reorganizations occurred during the introduction of, and adjustment to, the jet age.

The rate of technological progress has been extremely high in Air Transportation. This is typical of a rapidly expanding industry. The air traveling public benefits as air service continually improves. The improvement results in more safer, faster, larger and comfortable aircraft. To make these technological advances the carriers have had to use a large amount of capital. For the past twenty years the air industry has led all other United States industries, including public utilities, manufacturing and communications in the rate of increase in capital spending.

Technological advancements have created a reequipment cycle about every eight years. In addition to the capital spending required for these cycles, high costs are incurred in the hiring, training and retraining of personnel as well as buildings and other facilities to accommodate and maintain the new aircraft. Generally, one year is the introductory period for a new model aircraft and from two to three years before the air carrier can realize the full cost benefits of the new equipment. The large air carriers are now once again in a major reequipment cycle with the new wide-bodied jets; including the Boeing 747, Douglas DC-10 and the Lockheed L-1011. It is estimated that the major air carriers cost was nearly six billion dollars for the period from 1970 to 1973.

Nature of Costs

Costs fall into two general groups: fixed and variable. Fixed costs are those which do not change for a given volume of production, such as the quantity of revenue passengers carried. Fixed costs are usually those attributed to the rental and maintenance of land, buildings, hangars and terminal space. Utilities, insurance and taxes are examples of fixed costs. Interest expense on loans and payments to bondholders are also included in fixed costs.

Variable costs are those which do vary directly with production; examples are labor and materials. Total costs are the sum of fixed and variable.

The best test to determine if a cost is fixed or variable is to determine if it exists if the company is not in operation as occurs when the company is closed because of a strike. If the cost continues it is fixed, if it does not exist then the cost is a variable.

Because of the large amount of investment in capital items, manufacturing industries tend to have a high fixed cost. Also, railroads, for the same reason have a high fixed cost. This means that the major part of their total costs are of the fixed type. Since the major costs continues whether the train runs or not, the decision is made to run. The only added expense is the small amount of variable costs. The decision to operate the train is made if the expected income will cover the added variable cost. Any additional income above this can then be applied to the fixed cost. The result may well be a total loss by running the train but the loss would have been greater had the train not been run.

The economics of air carriers, in comparison with other types of transport industries and manufacturing, tend to have a relatively lower level of fixed costs. Conversely this means a substantial high variable costs. The decision to schedule a flight is predicated upon its anticipated income. On scheduled flights all seats are available but only about one-half are filled on a yearly average. Those seats not filled are wasted production. The costs of operating the flight are about the same regardless of how many seats are sold.

Part of the reason for the advantage of lower fixed costs is that airways control, navigation aids and even airport facilities are generally provided by government expense or borne by the public through taxation.

The high speed of aircraft lessens the amount of capital equipment required than would otherwise be needed.

Constant costs are variable costs that do not change with the volume of passengers carried. In this sense it satisfies the definition of a fixed cost although it is not. Constant costs are variable costs and sometimes called fixed-variable.

Examples of constant costs are air crew salaries; they are not paid according to the number of passengers that are carried on their flight. Fuel costs and even depreciation costs are of the constant type. The cost of ticketing a passenger and placing him aboard a flight is the same regardless of the income he generates by the price of the ticket he purchased. These are examples of variable costs which do not exist if their is no flight. However, they are practically unaffected once the flight departs. They are, in effect, a fixed type of variable cost which are constant costs.

Air carrier costs can also be looked upon from another direction entirely. Common and separable costs are categories necessary for management control. Common costs which are common to the different types of air carrier income; passengers, mail and air cargo. The cost of a flight carrying these various sources of income cannot be applied separately to the income source. For example: the pilots' ability and salary for flying the aircraft cannot be proportionately applied to the income from passengers, mail and air cargo.

Separable costs are those which can be applied to each type of income source. For example: the stewardess' salary as well as food service cost is attributed to passenger income only. The same is true in cargo handling costs attributed directly to air cargo income.

The economic future of the Air Transportation industry depends on its achieving financial and economic stability. This does not necessarily mean a constant rate of return on investment or the same rate for each individual company. It does, however, mean an adequate rate of return over a period of years.

Due to its high technological change and sensitivity to general economic conditions, the Air Transportation industry has eratic economic business cycles. These swings to highs and lows will even out as the industry further matures. This means that the industry will have to make adequate profits in good years in order to offset the years of poor earnings.

AIR CARRIER ORGANIZATION

The manner in which an air carrier produces its air transport service is by its organization. Organization can be defined as a structure. Buildings are physical structures in which activities take place. Likewise the human skeleton is a basic structure by means of which the human body can move about. Organization is the structure by which management can achieve its objectives. Industries and companies within an industry have different structures the same as people are physically different from each other.

Air carriers, due to their producing an air transport service, have certain common organizational structures. Air carrier organization, though basically the same, will vary from one company to another. This is due to several reasons, namely; historical growth, the influence of strong administrators, the classification of air carriers (see Chapter X), their route structures (domestic as opposed to international or local service, for example), as well as the size of the company.

The formal organization of a company is depicted by its organization chart. This chart shows the line of authority, chain of command and relationship of functions, among other things.

Regardless of their differences they all bear a family resemblance. Since they are producing an air transport service they would, of necessity, have a commonality. This commonality appears in both their line and staff department structure. The staff advisory and specialized department functions are indirectly related to the production and sale of air transport services. Beyond the staff departments are the line departments whose activities are directed toward the sale and delivery of air transportation.

That group of air carrier line departments having the responsibility of attracting, selling and placing the air passenger in the aircraft, is known as Marketing. Those line departments responsible for delivering the product to the passenger, or seeing to it that he gets that which he purchased, is known as Operations.

The purpose of the chart below is to describe the general functions of the various departments that constitute an air carrier. It would be of little value and very confusing to endeavour to describe any particular, or all air carrier organizations as they now exist. For this reason the organization chart presented is a composite of a typical, average air carrier. The titles used for the department names reflect the function that they perform. Actual company department names are not standardized and will be somewhat different from one air carrier to another. Actual department names are constantly changing due to the continuing reorganization that takes place. If the function performed by the departments are understood, then any actual air carrier organization chart will appear familiar and their activities recognizable.

Air carriers are private, profit making organizations. They are owned by the stockholders whose ownership represents equity. As in all large corporations, the stockholders elect a Board of Directors who designate one of their members as Chairman. The Board's main policy is to establish major objectives and goals of the company.

The Board employs the top administrative officer who is the President. It is his function to set major policies, make final decisions and to be ultimately responsible for the success of the company. The President must answer to the Board for his actions and that of all levels of the organization.

The President is aided in carrying out his responsibility by several Vice Presidents who are in charge of major areas. Some areas are more complex and larger in size than others and carry the higher rank of Executive or Senior Vice President.

The typical air carrier is a functionalized line of staff organization. It has several staff departments separated according to the function the department performs.

The line section of the air carriers is usually divided into two main divisions, although others of lesser importance may be established according to circumstances and individual company requirement. The lower levels of the line are spread throughout the air carrier's entire geographic route structure. Each line and staff department will have many subdepartments and branches.

STAFF DEPARTMENTS

All Staff departments are not only responsible for their particular area of specialization but also they act in an advisory capacity to the policy making administrative executives.

AIR CARRIER ORGANIZATION CHART

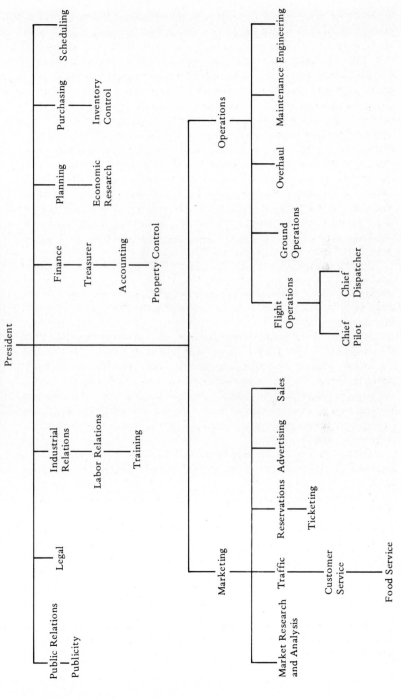

Public Relations Department

This department endeavours to interpret the company policies to the general public and to government agencies as well as the air carrier employees. Also, to present to the public the good image of the company. It is not paid advertising. This department is in continuous contact with the news media and supplies the newspaper and television with photographs and news items. Whenever a very important person (VIP) is an airline passenger, photos are taken which are submitted to the press. These photos will show the air carrier's name very inconspicuously somewhere in the background.

Some large air carriers have developed their public relations department to the extent of providing community services of many kinds. A few companies have developed large information centers which publish guide books and other sources of educational materials including extensive audiovisual aids. This department welcomes public groups to tour their facilities to learn about the workings of an air carrier. Public speakers are supplied to address civic groups on many subjects, usually relating to air transportation in some way.

Legal Department

All companies in the business world of today need advice and help in legal matters. The air carrier industry, unlike many other large industries, have a multiplicity of federal, state and local statutes, laws and regulations in addition to the economic and safety regulations to which they must unfalteringly adhere. Contracts of all types need the benefit of expert legal assistance.

Much of the responsibility for dealing with the public and other government agencies rests with the general counsel who heads this department. The legal department represents the company regarding legal actions, claims and suits both for and against the company. The department usually processes economic cases before the Civil Aeronautics Board for the company when such actions are required.

Industrial Relations Department

This function is the company's internal dealings with its employees. Included are recruiting, interviewing, hiring, training and placing new employees, wage and salary administration and employee services. Complete records and files are kept on all employees showing their history of performance with the company. Raises, advancements and promotions are compiled from these historical records.

Dealing with unions in labor relations is a very important part of this department; from hearing grievances to negotiating labor union contracts and complying with government labor laws. In these matters the legal department works in close relationship with this department.

Athletic teams and interdepartment sports competition is often established by this department to generate employee morale.

Finance Department

The control of the companys' money is the basic responsibility of this department. Included is budget formulation and budgetary control, the accounting and record keeping function, insurance, taxes and property control, are only some of the more important matters of financial responsibility.

Planning Department

To research and develop plans for the future operation of the company is the entire description of this department's function. This department assists the legal department in preparing exhibits for presentation to the Civil Aeronautics Board in economic proceedings. Formulation of statistical data for management needs in decision making is a part of this department's work.

Purchasing Department

The procuring of materials and supplies necessary to keep the company in operation is an important function resting in this department. Some specific responsibilities include:

> Processing purchase requisitions
> Maintaining a file of vendors or suppliers
> Material specification formulation
> Shipping and receiving
> Inventory control
> Issuance of purchase orders

Scheduling Department

This department is often found in almost any position in the company organization. In a larger air carrier it should be a separate staff function if only to allow it independence, thus freedom from pressures of line departments.

Scheduling flights is not a simple matter when consideration must be given to traffic needs, competition from other air carriers, flight crews and maintenance and overhaul of aircraft.

Scheduling is always a matter of compromise; never can there be an ideal, perfect schedule which satisfies all demands, yet this must be the objective of this department.

LINE DEPARTMENTS

As stated above, there are two major line functions:

Marketing—the function of selling and servicing the product of air service. The product being an available seat mile.

Operations—the function of delivering the product to the purchaser.

The Marketing function is carried out by several departments, some of which are presented below.

Market Research and Analysis Department

This department's responsibility includes determining what the customer wants and what he will buy. They seek out methods of expanding current markets of users of air service as well as expanding into new markets for air service. This department should have a complete description of the company's customers, available for management use, accumulated by an analysis of those who purchased the air carrier's product.

A major source of information is a short questionnaire to determine such facts as the frequency of flights made by passengers, the reason for the flight and information concerning service and rates. Surveys are made for the following objectives:

1. To measure the characteristics of the passenger.
2. To ascertain the group structure of air travelers.
3. To learn the preferences of air travelers.
4. To gain a basis for estimating the response to changes in rates.

Traffic Department

This department's responsibility is servicing the passenger and seeing to his needs and efficient handling. Food service and baggage handling is a large part of this department's function.

Reservations Department

This department's responsibility is that of maintaining the complicated system necessary to see to it that all space on the aircraft, scheduled for flight, is properly controlled. The ticketing function is the act of consumating the sale to the customer.

Advertising Department

Large air carriers maintain their own department while smaller companies find it economically feasible to contract this function to independent advertising agencies who specialize in this function. The large air carriers may go so far as conducting their own commercial art, drawing and print shops.

Advertising is the function of deliberately presenting the company's product before the public. This is done by the purchase of newspaper, magazine, radio and television services.

Sales Department

This department's principle responsibility is to obtain customers to purchase the company's product of air service. Large air carriers will divide this department into several levels of subdepartments. There will be those who will specialize in actively contacting and selling in the areas of passenger, conventions, charter, cargo, military, mail, interline, etc.

The Operation function is carried out by several departments, some of which are presented below.

Flight Operations Department

This department is responsible for all matters affecting the piloting and controlling of all the air carriers' flights. It is usually divided into two subdepartments having equal responsibility. They are the offices of chief pilot and chief dispatcher. An illustration of equal responsibility is that usually before a scheduled flight takes off, the pilot in command of the flight and the dispatcher on duty, must equally agree upon the disposition and plan for the flight. They are held equally responsible for the safe conduct and conclusion of the flight.

While the pilot is in the air, the dispatcher is in constant radio contact with the flight from the dispatch center on the ground. The dispatcher's job is to notify and assist the pilot on matters pertaining to the flight. The information includes fuel load and rate of consumption, weather conditions, reporting over check points, flight time and other important matters.

Ground Operations Department

This department is responsible for all activities which take place on the airport location assigned to the company. Included is the administration of stations, maintenance of aircraft other than at the home airport, servicing aircraft for flight and the operation of ground communication systems.

Overhaul Department

This department is responsible for the major replacement of parts and components which compose the aircraft structure.

No longer is the aircraft taken out of service for an extended period of time during which its expense continues while it is producing no income. A system known as "block overhaul" is now used. In this system the aircraft is under continuous overhaul. During the hours between flights, certain planned replacements of parts takes place.

It is surprising how efficient overhaul mechanics are in completely stripping an aircraft to the point where one would not only believe it could not be put back together but having it accomplished and ready for flight in an unbelievably short period of time.

Maintenance Department

Much credit must be given to the air carrier rank and file personnel who quite literally "keep them flying."

Maintenance is the hourly and daily care of the aircraft, its equipment and all its parts. No sooner has the aircraft wheels stopped and the engines winding down when the line maintenance crew are at work servicing and inspecting the aircraft in preparation for its next flight. Safety is not accidental, accidents are caused, they just do not happen. An interruption of a scheduled air carrier flight today is almost nonexistent, attesting to the high technological state of the art of aircraft construction and maintenance.

Engineering Department

This department is concerned with the improvement of the use of the aircraft. They continually study records as well as methods and parts to find a "better way." Engineering including, electrical, hydraulic, pneumatic, fuel, control, communication, etc., are some of the several areas involved. Standard operating procedures for flight, maintenance and overhaul are determined by the engineering department.

XIII

vvv

Economics of
Air Carrier Routes

The basic air carrier route structure in the United States today has progressed through many evolutionary stages and is continually changing. The air carrier route system presently in effect has been, and is currently influenced by, many factors. The most important of which are: the general economic-business conditions of the nation and the air industry, air carrier management policies, technological progress and government action.

The earliest air routes were determined by the requirements of the airmail. The early airmail routes were established between the large cities and areas of population which were separated by many miles. Not long after, transcontinental routes were developed. The rate of expansion of air routes in the decade of 1925 to 1935 was determined by the Post Office. It was not until after World War II that local routes and long international routes were developed.

Today, a large portion of the population in the United States have direct access to certificated air carrier routes. Many more people in the country are indirectly benefited by the service of air transportation.

Economics is a broad subject of study. It is a social science, with science meaning an organized body of knowledge or facts. The body of facts in a social science cannot be as exact as the physical sciences which have predictable results.

Economics as a social science is the study of the social aspects of business. It is a science that investigates the conditions affecting the production and use of labor, materials and equipment for the public interest.

In respect to air carrier routes, economics means management and regulation with regard to their productivity. Especial attention is given to the costs and revenues of producing the air route service for the commercial, postal and national defense needs of the United States.

Air Carrier Route Determinates

In general, the factors which determine air carrier routes fall within three areas, namely: economic, political and geography.

Economics include all of the activity of producing an air transportation service, not only to create, but also to satisfy a demand. The demand in this case includes that of air passengers for both business and pleasure reasons; all forms of air cargo including Air Express and Air Freight; and the need for mail transportation by air, including not only priority airmail, but also non-priority first class mail transported on a space availibility basis.

For want of a better term the word "political" is used to describe this air carrier route determinate. This includes all of the legislative and regulatory actions on the part of governments from local, state and federal to the relations of nations internationally. An air carrier may find it inexpedient to refuel its aircraft in one state rather than another because of the fuel tax levied. Taxes of all kinds tend to influence managment when they consider a location for the building of overhaul facilities. The treaties between nations in negotiating and granting reciprocal agreements also will affect the air carrier route structure.

The final route determinate, geography, though less important as formally due to the expanded capabilities of modern commercial aircraft, still bears important consideration. Our concepts of world geography have had to be changed. No longer can we think that the shortest route between the Pacific coast of the United States, and Tokyo, Japan, is a South-Southwest direction when in reality it is Northwest by way of Alaska. This is because of the globular shape of the earth, making it practical to follow the natural curve. This type of route which takes advantage of the earth's curve is known as the great-circle. It is the shortest distance between any two points on the surface of the earth. Air carriers are now carrying passengers in scheduled service on routes that cross over the top of the world. Many flights from the United States non-stop to Europe and Asia, follow this direct, much shorter route.

Meterology and the study of weather is a part of the natural science of geography. Pressure-pattern flying, high altitude flights, and within recent years the discovery and use of the jet streams, fast moving rivers of air criss-crossing the United States at extremely high altitudes and speeds, have caused a change in the geographical concepts of air carrier routes.

The interaction of these three route determinates have played and will continue to play a decisive role in formulating the air carrier route structure.

Economic Route Characteristics

There are several factors which determine the economic characteristics of an air carrier route. They are most all included when considering profitable, unprofitable and competition factors.

First of all must be considered those factors which tend to make a particular route economically successful. These profitable route factors are: the stage length of the route, the degree of density of traffic carried on that route, and the average length of haul.

By stage length is meant the overall physical length of the route in miles. The greater number of miles produced on a certain route by an aircraft will tend to decrease the per mile cost of operating the aircraft. A fixed cost for a given flight will remain fixed regardless of the total miles flown. This fixed cost, spread over more miles will result in a lower fixed cost per mile. This is recognized as a basic economic fact, that greater production will lower unit costs.

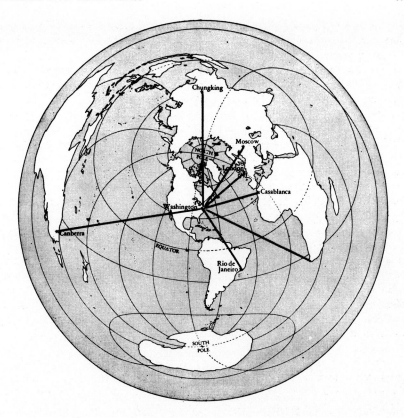

Great circle air routes are shown as straight lines on the azimuthal projection.

Density of traffic refers to the quantity of passengers or other traffic carried on a route. A route may be sufficiently long enough in miles but if the average density of traffic carried is low then this will offset the advantages of the lowered per mile cost. In fact, long routes and low densities are disastrous to profit.

The distance that the average passenger flies along an air carrier route is known as the average length of haul. A route may be a thousand miles long but if the average passenger disembarks after two or three hundred miles then his vacated seat may well remain empty for the remainder of the flight. This, of course, can be prevented by non-stop flights. The air carriers are most desirous of non-stop flights since the average length of haul would be equal to the stage length of the route. Non-stop routes are not always possible because air carriers must also serve intermediate points along their route as provided in their Certificate of Convenience and Necessity. The average length of haul has increased from 624 miles in 1960 to 776 miles in 1970.

All of these factors; stage length, density of traffic carried and the average length of haul, must be present for an air carrier route to be economically profitable, usually any two of these must be favorable if the company is to break-even. The degree to which any one of these factors are weak or lacking will be the cause of relatively unprofitable operations. A route may be relatively short but this disadvantage could be off-set if the density of traffic and the average length of haul is high. An example of this condition is the Boston-New York-Washington route.

A lesser degree of profitableness will exist if the size of the route is sufficient and the average length of haul is good but the density of traffic is low.

Likewise, poor financial operation will result if the size of the route is good and the density of traffic is high but the average length of haul is low. The weakening of any one of these three factors will tend to decrease the success or profitable nature of the air carrier route.

Air transportation is basically short-haul oriented. Fifty percent of all United States passenger trip lengths are 500 miles or less and seventy-five percent of all trips are 1000 miles or less. It would seem obvious that short-haul transportation is destined for an increasingly importan role in the total United States air transportation system. In this regard the F.A.A. has established a Quiet Short-Haul Air Transportation System (QSATS) department in its organization structure.

A recent CAB study, to determine the effect of stage length on local service operations, found that there is no way to avoid heavy losses on the short stage length trips that serve smaller cities. The CAB study stated that "As flight distance decreased, operating losses increased acutely. When the stage length fell below 100 miles the traffic, service and expense elements all combined to create an operating loss situation that no normal increase in traffic or fares, or decrease in expenses, could overcome."

While it is obviously true that the reverse of the factors which lead to an economically successful route will cause an uneconomic condition, specifically, uneconomic air carrier route factors are a result of one or more of the following: low load factors, cities too small in population or otherwise unable to generate sufficient air traffic to support air service, and unhealthy or excessive competition on the air carrier route from other air carriers or even surface carriers.

Load factor is expressed as a percentage which shows the relation between the production of an air carrier, usually available seat miles, and the sales or the revenue passenger miles that were actually sold. A break-even load factor is computed for any model or type of aircraft over any given route; this is equal to the percentage of the aircraft which must be filled by passengers or other traffic in order for the air carrier to cover its costs for the flight. This point must obviously be reached before a profit can be attained. It is consequential that if a scheduled flight does not achieve a sufficient load factor to cover costs for a route, then an uneconomic condition results.

This condition may be due to the second uneconomic route factor. If the cities along the route, which the air carrier serves, are too small in population or for some other reason do not have the ability to generate enough traffic, this would result in an unprofitable situation. This is particularly true in the case of the Local Service air carriers.

The third uneconomic route factor is excess competition. It has been the policy of the Civil Aeronautics Board, since its inception, to increase competition in order to produce better air service in the public interest. Since the United States air carrier route system was not planned on an over-all pattern, several instances have resulted in unhealthy competition. Unprofitableness results when there is simply not enough air traffic to support the air carriers that are serving a route. This situation has been further aggravated since the introduction of the wide jet transport aircraft. This type aircraft because of its greater capacity of seats than other jet aircraft, is able to produce a greater number of available seat miles; this, therefore, further aggravates the competition situation.

Because competition is perhaps the most direct cause of an uneconomic route, it bears further examining. There are three general factors which cause competition on air carrier routes. These are: the creation of new air carriers, the awarding of new routes to existing air carriers into areas already served by other air carriers, and lastly, mergers of companies or any type of route consolidations including interchanges and other operations.

There have been relatively few new air carriers permitted. There have been no new Domestic Truck air carriers certificated since 1938. In fact, the number of major air carriers has decreased due to the mergers that have taken place over the years. As the general economic inflation in the United States continues, costs will continue to rise. In order to lower costs through unduplication, more mergers will no doubt take place.

The Civil Aeronautics Board, early in its history, established the policy of balanced competition within each classification of air carriers. In determining the extent of competition necessary for adequate public service, consideration should be given to the total traffic potential which the route may be expected to produce. The result will indicate whether the route is sufficiently able to support one or more air carriers. The only justification for the duplication of air carriers on a route is when all of them can be expected to at least break-even with their load factors, and furthermore, to increase their volume of traffic in due course, thus allowing profits for all air carriers concerned.

The present economic condition of the United States air carrier industry is due to a multiplicity of causes and much attention is being given by the federal government in the area of economic activity.

Since the establishment of the air carrier industry, particularly with the passage of the Civil Aeronautics Act in 1938, air carrier routes have increased until they now criss-cross the United States in a web-like pattern.

A large percentage of these routes have a high degree of competition in that two or more air carriers serve them. This competition coupled with increased cost and declining profits has resulted in losses to the United States air carrier industry. The air carriers have consistently requested an increase in rates to offset the rising cost but the policy of the Civil Aeronautics Board pertaining to rates has been to not allow any substantial increases to offset these losses. Some air carriers have increased their route miles, by the acquisition of new routes, in order to alleviate their declining profits. These actions have resulted in creating more competition and further aggravating an already intense uneconomic condition. To acquire a new route is not necessarily the answer.

Public Utility Aspects of Air Carriers

The air transport industry has many characteristics like those of public utilities. Although they are responsible for air service in the public interest, they are not true public utilities according to the strict definition of the term.

A pure public utility is one which, although it is privately owned by the public stockholders, is subject to government regulatory control. This regulation covers three areas: geographic area of operational service, or routes in the case of air transport companies; the rates or fares charged to the public; and the percentage of return on profits.

Being a public utility usually implies a monopoly in that it is granted a franchise to conduct its business. This is true of electric, telephone and water companies; also intra-city bus companies. Most franchises are granted by the State Public Utilities Commission or equivalent State authority. Higher costs and rates would result if there were more than one public utility serving a city or area. The duplication of equipment would not be warranted.

The air transport industry operates in much the same way. The Civil Aeronautics Board grants the air carriers a franchise to serve a certain route. No air carrier can do so without the Civil Aeronautics Board approval. In this sense the air carriers are protected and are monopolies. The difference between air carriers and public utilities stops at that point. Within the air industry there is much competition, ask any air carrier administrator and the answer will be a resounding yes. Only the Civil Aeronautics Board will allow operation on air routes but encourages competition on these routes. The industry, or those air carriers serving a route, are monopolies as an industry, yet at the same time they compete with each other. This fact is the crux of the complaint against the Civil Aeronautics Board. The Civil Aeronautics Board's rationale is that they encourage competition to develop a better air service and lower fares in the public interest.

As contradictory as it may sound, nonetheless, the air carriers do conduct their business in a framework of monopolistic-competition. It is one of the very few industries that do so.

The advantage to a pure public utility to operate as a monopoly is offset by the disadvantage to it of having the rates it charges the public controlled by the government authority. This is true of air carriers. The Civil Aeronautics Board will disapprove a fare submitted to it if it feels in any way that the rate is either too high or too low. The low rate, which may or may not be below cost, would be unfair competition. The Civil Aeronautics Board sees to it that the same type of air service on the same route by competing air carriers will be just about the same. Competition will tend to equalize the fares anyhow.

Another offsetting disadvantage to being a public utility monopoly is that the amount of profit earned is controlled, limited or set by the government authority. In the air transport industry this is true. The Civil Aeronautics Board has established a percentage for a fair return on investment depending on the class of air carrier. Different routes of the same air carrier may even have different allowable percentages of profit or return on investment. The Board's opinion dealing with rate of return on investment stated in the Domestic Passenger-Fare Investigation* was that the fair and reasonable rate of return on investment for domestic passenger fare services of the Trunk air carriers was 12 per cent. This was based upon a 6.2 per cent cost of debt, a 16.75 per cent cost of equity and an optimum capital structure consisting of 45 per cent debt and 55 per cent equity. A loud factor of 55% is used as the basis for rates. The rate of return on investment for Local Service air carriers was 12.35 per cent, however.

Rate of Return on Investment
U.S. Scheduled Airlines

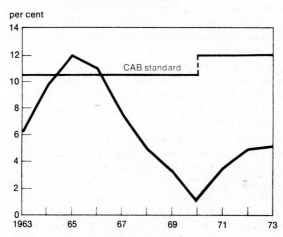

Source: Air Transport Association of America

*Civil Aeronautics Board, Docket 21866-8, April 9, 1971.

UNIT REVENUES AND COSTS

Passenger Revenues Compared

Average Revenue Per Revenue Passenger Mile—Intercity Common Carriers
(In Cents Per Mile)

	1973	1972	1971	1970	1969	1968	1967	1966	1965	1964	1963
U.S. Scheduled Airlines											
Domestic—First Class	8.93	8.70	8.58	8.31	7.78	7.32	7.24	7.24	7.33	7.26	7.17
Coach	6.11	5.88	5.81	5.46	5.27	5.11	5.13	5.28	5.52	5.58	5.62
Total	6.63	6.40	6.32	6.00	5.79	5.61	5.64	5.83	6.06	6.12	6.17
International—First Class	9.31	8.42	8.26	7.96	8.09	7.42	7.59	7.60	7.62	8.16	8.56
Tourist	4.98	4.66	4.79	4.68	4.82	4.65	4.71	4.85	5.00	5.12	5.47
Total	5.32	4.98	5.10	5.01	5.18	4.95	5.01	5.16	5.29	5.45	5.82
Total	6.34	6.08	6.05	5.79	5.68	5.46	5.49	5.67	5.87	5.95	6.09
Railroads, Class I											
First Class	—	4.56	4.72	4.27	4.08	3.88	3.76	3.84	3.87	3.91	4.00
Coach	5.19*	4.64	4.85	3.98	3.56	3.24	3.02	2.99	3.00	3.00	3.00
Motor Buses, Class I	4.05	3.98	3.83	3.60	3.39	3.18	2.98	2.89	2.88	2.74	2.72

* Includes first class and coach.

Freight Revenues Compared

Average Revenue Per Ton Mile—Intercity Common Carriers
(In Cents Per Mile)

	1973	1972	1971	1970	1969	1968	1967	1966	1965	1964	1963
U.S. Scheduled Airlines											
Domestic	23.31	22.75	22.58	21.91	21.03	19.97	19.89	20.21	20.46	20.97	21.72
International	19.89	19.70	19.73	19.36	18.29	18.83	19.63	19.92	20.76	23.60	24.78
Total	21.92	21.49	21.42	20.94	19.99	19.51	19.79	20.09	20.58	21.95	22.86
Railroads, Class I	1.62	1.62	1.59	1.43	1.35	1.31	1.27	1.26	1.27	1.28	1.31
Trucks, Class I	9.00^E	8.20	8.00	7.30	7.10	6.90	6.60	6.30	6.50	6.50	6.30

Airline Revenue, Cost and Profit per Revenue Ton Mile

(In Cents Per Mile)

	1973	1972	1971	1970	1969	1968	1967	1966	1965	1964	1963
Domestic Service											
Unit Revenue	58.02	55.51	54.76	51.74	49.74	49.66	49.90	51.79	54.48	56.58	57.75
Unit Cost	55.07	52.35	53.03	51.75	47.43	47.00	45.67	45.57	47.81	50.87	54.77
Operating Profit Margin	2.95	3.17	1.73	(00.01)	2.31	2.66	4.23	6.22	6.67	5.71	2.98
International and Territorial Service											
Unit Revenue	37.74	34.78	34.01	33.44	30.68	31.12	33.04	35.87	40.60	44.80	47.76
Unit Cost	36.47	33.52	32.73	32.74	29.60	27.82	28.01	29.63	33.56	38.59	41.06
Operating Profit Margin	1.27	1.26	1.28	00.70	1.08	3.30	5.03	6.24	7.04	6.21	6.70
Total Industry											
Unit Revenue	51.90	48.95	48.05	46.02	43.98	42.86	43.77	46.18	50.10	53.03	54.79
Unit Cost	49.46	46.39	46.47	45.81	42.04	39.96	39.26	39.95	43.31	47.17	50.72
Operating Profit Margin	2.44	2.56	1.59	00.21	1.94	2.90	4.51	6.23	6.79	5.86	4.07

E Estimated

Source: Air Transport Association of America

airline boardings top
200 million in 1973

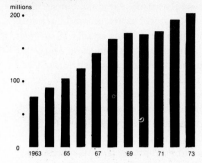

airline freight revenues set
$1 billion record in 1973

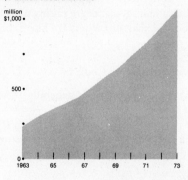

growth of airline capacity
and fuel consumption compared

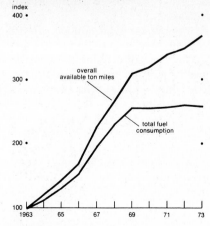

Source: Air Transport Association of
America

If the air carrier's percentage of profit return exceeds its limit set by the Civil Aeronautics Board, then fare reductions will surely result. An alert management will, in advance, see to it that any would be excess profits are plowed back into the company by expanding or improving its equipment. This results in a larger capital investment and therefore a higher dollar return for the same allowable percentage. The next result of expanded equipment is an expanded service and the cycle is complete and back to where it started but the circle is now larger. The public obviously is the beneficiary of these chain of events.

Strict public utilities that operate at a fixed return on investment can normally adjust upward or downward to maintain consistency in that return, because they are pure monopolies. The Civil Aeronautics Board sets a rate of return standard for airlines but few have been able to attain it. Since airlines are not pure monopolies and do not have consistent demand as does the local electric, gas or telephone company, pricing is a competitive tool. It cannot be used freely to make up rate of return deficiencies.

This is the way it is supposed to happen and usually does. However, some economists and air industry managements are raising questions.

In summary it can be said that air carriers are like public utilities with certain unique differences.

Establishment of Rates on Air Carrier Routes

The economic theory of rate making is generally in effect when considering how air carrier rates for service is determined.

Generally the rate on an air carrier route is supposed to be sufficient to allow the company to earn a fair rate of return on its investment. Only with such a return can they pay dividends to their stockholders, show capital gains and attract invested capital.

As in the establishment of any rate or product price, there are two considerations. The first is the cost of producing the service or product and the second is the demand, or the value, for that service or product. This is expressed in the formula $P = C + D$. "P" is the price or rate established, "C" is cost and "D" is demand.

The average total cost per unit of producing air service will decrease to a point and then increase as the "law of diminishing returns" takes effect.

The demand or value of the service to the air transport public is not a fixed quantity but rather several quantities of the service which the public will buy at various rate levels. A demand curve is simply a schedule of rates.

Generally, as air carrier rates are decreased, the quantity of purchases will increase. Air carriers have a high elasticity of demand, which means that normally they will experience a change in quantity or volume as rates are changed. The air industry is said to have a high demand sensitivity.

The graph below illustrates the typical condition in the air carrier industry for any given route on a per unit basis. The lower break-even is at point A. The upper break-even is at point B.

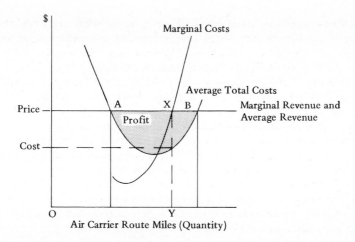

Air Carrier Route Miles (Quantity)

The quantity of miles that will yield the maximum profit is determined by the intersection of marginal cost and marginal revenue. This is XY on the graph. Any increase of quantity beyond that point will result in an increase in cost and a decrease in profit. When the upper break-even point is passed a loss occurs. The reason for this is that the marginal cost (the amount added to total cost for one more unit) increases while the marginal revenue (the amount added to total revenue for one more unit) remains constant.

For example:

If the horizontal axis were a flight from Miami to Boston, with the take off from Miami at point "O", the lower break-even point for the flight might be reached at Atlanta, point "A." The flight's termination at New York could be point "XY," thereby yielding the maximum profit. If the flight were to continue to Boston at point "B" the profit would be eliminated. If for some reason the flight continued beyond Boston a loss would occur.

The same example above can be expressed in hours of flight time and cost per hour. If the flight, when reaching its destination (point XY), is unable to land and must hold due to a back-up of air traffic for weather conditions or other reasons, the profit earned will be eliminated and loss will continue to mount as the holding time increases. This is the reason why "on time" arrivals are so important in an economic sense in addition to good service.

NEW ROUTE PROCEDURE

The processing of a new route case is a lengthly and complex task which is both costly and time consuming to the air carrier. Such an important procedure is nonetheless generally not understood except by those few specialized persons involved. It is therefore the purpose of the following discussion to summarize the procedural steps involved in a new route acquisition.

The Civil Aeronautics Act of 1938 and later the Federal Aviation Act of 1958 were passed to provide for the regulation and promotion of civil aviation. The Civil Aeronautics Board was the agency created for interpreting and carrying out the economic provisions of these Acts. Accordingly, the Civil Aeronautics Board created Economic Regulation, Part 302, "Rules of Practice in Economic Proceedings" which sets forth rules and regulations governing cases involved in processing and acquiring a new route.

"Rules of Practice in Economic Proceedings" is a standard operating procedure to be followed when dealing with the Civil Aeronautics Board in economic matters. Part 302 governs the conduct of all economic proceedings before the Board whether instituted by order of the Board or by the filing with the Board of an application by an air carrier.

In many respects the functions of the Board are similar to those of a court. Parties to cases appearing before the Civil Aeronautics Board are expected to conduct themselves with honor and dignity. Likewise, the Board and its employees who participate in the determination of cases are expected to conduct themselves with the same fidelity to standards of propriety that characterize a court and its staff. The standing and effectiveness of the Board, its personnel, and the representatives of air carriers are in direct relation to the observance of the highest standards of judicial and professional ethics.

Subpart "I," Part 302, of the Board's Rules of Practice in Economic Proceedings specifically contains the rules applicable to route proceedings under Sections 401 and 402 of the Federal Aviation Act.

The purpose of this subpart is to establish a procedure for the proceedings involving particular routes so that the Board may select the air carrier best suited to conduct the service in the public interest in the most efficient and expeditious manner.

The Civil Aeronautics Board considers four fundamental questions which govern the disposition of new route applications. These are:

1. Is the new service in the public need?
2. Can the public need be met by existing air carriers?
3. Can the applicant conduct the new service without impairing existing air carriers?
4. Will the cost of the new service to the government, if any, be worth it to the public?

This route case procedure is necessary to determine the answers to these questions.

Application

An application for a new route is filed by a certificated air carrier who is desirous of obtaining a regular route to engage in scheduled air service.

The statements contained in the application for a new route are restricted to significant and relevant facts; they cannot contain arguments or expressions of opinions except those pertinent to the position of the applicant.

Applications for authority to engage in interstate air transportation cannot also be included in requests for foreign or overseas air service.

Each application must contain full and adequate information regarding the request of the air carrier. In addition, it may contain additional data which the applicant deems necessary or appropriate in order to acquaint the Board with the particular circumstances of the route case involved.

The application need not contain all the evidence which the air carrier is prepared to present at the hearing or otherwise in support of its case. The application shall at least indicate the nature and result of the carrier's investigations and the character of the evidence that it will be prepared to present in support of its route request.

Each route, for which the application is filed, must be identified and specify the type of service to be rendered, each terminal city and intermediate point to be served. The type of aircraft which the air carrier proposes to use in the new service must also be given.

The Civil Aeronautics Board will include a brief summary of the application, together with its docket number and name of the applicant, in its Digest of Applications Filed, issued weekly. It is then the responsibility of any party (air carrier or civic body) to advise the Board that they are interested in receiving any and all documents filed in this docket.

Various periods of time will elapse before the application is placed upon the agenda of the Civil Aeronautics Board for a hearing. When this time is reached the Civil Aeronautics Board appoints an Administrative Law Judge from the Bureau of Administrative Law Judges and announces the date of the Prehearing Conference.

Petitions for Leave to Intervene

Any interested person may ask to intervene in a case and therefore become a party in the case if the Administrative Law Judge feels that such person has a property or financial interest which may not be adequately represented by existing parties.

A petition to be a party in the case can be filed by any person, including air carriers, who have a statutory right to be involved in the case. The petitioner must state the facts and the reasons why he should be permitted to intervene. These parties may include civic groups representing the cities on the route in question, industrial or professional groups and other air carriers.

In passing upon a Petition of Intervention the Board will consider the nature and extent of the interest of the petitioner.

All petitions must be filed before the Prehearing Conference. Petitioners may be opposed to, or in favor of, a particular applicant. If the Administrative Law Judge approves, then the petitioner is permitted to participate in the route case. He may be either for or against an applicant for the route.

Prehearing Conference

Before any formal Hearing is held there will ordinarily be a Prehearing conference before the Administrative Law Judge. Written notice of the conference will be sent to all parties involved in the route case.

The purpose of the Prehearing Conference is to define, simplify, and clarify the issues to be decided by the case, including the type of service and the definition of the area involved; also, to determine the ground rules for the conduct of the Hearing.

The Prehearing Conference allows all of the interested parties an opportunity to acquaint the Administrative Law Judge with their ideas and opinions as to what issues and areas should be included in the case.

In attendance at the Prehearing Conference is a representative from the Office of the General Counsel who circulates to all parties present a list of material which is recognized as legal sources of information. Also circulated to the parties is a list of information requests which the Bureau of Economics of the Civil Aeronautics Board desires that the applicants, and other interested parties furnish as part of their case. This information is determined by the Administrative Law Judge. Normally, the parties also exchange requests for information upon one another.

The General Counsel distributes a list of issues which the Administrative Law Judge feels should be determined in the case as well as the ideas and recommendations of the Bureau of Economics as to what should be the scope of the case. Since both the issues and the area are normally contested, the Administrative Law Judge will usually request that the parties advise him in writing as to their opinions on these two items and he refers these opinions, together with his own, to the Civil Aeronautics Board for final determination as to the issues and the scope of the case.

The Administrative Law Judge at the Prehearing Conference acts as a judge. In attendance are General Counsel (representing the Bureau of Economics), applicants and other interested parties. The Bureau of Economics operates independently and without instructions from the members of the Civil Aeronautics Board.

The purpose of the General Counsel is to see that all proceedings are carried out according to law and assist in the development of an adequate record.

The position of the Administrative Law Judge in the hearing is that of a judge in a court of law, except that the final decision of the case does not rest with him. It is his responsibility to conduct the Prehearing Conference. The Administrative Law Judge will issue a report of the Conference after it ends in which he will define the issues in the case and give an account of the results of the Conference.

Consolidation

Two or more proceedings involving substantially the same parties or issues, which are the same or closely related, may be consolidated for hearing by the Board if it finds that consolidating is conducive to the proper dispatch of business and to the ends of justice and will not unduly delay the proceedings.

A consolidation would take place when two or more air carriers make application for the same service or route.

A motion to consolidate applications has to be filed not later than the Prehearing Conference.

After the Prehearing Conference, the Civil Aeronautics Board determines which application should be consolidated and issues the consolidation order.

Exhibits (Written Evidence)

Exhibits-in-Chief

At the close of the Prehearing Conference the Administrative Law Judge sets the date for the filing of exhibits. One copy must be furnished to each of the parties in the case. All parties will exchange copies of exhibits at the earliest practical time before the Hearing.

The Exhibit-in-Chief is filed by the applicant. This consists of a written presentation designed to show the public need of the new route or service applied for. The data relied upon by the Civil Aeronautics Board in establishing public need is divided into two categories. The first is the "community of interest" and the second is the "economic characteristics."

The "community of interest" is that of the cities to be served along the new route. Such things as the volume of travel, commerce and communications, exchanged traffic requirements, and an estimate of the volume of traffic which would utilize the proposed new route. Such material used as evidence are long-distance telephone calls, telegrams, hotel reservations, etc., to substantiate the movement of traffic between the cities along the proposed route. One major source of information is the Civil Aeronautics Board "Domestic Origin—Destination Survey of Airline Passenger Traffic" which contains actual air traffic data.

"Economic characteristics" relate to such evidence as census figures to show population growth, retail sales volume, postal receipts, and income tax returns filed. Any other data peculiar to the economic characteristics of the particular cities may include the number of telephones, electric, water and gas meters; schools, building permits, sewer connections and volume of bank deposits in the community. Most important evidence is the proof of the need for the service in relation to the communities to be served. This information is obtained by the applicants by personal contact, research and analysis of the communities involved.

In the Exhibit-in-Chief the Applicant includes the following: an estimate of the total volume of traffic that is believed will move over the route, an estimate of the revenues they will receive from their share of the traffic; the expenses they anticipate in serving the traffic; and, the profit they expect to receive from the award of the new route. They normally show how the route will integrate into their current route systems and indicate the effect of their receipt of the route on the other applicants and/or parties. They show why they, among all the applicants, are best suited to provide the service, most qualified and why they need the additional authority more than does any other applicant.

Rebuttal Exhibits

After the Exhibits-in-Chief have been circulated to all interested parties, Rebuttal Exhibits are then filed. The purpose of these exhibits is to prove opposition to the new route proposed. These exhibits are also utilized to show where applicants or parties have made errors, miscalculations or significant omissions in their Exhibits-in-Chief. They are also utilized by all parties in order to point out deficiencies in the service proposals of other applicants.

Hearing

The Administrative Law Judge will give the parties reasonable notice of the date, place and nature of the Hearing to be held.

Every party has the right to present his case or defense by oral or documentary evidence, to submit evidence in rebuttal, and to conduct such cross-examination as may be required for a full and true disclosure of the facts pertaining to the route case.

The Board has established a policy to provide for excluding irrelevant, immaterial or repetitious evidence and to expedite the route proceedings.

At the Hearing, the Administrative Law Judge will give the parties adequate opportunity for the presentation of arguments in support of, or in opposition to, the route case being considered.

Evidence presented at the Hearing is limited to material evidence relevant to the issues defined as a result of the Prehearing Conference. Evidence is presented in written form by all parties wherever feasible as the Examiner may direct.

The Administrative Law Judge presides at the Hearing. All parties are usually represented by counsel. The order of presentation is as follows: cities, applicants, other interested parties and the General Counsel. Witnesses may be called upon to give evidence and support their exhibits, and they may be cross-examined.

The Administrative Law Judge will give the parties at the Hearing adequate opportunity during the course of the Hearing for a presentation of arguments. When, in the opinion of the Administrative Law Judge, the volume of importance of the evidence involved warrants, he may, by his own motion or at the request of a party, permit the presentation of oral argument.

All arguments and testimony are recorded and transcribed to be available to the Board for consideration in deciding the case. Copies of the transcript are supplied to the parties.

At the conclusion of the Hearing the General Counsel normally presents an affirmative case; that is, he takes the position as to whether the service proposed by the applicant is needed and which of the applicants, in the opinion of the Bureau of Economics, is best suited to perform the proposed service.

At the close of the Hearing, the Administrative Law Judge sets a date for filing briefs. A brief contains a concise, factual statement, it is a full discussion of the facts supporting the case.

Administrative Law Judge's Initial Decision

After receiving the briefs the Administrative Law Judge reviews and studies all of the evidence presented at the Hearing. He then makes his decision, which is his recommendation to the Board as to the outcome of the case.

The Administrative Law Judge's Initial Decision encompasses his decision pursuant to his delegation of authority on the merits of the proceeding and all issues at the close of the Hearing.

Unless a Petition for Discretionary Review is filed, or the Board issues an order to review upon its own initiative, the Administrative Law Judge's Initial Decision will become effective as the final order of the Board thirty days later.

If a Petition for Discretionary Review is filed, the effectiveness of the initial decision is stayed until further order of the Board.

Petition for Discretionary Review

An exception to the Administrative Law Judge's Initial Decision may be filed by a party to the case if he is dissatisfied with the Administrative Law Judge's decision.

Review by the Board is not a matter of right but of the sound discretion of the Board.

The Petition for Discretionary Review must be filed within twenty-one days after the Administrative Law Judge's decision is made public or the Board issues an order to review upon its own initiative.

If a Petition for Discretionary Review is filed or action to review is taken by the Board, the effectiveness of the initial decision is stayed until further order of the Board. The Petition must identify the exact parts of the decision by reference and state the grounds for the exceptions. Proof must accompany these exceptions.

Petitions for Discretionary Review can be filed only for one or more of the following reasons:

1. A material fact is in error.
2. A legal conclusion without governing precedent or is a departure from, or contrary to law, Board rules or precedent.
3. An important question of law, policy or discretion is involved.
4. A prejudicial error has occured.

Petitions usually cannot exceed twenty pages. Requests for oral argument on petitions will not be entertained by the Board.

The Board will either decline the petition or issue an order which will specify the issues to which review will be limited.

When the Board grants a Discretionary Review the party filing submits a brief to the Board supporting his exceptions to the decision and only on those issues specified in the Board's order. Briefs are filed within thirty days after the Board's order granting the review. In the Brief, the party attempts to present proof that the Administrative Law Judge's decision is in error and does not show a proper appraisal of the evidence.

Oral Argument

If any party desires to argue a case orally before the Board, he will request to do so in his Brief.

After the Exceptions have been dispensed with, the Oral Argument may take place. At the oral argument the five members of the Civil Aeronautics Board are in attendance. This constitutes an important step since it affords the only opportunity for the parties in the case to speak directly to the Board members. All parties avail themselves of the opportunity to present their argument. Civic parties are normally limited to five minutes each for their presentation. Air carrier applicants are normally limited to fifteen minutes each for their presentation. The Oral Argument is for the purpose of presenting the case of the parties based upon the record developed at the Hearing. No new material or evidence may be presented at the Oral Argument. It is a waste of time to plead with the Board for consideration. Not more than two or three important points are stressed. The argument should be straight-forward, convincing and a statement of the facts alone.

Final Decision of the Board

After the Oral Argument, the Board members review all evidence presented and issue an appropriate order. This order includes a statement of the reasons for its findings and conclusions. This order will be deemed the final order.

The Board's decision is final in all matters relative to civil aviation. The losing parties, if dissatisfied, may petition the Board for reconsideration within twenty days after the final order is issued. This is known as a Petition for Reconsideration and unless the Civil Aeronautics Board is shown where they have committed a legal error, or where they have not taken into consideration evidence already in the case and thereby arrived at a wrong decision, the petition is disallowed, thus concluding the case.

Judicial Review

Occasionally, after a party has had their Petition for Reconsideration denied, they will appeal the Board's decision to the Courts for review. These appeals are normally made upon legal points and not on error in facts. The Courts rarely give a favorable decision on these appeals and when they do it is where the Court determines the Civil Aeronautics Board has committed legal error.

CHAPTER
XIV
ᐯᐯᐯ
Air Carrier Accounting
and Financial Analysis

Accounting is the language of business; it is a primary means of reporting, measuring and communicating business data and information. All business enterprises practice various types of accounting procedures to keep record of their business transactions. Additionally, the United States government requires that records be accurately kept for tax reporting purposes. The air carrier industry is no exception. Accounting records are required for the needs of adequate managerial control.

Financial Statements reflect the information recorded in the accounting system or the records of transactions. The principle financial statements include the Balance Sheet and the Income Statement, traditionally known as Profit and Loss.

The Balance Sheet is a statement of financial condition of a business at one particular moment of time. It shows assets, liabilities and owner's equity. Assets represent what the company owns. Liabilities represnet obligations of a company, or what it owes. Owner's Equity represents the stockholders interest in the company; the excess of assets over liabilities.

The Income Statement shows activities of the company, during the period of time covered by the statement, including revenue, expense and profit or loss. Revenue is income from the sale of goods or services. Expense is cost incurred in the process of earning revenue. Profit or Loss is the resulting difference between revenue and expense.

The Income Statement is considered to be far more important than the Balance Sheet because of the greater emphasis upon earnings.

Since the air carrier industry functions in the public interest, they, like all other public utilities, are required to record and submit to the government, financial and statistical data.

The Federal Aviation Act charges the Civil Aeronautics Board with the responsibility for the economic regulation of the air carrier industry. Accordingly the Civil Aeronautics Board established Economic Regulation 241, known as the "Uniform System of Accounts and Reports for Certificated Air Carriers." This system is a standardized method so that all air carriers will keep financial data in the same manner. This data is then reported in a standard form to the Civil Aeronautics Board. The purpose of the system is to provide the Civil Aeronautics Board with information on air carrier's economic activity so that it may have the necessary financial information for its economic regulation of the air carrier industry.

The system of accounts and reports is designed to permit limited contraction or expansion to reflect the varying needs and capacities of different air carriers without impairing basic accounting comparability between air carriers.

Balance Sheet and Profit and Loss account groupings are designed, in general, to embrace all activities, both air transport and other than air transport, in which the air carrier engages.

In order to afford air carriers as much flexibility and freedom as possible in establishing ledger and subsidiary accounts to meet their individual needs, a minimum number of account subdivisions have been prescribed in the system of accounts. It is intended that each air carrier, in maintaining its accounting records, will provide subaccount and subsidiary account segregations of accounting elements which differ in nature of accounting characteristics, in a manner which will render individual elements readily discernible and traceable throughout the accounting system. This will provide for relating profit and loss elements to applicable balance sheet counterparts.

A four digit control number is assigned for each balance sheet and profit and loss account. Each balance sheet account is numbered sequentially designating basic balance sheet classification.

The first two digits assigned to each profit and loss account denote a detailed area of financial activity of functional operation. The second two digits denote objective classifications.

The general books of account and all books and records, which support in any way the entries therein, are kept in a manner to provide full information at any time relating to any account. The entries in each account must be supported by detailed information to render certainty to the identification of all facts. The books and records referred to include not only accounting records, but also all other records which develop the history of facts regarding any accounting or financial transaction.

The Uniform System of Accounts and Reports for Certificated Air Carriers is issued, prescribed and administered under provisions of the following sections of the Federal Aviation Act.

Section 204(a)

The Board is empowered to perform acts, to conduct investigations, to issue and amend orders, and to make rules, regulations and procedures, pursuant to and consistent with the Federal Aviation Act as it shall deem necessary to carry out and perform its powers and duties under the Act.

Section 407(a)

The Board is empowered to require annual, monthly, periodic and special reports from any air carrier; to prescribe the manner and form in which such reports shall be made; and to require from any air carrier specific answers to all questions upon which the Board may deem information to be necessary.

Section 407(b)

Each air carrier shall submit annually, and at such other times as the Board shall require, a list showing the names of each of its stockholders holding more than five per cent of the entire capital stock.

Section 407(d)

The Board shall prescribe the form of any and all accounts, records and memoranda to be kept by air carriers, including the accounts, records and memoranda of the movement of traffic, as well as the receipts and expenditures of money. It shall be unlawful for air carriers to keep any accounts or records other than those prescribed or approved by the Board. Any air carrier may keep additonal accounts or records if they do not impair the integrity of the accounts and records prescribed or approved by the Board and do not constitute an undue financial burden on such air carrier.

Section 407(e)

The Board shall at all times have access to all land, buildings, equipment, accounts and records required to be kept by air carriers; it may employ auditors to inspect and examine these at any time.

Balance Sheet

The Balance Sheet, of the Uniform System of Accounts, is designed to show the financial condition of the air carrier at a given date, reflecting the asset and liability balances carried forward subsequent to the closing of the air carrier's books of account.

The Balance Sheet items and their explanation follow:

Current Assets

Included in current assets are all resources which may reasonably be expected to be realized in cash or sold or consumed within one year, such as: unrestricted cash, assets that are readily convertible into cash or are held for current use in operations, and current claims against others that settlement is reasonably assured.

Investment and Special funds

Included are long term investments in securities of others exclusive of United States Government securities, securities which are not readily marketable, funds set aside for special purposes, contract performance deposits and other securities, receivables, or funds not available for current operations.

Property and Equipment

Included are all investments in land, tangible property and equipment. Property and Equipment is subclassified into:
1. Operating Property and Equipment.
   This encompasses items used in air transportation services.
2. Non-operating Property and Equipment.
   This encompasses investments in property and equipment not separately accounted for within a non-transport division but assigned to other than air transportation and its incidental services, and property and equipment held for future use.

Property and Equipment Depreciation and Overhaul

The Balance Sheet classification "depreciation reserves" include the accumulation of all provisions for losses occurring in property and equipment from use and obsolescence. It includes reserves for depreciation established to record current lessening in service value due to wear and tear from use and the action of time and the elements, as well as losses by obsolescence, change in popular demand or the requirement of public authority.

Each air carrier will adopt procedures of accounting for airframe and aircraft engine overhauls as will effectively result in the allocation of total maintenance expense between accounting periods in accordance with the use of airframes and aircraft engines. Each air carrier will file with the Civil Aeronautics Board a statement fully describing its plans of accounting for airframe and engine overhauls.

Deferred Charges

Included here are all debit balances in general clearing accounts including charges held in suspense pending receipt of information necessary for final disposition, prepayments chargeable against operations over a period of years, capitalized expenditures of an organizational character, copyrights and miscellaneous intangibles.

Current Liabilities

Included are all debts the payment of which is reasonably expected to be within one year. Current liabilities include payables incurred in the acquisition of materials.

Noncurrent Liabilities

Included are all debts the payment of which is not reasonably expected to require the use within one year of resources of a type which are classifiable as current assets or the creation of current liabilities.

Deferred Credits

Included are all credit balances in general clearing accounts including credits held in suspense pending receipt of information necessary for final disposition and premiums on long-term debt securities of the air carrier.

Stockholder Equity

Included are all items which record the aggregate interests of stockholders in assets owned by the air carrier. Subdivisions are:
1. Paid-in capital—direct contributions of the stockholders.
2. Retained earnings—income retained from the operation of the air carrier.
3. Treasury stock—the cost to the air carrier of capital stock issued which has been reacquired and is held for disposition.

PROFIT AND LOSS

The Profit and Loss accounts are designed to reflect the elements of income or loss accruing to the proprietary interests during each accounting period.

The system provides that profit and loss elements be grouped in accordance with their inherent characteristics within the following primary classifications:

Operating Revenues

This classification includes revenues ordinarily derived from the performance of air transportation, and net revenues from services performed incidental to it. Operating Revenues and their explanation follow:
1. Transportation Revenues
   Included are all revenues from the air transportation of traffic. Revenues are derived from direct aviation activity of:
   > Passengers
   > U.S. Mail (priority and non-priority)
   > Public Service Revenue
   > Air Express
   > Air Freight
2. Nontransportation Revenues
   Included are all revenues for providing air transportation facilities, but not as direct payment for the carriage of traffic, and all revenues (less expenses) directly associated with the performance of services that are incidental to air transportation services performed by the air carrier. Included is revenue from the operation of hotels, restaurants, food services, surface transportation, and services to other air carriers.

Operating Expenses

This classification includes expenses ordinarily incurred in performing air transportation services.

CHART OF BALANCE SHEET ACCOUNTS

Civil Aeronautics Board
Uniform System of Accounts and Reports
for Certificated Air Carriers

Name of account

Current assets:
 Cash . . . .
 Special deposits . . . .
 United States Government securities . . . .
 Other temporary cash investments . . . .
 Accounts receivable—U.S. Government . . . .
 Accounts receivable—foreign governments . . . .
 Accounts receivable—general traffic . . . .
 Notes and accounts receivable—associated companies . . . .
 Notes and accounts receivable—company personnel . . . .
 Notes and accounts receivable—other . . . .
 Reserve for uncollectible accounts . . . .
 Flight equipment expendable parts . . . .
 Obsolescence and deterioration reserves—expendable parts . . . . . .
 Miscellaneous materials and supplies . . . .
 Short-term prepayments . . . .
 Other current assets . . . .

 Investments and special funds:
  Investments in associated companies . . . .
   Investments in subsidiary companies . . . .
   Investments in other associated companies . . . .
  Advances to nontransport divisions . . . .
  Other investments and receivables . . . .
  Special funds—self-insurance . . . .
  Special funds—other . . . .

Property and equipment . . . .
 Airframes . . . .
 Aircraft engines . . . .
 Aircraft propellers . . . .
 Aircraft communications and navigational equipment . . . .
 Miscellaneous flight equipment . . . .
 Improvements to leased flight equipment . . . .
 Flight equipment rotatable parts and assemblies . . . .
  Airframe parts and assemblies . . . .
  Aircraft engine parts and assemblies . . . .
  Other parts and assemblies . . . .
 Flight equipment . . . .
 Reserve for depreciation—airframes . . . .
 Reserve for depreciation—aircraft engines . . . .

Chart of Balance Sheet Accounts (cont.)

    Reserve for depreciation—aircraft propellers . . . .

    Reserve for depreciation—aircraft communication and navigational
        equipment . . . .

    Reserve for depreciation—miscellaneous flight equipment . . . .

    Reserve for depreciation—improvements to leased flight equipment . . .

    Reserve for depreciation—flight equipment rotatable parts and assemblies .

        Airframe parts and assemblies . . . .

        Aircraft engine parts and assemblies . . . .

        Other parts and assemblies . . . .

    Reserve for depreciation—flight equipment . . . .

    Flight equipment airworthiness reserves . . . .

    Passenger service equipment . . . .

    Hotel, restaurant and food service equipment . . . .

    Ramp equipment . . . .

    Communication and meteorological equipment . . . .

    Maintenance and engineering equipment . . . .

    Surface transport vehicles and equipment . . . .

    Furniture, fixtures and office equipment . . . .

    Storage and distribution equipment . . . .

    Miscellaneous ground equipment . . . .

    Buildings and other improvements . . . .

        Maintenance buildings and improvements . . . .

        Other buildings and improvements . . . .

    Ground property and equipment . . . .

    Reserve for depreciation—passenger service equipment . . . .

    Reserve for depreciation—hotel, restaurant and food service equipment . .

    Reserve for depreciation—ramp equipment . . . .

    Reserve for depreciation—communication and meteorological equipment .

    Reserve for depreciation—maintenance and engineering equipment . . . .

    Reserve for depreciation—surface transport vehicles and equipment . . .

    Reserve for depreciation—furniture, fixtures and office equipment . . . .

    Reserve for depreciation—storage and distribution equipment . . . . . .

    Reserve for depreciation—miscellaneous ground equipment . . . .

    Reserve for depreciation—buildings and other improvements . . . . . .

        Maintenance buildings and improvements . . . .

        Other buildings and improvements . . . .

    Reserves for depreciation—ground property and equipment . . . .

    Land . . . .

    Construction work in progress . . . .

Deferred charges:

    Long-term prepayments . . . .

    Developmental and preoperating costs . . . .

    Unamortized discount and expense on debt . . . .

    Unamortized capital stock expense . . . .

Property acquisition adjustment . . . .
Other intangibles . . . .
Other deferred charges . . . .
Current liabilities:
    Current notes payable . . . .
    Accounts payable—general . . . .
    Collections as agent—traffic . . . .
    Collections as agent—other . . . .
    Notes and accounts payable—associated companies . . . .
    Accrued personnel compensation . . . .
    Accrued vacation liability . . . .
    Accrued Federal income taxes . . . .
    Other accrued taxes . . . .
    Dividends declared . . . .
    Air travel plan liability . . . .
    Unearned transportation revenue . . . .
    Other current liabilities . . . .
Noncurrent liabilities:
    Long-term debt . . . .
    Advances from associated companies . . . .
    Advances from nontransport divisions . . . .
    Pension liability . . . .
    Company stock purchase plan liability . . . .
    Other noncurrent liabilities . . . .
Deferred credits:
    Unamortized premium on debt . . . .
    Deferred Federal income taxes . . . .
    Deferred investment tax credits . . . .
    Reserve for self-insurance . . . .
    Other deferred credits . . . .
Stockholder equity:
    Preferred stock . . . .
    Common stock . . . .
    Capital stock subscribed and unissued . . . .
    Other paid-in capital . . . .
        Premium on capital stock . . . .
        Discount on capital stock . . . .
        Other capital stock transactions . . . .
        Miscellaneous paid-in capital . . . .
    Appropriations of retained earnings . . . .
    Unappropriated retained earnings . . . .
    Treasury stock . . . .

Operating Expenses and their explanation follow:

1. Flying Operations
    Included are expenses for salaries of flight personnel, aircraft fuels and
    oils, fuel taxes, rental of flight equipment, and insurance.
2. Maintenance
    Included are expenses identified with the repair and upkeep of equip-
    ment; expense of labor and materials.
3. General Services and Administration
    This is a general inclusive classification of expenses for Passenger Service,
    Aircraft and Traffic Servicing, Promotion and Sales, and Administration.
4. Depreciation and Amortization
    Included are expenses brought about by exhaustion of the serviceability
    of property and equipment due to use, wear and the passage of time.
    Separate accounts are maintained for the depreciation of airframe, en-
    gines, and their respective parts.

Nonoperating Income and Expense

This classification represents the net income or loss from ventures not directly related to the performance of air transportation service.

Income Taxes

This classification includes provisions for taxes for the current period, provisions for deferred federal income taxes, and investment tax credits deferred and
amortized.

Special Items

This classification includes extraordinary credits and debits, exclusive of
ordinary adjustments of a recurring nature, that are of sufficient magnitude to
materially distort the total operating revenues or total operating expenses and
permit misleading inferences to be drawn therefrom.

The resulting difference between the Revenues and Expenses is the profit or
loss for the period of time covered.

REPORTING SYSTEM

The Uniform System of Accounts and Reports for Certificated Air Carriers
contains two major divisions. The first, which has been covered in this chapter
pertains to accounting procedures. The second, pertaining to the procedures of
reporting financial and operating statistical data is presented below.

Every certificated air carrier must submit to the Civil Aeronautics Board,
monthly, quarterly, semiannual and annual reports of financial and operating
activity. The method used is known as Civil Aeronautics Board Form 41 Reports.

CHART OF PROFIT AND LOSS ACCOUNTS

Civil Aeronautics Board
Uniform System of Accounts and Reports
for Certificated Air Carriers

OPERATING REVENUES

01 Passenger.
    01.*1* Passenger—first class . . . .
    01.*2* Passenger—coach . . . .
02 United States mail.
    02.*1* Priority . . . .
    02.*2* Nonpriority . . . .
03 Foreign Mail . . . .
06 Property.
    06.*1* Express . . . .
    06.*2* Freight . . . .
    06.*3* Excess passenger baggage . . . .
07 Charter and special.
    07.*1* Passenger . . . .
    07.*2* Property . . . .
08 Section 406 subsidy . . . .
09 Foreign exchange fluctuation adjustments . . . .
10 Hotel, restaurant and food service.
    10.*1* Gross revenues . . . .
    10.*2* Depreciation expense . . . .
    10.*3* Other expenses . . . .
11 Rents.
    11.*1* Gross revenues . . . .
    11.*2* Depreciation expense . . . .
    11.*3* Other expenses . . . .
12 Limousine service.
    12.*1* Gross revenues . . . .
    12.*2* Depreciation expense . . . .
    12.*3* Other expenses . . . .
13 Interchange sales—associated companies.
    13.*1* Gross revenues . . . .
    13.*2* Depreciation expense . . . .
    13.*3* Other expenses . . . .
14 General service sales—associated companies.
    14.*1* Gross revenues . . . .
    14.*2* Depreciation expense . . . .
    14.*3* Other expenses . . . .
15 Interchange sales—outside.
    15.*1* Gross revenues . . . .
    15.*2* Depreciation expense . . . .
    15.*3* Other expenses . . . .

Chart of Profit and Loss Accounts (cont.)

16 General service sales—outside.
    16.1 Gross revenues . . . .
    16.2 Depreciation expense . . . .
    16.3 Other expenses . . . .
17 Air cargo services.
    17.1 Gross revenues . . . .
    17.2 Depreciation expense . . . .
    17.3 Other expenses . . . .
18 Other incidental revenues.
    18.1 Gross revenues . . . .
    18.2 Depreciation expense . . . .
    18.3 Other expenses . . . .
19 Other operating revenues.
    19.1 Reservations cancellation fees . . . .
    19.9 Miscellaneous operating revenues . . . .

OPERATING EXPENSES

21 General management personnel . . . .
23 Pilots and copilots . . . .
24 Other flight personnel . . . .
25 Maintenance labor.
    25.1 Labor—airframes . . . .
    25.2 Labor—aircraft engines . . . .
    25.3 Labor—other flight equipment . . . .
    25.6 Labor—flight equipment . . . .
    25.9 Labor—ground property and equipment . . . .
26 Aircraft and traffic handling personnel . . . .
    26.1 General aircraft and traffic handling personnel . . . .
    26.2 Aircraft control personnel . . . .
    26.3 Passenger handling personnel . . . .
    26.4 Cargo handling personnel . . . .
28 Trainees, instructors and unallocated shop labor.
    28.1 Trainees and instructors . . . .
    28.2 Unallocated shop labor . . . .
30 Communications personnel . . . .
31 Record keeping and statistical personnel . . . .
32 Lawyers and law clerks . . . .
33 Traffic solicitors . . . .
34 Purchasing personnel . . . .
35 Other personnel . . . .
36 Personnel expenses . . . .
37 Communications purchased . . . .
38 Light, heat, power and water . . . .
39 Traffic commissions . . . .
    39.1 Commissions—passenger . . . .

Chart of Profit and Loss Accounts (cont.)

64 Memberships . . . .
65 Corporate and fiscal expenses . . . .
66 Uncollectible accounts . . . .
67 Clearance, customs and duties . . . .
68 Taxes—payroll . . . .
69 Taxes—other than payroll . . . .
71 Other expenses . . . .
72 Flight equipment airworthiness provisions.
   72.1 Airworthiness reserve provisions—airframes . . . .
   72.2 Airworthiness reserve charges—airframes (credit) . . . .
   72.6 Airworthiness reserve provisions—aircraft engines . . . .
   72.7 Airworthiness reserve charges—aircraft engines (credit) . . . . .
73 Provisions for obsolescence and deterioration—expendable parts.
   73.1 Current provisions . . . .
   73.2 Inventory decline credits . . . .
74 Amortizations.
   74.1 Developmental and preoperating expenses . . . .
   74.2 Other intangibles . . . .
75 Depreciation.
   75.1 Airframes . . . .
   75.2 Aircraft engines . . . .
   75.3 Airframe parts . . . .
   75.4 Aircraft engine parts . . . .
   75.5 Other flight equipment . . . .
   75.6 Flight equipment . . . .
   75.8 Maintenance equipment and hangars . . . .
   75.9 General ground property . . . .
77 Uncleared expense credits.
   77.8 Uncleared interchange expense credits . . . .
   77.9 Other uncleared expense credits . . . .
78 Direct maintenance—flight equipment . . . .
79 Applied burden Dr/Cr.
   79.6 Flight equipment . . . .
   79.8 General ground property . . . .

NONOPERATING INCOME AND EXPENSES

80 Imputed interest capitalized.
   80.1 Imputed interest capitalized—credit . . . .
   80.2 Imputed interest deferred—debit . . . .
   80.3 Imputed interest deferred—credit . . . .
81 Capital gains and losses.
   81.1 Capital gains and losses—operating property . . . .
   81.2 Capital gains and losses—other . . . .
82 Unapplied cash discounts . . . .
83 Interest income . . . .

84   Income from subsidiary companies and dividend income.
     84.1 Income from subsidiary companies . . . .
     84.2 Dividend income—other than subsidiary companies . . . .
85   Foreign exchange adjustments . . . .
86   Income from nontransport ventures . . . .
87   Interest and debt expense.
     87.1 Interest on debt principal . . . .
     87.2 Interest capitalized—credit . . . .
     87.3 Amortization of discount and expense on debt . . . .
     87.4 Amortization of premium on debt . . . .
88   Miscellaneous nonoperating credits . . . .
89   Miscellaneous nonoperating debits . . . .

INCOME TAXES

91   Provision for income taxes.
     91.1 Income taxes before investment tax credits . . . .
     91.2 Investment tax credits utilized . . . .
92   Provisions for deferred Federal income taxes . . . .
     92.1 Current provisions for deferred taxes . . . .
     92.2 Application of deferred taxes . . . .
     92.3 Adjustment of deferred taxes . . . .
93   Investment tax credits deferred and amortized.
     93.1 Investment tax credits deferred . . . .
     93.2 Amortization of deferred investment tax credits . . . .

SPECIAL ITEMS

96   Special income credits and debits (net) . . . .
97   Special income tax credits and debits (net) . . . .

The reporting system provides for the submission, by each air carrier, of separate classes of financial and operating statistics. These individual schedules of Form 41 are:

	Code Letter
1. Certification	A
2. Balance Sheet Elements	B
3. Profit and Loss Elements	P
4. Traffic and Capacity Elements	T
5. General Corporate Elements	G
6. National Defense Elements	D

Each schedule is assigned a specific code letter. The numbers following the letter designate the particular schedule.

It is not the intention of this text to delve into the contents of the schedules required in the reporting system. For a further study the reader is referred to the actual system available from the Civil Aeronautics Board on a subscription basis.

The Form 41 Reporting Schedule, Balance Sheet and Income Statement follow for general information.

FORM 41—REPORT SCHEDULES

Civil Aeronautics Board
Uniform System of Accounts and Reports
for Certificated Air Carriers

Schedule No.

A . . . . . Certification . . . .

A-1 . . . . Status of Accounting Plans Required to be Filed . . . . .

B-1 . . . . Balance Sheet . . . .

B-2 . . . . Notes to Balance Sheet . . . .

B-3 . . . . Paid-in Capital; Self-Insurance Reserves and Appropriations of Retained Earnings; Deferred Income Taxes.

B-4 . . . . Reserve for Uncollectible Accounts; Accounts With Subsidiaries, Other Associated Companies and Nontransport Divisions.

B-5 . . . . Property and Equipment . . . .

B-7 . . . . Airframes and Aircraft Engines Acquired . . . .

B-7(a) . . . Reinvestment of Flight Equipment Capital Gains . . . . .

B-7(b) . . . Flight Equipment Acquired . . . .

B-8 . . . . Property and Equipment Retired . . . .

B-8(a) . . . Flight Equipment Capital Gains Invested or Deposited for Reinvestment in Flight Equipment.

B-9 . . . . Inventory of Flight Equipment Spare Parts and Assemblies .

B-10 . . . . Developmental and Preoperating Costs . . . .

B-41 . . . . Investments Held by, or for the Account of, Respondent . .

FORM 41—BALANCE SHEET

Civil Aeronautics Board
Uniform System of Accounts and Reports
for Certificated Air Carriers

ASSETS

Current Assets:

Cash	1010
Special deposits	1030
United States Government securities	1110
Other temporary cash investments	1120
Notes and accounts receivable:	
United states Government	1220
Foreign governments	1230
General traffic	1240
Associated companies	1250
Company personnel	1260
Other	1280
Total notes and accounts receivable	1289
Less: Reserve for uncollectible accounts	1290
Notes and accounts receivable—net	1299
Flight equipment—expendable parts	1310
Less: Obsolescence and deterioration reserves—expendable parts	1311
Miscellaneous materials and supplies	1330
Short-term prepayments	1410
Other current assets	1420
Total current assets	1499

Investments and Special Funds:

Investments in associated companies:	
Investments in subsidiary companies	1510.1
Investments in other associated companies	1510.2
Advances to nontransport divisions	1520
Other investments and receivables	1530
Special funds—self-insurance	1540
Special funds—other	1550
Total investments and special funds	1599

Operating Property and Equipment:

Flight equipment	1609
Less: Reserves for depreciation	1619
Flight equipment less depreciation reserves	1621
Less: Flight equipment airworthiness reserves	1629
Flight equipment—net	1629.9
Ground property and equipment	1649
Less: Reserves for depreciation	1669
Land	1679
Construction work in progress	1689
Operating property and equipment—net	1699

Non-Operating Property and Equipment: 1791

Less: Reserves for depreciation	1792
Non-operating property and equipment—net	1799

Deferred Charges:

Long-term prepayments	1820
Developmental and preoperating costs	1830
Unamortized discount and expense on debt	1840
Unamortized capital stock expense	1850
Property acquisition adjustment	1870
Other intangibles	1880
Other deferred charges	1890
Total deferred charges	1895

Total Assets 1899

LIABILITIES AND STOCKHOLDER EQUITY

Current Liabilities:

Notes and accounts payable:	
Current notes payable	2010
Accounts payable—general	2020
Collections as agent—traffic	2030
Collections as agent—other	2040
Associated companies	2050
Total notes and accounts payable	2059
Accrued personnel compensation	2110
Accrued vacation liability	2120
Accrued Federal income taxes	2131
Other accrued taxes	2139
Dividends declared	2140
Air travel plan liability	2150
Unearned transportation revenue	2160
Other current liabilities	2190
Total current liabilities	2199

Noncurrent Liabilities:

Long term debt	2210
Advances from. associated companies	2240
Advances from nontransport divisions	2245
Pension liability	2250
Company stock purchase plan liability	2260
Other noncurrent liabilities	2290
Total noncurrent liabilities	2299

Deferred Credits:

  Unamortized premium on debt 2330
  Deferred Federal income taxes 2340
  Deferred investment tax credits 2345
  Reserve for self-insurance.............. 2350
  Other deferred credits 2390
    Total deferred credits 2399

Stockholder Equity:

  Paid-in capital:
    Capital stock
      Preferred   shares issued ... 2820
      Common   shares issued ... 2840
      Subscribed and unissued 2860

       Total capital stock 2869
      Other paid-in capital 2890
        Paid-in capital—net................ 2899
    Retained earnings:
      Appropriated 2930
      Unappropriated 2940
      Net income—from January 1 2941
        Total retained earnings............. 2942
    Stockholder equity—gross 2943
    Less: Treasury stock ———— shares ... 2990
      Stockholder equity—net 2995

Total Liabilities and Stockholder Equity 2999

FORM 41—INCOME STATEMENT

Civil Aeronautics Board
Uniform System of Accounts and Reports
For Certificated Air Carriers

Operating Revenues

REF.

Transport:

		REF.	
Passenger		P-3	3901
United States mail		P-3	3902
Foreign mail		P-3	3903
Property		P-3	3906
Charter and special		P-3	3907
Other		P-3	3919
Total transport revenues			3999

Nontransport:

		REF.	
Federal subsidy			4100
Incidental revenues (net)		P-4	4600
Total nontransport revenues			4900
Total operating revenues			4999

Operating Expenses

	REF.	
Flying operations	.P-5.2	5100
Maintneance	P-6	5400
Passenger service	P-6	5500
Aircraft and traffic servicing	P-7 & P-8	6400
Promotion and sales	P-7 & P-8	6700
General and administrative	P-7	6800

Depreciation and amortization P-3   7000
    Total operating expenses   7199

    Operating profit or loss   7999

Nonoperating Income and
Expense—Net P-3   8100

    Net income before income taxes   8999

Income Taxes for Current Period   9100

    Net income before special items   9699

Special Items:
Special income credits and debits (net)   . . P-4   9796
Special income tax
    credits and debits (net) P-4   9797

    Net income after special items   9799

Unappropriated Retained
Earnings: 2940
Beginning of period   9810
Cash dividends and other
    asset distributions P-4   9830
Stock dividends and retained
    earnings adjustments P-4   9840
End of period (including net income)   9899

FINANCIAL ANALYSIS

Recording and reporting financial and operational activities is a subject in itself. However, in order to manage and control an air carrier it is necessary to analyze and to interpret the data shown in the financial statements when the financial condition or the progress of a company is to be determined. In doing so, three important factors are to be considered:

1. Solvency is a company having sufficient funds to meet its liabilities.
2. Financial Stability is the financial strength of a company and is a factor in appraising profitability.
3. Profitableness is success in realizing an appropriate amount of income in relation to the capital employed.

The most important interest in financial statements is evidenced by management who must plan, organize, and control the activities of the company to attain the desired objective, normally profit. Financial statements provide management with a tool or a blueprint by which they may determine the financial strength and weaknesses of their operation. Financial statements and their interpretation are essential to the successful management of an air carrier.

Interpretation and analysis of financial statements is used by management to:

1. Measure the costs of producing various incomes.
2. Determine efficiency of operations.
3. Measure profitability.
4. Measure performance.
5. Evaluate operations and to effect changes or improvements.
6. Make sound decisions.
7. Account to stockholders.
8. Establish future plans.

When interpreting financial statements, comparisons should be made between related items. The data of one company should be compared with similar companies or with the standard of the industry.

Statistics prepared are standards, ratios, trends, and percentages. They represent the financial and operating accomplishments of the company or the industry.

The analysis of financial statements consists of a study of relationships and trends to determine if the financial position, financial progress and the results of operations of a company are satisfactory.

The objective of analysis is to simplify or reduce the statistical data to understandable terms. The analyst must first compute and organize the data and then analyze and interpret it in order for it to be meaningful. Methods and techniques used in analyzing financial statements include:

Comparing:

>   Dollar amounts
>   Percentages
>   Increases and decreases in dollar amounts
>   Increases and decreases in percentages
>   Ratios
>   Percentages of totals

Computing:

>   Trend ratios of selected items

Data selected from financial statements may be compared and shown graphically. By studying charts the analyst may obtain an idea of the changes that have taken place. In comparison with reading a table of figures, a chart is more meaningful since variations are more noticeable.

Analysis of Air Carrier Financial Statements

The financial strength of an air carrier and the efficiency of its management may be measured and evaluated by comparisons with the company's data from year to year, and also in comparison with other air carriers of its class as well as the industry total. In order to make comparisons practical, the data obtained from accounting records and reports must be summarized into statistics that are comprehensive, comparable, readable, and understandable.

The key to the analysis of financial statements is the calculation of certain critical ratios. The analyzer must know the meaning of the data used in the ratios as well as their use.

Trend Ratios

The use of trend percentages (index numbers) is a valuable aid in analyzing financial and operating data.

Operating Ratio is determined by dividing the operating expenses by the operating revenues. The resulting operating ratio is regarded as an index of operating efficiency.

Comparisons of Operating Revenue and Operating Expense

Revenue and Expense can be compared from year to year for one company to show the percentage of change. Revenue and Expense of one air carrier can also be compared to that of other air carriers of like class and also to the total of the industry. The operating expense and revenue can be compared for the following items:

> The dollar amounts
> Cents per mile
> Percentage of operating revenue and expense
> Cents per mile flown (revenue and expense)

Current Ratio

The current ratio is a useful indication of the financial strength of the air carrier and is obtained by dividing current assets by current liabilities.

Return on Investment

Expressed as a percentage, return on investment is obtained by dividing the profit by the total assets of the company.

Profit Margin

A more exacting test of a company's operating success, for a period of time, is the profit margin. This is expressed as a percentage and is determined by dividing the profit by the revenue or income from sales. The higher the resulting percentage, the more successful the company has been. This ratio shows operating efficiency in a competitive situation and is considered a true test of management's ability.

Operating Cost

The operating cost percentage is the complement of the profit margin. If a company experienced a profit margin of ten percent then the operating cost figure is ninety percent. The lower this percentage the higher the profit margin.

Factors Affecting Air Carrier Financial Success

When making a complete and detailed analysis of an individual air carrier, consideration must be given to various external factors which are beyond control of the management. The most important of these are as follows:

1. Economic regulation by the Civil Aeronautics Board including routes, rates, competition, equipment and mergers.

2. Excessive competition is prevented through the control of establishing new routes, however, it has been the policy of the Civil Aeronautics Board to encourage healthy competition for the public interest. It should be understood that although economic regulation is necessary in the public interest it may also be so restrictive as to retard progress.

3. Business cycle. In analyzing air carrier trends, it is necessary to recognize the general business activity and economic condition of the country.

On the following pages are five examples of tables and graphs using the ratios stated above. Several pages of statistical data follow which can be used to prepare additional tables and graphs for analysis of several aspects of air carrier operation.

TREND RATIOS OF FINANCIAL STATEMENT ITEMS
(Index Numbers)

DOMESTIC TRUNK AIR CARRIERS
(In Thousands of Dollars)

	1965	1966	1967	1968	1969	1970	1971	1972	1973	1974	1975
Total Assets	4,165,869	5,417,909	6,911,951	8,106,198	8,970,709	9,579,112	9,768,047	10,469,239	13,005,244		
Percentages	100	130	165	194	215	229	234	251	312		
Total Liabilities	2,752,661	3,638,426	4,656,589	5,697,766	6,359,292	7,093,970	6,855,434	7,226,972	9,207,111		
Percentages	100	132	169	206	230	257	249	262	334		
Stockholder's Equity	1,386,207	1,779,483	2,255,362	2,408,432	2,611,418	2,485,143	2,912,612	3,241,268	3,798,132		
Percentages	100	128	162	173	188	179	210	233	274		
Total Operating Revenue	3,263,556	3,660,900	4,419,436	5,039,441	5,754,222	6,272,775	6,742,413	7,494,992	8,382,391		
Percentages	100	112	135	154	176	192	206	229	256		
Total Operating Expense	2,847,308	3,207,198	4,009,331	4,719,364	5,449,860	6,256,039	6,525,864	7,059,142	7,968,496		
Percentages	100	112	140	165	191	219	229	247	279		
Net Operating Income	416,249	453,703	410,106	320,077	304,362	16,736	216,549	435,850	413,895		
Percentages	100	130	96	77	73	4	52	104	99		
Net Profit or Loss	221,889	238,636	244,475	126,521	90,592	(100,414)	39,864	178,155	142,930		

Source: Air Transport Association of America

COMPARISON OF YEARLY CHANGE OF
OPERATING REVENUE AND OPERATING EXPENSE

DOMESTIC TRUNK AIR CARRIER
OPERATING REVENUE AND OPERATING EXPENSE
PERCENT OF TOTAL

	1975	1974	1973	1972	1971	1970	1969	1968	1967	1966	1965
Operating Revenue											
Transportation											
Passengers			89.5	90.2	89.8	90.0	90.0	90.0	90.6	90.2	90.4
Mail			1.9	1.9	2.1	2.2	2.2	2.4	2.2	2.3	2.1
Air Freight and											
Air Express			6.6	6.6	6.6	6.6	6.3	6.2	6.0	6.3	6.2
Public Service Revenue			–	–	–	–	–	–	.1	.1	.1
Nontransportation			2.0	1.3	1.5	1.2	1.5	1.4	1.1	1.1	1.2
			100.0	100.0	100.0	100.0	100.0	100.0	100.0	100.0	100.0
Operating Expense											
Flying Operations			28.5	28.6	29.9	29.2	29.1	28.4	27.4	27.1	26.9
Maintenance			15.1	14.9	14.9	15.5	15.8	17.0	18.3	18.5	19.8
General Services											
and Administration			46.7	46.5	44.7	44.4	44.2	44.4	44.2	44.0	42.7
Depreciation and											
Amortization			9.7	10.0	10.5	10.9	10.9	10.2	10.1	10.4	10.6
			100.0	100.0	100.0	100.0	100.0	100.0	100.0	100.0	100.0

Source: Air Transport Association of America

DOMESTIC TRUNK AIR CARRIERS
(THOUSANDS OF DOLLARS)

Year	Total Operating Revenue	Net Profit or Loss	Profit Margin
1963	2,451,915	13,117	.5
1964	2,790,877	134,362	4.8
1965	3,263,556	221,889	6.8
1966	3,660,900	238,636	6.5
1967	4,419,436	244,475	5.5
1968	5,039,441	126,521	2.5
1969	6,134,700	110,427	1.8
1970	6,272,775	(100,414)	—
1971	6,742,413	39,864	.6
1972	7,494,992	178,155	2.4
1973	8,382,391	142,930	1.7
1974			
1975			

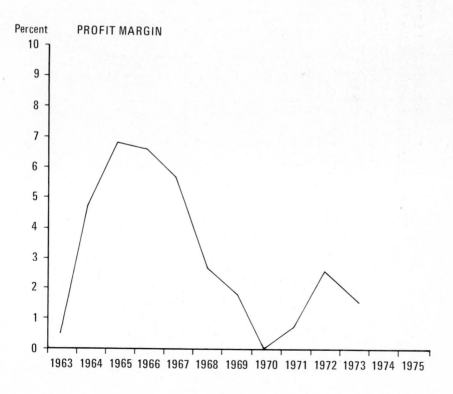

217

DOMESTIC TRUNK AIR CARRIERS

Year	Available Seat Miles (000)	Revenue Passenger Miles (000)	Load Factor
1963	67,601,302	36,383,756	53.8
1964	75,242,408	41,658,368	55.4
1965	88,731,152	48,986,972	55.2
1966	97,174,719	56,802,788	58.5
1967	124,141,624	70,990,141	57.2
1968	153,864,640	81,611,832	53.0
1969	190,064,498	95,657,705	50.3
1970	194,461,931	95,899,744	49.3
1971	205,509,471	97,756,113	48.3
1972	206,617,921	108,189,968	52.4
1973	222,446,581	115,352,180	51.9
1974			
1975			

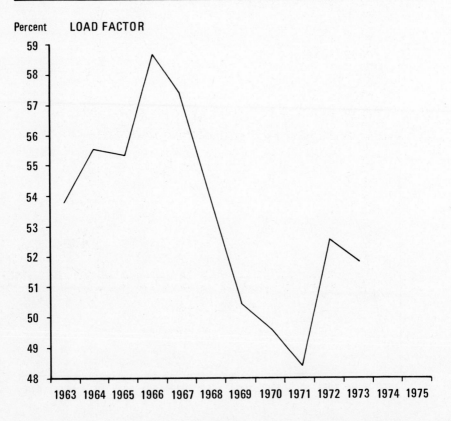

Percent   LOAD FACTOR

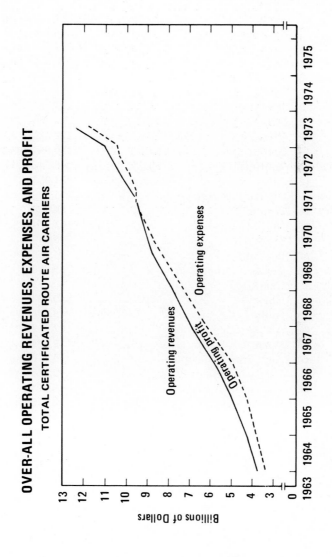

OVER-ALL OPERATING REVENUES, EXPENSES, AND PROFIT

TOTAL CERTIFICATED ROUTE AIR CARRIERS

Operating revenues

Operating expenses

Operating profit

Billions of Dollars

1963 1964 1965 1966 1967 1968 1969 1970 1971 1972 1973 1974 1975

Passenger Revenues   1973

(In Thousands of Dollars)

1.	United	$1,654,540
2.	American	1,296,318
3.	Trans World	1,154,069
4.	Eastern	1,130,276
5.	Pan American	1,049,914
6.	Delta	1,021,122
7.	Northwest	474,060
8.	National	382,959
9.	Western	379,824
10.	Braniff	370,954
11.	Continental	340,942
12.	Allegheny	294,953
13.	Hughes Airwest	108,609
14.	Frontier	104,688
15.	North Central	102,574
16.	Piedmont	90,839
17.	Southern	64,788
18.	Texas International	62,758
19.	Ozark	60,763
20.	Hawaiian	40,267
21.	Aloha	28,858
22.	Alaska	27,652
23.	Wien Air Alaska	12,804
24.	New York Helicopter	6,310
25.	Reeve Aleutian	5,228
26.	Caribbean-Atlantic	3,494
27.	San Francisco & Oakland Helicopter	2,426
28.	Aspen	1,984
29.	Wright	1,186
30.	Kodiak-Western Alaska	351
31.	Chicago Helicopter	159
32.	Western Alaska	19

*Note: Caribbean-Atlantic merged with Eastern
Air Lines on May 15, 1973 and Western Alaska
with Kodiak Airways on April 1, 1973.*

Source: Air Transport Association of America

Operating Revenues   1973

(In Thousands of Dollars)

1.	United	$1,940,963
2.	American	1,475,359
3.	Trans World	1,452,905
4.	Pan American	1,424,639
5.	Eastern	1,259,807
6.	Delta	1,122,971
7.	Northwest	584,748
8.	Braniff	428,099
9.	Western	414,717
10.	National	413,849
11.	Continental	387,332
12.	Allegheny	329,361
13.	Flying Tiger	174,538
14.	Hughes Airwest	130,107
15.	North Central	126,420
16.	Frontier	124,799
17.	Piedmont	107,484
18.	Southern	83,770
19.	Ozark	81,610
20.	Texas International	77,782
21.	Seaboard	74,809
22.	Hawaiian	44,822
23.	Airlift	37,899
24.	Alaska	36,876
25.	Aloha	30,613
26.	Wien Air Alaska	26,055
27.	Reeve Aleutian	6,845
28.	New York Helicopter	6,449
29.	Caribbean-Atlantic	3,880
30.	San Francisco & Oakland Helicopter	2,891
31.	Aspen	2,329
32.	Wright	1,722
33.	Kodiak-Western Alaska	1,465
34.	Chicago Helicopter	752
35.	Western Alaska	104

Source: Air Transport Association of America

TRAFFIC AND SERVICE

Total U.S. Scheduled Airlines	1973	1972	1971	1970	1969	1968	1967	1966	1965	1964	1963
Passenger Traffic											
Revenue passengers enplaned (000)	202,208	191,349	173,669	169,922	171,898	162,181	142,499	118,061	102,920	88,520	77,403
Revenue passenger miles (000)	161,957,307	152,406,276	135,657,702	131,710,018	125,420,120	113,958,321	98,746,641	79,889,246	68,676,459	58,493,654	50,362,042
Available seat miles (000)	310,597,107	287,411,214	279,823,351	265,119,871	250,845,929	216,445,750	174,818,524	137,844,486	124,319,945	106,315,777	94,844,743
Revenue passenger load factor (%)	52.1	53.0	48.5	49.7	50.0	52.6	56.5	58.0	55.2	55.0	53.1
Average length of haul (miles)	801	796	781	775	730	703	693	677	667	661	651
Cargo Traffic (Ton Miles)—Total (000)	6,035,200	5,495,072	5,108,659	4,984,197	4,690,355	4,167,064	3,426,117	2,900,941	2,303,131	1,751,106	1,453,967
Freight (000)	4,736,729	4,217,452	3,712,288	3,407,552	3,240,965	2,804,878	2,351,108	2,050,735	1,730,295	1,301,487	1,026,533
Express (000)	100,497	87,422	82,995	106,514	109,467	105,153	98,883	99,690	89,859	78,310	70,832
Priority U.S. Mail (000)	602,709	581,705	595,669	606,492	577,453	581,883	567,301	542,771	372,294	289,913	266,402
Nonpriority U.S. Mail (000)	595,265	608,493	717,707	863,639	762,470	675,168	408,825	207,745	110,683	81,396	90,200
Overall Traffic and Service											
Nonscheduled traffic—total ton miles (000)	1,685,764	2,059,180	2,220,658	2,019,832	3,091,193	2,865,022	2,648,005	1,754,930	909,401	582,369	514,169
Total revenue ton miles—all services (000)	23,927,638	22,805,371	20,905,968	20,185,500	19,989,409	18,114,334	15,684,289	12,440,854	9,894,985	8,015,941	6,860,302
Total available ton miles—all services (000)	51,443,617	48,680,473	47,255,550	44,298,170	42,779,192	37,223,333	30,785,135	23,505,292	19,660,993	16,302,481	13,930,752
Ton mile load factor (%)	46.5	46.8	44.2	45.6	46.7	48.7	46.4	52.9	50.3	49.2	49.2
Scheduled revenue aircraft departures	5,133,811	5,046,438	4,998,934	5,119,556	5,378,343	5,348,110	4,945,947	4,373,318	4,197,584	3,954,083	3,788,362
Scheduled revenue aircraft miles (000)	2,448,114	2,375,875	2,377,858	2,418,169	2,384,866	2,145,972	1,833,563	1,482,486	1,353,503	1,189,135	1,095,058
Scheduled revenue aircraft hours	5,898,575	5,728,496	5,725,925	5,846,195	5,895,772	5,521,311	4,924,613	4,233,467	4,071,943	3,774,772	3,606,638

Source: Air Transport Association of America

TRAFFIC AND SERVICE

Domestic Trunk Airlines	1973	1972	1971	1970	1969	1968	1967	1966	1965	1964	1963
Passenger Traffic											
Revenue passengers enplaned (000)	144,753	136,590	124,351	122,866	129,883	118,810	105,854	86,423	76,677	65,963	58,222
Revenue passenger miles (000)	115,352,180	108,189,968	97,756,113	95,899,744	95,657,705	81,611,832	70,990,141	56,802,788	48,986,972	41,658,368	36,383,756
Available seat miles (000)	222,446,581	206,617,921	202,509,471	194,461,930	190,064,198	153,864,640	124,141,624	97,174,719	88,731,152	75,242,408	67,601,302
Revenue passenger load factor (%)	51.9	52.4	48.3	49.3	50.3	53.0	57.2	58.5	55.2	55.4	53.8
Average length of haul (miles)	797	792	786	781	736	687	671	657	639	632	625
Cargo Traffic (Ton Miles)—Total (000)	2,961,808	2,779,389	2,593,965	2,555,646	2,622,526	2,072,466	1,666,721	1,353,051	1,131,081	902,733	752,609
Freight (000)	2,260,935	2,067,242	1,861,767	1,789,701	1,753,602	1,439,161	1,190,067	988,485	835,118	650,732	520,632
Express (000)	89,178	76,927	73,552	95,445	99,331	94,874	89,343	87,128	80,424	70,530	64,914
Priority U.S. Mail (000)	376,189	342,078	342,214	344,491	347,440	285,988	266,730	236,018	182,673	151,763	138,661
Nonpriority U.S. Mail (000)	235,506	293,142	316,432	326,009	422,153	252,443	120,581	41,420	32,866	29,708	28,402
Overall Traffic and Service											
Nonscheduled traffic—total ton miles (000)	401,864	447,622	432,442	443,083	806,533	425,942	498,919	287,753	165,401	45,251	24,230
Total revenue ton miles—all services (000)	14,899,500	14,046,278	12,801,877	12,589,056	12,647,138	10,321,322	8,969,988	7,083,014	5,983,537	4,928,807	4,257,567
Total available ton miles—all services (000)	33,695,886	31,703,285	30,977,903	29,623,686	29,165,115	23,097,750	18,769,379	14,403,764	12,850,594	10,752,433	9,222,953
Ton mile load factor (%)	44.2	44.3	41.3	42.5	43.4	44.7	47.8	49.2	46.6	45.8	46.2
Scheduled revenue aircraft departures	3,019,558	2,954,879	2,920,958	2,979,044	3,184,595	3,005,352	2,749,451	2,290,949	2,252,205	2,105,980	2,075,499
Scheduled revenue aircraft miles (000)	1,743,427	1,711,465	1,727,414	1,748,728	1,747,185	1,486,460	1,258,265	995,729	926,369	808,419	752,716
Scheduled revenue aircraft hours	4,013,888	3,922,530	3,954,387	4,008,837	4,073,520	3,597,467	3,134,676	2,589,592	2,541,328	2,354,069	2,288,840

Source: Air Transport Association of America

TRAFFIC AND SERVICE

Local Service Airlines	1973	1972	1971	1970	1969	1968	1967	1966	1965	1964	1963
Passenger Traffic											
Revenue passengers enplaned (000)	32,450	30,501	27,432	26,726	24,547	23,389	19,032	16,295	12,911	11,022	9,322
Revenue passenger miles (000)	9,829,603	8,899,388	7,851,515	7,430,666	6,312,630	5,489,224	4,114,304	3,467,510	2,621,201	2,244,488	1,868,988
Available seat miles (000)	20,178,505	18,074,128	17,335,816	17,024,403	14,722,390	12,153,585	8,862,400	6,908,077	5,545,691	4,836,305	4,266,886
Revenue passenger load factor (%)	48.7	49.2	45.3	43.6	42.9	45.2	46.4	50.2	47.3	46.4	43.8
Average length of haul (miles)	303	292	286	278	257	235	216	213	203	204	200
Cargo Traffic (Ton Miles)—Total (000)	114,432	101,456	86,206	86,264	70,440	59,036	41,277	35,701	27,801	22,008	17,687
Freight (000)	72,400	65,297	52,897	53,549	40,052	31,415	22,054	19,782	15,485	11,923	9,024
Express (000)	8,302	7,491	6,907	8,706	7,999	7,482	6,417	7,099	5,983	5,080	4,311
Priority U.S. Mail (000)	20,444	13,949	12,209	11,209	10,040	9,720	7,794	7,770.	5,520	4,350	3,765
Nonpriority U.S. Mail (000)	13,286	14,719	14,193	12,800	12,349	10,419	5,012	1,050	813	655	587
Overall Traffic and Service											
Nonscheduled traffic—total ton miles (000)	24,296	21,305	23,561	21,077	15,315	11,062	8,622	4,443	2,872	3,047	2,099
Total revenue ton miles—all services (000)	1,121,699	1,012,667	894,930	850,480	694,550	593,665	442,406	371,072	280,986	239,481	198,347
Total available ton miles—all services (000)	2,534,080	2,263,189	2,194,802	2,146,702	1,859,433	1,469,783	1,024,078	761,028	585,229	503,972	440,716
Ton mile load factor (%)	44.3	44.7	40.8	39.6	37.4	40.4	43.2	48.8	48.0	47.5	45.0
Scheduled revenue aircraft departures	1,526,880	1,516,473	1,515,651	1,554,585	1,585,363	1,620,940	1,561,417	1,479,063	1,376,203	1,304,837	1,238,138
Scheduled revenue aircraft miles (000)	270,677	249,561	241,911	242,471	227,603	211,203	185,041	165,281	145,175	133,532	121,292
Scheduled revenue aircraft hours	934,398	894,394	875,781	895,306	895,966	908,525	888,417	863,581	808,244	764,737	711,679

Source: Air Transport Association of America

TRAFFIC AND SERVICE

International and Territorial Airlines	1973	1972	1971	1970	1969	1968	1967	1966	1965	1964	1963
Passenger Traffic											
Revenue passengers enplaned (000)	18,936	18,897	17,474	16,260	13,493	16,407	14,020	12,272	10,847	9,381	8,037
Revenue passenger miles (000)	35,639,973	34,268,298	29,219,294	27,563,211	22,702,695	26,450,644	23,259,314	19,298,420	16,789,044	14,352,393	11,905,430
Available seat miles (000)	65,897,988	60,797,069	58,320,186	51,959,992	44,411,659	49,575,001	41,118,729	33,175,647	29,532,832	25,791,373	22,590,210
Revenue passenger load factor (%)	54.1	56.4	50.1	53.0	51.1	53.4	56.6	58.2	56.8	55.6	52.7
Average length of haul (miles)	1,882	1,813	1,672	1,695	1,683	1,612	1,659	1,573	1,548	1,530	1,481
Cargo Traffic (Ton Miles)—Total (000)	1,589,856	1,475,715	1,455,777	1,481,140	1,389,711	1,596,029	1,347,763	1,164,014	841,061	564,862	466,692
Freight (000)	1,237,861	1,113,373	1,009,254	941,563	936,110	926,091	795,858	720,627	596,416	393,858	295,610
Express (000)	723	731	531	445	444	1,159	1,106	982	908	823	794
Priority U.S. Mail (000)	155,345	171,644	189,400	200,444	195,477	273,239	277,909	283,742	173,158	124,768	115,810
Nonpriority U.S. Mail (000)	195,927	189,967	256,592	338,688	257,680	395,540	272,890	158,663	70,579	45,413	54,478
Overall Traffic and Service											
Nonscheduled traffic—total ton miles (000)	917,647	975,475	1,111,847	938,464	1,253,832	1,684,105	1,387,435	737,520	296,471	198,323	174,411
Total revenue ton miles—all services (000)	6,081,811	5,888,259	5,500,407	5,185,823	4,953,257	5,978,604	5,113,306	3,883,836	2,856,655	2,228,175	1,855,950
Total available ton miles—all services (000)	12,430,469	11,877,471	11,545,793	10,203,702	9,220,759	10,779,326	9,030,981	6,653,990	5,139,006	4,162,677	3,488,240
Ton mile load factor (%)	48.9	49.6	47.6	50.8	53.7	55.5	56.6	58.4	55.6	53.5	53.2
Scheduled revenue aircraft departures	297,153	292,995	292,515	299,529	295,489	367,960	298,573	280,481	257,377	238,886	213,508
Scheduled revenue aircraft miles (000)	361,481	350,163	350,744	369,870	359,476	408,136	350,719	285,711	247,766	214,375	192,140
Scheduled revenue aircraft hours	751,773	729,613	728,331	767,440	753,347	858,123	727,445	610,954	549,964	486,101	454,244

Source: Air Transport Association of America

OPERATING REVENUES AND EXPENSES
(In Thousands of Dollars)

Total U.S. Scheduled Airlines	1973	1972	1971	1970	1969	1968	1967	1966	1965	1964	1963
Operating Revenues—Total	12,418,771	11,163,271	10,045,577	9,289,658	8,790,951	7,753,211	6,864,726	5,745,038	4,957,851	4,250,838	3,759,051
Passenger	10,275,689	9,271,353	8,220,323	7,626,813	7,119,795	6,221,852	5,425,862	4,529,520	4,029,383	3,482,760	3,067,193
Freight	1,038,510	906,494	795,272	713,423	648,030	547,094	465,281	412,039	356,113	285,657	234,653
Priority U.S. Mail	190,430	169,204	169,512	175,248	168,358	162,763	184,232	189,252	138,238	122,746	117,916
Nonpriority U.S. Mail	103,237	94,415	110,152	123,311	120,015	104,466	76,082	43,481	25,234	19,050	21,086
Express	36,175	31,679	30,522	36,337	38,089	38,174	35,471	36,800	34,118	31,114	28,421
Charter	420,763	448,537	467,258	413,913	525,759	517,074	520,612	381,890	214,145	152,608	140,234
Public Service Revenue	68,930	68,881	63,392	45,857	40,003	46,745	59,912	65,619	80,622	82,806	82,222
Other*	285,037	172,707	189,147	154,752	130,903	115,044	97,273	86,439	79,997	74,098	67,327
Operating Expenses—Total	11,834,761	10,578,800	9,717,102	9,246,634	8,403,497	7,248,323	6,156,532	4,969,541	4,285,923	3,780,741	3,479,264
Flying Operations	3,389,637	3,021,942	2,901,373	2,705,106	2,468,714	2,080,537	1,733,888	1,368,532	1,157,945	1,029,893	949,417
Maintenance	1,745,702	1,571,081	1,417,547	1,402,009	1,302,001	1,193,639	1,087,177	900,306	815,958	749,367	665,006
General Services and Administration											
Passenger Service	1,269,402	1,125,545	989,709	939,681	830,681	716,056	578,639	458,887	381,860	309,389	263,185
Aircraft and Traffic Servicing	2,335,695	2,011,837	1,788,872	1,676,164	1,489,885	1,262,945	1,070,670	863,279	735,447	646,328	586,086
Promotion and Sales	1,424,741	1,294,161	1,151,562	1,112,409	1,035,401	900,940	776,304	645,574	551,134	479,203	419,978
Administrative	605,143	551,308	508,716	459,222	408,428	351,965	297,560	241,386	212,351	185,016	167,212
Total	5,634,981	4,982,851	4,438,859	4,187,476	3,764,394	3,231,906	2,723,173	2,209,126	1,880,793	1,619,936	1,436,462
Depreciation and Amortization	1,064,440	1,002,924	959,323	952,036	868,384	742,240	612,294	491,578	431,228	381,543	428,379
Net Operating Income	584,010	584,471	328,475	43,031	387,454	504,888	708,194	775,497	671,928	470,097	279,787

* Includes excess baggage, foreign mail, incidental revenues and other transport. For notes to statistical tables see page 35.

Source: Air Transport Association of America

OPERATING REVENUES AND EXPENSES
(In Thousands of Dollars)

Domestic Trunk Airlines	1973	1972	1971	1970	1969	1968	1967	1966	1965	1964	1963
Operating Revenues—Total	8,382,391	7,510,461	6,750,448	6,272,775	6,134,700	5,039,441	4,419,436	3,660,900	3,263,556	2,790,877	2,451,915
Passenger	7,363,558	6,664,950	5,959,062	5,536,144	5,350,986	4,451,341	3,901,528	3,233,095	2,908,045	2,504,861	2,208,430
Freight	524,589	462,076	414,972	387,120	365,015	284,707	235,774	201,289	174,150	140,962	116,466
Priority U.S. Mail	116,424	92,663	92,929	93,952	96,655	80,739	76,100	78,870	64,181	56,262	51,247
Nonpriority U.S. Mail	47,793	46,819	49,294	44,156	68,591	43,131	23,139	7,988	6,354	5,838	5,471
Express	31,111	26,822	26,332	31,257	33,317	33,146	30,752	31,601	29,703	27,247	25,246
Charter	125,037	119,656	107,933	100,294	147,482	87,475	104,962	70,429	44,375	17,629	12,420
Public Service Revenue	—	—				—	2,822	2,110	3,508	3,408	988
Other	173,879	97,475	99,926	79,851	72,655	58,902	44,360	35,518	33,240	34,668	31,648
Operating Expenses—Total	7,968,496	7,076,402	6,520,920	6,256,039	5,789,817	4,719,364	4,009,331	3,207,198	2,847,308	2,494,035	2,322,682
Flying Operations	2,273,665	2,025,229	1,953,216	1,830,972	1,690,242	1,341,342	1,101,480	869,925	767,902	676,974	626,708
Maintenance	1,197,031	1,058,338	963,835	974,254	908,489	802,853	735,445	596,269	566,413	514,552	464,803
General Services and Administration											
Passenger Service	890,389	789,761	684,211	653,762	600,072	488,635	396,449	311,564	266,279	213,988	179,890
Aircraft and Traffic Servicing	1,533,286	1,327,309	1,179,031	1,117,235	1,010,865	825,578	704,944	560,004	484,859	425,197	394,180
Promotion and Sales	935,224	839,904	747,115	728,402	701,427	579,244	501,987	410,282	348,223	299,629	261,691
Administrative	369,273	331,884	310,292	279,813	253,782	202,465	167,023	131,568	116,378	100,945	93,187
Total	3,728,172	3,288,857	2,920,650	2,779,212	2,566,147	2,095,921	1,770,403	1,413,418	1,215,739	1,039,759	928,949
Depreciation and Amortization	769,628	703,977	683,218	671,601	624,937	479,249	402,005	327,586	297,253	262,750	302,221
Net Operating Income	413,895	434,059	229,527	16,737	344,883	320,077	410,106	453,703	416,249	296,841	129,233

Source: Air Transport Association of America

227

OPERATING REVENUES AND EXPENSES
(In Thousands of Dollars)

Local Service Airlines	1973	1972	1971	1970	1969	1968	1967	1966	1965	1964	1963
Operating Revenues—Total	1,061,333	935,187	827,861	736,831	611,080	501,308	399,716	348,332	291,374	253,728	225,975
Passenger	889,973	789,767	688,938	627,590	520,806	414,732	313,833	264,949	203,423	169,244	143,171
Freight	43,864	37,966	31,478	29,794	22,630	17,477	13,053	10,961	8,764	6,698	5,031
Priority U.S. Mail	10,535	6,573	6,155	6,376	5,892	5,900	5,138	5,316	4,103	3,327	2,950
Nonpriority U.S. Mail	3,682	3,494	3,423	4,800	3,474	2,971	1,352	301	261	220	203
Express	3,931	3,876	3,602	4,281	3,957	3,967	3,545	3,729	3,196	2,781	2,508
Charter	14,376	12,912	12,930	12,099	9,252	6,837	5,565	3,516	2,115	2,294	1,531
Public Service Revenue	64,555	64,484	58,863	40,339	34,804	40,950	50,961	54,924	66,012	65,779	67,882
Other	30,417	16,114	22,472	11,552	10,266	8,476	6,266	4,637	3,499	3,385	2,698
Operating Expenses—Total	997,603	882,545	798,975	745,629	628,517	510,518	399,025	324,866	267,283	236,762	214,015
Flying Operations	287,884	256,549	242,577	226,809	189,916	146,193	109,656	88,985	74,233	66,787	60,846
Maintenance	173,970	156,463	137,585	128,332	108,272	91,971	79,323	69,475	59,837	52,735	47,256
General Services and Administration											
Passenger Service	71,100	59,070	52,711	47,970	38,751	30,613	21,995	17,307	13,426	11,739	10,660
Aircraft and Traffic Servicing	250,761	209,851	183,435	165,121	144,372	120,179	95,933	80,353	66,346	59,053	53,143
Promotion and Sales	100,542	85,406	77,219	69,502	58,329	46,467	36,107	29,472	23,469	20,639	18,617
Administrative	54,716	51,407	47,269	42,653	34,344	28,136	22,813	18,472	14,874	13,051	11,585
Total	477,120	405,734	360,634	325,246	275,795	225,396	176,849	145,604	118,114	104,482	94,004
Depreciation and Amortization	58,628	63,798	58,179	65,242	54,533	46,958	33,196	20,802	15,098	12,758	11,909
Net Operating Income	63,730	52,641	28,886	(8,798)	(17,436)	(9,210)	691	23,467	24,091	16,966	11,959

Source: Air Transport Association of America

OPERATING REVENUES AND EXPENSES
(In Thousands of Dollars)

International and Territorial Airlines

	1973	1972	1971	1970	1969	1968	1967	1966	1965	1964	1963
Operating Revenues—Total	2,526,878	2,284,300	2,080,262	1,913,592	1,689,387	1,949,766	1,769,682	1,474,480	1,210,875	1,040,020	931,452
Passenger	1,894,914	1,706,512	1,483,973	1,380,388	1,176,349	1,309,173	1,165,862	995,185	887,335	781,649	692,801
Freight	267,821	242,088	220,370	196,906	185,346	185,465	163,216	149,215	130,800	99,990	80,175
Priority U.S. Mail	45,576	50,202	52,295	54,126	54,103	68,815	94,055	96,683	63,170	56,943	57,697
Nonpriority U.S. Mail	25,790	27,176	37,893	49,176	37,666	55,922	49,596	33,373	16,989	11,527	13,613
Express	234	266	183	125	156	391	342	314	319	306	203
Charter	220,370	208,171	230,327	184,525	199,930	287,202	259,918	163,350	75,737	55,355	53,221
Public Service Revenue	—	—	—	—	—	2,606	1,400	1,753	1,999	2,851	2,679
Other	72,174	49,887	55,219	48,344	35,838	40,193	35,293	34,606	34,526	31,398	31,065
Operating Expenses—Total	2,459,448	2,233,879	2,050,095	1,894,391	1,638,275	1,747,946	1,496,540	1,220,894	1,001,362	896,187	799,462
Flying Operations	680,521	595,859	573,008	515,182	456,431	495,025	424,135	329,427	262,597	238,427	216,834
Maintenance	316,597	300,476	269,031	241,077	219,053	244,316	211,874	181,475	146,043	145,186	117,729
General Services and Administration											
Passenger Service	298,063	265,758	239,845	222,704	178,003	187,756	156,837	126,367	98,205	78,371	68,904
Aircraft and Traffic Servicing	460,235	395,554	360,715	332,268	278,708	281,377	238,244	194,943	161,691	142,773	122,803
Promotion and Sales	352,675	335,673	301,594	292,624	258,418	263,692	228,135	197,265	171,559	151,550	133,299
Administrative	137,584	128,650	115,681	102,644	90,641	94,899	81,298	67,894	61,198	51,729	44,383
Total	1,248,557	1,125,635	1,017,834	950,241	805,770	827,723	704,514	586,470	492,653	424,423	369,389
Depreciation and Amortization	213,772	211,908	190,220	187,889	157,019	180,881	156,017	123,521	100,070	88,151	95,510
Net Operating Income	67,430	50,421	30,167	19,202	51,113	201,820	273,142	253,586	209,513	143,833	131,991

Source: Air Transport Association of America

BALANCE SHEET
(In Thousands of Dollars)

Total U.S. Scheduled Airlines

	1973	1972	1968	1963
Assets				
Current Assets	3,147,810	2,812,678	2,170,058	1,174,711
Investments and Special Funds	1,172,176	1,301,952	1,281,929	282,477
Flight Equipment	12,910,010	11,917,922	9,021,381	3,974,866
Reserve for Depreciation and Airworthiness	(4,691,853)	(4,252,036)	(2,545,996)	(1,725,671)
Ground Property and Equipment	2,187,635	1,937,568	1,042,385	489,877
Reserve for Depreciation	(1,002,612)	(863,349)	(462,906)	(264,449)
Other Property	332,480	432,012	263,299	74,870
Deferred Charges	391,143	348,190	222,235	78,884
Total Assets	14,446,788	13,634,937	10,992,385	4,085,298
Liabilities				
Current Liabilities	2,901,297	2,574,853	1,747,639	950,537
Long-Term Debt	5,757,425	5,566,743	5,263,933	1,729,507
Other Non-Current Liabilities	323,277	368,513	22,814	21,024
Deferred Credit	1,254,200	1,141,163	835,959	305,042
Stockholders' Equity—Net of Treasury Stock	4,210,589	3,983,664	3,122,040	1,079,190
Preferred Stock	32,973	33,227	49,686	26,938
Common Stock	295,448	303,036	349,026	212,619
Other Paid-In Capital	2,076,427	2,046,251	1,054,438	461,040
Retained Earnings	1,806,401	1,601,811	1,670,864	381,429
Less: Treasury Stock	660	660	1,975	2,836
Total Liabilities and Equity	14,446,788	13,634,937	10,992,385	4,085,298

Domestic Trunk Airlines

	1973	1972	1968	1963
Assets				
Current Assets	2,739,100	2,044,272	1,576,569	873,744
Investments and Special Funds	1,017,113	975,505	831,219	178,513
Flight Equipment	11,923,593	9,618,346	6,956,181	3,050,528
Reserve for Depreciation and Airworthiness	(4,356,330)	(3,506,106)	(2,025,147)	(1,339,415)
Ground Property and Equipment	2,050,249	1,504,023	794,600	391,176
Reserve for Depreciation	(928,042)	(671,969)	(356,253)	(208,126)
Other Property	302,727	318,535	207,456	59,060
Deferred Charges	256,833	186,634	121,572	33,227
Total Assets	13,005,244	10,469,239	8,106,199	3,038,708
Liabilities				
Current Liabilities	2,538,177	1,901,398	1,202,723	657,478
Long-Term Debt	5,186,402	3,991,157	3,767,627	1,330,921
Other Non-Current Liabilities	279,199	320,594	16,386	15,932
Deferred Credit	1,203,333	1,014,823	711,030	239,774
Stockholders' Equity—Net of Treasury Stock	3,798,132	3,241,268	2,408,432	794,605
Preferred Stock	24,294	24,294	36,646	20,672
Common Stock	229,578	227,747	282,194	151,927
Other Paid-In Capital	1,751,748	1,499,480	770,795	353,187
Retained Earnings	1,793,166	1,489,748	1,319,737	270,425
Less: Treasury Stock	654	—	939	1,608
Total Liabilities and Equity	13,005,244	10,469,239	8,106,199	3,038,708

Source: Air Transport Association of America

BALANCE SHEET
(In Thousands of Dollars)

Local Service Airlines

	1973	1972	1968	1963
Assets				
Current Assets	261,346	221,252	173,435	55,114
Investments and Special Funds	17,262	26,887	48,658	10,203
Flight Equipment	735,109	655,559	609,357	121,011
Reserve for Depreciation and Airworthiness	(249,417)	(204,204)	(95,179)	(46,265)
Ground Property and Equipment	80,009	69,606	45,095	17,663
Reserve for Depreciation	(45,144)	(39,035)	(20,818)	(9,632)
Other Property	16,522	25,598	11,956	2,576
Deferred Charges	121,523	118,638	36,168	5,301
Total Assets	937,209	874,302	808,674	155,974
Liabilities				
Current Liabilities	252,186	216,815	167,886	51,047
Long-Term Debt	420,733	422,428	530,255	61,540
Other Non-Current Liabilities	7,943	6,447	231	479
Deferred Credit	5,678	5,348	5,257	2,555
Stockholders' Equity—Net of Treasury Stock	250,670	223,264	105,045	40,354
Preferred Stock	7,690	7,821	12,667	2,100
Common Stock	30,578	30,125	22,045	12,749
Other Paid-In Capital	225,268	224,621	72,151	10,816
Retained Earnings	(12,860)	(39,296)	(1,810)	14,798
Less: Treasury Stock	7	7	7	108
Total Liabilities and Equity	937,209	874,302	808,674	155,974

International and Territorial Airlines

		1973	1972	1968	1963
Assets					
Current Assets		424,764	329,091	203,892	
Investments and Special Funds		176,209	344,150	83,388	
Flight Equipment		1,370,924	1,101,919	602,852	
Reserve for Depreciation and Airworthiness		(461,334)	(325,804)	(271,755)	
Ground Property and Equipment		308,096	167,252	65,928	
Reserve for Depreciation		(125,091)	(72,525)	(38,682)	
Other Property		78,774	35,264	4,567	
Deferred Charges	Balance sheet	27,945	37,546	31,099	
Total Assets	data for	1,800,288	1,616,891	681,289	
Liabilities	this category reported in				
Current Liabilities	Domestic	353,118	294,831	198,760	
Long-Term Debt	Trunk	981,372	726,555	226,231	
Other Non-Current Liabilities	category.	5,678	3,466	1,863	
Deferred Credit		76,794	99,153	52,531	
Stockholders' Equity—Net of Treasury Stock		383,326	492,885	201,902	
Preferred Stock		—	—	—	
Common Stock		10,997	11,355	19,239	
Other Paid-In Capital		229,474	164,390	78,412	
Retained Earnings		143,510	317,925	105,369	
Less: Treasury Stock		654	785	1,115	
Total Liabilities and Equity		1,800,288	1,616,891	681,289	

Source: Air Transport Association of America

INCOME STATEMENT

Total U.S. Scheduled Airlines

	1973	1972	1971	1970	1969	1968	1967	1966	1965	1964	1963
Total Operating Revenues ($000)	12,418,771	11,163,271	10,045,577	9,289,658	8,790,951	7,753,211	6,864,726	5,745,038	4,957,851	4,250,838	3,759,051
Total Operating Expenses ($000)	11,834,761	10,578,800	9,717,102	9,246,634	8,403,497	7,248,323	6,156,532	4,969,541	4,285,923	3,780,741	3,479,264
Net Operating Income ($000)	584,010	584,471	328,475	43,031	387,454	504,888	708,194	775,497	671,928	470,097	279,787
Interest on Long-Term Debt ($000)	367,996	307,148	330,525	318,156	283,355	221,915	149,793	126,588	112,127	104,258	106,497
Income Taxes ($000)	143,453	98,402	21,423	(48,291)	94,898	135,240	236,231	279,570	234,740	174,088	114,105
Net Profit or (Loss) ($000)	222,847	214,850	28,006	(200,503)	52,723	209,952	415,388	427,633	367,119	223,172	78,480
Profit Margin on Sales (%)	1.8	1.9	0.3	—	0.6	2.8	6.1	7.4	7.4	5.3	2.1
Rate of Return on Investment (%)	5.1	4.9	3.5	1.2	3.3	4.9	7.6	11.0	12.0	9.8	6.1

Domestic Trunk Airlines

	1973	1972	1971	1970	1969	1968	1967	1966	1965	1964	1963
Total Operating Revenues ($000)	8,382,391	7,510,461	6,750,448	6,272,775	6,134,700	5,039,441	4,419,436	3,660,900	3,263,556	2,790,877	2,451,915
Total Operating Expenses ($000)	7,968,496	7,076,402	6,520,920	6,256,039	5,789,817	4,719,364	4,009,331	3,207,198	2,847,308	2,494,035	2,322,682
Net Operating Income ($000)	413,895	434,059	229,527	16,737	344,883	320,077	410,106	453,703	416,249	296,841	129,233
Interest on Long-Term Debt ($000)	219,438	178,261	189,207	173,748	169,005	131,174	88,475	81,065	73,222	69,260	70,103
Income Taxes ($000)	112,878	89,165	21,990	(41,131)	91,023	88,435	145,250	165,500	148,101	110,250	59,640
Net Profit or (Loss) ($000)	142,930	177,154	48,182	(100,412)	110,427	126,521	244,475	238,636	221,889	134,362	13,117
Profit Margin on Sales (%)	1.7	2.4	0.7	—	1.8	2.5	5.5	6.5	6.8	4.8	0.5
Rate of Return on Investment (%)	4.7	5.1	3.3	1.4	4.3	4.9	6.9	9.7	11.2	9.1	3.9

Local Service Airlines

	1973	1972	1971	1970	1969	1968	1967	1966	1965	1964	1963
Total Operating Revenues ($000)	1,061,333	935,187	827,861	736,831	611,080	501,308	399,716	348,332	291,374	253,728	225,975
Total Operating Expenses ($000)	997,603	882,545	798,975	745,629	628,517	510,518	399,025	324,866	267,283	236,762	214,015
Net Operating Income ($000)	63,730	52,641	28,886	(8,798)	(17,436)	(9,210)	691	23,467	24,091	16,966	11,959
Interest on Long-Term Debt ($000)	35,281	31,585	38,525	44,382	41,495	31,151	17,697	7,796	5,189	4,160	3,905
Income Taxes ($000)	4,980	4,579	198	(1,585)	(5,707)	(9,091)	(3,289)	6,558	8,353	5,948	4,374
Net Profit or (Loss) ($000)	29,634	15,669	(10,466)	(61,426)	(63,008)	(29,800)	(4,472)	10,376	12,722	7,776	4,872
Profit Margin on Sales (%)	2.8	1.7	—	—	—	—	—	3.0	4.4	3.1	2.2
Rate of Return on Investment (%)	8.9	5.5	3.7	(3.9)	(4.2)	(0.4)	2.4	7.2	10.4	9.4	8.8

International and Territorial Airlines

	1973	1972	1971	1970	1969	1968	1967	1966	1965	1964	1963
Total Operating Revenues ($000)	2,526,878	2,284,300	2,080,262	1,913,592	1,689,387	1,949,766	1,769,682	1,474,480	1,210,875	1,040,020	931,452
Total Operating Expenses ($000)	2,459,448	2,233,879	2,050,095	1,894,398	1,638,275	1,747,946	1,496,540	1,220,894	1,001,362	896,187	799,462
Net Operating Income ($000)	67,430	50,421	30,167	19,202	51,113	201,820	273,142	253,586	209,513	143,833	131,991
Interest on Long-Term Debt ($000)	99,105	81,646	83,389	74,930	49,928	50,366	36,941	30,641	25,896	22,980	24,234
Income Taxes ($000)	9,219	(10,657)	(11,792)	(11,735)	7,936	62,512	88,620	94,945	73,572	56,418	50,287
Net Profit or (Loss) ($000)	23,754	(3,749)	(18,161)	(18,035)	19,910	122,957	163,108	149,890	121,883	76,731	63,012
Profit Margin on Sales (%)	0.9	—	—	—	1.2	6.3	9.2	10.2	10.1	7.4	6.8
Rate of Return on Investment (%)	4.5	3.0	3.2	2.4	3.2	7.5	11.1	14.6	15.0	12.2	12.1

Net Profit or Loss. This figure is after "special items" and other non-operating income and expenses which are not shown.

Source: Air Transport Association of America

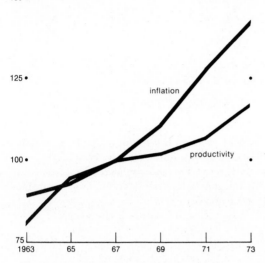

airline productivity and inflation compared

index 1967 = 100

Source: Air Transport Association of America

Net Income
U.S. Scheduled Airlines

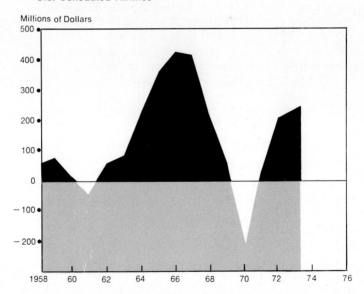

Source: Air Transport Association of America

XV

vvv

Legal Aspects
of Air Transportation*

The comparatively young field of aviation law has developed its own distinctive body of statutes, treaties, regulations, and case law. Nevertheless the cases in the field of aviation have borrowed from, and are related to, those other branches of the law that deal with transportation, railroads, admiralty, automobile, civil, military, international, and Federal.

A description of the specialized branches of aviation is the purpose of this chapter.

National Supremacy in Air Space

The United States is a Federation of States, and the authority of the Federal government is derived from the authority that is delegated by the several States to the Federal government. The specific authority that is delegated to the Federal government is set forth in the United States Constitution.

With the advent of air travel it soon became apparent that, in the matter of air travel and air regulation, there would be a conflict between the authority delegated to the Federal government, and the authority of the several States.

Some of the legal questions that arise in this area are:

1. Who has sovereignty over the airspace—the States or the Federal government?
2. It is acknowledged that the United States has sovereignty over the three nautical mile belt beyond the low water mark. How does this precedent in land and water rights affect the newer law of air rights?
3. Is there a difference between "Sovereignty" of air rights and "Ownership" of air rights?
4. What are the spheres of authority to tax aircraft which are constantly moving from one state to another? Can all states tax the property equally? Are the states preempted of their taxing authority, by the Federal government?

---

*This chapter consists of excerpts from the text "Aviation Law—Fundemental Cases," 1970 by Dr. Gerard Pucci.

5. Which branch of government has the jurisdiction over crimes on board aircraft? Are the State criminal laws violated? Are Federal criminal laws violated? Where is the crime committed when a plane is traveling at 600 miles per hour? Is the crime committed in one state, in a second state, or in both states?

This section sets forth the steps taken to delineate the responsibility and authority of these two branches of government.

Relationship of Federal and State Governments

The National responsibility for regulating air commerce has been acknowledged by the Congress of the United States and by the United States Supreme Court. Precedence for recognizing the Federal supremacy was developed from such cases as the Tidelands Oil Cases (U.S. v. Texas); and U.S. v. Causby.

Taxation

Taxation of aircraft, that were continually flying, landing, and being repaired in many different states, was an important question that had to be resolved. The authority of States in preference to the Federal government was decided. Then the question of which State could tax these aircrafts arose—was it the State in which the airline was domiciled or was it every State into which the aircraft flew? This question was resolved by many cases, two of which are: Northwest Airlines v. Minnesota, and Braniff Airways v. Nebraska. The States then further clarified the matter by agreeing to a Council of States Allocation Formula which allocated the percentage of taxes permitted to the different states based on the percentage of the number of stops, the tonnage, and the revenue originating in each state.

Crimes on Aircraft

Another area in which there was a conflict of responsibility between the two Branches of Government, was the commission of a crime on board an aircraft. There was little precedence for this area of aviation law. It was difficult to determine over exactly what location of land, the crime was committed in a moving aircraft. There were few parallels in the common law jurisprudence of criminal law.

The Federal government had to enact a body of laws that would cover these new crimes against society.

Airports and Liability

The question of liability of airports due to the noise which results by their use is considered.

The question raised is whether the noise created is a "taking" of the property of adjacent landowners, or whether the airport and airplane noise constitute a "tort" against the neighboring landowners.

A sovereign government can be sued only if it consents to be sued. The United States, by enactment of the Tucker Act in 1887, consented to be sued only in five situations, and expressly forbade lawsuits against the United States based on torts.

In 1946 the Federal Tort Claims Act was passed which, in general, permitted a citizen to sue the United States Governemnt for torts committed by a Federal employee while acting within the scope of his employment.

Similarly, a sovereign State of the United States, cannot be sued unless it consents to be sued. There are provisions in state constitutions which permit the state to be sued.

A state constitution may contain a provision for compensation for "taking," in which case if a court declares the state's airport noise as a commission of a tort, then the adjacent landowner could not recover. If, however, the state constitution mentioned "damages" then the landowner could recover on the grounds that lawsuits against the state were permitted for "torts" in which "damages" are the result. In cases involving a "taking," the landowner is considered entitled to compensation for the taking of an easement over his property, by operation of the airport. In this situation the "taking" by the airport constitutes depriving the landowner of one or more useful functions of the land, due to the noise resulting from the airport operation.

A distinction should be made between a "Tort" and a "Taking":

1. A "Tort" is any wrongful act (not involving contract) to which a civil action can be brought for damages.

2. A "Taking" exists where the owner of land is either prevented from his rightful use of his land, or his land is actually taken from him for public use. In either situation the owner must be compensated for the loss of his land or for the loss of the use of his land.

Damages and Injuries on Ground

This section examines the extent of liability of persons operating aircraft above land, and causing injury to persons and property on the land, by descent or ascent of the aircraft, or by dropping any object from the aircraft.

In the area of aerial agriculture, there are several cases that can be summarized here. The task of pinpointing liability is impeded, by the difficulty of establishing the source of the harmful spray and, in proving the negligence of the defendant.

The following are brief descriptions of cases, where it was held that the aircraft operation was liable for injury to plant life or animal stock on the ground.

1. The case of Hammond Ranch Corporation v. Dodson, 136 SW 2d 484 (Ark. 1940), involved the unauthorized spraying, with herbicides or pesticides, of the plaintiff's property adjacent to the property intended to be sprayed, and resulting in the death of the plaintiff's cattle.

2. The case of Burke V. Thomas 313 P 2d 1082 (Okla. 1957), involved the destruction of shade trees as a result of the unauthorized spraying with pesticides or herbicides.

Liability to Passengers and Others

The purpose of this section is to emphasize the legal considerations involved when a pilot, passenger, or employee is injured as a result of an aircraft crash or collision.

The legal questions that arise are:

1. Whether the passenger has the burden of proving that the carrier was negligent; or whether the carrier has the burden of proving that it was not negligent.

2. The second consideration is to determine whether the lawsuit should be tried under the laws of the State in which the accident occurred; or whether the lawsuit should be tried under the Laws of Admiralty, or the Death on the High Seas Act; or whether it should be tried under the laws of the foreign country in which the plane is registered; or whether the case is covered by Workmen's Compensation Laws in the case of an employee.

   This question is important because in some cases State laws make it easier for a plaintiff to recover damages; or the laws of the foreign country make it difficult for a plaintiff to recover damages; or the Workmen's Compensation cases limit the amount of damages that a plaintiff may recover for injuries.

3. A third question that must be resolved is whether the Federal Government is an employer and whether it is liable for the acts of its employees under the Federal Tort Claims Act. The United States Government is not liable under the Federal Tort Claims Act if the facts in the case considered, come within one of the exceptions set forth in the Act.

Admiralty Laws and Death on the High Seas Act

In 1920, Congress passed the Death on the High Seas Act (41 Stat. 537), and thereby created a remedy, or right of action, for death caused by wrongful act, neglect or default, on the high seas.

The First National Bank of Greenwich v. National Airlines, demonstrates how the courts resolved the question of whether to apply the State law or the Death on the High Seas Act. In this case the Court applied the Death on the High Seas Act because the crash occurred in the Gulf of Mexico beyond the three mile limit from the Alabama shore.

When the Death on the High Seas Act Created the right of action to sue for death occurring on the high seas, several other aspects arose.

The first task was to determine whether to apply the law of the United States or the laws of the foreign country in which the aircraft was registered.

The second task was to determine whether to afford the injured employee the relief of unlimited liability of employer, as provided by the Death on the High Seas Act; or whether to give the injured employee the limited liability of his employer as provided by the Workmen's Compensation laws.

The laws and rules of admiralty are old and settled. Some of these laws and rules have been made applicable to the law of aviation, and others have not.

United States and the Federal Tort Claims Act

A previous section discussed application of the Federal Tort Claims Act (1946) to airports and the liability of airports to their neighbors.

In this section the application of the Federal Tort Claims Act on the liability of the United States Government in military activities is examined.

The next several cases illustrate special applications of provisions of the Federal Tort Claims Act (FTCA):

1. FTCA Section 2680 (k) states that FTCA shall not apply to a claim arising in a foreign country. In U.S. v. Spelar, 338 U.S. 217 (1949), the court ruled that a military base in Newfoundland, leased to U.S. for a long term, was considered a foreign country for purposes of 2680 (k), and therefore U.S. was not liable.

2. In the case of Eastern Airlines V. Union Trust Co., 221 F. 2d 62 (1954), the executors of deceased bring the action for death arising out of a mid-air collision between a commercial airliner and a privately owned surplus fighter aircraft. The Airport was owned by the U.S. Government. It was determined that the negligence of the tower operator controlling aircraft movement was the proximate cause of the accident and of the death. The court held that the U.S. was liable because the tower operator was a Federal employee within the meaning of 1346 (b).

   In order to escape liability the defendant U.S. Government advanced two arguments:

   a. The airport was a discretionary function and therefore U.S. Government was not liable under FTCA Section 2680 (a).

   b. A private individual could not perform this function and therefore U.S. Government was not liable within the meaning of FTCA Section 2674.

   The court rejected both of the government's arguments and ruled that the government was liable because the airport function was not discretionary; and that anyone can operate an airport, hire tower operators, and get them certified by the Federal Government.

3. Another case in which the court held that the discretionary function provision of Section 2680 (a) did not preclude a suit under FTCA is:

   Bullock V. U.S., 133 F. Supp 885 (Utah 1955), in which the court ruled that the fallout damage to a flock of sheep as a result of nuclear tests conducted by the Atomic Energy Commission, did not prevent a suit under FTCA.

Tariffs—Limitation of Liability

A tariff is a list or schedule of charges, for services, and for transportation of goods and people; and the conditions therefor.

The study of tariffs in aviation cuts across many fields of study including the Warsaw Convention, and the Interstate Commerce Commission.

In the aviation industry, tariffs for air carriage must be filed with the Civil Aeronautics Board. Properly filed, tariffs become a part of the contract of the carriage between the carriers and the shipper, and therefore, are binding on both parties. Tariff rates and schedules have been held to be binding on all parties whether or not the shipper has knowledge of the tariff rates and schedules.

The United States Supreme Court has applied its Interstate Commerce Act tariff rulings, to cases under the FAA and under the CAB. Following are several cases decided by the United States Supreme Court under the Interstate Commerce Commission, as applicable to cases that might be brought under the Civil Aeronautics Board:

1. In the case of Texas & Pacific R.R. Company v. Mugg & Dryden, 202 U.S. 242, the shipper was quoted a lower rate than that filed with the Interstate Commerce Commission. The Supreme Court held that the shipper must pay the full rate recited in the tariff.

2. In Chicago & Atlantic R.R. Company v. Kirby, 255 U.S. 155 (1912), a carrier agreed to expedite a shipment of horses over its own lines in order to make connections with a fast freight train of a second carrier. The first carrier was not able to make the connection, and the shipper sued for recovery of damages for breach of an agreement. The Supreme Court held that the shipper could not recover damages for breach of an agreement, because the agreement constituted an unreasonable preference, forbidden by the Interstate Commerce Act. The shipper was charged only regular through rates with no provision for such service.

3. In Jones v. Northwest Airlines 157 P. 2d 728 (1945), the court applied the rulings under the ICC, to aviation cases and tariffs filed under CAB. The tariff in question permitted the carrier to cancel a flight at any time it deemed necessary and further stated that the carrier was not responsible for failure of the aircraft to depart or arrive on the scheduled time. The Court held that, even though the passenger claimed he had a special contract with carrier which recognized the limited time he had for the trip, the alleged contract was void because it was inconsistent with the terms of the tariff schedules. The court stated that the ticket was sold subject to tariff regulations, which regulations were in conflict with the alleged contract.

The general reasoning of many courts in cases similar to the above, is based, not on the fiction of constructive notice or of lack of contracts, but rather on the requirement for equality and uniformity of rates, and the application thereof.

Workmen's Compensation—Limitation of Liability

Workmen's compensation acts are within the province of the states and therefore are covered by state laws and statutes. Workmen's compensation acts provide benefits and care to employees who suffer injury or death in connection with their employment. The cost of these benefits is borne by the employer.

The primary task in workmen's compensation cases is to determine whether the injury or death of an employee occurred during the course of his employment. These are fact situations that are peculiar in themselves and cannot be readily applied to other cases.

The following are summaries of cases in which it was held that the injury or death of the employee occurred during the course of his employment and therefore the employee was covered by the Workmen's Compensation Act of his state:

1. In Markoholz v. General Electric Co., 243 N.Y.S. 2d 853 (1963), an employee was on a one-week personal visit to Italy, after attending a business conference in France. The court held that his death occurred while he was in the course of business and therefore covered by Workmen's Compensation Act.

2. In Dunham Co. v. Industrial Commission, 156 NE 2d 560 (Ill. 1959), an engineer was traveling as a passenger from Chicago to Seattle in a commercial airliner which was destroyed in mid-air by an act of sabotage. The court held that his death occurred during the course of his employment and therefore he was covered by the Workmen's Compensation Act of his state.

3. In Indiana Steel Products Company V. Leonard, 131 N.E. 2d 162 (Ind. 1956), a salesman piloting a rented aircraft to make a call on a customer, crashed the aircraft; and the court held he was covered by Workmen's Compensation Act.

The following are summaries of cases in which the courts held that the employee's injury or death did not occur within his duties of employment.

1. In Ruffi v. American Fly Away Service Inc. 104 N.W. 2d 37 (Ohio 1950), a pilot ferrying an aircraft, departed from flight altitude, buzzed a fishing boat and, as a consequence, crashed the aircraft. The court held that he was not acting within the scope of his employment and therefore not covered by Workmen's Compensation Law of his state.

2. In Lange v. Memphis, St. Paul Metropolitan Airports Commission 99 N.W. 2d 915 (Minn. 1959), an airport supervisor was instructed by his employer that flying aircraft was not a part of his duties and that flying was not permitted during working hours. The Supervisor, while flying in violation of these instructions, crashed the aircraft. The court held he was not covered by Workmen's Compensation Act of his state.

3. In Whitely v. King Radio Corporation 375 Pac. 2d 593 (Kansas 1962), an engineer was taking flying lessons at the expense of his employer. The flying, however, had no relationship to the duties of his employment. The court held he was not covered by Workmen's Compensation.

Warsaw Convention—Limitation of Liability

The Warsaw Convention of 1929 (The Convention for the Unification of Certain Rules Relating to International Transportation by Air), is a treaty to which the United States became a party on June 15, 1934, when the United States Senate gave its "advice and consent."

The purpose of the Warsaw Convention was to limit the liability of the Air Carriers in the fledgling aviation industry of the 1920's. It is felt, in some quarters, that the airline industry does not now need the protection that it was afforded in its young years.

There is legal opinion that the limited liability provision, (Article 22), and the venue provision, (Article 28), of the Warsaw Convention deny equal rights of American Citizens under the U.S. Constitution. In November 7, 1968, Judge Nicholas J. Bua of the Circuit Court of Cook County, Illinois handed down a lengthy Memorandum Opinion on this question (Burdell v. Canadian Pacific Airlines, No. 66L–10799, Cook County Circuit Court, Nov. 7, 1968). This case did not go to a higher court for appeal, because it was settled for $215,000 in favor of the plaintiff. The air carrier requested the court to withdraw that part of the ruling which related to constitutionality. The court granted the motion, but stated that, as concerns this case, the venue and damage limitation provisions of the Warsaw Convention were unconstitutional. This opinion, therefore, remains an important precedent on the constitutionality of Warsaw Articles 22, and 28. (Also refer to Illinois Bar Journal, February 1970, John J. Kennelly.)

The following summarized cases utilize and refer to several articles of the Warsaw Convention.

In Mertens v. Flying Tiger Lines, 8 CCH Av. Cases 18023 (Dec. 5, 1963), an aircraft, with crew, was chartered to the U.S. Government, and the tickets were not delivered to passengers until after the aircraft was airborne. The plaintiff passenger, in this case, asserted that there was not sufficient delivery of tickets under Warsaw Convention Article 3, and therefore the limited liability provisions of the Warsaw Convention did not apply to the air carrier. The court held that there was sufficient delivery and therefore the limited liability provisions of Warsaw Convention Article 22 was applicable.

In Kraus v. K.L.M., 92 N.Y.S. 2d (Oct. 17, 1949), an air freight "airwaybill" did not give a list of agreed stopping places as required by Warsaw Convention Article 8. However the air freight "airwaybill" did make reference to a timetable list of scheduled stopping places. The plaintiff shipper asserted that since the "airwaybill" did not set forth the stopping places, then Warsaw Convention Article 9 would apply and the carrier would not be able to use the limited liability provisions of the Convention. The court held that the reference to the timetable was sufficient compliance with Warsaw Convention Article 8, and therefore the limited liability provided by Article 20 would be applied in favor of the carrier defendant.

Liability of Manufacturers and Repairers

The liability of manufacturers and repairers to the buyers or passengers of their products is a dynamic aspect of aviation law. The two landmark cases, are MacPherson v. Buick, and Goldberg v. Kollsman.

The first question that must be resolved in manufacturer liability cases, is whether there is privity of contract between the buyer and the manufacturer; and whether that privity of contract is necessary to hold the manufacturer liable to the buyer for injury inflicted on the buyer from the manufacturer's products.

The courts have held that privity of contract is not necessary to hold the manufacturer liable.

The second question that must be resolved is whether the manufacturer is liable to the buyer on the legal theory that there is a tort, or on the theory that there is a breach of contract liability. This is an important question to be resolved.

If the manufacturer is liable on the basis of torts, then the plaintiff buyer has the burden of proving that the defendant manufacturer is negligent, because the manufacturer is presumed innocent until proved negligent. In addition, the defendant manufacturer has the following defenses by which he can wholly or partially escape liability:

1. The defendant can allege contributory negligence by the plaintiff buyer.
2. The defendant can allege that the plaintiff buyer assumed an unjustifiable risk.
3. The defendant can allege that the plaintiff violated a statute or ordinance.

If the manufacturer is liable on the contractual basis, whether it is actually written or implied, then the same manufacturer can be sued by the buyer on the basis that the manufacturer breached a warranty of contract. The warranty can be written or implied. Of course in this contractual situation the plaintiff is in a stronger position than in that of tort liability. If the plaintiff buyer can sue the defendant manufacturer on the basis that the manufacturer breached a warranty of contract, then the advantage to the plaintiff is threefold:

1. The plaintiff buyer does not have the burden of proving that defendant manufacturer is negligent.
2. The defendant manufacturer is presumed negligent and therefore has the burden of proving that he was not negligent.
3. The defendant does not have the three defenses set forth above in the theory of tort liability.

The case of MacPherson v. Buick covers the general analysis of the liability theories.

The case of Goldberg v. Kollsman applies the theory to the aircraft.

Appendix

The Appendix contains material for the purpose of reference and further study; it consists of reproductions from the Government Printing Office of the following Legislative Acts:

FEDERAL AVIATION ACT OF 1958

[*Act of August 23, 1958, 72 Stat. 731; as amended by Act of July 8, 1959, 73 Stat. 180; Act of August 25, 1959, 73 Stat. 427; Act of June 29, 1960, 74 Stat. 255; Act of July 12, 1960, 74 Stat. 445; Act of September 13, 1960, 74 Stat. 901; Act of July 20, 1961, 75 Stat. 210; Act of September 5, 1961, 75 Stat. 466; Act of September 13, 1961, 75 Stat. 497; Act of September 20, 1961, 75 Stat. 523; Act of October 4, 1961, 75 Stat. 785; Act of July 10, 1962, 76 Stat. 143; Act of October 11, 1962, 76 Stat. 832; Act of October 15, 1962, 76 Stat. 921; Act of October 15, 1962, 76 Stat. 936; Act of June 30, 1964, 78 Stat. 236; Act of August 14, 1964, 78 Stat. 400; Act of November 8, 1965, 79 Stat. 1310; Act of June 13, 1966, 80 Stat. 199; Act of October 15, 1966, 80 Stat. 931; Act of July 21, 1968, 82 Stat. 395; Act of September 26, 1968, 82 Stat. 867; Act of August 20, 1969, 83 Stat. 103; Act of May 21, 1970, 84 Stat. 219; Act of September 8, 1970, 84 Stat. 837; Act of October 14, 1970, 84 Stat. 921; and Act of October 15, 1970, 84 Stat. 922.*] [1]

AN ACT

To continue the Civil Aeronautics Board as an agency of the United States, to create a Federal Aviation Agency, to provide for the regulation and promotion of civil aviation in such manner as to best foster its development and safety, and to provide for the safe and efficient use of the airspace by both civil and military aircraft, and for other purposes.

Be it enacted by the Senate and House of Representatives of the United States of America in Congress assembled, That this Act, divided into titles and sections according to the following table of contents, may be cited as the "Federal Aviation Act of 1958":

TABLE OF CONTENTS

TITLE I—GENERAL PROVISIONS

Section 6(c)(1) of the Department of Transportation Act approved October 15, 1966; ffective April 1, 1967, transferred all functions, powers, and duties of the Federal Aviation Administrator and the Federal Aviation Agency to the Secretary of Transportation. Therefore, in accordance with a ruling of the General Counsel, Department of Transportation, this publication substitutes the words "Secretary of Transportation" for references to the Administrator, except where the context requires otherwise, and except for section 611 relating to noise abatement. The transfer to the Secretary is subject to the statutory requirement that the Administrator carry out the functions, powers, and duties of the Secretary relating to "aviation safety." The functions, powers, and duties previously exercised by the Civil Aeronautics Board under titles VI and VII of the Federal Aviation Act of 1958 were transferred by section 6(d) of the Department of Transportation Act to the National Transportation Safety Board established in the Department of Transportation. Section 3(e)(1) of the Department of Transportation Act also established the Federal Aviation Administration, headed by an Administrator, within the Department. These changes in the Federal Aviation Act of 1958, and in other statutes or Executive Orders, are indicated by appropriate footnotes to the provisions affected.

TITLE V—NATIONALITY AND OWNERSHIP OF AIRCRAFT

TITLE VI—SAFETY REGULATIONS OF CIVIL AERONAUTICS

TITLE X—PROCEDURE

TITLE XI—MISCELLANEOUS

TITLE XII—SECURITY PROVISIONS

[§ 101]

TITLE I—GENERAL PROVISIONS

DEFINITIONS

SEC. 101. [*72 Stat. 737, as amended by 75 Stat. 467, 76 Stat. 143, 82 Stat. 867, 84 Stat. 921, 49 U.S.C. 1301*] As used in this Act, unless the context otherwise requires—

(1) "Administrator"* means the Administrator of the Federal Aviation Administration.*

(2) "Aeronautics" means the science and art of flight.

(3) "Air carrier" means any citizen of the United States who undertakes, whether directly or indirectly or by a lease or any other arrangement, to engage in air transportation: *Provided*, That the Board may by order relieve air carriers who are not directly engaged in the operation of aircraft in air transportation from the provisions of this Act to the extent and for such periods as may be in the public interest.

(4) "Air commerce" means interstate, overseas, or foreign air commerce or the transportation of mail by aircraft or any operation or navigation of aircraft within the limits of any Federal airway or any operation or navigation of aircraft which directly affects, or which may endanger safety in, interstate, overseas, or foreign air commerce.

(5) "Aircraft" means any contrivance now known or hereafter invented, used, or designed for navigation of or flight in the air.

(6) "Aircraft engine" means an engine used, or intended to be used, for propulsion of aircraft and includes all parts, appurtenances, and accessories thereof other than propellers.

(7) "Airman" means any individual who engages, as the person in command or as pilot, mechanic, or member of the crew, in the navigation of aircraft while under way; and (except to the extent the Administrator may otherwise provide with respect to individuals employed outside the United States) any individual who is directly in charge of the inspection, maintenance, overhauling, or repair of aircraft, aircraft engines, propellers, or appliances; and any individual who serves in the capacity of aircraft dispatcher or air-traffic control-tower operator.

(8) "Air navigation facility" means any facility used in, available for use in, or designed for use in, aid of air navigation, including landing areas, lights, any apparatus or equipment for disseminating weather information, for signaling, for radio-directional finding, or for radio or other electrical communication, and any other structure

---

*See footnote 1.

or mechanism having a similar purpose for guiding or controlling flight in the air or the landing and take-off of aircraft.

(9) "Airport" means a landing area used regularly by aircraft for receiving or discharging passengers or cargo.

(10) "Air transportation" means interstate, overseas, or foreign air transportation or the transportation of mail by aircraft.

(11) "Appliances" means instruments, equipment, apparatus, parts, appurtenances, or accessories, of whatever description, which are used, or are capable of being or intended to be used, in the navigation, operation, or control of aircraft in flight (including parachutes and including communication equipment and any other mechanism or mechanisms installed in or attached to aircraft during flight), and which are not a part or parts of aircraft, aircraft engines, or propellers.

(12) "Board" means the Civil Aeronautics Board.

(13) "Citizen of the United States" means (a) an individual who is a citizen of the United States or of one of its possessions, or (b) a partnership of which each member is such an individual, or (c) a corporation or association created or organized under the laws of the United States or of any State, Territory, or possession of the United States, of which the president and two-thirds or more of the board of directors and other managing officers thereof are such individuals and in which at least 75 per centum of the voting interest is owned or controlled by persons who are citizens of the United States or of one of its possessions.

(14) "Civil aircraft" means any aircraft other than a public aircraft.

(15) "Civil aircraft of the United States" means any aircraft registered as provided in this Act.

(16) "Conditional sale" means (a) any contract for the sale of an aircraft, aircraft engine, propeller, appliance, or spare part under which possession is delivered to the buyer and the property is to vest in the buyer at a subsequent time, upon the payment of part or all of the price, or upon the performance of any other condition or the happening of any contingency; or (b) any contract for the bailment or leasing of an aircraft, aircraft engine, propeller, appliance, or spare part, by which the bailee or lessee contracts to pay as compensation a sum substantially equivalent to the value thereof, and by which it is agreed that the bailee or lessee is bound to become, or has the option of becoming, the owner thereof upon full compliance with the terms of the contract. The buyer, bailee, or lessee shall be deemed to be the person by whom any such contract is made or given.

(17) "Conveyance" means a bill of sale, contract of conditional sale, mortgage, assignment of mortgage, or other instrument affecting title to, or interest in, property.

(18) "Federal airway" means a portion of the navigable airspace of the United States designated by the Administrator as a Federal airway.

(19) "Foreign air carrier" means any person, not a citizen of the United States, who undertakes, whether directly or indirectly or by lease or any other arrangement, to engage in foreign air transportation.

[§ 101]

(20) "Interstate air commerce", "overseas air commerce", and "foreign air commerce", respectively, mean the carriage by aircraft of persons or property for compensation or hire, or the carriage of mail by aircraft, or the operation or navigation of aircraft in the conduct or furtherance of a business or vocation, in commerce between, respectively—

(a) a place in any State of the United States, or the District of Columbia, and a place in any other State of the United States, or the District of Columbia; or between places in the same State of the United States through the airspace over any place outside thereof; or between places in the same Territory or possession of the United States, or the District of Columbia;

(b) a place in any State of the United States, or the District of Columbia, and any place in a Territory or possession of the United States; or between a place in a Territory or possession of the United States, and a place in any other Territory or possession of the United States; and

(c) a place in the United States and any place outside thereof; whether such commerce moves wholly by aircraft or partly by aircraft and partly by other forms of transportation.

(21) "Interstate air transportation", "overseas air transportation", and "foreign air transportation", respectively, mean the carriage by aircraft of persons or property as a common carrier for compensation or hire or the carriage of mail by aircraft, in commerce between, respectively—

(a) a place in any State of the United States, or the District of Columbia, and a place in any other State of the United States, or the District of Columbia; or between places in the same State of the United States through the airspace over any place outside thereof; or between places in the same Territory or possession of the United States, or the District of Columbia;

(b) a place in any State of the United States, or the District of Columbia, and any place in a Territory or possession of the United States; or between a place in a Territory or possession of the United States, and a place in any other Territory or possession of the United States; and

(c) a place in the United States and any place outside thereof; whether such commerce moves wholly by aircraft or partly by aircraft and partly by other forms of transportation.

(22) "Landing area" means any locality, either of land or water, including airports and intermediate landing fields, which is used, or intended to be used, for the landing and take-off of aircraft, whether or not facilities are provided for the shelter, servicing, or repair of aircraft, or for receiving or discharging passengers or cargo.

(23) "Mail" means United States mail and foreign-transit mail.

(24) "Navigable airspace" means airspace above the minimum altitudes of flight prescribed by regulations issued under this Act, and shall include airspace needed to insure safety in take-off and landing of aircraft.

(25) "Navigation of aircraft" or "navigate aircraft" includes the piloting of aircraft.

(26) "Operation of aircraft" or "operate aircraft" means the use of aircraft, for the purpose of air navigation and includes the navigation of aircraft. Any person who causes or authorizes the operation of aircraft, whether with or without the right of legal control (in the capacity of owner, lessee, or otherwise) of the aircraft, shall be deemed to be engaged in the operation of aircraft within the meaning of this Act.

(27) "Person" means any individual, firm, copartnership, corporation, company, association, joint-stock association, or body politic; and includes any trustee, receiver, assignee, or other similar representative thereof.

(28) "Propeller" includes all parts, appurtenances, and accessories thereof.

(29) "Possessions of the United States" means (a) the Canal Zone, but nothing herein shall impair or affect the jurisdiction which has heretofore been, or may hereafter be, granted to the President in respect of air navigation in the Canal Zone; and (b) all other possessions of the United States. Where not otherwise distinctly expressed or manifestly incompatible with the intent thereof, references in this Act to possessions of the United States shall be treated as also referring to the Commonwealth of Puerto Rico.

(30) "Public aircraft" means an aircraft used exclusively in the service of any government or of any political subdivision thereof including the government of any State, Territory, or possession of the United States, or the District of Columbia, but not including any government-owned aircraft engaged in carrying persons or property for commercial purposes.

(31) "Spare parts" means parts, appurtenances, and accessories of aircraft (other than aircraft engines and propellers), of aircraft engines (other than propellers), of propellers and of appliances, maintained for installation or use in an aircraft, aircraft engine, propeller, or appliance, but which at the time are not installed therein or attached thereto.

(32) The term "special aircraft jurisdiction of the United States" includes the following aircraft while in flight—

    (a) civil aircraft of the United States;

    (b) aircraft of the national defense forces of the United States; and

    (c) any other aircraft—

        (i) within the United States, or

        (ii) outside the United States which has its next scheduled destination or last point of departure in the United States provided that in either case it next actually lands in the United States.

For the purpose of this definition, an aircraft is considered to be in flight from the moment when power is applied for the purpose of take-off until the moment when the landing run ends.

(33) "Supplemental air carrier" means an air carrier holding a certificate of public convenience and necessity authorizing it to engage in supplemental air transportation.

(34) "Supplemental air transportation" means charter trips, including inclusive tour charter trips, in air transportation, other than

[§ 102]

the transportation of mail by aircraft, rendered pursuant to a certificate of public convenience and necessity issued pursuant to section 401(d)(3) of this Act to supplement the scheduled service authorized by certificates of public convenience and necessity issued pursuant to sections 401(d) (1) and (2) of this Act. Nothing in this paragraph shall permit a supplemental air carrier to sell or offer for sale an inclusive tour in air transportation by selling or offering for sale individual tickets directly to members of the general public, or to do so indirectly by controlling, being controlled by, or under common control with, a person authorized by the Board to make such sales.[2]

(35) "Ticket agent" means any person, not an air carrier or a foreign air carrier and not a bona fide employee of an air carrier or foreign air carrier, who, as principal or agent, sells or offers for sale any air transportation, or negotiates for, or holds himself out by solicitation, advertisement, or otherwise as one who sells, provides, furnishes, contracts or arranges for, such transportation.

(36) "United States" means the several States, the District of Columbia, and the several Territories and possessions of the United States, including the territorial waters and the overlying airspace thereof.

DECLARATION OF POLICY: THE BOARD

SEC. 102. [*72 Stat. 740, 49 U.S.C. 1302*] In the exercise and performance of its powers and duties under this Act, the Board shall consider the following, among other things, as being in the public interest, and in accordance with the public convenience and necessity:

(a) The encouragement and development of an air-transportation system properly adapted to the present and future needs of the foreign and domestic commerce of the United States, of the Postal Service, and of the national defense;

(b) The regulation of air transportation in such manner as to recognize and preserve the inherent advantages of, assure the highest degree of safety in, and foster sound economic conditions in, such transportation, and to improve the relations between, and coordinate transportation by air carriers;

(c) The promotion of adequate, economical, and efficient service by air carriers at reasonable charges, without unjust discriminations, undue preferences or advantages, or unfair or destructive competitive practices;

(d) Competition to the extent necessary to assure the sound development of an air-transportation system properly adapted to the needs of the foreign and domestic commerce of the United States, of the Postal Service, and of the national defense;

(e) The promotion of safety in air commerce; and

(f) The promotion, encouragement, and development of civil aeronautics.

---

[2] The Act of September 26, 1968, 82 Stat. 867, which amended the definition of "supplemental air transportation," also provided that certificates of public convenience and necessity for supplemental air transportation and statements of authorizations issued by the Board were validated, ratified, and continued in effect according to their terms, notwithstanding any contrary determinations by any court that the Board lacked power to authorize performance of inclusive tour charter trips in air transportation.

DECLARATION OF POLICY: THE SECRETARY OF TRANSPORTATION*

SEC. 103. [*72 Stat. 740, 49 U.S.C. 1303*] In the exercise and performance of his powers and duties under this Act the Secretary of Transportation* shall consider the following, among other things, as being in the public interest:

(a) The regulation of air commerce in such manner as to best promote its development and safety and fulfill the requirements of national defense;

(b) The promotion, encouragement, and development of civil aeronautics;

(c) The control of the use of the navigable airspace of the United States and the regulation of both civil and military operations in such airspace in the interest of the safety and efficiency of both;

(d) The consolidation of research and development with respect to air navigation facilities, as well as the installation and operation thereof;

(e) The development and operation of a common system of air traffic control and navigation for both military and civil aircraft.

PUBLIC RIGHT OF TRANSIT

SEC. 104. [*72 Stat. 740, 49 U.S.C. 1304*] There is hereby recognized and declared to exist in behalf of any citizen of the United States a public right of freedom of transit through the navigable airspace of the United States.

TITLE II—CIVIL AERONAUTICS BOARD; GENERAL POWERS OF BOARD

CONTINUATION OF EXISTING BOARD

General

SEC. 201. [*72 Stat. 741, as amended by 78 Stat. 424, 49 U.S.C. 1321*] (a) (1) The Civil Aeronautics Board, created and established under the name "Civil Aeronautics Authority" by section 201 of the Civil Aeronautics Act of 1938 and redesignated as the "Civil Aeronautics Board" by Reorganization Plan No. IV of 1940, is hereby continued as an agency of the United States, and shall continue to be composed of five members appointed by the President, by and with the advice and consent of the Senate, for terms of six years, beginning upon the expiration of the terms for which their predecessors were appointed, except that any person appointed to fill a vacancy occurring prior to the expiration of the term for which his predecessor was appointed shall be appointed only for the remainder of such term; but upon the expiration of his term of office a member shall continue to serve until his successor is appointed and shall have qualified.

(2) The members of the Board may be removed by the President for inefficiency, neglect of duty, or malfeasance in office. No more than three of the members shall be appointed from the same political party.

*See footnote 1.

[§ 202]

The President shall designate annually one of the members of the Board to serve as chairman and one of the members to serve as vice chairman, who shall act as chairman in the absence or incapacity of the chairman.[3]

Qualifications of Members

(b) The members of the Board shall be appointed with due regard to their fitness for the efficient dispatch of the powers and duties vested in and imposed upon the Board by this Act. Each member of the Board shall be a citizen of the United States and no member of the Board shall have any pecuniary interest in or own any stock in or Bonds of any civil aeronautics enterprise. No member of the Board shall engage in any other business, vocation, or employment.

Quorum, Principal Office, and Seal

(c) Three of the members shall constitute a quorum of the Board. The principal office of the Board shall be in the District of Columbia where its general sessions shall be held, but whenever the convenience of the public or of the parties may be promoted, or delay or expense may be prevented, the Board may hold hearings or other proceedings at any other place. The Board shall have an official seal which shall be judicially noticed and which shall be preserved in the custody of the secretary of the Board.

MISCELLANEOUS

Officers and Employees

SEC. 202. [*72 Stat. 742, as amended by 75 Stat. 785, 49 U.S.C. 1322*] (a) The Board is authorized, without regard to the civil-service and classification laws,[4] to appoint and prescribe the duties and fix the compensation of a secretary of the Board, and to fix the compensation of a secretary and an administrative assistant for each member, and subject to the civil-service and classification laws, to select, employ, appoint, and fix the compensation of such officers, employees, attorneys, and agents as shall be necessary to carry out the provisions of this Act, and to define their authority and duties.

Supergrades

(b) [*Repealed by Act of October 4, 1961, 75 Stat. 785.*]

Temporary Personnel

(c) The Board may, from time to time, without regard to the provisions of the civil-service laws, engage for temporary service such duly qualified consulting engineers or agencies, or other qualified persons as are necessary in the exercise and performance of the powers and duties of each, and fix the compensation of such engineers, agen-

---

[3] See 5 U.S.C. 5314(17) and 5315(54) for annual compensation of the Chairman and Members of the Board.
[4] Classification Act of 1949, Act of Oct. 28, 1949, 63 Stat. 954, 5 U.S.C. 5101 *et seq.*

cies, or persons without regard to the Classification Act of 1949, as amended, and the expenses of such employment shall be paid out of sums appropriated for the expenses of the Board.

Cooperation With Other Federal Agencies

(d) The Board is authorized to use, with their consent, the available services, equipment, personnel, and facilities of other civilian or military agencies and instrumentalities of the Federal Government, on a reimbursable basis when appropriate, and on a similar basis to cooperate with such other agencies and instrumentalities in the establishment and use of services, equipment, and facilities of the Board.

AUTHORIZATION OF EXPENDITURES AND TRAVEL

General Authority

SEC. 203. [*72 Stat. 742, as amended by 76 Stat. 921, 49 U.S.C. 1323*] (a) The Board is empowered to make such expenditures at the seat of government and elsewhere as may be necessary for the exercise and performance of the powers and duties vested in and imposed upon the Board by law, and as from time to time may be appropriated for by Congress, including expenditures for (1) rent and personal services at the seat of government and elsewhere; (2) travel expenses; (3) office furniture, equipment and supplies, lawbooks, newspapers, periodicals, and books of reference (including the exchange thereof); (4) printing and binding; (5) membership in and cooperation with such organizations as are related to, or are part of the civil-aeronautics industry or the art of aeronautics in the United States or in any foreign country; (6) making investigations and conducting studies in matters pertaining to aeronautics; and (7) acquisition (including exchange), operation, and maintenance of passenger-carrying automobiles and aircraft, and such other property as is necessary in the exercise and performance of the powers and duties of the Board: *Provided,* That no aircraft or motor vehicle purchased under the provisions of this section, shall be used otherwise than for official business.

Travel

(b) Travel by personnel of the United States Government on commercial aircraft, domestic or foreign, including travel between airports and centers of population or posts of duty when incidental to travel on commercial aircraft, shall be allowed at public expense when authorized or approved by competent authority, and transportation requests for such travel may be issued upon such authorizations. Such expense shall be allowed without regard to comparative costs of transportation by aircraft with other modes of transportation.

Acceptance of Donations

(c) The Board, on behalf of the United States, is authorized to accept any gift or donation of money or personal property, or of services, where appropriate, for the purposes of its functions under

[§§ 204-205]

title VII of this Act.* For adequate compensation, by sale, lease, or otherwise, the Board, on behalf of the United States, is authorized to dispose of any such personal property or interest therein: *Provided,* That such disposition shall be made in accordance with the Federal Property and Administrative Services Act of 1949, as amended.

GENERAL POWERS AND DUTIES OF THE BOARD

General Powers

SEC. 204. [*72 Stat. 743, 49 U.S.C. 1324*] (a) The Board is empowered to perform such acts, to conduct such investigations, to issue and amend such orders, and to make and amend such general or special rules, regulations, and procedure, pursuant to and consistent with the provisions of this Act, as it shall deem necessary to carry out the provisions of, and to exercise and perform its powers and duties under this Act.

Cooperation With State Aeronautical Agencies

(b) The Board is empowered to confer with or to hold joint hearings with any State aeronautical agency, or other State agency, in connection with any matter arising under this Act within its jurisdiction, and to avail itself of the cooperation, services, records, and facilities of such State agencies as fully as may be practicable in the administration and enforcement of this Act.

Exchange of Information

(c) The Board is empowered to exchange with foreign governments, through appropriate agencies of the United States, information pertaining to aeronautics.

Publications

(d) Except as may be otherwise provided in this Act, the Board shall make a report in writing in all proceedings and investigations under this Act in which formal hearings have been held, and shall state in such report its conclusions together with its decision, order, or requirement in the premises. All such reports shall be entered of record and a copy thereof shall be furnished to all parties to the proceeding or investigation. The Board shall provide for the publication of such reports, and all other reports, orders, decisions, rules, and regulations issued by it under this Act in such form and manner as may be best adapted for public information and use. Publications purporting to be published by the Board shall be competent evidence of the orders, decisions, rules, regulations, and reports of the Board therein contained in all courts of the United States, and of the several States, Territories, and possessions thereof, and the District of Columbia, without further proof or authentication thereof.

ANNUAL REPORT

SEC. 205. [*72 Stat. 744, 49 U.S.C. 1325*] The Board shall make an annual report to the Congress, copies of which shall be distributed as

*See footnote 1.

are other reports transmitted to Congress. Such report shall contain in addition to a report of the work performed under this Act, such information and data collected by the Board as may be considered of value in the determination of questions connected with the development and regulation of civil aeronautics, together with such recommendations as to additional legislation relating thereto as the Board may deem necessary, and the Board may also transmit recommendations as to legislation at any other time.

TITLE III—ORGANIZATION OF ADMINISTRATION* AND POWERS AND DUTIES OF ADMINISTRATOR*

CREATION OF ADMINISTRATION*

General

SEC. 301. [*72 Stat. 744, as amended by 78 Stat. 424, 49 U.S.C. 1341*] (a) There is hereby established the Federal Aviation Administration.* referred to in this Act as the "Administration". The Administration shall be headed by an Administrator* who shall be appointed by the President, by and with the advice and consent of the Senate.[5] The Administrator shall be responsible for the exercise of all powers and the discharge of all duties of the Administration, and shall have authority and control over all personnel and activities thereof. In the exercise of his duties and the discharge of his responsibilities under this Act, the Administrator* shall not submit his decisions for the approval of, nor be bound by the decisions or recommendations of, any committee, board, or other organization created by Executive order.

Qualifications of Administrator

(b) The Administrator * shall be a citizen of the United States, and shall be appointed with due regard for his fitness for the efficient discharge of the powers and duties vested in and imposed upon him by this Act. At the time of his nomination he shall be a civilian and shall have had experience in a field directly related to aviation. The Administrator shall have no pecuniary interest in or own any stock in or bonds of any aeronautical enterprise nor shall he engage in any other business, vocation, or employment.[6]

Principal Office and Seal

(c) The principal office of the Administration* shall be in or near the District of Columbia, but it may act and exercise all its powers at any other place. The Administration* shall have an official seal which shall be judicially noticed.

---

*See footnote 1.
[5] See 5 U.S.C. 5313(19) for annual compensation of the Administrator of the Federal Aviation Administration.
[6] Qualifications of the Administrator specified in this subsection and qualifications and status of the Deputy Administrator specified in section 302(b) of this Act are made applicable, respectively, to the Administrator and Deputy Administrator of the Federal Aviation Administration by section 3(e)(2) of the Department of Transportation Act (80 Stat. 932, 49 U.S.C. 1652).

[§ 302]

ORGANIZATION OF ADMINISTRATION*

Deputy Administrator

SEC. 302. [*72 Stat. 744, as amended by 75 Stat. 785, 76 Stat. 864, 78 Stat. 424, 49 U.S.C. 1342, 1343*] (a) There shall be a Deputy Administrator of the Administration* who shall be appointed by the President by and with the advice and consent of the Senate. The Deputy Administrator shall perform such duties and exercise such powers as the Administrator shall prescribe. The Deputy Administrator shall act for, and exercise the powers of, the Administrator during his absence or disability.[7]

QUALIFICATIONS AND STATUS OF DEPUTY ADMINISTRATOR

(b) The Deputy Administrator shall be a citizen of the United States, and shall be appointed with due regard for his fitness for the efficient discharge of the powers and duties vested in and imposed upon him by this Act. At the time of his nomination he shall have had experience in a field directly related to aviation. He shall have no pecuniary interest in nor own any stocks in or bonds of any aeronautical enterprise, nor shall he engage in any other business, vocation, or employment. Nothing in this Act or other law shall preclude appointment to the position of Deputy Administrator of an officer on active duty with the armed services; except that if the Administrator is a former regular officer of any one of the armed services, the Deputy Administrator shall not be an officer on active duty with one of the armed services or a retired regular officer or a former regular officer of one of the armed services. Any officer on active duty or any retired officer, while serving as Deputy Administrator, shall continue to hold rank and grade not lower than that in which serving at the time of his appointment as Deputy Administrator, and shall be entitled to receive (1) the compensation provided for the Deputy Administrator by subsection (a) of this section, or (2) the military pay and allowances (including personal money allowance) or the retired pay, as the case may be, payable to a commissioned officer of his grade and length of service, whichever he may elect. Whenever any officer serving as Deputy Administrator elects to receive his military pay and allowances (including personal money allowance), or his retired pay, as the case may be, the appropriate department shall be reimbursed from any funds available to defray the expenses of the Agency.*

(c) (1) In order to insure that the interests of national defense are properly safeguarded and that the Administrator * is properly advised as to the needs and special problems of the armed services, the Administrator shall provide for participation of military personnel in carrying out his functions relating to regulation and protection of air traffic, including provision of air navigation facilities, and research and development with respect thereto, and the allocation of airspace. Members of the Army, the Navy, the Air Force, the Marine Corps, or the Coast Guard may be detailed by the appropriate Secretary, pursuant to cooperative agreements with the Administrator, including such agreement on reimbursement as may be deemed advisable by the

*See footnote 1.
[7] See 5 U.S.C. 5315(80) for annual compensation of the Deputy Administrator of the Federal Aviation Administration.

Administrator and the Secretary concerned, for service in the Agency to effect such participation.

(2) Appointment to, acceptance of, and service as Deputy Administrator or under such cooperative agreements shall in no way affect status, office, rank, or grade which commissioned officers or enlisted men may occupy or hold, or any emolument, perquisite, right, privilege, or benefit incident to or arising out of any such status, office, rank, or grade. No person so detailed or appointed shall be subject to direction by or control by the department from which detailed or appointed or by any agency or officer thereof directly or indirectly with respect to his responsibilities under this Act or within the Administration.*

(3) The Administrator, within six months of the effective date of this paragraph and semiannually thereafter, shall report in writing to the appropriate committees of the Congress on agreements entered into under this subsection, including the number, rank, and positions of members of the armed services detailed pursuant thereto, together with his evaluation of the effectiveness of such agreements and assignments of personnel thereunder in accomplishing the purposes of such subsection.

Exchange of Information

(d) In order to assist the Secretary of Transportation* further in the discharge of responsibilities under this Act, the Secretary of Transportation* and the Secretary of Defense, and the Secretary of Transportation* and the Administrator of the National Aeronautics and Space Administration, are directed to establish by cooperative agreement suitable arrangements for the timely exchange of information pertaining to their programs, policies, and requirements directly relating to such responsibilities.

Emergency Status [8]

(e) The Secretary of Transportation* shall develop, in consultation with the Department of Defense and other affected Government agencies, plans for the effective discharge of the responsibilities of the Agency in the event of war, and shall propose to Congress on or before January 1, 1960, legislation for such purpose: *Provided*, That in the event of war the President by the Executive order may transfer to the Department of Defense any functions (including powers, duties, activities, facilities, and parts of functions) of the Administration* prior to enactment of such proposed legislation. In connection with any such transfer, the President may provide for appropriate transfers of records, property, and personnel.

Officers and Employees

(f) The Secretary of Transportation* is authorized, subject to the civil-service and classification laws, to select, employ, appoint, and fix the compensation of such officers, employees, attorneys, and agents as shall be necessary to carry out the provisions of this Act, and to

---

*See footnote 1.

[8] See Executive Order 11161, p. 357.

define their authority and duties, except that the Secretary of Transportation* may fix the compensation for not more than twenty-three positions at rates not to exceed the highest rate of grade 18 of the General Schedule of the Classification Act of 1949, as amended.

Study of Special Personnel Problems

(g) The Secretary of Transportation* shall make a study, in consultation with other affected Government agencies, of personnel problems inherent in the functions of the Administration,* giving due consideration to the need for (1) special qualifications and training, (2) special provisions as to pay, retirement, and hours of service, and (3) special provisions to assure availability, responsiveness, and security status of essential personnel in fulfilling national defense requirements, and shall report the results thereof, and make recommendations for legislation thereon, to Congress on or before January 1, 1960.

Scientific Employees

(h) The Secretary of Transportation* is authorized to establish and fix the compensation for not to exceed twenty positions of officers and employees of the Administration* of a scientific or professional nature without regard to the Classification Act of 1949, as amended, each such position being established to effectuate those research, development, and related activities of the Administration* which require the services of specially qualified scientific or professional personnel. The rates of basic compensation for positions established pursuant to this subsection shall not exceed the maximum rate payable under the Act of August 1, 1947 (Public Law 313, Eightieth Congress), as amended, and Title V of the Act of July 31, 1956 (Public Law 854, Eighty-fourth Congress), and shall be subject to the approval of the Civil Service Commission. Positions created pursuant to this subsection shall be included in the classified civil service of the United States, but appointment to such positions shall be made without competitive examination upon approval of the proposed appointee's qualifications by the Civil Service Commission or such officers or agents as it may designate for this purpose.

Advisory Committees and Consultants

(i) The Secretary of Transportation* is authorized to appoint such advisory committees as shall be appropriate for the purpose of consultation with and advice to the Administration* in performance of its functions hereunder and to obtain services authorized by section 15 of the Administrative Expenses Act of 1946 (5 U.S.C. 55a), at rates not to exceed $100 per diem for individuals, and for not to exceed one hundred days in any calendar year in the case of any individual. Members of such committees shall be entitled to travel expenses and per diem as authorized by the Administrative Expenses Act of 1946 (5 U.S.C. 73b–2), for all persons employed intermittently as consultants or experts receiving compensation on a per diem basis.

---

*See footnote 1.

Supergrades

(j) [*Repealed by Act of October 9, 1961, 75 Stat. 785.*]

Cooperation With Other Agencies

(k) The Secretary of Transportation* is authorized to use with their consent the available services, equipment, personnel, and facilities of other civilian or military agencies and instrumentalities of the Federal Government, on a reimbursable basis when appropriate, and on a similar basis to cooperate with such other agencies and instrumentalities in the establishment and use of services, equipment, and facilities of the Administration.* The Secretary of Transportation* is further authorized to confer with and avail himself of the cooperation, services, records, and facilities of State, Territorial, municipal or other local agencies.

ADMINISTRATION OF THE ADMINISTRATION*

Authorization of Expenditures and Travel

SEC. 303 [*72 Stat. 747, as amended by 84 Stat. 234, 49 U.S.C. 1344*] (a) The Secretary of Transportation* is empowered to make such expenditures at the seat of government and elsewhere as may be necessary for the exercise and performance of the powers and duties vested in and imposed upon him by law, and as from time to time may be appropriated for by Congress, including expenditures for (1) rent and personal services at the seat of government and elsewhere; (2) travel expenses; (3) office furniture, equipment and supplies, lawbooks, newspapers, periodicals, and books of reference (including the exchange thereof); (4) printing and binding; (5) membership in and cooperation with such organizations as are related to, or are part of, the civil aeronautics industry or the art of aeronautics in the United States or in any foreign country; (6) payment of allowances and other benefits to employees stationed in foreign countries to the same extent as authorized from time to time for members of the Foreign Service of the United States of comparable grade; (7) making investigations and conducting studies in matters pertaining to aeronautics; and (8) acquisition (including exchange), operation and maintenance of passenger-carrying automobiles and aircraft, and such other property as is necessary in the exercise and performance of the powers and duties of the Administrator: *Provided,* That no aircraft or motor vehicles, purchased under the provisions of this section, shall be used otherwise than for official business.

Supplies and Materials for Overseas Installations

(b) When appropriations for any fiscal year for the Agency* have not been made prior to the first day of March preceding the beginning of such fiscal year, the Secretary of Transportation* may authorize such officer or officers as may be designated by him to incur obligations for the purchase and transportation of supplies and materials necessary to the proper execution of the Secretary of Transportation's

*See footnote 1.

[§ 303]

functions at installations outside the continental United States, including those in Alaska, in amounts not to exceed 75 per centum of the amount that had been made available for such purposes for the fiscal year then current, payments of these obligations to be made from the appropriations for the next succeeding fiscal year when they become available.

Acquisition and Disposal of Property

(c) The Secretary of Transportation,* on behalf of the United States, is authorized, where appropriate: (1) to accept any conditional or unconditional gift or donation of money or other property, real or personal, or of services; (2) within the limits of available appropriations made by the Congress therefor, to acquire by purchase, condemnation, lease, or otherwise, real property or interests therein, including, in the case of air navigation facilities (including airports) owned by the United States and operated under the direction of the Administrator, easements through or other interests in airspace immediately adjacent thereto and needed in connection therewith: *Provided*, That the authority herein granted shall not include authority for the acquisition of space in buildings for use by the Federal Aviation Administration*, suitable accommodations for which shall be provided by the Administrator of General Services, unless the Administrator of General Services determines, pursuant to section 1(d) of Reorganization Plan Numbered 18, 1950 (64 Stat. 1270) that the space to be acquired is to be utilized for the special purposes of the Federal Aviation Administration* and is not generally suitable for the use of other agencies; (3) for adequate compensation, by sale, lease, or otherwise, to dispose of any real or personal property or interest therein: *Provided*, That, except for airport and airway property and technical equipment used for the special purposes of the Agency, such disposition shall be made in accordance with the Federal Property and Administrative Services Act of 1949, as amended; and (4) to construct, improve, or renovate laboratories and other test facilities and to purchase or otherwise acquire real property required therefor. Any such acquisition by condemnation may be made in accordance with the provisions of the Act of August 1, 1888 (40 U.S.C. 257; 25 Stat. 357), the Act of February 26, 1931 (40 U.S.C. 258a–258e; 46 Stat. 1421), or any other applicable Act: *Provided*, That in the case of condemnations of easements through or other interests in airspace, in fixing condemnation awards, consideration may be given to the reasonable probable future use of the underlying land.

Delegation of Functions

(d) The Secretary of Transportation* may, subject to such regulations, supervision, and review as he may prescribe, from time to time make such provision as he shall deem appropriate authorizing the performance by any officer, employee, or administrative unit under his jurisdiction of any function under this Act; or, with its consent, authorizing the performance by any other Federal department or agency of any function under section 307(b) of this Act.

---

*See footnote 1.

Negotiation of Purchases and Contracts

(e) The Secretary of Transportation may negotiate without advertising purchases of and contracts for technical or special property related to, or in support of, air navigation that he determines to require a substantial initial investment or an extended period of preparation for manufacture, and for which he determines that formal advertising would be likely to result in additional cost to the Government by reason of duplication of investment or would result in duplication of necessary preparation which would unduly delay the procurement of the property. The Secretary shall, at the beginning of each fiscal year, report to the Committee on Interstate and Foreign Commerce of the House of Representatives and the Committee on Commerce of the Senate all transactions negotiated under this subsection during the preceding fiscal year.

AUTHORITY OF PRESIDENT TO TRANSFER CERTAIN FUNCTIONS

Sec. 304. [*72 Stat. 749, 49 U.S.C. 1345*] The President may transfer to the Secretary of Transportation* any functions (including powers, duties, activities, facilities, and parts of functions) of the executive departments or agencies of the Government or of any officer or organizational entity thereof which relate primarily to selecting, developing, testing, evaluating, establishing, operating and maintaining systems, procedures, facilities, or devices for safe and efficient air navigation and air traffic control. In connection with any such transfer, the President may provide for appropriate transfers of records, property, and for necessary civilian and military personnel to be made available from the other office, department, or other agency from which the transfer is made.

FOSTERING OF AIR COMMERCE

Sec. 305. [*72 Stat. 749, 49 U.S.C. 1346*] The Secretary of Transportation* is empowered and directed to encourage and foster the development of civil aeronautics and air commerce in the United States and abroad.

NATIONAL DEFENSE AND CIVIL NEEDS

Sec. 306. [*72 Stat. 749, 49 U.S.C. 1347*] In exercising the authority granted in, and discharging the duties imposed by, this Act, the Secretary of Transportation* shall give full consideration to the requirements of national defense, and of commercial and general aviation, and to the public right of freedom of transit through the navigable airspace.

AIRSPACE CONTROL AND FACILITIES

Use of Airspace

Sec. 307. [*72 Stat. 749, 49 U.S.C. 1348*] (a) The Secretary of Transportation* is authorized and directed to develop plans for and formulate policy with respect to the use of the navigable airspace; and

---

*See footnote 1.

[§ 307]

assign by rule, regulation, or order the use of the navigable airspace under such terms, conditions, and limitations as he may deem necessary in order to insure the safety of aircraft and the efficient utilization of such airspace. He may modify or revoke such assignment when required in the public interest.

Air Navigation Facilities

(b) The Secretary of Transportation* is authorized, within the limits of available appropriations made by the Congress, (1) to acquire, establish, and improve air-navigation facilities wherever necessary; (2) to operate and maintain such air-navigation facilities; (3) to arrange for publication of aeronautical maps and charts necessary for the safe and efficient movement of aircraft in air navigation utilizing the facilities and assistance of existing agencies of the Government so far as practicable; and (4) to provide necessary facilities and personnel for the regulation and protection of air traffic.

Air Traffic Rules

(c) The Secretary of Transportation* is further authorized and directed to prescribe air traffic rules and regulations governing the flight of aircraft, for the navigation, protection, and identification of aircraft, for the protection of persons and property on the ground, and for the efficient utilization of the navigable airspace including rules as to safe altitudes of flight and rules for the prevention of collision between aircraft, between aircraft and land or water vehicles, and between aircraft and airborne objects.

Applicability of Administrative Procedure Act [9]

(d) In the exercise of the rulemaking authority under subsections (a) and (c) of this section, the Secretary of Transportation* shall be subject to the provisions of the Administrative Procedure Act, notwithstanding any exception relating to military or naval functions in section 4 thereof.

Exemptions

(e) The Secretary of Transportation* from time to time may grant exemptions from the requirements of any rule or regulation prescribed under this title if he finds that such action would be in the public interest.

Exception for Military Emergencies

(f) When it is essential to the defense of the United States because of a military emergency or urgent military necessity, and when appropriate military authority so determines, and when prior notice thereof is given to the Secretary of Transportation,* such military authority may authorize deviation by military aircraft of the national defense forces of the United States from air traffic rules issued pursuant to

---

*See footnote 1.
[9] The provisions of the Administrative Procedure Act (60 Stat. 237, as amended) were repealed and superseded by Public Law 89–554, 80 Stat. 378, and are now codified in 5 U.S.C. 551 *et seq.* See p. 299.

this title. Such prior notice shall be given to the Secretary of Transportation* at the earliest time practicable and, to the extent time and circumstances permit, every reasonable effort shall be made to consult fully with the Secretary of Transportation* and to arrange in advance for the required deviation from the rules on a mutually acceptable basis.

EXPENDITURE OF FEDERAL FUNDS FOR CERTAIN AIRPORTS, ETC.

Airports for Other Than Military Purposes

SEC. 308. [*72 Stat. 750, 49 U.S.C. 1349*] (a) No Federal funds, other than those expended under this Act, shall be expended, other than for military purposes (whether or not in cooperation with State or other local governmental agencies), for the acquisition, establishment, construction, alteration, repair, maintenance, or operation of any landing area, or for the acquisition, establishment, construction, maintenance, or operation of air navigation facilities thereon, except upon written recommendation and certification by the Secretary of Transportation* that such landing area or facility is reasonably necessary for use in air commence or in the interests of national defense. Any interested person may apply to the Secretary of Transportation,* under regulations prescribed by him, for such recommendation and certification with respect to any landing area or air navigation facility proposed to be established, constructed, altered, repaired, maintained, or operated by, or in the interests of, such person. There shall be no exclusive right for the use of any landing area or air navigation facility upon which Federal funds have been expended.

Location of Airports, Landing Areas, and Missile and Rocket Sites

(b) In order to assure conformity to plans and policies for allocations of airspace by the Secretary of Transportation* under section 307 of this Act, no military airport or landing area, or missile or rocket site shall be acquired, established, or constructed, or any runway layout substantially altered, unless reasonable prior notice thereof is given the Secretary of Transportation* so that he may advise with the appropriate committees of the Congress and other interested agencies as to the effects of such acquisition, establishment, construction, or alteration on the use of airspace by aircraft. In case of a disagreement between the Secretary of Transportation* and the Department of Defense or the National Aeronautics and Space Administration the matter may be appealed to the President for final determination.

OTHER AIRPORTS

SEC. 309. [*72 Stat. 751, 49 U.S.C. 1350*] In order to assure conformity to plans and policies for, and allocations of, airspace by the Secretary of Transportation* under section 307 of this Act, no airport or landing area not involving expenditure of Federal funds shall be established, or constructed, or any runway layout substantially altered unless reasonable prior notice thereof is given the Secretary of Trans-

*See footnote 1.

[§§ 310–312]

portation,* pursuant to regulations prescribed by him, so that he may advise as to the effects of such construction on the use of airspace by aircraft.

METEOROLOGICAL SERVICE

SEC. 310. [*72 Stat. 751, 49 U.S.C. 1351*] The Secretary of Transportation* is empowered and directed to make recommendations to the Secretary of Commerce for providing meteorological service necessary for the safe and efficient movement of aircraft in air commerce. In providing meteorological services, the Secretary of Commerce shall cooperate with the Secretary of Transportation* and give full consideration to such recommendations.

COLLECTION AND DISSEMINATION OF INFORMATION

SEC. 311. [*72 Stat. 751, 49 U.S.C. 1352*] The Secretary of Transportation* is empowered and directed to collect and disseminate information relative to civil aeronautics (other than information collected and disseminated by the Board under titles IV and VII* of this Act) ; to study the possibilities of the development of air commerce and the aeronautical industry; and to exchange with foreign governments, through appropriate governmental channels, information pertaining to civil aeronautics.

DEVELOPMENT PLANNING

General

SEC. 312. [*72 Stat. 752, 49 U.S.C. 1353*] (a) The Secretary of Transportation* is directed to make long range plans for and formulate policy with respect to the orderly development and use of the navigable airspace, and the orderly development and location of landing areas, Federal airways, radar installations and all other aids and facilities for air navigation, as will best meet the needs of, and serve the interest of civil aeronautics and national defense, except for those needs of military agencies which are peculiar to air warfare and primarily of military concern.

Aircraft

(b) The Secretary of Transportation* is empowered to undertake or supervise such developmental work and service testing as tends to the creation of improved aircraft, aircraft engines, propellers, and appliances. For such purpose, the Secretary of Transportation* is empowered to make purchases (including exchange) by negotiation, or otherwise, of experimental aircraft, aircraft engines, propellers, and appliances, which seem to offer special advantages to aeronautics.

Research and Development

(c) The Secretary of Transportation* shall develop, modify, test, and evaluate systems, procedures, facilities, and devices, as well as define the performance characteristics thereof, to meet the needs for safe and efficient navigation and traffic control of all civil and mili-

---

*See footnote 1.   270

tary aviation except for those needs of military agencies which are peculiar to air warfare and primarily of military concern, and select such systems, procedures, facilities, and devices as will best serve such needs and will promote maximum coordination of air traffic control and air defense systems. Contracts may be entered into for this purpose without regard to section 3643 of the Revised Statutes, as amended (31 U.S.C. 529). When there is any substantial question as to whether a matter is of primary concern to the military, the Secretary of Transportation* is authorized and directed to determine whether he or the appropriate military agency shall have responsibility. Technical information concerning any research and development projects of the military agencies which have potential application to the needs of, or possible conflict with, the common system shall be furnished to the Secretary of Transportation* to the maximum extent necessary to insure that common system application potential is properly considered and potential future conflicts with the common system are eliminated.

OTHER POWERS AND DUTIES OF SECRETARY OF TRANSPORTATION*

General

SEC. 313. [*72 Stat. 752, as amended by 84 Stat. 235, 49 U.S.C. 1354*] (a) The Secretary of Transportation* is empowered to perform such acts, to conduct such investigations, to issue and amend such orders, and to make and amend such general or special rules, regulations, and procedures, pursuant to and consistent with the provisions of this Act, as he shall deem necessary to carry out the provisions of, and to exercise and perform his powers and duties under, this Act.

Publications

(b) Except as may be otherwise provided in this Act, the Secretary of Transportation* shall make a report in writing on all proceedings and investigations under this Act in which formal hearings have been held, and shall state in such report his conclusions together with his decisions, order, or requirement in the premises. All such reports shall be entered of record and a copy thereof shall be furnished to all parties to the proceeding or investigation. The Secretary of Transportation* shall provide for the publication of such reports, and all other reports, orders, decisions, rules, and regulations issued by him under this Act in such form and manner as may be best adapted for public information and use. Publications purporting to be published by the Secretary of Transportation* shall be competent evidence of the orders, decisions, rules, regulations, and reports of the Secretary of Transportation* therein contained in all courts of the United States, and of the several States, Territories, and possessions thereof, and the District of Columbia, without further proof or authentication thereof.

Power To Conduct Hearings and Investigations

(c) In the conduct of any public hearings or investigations authorized by this Act, the Federal Airport Act, or the Airport and Airway

---

*See footnote 1.

[§ 314]

Development Act of 1970, the Secretary of Transportation* shall have the same powers to take evidence, issue subpenas, take depositions, and compel testimony as are vested in members of the Board and its duly designated examiners by section 1004 of this Act. Actions of the Secretary of Transportation* in such cases shall be governed by the procedures specified in section 1004 and be enforced in the manner provided therein.

Training Schools

(d) The Secretary of Transportation* is empowered to conduct a school or schools for the purpose of training employees of the Agency in those subjects necessary for the proper performance of all authorized functions of the Administration.* He may also authorize attendance at courses given in such school or schools of other governmental personnel, and personnel of foreign governments, or personnel of the aeronautics industry: *Provided,* That in the event the attendance of such persons shall increase the cost of operation of such school or schools, the Secretary of Transportation* may require the payment or transfer of sufficient funds or other appropriate consideration to offset the additional costs. In providing any training to employees of the Administration* or of other agencies of the Federal Government, the Secretary of Transportation* shall be subject to the provisions of the Government Employees Training Act (72 Stat. 327). Funds received by the Secretary of Transportation* hereunder may be credited (1) to appropriations current at the time the expenditures are to be or have been paid, (2) to appropriations current at the time such funds are received, or (3) in part as provided under clause (1) and in part as provided under clause (2).

Annual Report

(e) The Secretary of Transportation* shall submit to the President and to the Congress an annual report. Such report shall contain, in addition to a report of the work performed under this Act, such information and data collected by the Secretary of Transportation* as may be considered of value in the determination of questions connected with the development and regulation of civil aeronautics, the utilization of national airspace, and the improvement of the air navigation and traffic control system, together with such recommendations as to additional legislation related thereto as the Secretary of Transportation* may deem necessary, and the Secretary of Transportation* may also transmit recommendations as to legislation at any other time.

DELEGATION OF POWERS AND DUTIES TO PRIVATE PERSONS

Delegation by Secretary of Transportation*

SEC. 314 [*72 Stat. 754, 49 U.S.C. 1355*] (a) In exercising the powers and duties vested in him by this Act, the Secretary of Trans-

---

*See footnote 1.

portation* may, subject to such regulations, supervision, and review as he may prescribe, delegate to any properly qualified private person, or to any employee or employees under the supervision of such person, any work, business, or function respecting (1) the examination, inspection, and testing necessary to the issuance of certificates under title VI of this Act, and (2) the issuance of such certificates in accordance with standards established by him. The Secretary of Transportation* may establish the maximum fees which such private persons may charge for their services and may rescind any delegation made by him pursuant to this subsection at any time and for any reason which he deems appropriate.

Application for Reconsideration

(b) Any person affected by any action taken by any private person exercising delegated authority under this section may apply for reconsideration of such action by the Secretary of Transportation.* The Secretary of Transportation* upon his own initiative, with respect to the authority granted under subsection (a), may reconsider the action of any private person either before or after it has become effective. If, upon reconsideration by the Secretary of Transportation*, it shall appear that the action in question is in any respect unjust or unwarranted, the Secretary of Transportation* shall reverse, change, or modify the same accordingly; otherwise such action shall be affirmed: *Provided,* That nothing in this subsection shall be construed as modifying, amending, or repealing any provisions of the Administrative Procedure Act.[10]

TITLE IV—AIR CARRIER ECONOMIC REGULATION

CERTIFICATE OF PUBLIC CONVENIENCE AND NECESSITY

Certificate Required

SEC. 401. [*72 Stat. 754, as amended by 76 Stat. 143, 82 Stat. 867, 49 U.S.C. 1371*] (a) No air carrier shall engage in any air transportation unless there is in force a certificate issued by the Board authorizing such air carrier to engage in such transportation.

Application for Certificate

(b) Application for a certificate shall be made in writing to the Board and shall be so verified, shall be in such form and contain such information, and shall be accompanied by such proof of service upon such interested persons, as the Board shall by regulation require.

Notice of Application

(c) Upon the filing of any such application, the Board shall give due notice thereof to the public by posting a notice of such application in the office of the secretary of the Board and to such other persons as the Board may by regulation determine. Any interested

---

*See footnote 1.
[10] Now codified in 5 U.S.C. 551, *et seq.* See p. 299.

[§ 401]

person may file with the Board a protest or memorandum of opposition to or in support of the issuance of a certificate. Such application shall be set for a public hearing, and the Board shall dispose of such application as speedily as possible.

Issuance of Certificate

(d) (1) The Board shall issue a certificate authorizing the whole or any part of the transportation covered by the application, if it finds that the applicant is fit, willing, and able to perform such transportation properly, and to conform to the provisions of this Act and the rules, regulations, and requirements of the Board hereunder, and that such transportation is required by the public convenience and necessity; otherwise such application shall be denied.

(2) In the case of an application for a certificate to engage in temporary air transportation, the Board may issue a certificate authorizing the whole or any part thereof for such limited periods as may be required by the public convenience and necessity, if it finds that the applicant is fit, willing, and able properly to perform such transportation and to conform to the provisions of this Act and the rules, regulations, and requirements of the Board hereunder.

(3) In the case of an application for a certificate to engage in supplemental air transportation, the Board may issue a certificate, to any applicant not holding a certificate under paragraph (1) or (2) of this subsection, authorizing the whole or any part thereof, and for such periods, as may be required by the public convenience and necessity, if it finds that the applicant is fit, willing, and able properly to perform the transportation covered by the application and to conform to the provisions of this Act and the rules, regulations, and requirements of the Board hereunder. Any certificate issued pursuant to this paragraph shall contain such limitations as the Board shall find necessary to assure that the service rendered pursuant thereto will be limited to supplemental air transportation as defined in this Act.

Terms and Conditions of Certificate

(e) (1) Each certificate issued under this section shall specify the terminal points and intermediate points, if any, between which the air carrier is authorized to engage in air transportation and the service to be rendered; and there shall be attached to the exercise of the privileges granted by the certificate, or amendment thereto, such reasonable terms, conditions, and limitations as the public interest may require.

(2) A certificate issued under this section to engage in foreign air transportation shall, insofar as the operation is to take place without the United States, designate the terminal and intermediate points only insofar as the Board shall deem practicable, and otherwise shall designate only the general route or routes to be followed. Any air carrier holding a certificate for foreign air transportation shall be authorized to handle and transport mail of countries other than the United States.

(3) A certificate issued under this section to engage in supplemental air transportation shall designate the terminal and intermediate points only insofar as the Board shall deem practicable and other-

wise shall designate only the geographical area or areas within or between which service may be rendered.

(4) No term, condition, or limitation of a certificate shall restrict the right of an air carrier to add to or change schedules, equipment, accommodations, and facilities for performing the authorized transportation and service as the development of the business and the demands of the public shall require; except that the Board may impose such terms, conditions, or limitations in a certificate for supplemental air transportation when required by subsection (d) (3) of this section.

(5) No air carrier shall be deemed to have violated any term, condition, or limitation of its certificate by landing or taking off during an emergency at a point not named in its certificate or by operating in an emergency, under regulations which may be prescribed by the Board, between terminal and intermediate points other than those specified in its certificate.

(6) Any air carrier, other than a supplemental air carrier, may perform charter trips (including inclusive tour charter trips) or any other special service, without regard to the points named in its certificate, or the type of service provided therein, under regulations prescribed by the Board.

Effective Date and Duration of Certificate

(f) Each certificate shall be effective from the date specified therein, and shall continue in effect until suspended or revoked as hereinafter provided, or until the Board shall certify that operation thereunder has ceased, or, if issued for a limited period of time under subsection (d) (2) of this section, shall continue in effect until the expiration thereof, unless, prior to the date of expiration, such certificate shall be suspended or revoked as provided herein, or the Board shall certify that operations thereunder have ceased: *Provided,* That if any service authorized by a certificate is not inaugurated within such period, not less than ninety days, after the date of the authorization as shall be fixed by the Board, or if, for a period of ninety days or such other period as may be designated by the Board any such service is not operated, the Board may by order, entered after notice and hearing, direct that such certificate shall thereupon cease to be effective to the extent of such service.

Authority to Modify, Suspend, or Revoke

(g) The Board upon petition or complaint or upon its own initiative, after notice and hearings, may alter, amend, modify, or suspend any such certificate, in whole or in part, if the public convenience and necessity so require, or may revoke any such certificate, in whole or in part, for intentional failure to comply with any provision of this title or any order, rule, or regulation issued hereunder or any term, condition, or limitation of such certificate: *Provided,* That no such certificate shall be revoked unless the holder thereof fails to comply, within a reasonable time to be fixed by the Board, with an order of the Board commanding obedience to the provision, or to the order (other than an order issued in accordance with this proviso), rule, regulation, term,

[§ 401]
condition, or limitation found by the Board to have been violated. Any interested person may file with the Board a protest or memorandum in support of or in opposition to the alteration, amendment, modification, suspension, or revocation of the certificate.

Transfer of Certificate

(h) No certificate may be transferred unless such transfer is approved by the Board as being consistent with the public interest.

Certain Rights Not Conferred by Certificate

(i) No certificate shall confer any proprietary, property, or exclusive right in the use of any airspace, Federal airway, landing area, or air-navigation facility.

Application for Abandonment

(j) No air carrier shall abandon any route, or part thereof, for which a certificate has been issued by the Board, unless, upon the application of such air carrier, after notice and hearing, the Board shall find such abandonment to be in the public interest. Any interested person may file with the Board a protest or memorandum of opposition to or in support of any such abandonment. The Board may, by regulations or otherwise, authorize such temporary suspension of service as may be in the public interest.

Compliance With Labor Legislation

(k) (1) Every air carrier shall maintain rates of compensation, maximum hours, and other working conditions and relations of all of its pilots and copilots who are engaged in interstate air transportation within the continental United States (not including Alaska) so as to conform with decision numbered 83 made by the National Labor Board on May 10, 1934, notwithstanding any limitation therein as to the period of its effectiveness.

(2) Every air carrier shall maintain rates of compensation for all of its pilots and copilots who are engaged in overseas or foreign air transportation or air transportation wholly within a Territory or possession of the United States, the minimum of which shall be not less, upon an annual basis, than the compensation required to be paid under said decision 83 for comparable service to pilots and copilots engaged in interstate air transportation within the continental United States (not including Alaska).

(3) Nothing herein contained shall be construed as restricting the right of any such pilots or copilots, or other employees, of any such air carrier to obtain by collective bargaining higher rates of compensation or more favorable working conditions or relations.

(4) It shall be a condition upon the holding of a certificate by any air carrier that such carrier shall comply with title II of the Railway Labor Act, as amended.

(5) The term "pilot" as used in this subsection shall mean an employee who is responsible for the manipulation of or who manipulates the flight controls of an aircraft while under way including take-off and landing of such aircraft, and the term "copilot" as used in this

subsection shall mean an employee any part of whose duty is to assist or relieve the pilot in such manipulation, and who is properly qualified to serve as, and holds a currently effective airman certificate authorizing him to serve as, such pilot or copilot.

Requirement as to Carriage of Mail

(l) Whenever so authorized by its certificate, any air carrier shall provide necessary and adequate facilities and service for the transportation of mail, and shall transport mail whenever required by the Postmaster General. Such air carrier shall be entitled to receive reasonable compensation therefor as hereinafter provided.

Application for New Mail Service

(m) Whenever, from time to time, the Postmaster General shall find that the needs of the Postal Service require the transportation of mail by aircraft between any points within the United States or between the United States and foreign countries, in addition to the transportation of mail authorized in certificates then currently effective, the Postmaster General shall certify such finding to the Board and file therewith a statement showing such additional service and the facilities necessary in connection therewith, and a copy of such certification and statement shall be posted for at least twenty days in the office of the secretary of the Board. The Board shall, after notice and hearing, and if found by it to be required by the public convenience and necessity, make provision for such additional service, and the facilities necessary in connection therewith, by issuing a new certificate or certificates or by amending an existing certificate or certificates in accordance with the provisions of this section.

Additional Powers and Duties of Board With Respect to Supplemental Air Carriers

(n) (1) No certificate to engage in supplemental air transportation, and no special operating authorization described in section 417 of this title, shall be issued or remain in effect unless the applicant for such certificate or the supplemental air carrier, as the case may be, complies with regulations or orders issued by the Board governing the filing and approval of policies of insurance, in the amount prescribed by the Board, conditioned to pay, within the amount of such insurance, amounts for which such applicant or such supplemental air carrier may become liable for bodily injuries to or the death of any person, or for loss of or damage to property of others, resulting from the negligent operation or maintenance of aircraft under such certificate or such special operating authorization.

(2) In order to protect travelers and shippers by aircraft operated by supplemental air carriers, the Board may require any supplemental air carrier to file a performance bond or equivalent security arrangement, in such amount and upon such terms as the Board shall prescribe, to be conditioned upon such supplemental air carrier's making appropriate compensation to such travelers and shippers, as prescribed by the Board, for failure on the part of such carrier to perform air transportation services in accordance with agreements therefor.

[§ 402]

(3) If any service authorized by a certificate to engage in supplemental air transportation is not performed to the minimum extent prescribed by the Board, it may by order, entered after notice and hearing, direct that such certificate shall thereupon cease to be effective to the extent of such service.

(4) The requirement that each applicant for a certificate to engage in supplemental air transportation must be found to be fit, willing, and able properly to perform the transportation covered by his application and to conform to the provisions of this Act and the rules, regulations, and requirements of the Board under this Act, shall be a continuing requirement applicable to each supplemental air carrier with respect to the transportation authorized by, and currently furnished or proposed to be furnished under, such carrier's certificate. The Board shall by order, entered after notice and hearing, modify, suspend, or revoke such certificate, in whole or in part, for failure of such carrier (A) to comply with the continuing requirement that such carrier be so fit, willing, and able, or (B) to file such reports as the Board may deem necessary to determine whether such carrier is so fit, willing, and able.

(5) In any case in which the Board determines that the failure of a supplemental air carrier to comply with the provisions of paragraph (1), (3), or (4) of this subsection, or regulations or orders of the Board thereunder, requires, in the interest of the rights, welfare, or safety of the public, immediate suspension of such carrier's certificate, the Board shall suspend such certificate, in whole or in part, without notice or hearing, for not more than thirty days. The Board shall immediately enter upon a hearing to determine whether such certificate should be modified, suspended, or revoked and, pending the completion of such hearing, the Board may further suspend such certificate for additional periods aggregating not more than sixty days. If the Board determines that a carrier whose certificate is suspended under this paragraph comes into compliance with the provisions of paragraphs (1), (3), and (4) of this subsection, and regulations and orders of the Board thereunder, the Board may immediately terminate the suspension of such certificate and any pending proceeding commenced under this paragraph, but nothing in this sentence shall preclude the Board from imposing on such carrier a civil penalty for any violation of such provisions, regulations, or orders.

(6) The Board shall prescribe such regulations and issue such orders as may be necessary to carry out the provisions of this subsection.

PERMITS TO FOREIGN AIR CARRIERS

Permit Required

SEC. 402. [*72 Stat. 757, 49 U.S.C. 1372*] (a) No foreign air carrier shall engage in foreign air transportation unless there is in force a permit issued by the Board authorizing such carrier so to engage.

Issuance of Permit

(b) The Board is empowered to issue such a permit if it finds that such carrier is fit, willing, and able properly to perform such air transportation and to conform to the provisions of this Act and the rules, regulations, and requirements of the Board hereunder, and that such transportation will be in the public interest.

Application for Permit

(c) Application for a permit shall be made in writing to the Board, shall be so verified, shall be in such form and contain such information, and shall be accompanied by such proof of service upon such interested persons, as the Board shall by regulation require.

Notice of Application

(d) Upon the filing of an application for a permit the Board shall give due notice thereof to the public by posting a notice of such application in the office of the secretary of the Board and to such other persons as the Board may by regulation determine. Any interested person may file with the Board a protest or memorandum of opposition to or in support of the issuance of a permit. Such application shall be set for public hearing and the Board shall dispose of such application as speedily as possible.

Terms and Conditions of Permit

(e) The Board may prescribe the duration of any permit and may attach to such permit such reasonable terms, conditions, or limitations as, in its judgment, the public interest may require.

Authority to Modify, Suspend, or Revoke

(f) Any permit issued under the provisions of this section may, after notice and hearing, be altered, modified, amended, suspended, canceled, or revoked by the Board whenever it finds such action to be in the public interest. Any interested person may file with the Board a protest or memorandum in support of or in opposition to the alteration, modification, amendment, suspension, cancellation, or revocation of a permit.

Transfer of Permit

(g) No permit may be transferred unless such transfer is approved by the Board as being in the public interest.

TARIFFS OF AIR CARRIERS

Filing of Tariffs Required

Sec. 403. [*72 Stat. 758, as amended by 74 Stat. 445, 49 U.S.C. 1373*] (a) Every air carrier and every foreign air carrier shall file with the Board, and print, and keep open to public inspection, tariffs showing all rates, fares, and charges for air transportation between points served by it, and between points served by it and points served by any other air carrier or foreign air carrier when through service and through rates shall have been established, and showing to the extent required by regulations of the Board, all classifications, rules, regula-

[§ 403]

tions, practices, and services in connection with such air transportation. Tariffs shall be filed, posted, and published in such form and manner, and shall contain such information, as the Board shall by regulation prescribe; and the Board is empowered to reject any tariff so filed which is not consistent with this section and such regulations. Any tariff so rejected shall be void. The rates, fares, and charges shown in any tariff shall be stated in terms of lawful money of the United States, but such tariffs may also state rates, fares, and charges in terms of currencies other than lawful money of the United States, and may, in the case of foreign air transportation, contain such information as may be required under the laws of any country in or to which an air carrier or foreign air carrier is authorized to operate.

Observance of Tariffs; Rebating Prohibited

(b) No air carrier or foreign air carrier shall charge or demand or collect or receive a greater or less or different compensation for air transportation, or for any service in connection therewith, than the rates, fares, and charges specified in its currently effective tariffs; and no air carrier or foreign air carrier shall, in any manner or by any device, directly or indirectly, or through any agent or broker, or otherwise, refund or remit any portion of the rates, fares, or charges so specified, or extend to any person any privileges or facilities, with respect to matters required by the Board to be specified in such tariffs, except those specified therein. Nothing in this Act shall prohibit such air carriers or foreign air carriers, under such terms and conditions as the Board may prescribe, from issuing or interchanging tickets or passes for free or reduced-rate transportation to their directors, officers, and employees (including retired directors, officers, and employees who are receiving retirement benefits from any air carrier or foreign air carrier), the parents and immediate families of such officers and employees, and the immediate families of such directors; widows, widowers, and minor children of employees who have died as a direct result of personal injury sustained while in the performance of duty in the service of such air carrier or foreign air carrier; witnesses and attorneys attending any legal investigation in which any such air carrier is interested; persons injured in aircraft accidents and physicians and nurses attending such persons; immediate families, including parents, of persons injured or killed in aircraft accidents where the object is to transport such persons in connection with such accident; and any person or property with the object of providing relief in cases of general epidemic, pestilence, or other calamitous visitation; and, in the case of overseas or foreign air transportation, to such other persons and under such other circumstances as the Board may by regulations prescribe. Any air carrier or foreign air carrier, under such terms and conditions as the Board may prescribe, may grant reduced-rate transportation to ministers of religion on a space-available basis.

Notice of Tariff Change

(c) No change shall be made in any rate, fare, or charge, or any classification, rule, regulation, or practice affecting such rate, fare, or charge, or the value of the service thereunder, specified in any effective tariff of any air carrier or foreign air carrier, except after thirty days' notice of the proposed change filed, posted, and published in accordance with subsection (a) of this section. Such notice shall plainly state the change proposed to be made and the time such change will take effect. The Board may in the public interest, by regulation or otherwise, allow such change upon notice less than that herein specified, or modify the requirements of this section with respect to filing and posting of tariffs, either in particular instances or by general order applicable to special or peculiar circumstances or conditions.

Filing of Divisions of Rates and Charges Required

(d) Every air carrier or foreign air carrier shall keep currently on file with the Board, if the Board so requires, the established divisions of all joint rates, fares, and charges for air transportation in which such air carrier or foreign air carrier participates.

RATES FOR CARRIAGE OF PERSONS AND PROPERTY

Carrier's Duty to Provide Service, Rates, and Divisions

SEC. 404. [*72 Stat. 760, 49 U.S.C. 1374*] (a) It shall be the duty of every air carrier to provide and furnish interstate and overseas air transportation, as authorized by its certificate, upon reasonable request therefor and to provide reasonable through service in such air transportation in connection with other air carriers; to provide safe and adequate service, equipment, and facilities in connection with such transportation; to establish, observe, and enforce just and reasonable individual and joint rates, fares, and charges, and just and reasonable classifications, rules, regulations, and practices relating to such air transportation; and, in case of such joint rates, fares, and charges, to establish just, reasonable, and equitable divisions thereof as between air carriers participating therein which shall not unduly prefer or prejudice any of such participating air carriers.

Discrimination

(b) No air carrier or foreign air carrier shall make, give, or cause any undue or unreasonable preference or advantage to any particular person, port, locality, or description of traffic in air transportation in any respect whatsoever or subject any particular person, port, locality, or description of traffic in air transportation to any unjust discrimination or any undue or unreasonable prejudice or disadvantage in any respect whatsoever.

TRANSPORTATION OF MAIL

Postal Rules and Regulations

SEC. 405. [*72 Stat. 760, 49 U.S.C. 1375*] (a) The Postmaster General is authorized to make such rules and regulations, not inconsistent with the provisions of this Act, or any order, rule, or regulation made by the Board thereunder, as may be necessary for the safe and expeditious carriage of mail by aircraft.

Mail Schedules

(b) Each air carrier shall, from time to time, file with the Board and the Postmaster General a statement showing the points between which such air carrier is authorized to engage in air transportation, and all schedules, and all changes therein, of aircraft regularly operated by the carrier between such points, setting forth in respect of each such schedule the points served thereby and the time of arrival and departure at each such point. The Postmaster General may designate any such schedule for the transportation of mail between the points between which the air carrier is authorized by its certificate to transport mail, and may, by order, require the air carrier to establish additional schedules for the transportation of mail between such points. No change shall be made in any schedules designated or ordered to be established by the Postmaster General except upon ten days' notice thereof filed as herein provided. The Postmaster General may by order disapprove any such change or alter, amend, or modify any such schedule or change. No order of the Postmaster General under this subsection shall become effective until ten days after its issuance. Any person who would be aggrieved by any such order of the Postmaster General under this subsection may, before the expiration of such ten-day period, apply to the Board, under such regulations as it may prescribe, for a review of such order. The Board may review, and, if the public convenience and necessity so require, amend, revise, suspend, or cancel such order; and, pending such review and the determination thereof, may postpone the effective date of such order. The Board shall give preference to proceedings under this subsection over all proceedings pending before it. No air carrier shall transport mail in accordance with any schedule other than a schedule designated or order to be established under this subsection for the transportation of mail.

Maximum Mail Load

(c) The Board may fix the maximum mail load for any schedule or for any aircraft or any type of aircraft; but, in the event that mail in excess of the maximum load is tendered by the Postmaster General for transportation by any air carrier in accordance with any schedule designated or ordered to be established by the Postmaster General under subsection (b) of this section for the transportation of mail, such air carrier shall, to the extent such air carrier is reasonably able as determined by the Board, furnish facilities sufficient to transport, and shall transport, such mail as nearly in accordance with such schedule as the Board shall determine to be possible.

Tender of Mail

(d) From and after the issuance of any certificate authorizing the transportation of mail by aircraft, the Postmaster General shall tender mail to the holder thereof, to the extent required by the Postal Service, for transportation between the points named in such certificate for the transportation of mail, and such mail shall be transported by the air carrier holding such certificate in accordance with such

[§ 405]

rules, regulations, and requirements as may be promulgated by the Postmaster General under this section.

Foreign Postal Arrangement

(e) (1) Nothing in this Act shall be deemed to abrogate or affect any arrangement made by the United States with the postal administration of any foreign country with respect to transportation of mail by aircraft, or to impair the authority of the Postmaster General to enter into any such arrangement with the postal administration of any foreign country.

(2) The Postmaster General may, in any case where service may be necessary by a person not a citizen of the United States who may not be obligated to transport the mail for a foreign country, make arrangements, without advertising, with such person for transporting mail by aircraft to or within any foreign country.

Transportation of Foreign Mail

(f) (1) Any air carrier holding a certificate to engage in foreign air transportation and transporting mails of foreign countries shall transport such mails subject to control and regulation by the United States. The Postmaster General shall from time to time fix the rates of compensation that shall be charged the respective foreign countries for the transportation of their mails by such air carriers, and such rates shall be put into effect by the Postmaster General in accordance with the provisions of the postal convention regulating the postal relations between the United States and the respective foreign countries, or as provided hereinafter in this subsection. In any case where the Postmaster General deems such action to be in the public interest, he may approve rates provided in arrangements between any such air carrier and any foreign country covering the transportation of mails of such country, under which mails of such country have been carried on scheduled operations prior to January 1, 1938, or in extensions or modifications of such arrangements, and may permit any such air carrier to enter into arrangements with any foreign country for the transportation of its mails at rates fixed by the Postmaster General in advance of the making of any such arrangement. The Postmaster General may authorize any such air carrier, under such limitations as the Postmaster General may prescribe, to change the rates to be charged any foreign country for the transportation of its mails by such air carrier within that country or between that country and another foreign country.

(2) In any case where such air carrier has an arrangement with any foreign country for transporting its mails, made or approved in accordance with the provisions of paragraph (1) of this subsection, it shall collect its compensation from the foreign country under its arrangement, and in case of the absence of any arrangement between the air carrier and the foreign country consistent with this subsection, the collections made from the foreign country by the United States shall be for the account of such air carrier: *Provided*, That no such air carrier shall be entitled to receive compensation both from

[§ 405]

such foreign country and from the United States in respect of the transportation of the same mail or the same mails of foreign countries.

Evidence of Performance of Mail Service

(g) Air carriers transporting or handling United States mail shall submit, under signature of a duly authorized official, when and in such form as may be required by the Postmaster General, evidence of the performance of mail service; and air carriers transporting or handling mails of foreign countries shall submit, under signature of a duly authorized official, when and in such form as may be required by the Postmaster General, evidence of the amount of such mails transported or handled, and the compensation payable and received therefor.

Emergency Mail Service

(h) In the event of emergency caused by flood, fire, or other calamitous visitation, the Postmaster General is authorized to contract, without advertising, for the transportation by aircraft of any or all classes of mail to or from localities affected by such calamity, where available facilities of persons authorized to transport mail to or from such localities are inadequate to meet the requirements of the Postal Service during such emergency. Such contracts may be only for such periods as may be necessitated, for the maintenance of mail service, by the inadequacy of such other facilities. No operation pursuant to any such contract, for such period, shall be air transportation within the purview of this Act. Payment of compensation for service performed under such contracts shall be made, at rates provided in such contracts, from appropriations for the transportation of mail by the means normally used for transporting the mail transported under such contracts.

Experimental Airmail Service

(i) Nothing contained in this Act shall be construed to repeal in whole or in part the provisions of section 6 of the Act entitled "An Act to provide for experimental airmail service, to further develop safety, efficiency, economy, and for other purposes", approved April 15, 1938, as amended. The transportation of mail under contracts entered into under such section shall not, except for sections 401(k) and 416(b), be deemed to be "air transportation" as used in this Act, and the rates of compensation for such transportation of mail shall not be fixed under this Act.

Free Travel for Postal Employees

(j) Every air carrier carrying the mails shall carry on any plane that it operates and without charge therefor, the persons in charge of the mails when on duty, and such duly accredited agents and officers of the Post Office Department, and post office inspectors, while traveling on official business relating to the transportation of mail by aircraft, as the Board may by regulation prescribe, upon the exhibition of their credentials.

Authority to Fix Rates

SEC. 406. [*72 Stat. 763, as amended by 76 Stat. 145, 80 Stat. 942, 49 U.S.C. 1376*] (a) The Board is empowered and directed, upon its own initiative or upon petition of the Postmaster General or an air carrier, (1) to fix and determine from time to time, after notice and hearing, the fair and reasonable rates of compensation for the transportation of mail by aircraft, the facilities used and useful therefor, and the services connected therewith (including the transportation of mail by an air carrier by other means than aircraft whenever such transportation is incidental to the transportation of mail by aircraft or is made necessary by conditions of emergency arising from aircraft operation), by each holder of a certificate authorizing the transportation of mail by aircraft, and to make such rates effective from such date as it shall determine to be proper; (2) to prescribe the method or methods, by aircraft-mile, pound-mile, weight, space, or any combination thereof, or otherwise, for ascertaining such rates of compensation for each air carrier or class of air carriers; and (3) to publish the same.

Rate Making Elements

(b) In fixing and determining fair and reasonable rates of compensation under this section, the Board, considering the conditions peculiar to transportation by aircraft and to the particular air carrier or class of air carriers, may fix different rates for different air carriers or classes of air carriers, and different classes of service. In determining the rate in each case, the Board shall take into consideration, among other factors, (1) the condition that such air carriers may hold and operate under certificates authorizing the carriage of mail only by providing necessary and adequate facilities and service for the transportation of mail; (2) such standards respecting the character and quality of service to be rendered by air carriers as may be prescribed by or pursuant to law; and (3) the need of each such air carrier (other than a supplemental air carrier) for compensation for the transportation of mail sufficient to insure the performance of such service, and, together with all other revenue of the air carrier, to enable such air carrier under honest, economical, and efficient management, to maintain and continue the development of air transportation to the extent and of the character and quality required for the commerce of the United States, the Postal Service, and the national defense. In applying clause (3) of this subsection, the Board shall take into consideration any standards and criteria prescribed by the Secretary of Transportation, for determining the character and quality of transportation required for the commerce of the United States and the national defense.

Payment

(c) The Postmaster General shall make payments out of appropriations for the transportation of mail by aircraft of so much of the total compensation as is fixed and determined by the Board under

[§ 406]

this section without regard to clause (3) of subsection (b) of this section. The Board shall make payments of the remainder of the total compensation payable under this section out of appropriations made to the Board for that purpose.

Treatment of Proceeds of Disposition of Certain Property

(d) In determining the need of an air carrier for compensation for the transportation of mail, and such carrier's "other revenue" for the purpose of this section, the Board shall not take into account—

(1) gains derived from the sale or other disposition of flight equipment if (A) the carrier notifies the Board in writing that it has invested or intends to reinvest the gains (less applicable expenses and taxes) derived from such sale or other disposition in flight equipment, and (B) submits evidence in the manner prescribed by the Board that an amount equal to such gains (less applicable expenses and taxes) has been expended for purchase of flight equipment or has been deposited in a special reequipment fund, or

(2) losses sustained from the sale or other disposition of flight equipment.

Any amounts so deposited in a reequipment fund as above provided shall be used solely for investment in flight equipment either through payments on account of the purchase price or construction of flight equipment or in retirement of debt contracted for the purchase or construction of flight equipment, and unless so reinvested within such reasonable time as the Board may prescribe, the carrier shall not have the benefit of this paragraph. Amounts so deposited in the reequipment fund shall not be included as part of the carrier's used and useful investment for purposes of section 406 until expended as provided above: *Provided*, That the flight equipment in which said gains may be invested shall not include equipment delivered to the carrier prior to April 6, 1956: *Provided further*, That the provisions of this subsection shall be effective as to all capital gains or losses realized on and after April 6, 1956, with respect to the sale or other disposition of flight equipment whether or not the Board shall have entered a final order taking account thereof in determining all other revenue of the air carrier.

Statement of Postmaster General and Carrier

(e) Any petition for the fixing of fair and reasonable rates of compensation under this section shall include a statement of the rate the petitioner believes to be fair and reasonable. The Postmaster General shall introduce as part of the record in all proceedings under this section a comprehensive statement of all service to be required of the air carrier and such other information in his possession as may be deemed by the Board to be material to the inquiry.

Weighing of Mail

(f) The Postmaster General may weigh the mail transported by aircraft and make such computations for statistical and administrative purposes as may be required in the interest of the mail service. The Postmaster General is authorized to employ such clerical and other assistance as may be required in connection with proceedings under this Act. If the Board shall determine that it is necessary or advisable, in order to carry out the provisions of this Act, to have additional and more frequent weighing of the mails, the Postmaster General, upon request of the Board shall provide therefor in like manner, but such weighing need not be for continuous periods of more than thirty days.

Availability of Appropriations

(g) Except as otherwise provided in section 405(h), the unexpended balances of all appropriations for the transportation of mail by aircraft pursuant to contracts entered into under the Air Mail Act of 1934, as amended, and the unexpended balances of all appropriations available for the transportation of mail by aircraft in Alaska, shall be available, in addition to the purposes stated in such appropriations, for the payment of compensation by the Postmaster General, as provided in this Act, for the transportation of mail by aircraft, the facilities used and useful therefor, and the services connected therewith, between points in the continental United States or between points in Hawaii or in Alaska or between points in the continental United States and points in Canada within one hundred and fifty miles of the international boundary line. Except as otherwise provided in section 405(h), the unexpended balances of all appropriations for the transportation of mail by aircraft pursuant to contracts entered into under the Act of March 8, 1928, as amended, shall be available, in addition to the purposes stated in such appropriations, for payment to be made by the Postmaster General, as provided by this Act, in respect of the transportation of mail by aircraft, the facilities used and useful therefor, and the services connected therewith, between points in the United States and points outside thereof, or between points in the continental United States and Territories or possessions of the United States, or between Territories or possessions of the United States.

Payments to Foreign Air Carriers

(h) In any case where air transportation is performed between the United States and any foreign country, both by aircraft owned or operated by one or more air carriers holding a certificate under this title and by aircraft owned or operated by one or more foreign air carriers, the Postmaster General shall not pay to or for the account of any such foreign air carrier a rate of compensation for transporting mail by aircraft between the United States and such foreign country, which, in his opinion, will result (over such reasonable period as the Postmaster General may determine, taking account of exchange fluctuations and other factors) in such foreign air carrier receiving a higher rate of compensation for transporting such mail than such foreign country pays to air carriers for transporting its mail by aircraft between such foreign country and the United States, or receiving a higher rate of compensation for transporting such mail than a rate determined by the Postmaster General to be comparable to the rate such foreign country pays to air carriers for transporting its mail by aircraft between such foreign country and intermediate country on the route of such air carrier between such foreign country and the United States.

ACCOUNTS, RECORDS, AND REPORTS

Filing of Reports

Sec. 407. [*72 Stat. 766, as amended by 83 Stat. 103, 49 U.S.C. 1377*] (a) The Board is empowered to require annual, monthly, periodical, and special reports from any air carrier; to prescribe the manner and form in which such reports shall be made; and to require from any air carrier specific answers to all questions upon which the Board may deem information to be necessary. Such reports shall be under oath whenever the Board so requires. The Board may also require any air carrier to file with it a true copy of each or any contract, agreement, understanding, or arrangement, between such air carrier and any other carrier or person, in relation to any traffic affected by the provisions of this Act.

Disclosure of Stock Ownership

(b) Each air carrier shall submit annually, and at such other times as the Board shall require, a list showing the names of each of its stockholders or members holding more than 5 per centum of the entire capital stock or capital, as the case may be, of such air carrier, together with the name of any person for whose account, if other than the holder, such stock is held; and a report setting forth a description of the shares of stock, or other interest, held by such air carrier, or for its account, in persons other than itself. Any person owning, beneficially or as trustee, more than 5 per centum of any class of the capital stock or capital, as the case may be, of an air carrier shall submit annually, and at such other times as the Board may require, a description of the shares of stock or other interest owned by such person, and the amount thereof.[11]

Disclosure of Stock Ownership by Officer or Director

(c) Each officer and director of an air carrier shall annually and at such other times as the Board shall require transmit to the Board a report describing the shares of stock or other interests held by him in any air carrier, any person engaged in any phase of aeronautics, or any common carrier, and in any person whose principal business, in purpose or in fact, is the holding of stock in, or control of, air carriers, other persons engaged in any phase of aeronautics, or common carriers.

Form of Accounts

(d) The Board shall prescribe the forms of any and all accounts, records, and memoranda to be kept by air carriers, including the accounts, records, and memoranda of the movement of traffic, as well as

---

[11] The Act of August 20, 1969, 83 Stat. 103, which added this sentence, provided that the amendment should take effect as of August 5, 1969.

of the receipts and expenditures of money, and the length of time such accounts, records, and memoranda shall be preserved; and it shall be unlawful for air carriers to keep any accounts, records, or memoranda other than those prescribed or approved by the Board: *Provided*, That any air carrier may keep additional accounts, records, or memoranda if they do not impair the integrity of the accounts, records, or memoranda prescribed or approved by the Board and do not constitute an undue financial burden on such air carrier.

Inspection of Accounts and Property

(e) The Board shall at all times have access to all lands, buildings, and equipment of any carrier and to all accounts, records, and memoranda, including all documents, papers, and correspondence, now or hereafter existing, and kept or required to be kept by air carriers; and it may employ special agents or auditors, who shall have authority under the orders of the Board to inspect and examine any and all such lands, buildings, equipment, accounts, records, and memoranda. The provisions of this section shall apply, to the extent found by the Board to be reasonably necessary for the administration of this Act, to persons having control over any air carrier, or affiliated with any air carrier within the meaning of section 5(8) of the Interstate Commerce Act, as amended.[12]

CONSOLIDATION, MERGER, AND ACQUISITION OF CONTROL

Acts Prohibited

SEC. 408. [*72 Stat. 767, as amended by 74 Stat. 901, 83 Stat. 103, 49 U.S.C. 1378*] (a) It shall be unlawful unless approved by order of the Board as provided in this section—

(1) For two or more air carriers, or for any air carrier and any other common carrier or any person engaged in any other phase of aeronautics, to consolidate or merge their properties, or any part thereof, into one person for the ownership, management, or operation of the properties theretofore in separate ownerships;

(2) For any air carrier, any person controlling an air carrier, any other common carrier, or any person engaged in any other phase of aeronautics, to purchase, lease, or contract to operate the properties, or any substantial part thereof, of any air carrier;

[12] [49 U.S.C. 5] Section 5(8) of the Interstate Commerce Act, as amended, relates to the jurisdiction of the district courts of the United States. Section 5(6) of the Interstate Commerce Act, as amended, is in substance the same as sec. 5(8) of the Interstate Commerce Act before it was restated by the Transportation Act of 1940, 54 Stat. 905, approved September 18, 1940, and is presumably the section to which reference was intended to be made. Section 5(6) provides: "For the purposes of this section a person shall be held to be affiliated with a carrier if, by reason of the relationship of such person to such carrier (whether by reason of the method of, or circumstances surrounding organization or operation, or whether established through common directors, officers, or stockholders, a voting trust or trusts, a holding or investment company or companies, or any other direct or indirect means), it is reasonable to believe that the affairs of any carrier of which control may be acquired by such person will be managed in the interest of such other carrier." Section 1(3)(b) provides: "For the purposes of section(s) 5, . . . , where reference is made to control (in referring to a relationship between any person or persons and another person or persons), such reference shall be construed to include actual as well as legal control, whether maintained or exercised through or by reason of the method of or circumstances surrounding organization or operation, through or by common directors, officers, or stockholders, a voting trust or trusts, a holding or investment company or companies, or through or by any other direct or indirect means; and to include the power to exercise control."

(3) For any air carrier or person controlling an air carrier to purchase, lease, or contract to operate the properties, or any substantial part thereof, of any person engaged in any phase of aeronautics otherwise than as an air carrier;

(4) For any foreign air carrier or person controlling a foreign air carrier to acquire control, in any manner whatsoever, of any citizen of the United States engaged in any phase of aeronautics;

(5) For any air carrier or person controlling an air carrier, any other common carrier, any person engaged in any other phase of aeronautics, or any other person to acquire control of any air carrier in any manner whatsoever: *Provided*, That the Board may by order exempt any such acquisition of a noncertificated air carrier from this requirement to the extent and for such periods as may be in the public interest; [13]

(6) For any air carrier or person controlling an air carrier to acquire control, in any manner whatsoever, of any person engaged in any phase of aeronautics otherwise than as an air carrier; or

(7) For any person to continue to maintain any relationship established in violation of any of the foregoing subdivisions of this subsection.

Power of Board

(b) Any person seeking approval of a consolidation, merger, purchase, lease, operating contract, or acquisition of control, specified in subsection (a) of this section, shall present an application to the Board, and thereupon the Board shall notify the persons involved in the consolidation, merger, purchase, lease, operating contract, or acquisition of control, and other persons known to have a substantial interest in the proceeding, of the time and place of a public hearing. Unless, after such hearing, the Board finds that the consolidation, merger, purchase, lease, operating contract, or acquisition of control will not be consistent with the public interest or that the conditions of this section will not be fulfilled, it shall by order approve such consolidation, merger, purchase, lease, operating contract, or acquisition of control, upon such terms and conditions as it shall find to be just and reasonable and with such modifications as it may prescribe: *Provided*, That the Board shall not approve any consolidation, merger, purchase, lease, operating contract, or acquisition of control which would result in creating a monopoly or monopolies and thereby restrain competition or jeopardize another air carrier not a party to the consolidation, merger, purchase, lease, operating contract, or acquisition of control: *Provided further*, That if the applicant is a carrier other than an air carrier, or a person controlled by a carrier other than an air carrier or affiliated therewith within the meaning of section 5(8) of the Interstate Commerce Act, as amended,[14] such applicant shall for the purposes of this section be considered an air carrier and the Board shall not enter such an order of approval unless it finds that the transaction proposed will promote the public interest by enabling such carrier other than an air carrier to use aircraft to

---

[13] The Act of August 20, 1969, 83 Stat. 103, which amended paragraph (5), provided that the amendment should take effect as of August 5, 1969.
[14] See footnote 12, *ante*.

public advantage in its operation and will not restrain competition: *Provided further,* That, in any case in which the Board determines that the transaction which is the subject of the application does not affect the control of an air carrier directly engaged in the operation of aircraft in air transportation, does not result in creating a monopoly, and does not tend to restrain competition, and determines that no person disclosing a substantial interest then currently is requesting a hearing, the Board, after publication in the Federal Register of notice of the Board's intention to dispose of such application without a hearing (a copy of which notice shall be furnished by the Board to the Attorney General not later than the day following the date of such publication), may determine that the public interest does not require a hearing and by order approve or disapprove such transaction.[15]

Interests in Ground Facilities

(c) The provisions of this section and section 409 shall not apply with respect to the acquisition or holding by any air carrier, or any officer or director thereof, of (1) any interest in any ticket office, landing area, hangar, or other ground facility reasonably incidental to the performance by such air carrier of any of its services, or (2) any stock or other interest or any office or directorship in any person whose principal business is the maintenance or operation of any such ticket office, landing area, hangar, or other ground facility.

Jurisdiction of Accounts of Noncarriers

(d) Whenever, after the effective date of this section, a person, not an air carrier, is authorized, pursuant to this section, to acquire control of an air carrier, such person thereafter shall, to the extent found by the Board to be reasonably necessary for the administration of this Act, be subject, in the same manner as if such person were an air carrier, to the provisions of this Act relating to accounts, records, and reports, and the inspection of facilities and records, including the penalties applicable in the case of violations thereof.

Investigation of Violations

(e) The Board is empowered, upon complaint or upon its own initiative, to investigate and, after notice and hearing, to determine whether any person is violating any provision of subsection (a) of this section. If the Board finds after such hearing that such person is violating any provision of such subsection, it shall by order require such person to take such action, consistent with the provisions of this Act, as may be necessary, in the opinion of the Board, to prevent further violation of such provision.

Presumption of Control

(f) For the purposes of this section, any person owning beneficially 10 per centum or more of the voting securities or capital, as the

---

[15] The Act of September 13, 1960, 74 Stat. 901, which adds this provision provides that it shall apply only with respect to applications submitted to the Civil Aeronautics Board on or after September 13, 1960.

[§ 409]

case may be, of an air carrier shall be presumed to be in control of such air carrier unless the Board finds otherwise. As used herein, beneficial ownership of 10 per centum of the voting securities of a carrier means ownership of such amount of its outstanding voting securities as entitles the holder thereof to cast 10 per centum of the aggregate votes which the holders of all the outstanding voting securities of such carrier are entitled to cast.[16]

PROHIBITED INTERESTS

Interlocking Relationships

SEC. 409. [*72 Stat. 768, 49 U.S.C. 1379*] (a) It shall be unlawful, unless such relationship shall have been approved by order of the Board upon due showing, in the form and manner prescribed by the Board, that the public interest will not be adversely affected thereby—

(1) For any air carrier to have and retain an officer or director who is an officer, director, or member, or who as a stockholder holds a controlling interest, in any other person who is a common carrier or is engaged in any phase of aeronautics.

(2) For any air carrier, knowingly and willfully, to have and retain an officer or director who has a representative or nominee who represents such officer or director as an officer, director, or member, or as a stockholder holding a controlling interest, in any other person who is a common carrier or is engaged in any phase of aeronautics.

(3) For any person who is an officer or director of an air carrier to hold the position of officer, director, or member, or to be a stockholder holding a controlling interest, or to have a representative or nominee who represents such person as an officer, director, or member, or as a stockholder holding a controlling interest, in any other person who is a common carrier or is engaged in any phase of aeronautics.

(4) For any air carrier to have and retain an officer or director who is an officer, director, or member, or who as a stockholder holds a controlling interest, in any person whose principal business, in purpose or in fact, is the holding of stock in, or control of, any other person engaged in any phase of aeronautics.

(5) For any air carrier, knowingly and willfully, to have and retain an officer or director who has a representative or nominee who represents such officer or director as an officer, director, or member, or as a stockholder holding a controlling interest, in any person whose principal business, in purpose or in fact, is the holding of stock in, or control of, any other person engaged in any phase of aeronautics.

(6) For any person who is an officer or director of an air carrier to hold the position of officer, director, or member, or to be a stockholder holding a controlling interest, or to have a representative or nominee who represents such person as an officer, director, or member, or as a stockholder holding a controlling interest, in any

---

[16] The Act of August 20, 1969, 83 Stat. 103, which added this subsection provided that the amendment should take effect as of August 5, 1969.

person whose principal business, in purpose or in fact, is the holding of stock in, or control of, any other person engaged in any phase of aeronautics.

Profit From Transfer of Securities

(b) It shall be unlawful for any officer or director of any air carrier to receive for his own benefit, directly or indirectly, any money or thing of value in respect of negotiation, hypothecation, or sale of any securities issued or to be issued by such carrier, or to share in any of the proceeds thereof.

LOANS AND FINANCIAL AID

SEC. 410. [*72 Stat. 769, as amended by 76 Stat. 936, 49 U.S.C. 1380*] The Board is empowered to approve or disapprove, in whole or in part, any and all applications made after the effective date of this section for or in connection with any loan or other financial aid from the United States or any agency thereof to, or for the benefit of, any air carrier. No such loan or financial aid shall be made or given without such approval, and the terms and conditions upon which such loan or financial aid is provided shall be prescribed by the Board. The provisions of this section shall not be applicable to the guaranty of loans by the Secretary of Commerce under the provisions of such Act of September 7, 1957, as amended, but the Secretary of Commerce shall consult with and consider the views and recommendations of the Board in making such guaranties.[17]

METHODS OF COMPETITION

SEC. 411. [*72 Stat. 769, 49 U.S.C. 1381*] The Board may, upon its own initiative or upon complaint by any air carrier, foreign air carrier, or ticket agent, if it considers that such action by it would be in the interest of the public, investigate and determine whether any air carrier, foreign air carrier, or ticket agent has been or is engaged in unfair or deceptive practices or unfair methods of competition in air transportation or the sale thereof. If the Board shall find, after notice and hearing, that such air carrier, foreign air carrier, or ticket agent is engaged in such unfair or deceptive practices or unfair methods of competition, it shall order such air carrier, foreign air carrier, or ticket agent to cease and desist from such practices or methods of competition.

POOLING AND OTHER AGREEMENTS

Filing of Agreements Required

SEC. 412. [*72 Stat. 770, 49 U.S.C. 1382*] (a) Every air carrier shall file with the Board a true copy, or, if oral, a true and complete memorandum, of every contract or agreement (whether enforceable by provisions for liquidated damages, penalties, bonds, or otherwise) affecting air transportation and in force on the effective date of this

---

[17] Functions, powers, and duties of the Secretary of Commerce under this section were transferred to the Secretary of Transportation by section 6(a)(3)(B) of the Department of Transportation Act (80 Stat. 937, 49 U.S.C. 1655).

section or hereafter entered into, or any modification or cancellation thereof, between such air carrier and any other air carrier, foreign air carrier, or other carrier for pooling or apportioning earnings, losses, traffic, service, or equipment, or relating to the establishment of transportation rates, fares, charges, or classifications, or for preserving and improving safety, economy, and efficiency of operation, or for controlling, regulating, preventing, or otherwise eliminating destructive, oppressive, or wasteful competition, or for regulating stops, schedules, and character of service, or for other cooperative working arrangements.

Approval by Board

(b) The Board shall by order disapprove any such contract or agreement, whether or not previously approved by it, that it finds to be adverse to the public interest, or in violation of this Act, and shall by order approve any such contract or agreement, or any modification or cancellation thereof, that it does not find to be adverse to the public interest, or in violation of this Act; except that the Board may not approve any contract or agreement between an air carrier not directly engaged in the operation of aircraft in air transportation and a common carrier subject to the Interstate Commerce Act, as amended, governing the compensation to be received by such common carrier for transportation services performed by it.

FORM OF CONTROL

SEC. 413. [*72 Stat. 770, 49 U.S.C. 1383*] For the purposes of this title, whenever reference is made to control, it is immaterial whether such control is direct or indirect.

LEGAL RESTRAINTS

SEC. 414. [*72 Stat. 770, 49 U.S.C. 1384*] Any person affected by any order made under sections 408, 409, or 412 of this Act shall be, and is hereby, relieved from the operations of the "antitrust laws", as designated in section 1 of the Act entitled "An Act to supplement existing laws against unlawful restraints and monopolies, and for other purposes", approved October 15, 1914, and of all other restraints or prohibitions made by, or imposed under, authority of law, insofar as may be necessary to enable such person to do anything authorized, approved, or required by such order.

INQUIRY INTO AIR CARRIER MANAGEMENT

SEC. 415. [*72 Stat. 770, 49 U.S.C. 1385*] For the purpose of exercising and performing its powers and duties under this Act, the Board is empowered to inquire into the management of the business of any air carrier and, to the extent reasonably necessary for any such inquiry, to obtain from such carrier, and from any person controlling or controlled by, or under common control with, such air carrier, full and complete reports and other information.

Classification

SEC. 416. [*72 Stat. 771, 49 U.S.C. 1386*] (a) The Board may from time to time establish such just and reasonable classifications or groups of air carriers for the purposes of this title as the nature of the services performed by such air carriers shall require; and such just and reasonable rules and regulations, pursuant to and consistent with the provisions of this title, to be observed by each such class or group, as the Board finds necessary in the public interest.

Exemptions

(b) (1) The Board, from time to time and to the extent necessary, may (except as provided in paragraph (2) of this subsection) exempt from the requirements of this title or any provision thereof, or any rule, regulation, term, condition, or limitation prescribed thereunder, any air carrier or class of air carriers, if it finds that the enforcement of this title or such provision, or such rule, regulation, term, condition, or limitation is or would be an undue burden on such air carrier or class of air carriers by reason of the limited extent of, or unusual circumstances affecting, the operations of such air carrier or class of air carriers and is not in the public interest.

(2) The Board shall not exempt any air carrier from any provision of subsection (k) of section 401 of this title, except that (A) any air carrier not engaged in scheduled air transportation, and (B), to the extent that the operations of such air carrier are conducted during daylight hours, any air carrier engaged in scheduled air transportation, may be exempted from the provisions of paragraphs (1) and (2) of such subsection if the Board finds, after notice and hearing, that, by reason of the limited extent of, or unusual circumstances affecting, the operations of any such air carrier, the enforcement of such paragraphs is or would be such an undue burden on such air carrier as to obstruct its development and prevent it from beginning or continuing operations, and that the exemption of such air carrier from such paragraphs would not adversely affect the public interest: *Provided*, That nothing in this subsection shall be deemed to authorize the Board to exempt any air carrier from any requirement of this title, or any provision thereof, or any rule, regulation, term, condition, or limitation prescribed thereunder which provides for maximum flying hours for pilots or copilots.

SPECIAL OPERATING AUTHORIZATIONS

Authority of Board to Issue

SEC. 417. [*76 Stat. 145, 49 U.S.C. 1387*] (a) If the Board finds upon an investigation conducted on its own initiative or upon request of an air carrier—

(1) that the capacity for air transportation being offered by the holder of a certificate of public convenience and necessity between particular points in the United States is, or will be,

temporarily insufficient to meet the requirements of the public or the postal service; or

(2) that there is a temporary requirement for air transportation between two points, one or both of which is not regularly served by any air carrier; and

(3) that any supplemental air carrier can provide the additional service temporarily required in the public interest; the Board may issue to such supplemental air carrier a special operating authorization to engage in air transportation between such points.

Terms of Authorization

(b) A special operating authorization issued under this section—

(1) shall contain such limitations or requirements as to frequency of service, size or type of equipment, or otherwise, as will assure that the service so authorized will alleviate the insufficiency which otherwise would exist, without significant diversion of traffic from the holders of certificates for the route;

(2) shall be valid for not more than thirty days and may be extended for additional periods aggregating not more than sixty days; and

(3) shall not be deemed a license within the meaning of section 9(b) of the Administrative Procedure Act (5 U.S.C. 1008(b)).

Procedure

(c) The Board shall by regulation establish procedures for the expeditious investigation and determination of requests for such special operating authorizations. Such procedures shall include written notice to air carriers certificated to provide service between the points involved, and shall provide for such opportunity to protest the application in writing, and at the Board's discretion to be heard orally in support of such protest, as will not unduly delay issuance of such special operating authorization, taking into account the degree of emergency involved.

TITLE V—NATIONALITY AND OWNERSHIP OF AIRCRAFT

REGISTRATION OF AIRCRAFT NATIONALITY

Registration Required

SEC. 501. [*72 Stat. 771, 49 U.S.C. 1401*] (a) It shall be unlawful for any person to operate or navigate any aircraft eligible for registration if such aircraft is not registered by its owner as provided in this section, or (except as provided in section 1108 of this Act) to operate or navigate within the United States any aircraft not eligible for registration: *Provided*, That aircraft of the national-defense forces of the United States may be operated and navigated without being so registered if such aircraft are identified, by the agency having jurisdiction over them, in a manner satisfactory to the Secretary of Transportation.* The Secretary of Transportation* may, by regulation, permit the operation and navigation of aircraft without registration by the owner for such reasonable periods after transfer of ownership thereof as the Secretary of Transportation* may prescribe.

Eligibility for Registration

(b) An aircraft shall be eligible for registration if, but only if—
(1) It is owned by a citizen of the United States and it is not registered under the laws of any foreign country; or
(2) It is an aircraft of the Federal Government, or of a State, Territory, or possession of the United States, or the District of Columbia, or of a political subdivision thereof.

Issuance of Certificate

(c) Upon request of the owner of any aircraft eligible for registration, such aircraft shall be registered by the Secretary of Transportation* and the Secretary of Transportation* shall issue to the owner thereof a certificate of registration.

Applications

(d) Applications for such certificates shall be in such form, be filed in such manner, and contain such information as the Secretary of Transportation* may require.

Suspension or Revocation

(e) Any such certificate may be suspended or revoked by the Secretary of Transportation* for any cause which renders the aircraft ineligible for registration.

Effect of Registration

(f) Such certificate shall be conclusive evidence of nationality for international purposes, but not in any proceeding under the laws of the United States. Registration shall not be evidence of ownership of aircraft in any proceeding in which such ownership by a particular person is, or may be, in issue.

REGISTRATION OF ENGINES, PROPELLERS, AND APPLIANCES

SEC. 502. [*72 Stat. 772, 49 U.S.C. 1402*] The Secretary of Transportation* may establish reasonable rules and regulations for registration and identification of aircraft engines, propellers, and appliances, in the interest of safety, and no aircraft engine, propeller, or appliance shall be used in violation of any such rule or regulation.

RECORDATION OF AIRCRAFT OWNERSHIP

Establishment of Recording System

SEC. 503. [*72 Stat. 772, as amended by 73 Stat. 180, 78 Stat. 236, 49 U.S.C. 1403*] (a) The Secretary of Transportation* shall establish and

*See footnote 1.

[§ 503]

maintain a system for the recording of each and all of the following:

(1) Any conveyance which affects the title to, or any interest in, any civil aircraft of the United States;

(2) Any lease, and any mortgage, equipment trust, contract of conditional sale, or other instrument executed for security purposes, which lease or other instrument affects the title to, or any interest in, any specifically identified aircraft engine or engines of seven hundred and fifty or more rated takeoff horsepower for each such engine or the equivalent of such horsepower, or any specifically identified aircraft propeller capable of absorbing seven hundred and fifty or more rated takeoff shaft horsepower, and also any assignment or amendment thereof or supplement thereto;

(3) Any lease, and any mortgage, equipment trust, contract of conditional sale, or other instrument executed for security purposes, which lease or other instrument affects the title to, or any interest in, any aircraft engines, propellers, or appliances maintained by or on behalf of an air carrier certificated under section 604(b) of this Act for installation or use in aircraft, aircraft engines, or propellers, or any spare parts maintained by or on behalf of such an air carrier, which instrument need only describe generally by types the engines, propellers, appliances, and spare parts covered thereby and designate the location or locations thereof; and also any assignment or amendment thereof or supplement thereto.

Recording of Releases

(b) The Secretary of Transportation* shall also record under the system provided for in subsection (a) of this section any release, cancellation, discharge, or satisfaction relating to any conveyance or other instrument recorded under said system.

Conveyances To Be Recorded

(c) No conveyance or instrument the recording of which is provided for by section 503(a) shall be valid in respect of such aircraft, aircraft engine or engines, propellers, appliances, or spare parts against any person other than the person by whom the conveyance or other instrument is made or given, his heir or devisee, or any person having actual notice thereof, until such conveyance or other instrument is filed for recordation in the office of the Secretary of Transportation*: *Provided*, That previous recording of any conveyance or instrument with the Administrator of the Civil Aeronautics Administration under the provisions of the Civil Aeronautics Act of 1938 shall have the same force and effect as though recorded as provided herein; and conveyances, the recording of which is provided for by section 503 (a) (1) made on or before August 21, 1938, and instruments, the recording of which is provided for by sections 503(a)(2) and 503 (a)(3) made on or before June 19, 1948, shall not be subject to the provisions of this subsection.

Effect of Recording

(d) Each conveyance or other instrument recorded by means of or under the system provided for in subsection (a) or (b) of this section

---

shall from the time of its filing for recordation be valid as to all persons without further or other recordation, except that an instrument recorded pursuant to section 503(a)(3) shall be effective only with respect to those of such items which may from time to time be situated at the designated location or locations and only while so situated: *Provided*, That an instrument recorded under section 503(a)(2) shall not be affected as to the engine or engines, or propeller or propellers, specifically identified therein, by any instrument theretofore or thereafter recorded pursuant to section 503(a)(3).

Form of Conveyances

(e) Except as the Secretary of Transportation* may by regulation prescribe, no conveyance or other instrument shall be recorded unless it shall have been acknowledged before a notary public or other officer authorized by the law of the United States, or of a State, territory, or possession thereof, or the District of Columbia, to take acknowledgment of deeds.

Index of Conveyances

(f) The Secretary of Transportation* shall keep a record of the time and date of the filing of conveyances and other instruments with him and of the time and date of recordation thereof. He shall record conveyances and other instruments filed with him in the order of their reception, in files to be kept for that purpose, and indexed according to—

(1) the identifying description of the aircraft, aircraft engine, or propeller, or in the case of an instrument referred to in section 503(a)(3), the location or locations specified therein; and

(2) the names of the parties to the conveyance or other instrument.

Regulations

(g) The Secretary of Transportation* is authorized to provide by regulation for the endorsement upon certificates of registration, or aircraft certificates, of information with respect to the ownership of the aircraft for which each certificate is issued, the recording of discharges and satisfactions of recorded instruments, and other transactions affecting title to or interest in aircraft, aircraft engines, propellers, appliances, or parts, and for such other records, proceedings, and details as may be necessary to facilitate the determination of the rights of parties dealing with civil aircraft of the United States, aircraft engines, propellers, appliances, or parts.

Previously Unrecorded Ownership

(h) The person applying for the issuance or renewal of an airworthiness certificate for an aircraft with respect to which there has been no recordation of ownership as provided in this section shall present with his application such information with respect to the ownership of the aircraft as the Secretary of Transportation* shall deem necessary to show the persons who are holders of property interests in such aircraft and the nature and extent of such interests.

LIMITATION OF SECURITY OWNERS LIABILITY

SEC. 504. *[72 Stat. 774, as amended by 73 Stat. 180, 49 U.S.C. 1404]*
No person having a security interest in, or security title to, any civil
aircraft, aircraft engine, or propeller under a contract of conditional
sale, equipment trust, chattel or corporate mortgage, or other instrument of similar nature, and no lessor of any such aircraft, aircraft
engine, or propeller under a bona fide lease of thirty days or more,
shall be liable by reason of such interest or title, or by reason of his
interest as lessor or owner of the aircraft, aircraft engine, or propeller
so leased, for any injury to or death of persons, or damage to or loss
of property, on the surface of the earth (whether on land or water)
caused by such aircraft, aircraft engine, or propeller, or by the ascent,
descent, or flight of such aircraft, aircraft engine, or propeller or by
the dropping or falling of an object therefrom, unless such aircraft,
aircraft engine, or propeller is in the actual possession or control of
such person at the time of such injury, death, damage, or loss.

DEALERS' AIRCRAFT REGISTRATION CERTIFICATES

SEC. 505. *[72 Stat. 774, 49 U.S.C. 1405]* The Secretary of Transportation* may, by such reasonable regulations as he may find to be
in the public interest, provide for the issuance, and for the suspension
or revocation, of dealers' aircraft registration certificates, and for
their use in connection with aircraft eligible for registration under
this Act by persons engaged in the business of manufacturing, distributing, or selling aircraft. Aircraft owned by holders of dealers'
aircraft registration certificates shall be deemed registered under this
Act to the extent that the Secretary of Transportation* may, by
regulation, provide. It shall be unlawful for any person to violate
any regulation, or any term, condition, or limitation contained in any
certificate, issued under this section.

LAW GOVERNING VALIDITY OF CERTAIN INSTRUMENTS

SEC. 506. *[Added by 78 Stat. 236, 49 U.S.C. 1406]* The validity of
any instrument the recording of which is provided for by section 503
of this Act shall be governed by the laws of the State, District of
Columbia, or territory or possession of the United States in which such
instrument is delivered, irrespective of the location or the place of
delivery of the property which is the subject of such instrument.
Where the place of intended delivery of such instrument is specified
therein, it shall constitute presumptive evidence that such instrument
was delivered at the place so specified.[18]

---

*See footnote 1.
[18] The Act of June 30, 1964, 78 Stat. 236, which added this section, provides that the
amendments made therein shall not (1) take precedence over the Convention on the
International Recognition of Rights in Aircraft (4 U.S.T. 1830) (see p. 495), or (2) be
applicable with respect to any instrument delivered before the date of enactment of such
Act.

TITLE VI—SAFETY REGULATION OF CIVIL AERONAUTICS

GENERAL SAFETY POWERS AND DUTIES

Minimum Standards; Rules and Regulations

SEC. 601. [*72 Stat. 775, 49 U.S.C. 1421*] (a) The Secretary of Transportation* is empowered and it shall be his duty to promote safety of flight of civil aircraft in air commerce by prescribing and revising from time to time:

(1) Such minimum standards governing the design, materials, workmanship, construction, and performance of aircraft, aircraft engines, and propellers as may be required in the interest of safety;

(2) Such minimum standards governing appliances as may be required in the interest of safety;

(3) Reasonable rules and regulations and minimum standards governing, in the interest of safety, (A) the inspection, servicing, and overhaul of aircraft, aircraft engines, propellers, and appliances; (B) the equipment and facilities for such inspection, servicing, and overhaul; and (C) in the discretion of the Secretary of Transportation,* the periods for, and the manner in, which such inspection, servicing, and overhaul shall be made, including provision for examinations and reports by properly qualified private persons whose examinations or reports the Secretary of Transportation* may accept in lieu of those made by its officers and employees;

(4) Reasonable rules and regulations governing the reserve supply of aircraft, aircraft engines, propellers, appliances, and aircraft fuel and oil, required in the interest of safety, including the reserve supply of aircraft fuel and oil which shall be carried in flight;

(5) Reasonable rules and regulations governing, in the interest of safety, the maximum hours or periods of service of airmen, and other employees, of air carriers; and

(6) Such reasonable rules and regulations, or minimum standards, governing other practices, methods, and procedure, as the Secretary of Transportation* may find necessary to provide adequately for national security and safety in air commerce.

Needs of Service To Be Considered; Classification of Standards, etc.

(b) In prescribing standards, rules, and regulations, and in issuing certificates under this title, the Secretary of Transportation* shall give full consideration to the duty resting upon air carriers to perform their services with the highest possible degree of safety in the public interest and to any differences between air transportation and other air commerce; and he shall make classifications of such standards, rules, regulations, and certificates appropriate to the differences between air transportation and other air commerce. The Secretary of Transportation* may authorize any aircraft, aircraft engine, propeller, or appliance, for which an aircraft certificate authorizing use thereof in air transportation has been issued, to be used in other air

---

*See footnote 1.

[§ 602]

commerce without the issuance of a further certificate. The Secretary of Transportation* shall exercise and perform his powers and duties under this Act in such manner as will best tend to reduce or eliminate the possibility of, or recurrence of, accidents in air transportation, but shall not deem himself required to give preference to either air transportation or other air commerce in the administration and enforcement of this title.

Exemptions

(c) The Secretary of Transportation* from time to time may grant exemptions from the requirements of any rule or regulation prescribed under this title if he finds that such action would be in the public interest.

AIRMAN CERTIFICATES

Power to Issue Certificate

SEC. 602. [72 Stat. 776, 49 U.S.C. 1422] (a) The Secretary of Transportation* is empowered to issue airman certificates specifying the capacity in which the holders thereof are authorized to serve as airmen in connection with aircraft.

Issuance of Certificate

(b) Any person may file with the Secretary of Transportation* an application for an airman certificate. If the Secretary of Transportation* finds, after investigation, that such person possesses proper qualifications for, and is physically able to perform the duties pertaining to, the position for which the airman certificate is sought, he shall issue such certificate, containing such terms, conditions, and limitations as to duration thereof, periodic or special examinations, tests of physical fitness, and other matters as the Secretary of Transportation* may determine to be necessary to assure safety in air commerce. Except in the case of persons whose certificates are, at the time of denial, under order of suspension or whose certificates have been revoked within one year of the date of such denial, any person whose application for the issuance or renewal of an airman certificate is denied may file with the Board* a petition for review of the Secretary of Transportation's* action. The Board shall thereupon assign such petition for hearing at a place convenient to the applicant's place of residence or employment. In the conduct of such hearing and in determining whether the airman meets the pertinent rules, regulations, or standards, the Board shall not be bound by findings of fact of the Secretary of Transportation.* At the conclusion of such hearing, the Board shall issue its decision as to whether the airman meets the pertinent rules, regulations, and standards and the Secretary of Transportation* shall be bound by such decision: *Provided*, That the Secretary of Transportation* may, in his discretion,

---

*See footnote 1.

[§ 603]

prohibit or restrict the issuance of airman certificates to aliens, or may make such issuance dependent on the terms of reciprocal agreements entered into with foreign governments.

Form and Recording of Certificate

(c) Each certificate shall be numbered and recorded by the Secretary of Transportation;* shall state the name and address of, and contain a description of, the person to whom the certificate is issued; and shall be entitled with the designation of the class covered thereby. Certificates issued to all pilots serving in scheduled air transportation shall be designated "airline transport pilot" of the proper class.

AIRCRAFT CERTIFICATES

Type Certificates

SEC. 603. [*72 Stat. 776, 49 U.S.C. 1423*] (a) (1) The Secretary of Transportation* is empowered to issue type certificates for aircraft, aircraft engines, and propellers; to specify in regulations the appliances for which the issuance of type certificates is reasonably required in the interest of safety; and to issue such certificates for appliances so specified.

(2) Any interested person may file with the Secretary of Transportation* an application for a type certificate for an aircraft, aircraft engine, propeller, or appliance specified in regulations under paragraph (1) of this subsection. Upon receipt of an application, the Secretary of Transportation* shall make an investigation thereof and may hold hearings thereon. The Secretary of Transportation* shall make, or require the applicant to make, such tests during manufacture and upon completion as the Secretary of Transportation* deems reasonably necessary in the interest of safety, including flight tests and tests of raw materials or any part or appurtenance of such aircraft, aircraft engine, propeller, or appliance. If the Secretary of Transportation* finds that such aircraft, aircraft engine, propeller, or appliance is of proper design, material, specification, construction, and performance for safe operation, and meets the minimum standards, rules, and regulations prescribed by the Secretary of Transportation,* he shall issue a type certificate therefor. The Secretary of Transportation* may prescribe in any such certificate the duration thereof and such other terms, conditions, and limitations as are required in the interest of safety. The Secretary of Transportation* may record upon any certificate issued for aircraft, aircraft engines, or propellers, a numerical determination of all of the essential factors relative to the performance of the aircraft, aircraft engine, or propeller for which the certificate is issued.

Production Certificate

(b) Upon application, and if it satisfactorily appears to the Secretary of Transportation* that duplicates of any aircraft, aircraft

*See footnote 1.

[§ 604]

engine, propeller, or appliance for which a type certificate has been issued will conform to such certificate, the Secretary of Transportation* shall issue a production certificate authorizing the production of duplicates of such aircraft, aircraft engines, propellers, or appliances. The Secretary of Transportation* shall make such inspection and may require such tests of any aircraft, aircraft engine, propeller, or appliance manufactured under a production certificate as may be necessary to assure manufacture of each unit in conformity with the type certificate or any amendment or modification thereof. The Secretary of Transportation* may prescribe in any such production certificate the duration thereof and such other terms, conditions, and limitations as are required in the interest of safety.

Airworthiness Certificate

(c) The registered owner of any aircraft may file with the Secretary of Transportation* an application for an airworthiness certificate for such aircraft. If the Secretary of Transportation* finds that the aircraft conforms to the type certificate therefor, and, after inspection, that the aircraft is in condition for safe operation, he shall issue an airworthiness certificate. The Secretary of Transporation* may prescribe in such certificate the duration of such certificate, the type of service for which the aircraft may be used, and such other terms, conditions, and limitations as are required in the interest of safety. Each such certificate shall be registered by the Secretary of Transportation* and shall set forth such information as the Secretary of Transportation* may deem advisable. The certificate number, or such other individual designation as may be required by the Secretary of Transportation,* shall be displayed upon each aircraft in accordance with regulations prescribed by the Secretary of Transportation.*

AIR CARRIER OPERATING CERTIFICATES

Power to Issue

SEC. 604. [*72 Stat. 778, 49 U.S.C. 1424*] (a) The Secretary of Transportation* is empowered to issue air carrier operating certificates and to establish minimum safety standards for the operation of the air carrier to whom any such certificate is issued.

Issuance

(b) Any person desiring to operate as an air carrier may file with the Secretary of Transportation* an application for an air carrier operating certificate. If the Secretary of Transportation* finds, after investigation, that such person is properly and adequately equipped and able to conduct a safe operation in accordance with the requirements of this Act and the rules, regulations, and standards prescribed thereunder, he shall issue an air carrier operating certificate to such

*See footnote 1.

person. Each air carrier operating certificate shall prescribe such terms, conditions, and limitations as are reasonably necessary to assure safety in air transportation, and shall specify the points to and from which, and the Federal airways over which, such person is authorized to operate as an air carrier under an air carrier operating certificate.

MAINTENANCE OF EQUIPMENT IN AIR TRANSPORTATION

Duty of Carriers and Airmen

SEC. 605. [*72 Stat. 778, 49 U.S.C. 1425*] (a) It shall be the duty of each air carrier to make, or cause to be made, such inspection, maintenance, overhaul, and repair of all equipment used in air transportation as may be required by this Act, or the orders, rules, and regulations of the Secretary of Transportation* issued thereunder. And it shall be the duty of every person engaged in operating, inspecting, maintaining, or overhauling equipment to observe and comply with the requirements of this Act relating thereto, and the orders, rules, and regulations issued thereunder.

Inspection

(b) The Secretary of Transportation* shall employ inspectors who shall be charged with the duty (1) of making such inspections of aircraft, aircraft engines, propellers, and appliances designed for use in air transportation, during manufacture, and while used by an air carrier in air transportation, as may be necessary to enable the Secretary of Transportation* to determine that such aircraft, aircraft engines, propellers, and appliances are in safe condition and are properly maintained for operation in air transportation; and (2) of advising and cooperating with each air carrier in the inspection and maintenance thereof by the air carrier. Whenever any inspector shall, in the performance of his duty, find that any aircraft, aircraft engine, propeller, or appliance, used or intended to be used by any air carrier in air transportation, is not in condition for safe operation, he shall so notify the carrier, in such form and manner as the Secretary of Transportation* may prescribe; and, for a period of five days thereafter, such aircraft, aircraft engine, propeller, or appliance shall not be used in air transportation, or in such manner as to endanger air transportation, unless found by the Secretary of Transportation* or his inspector to be in condition for safe operation.

AIR NAVIGATION FACILITY RATING

SEC. 606. [*72 Stat. 779, 49 U.S.C. 1426*] The Secretary of Transportation* is empowered to inspect, classify, and rate any air navigation facility available for the use of civil aircraft, as to its suitability for such use. The Secretary of Transportation* is empowered to issue a certificate for any such air navigation facility.

---

*See footnote 1.

AIR AGENCY RATING

SEC. 607. [*72 Stat. 779. 49 U.S.C. 1427*] The Secretary of Transportation* is empowered to provide for the examination and rating of (1) civilian schools giving instruction in flying or in the repair, alteration, maintenance, and overhaul of aircraft, aircraft engines, propellers, and appliances, as to the adequacy of the course of instruction, the suitability and airworthiness of the equipment, and the competency of the instructors; (2) repair stations or shops for the repair, alteration, maintenance, and overhaul of aircraft, aircraft engines, propellers, or appliances, as to the adequacy and suitability of the equipment, facilities, and materials for, and methods of, repair, alteration, maintenance, and overhaul of aircraft, aircraft engines, propellers, and appliances, and the competency of those engaged in the work or giving any instruction therein; and (3) such other air agencies as may, in his opinion, be necessary in the interest of the public. The Secretary of Transportation* is empowered to issue certificates for such schools, repair stations, and other agencies.

FORM OF APPLICATIONS

SEC. 608. [*72 Stat. 779, 49 U.S.C. 1428*] Applications for certificates under this title shall be in such form, contain such information, and be filed and served in such manner as the Secretary of Transportation* may prescribe, and shall be under oath whenever the Secretary of Transportation* so requires.

AMENDMENT, SUSPENSION, AND REVOCATION OF CERTIFICATES

SEC. 609. [*72 Stat. 779, 49 U.S.C. 1429*] The Secretary of Transportation* may, from time to time, reinspect any civil aircraft, aircraft engine, propeller, appliance, air navigation facility, or air agency, or may reexamine any civil airman. If, as a result of any such reinspection or reexamination, or if, as a result of any other investigation made by the Secretary of Transportation,* he determines that safety in air commerce or air transportation and the public interest requires, the Secretary of Transportation* may issue an order amending, modifying, suspending, or revoking, in whole or in part, any type certificate, production certificate, airworthiness certificate, airman certificate, air carrier operating certificate, air navigation facility certificate, or air agency certificate. Prior to amending, modifying, suspending, or revoking any of the foregoing certificates, the Secretary of Transportation* shall advise the holder thereof as to any charges or other reasons relied upon by the Secretary of Transportation* for his proposed action and, except in cases of emergency, shall provide the holder of such a certificate an opportunity to answer any charges and be heard as to why such certificate should not be amended, modified, suspended, or revoked. Any person whose certificate is affected by such an order of the Secretary of Transportation* under this section may appeal the Secretary of Transportation's* order to the Board* and the Board may, after notice and hearing, amend, modify, or reverse the Secretary of Transportation's* order if it finds that safety in air commerce or air transportation and the public interest do not require affirmation

*See footnote 1.

of the Secretary of Transportation's* order. In the conduct of its hearings the Board shall not be bound by findings of fact of the Secretary of Transportation.* The filing of an appeal with the Board shall stay the effectiveness of the Secretary of Transportation's* order unless the Secretary of Transportation* advises the Board that an emergency exists and safety in air commerce or air transportation requires the immediate effectiveness of his order, in which event the order shall remain effective and the Board shall finally dispose of the appeal within sixty days after being so advised by the Secretary of Transportation.* The person substantially affected by the Board's order may obtain judicial review of said order under the provisions of section 1006, and the Secretary of Transportation* shall be made a party to such proceedings.

PROHIBITIONS

Violations of Title

SEC. 610. [*72 Stat. 780, as amended by 84 Stat. 234, 49 U.S.C. 1430*]
(a) It shall be unlawful—

(1) For any person to operate in air commerce any civil aircraft for which there is not currently in effect an airworthiness certificate, or in violation of the terms of any such certificate;

(2) For any person to serve in any capacity as an airman in connection with any civil aircraft, aircraft engine, propeller or appliance used or intended for use, in air commerce without an airman certificate authorizing him to serve in such capacity, or in violation of any term, condition, or limitation thereof, or in violation of any order, rule, or regulation issued under this title;

(3) For any person to employ for service in connection with any civil aircraft used in air commerce an airman who does not have an airman certificate authorizing him to serve in the capacity for which he is employed;

(4) For any person to operate as an air carrier without an air carrier operating certificate, or in violation of the terms of any such certificate;

(5) For any person to operate aircraft in air commerce in violation of any other rule, regulation, or certificate of the Secretary of Transportation* under this title;

(6) For any person to operate a seaplane or other aircraft of United States registry upon the high seas in contravention of the regulations proclaimed by the President pursuant to section 1 of the Act entitled "An Act to authorize the President to proclaim regulations for preventing collisions at sea", approved October 11, 1951 (Public Law 172, Eighty-second Congress; 65 Stat. 406) ; [19]

(7) For any person holding an air agency or production certificate to violate any term, condition, or limitation thereof, or to violate any order, rule, or regulation under this title relating to the holder of such certificate; and

---

*See footnote 1.
[19] Repealed and superseded by Act of September 24, 1963 (Public Law 88–131, 77 Stat 194).

(8) For any person to operate an airport serving air carriers certificated by the Civil Aeronautics Board without an airport operating certificate, or in violation of the terms of any such certificate.[20]

Exemption of Foreign Aircraft and Airmen

(b) Foreign aircraft and airmen serving in connection therewith may, except with respect to the observance by such airmen of the air traffic rules, be exempted from the provisions of subsection (a) of this section, to the extent, and upon such terms and conditions, as may be prescribed by the Secretary of Transportation* as being in the interest of the public.

CONTROL AND ABATEMENT OF AIRCRAFT NOISE AND SONIC BOOM

Standards; Rules and Regulations [21]

SEC. 611. [*added by 82 Stat. 395, 49 U.S.C. 1431*] (a) In order to afford present and future relief and protection to the public from unnecessary aircraft noise and sonic boom, the Administrator of the Federal Aviation Administration, after consultation with the Secretary of Transportation, shall prescribe and amend standards for the measurement of aircraft noise and sonic boom and shall prescribe and amend such rules and regulations as he may find necessary to provide for the control and abatement of aircraft noise and sonic boom, including the application of such standards, rules, and regulations in the issuance, amendment, modification, suspension, or revocation of any certificate authorized by this title.

Considerations Determinative of Standards, Rules, and Regulations [21]

(b) In prescribing and amending standards, rules, and regulations under this section, the Administrator shall—

(1) consider relevant available data relating to aircraft noise and sonic boom, including the results of research, development, testing, and evaluation activities conducted pursuant to this Act and the Department of Transportation Act;

(2) consult with such Federal, State, and interstate agencies as he deems appropriate;

(3) consider whether any proposed standard, rule, or regulation is consistent with the highest degree of safety in air commerce or air transportation in the public interest;

(4) consider whether any proposed standard, rule, or regulation is economically reasonable, technologically practicable, and appropriate for the particular type of aircraft, aircraft engine, appliance, or certificate to which it will apply; and

(5) consider the extent to which such standard, rule, or regulation will contribute to carrying out the purposes of this section.

---

*See footnote 1.
[20] The Act of May 21, 1970, 84 Stat. 234, which added this paragraph, provided that the amendment should take effect upon the expiration of the two year period beginning on the date of enactment of the Act.
[21] Heading supplied.

[§§ 612, 701]

Modification, Suspension, or Revocation of Certificate [21]

(c) In any action to amend, modify, suspend, or revoke a certificate in which violation of aircraft noise or sonic boom standards, rules, or regulations is at issue, the certificate holder shall have the same notice and appeal rights as are contained in section 609, and in any appeal to the National Transportation Safety Board, the Board may amend, modify, or reverse the order of the Administrator if it finds that control or abatement of aircraft noise or sonic boom and the public interest do not require the affirmation of such order, or that such order is not consistent with safety in air commerce or air transportation.

AIRPORT OPERATING CERTIFICATES

Power to Issue

SEC. 612. [*added by 84 stat. 234*] (a) The Administrator is empowered to issue airport operating certificates to airports serving air carriers certificated by the Civil Aeronautics Board and to establish minimum safety standards for the operation of such airports.

Issuance

(b) Any person desiring to operate an airport serving air carriers certificated by the Civil Aeronautics Board may file with the Administrator an application for an airport operating certificate. If the Administrator finds, after investigation, that such person is properly and adequately equipped and able to conduct a safe operation in accordance with the requirements of this Act and the rules, regulations, and standards prescribed thereunder, he shall issue an airport operating certificate to such person. Each airport operating certificate shall prescribe such terms, conditions, and limitations as are reasonably necessary to assure safety in air transportation, including but not limited to, terms, conditions, and limitations relating to—

(1) the installation, operation, and maintenance of adequate air navigation facilities; and

(2) the operation and maintenance of adequate safety equipment, including firefighting and rescue equipment capable of rapid access to any portion of the airport used for the landing, takeoff, or surface maneuvering of aircraft.

TITLE VII—AIRCRAFT ACCIDENT INVESTIGATION

ACCIDENTS INVOLVING CIVIL AIRCRAFT

General Duties

SEC. 701. [*72 Stat. 781, as amended by 76 Stat. 921, 49 U.S.C. 1441*]
(a) It shall be the duty of the Board* to—

(1) Make rules and regulations governing notification and report of accidents involving civil aircraft;

(2) Investigate such accidents and report the facts, conditions, and circumstances relating to each accident and the probable cause thereof;

---

*See footnote 1.
[21] Heading supplied.

[§ 701]

(3) Make such recommendations to the Secretary of Transportation* as, in its opinion, will tend to prevent similar accidents in the future;

(4) Make such reports public in such form and manner as may be deemed by it to be in the public interest; and

(5) Ascertain what will best tend to reduce or eliminate the possibility of, or recurrence of, accidents by conducting special studies and investigations on matters pertaining to safety in air navigation and the prevention of accidents.

Temporary Personnel

(b) The Board* may, without regard to the civil-service laws, engage, for temporary service in the investigation of any accident involving aircraft, persons other than officers or employees of the United States and may fix their compensation without regard to the Classification Act of 1949, as amended; and may, with consent of the head of the executive department or independent establishment under whose jurisdiction the officer or employee is serving, secure for such service any officer or employee of the United States.

Conduct of Investigations

(c) In conducting any hearing or investigation, any member of the Board* or any officer or employee of the Board or any person engaged or secured under subsection (b) shall have the same powers as the Board has with respect to hearings or investigations conducted by it.

In carrying out its duties under this title, the Board* is authorized to examine and test to the extent necessary any civil aircraft, aircraft engine, propeller, appliance, or property aboard an aircraft involved in an accident in air commerce. In the case of any fatal accident, the Board is authorized to examine the remains of any deceased person aboard the aircraft at the time of the accident, who dies as a result of the accident, and to conduct autopsies or such other tests thereof as may be necessary to the investigation of the accident: *Provided*, That to the extent consistent with the needs of the accident investigation, provisions of local law protecting religious beliefs with respect to autopsies shall be observed.

Aircraft

(d) Any civil aircraft, aircraft engine, propeller, appliance, or property aboard an aircraft involved in an accident in air commerce, shall be preserved in accordance with, and shall not be moved except in accordance with, regulations prescribed by the Board.*

Use of Records and Reports as Evidence

(e) No part of any report or reports of the Board* relating to any accident or the investigation thereof, shall be admitted as evidence or used in any suit or action for damages growing out of any matter mentioned in such report or reports.

---

*See footnote 1.

Use of Agency in Accident Investigations

(f) Upon the request of the Board,* the Secretary of Transportation* is authorized to make investigations with regard to aircraft accidents and to report to the Board the facts, conditions, and circumstances thereof, and the Board is authorized to utilize such reports in making its determinations of probable cause under this title.

Participation by Agency

(g) In order to assure the proper discharge by the Secretary of Transportation* of his duties and responsibilities, the Board* shall provide for the appropriate participation of the Secretary of Transportation* and his representatives in any investigations conducted by the Board under this title: *Provided*, That the Secretary of Transportation* or his representatives shall not participate in the determination of probable cause by the Board under this title.

ACCIDENTS INVOLVING MILITARY AIRCRAFT

Sec. 702. [*72 Stat. 782, 49 U.S.C. 1442*] (a) In the case of accidents involving both civil and military aircraft, the Board* shall provide for participation in the investigation by appropriate military authorities.

(b) In the case of accidents involving solely military aircraft and in which a function of the Administrator is or may be involved, the military authorities shall provide for participation in the investigation by the Secretary of Transportation.*

(c) With respect to other accidents involving solely military aircraft, the military authorities shall provide the Secretary of Transportation* and the Board with any information with respect thereto which, in the judgment of the military authorities, would contribute to the promotion of air safety.

SPECIAL BOARDS OF INQUIRY

Sec. 703. [*72 Stat. 782, 49 U.S.C. 1443*] (a) In any accident which involves substantial questions of public safety in air transportation the Board* may establish a Special Board of Inquiry consisting of three members; one member of the Civil Aeronautics Board who shall act as Chairman of the Special Board of Inquiry; and two members representing the public who shall be appointed by the President upon notification of the creation of such Special Board of Inquiry by the Civil Aeronautics Board.

(b) Such public members of the Special Board of Inquiry shall be duly qualified by training and experience to participate in such inquiry and shall have no pecuniary interest in any aviation enterprise involved in the accident to be investigated.

(c) The Special Board of Inquiry when convened to investigate an accident certified to it by the Civil Aeronautics Board shall have all authority of the Civil Aeronautics Board as described in this title.

---

*See footnote 1.

[§§ 801–803]

TITLE VIII—OTHER ADMINISTRATIVE AGENCIES

THE PRESIDENT OF THE UNITED STATES

SEC. 801. [*72 Stat. 782, 49 U.S.C. 1461*] The issuance, denial, transfer, amendment, cancellation, suspension, or revocation of, and the terms, conditions, and limitations contained in, any certificate authorizing an air carrier to engage in overseas or foreign air transportation, or air transportation between places in the same Territory or possession, or any permit issuable to any foreign air carrier under section 402, shall be subject to the approval of the President. Copies of all applications in respect of such certificates and permits shall be transmitted to the President by the Board before hearing thereon, and all decisions thereon by the Board shall be submitted to the President before publication thereof.

THE DEPARTMENT OF STATE

SEC. 802. [*72 Stat. 783, 49 U.S.C. 1462*] The Secretary of State shall advise the Secretary of Transportation,* the Board, and the Secretary of Commerce, and consult with the Secretary of Transportation,* Board, or Secretary, as appropriate, concerning the negotiations of any agreement with foreign governments for the establishment or development of air navigation, including air routes and services.

WEATHER BUREAU

SEC. 803. [*72 Stat. 783, 49 U.S.C. 1463*] In order to promote safety and efficiency in air navigation to the highest possible degree, the Chief of the Weather Bureau, under the direction of the Secretary of Commerce, shall, in addition to any other functions or duties pertaining to weather information for other purposes, (1) make such observations, measurements, investigations, and studies of atmospheric phenomena, and establish such meteorological offices and stations, as are necessary or best suited for ascertaining, in advance, information concerning probable weather conditions; (2) furnish such reports, forecasts, warnings, and advices to the Secretary of Transportation,* and to such persons engaged in civil aeronautics as may be designated by the Secretary of Transportation,* and to such other persons as the Chief of the Weather Bureau may determine, and such reports shall be made in such manner and with such frequency as will best result in safety in and in facilitating air navigation; (3) cooperate with persons engaged in air commerce, or employees thereof, in meteorological service, establish and maintain reciprocal arrangements under which this provision is to be carried out and collect and disseminate weather reports available from aircraft in flight; (4) establish and coordinate the international exchanges of meteorological information required for the safety and efficiency or air navigation; (5) participate in the development of an international basic meteorological reporting network, including the establishment, operation, and maintenance of

---

*See footnote 1.

[§ 901]

reporting stations on the high seas, in polar regions, and in foreign countries in cooperation with other governmental agencies of the United States and the meteorological services of foreign countries and with persons engaged in air commerce; (6) coordinate meteorological requirements in the United States in order to maintain standard observations, promote efficient use of facilities and avoid duplication of services unless such duplication tends to promote the safety and efficiency of air navigation; and (7) promote and develop meteorological science and foster and support research projects in meteorology through the utilization of private and governmental research facilities and provide for the publication of the results of such research projects unless such publications would be contrary to the public interest.

TITLE IX—PENALTIES [22]

CIVIL PENALTIES

Safety, Economic, and Postal Offenses

SEC. 901. [*72 Stat. 783, as amended by 76 Stat. 149, 49 U.S.C. 1471*] (a) (1) Any person who violates (A) any provision of title III, IV, V, VI, VII, or XII of this Act, or any rule, regulation, or order issued thereunder, or under section 1002(i), or any term, condition, or limitation of any permit or certificate issued under title IV, or (B) any rule or regulation issued by the Postmaster General under this Act, shall be subject to a civil penalty of not to exceed $1,000 for each such violation. If such violation is a continuing one, each day of such violation shall constitute a separate offense: *Provided*, That this subsection shall not apply to members of the Armed Forces of the United States, or those civilian employees of the Department of Defense who are subject to the provisions of the Uniform Code of Military Justice, while engaged in the performance of their official duties; and the appropriate military authorities shall be responsible for taking any necessary disciplinary action with respect thereto and for making to the Secretary of Transportation* or Board, as appropriate, a timely report of any such action taken.

(2) Any such civil penalty may be compromised by the Secretary of Transportation* in the case of violations of titles III, V, VI, or XII, or any rule, regulation, or order issued thereunder, or by the Board in the case of violations of titles IV or VII, or any rule, regulation, or order issued thereunder, or under section 1002(i), or any term, condition, or limitation of any permit or certificate issued under title IV, or by the Postmaster General in the case of regulations issued by him. The amount of such penalty, when finally determined, or the amount agreed upon in compromise, may be deducted from any sums owing by the United States to the person charged.

---

*See footnote 1.
[22] Under this title, the penalties provided herein are applicable to violations of statutes or regulations administered by the Civil Aeronautics Board, the Secretary of Transportation, and the National Transportation Safety Board (see footnote 1,). Thus, whether a reference to "Board" means the "Civil Aeronautics Board" or the "National Transportation Safety Board" will depend upon whether the matters involved concern one or both of such agencies. As previously indicated, "Secretary of Transportation" is substituted for "Administrator", except where the context requires otherwise (see footnote 1,).

Liens

(b) In case an aircraft is involved in such violation and the violation is by the owner or person in command of the aircraft, such aircraft shall be subject to lien for the penalty: *Provided,* That this subsection shall not apply to a violation of a rule or regulation of the Postmaster General.

CRIMINAL PENALTIES

General

SEC. 902. [*72 Stat. 784, as amended by 75 Stat. 466, 76 Stat. 150, 76 Stat. 921, 84 Stat. 921, 49 U.S.C. 1472*] (a) Any person who knowingly and willfully violates any provision of this Act (except titles III, V, VI, VII, and XII), or any order, rule, or regulation issued by the Secretary of Transportation* or by the Board under any such provision or any term, condition, or limitation of any certificate or permit issued under title IV, for which no penalty is otherwise provided in this section or in section 904, shall be deemed guilty of a misdemeanor and upon conviction thereof shall be subject for the first offense to a fine of not more than $500, and for any subsequent offense to a fine of not more than $2,000. If such violation is a continuing one, each day of such violation shall constitute a separate offense.

Forgery of Certificates and False Marking of Aircraft

(b) Any person who knowingly and willfully forges, counterfeits, alters, or falsely makes any certificate authorized to be issued under this Act, or knowingly uses or attempts to use any such fraudulent certificate, and any person who knowingly and willfully displays or causes to be displayed on any aircraft, any marks that are false or misleading as to the nationality or registration of the aircraft, shall be subject to a fine of not exceeding $1,000 or to imprisonment not exceeding three years, or to both such fine and imprisonment.

Interference With Air Navigation

(c) A person shall be subject to a fine of not exceeding $5,000 or to imprisonment not exceeding five years, or to both such fine and imprisonment, who—

(1) with intent to interfere with air navigation within the United States, exhibits within the United States any light or signal at such place or in such manner that it is likely to be mistaken for a true light or signal established pursuant to this Act, or for a true light or signal in connection with an airport or other air navigation facility; or

(2) after due warning by the Secretary of Transportation,* continues to maintain any misleading light or signal; or

(3) knowingly removes, extinguishes, or interferes with the operation of any such true light or signal.

---

*See footnote 22.

Granting Rebates

(d) Any air carrier, foreign air carrier, or ticket agent, or any officer, agent, employee, or representative thereof, who shall, knowingly and willfully, offer, grant, or give, or cause to be offered, granted, or given, any rebate or other concession in violation of the provisions of this Act, or who, by any device or means, shall, knowingly and willfully, assist, or shall willingly suffer or permit, any person to obtain transportation or services subject to this Act at less than the rates, fares, or charges lawfully in effect, shall be deemed guilty of a misdemeanor and, upon conviction thereof, shall be subject for each offense to a fine of not less than $100 and not more than $5,000.

Failure to File Reports; Falsification of Records

(e) Any air carrier, or any officer, agent, employee, or representative thereof, who shall, knowingly and willfully, fail or refuse to make a report to the Board or Secretary of Transportation* as required by this Act, or to keep or preserve accounts, records, and memoranda in the form and manner prescribed or approved by the Board or Secretary of Transportation,* or shall, knowingly and willfully, falsify, mutilate, or alter any such report, account, record, or memorandum, or shall knowingly and willfully file any false report, account, record, or memorandum, shall be deemed guilty of a misdemeanor and, upon conviction thereof, be subject for each offense to a fine of not less than $100 and not more than $5,000.

Divulging Information

(f) If the Secretary of Transportation* or any member of the Board,* or any officer or employee of either, shall knowingly and willfully divulge any fact or information which may come to his knowledge during the course of an examination of the accounts, records, and memoranda of any air carrier, or which is withheld from public disclosure under section 1104, except as he may be directed by the Secretary of Transportation* or the Board in the case of information ordered to be withheld by either, or by a court of competent jurisdiction or a judge thereof, he shall upon conviction thereof be subject for each offense to a fine of not more than $5,000 or imprisonment for not more than two years, or both: *Provided*, That nothing in this section shall authorize the withholding of information by the Secretary of Transportation* or Board from the duly authorized committees of the Congress.

Refusal to Testify

(g) Any person who shall neglect or refuse to attend and testify, or to answer any lawful inquiry, or to produce books, papers, or documents, if in his power to do so, in obedience to the subpena or lawful requirement of the Board* or Secretary of Transportation,* shall

*See footnote 22.

[§ 902]

be guilty of a misdemeanor and, upon conviction thereof, shall be subject to a fine of not less than $100 nor more than $5,000, or imprisonment for not more than one year, or both.

Transportation of Explosives and Other Dangerous Articles [23]

(h) (1) Any person who knowingly delivers or causes to be delivered to an air carrier or to the operator of any civil aircraft for transportation in air commerce, or who causes the transportation in air commerce of, any shipment, baggage, or property, the transportation of which would be prohibited by any rule, regulation, or requirement prescribed by the Secretary of Transportation* under title VI of this Act, relating to the transportation, packing, marking, or description of explosives or other dangerous articles shall, upon conviction thereof for each such offense, be subject to a fine of not more than $1,000, or to imprisonment not exceeding one year, or to both such fine and imprisonment: *Provided*, That when death or bodily injury of any person results from an offense punishable under this subsection, the person or persons convicted thereof shall, in lieu of the foregoing penalty, be subject to a fine of not more than $10,000 or to imprisonment not exceeding ten years, or to both such fine and imprisonment.

(2) In the exercise of his authority under title VI of this Act, the Secretary of Transportation* may provide by regulation for the application in whole or in part of the rules or regulations of the Interstate Commerce Commission (including future amendments and additions thereto) relating to the transportation, packing, marking, or description of explosives or other dangerous articles for surface transportation, to the shipment and carriage by air of such articles.[24] Such applicability may be terminated by the Secretary of Transportation* at any time. While so made applicable, any such rule or regulation, or part thereof, of the Interstate Commerce Commission shall for the purposes of this Act be deemed to be a regulation of the Secretary of Transportation* prescribed under title VI.

Aircraft Piracy

(i) (1) Whoever commits or attempts to commit aircraft piracy, as herein defined, shall be punished—

(A) by death if the verdict of the jury shall so recommend, or, in the case of a plea of guilty, or a plea of not guilty where the defendant has waived a trial by jury, if the court in its discretion shall so order; or

(B) by imprisonment for not less than twenty years, if the death penalty is not imposed.

(2) As used in this subsection, the term "aircraft piracy" means any seizure or exercise of control, by force or violence or threat of

---

* See footnote 22.
[23] See also Act of July 14, 1956, 70 Stat. 538, p. 272, which amends Title 18, U.S.C., to provide penalties for the willful damaging or destroying of aircraft or motor vehicles, and their facilities.
[24] Functions, powers, and duties of the Interstate Commerce Commission under section 831–835 of title 18, United States Code, as amended, relating generally to explosives and other dangerous articles, were transferred by section 6(e)(4) of the Department of Transportation Act (80 Stat. 939, 49 U.S.C. 1655) to the Secretary of Transportation.

force or violence and with wrongful intent, of an aircraft within the special aircraft jurisdiction of the United States.

Interference With Flight Crew Members or Flight Attendants

(j) Whoever, while aboard an aircraft within the special aircraft jurisdiction of the United States, assaults, intimidates, or threatens any flight crew member or flight attendant (including any steward or stewardess) of such aircraft, so as to interfere with the performance by such member or attendant of his duties or lessen the ability of such member or attendant to perform his duties, shall be fined not more than $10,000 or imprisoned not more than twenty years, or both. Whoever in the commission of any such act uses a deadly or dangerous weapon shall be imprisoned for any term of years or for life.

Certain Crimes Aboard Aircraft in Flight

(k) (1) Whoever, while aboard an aircraft within the special aircraft jurisdiction of the United States, commits an act which, if committed within the special maritime and territorial jurisdiction of the United States, as defined in section 7 of title 18, United States Code, would be in violation of section 113, 114, 661, 662, 1111, 1112, 1113, 2031, 2032, or 2111 of such title 18 shall be punished as provided therein.

(2) Whoever, while aboard an aircraft within the special aircraft jurisdiction of the United States, commits an act, which, if committed in the District of Columbia would be in violation of section 9 of the Act entitled "An Act for the preservation of the public peace and the protection of property within the District of Columbia," approved July 29, 1892, as amended (D.C. Code, sec. 22–1112), shall be punished as provided therein.

Carrying Weapons Aboard Aircraft

(l) Except for law enforcement officers of any municipal or State government, or the Federal Government, who are authorized or required to carry arms, and except for such other persons as may be so authorized under regulations issued by the Secretary of Transportation,* whoever, while aboard an aircraft being operated by an air carrier in air transportation, has on or about his person a concealed deadly or dangerous weapon, or whoever attempts to board such an aircraft while having on or about his person a concealed deadly or dangerous weapon, shall be fined not more than $1,000 or imprisoned not more than one year, or both.

False Information

(m) (1) Whoever imparts or conveys or causes to be imparted or conveyed false information, knowing the information to be false, concerning an attempt or alleged attempt being made or to be made,

*See footnote 22.

317

[§ 903]

to do any act which would be a crime prohibited by subsection (i), (j), (k), or (l) of this section, shall be fined not more than $1,000 or imprisoned not more than one year, or both.

(2) Whoever willfully and maliciously, or with reckless disregard for the safety of human life, imparts or conveys or causes to be imparted or conveyed false information, knowing the information to be false, concerning an attempt or alleged attempt being made or to be made, to do any act which would be a crime prohibited by subsection (i), (j), (k), or (l) of this section, shall be fined not more than $5,000 or imprisoned not more than five years, or both.

Investigations by Federal Bureau of Investigation

(n) Violations of subsections (i) through (m), inclusive, of this section shall be investigated by the Federal Bureau of Investigation of the Department of Justice.

Interference With Aircraft Accident Investigation

(o) Any person who knowingly and without authority removes, conceals, or withholds any part of a civil aircraft involved in an accident, or any property which was aboard such aircraft at the time of the accident, shall be subject to a fine of no less than $100 nor more than $5,000, or imprisonment for not more than one year, or both.

VENUE AND PROSECUTION OF OFFENSES

Venue

SEC. 903. [*72 Stat. 786, as amended by 75 Stat. 467, 49 U.S.C. 1473*] (a) The trial of any offense under this Act shall be in the district in which such offense is committed; or, if the offense is committed out of the jurisdiction of any particular State or district, the trial shall be in the district where the offender, or any one of two or more joint offenders, is arrested or is first brought. If such offender or offenders are not so arrested or brought into any district, an indictment or information may be filed in the district of the last known residence of the offender or of any one of two or more joint offenders, or if no such residence is known the indictment or information may be filed in the District of Columbia. Whenever the offense is begun in one jurisdiction and completed in another, or committed in more than one jurisdiction, it may be dealt with, inquired of, tried, determined, and punished in any jurisdiction in which such offense was begun, continued, or completed, in the same manner as if the offense had been actually and wholly committed therein.

Procedure in Respect of Civil Penalties

(b)(1) Any civil penalty imposed under this Act may be collected by proceedings in personam against the person subject to the penalty and, in case the penalty is a lien, by proceedings in rem against the aircraft, or by either method alone. Such proceedings shall conform as nearly as may be to civil suits in admiralty, except that either party may demand trial by jury of any issue of fact, if the value in controversy exceeds $20, and the facts so tried shall not be reexamined other than in accordance with the rules of the common law. The fact that in a libel in rem the seizure is made at a place not upon the high seas or navigable waters of the United States shall not be held in any way to limit the requirement of the conformity of the proceedings to civil suits in rem in admiralty.

(2) Any aircraft subject to such lien may be summarily seized by and placed in the custody of such persons as the Board or Secretary of Transportation* may by regulation prescribe, and a report of the cause shall thereupon be transmitted to the United States attorney for the judicial district in which the seizure is made. The United States attorney shall promptly institute proceedings for the enforcement of the lien or notify the Board* or Secretary of Transportation* of his failure to so act.

(3) The aircraft shall be released from such custody upon payment of the penalty or the amount agreed upon in compromise; or seizure in pursuance of process of any court in proceedings in rem for enforcement of the lien, or notification by the United States attorney of failure to institute such proceedings; or deposit of a bond in such amount and with such sureties as the Board or Secretary of Transportation* may prescribe, conditioned upon the payment of the penalty or the amount agreed upon in compromise.

(4) The Supreme Court of the United States, and under its direction other courts of the United States, may prescribe rules regulating such proceedings in any particular not provided by law.

VIOLATIONS OF SECTION 1109

SEC. 904. [*72 Stat. 787, 49 U.S.C. 1474*] (a) Any person who (1) violates any entry or clearance regulation made under section 1109(c) of this Act, or (2) any immigration regulations made under such section, shall be subject to a civil penalty of $500 which may be remitted or mitigated by the Secretary of the Treasury, or the Attorney General, respectively, in accordance with such proceedings as the Secretary or Attorney General shall by regulation prescribe Any person violating any customs regulation made under section 1109(b) of this Act, or any provision of the customs or public-health laws or regulations thereunder made applicable to aircraft by regulation under such section shall be subject to a civil penalty of $500, and any aircraft used in connection with any such violation shall be subject to seizure and forfeiture as provided for in such customs laws, which penalty and forfeiture may be remitted or mitigated by the Secretary of the Treasury. In case the violation is by the owner or person in command of the aircraft, the penalty shall be a lien against the aircraft. Any person violating any provision of the laws and regulations relating to animal and plant quarantine made applicable to civil air navigation by regulation in accordance with section 1109(d) of this Act shall be subject to the same penalties as those provided by the said laws for

---

*See footnote 22.

[§ 1001]

violations thereof. Any civil penalty imposed under this section may
be collected by proceedings in personam against the person subject to
the penalty and/or in case the penalty is a lien, by proceedings in rem
against the aircraft. Such proceedings shall conform as nearly as
may be to civil suits in admiralty; except that either party may demand
trial by jury of any issue of fact, if the value in controversy exceeds
$20, and facts so tried shall not be reexamined other than in accordance
with the rules of the common law. The fact that in a libel in rem
the seizure is made at a place not upon the high seas or navigable
waters of the United States, shall not be held in any way to limit the
requirement of the conformity of the proceedings to civil suits in rem
in admiralty. The Supreme Court of the United States, and under
its direction other courts of the United States, are authorized to prescribe rules regulating such proceedings in any particular not provided
by law. The determination under this section as to the remission
or mitigation of a civil penalty imposed under this section shall be
final. In case libel proceedings are pending at any time during the
pendency of remission or mitigation proceedings, the Secretary or
Attorney General shall give notice thereof to the United States
attorney prosecuting the libel proceedings.

(b) Any aircraft subject to a lien for any civil penalty imposed
under this section may be summarily seized by and placed in the custody of such persons as the appropriate Secretary or Attorney General may by regulation prescribe and a report of the case thereupon
transmitted to the United States attorney for the judicial district in
which the seizure is made. The United States attorney shall promptly
institute proceedings for the enforcement of the lien or notify the
Secretary of his failure so to act. The aircraft shall be released from
such custody upon (1) payment of the penalty or so much thereof as
is not remitted or mitigated, (2) seizure in pursuance of process of
any court in proceedings in rem for enforcement of the lien, or notification by the United States attorney of failure to institute such
proceedings, or (3) deposit of a bond in such amount and with such
sureties as the Secretary or Attorney General may prescribe, conditioned upon the payment of the penalty or so much thereof as is not
remitted or mitigated.

TITLE X—PROCEDURE [25]

CONDUCT OF PROCEEDINGS

SEC. 1001. [*72 Stat. 788, 49 U.S.C. 1481*] The Board and the Secretary of Transportation,* subject to the provisions of this Act and
the Administrative Procedure Act, may conduct their proceedings in
such manner as will be conducive to the proper dispatch of business

---

*See footnote 1.

[25] The provisions of this title are applicable to the procedural and substantive aspects
of the work of the Civil Aeronautics Board, the Administrator of the Federal Aviation
Administration and the National Transportation Safety Board, including judicial review
of administrative orders and the like (see footnote 1.). Thus, whether the term
"Board" means the "Civil Aeronautics Board" or the "National Transportation Safety
Board," or both, in a particular instance will depend upon whether the work involved
is that of one or both of such agencies. As previously indicated, "Secretary of Transportation" is substituted for "Administrator", except where the context requires otherwise
(see footnote 1,).

[§ 1002]

and to the ends of justice. No member of the Board or Administration* shall participate in any hearing or proceeding in which he has a pecuniary interest. Any person may appear before the Board or Administration* and be heard in person or by attorney. The Board, in its discretion, may enter its appearance and participate as an interested party in any proceeding conducted by the Secretary of Transportation* under title III of this Act, and in any proceeding conducted by the Secretary of Transportation* under title VI of this Act from which no appeal is provided to the Board. Every vote and official act of the Board and the Administration* shall be entered of record, and the proceedings thereof shall be open to the public upon request of any interested party, unless the Board or the Secretary of Transportation* determines that secrecy is requisite on grounds of national defense.

COMPLAINTS TO AND INVESTIGATIONS BY THE SECRETARY OF TRANSPORTA-
TION* AND THE BOARD

Filing of Complaints Authorized

SEC. 1002. [*72 Stat. 788, 49 U.S.C. 1482*] (a) Any person may file with the Secretary of Transportation* or the Board,* as to matters within their respective jurisdictions, a complaint in writing with respect to anything done or omitted to be done by any person in contravention of any provisions of this Act, or of any requirement established pursuant thereto. If the person complained against shall not satisfy the complaint and there shall appear to be any reasonable ground for investigating the complaint, it shall be the duty of the Secretary of Transportation* or the Board to investigate the matters complained of. Whenever the Secretary of Transportation* or the Board is of the opinion that any complaint does not state facts which warrant an investigation or action, such complaint may be dismissed without hearing. In the case of complaints against a member of the Armed Forces of the United States acting in the performance of his official duties, the Secretary of Transportation* or the Board, as the case may be, shall refer the complaint to the Secretary of the department concerned for action. The Secretary shall, within ninety days after receiving such a complaint, inform the Secretary of Transportation* or the Board of his disposition of the complaint, including a report as to any corrective or disciplinary actions taken.

Investigations on Initiative of Secretary of Transportation* or Board

(b) The Secretary of Transportation* or Board,* with respect to matters within their respective jurisdictions, is empowered at any time to institute an investigation, on their own initiative, in any case and as to any matter or thing within their respective jurisdictions, concerning which complaint is authorized to be made to or before the Secretary of Transportation* or Board by any provision of this Act, or concerning which any question may arise under any of the provisions of this Act, or relating to the enforcement of any of the

*See footnote 1.

provisions of this Act. The Secretary of Transportation* or the Board shall have the same power to proceed with any investigation instituted on their own motion as though it had been appealed to by complaint.

Entry of Orders for Compliance With Act

(c) If the Secretary of Transportation* or the Board* finds, after notice and hearing, in any investigation instituted upon complaint or upon their own initiative, with respect to matters within their jurisdiction, that any person has failed to comply with any provision of this Act or any requirement established pursuant thereto, the Secretary of Transportation* or the Board shall issue an appropriate order to compel such person to comply therewith.

Power to Prescribe Rates and Practices of Air Carriers

(d) Whenever, after notice and hearing, upon complaint, or upon its own initiative, the Board* shall be of the opinion that any individual or joint rate, fare, or charge demanded, charged, collected or received by any air carrier for interstate or overseas air transportation, or any classification, rule, regulation, or practice affecting such rate, fare, or charge, or the value of the service thereunder, is or will be unjust or unreasonable, or unjustly discriminatory, or unduly preferential, or unduly prejudicial, the Board shall determine and prescribe the lawful rate, fare, or charge (or the maximum or minimum, or the maximum and minimum thereof) thereafter to be demanded, charged, collected, or received, or the lawful classification, rule, regulation, or practice thereafter to be made effective: *Provided*, That as to rates, fares, and charges for overseas air transportation, the Board shall determine and prescribe only a just and reasonable maximum or minimum, or maximum and minimum rate, fare, or charge.

Rule of Ratemaking

(e) In exercising and performing its powers and duties with respect to the determination of rates for the carriage of persons or property, the Board* shall take into consideration, among other factors—

(1) The effect of such rates upon the movement of traffic:

(2) The need in the public interest of adequate and efficient transportation of persons and property by air carriers at the lowest cost consistent with the furnishing of such service;

(3) Such standards respecting the character and quality of service to be rendered by air carriers as may be prescribed by or pursuant to law;

(4) The inherent advantages of transportation by aircraft; and

(5) The need of each air carrier for revenue sufficient to enable such air carrier, under honest, economical, and efficient management, to provide adequate and efficient air carrier service.

*See footnote 25.

Removal of Discrimination in Foreign Air Transportation

(f) Whenever, after notice and hearing, upon complaint, or upon its own initiative, the Board* shall be of the opinion that any individual or joint rate, fare, or charge demanded, charged, collected, or received by any air carrier or foreign air carrier for foreign air transportation, or any classification, rule, regulation, or practice affecting such rate, fare, or charge, or the value of the service thereunder, is or will be unjustly discriminatory, or unduly preferential, or unduly prejudicial, the Board may alter the same to the extent necessary to correct such discrimination, preference, or prejudice and make an order that the air carrier or foreign air carrier shall discontinue demanding, charging, collecting, or receiving any such discriminatory, preferential, or prejudicial rate, fare, or charge or enforcing any such discriminatory, preferential, or prejudicial classification, rule, regulation, or practice.

Suspension of Rates

(g) Whenever any air carrier shall file with the Board* a tariff stating a new individual or joint (between air carriers) rate, fare, or charge for interstate or overseas air transportation or any classification, rule, regulation, or practice affecting such rate, fare, or charge, or the value of the service thereunder, the Board is empowered, upon complaint or upon its own initiative, at once, and, if it so orders, without answer or other formal pleading by the air carrier, but upon reasonable notice, to enter upon a hearing concerning the lawfulness of such rate, fare, or charge, or such classification, rule, regulation, or practice; and pending such hearing and the decision thereon, the Board, by filing with such tariff, and delivering to the air carrier affected thereby, a statement in writing of its reasons for such suspension, may suspend the operation of such tariff and defer the use of such rate, fare, or charge, or such classification, rule, regulation, or practice, for a period of ninety days, and, if the proceeding has not been concluded and a final order made within such period, the Board may, from time to time, extend the period of suspension, but not for a longer period in the aggregate than one hundred and eighty days beyond the time when such tariff would otherwise go into effect; and, after hearing, whether completed before or after the rate, fare, charge, classification, rule, regulation, or practice goes into effect, the Board may make such order with reference thereto as would be proper in a proceeding instituted after such rate, fare, charge, classification, rule, regulation, or practice had become effective. If the proceeding has not been concluded and an order made within the period of suspension, the proposed rate, fare, charge, classification, rule, regulation, or practice shall go into effect at the end of such period: *Provided*, That this subsection shall not apply to any initial tariff filed by any air carrier.

Power to Prescribe Divisions of Rates

(h) Whenever, after notice and hearing, upon complaint or upon its own initiative, the Board* is of the opinion that the divisions of

*Means "Civil Aeronautics Board."   See footnote 25.

[§ 1003]

joint rates, fares, or charges for air transportation are or will be unjust, unreasonable, inequitable, or unduly preferential or prejudicial as between the air carriers or foreign air carriers parties thereto. the Board shall prescribe the just, reasonable, and equitable divisions thereof to be received by the several air carriers. The Board may require the adjustment of divisions between such air carriers from the date of filing the complaint or entry of order of investigation, or such other date subsequent thereto as the Board finds to be just, reasonable, and equitable.

Power to Establish Through Air Transportation Service

(i) The Board* shall, whenever required by the public convenience and necessity, after notice and hearing, upon complaint or upon its own initiative, establish through service and joint rates, fares, or charges (or the maxima or minima, or the maxima and minima thereof) for interstate or overseas air transportation, or the classifications, rules, regulations, or practices affecting such rates, fares, or charges, or the value of the service thereunder, and the terms and conditions under which such through service shall be operated: *Provided*, That as to joint rates, fares, and charges for overseas air transportation the Board shall determine and prescribe only just and reasonable maximum or minimum or maximum and minimum joint rates, fares, or charges.

JOINT BOARDS

Designation of Boards

SEC. 1003. [*72 Stat. 791, 49 U.S.C. 1483*] (a) The Board* and the Interstate Commerce Commission shall direct their respective chairmen to designate, from time to time, a like number of members of each to act as a joint board to consider and pass upon matters referred to such board as provided in subsection (c) of this section.

Through Service and Joint Rates

(b) Air carriers may establish reasonable through service and joint rates, fares, and charges with other common carriers; except that with respect to transportation of property, air carriers not directly engaged in the operation of aircraft in air transportation (other than companies engaged in the air express business) may not establish joint rates or charges, under the provisions of this subsection, with common carriers subject to the Interstate Commerce Act. In case of through service by air carriers and common carriers subject to the Interstate Commerce Act, it shall be the duty of the carriers parties thereto to establish just and reasonable rates, fares, or charges and just and reasonable classifications, rules, regulations, and practices affecting such rates, fares, or charges, or the value of the service thereunder, and if joint rates, fares, or charges shall have been established with respect to such through service, just, reasonable, and equitable divisions of such joint rates, fares, or charges as between the carriers partici-

---

*Means "Civil Aeronautics Board." See footnote 25.

pating therein. Any air carrier, and any common carrier subject to the Interstate Commerce Act, which is participating in such through service and joint rates, fares, or charges. shall include in its tariffs, filed with the Civil Aeronautics Board or the Interstate Commerce Commission, as the case may be, a statement showing such through service and joint rates, fares, or charges.

Jurisdiction of Boards

(c) Matters relating to such through service and joint rates, fares, or charges may be referred by the Board* or the Interstate Commerce Commission, upon complaint or upon its own initiative, to a joint board created as provided in subsection (a). Complaints may be made to the Interstate Commerce Commission or the Board with respect to any matter which may be referred to a joint board under this subsection.

Power of Boards

(d) With respect to matters referred to any joint board as provided in subsection (c), if such board finds, after notice and hearing, that any such joint rate, fare, or charge, or classification, rule, regulation, or practice, affecting such joint rate, fare, or charge or the value of the service thereunder is or will be unjust, unreasonable, unjustly discriminatory, or unduly preferential or prejudicial, or that any division of any such joint rate, fare, or charge, is or will be unjust, unreasonable, inequitable, or unduly preferential or prejudicial as between the carriers parties thereto, it is authorized and directed to take the same action with respect thereto as the Board is empowered to take with respect to any joint rate, fare, or charge, between air carriers, or any divisions thereof, or any classification, rule, regulation, or practice affecting such joint rate, fare, or charge or the value of the service thereunder.

Judicial Enforcement and Review

(e) Orders of the joint boards shall be enforceable and reviewable as provided in this Act with respect to orders of the Board.

EVIDENCE

Power to Take Evidence

SEC. 1004. [*72 Stat. 792, as amended by 84 Stat. 922, 49 U.S.C. 1484*] (a) Any member or examiner of the Board,* when duly designated by the Board for such purpose, may hold hearings, sign and issue subpenas, administer oaths, examine witnesses, and receive evidence at any place in the United States designated by the Board. In all cases heard by an examiner or a single member the Board shall hear or receive argument on request of either party.

Power to Issue Subpena

(b) For the purposes of this Act the Board* shall have the power to require by subpena the attendance and testimony of witnesses and the

---

*See footnote 25.

[§ 1004]
production of all books, papers, and documents relating to any matter under investigation. Witnesses summoned before the Board shall be paid the same fees and mileage that are paid witnesses in the courts of the United States.

Enforcement of Subpena

(c) The attendance of witnesses, and the production of books, papers, and documents, may be required from any place in the United States, at any designated place of hearing. In case of disobedience to a subpena, the Board,* or any party to a proceeding before the Board, may invoke the aid of any court of the United States in requiring attendance and testimony of witnesses and the production of such books, papers, and documents under the provisions of this section.

Contempt

(d) Any court of the United States within the jurisdiction of which an inquiry is carried on may, in case of contumacy or refusal to obey a subpena issued to any person, issue an order requiring such person to appear before the Board (and produce books, papers, or documents if so ordered) and give evidence touching the matter in question; and any failure to obey such order of the court may be punished by such court as a contempt thereof.

Deposition

(e) The Board* may order testimony to be taken by deposition in any proceeding or investigation pending before it, at any stage of such proceeding or investigation. Such depositions may be taken before any person designated by the Board and having power to administer oaths. Reasonable notice must first be given in writing by the party or his attorney proposing to take such deposition to the opposite party or his attorney of record, which notice shall state the name of the witness and the time and place of the taking of his deposition. Any person may be compelled to appear and depose, and to produce books, papers, or documents, in the same manner as witnesses may be compelled to appear and testify and produce like documentary evidence before the Board, as hereinbefore provided.

Method of Taking Depositions

(f) Every person deposing as herein provided shall be cautioned and shall be required to swear (or affirm, if he so requests) to testify the whole truth, and shall be carefully examined. His testimony shall be reduced to writing by the person taking the deposition, or under his direction, and shall, after it has been reduced to writing, be subscribed by the deponent. All depositions shall be promptly filed with the Board.*

---

*See footnote 25.

Foreign Depositions

(g) If a witness whose testimony may be desired to be taken by deposition be in a foreign country, the deposition may be taken, provided the laws of the foreign country so permit, by a consular officer or other person commissioned by the Board,* or agreed upon by the parties by stipulation in writing to be filed with the Board, or may be taken under letters rogatory issued by a court of competent jurisdiction at the request of the Board.

Fees

(h) Witnesses whose depositions are taken as authorized in this Act, and the persons taking the same, shall severally be entitled to the same fees as are paid for like services in the courts of the United States: *Provided*, That with respect to commissions or letters rogatory issued at the initiative of the Board,* executed in foreign countries, the Board shall pay such fees, charges, or expenses incidental thereto as may be found necessary, in accordance with regulations on the subject to be prescribed by the Board.

Compelling Testimony

(i) [Repealed by Act of October 15, 1970, 84 Stat. 922, effective December 14, 1970]

ORDERS, NOTICES, AND SERVICE

Effective Date of Orders; Emergency Orders

SEC. 1005. [*72 Stat. 794, as amended by 73 Stat. 427, 49 U.S.C. 1485*] (a) Except as otherwise provided in this Act, all orders, rules, and regulations of the Board* or the Secretary of Transportation* shall take effect within such reasonable time as the Board or Secretary of Transportation* may prescribe, and shall continue in force until their further order, rule, or regulation, or for a specified period of time, as shall be prescribed in the order, rule, or regulation: *Provided*, That whenever the Secretary of Transportation* is of the opinion that an emergency requiring immediate action exists in respect of safety in air commerce, the Secretary of Transportation* is authorized, either upon complaint or his own initiative without complaint, at once, if he so orders, without answer or other form of pleading by the interested person or persons, and with or without notice, hearing, or the making or filing of a report, to make such just and reasonable orders, rules, or regulations, as may be essential in the interest of safety in air commerce to meet such emergency: *Provided further*, That the Secretary of Transportation* shall immediately initiate proceedings relating to the matters embraced in any such order, rule, or regulation, and shall, insofar as practicable, give preference to such proceedings over all others under this Act.

---

*See footnote 25.

[§ 1005]

Designation of Agent for Service

(b) It shall be the duty of every air carrier and foreign air carrier to designate in writing an agent upon whom service of all notices and process and all orders, decisions, and requirements of the Board* and the Secretary of Transportation* may be made for and on behalf of said carrier, and to file such designation with the Secretary of Transportation* and in the office of the secretary of the Board, which designation may from time to time be changed by like writing similarly filed. Service of all notices and process and orders, decisions, and requirements of the Secretary of Transportation* or the Board may be made upon such carrier by service upon such designated agent at his office or usual place of residence with like effect as if made personally upon such carrier, and in default of such designation of such agent, service of any notice or other process in any proceedings before said Secretary of Transportation* or Board or of any order, decision, or requirements of the Secretary of Transportation* or Board, may be made by posting such notice, process, order, requirement, or decision in the office of the Secretary of Transportation* or with the secretary of the Board.

Other Methods of Service

(c) Service of notices, processes, orders, rules, and regulations upon any person may be made by personal service, or upon an agent designated in writing for the purpose, or by registered or certified mail addressed to such person or agent. Whenever service is made by registered or certified mail, the date of mailing shall be considered as the time when service is made.

Suspension or Modification of Order

(d) Except as otherwise provided in this Act, the Secretary of Transportation* or the Board is empowered to suspend or modify their orders upon such notice and in such manner as they shall deem proper.

Compliance with Order Required

(e) It shall be the duty of every person subject to this Act, and its agents and employees, to observe and comply with any order, rule, regulation, or certificate issued by the Secretary of Transportation* or the Board* under this Act affecting such person so long as the same shall remain in effect.

Form and Service of Orders

(f) Every order of the Secretary of Transportation* or the Board* shall set forth the findings of fact upon which it is based, and shall be served upon the parties to the proceeding and the persons affected by such order.

*See footnote 25.

JUDICIAL REVIEW OF ORDERS

Orders of Board and Secretary of Transportation* subject to Review

SEC. 1006. [*72 Stat. 795, as amended by 74 Stat. 255, 75 Stat. 497, 49 U.S.C. 1486*] (a) Any order, affirmative or negative, issued by the Board* or Secretary of Transportation* under this Act, except any order in respect of any foreign air carrier subject to the approval of the President as provided in section 801 of this Act, shall be subject to review by the courts of appeals of the United States or the United States Court of Appeals for the District of Columbia upon petition, filed within sixty days after the entry of such order, by any person disclosing a substantial interest in such order. After the expiration of said sixty days a petition may be filed only by leave of court upon a showing of reasonable grounds for failure to file the petition theretofore.

Venue

(b) A petition under this section shall be filed in the court for the circuit wherein the petitioner resides or has his principal place of business or in the United States Court of Appeals for the District of Columbia.

Notice to Board or Secretary of Transportation*; Filing of Transcript

(c) A copy of the petition shall, upon filing, be forthwith transmitted to the Board* or Secretary of Transportation* by the clerk of the court, and the Board or Secretary of Transportation* shall thereupon file in the court the record, if any, upon which the order complained of was entered, as provided in section 2112 of title 28, United States Code.

Power of Court

(d) Upon transmittal of the petition to the Board* or Secretary of Transportation,* the court shall have exclusive jurisdiction to affirm, modify, or set aside the order complained of, in whole or in part, and if need be, to order further proceedings by the Board or Secretary of Transportation.* Upon good cause shown and after reasonable notice to the Board or Secretary of Transportation,* interlocutory relief may be granted by stay of the order or by such mandatory or other relief as may be appropriate.

Findings of Fact Conclusive

(e) The findings of facts by the Board* or Secretary of Transportation,* if supported by substantial evidence, shall be conclusive. No objection to an order of the Board or Secretary of Transportation* shall be considered by the court unless such objection shall have been urged before the Board or Secretary of Transportation* or if it was not so urged, unless there were reasonable grounds for failure to do so.

*See footnote 25.

Certification or Certiorari

(f) The judgment and decree of the court affirming, modifying, or setting aside any such order of the Board* or Secretary of Transportation* shall be subject only to review by the Supreme Court of the United States upon certification or certiorari as provided in section 1254 of title 28, United States Code.

JUDICIAL ENFORCEMENT

Jurisdiction of Court

SEC. 1007. [*72 Stat. 796, 49 U.S.C. 1487*] (a) If any person violates any provision of this Act, or any rule, regulation, requirement, or order thereunder, or any term, condition, or limitation of any certificate or permit issued under this Act, the Board* or Secretary of Transportation,* as the case may be, their duly authorized agents, or, in the case of a violation of section 401(a) of this Act, any party in interest may apply to the district court of the United States, for any district wherein such person carries on his business or wherein the violation occurred, for the enforcement of such provision of this Act, or of such rule, regulation, requirement, order, term, condition, or limitation; and such court shall have jurisdiction to enforce obedience thereto by a writ of injunction or other process, mandatory or otherwise, restraining such person, his officers, agents, employees, and representatives, from further violation of such provision of this Act or of such rule, regulation, requirement, order, term, condition, or limitation, and requiring their obedience thereto.

Application for Enforcement

(b) Upon the request of the Board* or Secretary of Transportation,* any district attorney of the United States to whom the Board or Secretary of Transportation* may apply is authorized to institute in the proper court and to prosecute under the direction of the Attorney General all necessary proceedings for the enforcement of the provisions of this Act or any rule, regulation, requirement, or order thereunder, or any term, condition, or limitation of any certificate or permit, and for the punishment of all violations thereof, and the costs and expenses of such prosecutions shall be paid out of the appropriations for the expenses of the courts of the United States.

PARTICIPATION IN COURT PROCEEDINGS

SEC. 1008 [*72 Stat. 796, 49 U.S.C. 1488*] Upon request of the Attorney General, the Board* or Secretary of Transportation,* as the case may be, shall have the right to participate in any proceeding in court under the provisions of this Act.

JOINDER OF PARTIES

SEC. 1009. [*72 Stat. 796, 49 U.S.C. 1489*] In any proceeding for the enforcement of the provisions of this Act, or any rule, regulation,

---

*See footnote 25.

requirement, or order thereunder, or any term, condition, or limitation of any certificate or permit, whether such proceedings be instituted before the Board* or be begun originally in any court of the United States, it shall be lawful to include as parties, or to permit the intervention of, all persons interested in or affected by the matter under consideration; and inquiries, investigations, orders, and decrees may be made with reference to all such parties in the same manner, to the same extent, and subject to the same provisions of law as they may be made with respect to the persons primarily concerned.

TITLE XI—MISCELLANEOUS [26]

HAZARDS TO AIR COMMERCE [27]

SEC. 1101. [*72 Stat. 797, 49 U.S.C. 1501*] The Secretary of Transportation* shall, by rules and regulations, or by order where necessary, require all persons to give adequate public notice, in the form and manner prescribed by the Secretary of Transportation,* of the construction or alteration, or of the proposed construction or alteration, of any structure where notice will promote safety in air commerce.

INTERNATIONAL AGREEMENTS

SEC. 1102. [*72 Stat. 797, 49 U.S.C. 1502*] In exercising and performing their powers and duties under this Act, the Board and the Secretary of Transportation* shall do so consistently with any obligation assumed by the United States in any treaty, convention, or agreement that may be in force between the United States and any foreign country or foreign countries, and shall take into consideration any applicable laws and requirements of foreign countries and the Board* shall not, in exercising and performing its powers and duties with respect to certificates of convenience and necessity, restrict compliance by any air carrier with any obligation, duty, or liability imposed by any foreign country: *Provided*, That this section shall not apply to any obligation, duty, or liability arising out of a contract or other agreement, heretofore or hereafter entered into between an air carrier, or any officer or representative thereof, and any foreign country, if such contract or agreement is disapproved by the Board as being contrary to the public interest.

NATURE AND USE OF DOCUMENTS FILED

SEC. 1103. [*72 Stat. 797, 49 U.S.C. 1503*] The copies of tariffs and of all contracts, agreements, understandings, and arrangements filed with the Board* as herein provided, and the statistics, tables, and

---

[26] Certain provisions of this title would appear to be applicable to both the Civil Aeronautics Board and the National Transportation Safety Board, as well as the Secretary of Transportation (see footnote 1). Thus, the term "Board" may mean the "Civil Aeronautics Board" or the "National Transportation Safety Board," or both, depending upon whether the matter involved concerns one or both of such agencies. As previously indicated, "Secretary of Transportation" has been substituted for "Administrator," except where the context requires otherwise (see footnote 1).

[27] See section 303(q) of the Federal Communications Act of 1934, p. 292.

*See footnote 26.

[§§ 1104–1105]

figures contained in the annual or other reports of air carriers and other persons made to the Board as required under the provisions of this Act shall be preserved as public records (except as otherwise provided in this Act) in the custody of the secretary of the Board, and shall be received as prima facie evidence of what they purport to be for the purpose of investigations by the Board and in all judicial proceedings; and copies of, and extracts from, any of such tariffs, contracts, agreements, understandings, arrangements, or reports, certified by the secretary of the Board, under the seal of the Board, shall be received in evidence with like effect as the originals.

WITHHOLDING OF INFORMATION

Sec. 1104. [*72 Stat. 797, 49 U.S.C. 1504*] Any person may make written objection to the public disclosure of information contained in any application, report, or document filed pursuant to the provisions of this Act or of information obtained by the Board* or the Secretary of Transportation,* pursuant to the provisions of this Act, stating the grounds for such objection. Whenever such objection is made, the Board or Secretary of Transportation* shall order such information withheld from public disclosure when, in their judgment, a disclosure of such information would adversely affect the interests of such person and is not required in the interest of the public. The Board or Secretary of Transportation* shall be responsible for classified information in accordance with appropriate law: *Provided,* That nothing in this section shall authorize the withholding of information by the Board or Secretary of Transportation* from the duly authorized committees of the Congress.

COOPERATION WITH GOVERNMENT AGENCIES

Sec. 1105. [*72 Stat. 798, as amended by 76 Stat. 921, 49 U.S.C. 1505*] The Board* and the Secretary of Transportation* may avail themselves of the assistance of the National Aeronautics and Space Administration and any research or technical agency of the United States on matters relating to aircraft fuel and oil and to the design, materials, workmanship, construction, performance, maintenance, and operation of aircraft, aircraft engines, propellers, appliances, and air navigation facilities. The Board may avail itself of the assistance of the Federal Bureau of Investigation and of any investigatory or intelligence agency of the United States in the investigation of the activities of any person in connection with an aircraft accident. The Board may avail itself of the assistance of any medical agency of the United States in the conduct of such autopsies or tests on the remains of deceased persons aboard the aircraft at the time of the accident who die as a result of the accident, as may be necessary to aid the Board in the investigation of an aircraft accident. Each such agency is authorized to conduct such scientific and technical researches, investigations, and tests as may be necessary to aid the Board and Secretary of Transportation* in the exercise and performance of their

---

*See footnote 26.

powers and duties. Nothing contained in this Act shall be construed to authorize the duplication of the laboratory research activities of any existing governmental agency.

REMEDIES NOT EXCLUSIVE

SEC. 1106. [*72 Stat. 798, 49 U.S.C. 1506*] Nothing contained in this Act shall in any way abridge or alter the remedies now existing at common law or by statute, but the provisions of this Act are in addition to such remedies.

PUBLIC USE OF FACILITIES

SEC. 1107. [*72 Stat. 798, 49 U.S.C. 1507*] (a) Air navigation facilities owned or operated by the United States may be made available for public use under such conditions and to such extent as the head of the department or other agency having jurisdiction thereof deems advisable and may by regulation prescribe.

(b) The head of any Government department or other agency having jurisdiction over any airport or emergency landing field owned or operated by the United States may provide for the sale to any aircraft of fuel, oil, equipment, and supplies, and the furnishing to it of mechanical service, temporary shelter, and other assistance under such regulations as the head of the department or agency may prescribe, but only if such action is by reason of an emergency necessary to the continuance of such aircraft on its course to the nearest airport operated by private enterprise. All such articles shall be sold and such assistance furnished at the fair market value prevailing locally as ascertained by the head of such department or agency. All amounts received under this subsection shall be covered into the Treasury; but that part of such amounts which, in the judgment of the head of the department or agency, is equivalent to the cost of the fuel, oil, equipment, supplies, services, shelter, or other assistance so sold or furnished shall be credited to the appropriation from which such cost was paid, and the balance, if any, shall be credited to miscellaneous receipts.

FOREIGN AIRCRAFT

SEC. 1108. [*72 Stat. 798, 49 U.S.C. 1508*] (a) The United States of America is hereby declared to possess and exercise complete and exclusive national sovereignty in the airspace of the United States, including the airspace above all inland waters and the airspace above those portions of the adjacent marginal high seas, bays, and lakes, over which by international law or treaty or convention the United States exercises national jurisdiction. Aircraft of the armed forces of any foreign nation shall not be navigated in the United States, including the Canal Zone, except in accordance with an authorization granted by the Secretary of State.

(b) Foreign aircraft, which are not a part of the armed forces of a foreign nation, may be navigated in the United States by airmen holding certificates or licenses issued or rendered valid by the United States or by the nation in which the aircraft is registered if such for-

[§ 1109]

eign nation grants a similar privilege with respect to aircraft of the United States and only if such navigation is authorized by permit, order, or regulation issued by the Board hereunder, and in accordance with the terms, conditions, and limitations thereof. The Board shall issue such permits, orders, or regulations to such extent only as it shall find such action to be in the interest of the public: *Provided, however,* That in exercising its powers hereunder, the Board shall do so consistently with any treaty, convention, or agreement which may be in force between the United States and any foreign country or countries. Foreign civil aircraft permitted to navigate in the United States under this subsection may be authorized by the Board to engage in air commerce within the United States except that they shall not take on at any point within the United States, persons, property, or mail carried for compensation or hire and destined for another point within the United States. Nothing contained in this subsection (b) shall be deemed to limit, modify, or amend section 402 of this Act, but any foreign air carrier holding a permit under said section 402 shall not be required to obtain additional authorization under this subsection with respect to any operation authorized by said permit.

APPLICATION OF EXISTING LAWS RELATING TO FOREIGN COMMERCE

SEC. 1109. [*72 Stat. 799, as amended by 75 Stat. 527, 49 U.S.C. 1509*] (a) Except as specifically provided in the Act entitled "An Act to authorize the President to proclaim regulations for preventing collisions at sea", approved October 11, 1951 (Public Law 172, Eighty-second Congress; 65 Stat. 406), the navigation and shipping laws of the United States, including any definition of "vessel" or "vehicle" found therein and including the rules for the prevention of collisions, shall not be construed to apply to seaplanes or other aircraft or to the navigation of vessels in relation to seaplanes or other aircraft.

(b) The Secretary of the Treasury is authorized to (1) designate places in the United States as ports of entry for civil aircraft arriving in the United States from any place outside thereof and for merchandise carried on such aircraft, (2) detail to ports of entry for civil aircraft such officers and employees of the customs service as he may deem necessary, and to confer or impose upon any officer or employee of the United States stationed at any such port of entry (with the consent of the head of the Government department or other agency under whose jurisdiction the officer or employee is serving) any of the powers, privileges, or duties conferred or imposed upon officers or employees of the customs service, and (3) by regulation to provide for the application to civil air navigation of the laws and regulations relating to the administration of the customs laws to such extent and upon such conditions as he deems necessary.

(c) The Secretary of the Treasury is authorized by regulation to provide for the application to civil aircraft of the laws and regulations relating to the entry and clearance of vessels to such extent and upon such conditions as he deems necessary.

(d) The Secretary of Agriculture is authorized by regulation to provide for the application to civil air navigation of the laws and regulations related to animal and plant quarantine, including the importation, exportation, transportation, and quarantine of animals, plants, animal and plant products, insects, bacterial and fungus cultures, viruses, and serums, to such extent and upon such conditions as he deems necessary.

(e) There are authorized to be appropriated such sums as may be necessary to enable the head of any department or agency of the Federal Government charged with any duty of inspection, clearance, collection of taxes or duties, or other similar function, with respect to persons or property moving in air commerce, to acquire such space at public airports (as defined in the Airport and Airway Development Act of 1970) as he determines, after consultation with the Secretary of Transportation,* to be necessary for the performance of such duty. In acquiring any such space, the head of such department or agency shall act through the Administrator of General Services in accordance with the procedures established by law which are generally applicable to the acquisition of space to be used by departments and agencies of the Federal Government.

GEOGRAPHICAL EXTENSION OF JURISDICTION [28]

SEC. 1110. [*72 Stat. 800, 49 U.S.C. 1510*] Whenever the President determines that such action would be in the national interest, he may, to the extent, in the manner, and for such periods of time as he may consider necessary, extend the application of this Act to any areas of land or water outside of the United States and the overlying airspace thereof in which the Federal Government of the United States, under international treaty, agreement or other lawful arrangement has the necessary legal authority to take such action.

AUTHORITY TO REFUSE TRANSPORTATION

SEC. 1111. [*72 Stat. 800, 49 U.S.C. 1511*] Subject to reasonable rules and regulations prescribed by the Secretary of Transportation,* any air carrier is authorized to refuse transportation to a passenger or to refuse to transport property when, in the opinion of the air carrier, such transportation would or might be inimical to safety of flight.

TITLE XII—SECURITY PROVISIONS

PURPOSE

SEC. 1201. [*72 Stat. 800, 49 U.S.C. 1521*] The purpose of this title is to establish security provisions which will encourage and permit the maximum use of the navigable airspace by civil aircraft consistent with the national security.

SECURITY CONTROL OF AIR TRAFFIC

SEC. 1202. [*72 Stat. 800, 49 U.S.C. 1522*] In the exercise of his authority under section 307(a) of this Act, the Secretary of Transportation,* in consultation with the Department of Defense, shall establish such zones or areas in the airspace of the United States as

---

*See footnote 1.
[28] See Executive Order No. 10854.

[§§ 1203, 1301–1302]

he may find necessary in the interests of national defense, and by rule, regulation, or order restrict or prohibit the flight of civil aircraft, which he cannot identify, locate, and control with available facilities, within such zones or areas.

PENALTIES

SEC. 1203. [*72 Stat. 800, 49 U.S.C. 1523*] In addition to the penalties otherwise provided for by this Act, any person who knowingly or willfully violates any provision of this title, or any rule, regulation, or order issued thereunder shall be deemed guilty of a misdemeanor, and upon conviction thereof, shall be subject to a fine of not exceeding $10,000 or to imprisonment not exceeding one year, or to both such fine and imprisonment.

TITLE XIII—WAR RISK INSURANCE [29]

DEFINITIONS

American Aircraft

SEC. 1301. [*72 Stat. 800, 49 U.S.C. 1531*] As used in this title—

(a) The term "American aircraft" means "civil aircraft of the United States" as defined in section 101(15) of this Act, and any aircraft owned or chartered by or made available to the United States, or any department or agency thereof, or the government of any State, Territory, or possession of the United States, or any political subdivision thereof, or the District of Columbia.

War Risks

(b) The term "war risks" includes, to such extent as the Secretary may determine, all or any part of those risks which are described in "free of capture and seizure" clauses, or analogous clauses.

Secretary

(c) The term "Secretary" means the Secretary of Transportation.*

Insurance Company and Insurance Carrier

(d) The terms "insurance company" and "insurance carrier" in sections 1305 (a) and (b) and in section 1307(d) shall include any mutual or stock insurance company, reciprocal insurance association, and any group or association authorized to do an aviation insurance business in any State of the United States.

AUTHORITY TO INSURE

Power of Secretary

SEC. 1302. [*72 Stat. 801, 49 U.S.C. 1532*] (a) The Secretary, with the approval of the President, and after such consultation with inter-

---

[29] Functions, powers, and duties of the Secretary of Commerce under this title transferred to the Secretary of Transportation by section 6(a)(3)(C) of the Department of Transportation Act (80 Stat. 937, 49 U.S.C. 1655). Accordingly, on advice from the General Counsel, Department of Transportation, the publication substitutes the words "Secretary of Transportation" for "Secretary of Commerce" in section 1301(c).
*See footnote 29.

ested agencies of the Government as the President may require, may provide insurance and reinsurance against loss or damage arising out of war risks in the manner and to the extent provided in this title, whenever it is determined by the Secretary that such insurance adequate for the needs of the air commerce of the United States cannot be obtained on reasonable terms and conditions from companies authorized to do an insurance business in a State of the United States: *Provided,* That no insurance shall be issued under this title to cover war risks on persons or property engaged or transported exclusively in air commerce within the several States of the United States and the District of Columbia.

Basis of Insurance

(b) Any insurance or reinsurance issued under any of the provisions of this title shall be based, insofar as practicable, upon consideration of the risk involved.

INSURABLE PERSONS, PROPERTY, OR INTERESTS

SEC. 1303. [*72 Stat. 801, 49 U.S.C. 1533*] The Secretary may provide the insurance and reinsurance, authorized by section 1302 with respect to the following persons, property, or interest:

Aircraft

(a) American aircraft, and those foreign-flag aircraft engaged in aircraft operations deemed by the Secretary to be in the interest of the national defense or the national economy of the United States, when so engaged.

Cargo

(b) Cargoes transported or to be transported on any such aircraft, including shipments by express or registered mail; air cargoes owned by citizens or residents of the United States, its Territories, or possessions; air cargoes imported to, or exported from, the United States, its Territories, or possessions and air cargoes sold or purchased by citizens or residents of the United States, its Territories, or possessions, under contracts of sale or purchase by the terms of which the risk of loss by war risks or the obligation to provide insurance against such risks is assumed by or falls upon a citizen or resident of the United States, its Territories, or possessions; air cargoes transported between any point in the United States and any point in a Territory or possession of the United States, between any point in any such Territory or possession and any point in any other such Territory or possession, or between any point in any such Territory or possession and any other point in the same Territory or possession.

Personal Effects and Baggage

(c) The personal effects and baggage of the captains, pilots, officers, members of the crews of such aircraft, and of other persons employed or transported on such aircraft.

Persons

(d) Captains, pilots, officers, members of the crews of such aircraft, and other persons employed or transported thereon against loss of life, injury, or detention.

Other Interests

(e) Statutory or contractual obligations or other liabilities of such aircraft or of the owner or operator of such aircraft of the nature customarily covered by insurance.

INSURANCE FOR DEPARTMENTS AND AGENCIES

Exception

SEC. 1304. [*72 Stat. 802, 49 U.S.C. 1534*] (a) Any department or agency of the United States may, with the approval of the President, procure from the Secretary any of the insurance provided under this title, except with respect to valuables covered by sections 1 and 2 of the Act of July 8, 1937 (50 Stat. 479).

Indemnity Agreements

(b) The Secretary is authorized with such approval to provide such insurance at the request of the Secretary of Defense, and such other agencies as the President may prescribe, without premium in consideration of the agreement of the Secretary of Defense or such agency to indemnify the Secretary against all losses covered by such insurance, and the Secretary of Defense and such other agencies are authorized to execute such indemnity agreement with the Secretary.

REINSURANCE

Who May Be Reinsured

SEC. 1305. [*72 Stat. 802, 49 U.S.C. 1535*] (a) To the extent that he is authorized by this title to provide insurance, the Secretary may reinsure, in whole or in part, any company authorized to do an insurance business in any State of the United States. The Secretary may reinsure with, or cede or retrocede to, any such company, any insurance or reinsurance provided by the Secretary in accordance with the provisions of this title.

Rates for Reinsurance

(b) Reinsurance shall not be provided by the Secretary at rates less than nor obtained by the Secretary at rates more than the rates established by the Secretary on the same or similar risks or the rates charged by the insurance carrier for the insurance so reinsured, whichever is most advantageous to the Secretary, except that the Secretary may make to the insurance carrier such allowances for expenses on account of the cost of services rendered or facilities furnished as he deems reasonably to accord with good business practice, but such allowance to the carrier shall not provide for any payment by the carrier on account of solicitation for or stimulation of insurance business.

COLLECTION AND DISBURSEMENT OF FUNDS

Treasury Revolving Fund

SEC. 1306. [*72 Stat. 803, 49 U.S.C. 1536*] (a) Moneys appropriated by Congress to carry out the provisions of this title and all moneys received from premiums, salvage, or other recoveries and all receipts in connection with this title shall be deposited in a revolving fund in the Treasury of the United States. Payments of return premiums, losses, settlements, judgments, and all liabilities incurred by the United States under this title shall be made from such funds through the disbursing facilities of the Treasury Department.

Appropriations

(b) Such sums as shall be necessary to carry out the provisions of this title are authorized to be appropriated to such fund.

Revolving Fund Excess

(c) At least annually, any balance in the revolving fund in excess of an amount determined by the Secretary to be necessary for the requirements of the fund, and for reasonable reserves to maintain the solvency of the fund shall be paid into the Treasury as miscellaneous receipts.

Annual Payment of Costs

(d) Annual payments shall be made by the Secretary to the Treasury of the United States as miscellaneous receipts by reason of costs incurred by the Government through the employment of appropriated funds by the Secretary in carrying out the provisions of this title. These payments shall be computed by applying to the average monthly balance of appropriated funds retained in the revolving fund a percentage determined annually in advance by the Secretary of the Treasury. Such percentage shall not be less than the current average rate which the Treasury pays on its marketable obligations.

Civil Service Retirement System

(e) The Secretary shall contribute to the Civil Service Retirement and Disability Fund, on the basis of annual billings as determined by the Civil Service Commission, for the Government's share of the cost of the Civil Service Retirement System applicable to the employees engaged in carrying out the provisions of this title. The Secretary shall also contribute to the employees' compensation fund, on the basis of annual billings as determined by the Secretary of Labor for the benefit payments made from such fund on account of the employees engaged in carrying out the provisions of this title. The annual billings shall also include a statement of the fair portion of the cost of the administration of the respective funds, which shall be paid by the Secretary into the Treasury as miscellaneous receipts.

Regulatory and Settlement

SEC. 1307. [*72 Stat. 803, 49 U.S.C. 1537*] (a) The Secretary, in the administration of this title, may issue such policies, rules, and regulations as he deems proper and, subject to the following provisions of this subsection, may adjust and pay losses, compromise and settle claims, whether in favor of or against the United States and pay the amount of any judgment rendered against the United States in any suit, or the amount of any settlement agreed upon, in respect of any claim under insurance authorized by this title. In the case of any aircraft which is insured under the provisions of this title, (1) the policy shall specify a stated amount to be paid in the event of total loss, and such stated amount shall not exceed an amount determined by the Secretary, after consultation with the Civil Aeronautics Board, to represent the fair and reasonable value of the aircraft, and (2) the amount of any claim which is compromised, settled, adjusted, or paid shall in no event exceed such stated amount.

Forms, Policies, Amounts Insured, and Rates

(b) The Secretary may prescribe and change forms and policies, and fix, adjust, and change the amounts insured and rates of premium provided for in this title: *Provided,* That with respect to policies in effect at the time any such change is made, such change shall apply only with the consent of the insured.

Manner of Administration

(c) The Secretary, in administering this title, may exercise his powers, perform his duties and functions, and make his expenditures in accordance with commercial practice in the aviation insurance business. Except as authorized in subsection (d) of this section, no insurance broker or other person acting in a similar intermediary capacity shall be paid any fee or other consideration by the Secretary by virtue of his participation in arranging any insurance wherein the Secretary directly insures any of the risk thereof.

Employment of Aviation Insurance Companies and Agents

(d) The Secretary may, and whenever he finds it practical to do so shall, employ companies or groups of companies authorized to do an aviation insurance business in any State of the United States, to act as his underwriting agent. The Secretary may allow such companies or groups of companies fair and reasonable compensation for servicing insurance written by such companies or groups of companies as underwriting agent for the Secretary. The services of such underwriting agents may be utilized in the adjustment of claims under insurance provided by this title, but no claim shall be paid unless and until it has been approved by the Secretary. Such compensation may include an allowance for expenses reasonably incured by such agent, but such allowance shall not include any payment by such agent on account of solicitation for or stimulation of insurance business.

Cooperation With Other Agencies

(e) The Secretary with the consent of any executive department, independent establishment, or other agency of the Government, including any field service thereof, may avail himself of the use of information, services, facilities, officers, and employees thereof in carrying out the provisions of this title.

Budget Program and Accounts

(f) The Secretary, in the performance of, and with respect to, the functions, powers, and duties vested in him by this title, shall prepare annually and submit a budget program as provided for wholly owned Government corporations by the Government Corporation Control Act, as amended (59 Stat. 597; 31 U.S.C. 841). The Secretary shall maintain an integral set of accounts which shall be audited annually by the General Accounting Office in accordance with principles and procedures applicable to commercial transactions as provided by the said Government Corporation Control Act: *Provided*, That, because of the business activities authorized by this title, the Secretary may exercise the powers conferred in said title, perform the duties and functions, and make expenditures required in accordance with commercial practice in the aviation insurance business, and the General Accounting Office shall allow credit for such expenditures when shown to be necessary because of the nature of such authorized activities.

RIGHTS OF AIRMEN UNDER EXISTING LAW

SEC. 1308. [*72 Stat. 805, 49 U.S.C. 1538*] This title shall not affect rights of airmen under existing law.

ANNUAL REPORTS TO CONGRESS

SEC. 1309. [*72 Stat. 805, as amended by 79 Stat. 1310, 49 U.S.C. 1539*] The Secretary shall include in his annual report to Congress a detailed statement of all activities and of all expenditures and receipts under this title for the period covered by such report.

JUDICIAL REVIEW OF CLAIMS

SEC. 1310. [*72 Stat. 805, 49 U.S.C. 1540*] Upon disagreement as to a loss insured under this title, suit may be maintained against the United States in the United States District Court for the District of Columbia or in the United States district court in and for the district in which the claimant or his agent resides, notwithstanding the amount of the claim and any provision of existing law as to the jurisdiction of United States district courts, and this remedy shall be exclusive of any other action by reason of the same subject matter against any agent or employee of the United States employed or retained under this title. If the claimant has no residence in the United States, suit may be brought in the United States District Court for the District of Columbia or in any other United States district court in which the Attorney General of the United States agrees to accept service. The procedure in such suits shall otherwise be the same as that provided for suits in the district courts by title 28, United States Code, section 1346(a)(2), so far as applicable. All persons having or claiming or who might have an interest in such insurance may be made parties either initially or upon the motion of either party. In any case where the Secretary acknowledges the indebtedness of the United States on account of such insurance, and there is a dispute as to the persons entitled to receive payment, the United States may bring an action in the nature of a bill of interpleader against such parties, in the United States District Court for the District of Columbia, or in the United States district court of the district in which any such person resides. In such actions any party, if not a resident of or found within the district, may be brought in by order of court served in such reasonable manner as the court directs. If the court is satisfied that persons unknown might assert a claim on account of such insurance, it may direct service upon such persons unknown by publication in the Federal Register. Judgment in any such suit shall discharge the United States from further liability to any parties to such action, and to all persons when service by publication upon persons unknown is directed by the court. The period within which suits may be commenced contained in said Act providing for bringing of suits against the United States shall, if claim be filed therefor within such period, be suspended from such time of filing until the claim shall have been administratively denied by the Secretary and for sixty days thereafter: *Provided, however*, That such claim shall be deemed to have been administratively denied if not acted upon within six months after the time of filing, unless the Secretary for good cause shown shall have otherwise agreed with the claimant.

INSURANCE OF EXCESS WITH OTHER UNDERWRITERS

Sec. 1311. [*72 Stat. 806, 49 U.S.C. 1541*] A person having an insurable interest in an aircraft may, with the approval of the Secretary, insure with other underwriters in an amount in excess of the amount insured with the Secretary, and, in that event, the Secretary shall not be entitled to the benefit of such insurance, but nothing in this section shall prevent the Secretary from entering into contracts of coinsurance.

TERMINATION OF TITLE

Sec. 1312. [*72 Stat. 806, as amended by 75 Stat. 210, 80 Stat. 199, 84 Stat. 837, 49 U.S.C. 1542*] The authority of the Secretary to provide insurance and reinsurance under this title shall expire at the termination of September 7, 1975.

TITLE XIV—REPEALS AND AMENDMENTS

REPEALS

Sec. 1401. [*72 Stat. 806*] (a) The Act of May 20, 1926 (Air Commerce Act of 1926, 44 Stat. 568), as amended, is hereby repealed.

[§ 1402]

(b) The Act of June 23, 1938 (Civil Aeronautics Act of 1938, 52 Stat. 973), as amended, is hereby repealed, except that the repeal by this subsection of subsections (b) and (c) of section 307 and clause (8) of section 803 of such Act shall not take effect in such manner as to impair the operation of the deferred repeal of such subsections and such clause as provided in section 21 of the Government Employees Training Act.

(c) [*72 Stat. 806; 5 U.S.C. 133t note; 49 U.S.C. 486 note, 1343 note*] Section 7 of Reorganization Plan Numbered III (54 Stat. 1233) and section 7 of Reorganization Plan Numbered IV (54 Stat. 1235-1236), which became effective on June 30, 1940 (54 Stat. 231), and Reorganization Plan No. 10, which became effective October 1, 1953 (67 Stat. 644), are hereby repealed. No function vested in the Secretary of Transportation* by this Act shall hereafter be subject to the provisions of section 1(a) of Reorganization Plan No. 5 of 1950 (64 Stat. 1263).

(d) The Act of August 14, 1957 (Airways Modernization Act of 1957, 71 Stat. 349), is hereby repealed.[30]

(e) [*72 Stat. 806, 49 U.S.C. 1301 note*] All other Acts or parts of Acts inconsistent with any provision of this Act are hereby repealed.

AMENDMENTS TO ACTS RELATING TO AIRPORTS

Act Relating to Public Airports

SEC. 1402. [*72 Stat. 806*] (a) [*72 Stat. 806, 49 U.S.C. 211 (b), (c)*] The Act of May 24, 1928, as amended (45 Stat. 728), is further amended by striking out the words "Civil Aeronautics Authority" wherever they appear and inserting in lieu thereof the words "Administrator of the Federal Aviation Agency".

Federal Airport Act

(b) The Act of May 13, 1946, as amended (60 Stat. 170), is further amended as follows:

(1) [*72 Stat. 806, 49 U.S.C. 1101(a)(1)*] By striking the words "Administrator of Civil Aeronautics" wherever they appear and inserting in lieu thereof the words "Administrator of the Federal Aviation Agency";

(2) [*72 Stat. 807, 49 U.S.C. 1102(a), 1105, 1116(d), (e)*] By striking the word "Secretary" where it appears in sections 3(a), 6, and 17, and inserting in lieu thereof the word "Administrator"; and

(3) [*72 Stat. 807, 49 U.S.C. 1103, 1108 (a), (d), 1111*] By striking the words "Secretary of Commerce" wherever they appear and inserting in lieu thereof the word "Administrator".

Government Surplus Airports and Equipment Act

(c) [*72 Stat. 807, 50 U.S.C. App. 1622(g), 1622a, 1622b, 1622c*] The Act of July 30, 1947 (61 Stat. 678), as amended, including the

---

*See footnote 1,
[30] Functions, property, etc. of Airways Modernization Board were transferred to Administrator, Federal Aviation Agency on November 1, 1958 (Executive Order No. 10786, 23 Fed. Reg. 8573).

[§ 1402]

Act of October 1, 1949 (63 Stat. 700), is further amended by striking the words "Administrator of Civil Aeronautics" wherever they appear and inserting in lieu thereof the words "Administrator of the Federal Aviation Agency".

Alaskan Airports Act

(d) The Act of May 28, 1948, as amended (62 Stat. 277), is amended as follows:

(1) [*72 Stat. 807*, *48 U.S.C. 485*] By striking the words "Administrator of Civil Aeronautics" and inserting in lieu thereof the words "Administrator of the Federal Aviation Agency";

(2) [*72 Stat. 807*, *48 U.S.C. 485c*] By striking the words "Civil Aeronautics Administration" and inserting in lieu thereof the words "Federal Aviation Agency";

(3) [*72 Stat. 807*, *48 U.S.C. 485d*] By striking the words "Secretary of Commerce" and inserting in lieu thereof the words "Administrator of the Federal Aviation Agency".

Department of Interior Airports Act

(e) [*72 Stat. 807*, *16 U.S.C. 7a*] The Act of March 18, 1950 (64 Stat. 27), is amended by striking the words "Administrator of Civil Aeronautics" and inserting in lieu thereof the words "Administrator of the Federal Aviation Agency".

Washington National Airport Act

(f) The Act of June 29, 1940 (54 Stat. 686), as amended, is further amended by striking out the words "Administrator of the Civil Aeronautics Authority" in subsection (a) of section 1 and inserting in lieu thereof the words "Administrator of the Federal Aviation Agency", and by striking out the words "Civil Aeronautics Administration" in subsection (a) of section 4 and inserting in lieu thereof the words "Federal Aviation Agency".

Second Washington Airport Act

(g) The Act of September 7, 1950 (64 Stat. 770), is amended by striking the word "Secretary" wherever it appears except in subsection (c) of section 8 and inserting in lieu thereof the word "Administrator"; by striking the words "Secretary of Commerce" from the first section of such Act and inserting in lieu thereof the words "Administrator of the Federal Aviation Agency"; by striking the words "Department of Commerce" wherever they appear and inserting in lieu thereof the words "Federal Aviation Agency"; and by striking subsection (c) of section 8 and inserting in lieu thereof a new subsection as follows:

"(c) The United States Park Police may, at the request of the Administrator, be assigned by the Secretary of the Interior, in his discretion, to patrol any area of the airport, and any members of the United States Park Police so assigned are hereby authorized and empowered to make arrests within the limits of the airport for the same offenses and in the same manner and circumstances as are provided in this section with respect to employees designated by the Administrator."

AMENDMENTS TO THE INTERNATIONAL AVIATION FACILITIES ACT

SEC. 1403. [*72 Stat. 808, 49 U.S.C. 1151, 1152, 1155, 1157 (a), (b), 1160*] The Act of June 16, 1948 (62 Stat. 450), as amended, is further amended by striking the words "Administrator of Civil Aeronautics" and inserting in lieu thereof the words "Administrator of the Federal Aviation Agency", and by striking the words "Civil Aeronautics Administration" and inserting in lieu thereof the words "Federal Aviation Agency"; by striking paragraph (1) of section 2 and renumbering subsequent subsections; by striking the phrase "After consultation with the Air Coordinating Committee and" from section 3; by striking the phrase "with the unanimous approval of the Air Coordinating Committee," from section 6; and by striking the sentence reading "Transfer of property in foreign territory shall be made hereunder only after consultation with the Air Coordinating Committee." wherever it appears in section 8.

AMENDMENTS TO ACT RELATING TO COAST GUARD AIDS TO NAVIGATION AND OCEAN STATIONS

SEC. 1404. [*72 Stat. 808, 14 U.S.C. prec. 81, 82, 90(b)*] The Act of August 4, 1949 (63 Stat. 495), as amended, is further amended by striking the words "Administrator of Civil Aeronautics" wherever they appear and inserting in lieu thereof the words "Administrator of the Federal Aviation Agency", and by striking the words "Civil Aeronautics Administration" wherever they appear and inserting in lieu thereof the words "Federal Aviation Agency".

AMENDMENTS TO FEDERAL EXPLOSIVES ACT

SEC. 1405. [*72 Stat. 808, 50 U.S.C. 123*] The Act of November 24, 1942 (56 Stat. 1022), is amended by striking the words "Civil Aeronautics Board" and inserting in lieu thereof the words "Administrator of the Federal Aviation Agency".

AMENDMENTS TO FEDERAL PROPERTY AND ADMINISTRATIVE SERVICES ACT OF 1949

SEC. 1406. [*72 Stat. 808, 40 U.S.C. 474(14)*] The Federal Property and Administrative Services Act of 1949, as amended, is further amended by striking the phrase "Administrator of Civil Aeronautics" in section 602(d) (40 U.S.C. 474(14)), and inserting in lieu thereof the phrase "Administrator of the Federal Aviation Agency".

AMENDMENTS TO ACT RELATING TO PURCHASE AND MANUFACTURE OF MATERIALS AND SUPPLIES

SEC. 1407. [*72 Stat. 808, 31 U.S.C. 686(a)*] The Act of March 4, 1915, as amended, (31 U.S.C. 686), is further amended by striking the phrase "Civil Aeronautics Administration" and inserting in lieu thereof the phrase "Federal Aviation Agency".

AMENDMENTS TO EXPERIMENTAL AIR MAIL ACT

SEC. 1408. [*72 Stat. 808, 39 U.S.C. 470*] The Act of April 15, 1938, as amended (39 U.S.C. 470), is further amended by striking the phrase "Civil Aeronautics Act of 1938" and inserting in lieu thereof the phrase "Federal Aviation Act of 1958".

AMENDMENTS TO TRANSPORTATION OF FOREIGN MAIL BY AIRCRAFT ACT

SEC. 1409. [*72 Stat. 809, 49 U.S.C. 485a, 485b*] The Act of August 27, 1940, as amended (49 U.S.C. 485a), is further amended by striking the phrase "Civil Aeronautics Act of 1938" and inserting in lieu thereof the phrase "Federal Aviation Act of 1958".

AMENDMENTS TO ACT RELATING TO TRANSPORTATION OF REGULAR MAIL TO ALASKA BY AIR

SEC. 1410. [*72 Stat. 809, 39 U.S.C. 488a*] The Act of October 14, 1940, as amended (39 U.S.C. 488a), is further amended by striking the phrase "Civil Aeronautics Act of 1938" and inserting in lieu thereof the phrase "Federal Aviation Act of 1958".

AMENDMENT TO PROVISION IN THE FEDERAL TRADE COMMISSION ACT

SEC. 1411. [*72 Stat. 809, 15 U.S.C. 45*(a)(*6*)] Section 5(a)(6) of the Act of September 26, 1914, as amended (15 U.S.C. 45), is further amended by striking the phrase "Civil Aeronautics Act of 1938" and inserting in lieu thereof the phrase "Federal Aviation Act of 1958".

TITLE XV—SAVING PROVISIONS AND EFFECTIVE DATE

EFFECT OF TRANSFERS, REPEALS, AND AMENDMENTS

Existing Rules, Regulations, Orders, and so forth

SEC. 1501. [*72 Stat. 809, 49 U.S.C. 1301 note*] (a) All orders, determinations, rules, regulations, permits, contracts, certificates, licenses, rates, and privileges which have been issued, made, or granted, or allowed to become effective, by the President, the Department of Commerce, the Secretary of Commerce, the Administrator of Civil Aeronautics, the Civil Aeronautics Board, the Airways Modernization Board, the Secretary of the Treasury, the Secretary of Agriculture, or the Postmaster General, or any court of competent jurisdiction, under any provision of law repealed or amended by this Act, or in the exercise of duties, powers, or functions which, under this Act, are vested in the Administrator of the Federal Aviation Agency or the Civil Aeronautics Board, and which are in effect at the time this section takes effect, shall continue in effect according to their terms until modified, terminated, superseded, set aside, or repealed by the Administrator or the Board, as the case may be, or by any court of competent jurisdiction, or by operation of law.

Pending Administrative Proceedings

(b) The provisions of this Act shall not affect any proceedings pending at the time this section takes effect before the Secretary of Commerce, the Administrator of Civil Aeronautics, the Civil Aeronautics Board, the Chairman of the Airways Modernization Board, the Secretary of the Treasury, or the Secretary of Agriculture; but any such proceedings shall be continued before the successor agency, orders therein issued, appeals therefrom taken, and payments made pursuant to such orders, as if this Act had not been enacted; and orders issued in any such proceedings shall continue in effect until modified, terminated, superseded, or repealed by the Administrator, the Civil Aeronautics Board, the Secretary of the Treasury, or the Secretary of Agriculture or by operation of law.

Pending Judicial Proceedings

(c) The provisions of this Act shall not affect suits commenced prior to the date on which this section takes effect; and all such suits shall be continued by the successor agency, proceedings therein had, appeals therein taken, and judgments therein rendered, in the same manner and with the same effect as if this Act had not been passed. No suit, action, or other proceeding lawfully commenced by or against any agency or officer of the United States, in relation to the discharge of official duties, shall abate by reason of any transfer of authority, power, or duties from such agency or officer to the Administrator or the Board under the provisions of this Act, but the court, upon motion or supplemental petition filed at any time within twelve months, after such transfer, showing the necessity for a survival of such suit, action, or other proceeding to obtain a settlement of the questions involved, may allow the same to be maintained by or against the Administrator or the Board.

PERSONNEL, PROPERTY, AND APPROPRIATIONS

SEC. 1502. [*72 Stat. 810, 49 U.S.C. 1341 note*] (a) The officers, employees, and property (including office equipment and official records) of the Civil Aeronautics Administration of the Department of Commerce, and of the Airways Modernization Board, and such employees and property (including office equipment and official records) as the President, after consultation with the Civil Aeronautics Board, shall determine to have been employed by the Civil Aeronautics Board, in the exercise and performance of those powers and duties vested in and imposed upon it by the Civil Aeronautics Act of 1938, as amended, and which are vested by this Act in the Agency, shall be transferred to the Agency upon such date or dates as the President shall specify: *Provided*, That the transfer of such personnel shall be without reduction in classification or compensation, except that this requirement shall not operate after the end of the fiscal year during which such transfer is made to prevent the adjust-

[§§ 1503–1505]

ment of classification or compensation to conform to the duties to which such transferred personnel may be assigned.

(b) Such of the unexpended balances of appropriations available for use by the Civil Aeronautics Administration of the Department of Commerce and by the Airways Modernization Board, and such of the unexpended balances of appropriations available for use by the Civil Aeronautics Board in the exercise and performance of those powers and duties vested in and imposed upon it by the Civil Aeronautics Act of 1938, as amended, and which are vested by this Act in the Administrator, shall be transferred to the Agency upon such date or dates as the President shall specify, and shall be available for use in connection with the exercise and performance of the powers and duties vested in and imposed upon the Administrator by this Act. Where provisions of this Act which are to be administered by the Board are in substance reenactments (with or without modifications) of provisions of the Civil Aeronautics Act of 1938, as amended, administered by the Board at the time this section takes effect, the Board, in carrying out such provisions of this Act, may utilize unexpended balances of appropriations made for carrying out such provisions of the Civil Aeronautics Act of 1938, as amended.

(c) All records transferred to the Administrator under this Act shall be available for use by him to the same extent as if such records were originally records of the Administrator.

MEMBERS, OFFICERS, AND EMPLOYEES OF THE BOARD

SEC. 1503. [*72 Stat. 811, 49 U.S.C. 1321 note*] Nothing in this Act (1) shall affect the tenure of office of any individual who is a member of the Civil Aeronautics Board at the time title IV of this Act takes effect, or to nullify any action theretofore taken by the President in designating any such person as chairman or vice chairman of the Board, or (2) subject to section 1502(a), change the status of the officers and employees under the jurisdiction of the Board at that time.

SEPARABILITY

SEC. 1504. [*72 Stat. 811, 49 U.S.C. 1301 note*] If any provision of this Act or the application thereof to any person or circumstance is held invalid, the remainder of the Act and the application of such provision to other persons or circumstances shall not be affected thereby.

EFFECTIVE DATE

SEC. 1505. [*72 Stat. 811, 49 U.S.C. 1301 note*] The provisions of this Act shall become effective as follows:

(1) Section 301, section 302 (a), (b), (c), (f), (i), and (k), section 303(a), section 304, and section 1502, shall become effective on the date of enactment of this Act; and

(2) The remaining provisions shall become effective on the 60th day following the date on which the Administrator of the Federal Aviation Agency first appointed under this Act qualifies and takes office.[31]

---

[31] The first appointed Administrator qualified and took office on November 1, 1958. The remaining provisions of the Act became effective December 31, 1958.

Department of Transportation
Act - 1966

Public Law 89-670
89th Congress, H. R. 15963
October 15, 1966

𝔄𝔫 𝔄𝔠𝔱

To establish a Department of Transportation, and for other purposes.

Be it enacted by the Senate and House of Representatives of the United States of America in Congress assembled, That this Act may be cited as the "Department of Transportation Act".

DECLARATION OF PURPOSE

SEC. 2. (a) The Congress hereby declares that the general welfare, the economic growth and stability of the Nation and its security require the development of national transportation policies and programs conducive to the provision of fast, safe, efficient, and convenient transportation at the lowest cost consistent therewith and with other national objectives, including the efficient utilization and conservation of the Nation's resources.

(b)(1) The Congress therefore finds that the establishment of a Department of Transportation is necessary in the public interest and to assure the coordinated, effective administration of the transportation programs of the Federal Government; to facilitate the development and improvement of coordinated transportation service, to be provided by private enterprise to the maximum extent feasible; to encourage cooperation of Federal, State, and local governments, carriers, labor, and other interested parties toward the achievement of national transportation objectives; to stimulate technological advances in transportation; to provide general leadership in the identification and solution of transportation problems; and to develop and recommend to the President and the Congress for approval national transportation policies and programs to accomplish these objectives with full and appropriate consideration of the needs of the public, users, carriers, industry, labor, and the national defense.

(2) It is hereby declared to be the national policy that special effort should be made to preserve the natural beauty of the countryside and public park and recreation lands, wildlife and waterfowl refuges, and historic sites.

SEC. 3. (a) There is hereby established at the seat of government an executive department to be known as the Department of Transportation (hereafter referred to in this Act as the "Department"). There shall be at the head of the Department a Secretary of Transportation (hereafter referred to in this Act as the "Secretary"), who shall be appointed by the President, by and with the advice and consent of the Senate.

(b) There shall be in the Department an Under Secretary, who shall be appointed by the President, by and with the advice and consent of the Senate. The Under Secretary (or, during the absence or disability of the Under Secretary, or in the event of a vacancy in the office of Under Secretary, an Assistant Secretary or the General Counsel, determined according to such order as the Secretary shall prescribe) shall act for, and exercise the powers of the Secretary, during the absence or disability of the Secretary or in the event of a vacancy in the office of Secretary. The Under Secretary shall perform such functions, powers, and duties as the Secretary shall prescribe from time to time.

(c) There shall be in the Department four Assistant Secretaries and a General Counsel, who shall be appointed by the President, by and with the advice and consent of the Senate, and who shall perform such functions, powers, and duties as the Secretary shall prescribe from time to time.

(d) There shall be in the Department an Assistant Secretary for Administration, who shall be appointed, with the approval of the President, by the Secretary under the classified civil service who shall perform such functions, powers, and duties as the Secretary shall prescribe from time to time.

(e) (1) There is hereby established within the Department a Federal Highway Administration; a Federal Railroad Administration; and a Federal Aviation Administration. Each of these components shall be headed by an Administrator, and in the case of the Federal Aviation Administration there shall also be a Deputy Administrator. The Administrators and the Deputy Federal Aviation Administrator shall be appointed by the President, by and with the advice and consent of the Senate.

(2) The qualifications of the Administrator of the Federal Aviation Agency specified in section 301(b) of the Federal Aviation Act of 1958, as amended (72 Stat. 744; 49 U.S.C. 1341), and the qualifications and status of the Deputy Administrator specified in section 302(b) of the Federal Aviation Act of 1958, as amended (72 Stat. 744; 49 U.S.C. 1342), shall apply, respectively, to the Administrator and Deputy Administrator of the Federal Aviation Administration. However, nothing in this Act shall be construed to preclude the appointment of the present Administrator of the Federal Aviation Agency as Administrator of the Federal Aviation Administration in accordance with the provisions of the Act of June 22, 1965, as amended (79 Stat. 171).

(3) In addition to such functions, powers, and duties as are specified in this Act to be carried out by the Administrators, the Administrators and the Commandant of the Coast Guard shall carry out such additional functions, powers, and duties as the Secretary may prescribe.

The Administrators and the Commandant of the Coast Guard shall report directly to the Secretary.

(4) The functions, powers, and duties specified in this Act to be carried out by each Administrator shall not be transferred elsewhere in the Department unless specifically provided for by reorganization plan submitted pursuant to provisions of chapter 9 of title 5, United States Code, or by statute.

(f)(1) The Secretary shall carry out the provisions of the National Traffic and Motor Vehicle Safety Act of 1966 (80 Stat. 718) through a National Traffic Safety Bureau (hereafter referred to in this paragraph as "Bureau"), which he shall establish in the Department of Transportation. The Bureau shall be headed by a Director who shall be appointed by the President, by and with the advice and consent of the Senate, and shall be compensated at the rate prescribed for level V of the Executive Schedule. All other provisions of the National Traffic and Motor Vehicle Safety Act of 1966 shall apply.

(2) The Secretary shall carry out the provisions of the Highway Safety Act of 1966 (80 Stat. 731) (including chapter 4 of title 23 of the United States Code) through a National Highway Safety Bureau (hereafter referred to in this paragraph as "Bureau"), which he shall establish in the Department of Transportation. The Bureau shall be headed by a Director who shall be appointed by the President, by and with the advice and consent of the Senate, who shall be compensated at the rate prescribed for level V of the Executive Schedule. All other provisions of the Highway Safety Act of 1966 shall apply.

(3) The President is authorized, as provided in section 201 of the Highway Safety Act of 1966, to carry out the provisions of the National Traffic and Motor Vehicle Safety Act of 1966 through the Bureau and Director authorized by section 201 of the Highway Safety Act of 1966.

(4) The office of Federal Highway Administrator, created by section 303 of title 23, United States Code, is hereby transferred to and continued within the Department under the title Director of Public Roads. The Director shall be the operating head of the Bureau of Public Roads, or any other agency created within the Department to carry out the primary functions carried out immediately before the effective date of this Act by the Bureau of Public Roads.

GENERAL PROVISIONS

SEC. 4. (a) The Secretary in carrying out the purposes of this Act shall, among his responsibilities, exercise leadership under the direction of the President in transportation matters, including those affecting the national defense and those involving national or regional emergencies; provide leadership in the development of national transportation policies and programs, and make recommendations to the President and the Congress for their consideration and implementation; promote and undertake development, collection, and dissemination of technological, statistical, economic, and other information relevant to domestic and international transportation; consult and cooperate with the Secretary of Labor in gathering information regarding the status of labor-management contracts and other labor-management problems and in promoting industrial harmony and stable employment conditions in all modes of transportation; promote and undertake research and development relating to transportation, including noise abatement, with particular attention to aircraft noise; consult with the heads of other Federal departments and agencies on the transportation requirements of the Government, including the procurement of transportation or the operation of their own transport services in order to encourage them to establish and observe policies consistent with the maintenance of a coordinated transportation system; and consult and cooperate with State and local governments, carriers, labor, and other interested parties; including, when appropriate, holding informal public hearings.

(b)(1) In carrying out his duties and responsibilities under this Act, the Secretary shall be governed by all applicable statutes including the policy standards set forth in the Federal Aviation Act of 1958, as amended (49 U.S.C. 1301 et seq.); the national transportation policy of the Interstate Commerce Act, as amended (49 U.S.C., preceding §§ 1, 301, 901, and 1001); title 23, United States Code, relating to Federal-aid highways; and title 14 U.S.C., titles LII and LIII of the Revised Statutes (46 U.S.C., chs. 2A, 7, 11, 14, 15, and 18), the Act of April 25, 1940, as amended (54 Stat. 163; 46 U.S.C. 526–526u), and the Act of September 2, 1958, as amended (72 Stat. 1754; 46 U.S.C. 527–527h), relating to the United States Coast Guard.

(2) Nothing in this Act shall be construed to authorize, without appropriate action by Congress, the adoption, revision, or implementation of—

(A) any transportation policy, or

(B) any investment standards or criteria.

(3) In exercising the functions, powers, and duties conferred on and transferred to the Secretary by this Act, the Secretary shall give full consideration to the need for operational continuity of the functions transferred, to the need for effectiveness and safety in transportation systems, and to the needs of the national defense.

(c) Orders and actions of the Secretary or the National Transportation Safety Board in the exercise of functions, powers, and duties transferred under this Act, and orders and actions of the Administrators pursuant to the functions, powers, and duties specifically assigned to them by this Act, shall be subject to judicial review to the same extent and in the same manner as if such orders and actions had been by the department or agency exercising such functions, powers, and duties immediately preceding their transfer. Any statutory requirements relating to notice, hearings, action upon the record, or administrative review that apply to any function transferred by this Act shall apply to the exercise of such functions by the Secretary, the Administrators, or the National Transportation Safety Board.

(d) In the exercise of the functions, powers, and duties transferred under this Act, the Secretary, the Administrators, and the National Transportation Safety Board shall have the same authority as that vested in the department or agency exercising such functions, powers, and duties immediately preceding their transfer, and their actions in exercising such functions, powers, and duties shall have the same force and effect as when exercised by such department or agency.

(e) It shall be the duty of the Secretary—

(1) to promptly investigate the safety compliance records in the Department of each applicant seeking operating authority from the Interstate Commerce Commission (referred to in this subsection as the "Commission") and to report his findings to the Commission;

(2) when the safety record of an applicant for permanent operating authority, or for approval of a proposed transaction involving transfer of operating authority, fails to satisfy the Secretary, to intervene and present evidence of such applicant's fitness in Commission proceedings;

(3) to furnish promptly upon request of the Commission a statement regarding the safety record of any applicant seeking temporary operating authority from the Commission; and

(4) (A) to furnish upon request of the Commission a complete report of the safety compliance of any carrier, (B) to have made such additional inspections or safety compliance surveys which the Commission deems necessary or desirable in order to process an application or to determine the fitness of a carrier, and (C) if the Commission so requests, to intervene and present evidence in any proceeding in which a determination of fitness is required.

(f) The Secretary shall cooperate and consult with the Secretaries of the Interior, Housing and Urban Development, and Agriculture, and with the States in developing transportation plans and programs that include measures to maintain or enhance the natural beauty of the lands traversed. After the effective date of this Act, the Secretary shall not approve any program or project which requires the use of any land from a public park, recreation area, wildlife and waterfowl refuge, or historic site unless (1) there is no feasible and prudent alternative to the use of such land, and (2) such program includes all possible planning to minimize harm to such park, recreational area, wildlife and waterfowl refuge, or historic site resulting from such use.

(g) The Secretary and the Secretary of Housing and Urban Development shall consult and exchange information regarding their respective transportation policies and activities; carry on joint planning, research and other activities; and coordinate assistance for local transportation projects. They shall jointly study how Federal policies and programs can assure that urban transportation systems most effectively serve both national transportation needs and the comprehensively planned development of urban areas. They shall, within one year after the effective date of this Act, and annually thereafter, report to the President, for submission to the Congress, on their studies and other activities under this subsection, including any legislative recommendations which they determine to be desirable. The Secretary and the Secretary of Housing and Urban Development shall study and report within one year after the effective date of this Act to the President and the Congress on the logical and efficient organization and location of urban mass transportation functions in the Executive Branch.

NATIONAL TRANSPORTATION SAFETY BOARD

SEC. 5. (a) There is hereby established within the Department a National Transportation Safety Board (referred to hereafter in this Act as "Board").

(b) There are hereby transferred to, and it shall be the duty of the Board to exercise, the functions, powers, and duties transferred to the Secretary by sections 6 and 8 of this Act with regard to—

(1) determining the cause or probable cause of transportation accidents and reporting the facts, conditions, and circumstances relating to such accidents; and

(2) reviewing on appeal the suspension, amendment, modification, revocation, or denial of any certificate or license issued by the Secretary or by an Administrator.

(c) The Board shall exercise the functions, powers, and duties relating to aircraft accident investigations transferred to the Secretary by section 6(d) of this Act.

(d) The Board is further authorized to—

(1) make such recommendations to the Secretary or Administrators on the basis of the exercise of its functions, powers, and duties which, in its opinion, will tend to prevent transportation accidents and promote transportation safety;

(2) conduct special studies on matters pertaining to safety in transportation and the prevention of accidents;

(3) insure that in cases in which it is required to determine cause or probable cause, reports of investigation adequately state the circumstances of the accident involved;

(4) initiate on its own motion or conduct rail, highway, or pipeline accident investigations as the Board deems necessary or appropriate;

(5) make recommendations to the Secretary or Administrators concerning rules, regulations, and procedures for the conduct of accident investigations;

(6) request the Secretary or Administrators to initiate specific accident investigations or conduct further investigations as the Board determines to be necessary or appropriate;

(7) arrange for the personal participation of members or other personnel of the Board in accident investigations conducted by the Secretary or Administrators in such cases as it deems appropriate; and

(8) request from the Secretary or Administrators notification of transportation accidents and reports of such accidents as the Board deems necessary.

(e) Except as otherwise provided by statute, the Board shall make public all reports, orders, decisions, rules, and regulations issued pursuant to sections 5(b)(1) and 5(b)(2), and the Board shall also make public—

(1) every recommendation made to the Secretary or an Administrator;

(2) every special study conducted; and

(3) every action of the Board requesting the Secretary or an Administrator to take action,

pursuant to section 5(d)(1), (2), (3), (5), (6), or (8).

(f) In the exercise of its functions, powers, and duties, the Board shall be independent of the Secretary and the other offices and officers of the Department.

(g) The Board shall report to the Congress annually on the conduct of its functions under this Act and the effectiveness of accident investigations in the Department, together with such recommendations for legislation as it may deem appropriate.

(h) The Board shall consist of five members to be appointed by the President, by and with the advice and consent of the Senate. No more than three members of the Board shall be of the same political party. Members of the Board shall be appointed with due regard to their fitness for the efficient dispatch of the functions, powers, and duties vested in and imposed upon the Board, and may be removed by the President for inefficiency, neglect of duty, or malfeasance in office.

(i) Members of the Board shall be appointed for terms of five years, except that (1) any member appointed to fill a vacancy occurring prior to the expiration of the term for which his predecessor was appointed shall be appointed only for the remainder of such term, and (2) the five members first appointed shall serve for terms (designated by the President at the time of appointment) ending on the last day of the first, second, third, fourth, and fifth calendar years beginning after the year of enactment of this Act. Upon the expiration of his term of office, a member shall continue to serve until his successor is appointed and shall have qualified.

(j) The President shall designate from time to time one of the members of the Board as Chairman and one of the members as Vice Chairman, who shall act as Chairman in the absence or incapacity of the Chairman, or in the event of a vacancy in the office of the Chairman. The Chairman shall be the chief executive and administrative officer of the Board and shall exercise the responsibility of the Board with respect to (1) the appointment and supervision of personnel employed by the Board; (2) the distribution of business among the Board's personnel; and (3) the use and expenditure of funds. In executing and administering the functions of the Board on its behalf, the Chairman shall be governed by the general policies of the Board and by its decisions, findings, and determinations. Three of the members shall constitute a quorum of the Board.

(k) The Board is authorized to establish such rules, regulations, and procedures as are necessary to the exercise of its functions.

(l) In carrying out its functions, the Board (or, upon the authorization of the Board, any member thereof or any hearing examiner assigned to or employed by the Board) shall have the same powers as are vested in the Secretary to hold hearings, sign and issue subpenas, administer oaths, examine witnesses, and receive evidence at any place in the United States it may designate.

(m) The Board may delegate to any officer or official of the Board, or, with the approval of the Secretary, to any officer or official of the Department such of its functions as it may deem appropriate, except that—

(1) with respect to aviation, the proviso in section 701(g) of the Federal Aviation Act of 1958, as amended (72 Stat. 782; 49 U.S.C. 1441(g)) shall apply to the Secretary, the Federal Aviation Administrator and their representatives, and

(2) the Board shall not delegate the appellate or determination of probable cause functions transferred to it by section 6(d) of this Act.

(n) Subject to the civil service and classification laws, the Board is authorized to select, appoint, employ, and fix compensation of such officers and employees, including investigators, attorneys and hearing examiners, as shall be necessary to carry out its powers and duties under this Act.

(o) The Board is authorized, on a reimbursable basis when appropriate, to use the available services, equipment, personnel, and facilities of the Department and of other civilian or military agencies and instrumentalities of the Federal Government, and to cooperate with the Department and such other agencies and instrumentalities in the establishment and use of services, equipment, and facilities of the Board. The Board is further authorized to confer with and avail itself of the cooperation, services, records, and facilities of State, territorial, municipal, or other local agencies.

TRANSFERS TO DEPARTMENT

SEC. 6. (a) There are hereby transferred to and vested in the Secretary all functions, powers, and duties of the Secretary of Commerce and other offices and officers of the Department of Commerce under—

(1) the following laws and provisions of law relating generally to highways:

(A) Title 23, United State Code, as amended.

(B) The Federal-Aid Highway Act of 1966 (80 Stat. 766).

(C) The Federal-Aid Highway Act of 1962, as amended (76 Stat. 1145; 23 U.S.C. 307 note).

(D) The Act of July 14, 1960, as amended (74 Stat. 526; 23 U.S.C. 313 note).

(E) The Federal-Aid Highway Act of 1954, as amended (68 Stat. 70).

(F) The Act of September 26, 1961, as amended (75 Stat. 670).

(G) The Highway Revenue Act of 1956, as amended (70 Stat. 387; 23 U.S.C. 120 note).

(H) The Highway Beautification Act of 1965, as amended (79 Stat. 1028; 23 U.S.C. 131 et seq. notes).

(I) The Alaska Omnibus Act, as amended (73 Stat. 141; 48 U.S.C. 21 note prec.).

(J) The Joint Resolution of August 28, 1965, as amended (79 Stat. 578; 23 U.S.C. 101 et seq. notes).

(K) Section 502(c) of the General Bridge Act of 1946, as amended (60 Stat. 847; 33 U.S.C. 525(c)).

(L) The Act of April 27, 1962, as amended (76 Stat. 59).

(M) Reorganization Plan No. 7 of 1949 (63 Stat. 1070; 5 U.S.C. 133z–15 note).

(2) the following laws and provisions of law relating generally to ground transportation:

(A) The Act of September 30, 1965, as amended (79 Stat. 893; 49 U.S.C. 1631 et seq.).

(B) The Urban Mass Transportation Act of 1964, as amended (78 Stat. 306, 49 U.S.C. 1607).

(3) the following laws and provisions of law relating generally to aircraft:

(A) The Act of September 7, 1957, as amended (71 Stat. 629; 49 U.S.C. 1324 note).

(B) Section 410 of the Federal Aviation Act of 1958, as amended (72 Stat. 769; 49 U.S.C. 1380).

(C) Title XIII of the Federal Aviation Act of 1958, as amended (72 Stat. 800; 49 U.S.C. 1531 et seq.).

(4) the following law relating generally to pilotage: The Great Lakes Pilotage Act of 1960, as amended (74 Stat. 259; 46 U.S.C. 216 et seq.).

(5) the following law to the extent it authorizes scientific and professional positions which relate primarily to functions transferred by this subsection: The Act of August 1, 1947, as amended (61 Stat. 715; 5 U.S.C. 1161).

(6) the following laws relating generally to traffic and highway safety:

(A) The National Traffic and Motor Vehicle Safety Act of 1966 (80 Stat. 718).

(B) The Highway Safety Act of 1966 (80 Stat. 731).

(b)(1) The Coast Guard is hereby transferred to the Department, and there are hereby transferred to and vested in the Secretary all functions, powers, and duties, relating to the Coast Guard, of the Secretary of the Treasury and of other officers and offices of the Department of the Treasury.

(2) Notwithstanding the transfer of the Coast Guard to the Department and the transfer to the Secretary of the functions, powers, and duties, relating to the Coast Guard, of the Secretary of the Treasury and of other officers and offices of the Department of the Treasury, effected by the provisions of paragraph (1) of this subsection, the Coast Guard, together with the functions, powers, and duties relating thereto, shall operate as a part of the Navy, subject to the orders of the Secretary of the Navy, in time of war or when the President shall so direct, as provided in section 3 of title 14, United States Code, as amended.

(3) Notwithstanding any other provision of this Act, the functions, powers, and duties of the General Counsel of the Department of the Treasury set out in chapter 47 of title 10, United States Code, as amended (Uniform Code of Military Justice), are hereby transferred to and vested in the General Counsel of the Department.

(c)(1) There are hereby transferred to and vested in the Secretary all functions, powers, and duties of the Federal Aviation Agency, and of the Administrator and other officers and offices thereof, including the development and construction of a civil supersonic aircraft: *Provided, however,* That there are hereby transferred to the Federal Aviation Administrator, and it shall be his duty to exercise the functions, powers, and duties of the Secretary pertaining to aviation safety as set forth in sections 306, 307, 308, 309, 312, 313, 314, 1101, 1105, and 1111, and titles VI, VII, IX, and XII of the Federal Aviation Act of 1958, as amended. In exercising these enumerated functions, powers, and duties, the Administrator shall be guided by the declaration of policy in section 103 of the Federal Aviation Act of 1958, as amended. Decisions of the Federal Aviation Administrator made pursuant to the exercise of the functions, powers, and duties enumerated in this subsection to be exercised by the Administrator shall be administratively final, and appeals as authorized by law or this Act shall be taken directly to the National Transportation Safety Board or to the courts, as appropriate.

(2) Nothing in this Act shall affect the power of the President under section 302(e) of the Federal Aviation Act of 1958 (72 Stat. 746, 49 U.S.C. 1343(c)) to transfer, to the Department of Defense in the event of war, any functions transferred by this Act from the Federal Aviation Agency.

(d) There are hereby transferred to and vested in the Secretary all functions, powers, and duties of the Civil Aeronautics Board, and of the Chairman, members, officers, and offices thereof under titles VI (72 Stat. 775; 5 U.S.C. 1421 et seq.) and VII (72 Stat. 781; 49 U.S.C. 1441 et seq.) of the Federal Aviation Act of 1958, as amended: *Provided, however,* That these functions, powers, and duties are hereby transferred to and shall be exercised by the National Transportation Safety Board. Decisions of the National Transportation Safety Board made pursuant to the exercise of the functions, powers, and duties enumerated in this subsection shall be administratively final, and appeals as authorized by law or this Act shall be taken directly to the courts.

(e) There are hereby transferred to and vested in the Secretary all functions, powers, and duties of the Interstate Commerce Commission, and of the Chairman, members, officers, and offices thereof, under—

(1) the following laws relating generally to safety appliances and equipment on railroad engines and cars, and protection of employees and travelers:

(A) The Act of March 2, 1893, as amended (27 Stat. 531; 45 U.S.C. 1 et seq.).

(B) The Act of March 2, 1903, as amended (32 Stat. 943; 45 U.S.C. 8 et seq.).

(C) The Act of April 14, 1910, as amended (36 Stat. 298; 45 U.S.C. 11 et seq.).

(D) The Act of May 30, 1908, as amended (35 Stat. 476; 45 U.S.C. 17 et seq.).

(E) The Act of February 17, 1911, as amended (36 Stat. 913; 45 U.S.C. 22 et seq.).

(F) The Act of March 4, 1915, as amended (38 Stat. 1192; 45 U.S.C. 30).

(G) Reorganization Plan No. 3 of 1965 (79 Stat. 1320).

(H) Joint Resolution of June 30, 1906, as amended (34 Stat. 838; 45 U.S.C. 35).

(I) The Act of May 27, 1908, as amended (35 Stat. 325; 45 U.S.C. 36 et seq.).

(J) The Act of March 4, 1909, as amended (35 Stat. 965; 45 U.S.C. 37).

(K) The Act of May 6, 1910, as amended (36 Stat. 350; 45 U.S.C. 38 et seq.).

(2) the following law relating generally to hours of service of employees: The Act of March 4, 1907, as amended (34 Stat. 1415; 45 U.S.C. 61 et seq.).

(3) the following law relating generally to medals for heroism: The Act of February 23, 1905, as amended (33 Stat. 743; 49 U.S.C. 1201 et seq.).

(4) the following provisions of law relating generally to explosives and other dangerous articles: Sections 831–835 of title 18, United States Code, as amended.

(5) the following laws relating generally to standard time zones and daylight saving time:

(A) The Act of March 19, 1918, as amended (40 Stat. 450; 15 U.S.C. 261 et seq.).

(B) The Act of March 4, 1921, as amended (41 Stat. 1446; 15 U.S.C. 265).

(C) The Uniform Time Act of 1966, as amended (80 Stat. 107).

(6) the following provisions of the Interstate Commerce Act, as amended—

(A) relating generally to safety appliances methods and systems: Section 25 (49 U.S.C. 26).

(B) relating generally to investigation of motor vehicle sizes, weights, and service of employees: Section 226 (49 U.S.C. 325).

(C) relating generally to qualifications and maximum hours of service of employees and safety of operation and equipment: Sections 204(a) (1) and (2), to the extent that they relate to qualifications and maximum hours of service of employees and safety of operation and equipment; and sections 204(a) (3), (3a), and (5) (49 U.S.C. 304).

(D) to the extent they relate to private carriers of property by motor vehicle and carriers of migrant workers by motor vehicle other than contract carriers: Sections 221(a), 221(c), and 224 (49 U.S.C. 321 et seq.).

(f)(1) Nothing in subsection (e) shall diminish the functions, powers, and duties of the Interstate Commerce Commission under sections 1(6), 206, 207, 209, 210a, 212, and 216 of the Interstate Commerce Act, as amended (49 U.S.C. 1(6), 306 et seq.), or under any other section of that Act not specifically referred to in subsection (e).

(2)(A) With respect to any function which is transferred to the Secretary by subsection (e) and which was vested in the Interstate Commerce Commission preceding such transfer, the Secretary shall have the same administrative powers under the Interstate Commerce Act as the Commission had before such transfer with respect to such transferred function. After such transfer, the Commission may exercise its administrative powers under the Interstate Commerce Act only with respect to those of its functions not transferred by subsection (e).

(B) For purposes of this paragraph—

(i) the term "function" includes power and duty, and

(ii) the term "administrative powers under the Interstate Commerce Act" means any functions under the following provisions of the Interstate Commerce Act, as amended: Sections 12, 13(1), 13(2), 14, 16(12), the last sentence of 18(1), sections 20 (except clauses (3), (4), (11), and (12) thereof), 204(a) (6) and (7), 204(c), 204(d), 205(d), 205(f), 220 (except subsection (c) and the proviso of subsection (a) thereof), 222 (except subsections (b) (2) and (b) (3) thereof), and 417(b) (1) (49 U.S.C. 12 et seq., 304 et seq., and 1017).

(3)(A) The Federal Railroad Administrator shall carry out the functions, powers, and duties of the Secretary pertaining to railroad and pipeline safety as set forth in the statutes transferred to the Secretary by subsection (e) of this section.

(B) The Federal Highway Administrator shall carry out the functions, powers, and duties of the Secretary pertaining to motor carrier safety as set forth in the statutes transferred to the Secretary by subsection (e) of this section.

(C) Decisions of the Federal Railroad Administrator and the Federal Highway Administrator (i) which are made pursuant to the exercise of the functions, powers, and duties enumerated in subparagraphs (A) and (B) of this paragraph to be carried out by the Administrators, and (ii) which involve notice and hearing required by law, shall be administratively final, and appeals as authorized by law or this Act shall be taken directly to the National Transportation Safety Board or the courts, as appropriate.

(g) There are hereby transferred to and vested in the Secretary all functions, powers, and duties of the Secretary of the Army and other officers and offices of the Department of the Army under—

    (1) the following law and provisions of law relating generally to water vessel anchorages:

        (A) Section 7 of the Act of March 4, 1915, as amended (38 Stat. 1053; 33 U.S.C. 471).

        (B) Article 11 of section 1 of the Act of June 7, 1897, as amended (30 Stat. 98; 33 U.S.C. 180).

        (C) Rule 9 of section 1 of the Act of February 8, 1895, as amended (28 Stat. 647; 33 U.S.C. 258).

        (D) Rule numbered 13 of section 4233 of the Revised Statutes, as amended (33 U.S.C. 322).

    (2) the following provision of law relating generally to drawbridge operating regulations: Section 5 of the Act of August 18, 1894, as amended (28 Stat. 362; 33 U.S.C. 499).

    (3) the following law relating generally to obstructive bridges: The Act of June 21, 1940, as amended (54 Stat. 497; 33 U.S.C. 511 et seq.).

    (4) the following laws and provisions of law relating generally to the reasonableness of tolls:

        (A) Section 4 of the Act of March 23, 1906, as amended (34 Stat. 85; 33 U.S.C. 494).

        (B) Section 503 of the General Bridge Act of 1946, as amended (60 Stat. 847; 33 U.S.C. 526).

        (C) Section 17 of the Act of June 10, 1930, as amended (46 Stat. 552; 33 U.S.C. 498a).

        (D) The Act of June 27, 1930, as amended (46 Stat. 821; 33 U.S.C. 498b).

        (E) The Act of August 21, 1935, as amended (49 Stat. 670; 33 U.S.C. 503 et seq.).

    (5) the following law relating to prevention of pollution of the sea by oil: The Oil Pollution Act, 1961, as amended (75 Stat. 402; 33 U.S.C. 1001 et seq.).

    (6) the following laws and provision of law to the extent that they relate generally to the location and clearances of bridges and causeways in the navigable waters of the United States:

        (A) Section 9 of the Act of March 3, 1899, as amended, (30 Stat. 1151; 33 U.S.C. 401).

        (B) The Act of March 23, 1906, as amended (34 Stat. 84; 33 U.S.C. 491 et seq.).

(C) The General Bridge Act of 1946; as amended (60 Stat. 847; 33 U.S.C. 525 et seq.).

(h) The provisions of subchapter II of chapter 5 and of chapter 7 of title 5, United States Code, shall be applicable to proceedings by the Department and any of the administrations or boards within the Department established by this Act except that notwithstanding this or any other provision of this Act, the transfer of functions, powers, and duties to the Secretary or any other officer in the Department shall not include functions vested by subchapter II of chapter 5 of title 5, United States Code, in hearing examiners employed by any department, agency, or component thereof whose functions are transferred under the provisions of this Act.

(i) The administration of the Alaska Railroad, established pursuant to the Act of March 12, 1914, as amended (38 Stat. 308), and all of the functions authorized to be carried out by the Secretary of the Interior pursuant to Executive Order Numbered 11107, April 25, 1963 (28 F.R. 4225), relative to the operation of said Railroad, are hereby transferred to and vested in the Secretary of Transportation who shall exercise the same authority with respect thereto as is now exercised by the Secretary of the Interior pursuant to said Executive order.

TRANSPORTATION INVESTMENT STANDARDS

SEC. 7. (a) The Secretary, subject to the provisions of section 4 of this Act, shall develop and from time to time in the light of experience revise standards and criteria consistent with national transportation policies, for the formulation and economic evaluation of all proposals for the investment of Federal funds in transportation facilities or equipment, except such proposals as are concerned with (1) the acquisition of transportation facilities or equipment by Federal agencies in providing transportation services for their own use; (2) an interoceanic canal located outside the contiguous United States; (3) defense features included at the direction of the Department of Defense in the design and construction of civil air, sea, and land transportation; (4) programs of foreign assistance; (5) water resource projects; or (6) grant-in-aid programs authorized by law. The standards and criteria developed or revised pursuant to this subsection shall be promulgated by the Secretary upon their approval by the Congress.

The standards and criteria for economic evaluation of water resource projects shall be developed by the Water Resources Council established by Public Law 89–80. For the purpose of such standards and criteria, the primary direct navigation benefits of a water resource project are defined as the product of the savings to shippers using the waterway and the estimated traffic that would use the waterway; where the savings to shippers shall be construed to mean the difference between (a) the freight rates or charges prevailing at the time of the study for the movement by the alternative means and (b) those which would be charged on the proposed waterway; and where the estimate of traffic that would use the waterway will be based on such freight rates, taking into account projections of the economic growth of the area.

The Water Resources Council established under section 101 of Public Law 89–80 is hereby expanded to include the Secretary of Transportation on matters pertaining to navigation features of water resource projects.

(b) Every survey, plan, or report formulated by a Federal agency which includes a proposal as to which the Secretary has promulgated standards and criteria pursuant to subsection (a) shall be (1) prepared in accord with such standards and criteria and upon the basis of information furnished by the Secretary with respect to projected growth of transportation needs and traffic in the affected area, the relative efficiency of various modes of transport, the available transportation services in the area, and the general effect of the proposed investment on existing modes, and on the regional and national economy; (2) coordinated by the proposing agency with the Secretary and, as appropriate, with other Federal agencies, States, and local units of government for inclusion of his and their views and comments; and (3) transmitted thereafter by the proposing agency to the President for disposition in accord with law and procedures established by him.

AMENDMENTS TO OTHER LAWS

SEC. 8. (a) Section 406(b) of the Federal Aviation Act of 1958, as amended (72 Stat. 763; 49 U.S.C. 1376(b)), is amended by adding the following sentence at the end thereof: "In applying clause (3) of this subsection, the Board shall take into consideration any standards and criteria prescribed by the Secretary of Transportation, for determining the character and quality of transportation required for the commerce of the United States and the national defense."

(b) Section 201 of the Appalachian Regional Development Act of 1965, as amended (79 Stat. 10; 40 U.S.C. App. 206) is amended as follows:

(1) The first sentence of subsection (a) of that section is amended by striking the words "Commerce (hereafter in this section referred to as the 'Secretary')" and inserting in lieu thereof "Transportation".

(2) The last sentence of subsection (a) of that section is amended by inserting after the word "Secretary", the words "of Transportation".

(3) Subsection (b) of that section is amended by inserting after the word "Secretary", the words "of Commerce".

(4) Subsection (c) of that section is amended by striking the first sentence and inserting in lieu thereof the following sentence: "Such recommendations as are approved by the Secretary of Commerce shall be transmitted to the Secretary of Transportation for his approval."

(5) The second sentence of subsection (c) of that section is amended by inserting after the word "Secretary" the words "of Transportation".

(6) Subsection (e) of that section is amended by inserting after the word "Secretary" the words "of Transportation".

(7) Subsection (f) of that section is amended by inserting after the word "Secretary", the words "of Commerce and the Secretary of Transportation". Subsection (f) of that section is further amended by striking the word "determines" and inserting in lieu thereof "determine".

(8) Subsection (g) of that section is amended by striking the period at the end thereof and adding the following: "to the Secretary of Commerce, who shall transfer funds to the Secretary of Transportation for adminstration of projects approved by both Secretaries."

(c) Section 206(c) of the Appalachian Regional Development Act of 1965, as amended (79 Stat. 15; 40 U.S.C. App. 206), is amended by inserting after "Interior," the words "Secretary of Transportation,".

(d) Section 212(a) of the Interstate Commerce Act, as amended (49 Stat. 555), is amended by striking "of the Commission" the second, third, and fourth times those words occur.

(e) Section 13(b)(1) of the Fair Labor Standards Act of 1938, as amended (52 Stat. 1067), is amended by striking the words "Interstate Commerce Commission" and inserting in lieu thereof "Secretary of Transportation".

(f) The second sentence of section 3 of the Federal Explosives Act, as amended (40 Stat. 386; 50 U.S.C. 123) is amended to read as follows: "This Act shall not apply to explosives or ingredients which are in transit upon vessels, railroad cars, aircraft, or other conveyances in conformity with statutory law or with the rules and regulations of the Secretary of Transportation."

(g)(1) Section 1 of the Act of May 13, 1954, as amended (68 Stat. 93; 33 U.S.C. 981), is amended to read as follows:

"SECTION 1. There is hereby created, subject to the direction and supervision of the Secretary of Transportation, a body corporate to be known as the Saint Lawrence Seaway Development Corporation (hereinafter referred to as the 'Corporation')."

(2) Notwithstanding any other provision of this Act, the Administrator of the Saint Lawrence Seaway Development Corporation shall report directly to the Secretary.

(h) Section 201 of the Highway Safety Act of 1966 (80 Stat. 731) is amended by striking the words "Federal Highway Administrator" and inserting in lieu thereof the words "Director of Public Roads", by striking the word "Agency" wherever it occurs in such section and inserting in lieu thereof the word "Bureau", and by striking "an Administrator" or "Administrator", wherever appearing therein, and inserting in lieu thereof "a Director" or "Director", respectively.

(i) Section 115 of the National Traffic and Motor Vehicle Safety Act of 1966 (80 Stat. 718) is amended by striking the word "Agency" wherever it occurs in such section and inserting in lieu thereof the word "Bureau", and by striking the word "Administrator" wherever it occurs in such section and inserting in lieu thereof the word "Director".

(j) Section 3(a) of the Marine Resources and Engineering Development Act of 1966 (80 Stat. 204) is amended by striking the words "the Treasury" and inserting in lieu thereof "Transportation".

(k) Section 2(e) of the Act of September 22, 1966, Public Law 89-599, is amended by striking the words "of Commerce" and inserting in lieu thereof the words "of Transportation".

ADMINISTRATIVE PROVISIONS

SEC. 9. (a) In addition to the authority contained in any other Act which is transferred to and vested in the Secretary, the National Transportation Safety Board, or any other officer in the Department, the Secretary is authorized, subject to the civil service and classification laws, to select, appoint, employ, and fix the compensation of such officers and employees, including investigators, attorneys, and hearing examiners, as are necessary to carry out the provisions of this Act and to prescribe their authority and duties.

(b) The Secretary may obtain services as authorized by section 3109 of title 5 of the United States Code, but at rates not to exceed $100 per diem for individuals unless otherwise specified in an appropriation Act.

(c) The Secretary is authorized to provide for participation of military personnel in carrying out the functions of the Department. Members of the Army, the Navy, the Air Force, or the Marine Corps may be detailed for service in the Department by the appropriate Secretary, pursuant to cooperative agreements with the Secretary of Transportation.

(d)(1) Appointment, detail, or assignment to, acceptance of, and service in any appointive or other position in the Department under the authority of section 9(c) and section 9(p) shall in no way affect status, office, rank, or grade which officers or enlisted men may occupy or hold or any emolument, perquisite, right, privilege, or benefit incident to or arising out of any such status, office, rank, or grade, nor shall any member so appointed, detailed, or assigned be charged against any statutory limitation on grades or strengths applicable to the Armed Forces. A person so appointed, detailed, or assigned shall not be subject to direction by or control by his armed force or any officer thereof directly or indirectly with respect to the responsibilities exercised in the position to which appointed, detailed, or assigned.

(2) The Secretary shall report annually in writing to the appropriate committees of the Congress on personnel appointed and agreements entered into under subsection (c) of this section, including the number, rank, and positions of members of the armed services detailed pursuant thereto.

(e)(1) Except where this Act vests in any administration, agency or board, specific functions, powers, and duties, the Secretary may, in addition to the authority to delegate and redelegate contained in any other Act in the exercise of the functions transferred to or vested in the Secretary in this Act, delegate any of his residual functions, powers and duties to such officers and employees of the Department as he may designate, may authorize such successive redelegations of such functions, powers, and duties as he may deem desirable, and may make such rules and regulations as may be necessary to carry out his functions, powers, and duties.

(2) In addition to the authority to delegate and redelegate contained in any other Act, in the exercise of the functions transferred to or specified by this Act to be carried out by any officer in the Department, such officer may delegate any of such functions, powers, and duties to such other officers and employees of the Department as he may designate; may authorize such successive redelegations of such functions, powers, and duties as he may deem desirable; and may make such rules and regulations as may be necessary to carry out such functions, powers, and duties.

(3) The Administrators established by section 3(e) of this Act may not delegate any of the statutory duties and responsibilities specifically assigned to them by this Act outside of their respective administrations.

(f) The personnel, assets, liabilities, contracts, property, records, and unexpended balances of appropriations, authorizations, allocations, and other funds employed, held, used, arising from, available or to be made available, of the Federal Aviation Agency, and of the head and other officers and offices thereof, are hereby transferred to the Secretary: *Provided, however,* That the personnel, assets, liabilities, contracts, property, records, and unexpended balances of appropriations, authorizations, allocations, and other funds employed, held, used, arising from, available, or to be made available in carrying out the duties and functions transferred by this Act to the Secretary which are specified by this Act to be carried out by the Federal Aviation Administrator shall be assigned by the Secretary to the Federal Aviation Administrator for these purposes.

(g) So much of the positions, personnel, assets, liabilities, contracts, property, records, and unexpended balances of appropriations, authorizations, allocations, and other funds employed, held, used, arising from, available or to be made available in connection with the functions, powers, and duties transferred by sections 6 (except section 6(c)) and 8 (d) and (e) of this Act as the Director of the Bureau of the Budget shall determine shall be transferred to the Secretary: *Provided, however,* That the positions, personnel, assets, liabilities, contracts, property, records, and unexpended balances of appropriations, authorizations, allocations, and other funds employed, held, used, arising from, available, or to be made available, by the Civil Aeronautics Board in carrying out the duties transferred by this Act to be exercised by the National Transportation Safety Board shall be transferred to the National Transportation Safety Board. Except as provided in subsection (h), personnel engaged in functions, powers, and duties transferred under this Act shall be transferred in accordance with applicable laws and regulations relating to transfer of functions.

(h) The transfer of personnel pursuant to subsections (f) and (g) of this section shall be without reduction in classification or compensation for one year after such transfer.

(i) In any case where all of the functions, powers, and duties of any office or agency, other than the Coast Guard, are transferred pursuant to this Act, such office or agency shall lapse. Any person who, on the effective date of this Act, held a position compensated in accordance with the Executive Schedule, and who, without a break in service, is appointed in the Department to a position having duties comparable to those performed immediately preceding his appointment shall continue to be compensated in his new position at not less than the rate provided for his previous position, for the duration of his service in his new position.

(j) The Secretary is authorized to establish a working capital fund, to be available without fiscal year limitation, for expenses necessary for the maintenance and operation of such common administrative services as he shall find to be desirable in the interest of economy and efficiency in the Department, including such services as a central supply service for stationery and other supplies and equipment for which adequate stocks may be maintained to meet in whole or in part the requirements of the Department and its agencies; central messenger, mail, telephone, and other communications services; office space, central services for document reproduction, and for graphics and visual aids; and a central library service. The capital of the fund shall consist of any appropriations made for the purpose of providing capital (which appropriations are hereby authorized) and the fair and reasonable value of such stocks of supplies, equipment, and other assets and inventories on order as the Secretary may transfer to the fund, less the related liabilities and unpaid obligations. Such funds shall be reimbursed in advance from available funds of agencies and offices in the Department, or from other sources, for supplies and services at rates which will approximate the expense of operation, including the accrual of annual leave and the depreciation of equipment. The fund shall also be credited with receipts from sale or exchange of property and receipts in payment for loss or damage to property owned by the fund. There shall be covered into the United States Treasury as miscellaneous receipts any surplus found in the fund (all assets, liabilities, and prior losses considered) above the amounts transferred or appropriated to establish and maintain said fund.

(k) The Secretary shall cause a seal of office to be made for the Department of such device as he shall approve, and judicial notice shall be taken of such seal.

(l) In addition to the authority contained in any other Act which is transferred to and vested in the Secretary, the National Transportation Safety Board, or other officer in the Department, as necessary, and when not otherwise available, the Secretary is authorized to provide for, construct, or maintain the following for employees and their dependents stationed at remote localities:

(1) Emergency medical services and supplies;

(2) Food and other subsistence supplies;

(3) Messing facilities;

(4) Motion picture equipment and film for recreation and training;

(5) Reimbursement for food, clothing, medicine, and other supplies furnished by such employees in emergencies for the temporary relief of distressed persons; and

(6) Living and working quarters and facilities.

The furnishing of medical treatment under paragraph (1) and the furnishing of services and supplies under paragraphs (2) and (3) of this subsection shall be at prices reflecting reasonable value as determined by the Secretary, and the proceeds therefrom shall be credited to the appropriation from which the expenditure was made.

(m)(1) The Secretary is authorized to accept, hold, administer, and utilize gifts and bequests of property, both real and personal, for the purpose of aiding or facilitating the work of the Department. Gifts and bequests of money and the proceeds from sales of other property received as gifts or bequests shall be deposited in the Treasury in a separate fund and shall be disbursed upon order of the Secretary. Property accepted pursuant to this paragraph, and the proceeds thereof, shall be used as nearly as possible in accordance with the terms of the gift or bequest.

(2) For the purpose of Federal income, estate, and gift taxes, property accepted under paragraph (1) shall be considered as a gift or bequest to or for use of the United States.

(3) Upon the request of the Secretary, the Secretary of the Treasury may invest and reinvest in securities of the United States or in securities guaranteed as to principal and interest by the United States any moneys contained in the fund provided for in paragraph (1). Income accruing from such securities, and from any other property held by the

Secretary pursuant to paragraph (1) shall be deposited to the credit of the fund, and shall be disbursed upon order of the Secretary.

(n) (1) The Secretary is authorized, upon the written request of any person, or any State, territory, possession, or political subdivision thereof, to make special statistical studies relating to foreign and domestic transportation, and special studies relating to other matters falling within the province of the Department, to prepare from its records special statistical compilations, and to furnish transcripts of its studies, tables, and other records upon the payment of the actual cost of such work by the person or body requesting it.

(2) All moneys received by the Department in payment of the cost of work under paragraph (1) shall be deposited in a separate account to be administered under the direction of the Secretary. These moneys may be used, in the discretion of the Secretary, for the ordinary expenses incidental to the work and/or to secure in connection therewith the special services of persons who are neither officers nor employees of the United States.

(o) The Secretary is authorized to appoint, without regard to the civil service laws, such advisory committees as shall be appropriate for the purpose of consultation with and advice to the Department in performance of its functions. Members of such committees, other than those regularly employed by the Federal Government, while attending meetings of such committees or otherwise serving at the request of the Secretary, may be paid compensation at rates not exceeding those authorized for individuals under subsection (b) of this section, and while so serving away from their homes or regular places of business, may be allowed travel expenses, including per diem in lieu of subsistence, as authorized by section 5703 of title 5, United States Code, for persons in the Government service employed intermittently.

(p) (1) Notwithstanding any provision of this Act or other law, a member of the Coast Guard on active duty may be appointed, detailed, or assigned to any position in the Department other than Secretary, Under Secretary, and Assistant Secretary for Administration.

(2) Subject to the provisions of title 5, United States Code, a retired member of the Coast Guard may be appointed to any position in the Department.

(q) (1) The Secretary is authorized to enter into contracts with educational institutions, public or private agencies or organizations, or persons for the conduct of scientific or technological research into any aspect of the problems related to the programs of the Department which are authorized by statute.

(2) The Secretary shall require a showing that the institutions, agencies, organizations, or persons with which he expects to enter into contracts pursuant to this subsection have the capability of doing effective work. He shall furnish such advice and assistance as he believes will best carry out the mission of the Department, participate in coordinating all research initiated under this subsection, indicate the lines of inquiry which seem to him most important, and encourage and assist in the establishment and maintenance of cooperation by and between the institutions, agencies, organizations, or persons and between them and other research organizations, the Department, and other Federal agencies.

(3) The Secretary may from time to time disseminate in the form of reports or publications to public or private agencies or organizations, or individuals such information as he deems pertinent on the research carried out pursuant to this section.

(4) Nothing contained in this subsection is intended to amend, modify, or repeal any provisions of law administered by the Department which authorize the making of contracts for research.

CONFORMING AMENDMENTS TO OTHER LAWS

SEC. 10. (a) Section 19(d)(1) of title 3, United States Code, as amended, is hereby amended by striking out the period at the end thereof and inserting a comma and the following: "Secretary of Transportation."

(b) Section 101 of title 5 of the United States Code is amended by inserting at the end thereof the following:

"The Department of Housing and Urban Development.

"The Department of Transportation".

(c) The amendment made by subsection (b) of this section shall not be construed to make applicable to the Department any provision of law inconsistent with this Act.

(d) Subchapter II (relating to executive schedule pay rates) of chapter 53 of title V of the United States Code is amended as follows:

(1) Section 5312 is amended by adding at the end thereof the following:

"(11) Secretary of Housing and Urban Development.

"(12) Secretary of Transportation."

(2) Section 5313 is amended by striking out "(7) Administrator of the Federal Aviation Agency" and inserting in lieu thereof "(7) Under Secretary of Transportation", and by adding at the end thereof the following:

"(19) Administrator, Federal Aviation Administration."

(3) Section 5314 is amended by adding at the end thereof the following:

"(46) Administrator, Federal Highway Administration.

"(47) Administrator, Federal Railroad Administration.

"(48) Chairman, National Transportation Safety Board."

(4) Section 5315 is amended by adding at the end thereof the following:

"(78) Members, National Transportation Safety Board.

"(79) General Counsel, Department of Transportation.

"(80) Deputy Administrator, Federal Aviation Administration.

"(81) Assistant Secretaries of Transportation (4).

"(82) Director of Public Roads.

"(83) Administrator of the St. Lawrence Seaway Development Corporation."

(5) Section 5316 is amended by adding at the end thereof the following:

"(117) Assistant Secretary for Administration, Department of Transportation."

(6) Section 5317 is amended by striking out "thirty" and inserting in lieu thereof "thirty-four".

(e) Subsections 5314(6), 5315(2), and 5316 (10), (12), (13), (14), (76), and (82) of title 5 of the United States Code are repealed, subject to the provisions of section 9 of this Act.

(f) Title 18, United States Code, section 1020, as amended, is amended by striking the words "Secretary of Commerce" where they appear therein and inserting in lieu thereof "Secretary of Transportation".

(g) Subsection (1) of section 801, title 10, United States Code, as amended, is amended by striking out "the General Counsel of the Department of the Treasury" and inserting in lieu thereof "the General Counsel of the Department of Transportation".

ANNUAL REPORT

Sec. 11. The Secretary shall, as soon as practicable after the end of each fiscal year, make a report in writing to the President for submission to the Congress on the activities of the Department during the preceding fiscal year.

SAVINGS PROVISIONS

Sec. 12. (a) All orders, determinations, rules, regulations, permits, contracts, certificates, licenses, and privileges—
(1) which have been issued, made, granted, or allowed to become effective—
(A) under any provision of law amended by this Act, or
(B) in the exercise of duties, powers, or functions which are transferred under this Act,
by (i) any department or agency, any functions of which are transferred by this Act, or (ii) any court of competent jurisdiction, and
(2) which are in effect at the time this Act takes effect,
shall continue in effect according to their terms until modified, terminated, superseded, set aside, or repealed by the Secretary, Administrators, Board, or General Counsel (in the exercise of any authority respectively vested in them by this Act), by any court of competent jurisdiction, or by operation of law.

(b) The provisions of this Act shall not affect any proceedings pending at the time this section takes effect before any department or agency (or component thereof), functions of which are transferred by this Act; but such proceedings, to the extent that they relate to functions so transferred, shall be continued before the Department. Such proceedings, to the extent they do not relate to functions so transferred, shall be continued before the department or agency before which they were pending at the time of such transfer. In either case orders shall be issued in such proceedings, appeals shall be taken therefrom, and payments shall be made pursuant to such orders, as if this Act had not been enacted; and orders issued in any such proceedings shall continue in effect until modified, terminated, superseded, or repealed by the Secretary, Administrators, Board, or General Counsel (in the exercise of any authority respectively vested in them by this Act), by a court of competent jurisdiction, or by operation of law.

(c) (1) Except as provided in paragraph (2)—
(A) the provisions of this Act shall not affect suits commenced prior to the date this section takes effect, and

(B) in all such suits proceedings shall be had, appeals taken, and judgments rendered, in the same manner and effect as if this Act had not been enacted.

No suit, action, or other proceeding commenced by or against any officer in his official capacity as an officer of any department or agency, functions of which are transferred by this Act, shall abate by reason of the enactment of this Act. No cause of action by or against any department or agency, functions of which are transferred by this Act, or by or against any officer thereof in his official capacity shall abate by reason of the enactment of this Act. Causes of actions, suits, actions, or other proceedings may be asserted by or against the United States or such official of the Department as may be appropriate and, in any litigation pending when this section takes effect, the court may at any time, on its own motion or that of any party, enter an order which will give effect to the provisions of this subsection.

(2) If before the date on which this Act takes effect, any department or agency, or officer thereof in his official capacity, is a party to a suit, and under this Act—

(A) such department or agency is transferred to the Secretary, or

(B) any function of such department, agency, or officer is transferred to the Secretary,

then such suit shall be continued by the Secretary (except in the case of a suit not involving functions transferred to the Secretary, in which case the suit shall be continued by the department, agency, or officer which was a party to the suit prior to the effective date of this Act).

(d) With respect to any function, power, or duty transferred by this Act and exercised after the effective date of this Act, reference in any other Federal law to any department or agency, officer or office so transferred or functions of which are so transferred shall be deemed to mean the officer or agency in which this Act vests such function after such transfer.

SEPARABILITY

SEC. 13. If any provision of this Act or the application thereof to any person or circumstances is held invalid, the remainder of this Act, and the application of such provision to other persons or circumstances shall not be affected thereby.

CODIFICATION

SEC. 14. The Secretary is directed to submit to the Congress within two years from the effective date of this Act, a proposed codification of all laws that contain the powers, duties, and functions transferred to or vested in the Secretary or the Department by this Act.

EFFECTIVE DATE; INITIAL APPOINTMENT OF OFFICERS

SEC. 15. (a) This Act shall take effect ninety days after the Secretary first takes office, or on such prior date after enactment of this Act as the President shall prescribe and publish in the Federal Register.

(b) Any of the officers provided for in this Act may (notwith-standing subsection (a)) be appointed in the manner provided for in this Act, at any time after the date of enactment of this Act. Such officers shall be compensated from the date they first take office, at the rates provided for in this Act. Such compensation and related expenses of their offices shall be paid from funds available for the functions to be transferred to the Department pursuant to this Act.

Approved October 15, 1966, 1:25 p. m.

Public Law 91-258
91st Congress, H. R. 14465
May 21, 1970

An Act

84 STAT. 219

To provide for the expansion and improvement of the Nation's airport and airway system, for the imposition of airport and airway user charges, and for other purposes.

Be it enacted by the Senate and House of Representatives of the United States of America in Congress assembled,

Aviation facilities, expansion and improvement; revenue.

TITLE I—AIRPORT AND AIRWAY DEVELOPMENT ACT OF 1970

PART I—SHORT TITLE, ETC.

SECTION 1. SHORT TITLE.

This title may be cited as the "Airport and Airway Development Act of 1970".

Citation of title.

SEC. 2. DECLARATION OF POLICY.

The Congress hereby finds and declares—

That the Nation's airport and airway system is inadequate to meet the current and projected growth in aviation.

That substantial expansion and improvement of the airport and airway system is required to meet the demands of interstate commerce, the postal service, and the national defense.

That the annual obligational authority during the period July 1, 1970, through June 30, 1980, for the acquisition, establishment, and improvement of air navigational facilities under the Federal Aviation Act of 1958 (49 U.S.C. 1301 et seq.), should be no less than $250,000,000.

72 Stat. 731.

That the obligational authority during the period July 1, 1970, through June 30, 1980, for airport assistance under this title should be $2,500,000,000.

SEC. 3. NATIONAL TRANSPORTATION POLICY.

(a) FORMULATION OF POLICY.—Within one year after the date of enactment of this title, the Secretary of Transportation shall formulate and recommend to the Congress for approval a national transportation policy. In the formulation of such policy, the Secretary shall take into consideration, among other things—

(1) the coordinated development and improvement of all modes of transportation, together with the priority which shall be assigned to the development and improvement of each mode of transportation; and

(2) the coordination of recommendations made under this title relating to airport and airway development with all other recommendations to the Congress for the development and improvement of our national transportation system.

(b) ANNUAL REPORT.—The Secretary shall submit an annual report to the Congress on the implementation of the national transportation policy formulated under subsection (a) of this section. Such report shall include the specific actions taken by the Secretary with respect to (1) the coordination of the development and improvement of all modes of transportation, (2) the establishment of priorities with respect to the development and improvement of each mode of transportation, and (3) the coordination of recommendations under this title relating to airport and airway development with all other recommendations to the Congress for the development and improvement of our national transportation system.

Report to Congress.

SEC. 4. COST ALLOCATION STUDY.

The Secretary of Transportation shall conduct a study respecting the appropriate method for allocating the cost of the airport and airway system among the various users, and shall identify the cost to the Federal Government that should appropriately be charged to the system and the value to be assigned to any general public benefit, including military, which may be determined to exist. In conducting the study the Secretary shall consult fully with and give careful consideration to the views of the users of the system. The Secretary shall report the results of the study to Congress within two years from the date of enactment of this title.

Report to
Congress.

PART II—AIRPORT AND AIRWAY DEVELOPMENT

SEC. 11. DEFINITIONS.

As used in this part—

(1) "Airport" means any area of land or water which is used, or intended for use, for the landing and takeoff of aircraft, and any appurtenant areas which are used, or intended for use, for airport buildings or other airport facilities or rights-of-way, together with all airport buildings and facilities located thereon.

(2) "Airport development" means (A) any work involved in constructing, improving, or repairing a public airport or portion thereof, including the removal, lowering, relocation, and marking and lighting of airport hazards, and including navigation aids used by aircraft landing at, or taking off from, a public airport, and including safety equipment required by rule or regulation for certification of the airport under section 612 of the Federal Aviation Act of 1958, and (B) any acquisition of land or of any interest therein, or of any easement through or other interest in airspace, including land for future airport development, which is necessary to permit any such work or to remove or mitigate or prevent or limit the establishment of, airport hazards.

Post, p. 234.

(3) "Airport hazard" means any structure or object of natural growth located on or in the vicinity of a public airport, or any use of land near such airport, which obstructs the airspace required for the flight of aircraft in landing or taking off at such airport or is otherwise hazardous to such landing or taking off of aircraft.

(4) "Airport master planning" means the development for planning purposes of information and guidance to determine the extent, type, and nature of development needed at a specific airport. It may include the preparation of an airport layout plan and feasibility studies, and the conduct of such other studies, surveys, and planning actions as may be necessary to determine the short-, intermediate-, and long-range aeronautical demands required to be met by a particular airport as a part of a system of airports.

(5) "Airport system planning" means the development for planning purposes of information and guidance to determine the extent, type, nature, location, and timing of airport development needed in a specific area to establish a viable and balanced system of public airports. It includes identification of the specific aeronautical role of each airport within the system, development of estimates of system-wide development costs, and the conduct of such studies, surveys, and other planning actions as may be necessary to determine the short-, intermediate-, and long-range aeronautical demands required to be met by a particular system of airports.

(6) "Landing area" means that area used or intended to be used for the landing, takeoff, or surface maneuvering of aircraft.

(7) "Government aircraft" means aircraft owned and operated by the United States.

(8) "Planning agency" means any planning agency designated by the Secretary which is authorized by the laws of the State or States (including the Commonwealth of Puerto Rico, the Virgin Islands, and Guam) or political subdivisions concerned to engage in areawide planning for the areas in which assistance under this part is to be used.

(9) "Project" means a project for the accomplishment of airport development, airport master planning, or airport system planning.

(10) "Project costs" means any costs involved in accomplishing a project.

(11) "Public agency" means a State, the Commonwealth of Puerto Rico, the Virgin Islands, or Guam or any agency of any of them; a municipality or other political subdivision; or a tax-supported organization; or an Indian tribe or pueblo.

(12) "Public airport" means any airport which is used or to be used for public purposes, under the control of a public agency, the landing area of which is publicly owned.

(13) "Secretary" means the Secretary of Transportation.

(14) "Sponsor" means any public agency which, either individually or jointly with one or more other public agencies, submits to the Secretary, in accordance with this part, an application for financial assistance.

(15) "State" means a State of the United States or the District of Columbia.

(16) "Terminal area" means that area used or intended to be used for such facilities as terminal and cargo buildings, gates, hangars, shops, and other service buildings; automobile parking, airport motels, and restaurants, and garages and automobile service facilities used in connection with the airport; and entrance and service roads used by the public within the boundaries of the airport.

(17) "United States share" means that portion of the project costs of projects for airport development approved pursuant to section 16 of this part which is to be paid from funds made available for the purposes of this part.

SEC. 12. NATIONAL AIRPORT SYSTEM PLAN.

(a) FORMULATION OF PLAN.—The Secretary is directed to prepare and publish, within two years after the date of enactment of this part, and thereafter to review and revise as necessary, a national airport system plan for the development of public airports in the United States. The plan shall set forth, for at least a ten-year period, the type and estimated cost of airport development considered by the Secretary to be necessary to provide a system of public airports adequate to anticipate and meet the needs of civil aeronautics, to meet requirements in support of the national defense as determined by the Secretary of Defense, and to meet the special needs of the postal service. The plan shall include all types of airport development eligible for Federal aid under section 14 of this part, and terminal area development considered necessary to provide for the efficient accommodation of persons and goods at public airports, and the conduct of functions in operational support of the airport. Airport development identified by the plan shall not be limited to the requirements of any classes or categories of public airports. In preparing the plan, the Secretary shall consider the needs of all segments of civil aviation.

(b) CONSIDERATION OF OTHER MODES OF TRANSPORTATION.—In formulating and revising the plan, the Secretary shall take into consideration, among other things, the relationship of each airport to the rest of the transportation system in the particular area, to the forecasted technological developments in aeronautics, and to developments forecasted in other modes of intercity transportation.

(c) FEDERAL, STATE, AND OTHER AGENCIES.—In developing the national airport system plan, the Secretary shall to the extent feasible consult with the Civil Aeronautics Board, the Post Office Department, the Department of the Interior regarding conservation and natural resource values, and other Federal agencies, as appropriate; with planning agencies, and airport operators; and with air carriers, aircraft manufacturers, and others in the aviation industry. The Secretary shall provide technical guidance to agencies engaged in the conduct of airport system planning and airport master planning to insure that the national airport system plan reflects the product of interstate, State, and local airport planning.

(d) COOPERATION WITH FEDERAL COMMUNICATIONS COMMISSION.— The Secretary shall, to the extent possible, consult, and give consideration to the views and recommendations of the Federal Communications Commission, and shall make all reasonable efforts to cooperate with that Commission for the purpose of eliminating, preventing, or minimizing airport hazards caused by the construction or operation of any radio or television station. In carrying out this section, the Secretary may make any necessary surveys, studies, examinations, and investigations.

(e) CONSULTATION WITH DEPARTMENT OF DEFENSE.—The Department of Defense shall make military airports and airport facilities available for civil use to the extent feasible. In advising the Secretary of national defense requirements pursuant to subsection (a) of this section, the Secretary of Defense shall indicate the extent to which military airports and airport facilities will be available for civil use.

(f) CONSULTATION CONCERNING ENVIRONMENTAL CHANGES.—In carrying out this section, the Secretary shall consult with and consider the views and recommendations of the Secretary of the Interior, the Secretary of Health, Education, and Welfare, the Secretary of Agriculture, and the National Council on Environmental Quality. The recommendations of the Secretary of the Interior, the Secretary of Health, Education, and Welfare, the Secretary of Agriculture, and the National Council on Environmental Quality, with regard to the preservation of environmental quality, shall, to the extent that the Secretary of Transportation determines to be feasible, be incorporated in the national airport system plan.

(g) COOPERATION WITH THE FEDERAL POWER COMMISSION.—The Secretary shall, to the extent possible, consult, and give consideration to the views and recommendations of the Federal Power Commission, and shall make all reasonable efforts to cooperate with that Commission for the purpose of eliminating, preventing, or minimizing airport hazards caused by the construction or operation of power facilities. In carrying out this section, the Secretary may make any necessary surveys, studies, examinations, and investigations.

(h) AVIATION ADVISORY COMMISSION.—

Establishment; membership.

(1) There is established an Aviation Advisory Commission (hereafter in this subsection referred to as the "Commission"). The Commission shall be composed of nine members appointed by the President from private life as follows:

(A) One person to serve as Chairman of the Commission who is specially qualified to serve as Chairman by virtue of his education, training, or experience.

(B) Eight persons who are specially qualified to serve on such Commission from among representatives of the commercial air carriers, general aviation, aircraft manufacturers, airport sponsors, State aeronautics agencies, and three major organizations concerned with conservation or regional planning.

Not more than five members of the Commission shall be from the same political party. Any vacancy in the Commission shall not affect its powers but shall be filled in the same manner in which the original appointment was made, and subject to the same limitations with respect to party affiliations. Five members shall constitute a quorum.

(2) It shall be the duty of the Commission— Duties.

(A) to formulate recommendations concerning the long-range needs of aviation, including but not limited to, future airport requirements and the national airport system plan described in subsection (a) of this section, and recommendations concerning surrounding land uses, ground access, airways, air service, and aircraft compatible with such plan;

(B) to facilitate consideration of other modes of transportation and cooperation with other agencies and community and industry groups as provided in subsections (b) through (g) of this section. In carrying out its duties under this subsection, the Commission shall establish such task forces as are necessary to include technical representation from the organizations referred to in this subsection, from Federal agencies, and from such other organizations and agencies as the Commission considers appropriate.

(3) Each member of the Commission shall, while serving on the business of the Commission, be entitled to receive compensation at a rate fixed by the President, but not exceeding $100 per day, including travel time; and, while so serving away from his home or regular place of business, may be allowed travel expenses, including per diem in lieu of subsistence, as authorized by section 5703 of title 5 of the United States Code for persons in the Government service employed intermittently. Compensation; travel expenses.
83 Stat. 190.

(4)(A) The Commission is authorized, without regard to the provisions of title 5, United States Code, governing appointments in the competitive service, and without regard to the provisions of chapter 51 and subchapter III of chapter 53 of such title relating to classification and General Schedule pay rates, to appoint and fix the compensation of such personnel as may be necessary to carry out the functions of the Commission, but no individual so appointed shall receive compensation in excess of the rate authorized for GS-18 by section 5332 of such title. 80 Stat. 443, 467.
5 USC 5101-5115, 5331-5338.
35 F. R. 6247.

(B) The Commission is authorized to obtain the services of experts and consultants in accordance with the provisions of section 3109 of title 5, United States Code, but at rates for individuals not to exceed $100 per diem. 80 Stat. 416.

(C) Administrative services shall be provided the Commission by the General Services Administration on a reimbursable basis.

(D) The Commission is authorized to request from any department, agency, or independent instrumentality of the Government any information and assistance it deems necessary to carry out its functions under this subsection; and each such department, agency, and instrumentality is authorized to cooperate with the Commission and, to the extent permitted by law, to furnish such information and assistance to the Commission upon request made by the Chairman.

(5) The Commission shall submit to the President and to the Congress, or or before January 1, 1972, a final report containing the recommendations formulated by it under this subsection. The Commission shall cease to exist 60 days after the date of the submission of its final report. Report to President and Congress.
Termination.

(6) There are authorized to be appropriated from the Airport and Airway Trust Fund such sums, not to exceed $2,000,000, as may be necessary to carry out the provisions of this subsection. Appropriation.

Pub. Law 91-258   May 21, 1970

SEC. 13. PLANNING GRANTS.

(a) AUTHORIZATION TO MAKE GRANTS.—In order to promote the effective location and development of airports and the development of an adequate national airport system plan, the Secretary may make grants of funds to planning agencies for airport system planning, and to public agencies for airport master planning.

(b) AMOUNT AND APPORTIONMENT OF GRANTS.—The award of grants under subsection (a) of this section is subject to the following limitations:

(1) The total funds obligated for grants under this section may not exceed $75,000,000 and the amount obligated in any one fiscal year may not exceed $15,000,000.

(2) No grant under this section may exceed two-thirds of the cost incurred in the accomplishment of the project.

(3) No more than 7.5 per centum of the funds made available under this section in any fiscal year may be allocated for projects within a single State, the Commonwealth of Puerto Rico, the Virgin Islands, or Guam. Grants for projects encompassing an area located in two or more States shall be charged to each State in the proportion which the number of square miles the project encompasses in each State bears to the square miles encompassed by the entire project.

(c) REGULATIONS; COORDINATION WITH SECRETARY OF HOUSING AND URBAN DEVELOPMENT.—The Secretary may prescribe such regulations as he deems necessary governing the award and administration of grants authorized by this section. The Secretary and the Secretary of Housing and Urban Development shall develop jointly procedures designed to preclude duplication of their respective planning assistance activities and to ensure that such activities are effectively coordinated.

SEC. 14. AIRPORT AND AIRWAY DEVELOPMENT PROGRAM.

Grants.

(a) GENERAL AUTHORITY.—In order to bring about, in conformity with the national airport system plan, the establishment of a nation-wide system of public airports adequate to meet the present and future needs of civil aeronautics, the Secretary is authorized to make grants for airport development by grant agreements with sponsors in aggregate amounts not less than the following:

(1) For the purpose of developing in the several States, the Commonwealth of Puerto Rico, Guam, and the Virgin Islands, airports served by air carriers certificated by the Civil Aeronautics Board, and airports the primary purpose of which is to serve general aviation and to relieve congestion at airports having a high density of traffic serving other segments of aviation, $250,000,000 for each of the fiscal years 1971 through 1975.

(2) For the purpose of developing in the several States, the Commonwealth of Puerto Rico, Guam, and the Virgin Islands, airports serving segments of aviation other than air carriers certificated by the Civil Aeronautics Board, $30,000,000 for each of the fiscal years 1971 through 1975.

(b) OBLIGATIONAL AUTHORITY.—To facilitate orderly long-term planning by sponsors, the Secretary is authorized, effective on the date of enactment of this title, to incur obligations to make grants for airport development from funds made available under this part for the fiscal year ending June 30, 1971, and the succeeding four fiscal years in a total amount not to exceed $840,000,000. No obligation shall be incurred under this subsection for a period of more than three fiscal years and no such obligation shall extend beyond June 30, 1975. The Secretary shall not incur more than one obligation under this subsection with respect to any single project for airport development. Obligations incurred under this subsection shall not be liquidated in an aggregate amount exceeding $280,000,000 prior to June 30, 1971, an aggregate amount exceeding $560,000,000 prior to June 30, 1972, and an aggregate amount exceeding $840,000,000 prior to June 30, 1973.

(c) AIRWAY FACILITIES.—For the purpose of acquiring, establishing, and improving air navigation facilities under section 307(b) of the Federal Aviation Act of 1958, the Secretary is authorized, within the limits established in appropriations Acts, to obligate for expenditure not less than $250,000,000 for each of the fiscal years 1971 through 1975.

72 Stat. 750.
49 USC 1348.

(d) OTHER EXPENSES.—The balance of the moneys available in the trust fund shall be allocated for the necessary administrative expenses incident to the administration of programs for which funds are to be allocated as set forth in subsections (a) and (b) of this section, and for the maintenance and operation of air navigation facilities and the conduct of other functions under section 307(b) of the Federal Aviation Act of 1958, not otherwise provided for in subsection (c) of this section, and for research and development activities under section 312(c) (as it relates to safety in air navigation) of the Federal Aviation Act of 1958. The initial $50,000,000 of any sums appropriated to the trust fund pursuant to subsection (d) of section 208 of the Airport and Airway Revenue Act of 1970 shall be allocated to such research and development activities.

49 USC 1353.

Post, p. 250.

SEC. 15. DISTRIBUTION OF FUNDS; STATE APPORTIONMENT.

(a) APPORTIONMENT OF FUNDS.—

(1) As soon as possible after July 1 of each fiscal year for which any amount is authorized to be obligated for the purposes of paragraph (1) of section 14(a) of this part, the amount made available for that year shall be apportioned by the Secretary as follows:

(A) One-third to be distributed as follows:

(i) 97 per centum of such one-third for the several States, one-half in the proportion which the population of each State bears to the total population of all the States, and one-half in the proportion which the area of each State bears to the total area of all the States.

(ii) 3 per centum of such one-third for Hawaii, the Commonwealth of Puerto Rico, Guam, and the Virgin Islands, to be distributed in shares of 35 per centum, 35 per centum, 15 per centum, and 15 per centum, respectively.

(B) One-third to be distributed to sponsors of airports served by air carriers certificated by the Civil Aeronautics Board in the same ratio as the number of passengers enplaned at each airport of the sponsor bears to the total number of passengers enplaned at all such airports.

(C) One-third to be distributed at the discretion of the Secretary.

(2) As soon as possible after July 1 of each fiscal year for which any amount is authorized to be obligated for the purposes of paragraph (2) of section 14(a) of this part, the amount made available for that year shall be apportioned by the Secretary as follows:

(A) Seventy-three and one-half per centum for the several States, one-half in the proportion which the population of each State bears to the total population of all the States, and one-half in the proportion which the area of each State bears to the total area of all the States.

(B) One and one-half per centum for Hawaii, the Commonwealth of Puerto Rico, Guam, and the Virgin Islands, to be distributed in shares of 35 per centum, 35 per centum, 15 per centum, and 15 per centum, respectively.

(C) Twenty-five per centum to be distributed at the discretion of the Secretary.

(3) Each amount apportioned to a State under paragraph (1) (A) (i) or (2) (A) of this subsection shall, during the fiscal year for which it was first authorized to be obligated and the fiscal year immediately following, be available only for approved airport development projects located in that State, or sponsored by that State or some public agency thereof but located in an adjoining State. Each amount apportioned to a sponsor of an airport under paragraph (1) (B) of this subsection shall, during the fiscal year for which it was first authorized to be obligated and the two fiscal years immediately following, be available only for approved airport development projects located at airports sponsored by it. Any amount apportioned as described in this paragraph which has not been obligated by grant agreement at the expiration of the period of time for which it was so apportioned shall be added to the discretionary fund established by subsection (b) of this section.

"Passengers enplaned."
(4) For the purposes of this section, the term "passengers enplaned" shall include United States domestic, territorial, and international revenue passenger enplanements in scheduled and nonscheduled service of air carriers and foreign air carriers in intrastate and interstate commerce as shall be determined by the Secretary pursuant to such regulations as he shall prescribe.

(b) DISCRETIONARY FUND.—(1) The amounts authorized by subsection (a) of this section to be distributed at the discretion of the Secretary shall constitute a discretionary fund.

(2) The discretionary fund shall be available for such approved projects for airport development in the several States, the Commonwealth of Puerto Rico, the Virgin Islands, and Guam as the Secretary considers most appropriate for carrying out the national airport system plan regardless of the location of the projects. In determining the projects for which the fund is to be used, the Secretary shall consider the existing airport facilities in the several States, the Commonwealth of Puerto Rico, the Virgin Islands, and Guam, and the need for or lack of development of airport facilities in the several States, the Commonwealth of Puerto Rico, the Virgin Islands, and Guam. Amounts placed in the discretionary fund pursuant to subsection (a) of this section, including amounts added to the discretionary fund pursuant to paragraph (3) of such subsection (a), may be used only in accordance with the purposes for which originally appropriated.

(c) NOTICE OF APPORTIONMENT; DEFINITION OF TERMS.—Upon making an apportionment as provided in subsection (a) of this section, the Secretary shall inform the executive head of each State, and any public agency which has requested such information, as to the amounts apportioned to each State. As used in this section, the term "population" means the population according to the latest decennial census of the United States and the term "area" includes both land and water.

SEC. 16. SUBMISSION AND APPROVAL OF PROJECTS FOR AIRPORT DEVELOPMENT.

(a) SUBMISSION.—Subject to the provisions of subsection (b) of this section, any public agency, or two or more public agencies acting jointly, may submit to the Secretary a project application, in a form and containing such information, as the Secretary may prescribe, setting forth the airport development proposed to be undertaken. No project application shall propose airport development other than that included in the then current revision of the national airport system plan formulated by the Secretary under this part, and all proposed development shall be in accordance with standards established by the Secretary, including standards for site location, airport layout, grading, drainage, seeding, paving, lighting, and safety of approaches.

(b) PUBLIC AGENCIES WHOSE POWERS ARE LIMITED BY STATE LAW.—Nothing in this part shall authorize the submission of a project application by any municipality or other public agency which is subject to the law of any State if the submission of the project application by the municipality or other public agency is prohibited by the law of that State.

(c) APPROVAL.—

(1) All airport development projects shall be subject to the approval of the Secretary, which approval may be given only if he is satisfied that—

(A) the project is reasonably consistent with plans (existing at the time of approval of the project) of planning agencies for the development of the area in which the airport is located and will contribute to the accomplishment of the purposes of this part;

(B) sufficient funds are available for that portion of the project costs which are not to be paid by the United States under this part;

(C) the project will be completed without undue delay;

(D) the public agency or public agencies which submitted the project application have legal authority to engage in the airport development as proposed; and

(E) all project sponsorship requirements prescribed by or under the authority of this part have been or will be met.

No airport development project may be approved by the Secretary with respect to any airport unless a public agency holds good title, satisfactory to the Secretary, to the landing area of the airport or the site therefor, or gives assurance satisfactory to the Secretary that good title will be acquired.

(2) No airport development project may be approved by the Secretary which does not include provision for installation of the landing aids specified in subsection (d) of section 17 of this part and determined by him to be required for the safe and efficient use of the airport by aircraft taking into account the category of the airport and the type and volume of traffic utilizing the airport.

(3) No airport development project may be approved by the Secretary unless he is satisfied that fair consideration has been given to the interest of communities in or near which the project may be located.

(4) It is declared to be national policy that airport development projects authorized pursuant to this part shall provide for the protection and enhancement of the natural resources and the quality of environment of the Nation. In implementing this policy, the Secretary shall consult with the Secretaries of the Interior and Health, Education, and Welfare with regard to the effect that any project involving airport location, a major runway extension, or runway location may have on natural resources including, but not limited to, fish and wildlife, natural, scenic, and recreation assets, water and air quality, and other factors affecting the environment, and shall authorize no such project found to have adverse effect unless the Secretary shall render a finding, in writing, following a full and complete review, which shall be a matter of public record, that no feasible and prudent alternative exists and that all possible steps have been taken to minimize such adverse effect.

(d) HEARINGS.—

(1) No airport development project involving the location of an airport, an airport runway, or a runway extension may be approved by the Secretary unless the public agency sponsoring the project certifies to the Secretary that there has been afforded the opportunity for public hearings for the purpose of considering the economic, social, and environmental effects of the airport location and its consistency with the goals and objectives of such urban planning as has been carried out by the community.

Pub. Law 91-258   May 21, 1970

(2) When hearings are held under paragraph (1) of this subsection, the project sponsor shall, when requested by the Secretary, submit a copy of the transcript to the Secretary.

(e) AIR AND WATER QUALITY.—

(1) The Secretary shall not approve any project application for a project involving airport location, a major runway extension, or runway location unless the Governor of the State in which such project may be located certifies in writing to the Secretary that there is reasonable assurance that the project will be located, designed, constructed, and operated so as to comply with applicable air and water quality standards. In any case where such standards have not been approved or where such standards have been promulgated by the Secretary of the Interior or the Secretary of Health, Education, and Welfare, certification shall be obtained from the appropriate Secretary. Notice of certification or of refusal to certify shall be provided within sixty days after the project application is received by the Secretary.

(2) The Secretary shall condition approval of any such project application on compliance during construction and operation with applicable air and water quality standards.

(f) AIRPORT SITE SELECTION.—

(1) Whenever the Secretary determines (A) that a metropolitan area comprised of more than one unit of State or local government is in need of an additional airport to adequately meet the air transportation needs of such area, and (B) that an additional airport for such area is consistent with the national airport system plan prepared by the Secretary, he shall notify, in writing, the governing authorities of the area concerned of the need for such additional airport and request such authorities to confer, agree upon a site for the location of such additional airport, and notify the Secretary of their selection. In order to facilitate the selection of a site for an additional airport under the preceding sentence, the Secretary shall exercise such of his authority under this part as he may deem appropriate to carry out the provisions of this paragraph. For the purposes of this subsection, the term "metropolitan area" means a standard metropolitan statistical area as established by the Bureau of the Budget, subject however to such modifications and extensions as the Secretary may determine to be appropriate for the purposes of this subsection.

"Metropolitan area."

(2) In the case of a proposed new airport serving any area, which does not include a metropolitan area, the Secretary shall not approve any airport development project with respect to any proposed airport site not approved by the community or communities in which the airport is proposed to be located.

SEC. 17. UNITED STATES SHARE OF PROJECT COSTS.

(a) GENERAL PROVISION.—Except as provided in subsections (b), (c), and (d) of this section, the United States share payable on account of any approved airport development project submitted under section 16 of this part may not exceed 50 per centum of the allowable project costs.

(b) PROJECTS IN PUBLIC LAND STATES.—In the case of any State containing unappropriated and unreserved public lands and nontaxable Indian lands (individual and tribal) exceeding 5 per centum of the total area of all lands therein, the United States share under subsection (a) shall be increased by whichever is the smaller of the following percentages thereof: (1) 25 per centum, or (2) a percentage equal to one-half of the percentage that the area of all such lands in that State is of its total area.

(c) PROJECTS IN THE VIRGIN ISLANDS.—The United States share payable on account of any approved project for airport development in the Virgin Islands shall be any portion of the allowable project costs of the project, not to exceed 75 per centum, as the Secretary considers appropriate for carrying out the provisions of this part.

(d) LANDING AIDS.—To the extent that the project costs of an approved project for airport development represent the cost of (1) land required for the installation of approach light systems, (2) touchdown zone and centerline runway lighting, or (3) high intensity runway lighting, the United States share shall be not to exceed 82 per centum of the allowable costs thereof.   Cost limitation.

SEC. 18. PROJECT SPONSORSHIP.

As a condition precedent to his approval of an airport development project under this part, the Secretary shall receive assurances in writing, satisfactory to him, that—

(1) the airport to which the project for airport development relates will be available for public use on fair and reasonable terms and without unjust discrimination;

(2) the airport and all facilities thereon or connected therewith will be suitably operated and maintained, with due regard to climatic and flood conditions;

(3) the aerial approaches to the airport will be adequately cleared and protected by removing, lowering, relocating, marking, or lighting or otherwise mitigating existing airport hazards and by preventing the establishment or creation of future airport hazards;

(4) appropriate action, including the adoption of zoning laws, has been or will be taken, to the extent reasonable, to restrict the use of land adjacent to or in the immediate vicinity of the airport to activities and purposes compatible with normal airport operations, including landing and takeoff of aircraft;

(5) all of the facilities of the airport developed with Federal financial assistance and all those usable for landing and takeoff of aircraft will be available to the United States for use by Government aircraft in common with other aircraft at all times without charge, except, if the use by Government aircraft is substantial, a charge may be made for a reasonable share, proportional to such use, of the cost of operating and maintaining the facilities used;

(6) the airport operator or owner will furnish without cost to the Federal Government for use in connection with any air traffic control activities, or weather-reporting and communication activities related to air traffic control, any areas of land or water, or estate therein, or rights in buildings of the sponsor as the Secretary considers necessary or desirable for construction at Federal expense of space or facilities for such purposes;

(7) all project accounts and records will be kept in accordance with a standard system of accounting prescribed by the Secretary after consultation with appropriate public agencies;

(8) the airport operator or owner will maintain a fee and rental structure for the facilities and services being provided the airport users which will make the airport as self-sustaining as possible under the circumstances existing at that particular airport, taking into account such factors as the volume of traffic and economy of collection;

(9) the airport operator or owner will submit to the Secretary such annual or special airport financial and operations reports as the Secretary may reasonably request; and   Reports.

(10) the airport and all airport records will be available for inspection by any duly authorized agent of the Secretary upon reasonable request.   Availability of records.

Compliance.

Contract
authority.

60 Stat. 170;
Post, p. 235.
49 USC 1101
note.

To insure compliance with this section, the Secretary shall prescribe such project sponsorship requirements, consistent with the terms of this part, as he considers necessary. Among other steps to insure such compliance the Secretary is authorized to enter into contracts with public agencies, on behalf of the United States. Whenever the Secretary obtains from a sponsor any area of land or water, or estate therein, or rights in buildings of the sponsor and constructs space or facilities thereon at Federal expense, he is authorized to relieve the sponsor from any contractual obligation entered into under this part or the Federal Airport Act to provide free space in airport buildings to the Federal Government to the extent he finds that space no longer required for the purposes set forth in paragraph (6) of this section.

SEC. 19. GRANT AGREEMENTS.

Upon approving a project application for airport development, the Secretary, on behalf of the United States, shall transmit to the sponsor or sponsors of the project application an offer to make a grant for the United States share of allowable project costs. An offer shall be made upon such terms and conditions as the Secretary considers necessary to meet the requirements of this part and the regulations prescribed thereunder. Each offer shall state a definite amount as the maximum obligation of the United States payable from funds authorized by this part, and shall stipulate the obligations to be assumed by the sponsor or sponsors. If and when an offer is accepted in writing by the sponsor, the offer and acceptance shall comprise an agreement constituting an obligation of the United States and of the sponsor. Thereafter, the amount stated in the accepted offer as the maximum obligation of the United States may not be increased by more than 10 per centum. Unless and until an agreement has been executed, the United States may not pay, nor be obligated to pay, any portion of the costs which have been or may be incurred.

SEC. 20. PROJECT COSTS.

(a) ALLOWABLE PROJECT COSTS.—Except as provided in section 21 of this part, the United States may not pay, or be obligated to pay, from amounts appropriated to carry out the provisions of this part, any portion of a project cost incurred in carrying out a project for airport development unless the Secretary has first determined that the cost is allowable. A project cost is allowable if—

(1) it was a necessary cost incurred in accomplishing airport development in conformity with approved plans and specifications for an approved airport development project and with the terms and conditions of the grant agreement entered into in connection with the project;

(2) it was incurred subsequent to the execution of the grant agreement with respect to the project, and in connection with airport development accomplished under the project after the execution of the agreement. However, the allowable costs of a project may include any necessary costs of formulating the project (including the costs of field surveys and the preparation of plans and specifications, the acquisition of land or interests therein or easements through or other interests in airspace, and any necessary administrative or other incidental costs incurred by the sponsor specifically in connection with the accomplishment of the project for airport development, which would not have been incurred otherwise) which were incurred subsequent to May 13, 1946;

(3) in the opinion of the Secretary it is reasonable in amount, and if the Secretary determines that a project cost is unreasonable in amount, he may allow as an allowable project cost only so much of such project cost as he determines to be reasonable; except that

384

in no event may he allow project costs in excess of the definite amount stated in the grant agreement; and

(4) it has not been included in any project authorized under section 13 of this part.

The Secretary is authorized to prescribe such regulations, including   Regulations. regulations with respect to the auditing of project costs, as he considers necessary to effectuate the purposes of this section.

(b) COSTS NOT ALLOWED.—The following are not allowable project costs: (1) the cost of construction of that part of an airport development project intended for use as a public parking facility for passenger automobiles; or (2) the cost of construction, alteration, or repair of a hangar or of any part of an airport building except such of those buildings or parts of buildings intended to house facilities or activities directly related to the safety of persons at the airport.

SEC. 21. PAYMENTS UNDER GRANT AGREEMENTS.

The Secretary, after consultation with the sponsor with which a grant agreement has been entered into, may determine the times and amounts in which payments shall be made under the terms of a grant agreement for airport development. Payments in an aggregate amount not to exceed 90 per centum of the United States share of the total estimated allowable project costs may be made from time to time in advance of accomplishment of the airport development to which the payments relate, if the sponsor certifies to the Secretary that the aggregate expenditures to be made from the advance payments will not at any time exceed the cost of the airport development work which has been performed up to that time. If the Secretary determines that the aggregate amount of payments made under a grant agreement at any time exceeds the United States share of the total allowable project costs, the United States shall be entitled to recover the excess. If the Secretary finds that the airport development to which the advance payments relate has not been accomplished within a reasonable time or the development is not completed, the United States may recover any part of the advance payment for which the United States received no benefit. Payments under a grant agreement shall be made to the official or depository authorized by law to receive public funds and designated by the sponsor.

SEC. 22. PERFORMANCE OF CONSTRUCTION WORK.

(a) REGULATIONS.—The construction work on any project for airport development approved by the Secretary pursuant to section 16 of this part shall be subject to inspection and approval by the Secretary and in accordance with regulations prescribed by him. Such regulations shall require such cost and progress reporting by the sponsor or sponsors of such project as the Secretary shall deem necessary. No such regulation shall have the effect of altering any contract in connection with any project entered into without actual notice of the regulation.

(b) MINIMUM RATES OF WAGES.—All contracts in excess of $2,000 for work on projects for airport development approved under this part which involve labor shall contain provisions establishing minimum rates of wages, to be predetermined by the Secretary of Labor, in accordance with the Davis-Bacon Act, as amended (40 U.S.C. 276a— 276a–5), which contractors shall pay to skilled and unskilled labor, and   49 Stat. 1011. such minimum rates shall be stated in the invitation for bids and shall be included in proposals or bids for the work.

(c) OTHER PROVISIONS AS TO LABOR.—All contracts for work on projects for airport development approved under this part which involve labor shall contain such provisions as are necessary to insure (1) that no convict labor shall be employed; and (2) that, in the employment of labor (except in executive, administrative, and supervisory positions), preference shall be given, where they are qualified, to individuals who have served as persons in the military service of the United States, as defined in section 101(1) of the Soldiers' and Sailors'

54 Stat. 1179.   Civil Relief Act of 1940, as amended (50 App. U.S.C. 511(1)), and who have been honorably discharged from such service. However, this preference shall apply only where the individuals are available and qualified to perform the work to which the employment relates.

SEC. 23. USE OF GOVERNMENT-OWNED LANDS.

(a) REQUESTS FOR USE.—Subject to the provisions of subsection (c) of this section, whenever the Secretary determines that use of any lands owned or controlled by the United States is reasonably necessary for carrying out a project for airport development under this part, or for the operation of any public airport, including lands reasonably necessary to meet future development of an airport in accordance with the national airport system plan, he shall file with the head of the department or agency having control of the lands a request that the necessary property interests therein be conveyed to the public agency sponsoring the project in question or owning or controlling the airport. The property interest may consist of the title to, or any other interest in, land or any easement through or other interest in airspace.

(b) MAKING OF CONVEYANCES.—Upon receipt of a request from the Secretary under this section, the head of the department or agency having control of the lands in question shall determine whether the requested conveyance is inconsistent with the needs of the department or agency, and shall notify the Secretary of his determination within a period of four months after receipt of the Secretary's request. If the department or agency head determines that the requested conveyance is not inconsistent with the needs of that department or agency, the department or agency head is hereby authorized and directed, with the approval of the President and the Attorney General of the United States, and without any expense to the United States, to perform any acts and to execute any instruments necessary to make the conveyance requested. A conveyance may be made only on the condition that, at the option of the Secretary, the property interest conveyed shall revert to the United States in the event that the lands in question are not developed for airport purposes or used in a manner consistent with the terms of the conveyance. If only a part of the property interest conveyed is not developed for airport purposes, or used in a manner consistent with the terms of the conveyance, only that particular part shall at the option of the Secretary, revert to the United States.

(c) EXEMPTION OF CERTAIN LANDS.—Unless otherwise specifically provided by law, the provisions of subsections (a) and (b) of this section shall not apply with respect to lands owned or controlled by the United States within any national park, national monument, national recreation area, or similar area under the administration of the National Park Service; within any unit of the National Wildlife Refuge System or similar area under the jurisdiction of the Bureau of Sport Fisheries and Wildlife; or within any national forest or Indian reservation.

SEC. 24. REPORTS TO CONGRESS.

On or before the third day of January of each year the Secretary shall make a report to the Congress describing his operations under this part during the preceding fiscal year. The report shall include a detailed statement of the airport development accomplished, the status of each project undertaken, the allocation of appropriations, and an itemized statement of expenditures and receipts.

SEC. 25. FALSE STATEMENTS.

Any officer, agent, or employee of the United States, or any officer, agent, or employee of any public agency, or any person, association, firm, or corporation who, with intent to defraud the United States—

(1) knowingly makes any false statement, false representation, or false report as to the character, quality, quantity, or cost of the material used or to be used, or the quantity or quality of the work performed or to be performed, or the costs thereof, in connection with the submission of plans, maps, specifications, contracts, or estimates of project costs for any project submitted to the Secretary for approval under this part;

(2) knowingly makes any false statement, false representation, or false report or claim for work or materials for any project approved by the Secretary under this part; or

(3) knowingly makes any false statement or false representation in any report required to be made under this part;

shall, upon conviction thereof, be punished by imprisonment for not   Penalty. to exceed five years or by a fine of not to exceed $10,000, or by both.

SEC. 26. ACCESS TO RECORDS.

(a) RECORDKEEPING REQUIREMENTS.—Each recipient of a grant under this part shall keep such records as the Secretary may prescribe, including records which fully disclose the amount and the disposition by the recipient of the proceeds of the grant, the total cost of the plan or program in connection with which the grant is given or used, and the amount and nature of that portion of the cost of the plan or program supplied by other sources, and such other records as will facilitate an effective audit.

(b) AUDIT AND EXAMINATION.—The Secretary and the Comptroller General of the United States, or any of their duly authorized representatives, shall have access for the purpose of audit and examination to any books, documents, papers, and records of the recipient that are pertinent to grants received under this part.

(c) AUDIT REPORTS.—In any case in which an independent audit is made of the accounts of a recipient of a grant under this part relating to the disposition of the proceeds of such grant or relating to the plan or program in connection with which the grant was given or used, the recipient shall file a certified copy of such audit with the Comptroller General of the United States not later than six months following the close of the fiscal year for which the audit was made. On or before January 3 of each year the Comptroller General shall make a report   Report to to the Congress describing the results of each audit conducted or   Congress. reviewed by him under this section during the preceding fiscal year. The Comptroller General shall prescribe such regulations as he may   Regulations. deem necessary to carry out the provisions of this subsection.

(d) WITHHOLDING INFORMATION.—Nothing in this section shall authorize the withholding of information by the Secretary or the Comptroller General of the United States, or any officer or employee under the control of either of them, from the duly authorized committees of the Congress.

SEC. 27. GENERAL POWERS.

The Secretary is empowered to perform such acts, to conduct such investigations and public hearings, to issue and amend such orders, and to make and amend such regulations and procedures, pursuant to and consistent with the provisions of this part, as he considers necessary to carry out the provisions of, and to exercise and perform his powers and duties under, this part.

PART III—MISCELLANEOUS

SEC. 51. AMENDMENTS TO FEDERAL AVIATION ACT OF 1958.

72 Stat. 747.

(a)(1) PROCUREMENT PROCEDURES.—Section 303 of the Federal Aviation Act of 1958 (49 U.S.C. 1344) is amended by adding at the end thereof the following new subsection:

"NEGOTIATION OF PURCHASES AND CONTRACTS

"(e) The Secretary of Transportation may negotiate without advertising purchases of and contracts for technical or special property related to, or in support of, air navigation that he determines to require a substantial initial investment or an extended period of preparation for manufacture, and for which he determines that formal advertising would be likely to result in additional cost to the Government by reason of duplication of investment or would result in duplication of necessary preparation which would unduly delay the procurement of the property. The Secretary shall, at the beginning of each fiscal year, report to the Committee on Interstate and Foreign Commerce of the House of Representatives and the Committee on Commerce of the Senate all transactions negotiated under this subsection during the preceding fiscal year."

Report to congressional committees.

(2) TABLE OF CONTENTS.—That portion of the table of contents contained in the first section of the Federal Aviation Act of 1958 which appears under the side heading "Sec. 303. Administration of the Agency." is amended by adding at the end thereof the following:

"(e) Negotiation of purchases and contracts.".

72 Stat. 775;
82 Stat. 395.

(b)(1) AIRPORT CERTIFICATION.—Title VI of the Federal Aviation Act of 1958 (49 U.S.C. 1421–1431), relating to safety regulation of civil aeronautics, is amended by adding at the end thereof the following new section:

"AIRPORT OPERATING CERTIFICATES

"POWER TO ISSUE

"SEC. 612. (a) The Administrator is empowered to issue airport operating certificates to airports serving air carriers certificated by the Civil Aeronautics Board and to establish minimum safety standards for the operation of such airports.

"ISSUANCE

"(b) Any person desiring to operate an airport serving air carriers certificated by the Civil Aeronautics Board may file with the Administrator an application for an airport operating certificate. If the Administrator finds, after investigation, that such person is properly and adequately equipped and able to conduct a safe operation in accordance with the requirements of this Act and the rules, regulations, and standards prescribed thereunder, he shall issue an airport operating certificate to such person. Each airport operating certificate shall prescribe such terms, conditions, and limitations as are reasonably necessary to assure safety in air transportation, including but not limited to, terms, conditions, and limitations relating to—

Terms and conditions.

"(1) the installation, operation, and maintenance of adequate air navigation facilities; and

"(2) the operation and maintenance of adequate safety equipment, including firefighting and rescue equipment capable of rapid access to any portion of the airport used for the landing, takeoff, or surface maneuvering of aircraft."

(2) TABLE OF CONTENTS.—That portion of the table of contents contained in the first section of the Federal Aviation Act of 1958 which appears under the center heading "TITLE VI—SAFETY REGULATION OF CIVIL AERONAUTICS" is amended by adding at the end thereof the following:

72 Stat. 731.

"Sec. 612. Airport operating certificates.
    "(a) Power to issue.
    "(b) Issuance.".

(3) PROHIBITIONS.—Section 610(a) of such Act (49 U.S.C. 1430 (a)), relating to prohibitions, is amended—

72 Stat. 780.

(A) by striking out "and" at the end of paragraph (6);
(B) by striking out the period at the end of paragraph (7) and inserting in lieu thereof "; and"; and
(C) by adding at the end thereof the following new paragraph:
"(8) For any person to operate an airport serving air carriers certificated by the Civil Aeronautics Board without an airport operating certificate, or in violation of the terms of any such certificate."

(4) EFFECTIVE DATE.—The amendments made by paragraph (3) of this subsection shall take effect upon the expiration of the two-year period beginning on the date of their enactment.

SEC. 52. REPEAL; CONFORMING AMENDMENTS; SAVING PROVISIONS; AND SEPARABILITY.

(a) REPEAL.—The Federal Airport Act (49 U.S.C. 1101 et seq.) is repealed as of the close of June 30, 1970.

60 Stat. 170.

(b) CONFORMING AMENDMENTS.—

(1) The first section of the Act of March 18, 1950, relating to Department of the Interior Airports (16 U.S.C. 7a), is amended by striking out "Administrator of the Federal Aviation Agency" each place it appears and inserting in lieu thereof at each such place "Secretary of Transportation".

64 Stat. 27;
72 Stat. 807.

(2) Section 509(c) of the Public Works and Economic Development Act of 1965 (42 U.S.C. 3188a) is amended by inserting "Airport and Airway Development Act of 1970;" immediately after "Federal Airport Act;".

81 Stat. 267;
83 Stat. 218.

(3) Section 208(2) of the Demonstration Cities and Metropolitan Development Act of 1966 (42 U.S.C. 3338(2)) is amended by inserting "section 19 of the Airport and Airway Development Act of 1970;" immediately after "section 12 of the Federal Airport Act;".

80 Stat. 1265.

(4) The Federal Aviation Act of 1958 (49 U.S.C. 1301 et seq.) is amended—

(A) by striking out "or by the Federal Airport Act" in section 313(c) and inserting in lieu thereof ", the Federal Airport Act, or the Airport and Airway Development Act of 1970"; and

49 USC 1354.

(B) by striking out "Federal Airport Act" in section 1109(e) and inserting in lieu thereof "Airport and Airway Development Act of 1970".

75 Stat. 527.
49 USC 1509.

(5) Section 214(c) of the Appalachian Regional Development Act of 1965 (40 App. U.S.C. 214(c)) is amended by inserting "Airport and Airway Development Act of 1970;" immediately after "Federal Airport Act;".

81 Stat. 263;
83 Stat. 215.

(6) Section 13(g)(1) of the Surplus Property Act of 1944 (50 App. U.S.C. 1622(g)(1)) is amended by striking out "Federal Airport Act (60 Stat. 170)" and inserting in lieu thereof "Airport and Airway Development Act of 1970".

61 Stat. 678.

(7) Reorganization Plan Numbered 14 of 1950 (64 Stat. 1267) is amended by striking out "and (h)" and inserting in lieu thereof "(h) the Airport and Airway Development Act of 1970; and (i)".

(c) SAVING PROVISIONS.—All orders, determinations, rules, regulations, permits, contracts, certificates, licenses, grants, rights, and privileges which have been issued, made, granted, or allowed to become effective by the President, the Secretary of Transportation, or any court of competent jurisdiction under any provision of the Federal Airport Act, as amended, which are in effect at the time this section takes effect, are continued in effect according to their terms until modified, terminated, superseded, set aside, or repealed by the Secretary of Transportation or by any court of competent jurisdiction, or by operation of law.

(d) SEPARABILITY.—If any provision of this title or the application thereof to any person or circumstances is held invalid, the remainder of the title and the application of the provision to other persons or circumstances is not affected thereby.

SEC. 53. MAXIMUM CHARGES FOR CERTAIN OVERTIME SERVICES.

(a) Notwithstanding the provisions of section 451 of the Tariff Act of 1930 (19 U.S.C. 1451) or any other provisions of law, the maximum amount payable by the owner, operator, or agent of any private aircraft or private vessel for services performed on or after July 1, 1970, upon the request of such owner, operator, or agent, by officers and employees of the Customs Service, by officers and employees of the Immigration and Naturalization Service, by officers and employees (including an independent contractor performing inspectional services) of the Public Health Service, and by officers and employees of the Department of Agriculture, on a Sunday or holiday, or at any time after 5 o'clock postmeridian or before 8 o'clock antemeridian on a week day, in connection with the arrival in or departure from the United States of such private aircraft or vessel, shall not exceed $25.

46 Stat. 715;
58 Stat. 269.

(b) Notwithstanding any other provision of law, no payment shall be required for services described in subsection (a) if such services are performed on a week day and an officer or employee stationed on his regular tour of duty at the place of arrival or departure is available to perform such services.

(c) Amounts payable for services described in subsection (a) shall be collected by the Department or agency providing the services and shall be deposited into the Treasury of the United States to the credit of the appropriation of that agency charged with the expense of such services.

Definitions.

(d) As used in this section—

(1) the term "private aircraft" means any civilian aircraft not being used to transport persons or property for compensation or hire, and

(2) the term "private vessel" means any civilian vessel not being used (A) to transport persons or property for compensation or hire, or (B) in fishing operations or in processing of fish or fish products.

TITLE II—AIRPORT AND AIRWAY REVENUE ACT OF 1970

Citation of
title.

SEC. 201. SHORT TITLE, ETC.

(a) SHORT TITLE.—This title may be cited as the "Airport and Airway Revenue Act of 1970".

(b) AMENDMENT OF 1954 CODE.—Except as otherwise expressly provided, whenever in this title an amendment or repeal is expressed in terms of an amendment to, or repeal of, a section or other provision, the reference shall be considered to be made to a section or other provision of the Internal Revenue Code of 1954.

68A Stat. 3.
26 USC 1 et seq.

SEC. 202. TAX ON AVIATION FUEL.

(a) IMPOSITION OF TAX.—Section 4041 (relating to tax on special fuels) is amended by striking out subsections (c), (d), and (e) and inserting after subsection (b) the following new subsections:

"(c) NONCOMMERCIAL AVIATION.—

"(1) IN GENERAL.—There is hereby imposed a tax of 7 cents a gallon upon any liquid (other than any product taxable under section 4081)—

"(A) sold by any person to an owner, lessee, or other operator of an aircraft, for use as a fuel in such aircraft in noncommercial aviation; or

"(B) used by any person as a fuel in an aircraft in noncommercial aviation, unless there was a taxable sale of such liquid under this section.

"(2) GASOLINE.—There is hereby imposed a tax (at the rate specified in paragraph (3)) upon any product taxable under section 4081—

"(A) sold by any person to an owner, lessee, or other operator of an aircraft, for use as a fuel in such aircraft in noncommercial aviation; or

"(B) used by any person as a fuel in an aircraft in noncommercial aviation, unless there was a taxable sale of such product under subparagraph (A).

The tax imposed by this paragraph shall be in addition to any tax imposed under section 4081.

"(3) RATE OF TAX.—The rate of tax imposed by paragraph (2) is as follows:

"3 cents a gallon for the period ending September 30, 1972; and

"5½ cents a gallon for the period after September 30, 1972.

"(4) DEFINITION OF NONCOMMERCIAL AVIATION.—For purposes of this chapter, the term 'noncommercial aviation' means any use of an aircraft, other than use in a business of transporting persons or property for compensation or hire by air. The term also includes any use of an aircraft, in a business described in the preceding sentence, which is properly allocable to any transportation exempt from the taxes imposed by sections 4261 and 4271 by reason of section 4281 or 4282.

"(5) TERMINATION.—On and after July 1, 1980, the taxes imposed by paragraphs (1) and (2) shall not apply.

"(d) ADDITIONAL TAX.—If a liquid on which tax was imposed on the sale thereof is taxable at a higher rate under subsection (c)(1) of this section on the use thereof, there is hereby imposed a tax equal to the difference between the tax so imposed and the tax payable at such higher rate.

"(e) RATE REDUCTION.—On and after October 1, 1972—

"(1) the taxes imposed by subsections (a) and (b) shall be 1½ cents a gallon, and

"(2) the second and third sentences of subsections (a) and (b) shall not apply.

"(f) EXEMPTION FOR FARM USE.—

"(1) EXEMPTION.—Under regulations prescribed by the Secretary or his delegate, no tax shall be imposed under this section on any liquid sold for use or used on a farm for farming purposes.

"(2) USE ON A FARM FOR FARMING PURPOSES.—For purposes of paragraph (1) of this subsection, use on a farm for farming purposes shall be determined in accordance with paragraphs (1), (2), and (3) of section 6420(c).

"(g) EXEMPTION FOR USE AS SUPPLIES FOR VESSELS.—Under regulations prescribed by the Secretary or his delegate, no tax shall be

Margin notes:
70 Stat. 89, 388; 72 Stat. 1286.
26 USC 4041.

70 Stat. 389.

Post, pp. 238, 239, 241.

70 Stat. 87.

72 Stat. 1282.
26 USC 4221.
imposed under this section on any liquid sold for use or used as supplies for vessels or aircraft (within the meaning of section 4221(d)(3)).

"(h) REGISTRATION.—If any liquid is sold by any person for use as a fuel in an aircraft, it shall be presumed for purposes of this section that a tax imposed by this section applies to the sale of such liquid unless the purchaser is registered in such manner (and furnishes such information in respect of the use of the liquid) as the Secretary or his delegate shall by regulations provide."

68A Stat. 478;
70 Stat. 388.
(b) CONFORMING AND TECHNICAL AMENDMENTS.—Section 4041(b) (relating to imposition of tax on special motor fuels) is amended—

(1) by striking out "motor vehicle, motorboat, or airplane" each place it appears and inserting in lieu thereof "motor vehicle or motorboat", and

(2) by striking out "for the propulsion of" each place it appears and inserting in lieu thereof "in".

SEC. 203. TAX ON TRANSPORTATION OF PERSONS BY AIR.

(a) IMPOSITION OF TAX.—Section 4261 (relating to imposition of
76 Stat. 115.
tax on transportation of persons by air) is amended to read as follows:

"SEC. 4261. IMPOSITION OF TAX.

Infra.
"(a) IN GENERAL.—There is hereby imposed upon the amount paid for taxable transportation (as defined in section 4262) of any person which begins after June 30, 1970, a tax equal to 8 percent of the amount so paid. In the case of amounts paid outside of the United States for taxable transportation, the tax imposed by this subsection shall apply only if such transportation begins and ends in the United States.

"(b) SEATS, BERTHS, ETC.—There is hereby imposed upon the amount paid for seating or sleeping accommodations in connection with transportation which begins after June 30, 1970, and with respect to which a tax is imposed by subsection (a), a tax equal to 8 percent of the amount so paid.

"(c) USE OF INTERNATIONAL TRAVEL FACILITIES.—There is hereby imposed a tax of $3 upon any amount paid (whether within or without the United States) for any transportation of any person by air, if such transportation begins in the United States and begins after June 30, 1970. This subsection shall not apply to any transportation all of which is taxable under subsection (a) (determined without
Post, p. 241.
regard to sections 4281 and 4282).

"(d) BY WHOM PAID.—Except as provided in section 4263 (a), the taxes imposed by this section shall be paid by the person making the payment subject to the tax.

"(e) REDUCTION, ETC., OF RATES.—Effective with respect to transportation beginning after June 30, 1980—

"(1) the rate of the taxes imposed by subsections (a) and (b) shall be 5 percent, and

"(2) the tax imposed by subsection (c) shall not apply."

(b) DEFINITION OF TAXABLE TRANSPORTATION.—Section 4262 (relating to definition of taxable transportation) is amended—

(1) by striking out "subchapter" in subsections (a) and (b) and inserting in lieu thereof "part";

(2) by striking out "transportation" in subsection (a)(1) and inserting in lieu thereof "transportation by air";

(3) by striking out "in the case of transportation" in subsection (a)(2) and inserting in lieu thereof "in the case of transportation by air";

(4) by striking out "any transportation which" in subsection (b) and inserting in lieu thereof "any transportation by air which"; and

(5) by adding at the end thereof the following new subsection:

"(d) TRANSPORTATION.—For purposes of this part, the term 'trans-   "Transportation."
portation' includes layover or waiting time and movement of the aircraft in deadhead service."

(c) REQUIREMENTS WITH RESPECT TO AIRLINE TICKETS AND
ADVERTISING.—

(1) Subchapter B of chapter 75 (relating to other offenses) is   68A Stat. 862;
amended by adding at the end thereof the following new section: 79 Stat. 155.
                                                                  26 USC 7261-
"SEC. 7275. PENALTY FOR OFFENSES RELATING TO CERTAIN AIRLINE   7274.
TICKETS AND ADVERTISING.

"(a) TICKETS.—In the case of transportation by air all of which is
taxable transportation (as defined in section 4262), the ticket for such   Ante, p. 238.
transportation—

"(1) shall show the total of (A) the amount paid for such transportation and (B) the taxes imposed by sections 4261 (a) and (b),   Ante, p. 238.

"(2) shall not show separately the amount paid for such transportation nor the amount of such taxes, and

"(3) if the ticket shows amounts paid with respect to any segment of such transportation, shall comply with paragraphs (1)
and (2) with respect to such segments as well as with respect to
the sum of the segments.

"(b) ADVERTISING.—In the case of transportation by air all of which
is taxable transportation (as defined in section 4262) or would be taxable transportation if section 4262 did not include subsection (b)
thereof, any advertising made by or on behalf of any person furnishing
such transportation (or offering to arrange such transportation) which
states the cost of such transportation shall—

"(1) state such cost only as the total of (A) the amount to be
paid for such transportation, and (B) the taxes imposed by sections 4261 (a), (b), and (c), and

"(2) shall not state separately the amount to be paid for such
transportation nor the amount of such taxes.

"(c) PENALTY.—Any person who violates any provision of subsection (a) or (b) is, for each violation, guilty of a misdemeanor, and
upon conviction thereof shall be fined not more than $100."

(2) The table of sections for such subchapter B is amended by adding
at the end thereof the following:

"Sec. 7275. Penalty for offenses relating to certain airline tickets and advertising."

SEC. 204. TAX ON TRANSPORTATION OF PROPERTY BY AIR.

Subchapter C of chapter 33 (relating to transportation by air)   Ante, p. 238.
is amended by adding at the end thereof the following new part: 72 Stat. 260.
                                                                  26 USC 4261-
                                                                  4264.

"PART II—PROPERTY

"Sec. 4271. Imposition of tax.
"Sec. 4272. Definition of taxable transportation, etc.

"SEC. 4271. IMPOSITION OF TAX.

"(a) IN GENERAL. —There is hereby imposed upon the amount paid
within or without the United States for the taxable transportation
(as defined in section 4272) of property which begins after June 30,
1970, a tax equal to 5 percent of the amount so paid for such transportation. The tax imposed by this subsection shall apply only to amounts
paid to a person engaged in the business of transporting property by
air for hire.

"(b) BY WHOM PAID.—

"(1) IN GENERAL.—Except as provided by paragraph (2), the
tax imposed by subsection (a) shall be paid by the person making
the payment subject to tax.

Pub. Law 91-258   May 21, 1970

"(2) PAYMENTS MADE OUTSIDE THE UNITED STATES.—If a payment subject to tax under subsection (a) is made outside the United States and the person making such payment does not pay such tax, such tax—

"(A) shall be paid by the person to whom the property is delivered in the United States by the person furnishing the last segment of the taxable transportation in respect of which such tax is imposed, and

"(B) shall be collected by the person furnishing the last segment of such taxable transportation.

"(c) DETERMINATION OF AMOUNTS PAID IN CERTAIN CASES.—For purposes of this section, in any case in which a person engaged in the business of transporting property by air for hire and one or more other persons not so engaged jointly provide services which include taxable transportation of property, and the person so engaged receives, for the furnishing of such taxable transportation, a portion of the receipts from the joint providing of such services, the amount paid for the taxable transportation shall be treated as being the sum of (1) the portion of the receipts so received, and (2) any expenses incurred by any of the persons not so engaged which are properly attributable to such taxable transportation and which are taken into account in determining the portion of the receipts so received.

Termination date.

"(d) TERMINATION.—Effective with respect to transportation beginning after June 30, 1980, the tax imposed by subsection (a) shall not apply.

"SEC. 4272. DEFINITION OF TAXABLE TRANSPORTATION, ETC.

"(a) IN GENERAL.—For purposes of this part, except as provided in subsection (b), the term 'taxable transportation' means transportation by air which begins and ends in the United States.

"(b) EXCEPTIONS.—For purposes of this part, the term 'taxable transportation' does not include—

76 Stat. 116;
Ante, p. 238.
26 USC 4262.

"(1) that portion of any transportation which meets the requirements of paragraphs (1), (2), (3), and (4) of section 4262(b), or

"(2) under regulations prescribed by the Secretary or his delegate, transportation of property in the course of exportation (including shipment to a possession of the United States) by continuous movement, and in due course so exported.

"(c) EXCESS BAGGAGE OF PASSENGERS.—For purposes of this part, the term 'property' does not include excess baggage accompanying a passenger traveling on an aircraft operated on an established line.

"(d) TRANSPORTATION.—For purposes of this part, the term 'transportation' includes layover or waiting time and movement of the aircraft in deadhead service."

SEC. 205. MISCELLANEOUS AMENDMENTS RELATING TO TAXES ON TRANSPORTATION BY AIR.

(a) EXEMPTIONS AND SPECIAL RULES.—

Ante, p. 239;
72 Stat. 260.

(1) Subchapter C of chapter 33 (relating to transportation by air) is amended by adding at the end thereof the following new part:

"PART III—SPECIAL PROVISIONS APPLICABLE TO TAXES ON TRANSPORTATION BY AIR

"Sec. 4281. Small aircraft on nonestablished lines.
"Sec. 4282. Transportation by air for other members of affiliated group.

"SEC. 4281. SMALL AIRCRAFT ON NONESTABLISHED LINES.

"The taxes imposed by sections 4261 and 4271 shall not apply to Ante, pp. 238, transportation by an aircraft having a maximum certificated takeoff 239. weight (as defined in section 4492(b)) of 6,000 pounds or less, except Post, p. 243. when such aircraft is operated on an established line.

"SEC. 4282. TRANSPORTATION BY AIR FOR OTHER MEMBERS OF AFFILIATED GROUP.

"(a) GENERAL RULE.—Under regulations prescribed by the Secretary or his delegate, if—

"(1) one member of an affiliated group is the owner or lessee of an aircraft, and

"(2) such aircraft is not available for hire by persons who are not members of such group,

no tax shall be imposed under section 4261 or 4271 upon any payment received by one member of the affiliated group from another member of such group for services furnished to such other member in connection with the use of such aircraft.

"(b) AFFILIATED GROUP.—For purposes of subsection (a), the term "Affiliated 'affiliated group' has the meaning assigned to such term by section group." 1504(a), except that all corporations shall be treated as includible 68A Stat. 369; corporations (without any exclusion under section 1504(b))." 80 Stat. 116.

(2) Section 4292 (relating to State and local governmental 26 USC 1504. exemption) is amended by striking out "or 4261". 72 Stat. 260.

(3) Section 4293 (relating to exemption for United States and 68A Stat. 511. possessions) is amended by striking out "subchapters B and C" and inserting in lieu thereof "subchapter B".

(4) Section 4294(a) (relating to exemption for nonprofit edu- 72 Stat. 1292. cational organizations) is amended by striking out "or 4261".

(b) CREDITS AND REFUNDS.—

(1)(A) Section 6421(a) (relating to nonhighway use of gaso- 70 Stat. 394; line) is amended by adding the following sentence at the end 73 Stat. 615. thereof: "Except as provided in paragraph (3) of subsection (e) of this section, in the case of gasoline used after June 30, 1970, as Infra. a fuel in an aircraft, the Secretary or his delegate shall pay (without interest) to the ultimate purchaser of such gasoline an amount equal to the amount determined by multiplying the number of gallons of gasoline so used by the rate at which tax was imposed on such gasoline under section 4081." 70 Stat. 389;

(B) Section 6421(e) (relating to exempt sales; other payments 75 Stat. 123. or refunds available) is amended by adding at the end thereof the 70 Stat. 394. following new paragraph:

"(3) GASOLINE USED IN NONCOMMERCIAL AVIATION.—This section shall not apply in respect of gasoline which is used after June 30, 1970, as a fuel in an aircraft in noncommercial aviation (as defined in section 4041(c)(4))." Ante, p. 237.

(2) Section 6415 (relating to credits or refunds to persons who 68A Stat. 798. collected certain taxes) is amended by striking out "section 4251 or 4261" each place it appears and inserting in lieu thereof "section 4251, 4261, or 4271".

72 Stat. 1306.
26 USC 6416.

(3) Subparagraph (A) of section 6416(a)(2) (relating to exceptions) is amended by striking out "section 4041 (a)(2) or (b)(2) (use of diesel and special motor fuels)" and inserting in lieu thereof "section 4041 (relating to tax on special fuels) on the use of any liquid".

(4) Subparagraph (M) of section 6416(b)(2) (relating to special cases in which tax payments constitute overpayments) is amended to read as follows:

"(M) in the case of gasoline, used or sold for use in the production of special fuels referred to in section 4041;".

(c) OTHER TECHNICAL AND CLERICAL AMENDMENTS.—

Repeal.
76 Stat. 117.

(1) Section 4263 (relating to exemptions) is hereby repealed.
(2) Section 4264 (relating to special rules) is redesignated as section 4263.

79 Stat. 148.

(3) Section 4291 is amended by striking out "section 4264(a)" and inserting in lieu thereof "section 4263(a)".

(4) So much of subchapter C of chapter 33 (relating to transportation of persons) as precedes section 4261 is amended to read as follows:

"Subchapter C—Transportation by Air

"Part I. Persons.
"Part II. Property.
"Part III. Special provisions relating to taxes on transportation by air.

"PART I—PERSONS

"Sec. 4261. Imposition of tax.
"Sec. 4262. Definition of taxable transportation.
"Sec. 4263. Special rules."

(5) The table of subchapters for chapter 33 is amended by striking out "SUBCHAPTER C—Transportation of Persons by Air." and inserting in lieu thereof "SUBCHAPTER C—Transportation by Air."

68A Stat. 483.

(6) Section 4082(c) (relating to certain uses defined as sales) is amended by striking out "or of special motor fuels referred to in section 4041(b)" and inserting in lieu thereof "or of special fuels referred to in section 4041".

70 Stat. 87;
79 Stat. 165.

(7) Section 6420(i)(1) (relating to cross references) is amended—

(A) by striking out "diesel fuel and special motor fuels" and inserting in lieu thereof "special fuels", and

(B) by striking out "section 4041(d)" and inserting in lieu thereof "section 4041(f)".

(8) Section 6421(j) (relating to cross references) is amended to read as follows:

"(j) CROSS REFERENCES.—

"(1) For rate of tax in case of special fuels used in noncommercial aviation or for nonhighway purposes, see section 4041.

"(2) For civil penalty for excessive claims under this section, see section 6675.

"(3) For fraud penalties, etc., see chapter 75 (section 7201 and following, relating to crimes, other offenses, and forfeitures)."

SEC. 206. TAX ON USE OF AIRCRAFT.

26 USC 4461
et seq.

(a) IMPOSITION OF TAX.—Chapter 36 (relating to certain other excise taxes) is amended by adding at the end thereof the following new subchapter:

"Subchapter E—Tax on Use of Civil Aircraft

"Sec. 4491.Imposition of tax.
"Sec. 4492. Definitions.
"Sec. 4493. Special rules.
"Sec. 4494. Cross reference.

"SEC. 4491. IMPOSITION OF TAX.

"(a) IMPOSITION OF TAX.—A tax is hereby imposed on the use of any taxable civil aircraft during any year at the rate of—

"(1) $25, plus

"(2) (A) in the case of an aircraft (other than a turbine engine powered aircraft) having a maximum certificated takeoff weight of more than 2,500 pounds, 2 cents a pound for each pound of the maximum certificated takeoff weight, or (B) in the case of any turbine engine powered aircraft, 3½ cents a pound for each pound of the maximum certificated takeoff weight.

"(b) BY WHOM PAID.—Except as provided in section 4493(a), the tax imposed by this section shall be paid—

"(1) in the case of a taxable civil aircraft described in section 4492(a)(1), by the person in whose name the aircraft is, or is required to be, registered, or

"(2) in the case of a taxable civil aircraft described in section 4492(a)(2), by the United States person by or for whom the aircraft is owned.

"(c) PRORATION OF TAX.—If in any year the first use of the taxable civil aircraft is after the first month in such year, that portion of the tax which is determined under subsection (a)(2) shall be reckoned proportionately from the first day of the month in which such use occurs to and including the last day in such year.

"(d) ONE TAX LIABILITY PER YEAR.—

"(1) IN GENERAL.—To the extent that the tax imposed by this section is paid with respect to any taxable civil aircraft for any year, no further tax shall be imposed by this section for such year with respect to such aircraft.

"(2) CROSS REFERENCE.—

"For privilege of paying tax imposed by this section in installments, see section 6156.

"(e) TERMINATION.—On and after July 1, 1980, the tax imposed by subsection (a) shall not apply.

"SEC. 4492. DEFINITIONS.

"(a) TAXABLE CIVIL AIRCRAFT.—For purposes of this subchapter, the term 'taxable civil aircraft' means any engine driven aircraft—

"(1) registered, or required to be registered, under section 501(a) of the Federal Aviation Act of 1958 (49 U.S.C., sec. 1401(a)), or

72 Stat. 771.

"(2) which is not described in paragraph (1) but which is owned by or for a United States person.

"(b) WEIGHT.—For purposes of this subchapter, the term 'maximum certificated takeoff weight' means the maximum such weight contained in the type certificate or airworthiness certificate.

"(c) OTHER DEFINITIONS.—For purposes of this subchapter—

"(1) YEAR.—The term 'year' means the one-year period beginning on July 1.

"(2) USE.—The term 'use' means use in the navigable airspace of the United States.

397

"(3) NAVIGABLE AIRSPACE OF THE UNITED STATES.—The term 'navigable airspace of the United States' has the definition given to such term by section 101(24) of the Federal Aviation Act of 1958 (49 U.S.C., sec. 1301(24)), except that such term does not include the navigable airspace of the Commonwealth of Puerto Rico or of any possession of the United States.

72 Stat. 737.

"SEC. 4493. SPECIAL RULES.

"(a) PAYMENT OF TAX BY LESSEE.—

"(1) IN GENERAL.—Any person who is the lessee of any taxable civil aircraft on the day in any year on which occurs the first use which subjects such aircraft to the tax imposed by section 4491 for such year may, under regulations prescribed by the Secretary or his delegate, elect to be liable for payment of such tax. Notwithstanding any such election, if such lessee does not pay such tax, the lessor shall also be liable for payment of such tax.

"(2) EXCEPTION.—No election may be made under paragraph (1) with respect to any taxable civil aircraft which is leased from a person engaged in the business of transporting persons or property for compensation or hire by air.

Foreign air commerce.

"(b) CERTAIN PERSONS ENGAGED IN FOREIGN AIR COMMERCE.—

"(1) ELECTION TO PAY TENTATIVE TAX.—Any person who is a significant user of taxable civil aircraft in foreign air commerce may, with respect to that portion of the tax imposed by section 4491 which is determined under section 4491(a)(2) on any taxable civil aircraft for any year beginning on or after July 1, 1970, elect to pay the tentative tax determined under paragraph (2). The payment of such tentative tax shall not relieve such person from payment of the net liability for the tax imposed by section 4491 on such taxable civil aircraft (determined as of the close of such year).

"(2) TENTATIVE TAX.—For purposes of paragraph (1), the tentative tax with respect to any taxable civil aircraft for any year is an amount equal to that portion of the tax imposed by section 4491 on such aircraft for such year which is determined under section 4491(a)(2), reduced by a percentage of such amount equal to the percentage which the aggregate of the payments to which such person was entitled under section 6426 (determined without regard to section 6426(c)(2)) with respect to the preceding year is of the aggregate of the taxes imposed by section 4491 for which such person was liable for payment for the preceding year. In the case of the year beginning on July 1, 1970, this subsection shall apply only if the person electing to pay the tentative tax establishes what the tentative tax would have been for such year if section 4491 had taken effect on July 1, 1969.

Post, p. 245.

"(3) SIGNIFICANT USERS OF AIRCRAFT IN FOREIGN AIR COMMERCE.—For purposes of paragraph (1), a person is a significant user of taxable civil aircraft in foreign air commerce for any year only if the aggregate of the payments to which such person was entitled under section 6426 (determined without regard to section 6426(c)(2)) with respect to the preceding year was at least 10 percent of the aggregate of the taxes imposed by section 4491 for which such person was liable for payment for the preceding year.

"(4) NET LIABILITY FOR TAX.—For purposes of paragraph (1), the net liability for the tax imposed by section 4491 with respect to any taxable civil aircraft for any year is—

"(A) the amount of the tax imposed by such section, reduced by

398

"(B) the amount payable under section 6426 with respect to such aircraft for the year (determined without regard to section 6426(c)(2)).

"SEC. 4494. CROSS REFERENCE.

"**For penalties and administrative provisions applicable to this subchapter, see subtitle F.**"

(b) INSTALLMENT PAYMENT OF TAX.—

(1) Section 6156(a) (relating to installment payments of tax 75 Stat. 125. on use of highway motor vehicles) is amended by inserting "or 4491" after "4481".

(2) Paragraph (2) of section 6156(e) is amended to read as follows:

"(2) July, August, or September of 1972, in the case of the tax imposed by section 4481."

(c) REFUND FOR CERTAIN FOREIGN AIR COMMERCE.—Subchapter B of chapter 65 (relating to rules of special application) is amended by 68A Stat. 794; adding at the end thereof the following new section: 82 Stat. 262.

"SEC. 6426. REFUND OF AIRCRAFT USE TAX WHERE PLANE TRANS- 26 USC 6411-
PORTS FOR HIRE IN FOREIGN AIR COMMERCE. 6425.

"(a) GENERAL RULE.—In the case of any aircraft used in the business of transporting persons or property for compensation or hire by air, if any of such transportation during any period is transportation in foreign air commerce, the Secretary or his delegate shall pay (without interest) to the person who paid the tax under section 4491 for Ante, p. 243. such period the amount determined by multiplying that portion of the amount so paid for such period which is determined under section 4491(a)(2) with respect to such aircraft by a fraction—

"(1) the numerator of which is the number of airport-to-airport miles such aircraft traveled in foreign air commerce during such period while engaged in such business, and

"(2) the denominator of which is the total number of airport-to-airport miles such aircraft traveled during such period.

"(b) DEFINITIONS.—For purposes of this section—   Definitions.

"(1) FOREIGN AIR COMMERCE.—The term 'foreign air commerce' means any movement by air of the aircraft which does not begin and end in the United States; except that any segment of such movement in which the aircraft traveled between two ports or stations in the United States shall be treated as travel which is not foreign air commerce.

"(2) AIRPORT-TO-AIRPORT MILES.—The term 'airport-to-airport miles' means the official mileage distance between airports as determined under regulations prescribed by the Secretary or his delegate.

"(c) PAYMENTS TO PERSONS PAYING TENTATIVE TAX.—In the case of any person who paid a tentative tax determined under section 4493(b) with respect to any aircraft for any period, the amount payable under subsection (a) with respect to such aircraft for such period—

"(1) shall be computed with reference to that portion of the tax imposed under section 4491 for such period which is determined under section 4491(a)(2), and

"(2) as so computed, shall be reduced by an amount equal to—

"(A) the amount by which that portion of the tax imposed under section 4491 for such period which is determined under section 4491(a)(2), exceeds

"(B) the amount of the tentative tax determined under section 4493(b) paid for such period.

"(d) TIME FOR FILING CLAIM.—Not more than one claim may be filed under this section by any person with respect to any year. No

claim shall be allowed under this subsection with respect to any year
unless filed on or before the first September 30 after the end of such
year.

"(e) REGULATIONS.—The Secretary or his delegate may by regulations prescribe the conditions, not inconsistent with the provisions of
this section, under which payments may be made under this section or
the amount to which any person is entitled under this section with
respect to any period may be treated by such person as an overpayment
which may be credited against the tax imposed by section 4491 with
respect to such period."

(d) CLERICAL AMENDMENTS.—

(1) The table of subchapters for chapter 36 is amended by adding at the end thereof the following:

"SUBCHAPTER E. Tax on use of civil aircraft."

(2) The heading for section 6156 is amended by inserting "**AND
CIVIL AIRCRAFT**" after "**HIGHWAY MOTOR VEHICLES**".

(3) The table of sections for subchapter A of chapter 62 is
amended by inserting "and civil aircraft" after "highway motor
vehicles" in the item relating to section 6156.

(4) The table of sections for subchapter B of chapter 65 is
amended by adding at the end thereof the following:

"Sec. 6426. Refund of aircraft use tax where plane transports for hire in foreign air commerce."

SEC. 207. PAYMENTS WITH RESPECT TO CERTAIN USES OF GASOLINE AND SPECIAL FUELS.

(a) PAYMENTS WITH RESPECT TO CERTAIN NONTAXABLE USES OF
FUELS.—Subchapter B of chapter 65 (relating to rules of special
application) is amended by adding after section 6426 (as added by sec-
Ante, p. 245. tion 406 (c) of this title) the following new section:

"**SEC. 6427. FUELS NOT USED FOR TAXABLE PURPOSES.**

"(a) NONTAXABLE USES.—Except as provided in subsection (f), if
75 Stat. 123;
Ante, p. 237. tax has been imposed under section 4041 (a), (b), or (c) on the sale
of any fuel and, after June 30, 1970, the purchaser uses such fuel other
than for the use for which sold, or resells such fuel, the Secretary or
his delegate shall pay (without interest) to him an amount equal to—

"(1) the amount of tax imposed on the sale of the fuel to him,
reduced by

"(2) if he uses the fuel, the amount of tax which would have
been imposed under section 4041 on such use if no tax under section
4041 had been imposed on the sale of the fuel.

"(b) LOCAL TRANSIT SYSTEMS.—

"(1) ALLOWANCE.—Except as provided in subsection (f) if any
fuel on the sale of which tax was imposed under section 4041 (a)
or (b) is, after June 30, 1970, used by the purchaser during any
calendar quarter in vehicles while engaged in furnishing scheduled common carrier public passenger land transportation service along regular routes, the Secretary or his delegate shall, subject to the provisions of paragraph (2), pay (without interest) to
the purchaser the amount determined by multiplying—

"(A) 2 cents for each gallon of fuel so used on which tax
was imposed at the rate of 4 cents a gallon, by

"(B) the percentage which the purchaser's commuter fare
76 Stat. 119. revenue (as defined in section 6421(d)(2)) derived from
such scheduled service during the quarter was of his total
passenger fare revenue derived from such scheduled service
during the quarter.

"(2) LIMITATION.—Paragraph (1) shall apply in respect of
fuel used during any calendar quarter only if at least 60 percent
of the total passenger fare revenue derived during the quarter

from scheduled service described in paragraph (1) by the purchaser was attributable to commuter fare revenue derived during the quarter by the purchaser from such scheduled service.

"(c) USE FOR FARMING PURPOSES.—Except as provided in subsection (f), if any fuel on the sale of which tax was imposed under section 4041 (a), (b), or (c) is, after June 30, 1970, used on a farm for farming purposes (within the meaning of section 6420(c)), the Secretary or his delegate shall pay (without interest) to the purchaser an amount equal to the amount of the tax imposed on the sale of the fuel. For purposes of this subsection, if fuel is used on a farm by any person other than the owner, tenant, or operator of such farm, such owner, tenant, or operator shall be treated as the user and purchaser of such fuel. 75 Stat. 123;
Ante, p. 237.
70 Stat. 87.

"(d) TIME FOR FILING CLAIMS; PERIOD COVERED.—

"(1) GENERAL RULE.—Except as provided in paragraph (2), not more than one claim may be filed under subsection (a), (b), or (c), by any person with respect to fuel used during his taxable year; and no claim shall be allowed under this paragraph with respect to fuel used during any taxable year unless filed by the purchaser not later than the time prescribed by law for filing a claim for credit or refund of overpayment of income tax for such taxable year. For purposes of this paragraph, a person's taxable year shall be his taxable year for purposes of subtitle A.

"(2) EXCEPTION.—If $1,000 or more is payable under subsections (a) and (b) to any person with respect to fuel used during any of the first three quarters of his taxable year, a claim may be filed under this section by the purchaser with respect to fuel used during such quarter. No claim filed under this paragraph shall be allowed unless filed on or before the last day of the first quarter following the quarter for which the claim is filed.

"(e) APPLICABLE LAWS.—

"(1) IN GENERAL.—All provisions of law, including penalties, applicable in respect of the taxes imposed by section 4041 shall, insofar as applicable and not inconsistent with this section, apply in respect of the payments provided for in this section to the same extent as if such payments constituted refunds of overpayments of the tax so imposed.

"(2) EXAMINATION OF BOOKS AND WITNESSES.—For the purpose of ascertaining the correctness of any claim made under this section, or the correctness of any payment made in respect of any such claim, the Secretary or his delegate shall have the authority granted by paragraphs (1), (2), and (3) of section 7602 (relating to examination of books and witnesses) as if the claimant were the person liable for tax. 68A Stat. 901.

"(f) INCOME TAX CREDIT IN LIEU OF PAYMENT.—

"(1) PERSONS NOT SUBJECT TO INCOME TAX.—Payment shall be made under this section only to—

"(A) the United States or an agency or instrumentality thereof, a State, a political subdivision of a State, or any agency or instrumentality of one or more States or political subdivisions, or

"(B) an organization exempt from tax under section 501 (a) (other than an organization required to make a return of the tax imposed under subtitle A for its taxable year). 26 USC 501.

"(2) EXCEPTION.—Paragraph (1) shall not apply to a payment of a claim filed under subsection (d)(2).

"(3) ALLOWANCE OF CREDIT AGAINST INCOME TAX.—

"For allowances of credit against the income tax imposed by subtitle A for fuel used or resold by the purchaser, see section 39.

"(g) REGULATIONS.—The Secretary or his delegate may by regulations prescribe the conditions, not inconsistent with the provisions of this section, under which payments may be made under this section.

"(h) CROSS REFERENCES.—

"(1) For civil penalty for excessive claims under this section, see section 6675.
"(2) For fraud penalties, etc., see chapter 75 (section 7201 and following, relating to crimes, other offenses, and forfeitures)."

79 Stat. 165.

(b) TIME FOR FILING CLAIMS.—Section 6420(b)(2)(B) (relating to gasoline used on farms), section 6421(c)(3)(A)(ii) (relating to gasoline used for certain nonhighway purposes or by local transit

79 Stat. 137.

systems), and section 6424(b)(1) (relating to lubricating oil not used in highway vehicles) are each amended by striking out "time prescribed by law for filing an income tax return for such taxable year" and inserting in lieu thereof "time prescribed by law for filing a claim for credit or refund of overpayment of income tax for such taxable year".

79 Stat. 167.
26 USC 39.

(c) CREDIT AGAINST INCOME TAX.—Section 39 (relating to certain uses of gasoline and lubrication oil) is amended—
(1) by inserting ", **SPECIAL FUELS**," after "**GASOLINE**" in the heading of such section;
(2) by striking out "and" at the end of subsection (a)(2), by striking out the period at the end of subsection (a)(3) and inserting in lieu thereof ", and", and by adding at the end of subsection (a) the following new paragraph:

Ante, p. 246.

"(4) under section 6427 with respect to fuels used for nontaxable purposes or resold during the taxable year (determined without regard to section 6427(f)).";
(3) by striking out "6421 or 6424" in subsection (c) and inserting in lieu thereof "6421, 6424, or 6427"; and
(4) by striking out "6421(i) or 6424(g)" in subsection (c) and inserting in lieu thereof "6421(i), 6424(g), or 6427(f)".

(d) TECHNICAL AND CONFORMING AMENDMENTS.—

79 Stat. 167,
168.

(1) Sections 874(a), 6201(a)(4), and 6401(b) are each amended by striking out "uses of gasoline and lubricating oil" and inserting in lieu thereof "uses of gasoline, special fuels, and lubricating oil"
(2) The heading of section 6201(a)(4) is amended by striking out "FOR USE OF GASOLINE" and inserting in lieu thereof "UNDER SECTION 39".

79 Stat. 139.

(3) Section 6206 is amended—
(A) by striking out "**AND 6424**" in the heading of such section and inserting in lieu thereof "**6424, AND 6427**";
(B) by striking out "or 6424" each place it appears in the text of such section and inserting in lieu thereof "6424, or 6427"; and
(C) by striking out "by section 4081 (or, in the case of lubricating oil, by section 4091)" and inserting in lieu thereof "by section 4081 (with respect to payments under sections 6420 and 6421), 4091 (with respect to payments under section 6424), or 4041 (with respect to payments under section 6427)".

72 Stat. 1307.

(4) Section 6416(b)(2)(G) is amended by inserting "before July 1, 1970" after "if".

(5) Section 6416(b)(2)(H) is amended by inserting "beginning before July 1, 1970," after "during any calendar quarter". 72 Stat. 1306. 26 USC 6416.

(6) Section 6416(b)(2)(I) is amended by inserting "before July 1, 1970," after "used or resold for use".

(7) Section 6416(b)(2)(J) is amended by inserting "before July 1, 1970," after "used or resold for use".

(8) Section 6675 is amended— 70 Stat. 90.

(A) by striking out "**GASOLINE**" in the heading of such section and inserting in lieu thereof "**FUELS**";

(B) by striking out "or" before "6424" in subsection (a), and by inserting after "motor vehicles)" in such subsection ", or 6427 (relating to fuels not used for taxable purposes)"; and

(C) by striking out "or 6424" in subsection (b)(1) and inserting in lieu thereof "6424, or 6427".

(9) Sections 7210, 7603, and 7604, and the first sentence of section 7605(a) are each amended by inserting "6427(e)(2)," after "6424(d)(2),". The second sentence of section 7605(a) is amended by striking out "or 6424(d)(2)" and inserting in lieu thereof "6424(d)(2), or 6427(e)(2)". 68A Stat. 854-902.

(10) The table of sections for subpart A of part IV of subchapter A of chapter 1 is amended by inserting ", special fuels," after "gasoline" in the item relating to section 39.

(11) The table of sections for subchapter A of chapter 63 is amended by striking out "and 6424" in the item relating to section 6206 and inserting in lieu thereof "6424, and 6427".

(12) The table of sections for subchapter B of chapter 65 is amended by adding at the end thereof the following new item:

"Sec. 6427. Fuels not used for taxable purposes."

(13) The table of sections for subchapter B of chapter 68 is amended by striking out "gasoline" in the item relating to section 6675 and inserting in lieu thereof "fuels".

(e) Highway Trust Fund Amendments.—Subsection (f) of section 209 of the Highway Revenue Act of 1956 (23 U.S.C., sec. 120 note) is amended— 70 Stat. 399.

(1) by inserting at the end of paragraph (3) the following new sentence: "This paragraph shall not apply to amounts estimated by the Secretary of the Treasury as paid under sections 6420 and 6421 of such Code with respect to gasoline used after June 30, 1970, in aircraft."; Ante, p. 241.

(2) by striking out "GASOLINE AND LUBRICATING OIL" in the heading of paragraph (6) and inserting in lieu thereof "GASOLINE, SPECIAL FUELS, AND LUBRICATING OIL"; 79 Stat. 168.

(3) by striking out "(relating to credit for certain uses of gasoline and lubricating oil) with respect to gasoline and lubricating oil" in the first sentence of paragraph (6) and inserting in lieu thereof "(relating to credit for certain uses of gasoline, special fuels, and lubricating oil) with respect to gasoline, special fuels, and lubricating oil";

(4) by adding at the end of paragraph (6) the following new sentence: "This paragraph shall not apply to amounts estimated by the Secretary of the Treasury as attributable to the use after June 30, 1970, of gasoline and special fuels in aircrafts."; and

(5) by adding after paragraph (6) the following new paragraph:

"(7) Transfers from trust fund for nontaxable uses of fuels.—The Secretary of the Treasury shall pay from time to time from the Trust Fund into the general fund of the Treasury amounts equivalent to the amounts paid before July 1, 1973, under

Ante, p. 246.

section 6427 of the Internal Revenue Code of 1954 (relating to fuels not used for taxable purposes) on the basis of claims filed for fuels used before October 1, 1972. This paragraph shall not apply to amounts estimated by the Secretary of the Treasury as paid under such section 6427 with respect to fuels used in aircraft."

SEC. 208. AIRPORT AND AIRWAY TRUST FUND.

(a) CREATION OF TRUST FUND.—There is established in the Treasury of the United States a trust fund to be known as the "Airport and Airway Trust Fund" (hereinafter in this section referred to as the "Trust Fund"), consisting of such amounts as may be appropriated or credited to the Trust Fund as provided in this section.

(b) TRANSFER TO TRUST FUND OF AMOUNTS EQUIVALENT TO CERTAIN TAXES.—There is hereby appropriated to the Trust Fund—

(1) amounts equivalent to the taxes received in the Treasury after June 30, 1970, and before July 1, 1980, under subsections

Ante, p. 237.
Ante, pp. 238, 239, 243.

(c) and (d) of section 4041 (taxes on aviation fuel) and under sections 4261, 4271, and 4491 (taxes on transportation by air and on use of civil aircraft) of the Internal Revenue Code of 1954;

68A Stat. 483;
75 Stat. 123.
26 USC 4081.

(2) amounts determined by the Secretary of the Treasury to be equivalent to the taxes received in the Treasury after June 30, 1970, and before July 1, 1980, under section 4081 of such Code, with respect to gasoline used in aircraft; and

(3) amounts determined by the Secretary of the Treasury to be equivalent to the taxes received in the Treasury after June 30, 1970, and before July 1, 1980, under paragraphs (2) and (3) of

70 Stat. 388;
75 Stat. 124.

section 4071(a) of such Code, with respect to tires and tubes of the types used on aircraft.

The amounts appropriated by paragraphs (1), (2), and (3) shall be transferred at least quarterly from the general fund of the Treasury to the Trust Fund on the basis of estimates made by the Secretary of the Treasury of the amounts referred to in paragraphs (1), (2), and (3) received in the Treasury. Proper adjustments shall be made in the amounts subsequently transferred to the extent prior estimates were in excess of or less than the amounts required to be transferred.

(c) TRANSFER OF UNEXPENDED FUNDS.—At the close of June 30, 1970, there shall be transferred to the Trust Fund all unexpended funds which have been appropriated before July 1, 1970, out of the general fund of the Treasury to meet obligations of the United States (1) described in subparagraph (B) or (C) of subsection (f)(1) of this section, or (2) incurred under the Federal Airport Act (49

60 Stat. 170.

U.S.C., sec. 1101 et seq.).

(d) APPROPRIATION OF ADDITIONAL SUMS.—There are hereby authorized to be appropriated to the Trust Fund such additional sums as may be required to make the expenditures referred to in subsection (f) of this section.

(e) MANAGEMENT OF TRUST FUND.—

Report to
Congress.

(1) REPORT.—It shall be the duty of the Secretary of the Treasury to hold the Trust Fund, and (after consultation with the Secretary of Transportation) to report to the Congress each year on the financial condition and the results of the operations of the Trust Fund during the preceding fiscal year and on its expected condition and operations during the next five fiscal years. Such report shall be printed as a House document of the session of the Congress to which the report is made.

(2) Investment.—

(A) In general.—It shall be the duty of the Secretary of the Treasury to invest such portion of the Trust Fund as is not, in his judgment, required to meet current withdrawals. Such investments may be made only in interest-bearing obligations of the United States or in obligations guaranteed as to both principal and interest by the United States. For such purpose, such obligations may be acquired (i) on original issue at the issue price, or (ii) by purchase of outstanding obligations at the market price. The purposes for which obligations of the United States may be issued under the Second Liberty Bond Act, as amended, are hereby extended to authorize the issuance at par of special obligations exclusively to the Trust Fund. Such special obligations shall bear interest at a rate equal to the average rate of interest, computed as to the end of the calendar month next preceding the date of such issue, borne by all marketable interest-bearing obligations of the United States then forming a part of the Public Debt; except that where such average rate is not a multiple of one-eighth of 1 percent, the rate of interest of such special obligations shall be the multiple of one-eighth of 1 percent next lower than such average rate. Such special obligations shall be issued only if the Secretary of the Treasury determines that the purchase of other interest-bearing obligations of the United States, or of obligations guaranteed as to both principal and interest by the United States on original issue or at the market price, is not in the public interest. 40 Stat. 288.
31 USC 774.

(B) Sale of obligations.—Any obligation acquired by the Trust Fund (except special obligations issued exclusively to the Trust Fund) may be sold by the Secretary of the Treasury at the market price, and such special obligations may be redeemed at par plus accrued interest.

(C) Interest on certain proceeds.—The interest on, and the proceeds from the sale or redemption of, any obligations held in the Trust Fund shall be credited to and form a part of the Trust Fund.

(3) Applicability of paragraph (2).—Paragraph (2) of this subsection shall not apply until the beginning of the fiscal year immediately following the first fiscal year beginning after June 30, 1970, in which the receipts of the Trust Fund under subsection (b) exceed 80 percent of the expenditures from the Trust Fund under subsection (f)(1).

(f) Expenditures From Trust Fund.—

(1) Airport and airway program.—Amounts in the Trust Fund shall be available, as provided by appropriation Acts, for making expenditures after June 30, 1970, and before July 1, 1980, to meet those obligations of the United States—

(A) hereafter incurred under title I of this Act (as in effect on the date of the enactment of this Act), or incurred at any time before July 1, 1970, under the Federal Airport Act (49 U.S.C., sec. 1101 et seq.); Ante, p. 219.
60 Stat. 170.

(B) heretofore or hereafter incurred under the Federal Aviation Act of 1958, as amended (49 U.S.C., sec. 1301 et seq.), which are attributable to planning, research and 72 Stat. 731.

development, construction, or operation and maintenance of—

(i) air traffic control,
(ii) air navigation,
(iii) communications, or
(iv) supporting services,

for the airway system; or

(C) for those portions of the administrative expenses of the Department of Transportation which are attributable to activities described in subparagraph (A) or (B).

(2) TRANSFERS FROM TRUST FUND ON ACCOUNT OF CERTAIN REFUNDS.—The Secretary of the Treasury shall pay from time to time from the Trust Fund into the general fund of the Treasury amounts equivalent to—

70 Stat. 87;
79 Stat. 165.
Ante, p. 241.

Ante, p. 246.
Ante, p. 245.

(A) the amounts paid after June 30, 1970, and before July 1, 1980, in respect of fuel used in aircraft, under sections 6420 (relating to amounts paid in respect of gasoline used on farms), 6421 (relating to amounts paid in respect of gasoline used for certain nonhighway purposes), and 6427 (relating to fuels not used for taxable purposes) of the Internal Revenue Code of 1954, and

(B) the amounts paid under section 6426 of such Code (relating to refund of aircraft use tax where plane transports for hire in foreign air commerce),

on the basis of claims filed for periods beginning after June 30, 1970.

(3) TRANSFERS FROM TRUST FUND ON ACCOUNT OF CERTAIN SECTION 39 CREDITS.—The Secretary of the Treasury shall pay from time to time from the Trust Fund into the general fund of the Treasury amounts equivalent to the credits allowed under section

Ante, p. 248.

39 of the Internal Revenue Code of 1954 with respect to fuel used in aircraft during taxable years ending after June 30, 1970, and beginning before July 1, 1980, and attributable to use after June 30, 1970, and before July 1, 1980. Such amounts shall be transferred on the basis of estimates by the Secretary of the Treasury, and proper adjustments shall be made in amounts subsequently transferred to the extent prior estimates were in excess of or less than the credits allowed.

70 Stat. 397.

(g) HIGHWAY TRUST FUND AMENDMENT.—Subsection (c) of section 209 of the Highway Revenue Act of 1956 (23 U.S.C., sec. 120 note) is amended by adding at the end thereof the following new paragraph:

"(5) ADJUSTMENTS FOR AVIATION USES.—The amounts described in paragraphs (1)(A) and (3)(A) with respect to any period shall (before the application of this subsection) be reduced by appropriate amounts to reflect any amounts transferred to the Airport and Airway Trust Fund under section 208(b) of the

Ante, p. 250.

Airport and Airway Revenue Act of 1970 with respect to such period. The amounts described in paragraphs (1)(E) and (3)(C) with respect to any period shall (before the application of this subsection) be reduced by appropriate amounts to reflect any amounts transferred to the Airport and Airway Trust Fund under section 208(b)(3) of the Airport and Airway Revenue Act of 1970 with respect to such period."

SEC. 209. INVESTIGATION AND REPORT TO CONGRESS.

(a) STUDY AND INVESTIGATION.—The Secretary of Transportation is hereby authorized and directed, in cooperation with such other Federal officers and agencies as may be designated by the President and through full consultation with and consideration of the views of the users of the system, to make a study and investigation to make available to the Congress information on the basis of which it may determine what revisions, if any, of the taxes imposed by the United States should be made in order to assure, insofar as practicable, an equitable distribution of the tax burden among the various classes of persons using the airports and airways of the United States or otherwise deriving benefits from such airports and airways.

(b) REPORTS.—The Secretary of Transportation shall report to the Congress the results of the study and investigation required by subsection (a). The final report shall be made as soon as possible but in no event later than March 1, 1972. On or before March 1, 1971, the Secretary of Transportation shall report to the Congress the progress that has been made in carrying out the study and investigation required by subsection (a). Each such report shall be printed as a House document of the session of the Congress to which the report is made. In addition, the Secretary of Transportation shall identify the costs to the Federal Government that should appropriately be charged to the system and the value to be appropriately assigned to the general public benefit.

Reports to Congress.

(c) FUNDS FOR STUDY AND INVESTIGATION.—There are hereby authorized to be appropriated out of the Airport and Airway Trust Fund such sums as may be necessary to enable the Secretary of Transportation to carry out the provisions of this section.

Appropriations.

SEC. 210. APPLICATION OF CERTAIN OTHER TAX PROVISIONS.

(a) Nothing in this title or in any other law of the United States shall prevent the application of sections 104 through 110 of title 4 of the United States Code to civil airports owned by the United States.

61 Stat. 644; 70 Stat. 799.

(b) Subsection (a) shall not apply to—

(1) sales or use taxes in respect of fuels for aircraft or in respect of other servicing of aircraft, or

(2) taxes, fees, head charges, or other charges in respect of the landing or taking off of aircraft or aircraft passengers or freight.

(c) In the case of any lease in effect on September 28, 1969, subsection (a) shall not authorize the levy or collection of any tax in respect of any transaction occurring, or any service performed, pursuant to such lease before the expiration of such lease (determined without regard to any renewal or extension of such lease made after September 28, 1969). For purposes of the preceding sentence, the term "lease" includes a contract.

"Lease."

SEC. 211. EFFECTIVE DATES.

(a) GENERAL RULE.—Except as provided in subsection (b), the amendments made by this title shall take effect on July 1, 1970.

(b) EXCEPTIONS.—The amendments made by sections 203 and 204 shall apply to transportation beginning after June 30, 1970. The amendments made by subsections (a), (b), and (c) of section 207 shall apply with respect to taxable years ending after June 30, 1970.

Approved May 21, 1970.

LEGISLATIVE HISTORY:

HOUSE REPORTS: No. 91-601 (Interstate and Foreign Commerce) and
　　　　　　　No. 91-1074 (Comm. of Conference).
SENATE REPORTS: No. 91-565 accompanying S. 3108 (Comm. on Commerce)
　　　　　　　and No. 91-706 (Comm. on Finance).
CONGRESSIONAL RECORD:
　　　Vol. 115 (1969): Nov. 6, considered and passed House.
　　　Vol. 116 (1970): Feb. 24-26, considered and passed Senate,
　　　　　　　　　amended.
　　　　　　　　May 12, Senate agreed to conference report.
　　　　　　　　May 13, House agreed to conference report.

CONVENTION FOR THE SUPPRESSION OF UNLAWFUL SEIZURE OF AIRCRAFT (HIJACKING CONVENTION)

Convention done at The Hague, December 16, 1970.

Ratification advised by the Senate of the United States of America September 8, 1971.

Ratified by the President of the United States September 14, 1971.

Ratification of the United States of America deposited at Washington September 14, 1971.

Proclaimed by the President of the United States of America October 18, 1971

Entered into Force October 14, 1971.

Treaties and Other International Acts Series 7192.

THE STATES PARTIES TO THIS CONVENTION

CONSIDERING that unlawful acts of seizure or exercise of control of aircraft in flight jeopardize the safety of persons and property, seriously affect the operation of air services, and undermine the confidence of the peoples of the world in the safety of civil aviation;

CONSIDERING that the occurrence of such acts is a matter of grave concern;

CONSIDERING that, for the purpose of deterring such acts, there is an urgent need to provide appropriate measures for punishment of offenders;

HAVE AGREED AS FOLLOWS:

Article 1

Any person who on board an aircraft in flight:

(a) unlawfully, by force or threat thereof, or by any other form of intimidation, seizes, or exercises control of that aircraft, or attempts to perform any such act, or

(b) is an accomplice of a person who performs or attempts to perform any such act, commits an offense (hereinafter referred to as "the offense").

Article 2

Each Contracting State undertakes to make the offense punishable by severe penalties.

Article 3

1. For the purpose of this Convention, an aircraft is considered to be in flight at any time from the moment when all its external doors are closed following embarkation until the moment when any such door is opened for disembarkation. In the case of a forced landing, the flight shall be deemed to continue until the competent authorities take over the responsibility for the aircraft and for persons and property on board.

2. This Convention shall not apply to aircraft used in military, customs or police services.

3. This Convention shall apply only if the place of take-off or the place of actual landing of the aircraft on board which the offence is committed is situated outside the territory of the State of registration of that aircraft; it shall be immaterial whether the aircraft is engaged in an international or domestic flight.

4. In the cases mentioned in Article 5, this Convention shall not apply if the place of take-off and the place of actual landing of the aircraft on board which the offence is committed are situated within the territory of the same State where that State is one of these referred to in that Article.

5. Notwithstanding paragraphs 3 and 4 of this Article, Articles 6, 7, 8 and 10 shall apply whatever the place of take-off or the place of actual landing of the aircraft, if the offender or the alleged offender is found in the territory of a State other than the State of registration of that aircraft.

Article 4

1. Each Contracting State shall likewise take such measures as may be necessary to establish its jurisdiction over the offence and any other act of violence against passengers or crew committed by the alleged offender in connection with the offence, in the following cases:

(a) when the offence is committed on board an aircraft registered in that State;

(b) when the aircraft on board which the offence is committed lands in its territory with the alleged offender still on board;

(c) when the offence is committed on board an aircraft leased without crew to a lessee who has his principal place of business or, if the lessee has no such place of

409

business, his permanent residence, in that State.

2. Each Contracting State shall likewise take such measures as may be necessary to establish its jurisdiction over the offence in the case where the alleged offender is present in its territory and it does not extradite him pursuant to Article 8 to any of the States mentioned in paragraph 1 of this Article.

3. This Convention does not exclude any criminal jurisdiction exercised in accordance with national law.

Article 5

The Contracting States which establish joint air transport operating organizations or international operating agencies, which operate aircraft which are subject to joint or international registration shall, by appropriate means, designate for each aircraft the State among them which shall exercise the jurisdiction and have the attributes of the State of registration for the purpose of this Convention and shall give notice thereof to the International Civil Aviation Organization which shall communicate the notice to all States parties to this Convention.

Article 6

1. Upon being satisfied that the circumstances so warrant, any Contracting State in the territory of which the offender or the alleged offender is present, shall take him into custody or take other measures to ensure his presence. The custody and other measures shall be as provided in the law of that State but may only be continued for such time as is necessary to enable any criminal or extradition proceedings to be instituted.

2. Such State shall immediately make a preliminary enquiry into the facts.

3. Any person in custody pursuant to paragraph 1 of this Article shall be assisted in communicating immediately with the nearest appropriate representative of the State of which he is a national.

4. When a State, pursuant to this Article, has taken a person into custody, it shall immediately notify the State of registration of the aircraft, the State mentioned in Article 4, paragraph 1(c), the State of nationality of the detained person and, if it considers it advisable, any other interested States of the fact that such person is in custody and of the circumstances which warrant his detention. The State which makes the preliminary enquiry contemplated in paragraph 2 of this Article

shall promptly report its findings to the said States and shall indicate whether it intends to exercise jurisdiction.

Article 7

The Contracting State in the territory of which the alleged offender is found shall, if it does not extradite him, be obliged, without exception whatsoever, and whether or not the offense was committed in its territory, to submit the case to its competent authorities for the purpose of prosecution. Those authorities shall take their decision in the same manner as in the case of any ordinary offence of a serious nature under the law of that State.

Article 8

1. The offence shall be deemed to be included as an extraditable offence in any extradition treaty existing between Contracting States. Contracting States undertake to include the offence as an extraditable offence in every extradition treaty to be concluded between them.

2. If a Contracting State which makes extradition conditional on the existence of a treaty receives a request for extradition from another Contracting State with which it has no extradition treaty, it may at its option consider this Convention as the legal basis for extradition in respect of the offence. Extradition shall be subject to the other conditions provided by the law of the requested State.

3. Contracting States which do not make extradition conditional on the existence of a treaty shall recognize the offence as an extraditable offence between themselves subject to the conditions provided by the law of the requested State.

4. The offence shall be treated, for the purpose of extradition between Contracting States, as if it had been committed not only in the place in which it occurred but also in the territories of the States required to establish their jurisdiction in accordance with Article 4, paragraph 1.

Article 9

1. When any of the acts mentioned in Article 1(a) has occurred or is about to occur[,] Contracting States shall take all appropriate measures to restore control of the aircraft to its lawful commander or to preserve his control of the aircraft.

2. In the cases contemplated by the preceding paragraph, any Contracting State

in which the aircraft or its passengers or crew are present shall facilitate the continuation of the journey of the passengers and crew as soon as practicable, and shall without delay return the aircraft and its cargo to the persons lawfully entitled to possession.

Article 10

1. Contracting States shall afford one another the greatest measure of assistance in connection with criminal proceedings brought in respect of the offence and other acts mentioned in Article 4. The law of the State requested shall apply in all cases.

2. The provisions of paragraph 1 of this Article shall not affect obligations under any other treaty, bilateral or multilateral, which governs or will govern, in whole or in part, mutual assistance in criminal matters.

Article 11

Each Contracting State shall in accordance with its national law report to the Council of the International Civil Aviation Organization as promptly as possible any relevant information in its possession concerning:

(a) the circumstances of the offence;

(b) the action taken pursuant to Article 9;

(c) the measures taken in relation to the offender or the alleged offender, and, in particular, the results of any extradition proceedings or other legal proceedings.

Article 12

1. Any dispute between two or more Contracting States concerning the interpretation or application of this Convention which cannot be settled through negotiation, shall, at the request of one of them, be submitted to arbitration. If within six months from the date of the request for arbitration the Parties are unable to agree on the organization of the arbitration, any one of those Parties may refer the dispute to the International Court of Justice by request in conformity with the statute of that court.

2. Each State may at the time of signature or ratification of this Convention or accession thereto, declare that it does not consider itself bound by the preceding paragraph. The other Contracting States shall not be bound by the preceding paragraph with respect to any Contracting States having made such a reservation.

3. Any Contracting State having made a reservation in accordance with the pre-

ceding paragraph may at any time withdraw this reservation by notification to the Depositary Governments.

Article 13

1. This Convention shall be open for signature at The Hague on 16 December 1970, by States participating in the International Conference on Air Law held at The Hague from 1 to 16 December 1970 (hereinafter referred to as The Hague Conference). After 31 December 1970, the Convention shall be open to all States for signature in Moscow, London and Washington. Any State which does not sign this Convention before its entry into force in accordance with paragraph 3 of this Article may accede to it at any time.

2. This Convention shall be subject to ratification by the signatory States. Instruments of ratification and instruments of accession shall be deposited with the Governments of the Union of Soviet Socialist Republics, the United Kingdom of Great Britain and Northern Ireland, and the United States of America, which are hereby designated the Depositary Governments.

3. This Convention shall enter into force thirty days following the date of the deposit of instruments of ratification by ten States signatory to this Convention which participated in The Hague Conference.

4. For other States, this Convention shall enter into force on the date of entry into force of this Convention in accordance with paragraph 3 of this Article, or thirty days following the date of deposit of their instruments of ratification or accession, whichever is later.

5. The Depositary Governments shall promptly inform all signatory and acceding States of the date of each signature, the date of deposit of each instrument of ratification or accession, the date of entry into force of this Convention and other notices.

6. As soon as this Convention comes into force, it shall be registered by the Depositary Governments pursuant to Article 102 of the Charter of the United Nations and pursuant to Article 83 of the Convention on International Civil Aviation (Chicago, 1944).

Article 14

1. Any Contracting State may denounce this Convention by written notification to the Depositary Governments.

2. Denunciation shall take effect six months following the date on which notification is received by the Depositary Governments.

IN WITNESS WHEREOF the undersigned Plenipotentiaries, being duly authorized thereto by their Governments, have signed this Convention.

DONE at The Hague, this sixteenth day of December, one thousand nine hundred and seventy, in three originals, each being drawn up in four authentic texts in the English, French, Russian and Spanish languages.

Ratification or Accession Deposited

Brazil
Bulgaria
Costa Rica
Dahomey
Ecuador
Finland
Gabon
German Democratic Republic
Hungary
Iraq
Israel
Japan
Jordan
Mali
Mongolia
Niger
Norway
Panama
Paraguay
Poland
Sweden
Switzerland
Trinidad and Tobago
Union of Soviet Socialist Reps.
United Kingdom
United States

CONVENTION FOR THE SUPPRESSION OF UNLAWFUL ACTS AGAINST THE SAFETY OF CIVIL AVIATION (MONTREAL CONVENTION)

Convention done at Montreal, September 23, 1971.
Ratification advised by the Senate of the United States October 3, 1972.
Ratified by the President of the United States, November 1, 1972.
Entered into Force January 26, 1973.

THE STATES PARTIES TO THIS CONVENTION

CONSIDERING that unlawful acts against the safety of civil aviation jeopardize the safety of persons and property, seriously affect the operation of air services, and undermine the confidence of the peoples of the world in the safety of civil aviation;

CONSIDERING that the occurrence of such acts is a matter of grave concern;

CONSIDERING that, for the purpose of deterring such acts, there is an urgent need to provide appropriate measures for punishment of offenders;

HAVE AGREED AS FOLLOWS:

Article 1

1. Any person commits an offence if he unlawfully and intentionally:

(a) performs an act of violence against a person on board an aircraft in flight if that act is likely to endanger the safety of that aircraft; or

(b) destroys an aircraft in service or causes damage to such an aircraft which renders it incapable of flight or which is likely to endanger its safety in flight; or

(c) places or causes to be placed on an aircraft in service, by any means whatsoever, a device or substance which is likely to destroy that aircraft, or to cause damage to it which renders it incapable of flight, or to cause damage to it which is likely to endanger its safety in flight; or

(d) destroys or damages air navigation facilities or interferes with their operation, if any such act is likely to endanger the safety of aircraft in flight; or

(e) communicates information which he knows to be false, thereby endangering the safety of an aircraft in flight.

2. Any person also commits an offence if he:

(a) attempts to commit any of the offences mentioned in paragraph 1 of this Article; or

(b) is an accomplice of a person who commits or attempts to commit any such offence.

Article 2

For the purpose of this Convention:

(a) an aircraft is considered to be in flight at any time from the moment when all its external doors are closed following embarkation until the moment when any such door is opened for disembarkation; in the case of a forced landing, the flight shall be deemed to continue until the competent authorities take over the responsibility for the aircraft and for persons and property on board;

(b) an aircraft is considered to be in service from the beginning of the preflight preparation of the aircraft by ground personnel or by the crew for a specific flight until twenty-four hours after any landing; the period of service shall, in any event, extend for the entire period during which the aircraft is in flight as defined in paragraph (a) of this Article.

Article 3

Each Contracting State undertakes to make the offences mentioned in Article 1 punishable by severe penalties.

Article 4

1. This Convention shall not apply to aircraft used in military, customs or police services.

2. In the cases contemplated in subparagraphs (a), (b), (c) and (e) of paragraph 1 of Article 1, this Convention shall apply, irrespective of whether the aircraft is engaged in an international or domestic flight, only if:

(a) the place of take-off or landing, actual or intended, of the aircraft is situated outside the territory of the State of registration of that aircraft; or

(b) the offence is committed in the territory of a State other than the State of registration of the aircraft.

3. Notwithstanding paragraph 2 of this Article, in the cases contemplated in subparagraphs (a), (b), (c) and (e) of paragraph 1 of Article 1, this Convention shall also apply if the offender or the alleged offender is found in the territory of a State

other than the State of registration of the aircraft.

4. With respect to the States mentioned in Article 9 and in the cases mentioned in subparagraphs (a), (b), (c) and (e) of paragraph 1 of Article 1, this Convention shall not apply if the places referred to in subparagraph (a) of paragraph 2 of this Article are situated within the territory of the same State where that State is one of those referred to in Article 9, unless the offence is committed or the offender or alleged offender is found in the territory of a State other than that State.

5. In the cases contemplated in subparagraph (d) of paragraph 1 of Article 1, this Convention shall apply only if the air navigation facilities are used in international air navigation.

6. The provisions of paragraphs 2, 3, 4 and 5 of this Article shall also apply in the cases contemplated in paragraph 2 of Article 1.

Article 5

1. Each Contracting State shall take such measures as may be necessary to establish its jurisdiction over the offences in the following cases:

(a) when the offence is committed in the territory of that State;

(b) when the offence is committed against or on board an aircraft registered in that State;

(c) when the aircraft on board which the offence is committed lands in its territory with the alleged offender still on board;

(d) when the offence is committed against or on board an aircraft leased without crew to a lessee who has his principal place of business or, if the lessee has no such place of business, his permanent residence, in that State.

1. Each Contracting State shall take such

2. Each Contracting State shall likewise take such measures as may be necessary to establish its jurisdiction over the offences mentioned in Article 1, paragraph 1(a), (b) and (c), and in Article 1, paragraph 2, in so far as that paragraph relates to those offences, in the case where the alleged offender is present in its territory and it does not extradite him pursuant to Article 8 to any of the States mentioned in paragraph 1 of this Article.

3. This Convention does not exclude any criminal jurisdiction exercised in accordance with national law.

Article 6

1. Upon being satisfied that the circumstances so warrant, any Contracting State in the territory of which the offender or the alleged offender is present, shall take him into custody or take other measures to ensure his presence. The custody and other measures shall be as provided in the law of that State but may only be continued for such time as is necessary to enable any criminal or extradition proceedings to be instituted.

2. Such State shall immediately make a preliminary inquiry into the facts.

3. Any person in custody pursuant to paragraph 1 of this Article shall be assisted in communicating immediately with the nearest appropriate representative of the State of which he is a national.

4. When a State, pursuant to this Article, has taken a person into custody, it shall immediately notify the States mentioned in Article 5, paragraph 1, the State of nationality of the detained person and, if it considers it advisable, any other interested States of the fact that such person is in custody and of the circumstances which warrant his detention. The State which makes the preliminary enquiry contemplated in paragraph 2 of this Article shall promptly report its findings to the said States and shall indicate whether it intends to exercise jurisdiction.

Article 7

The Contracting State in the territory of which the alleged offender is found shall, if it does not extradite him, be obliged, without exception whatsoever and whether or not the offence was committed in its territory, to submit the case to its competent authorities for the purpose of prosecution. Those authorities shall take their decision in the same manner as in the case of any ordinary offence of a serious nature under the law of that State.

Article 8

1. The offences shall be deemed to be included as extraditable offences in any extradition treaty existing between Contracting States. Contracting States undertake to include the offences as extraditable offences in every extradition treaty to be concluded between them.

2. If a Contracting State which makes extradition conditional on the existence of a treaty receives a request for extradition from another Contracting State with which it has no extradition treaty, it may at its option consider this Convention as the legal basis for extradition in respect of the offences. Extradition shall be subject to the other conditions provided by the law of the requested State.

3. Contracting States which do not make extradition conditional on the existence of a treaty shall recognize the offences as extraditable offences between themselves subject to the conditions provided by the law of the requested State.

4. Each of the offences shall be treated, for the purpose of extradition between Contracting States, as if it had been committed not only in the place in which it occurred but also in the territories of the States required to establish their jurisdiction in accordance with Article 5, paragraph 1(b), (c) and (d).

Article 9

The Contracting States which establish joint air transport operating organizations or international operating agencies, which operate aircraft which are subject to joint or international registration shall, by appropriate means, designate for each aircraft the State among them which shall exercise the jurisdiction and have the attributes of the State of registration for the purpose of this Convention and shall give notice thereof to the International Civil Aviation Organization which shall communicate the notice to all States Parties to this Convention.

Article 10

1. The Contracting States shall, in accordance with international and national law, endeavor to take all practicable measures for the purpose of preventing the offences mentioned in Article 1.

2. When, due to the commission of one of the offences mentioned in Article 1, a flight has been delayed or interrupted, any Contracting State in whose territory the aircraft or passengers or crew are present shall facilitate the continuation of the journey of the passengers and crew as soon as practicable, and shall without delay return the aircraft and its cargo to the persons lawfully entitled to possession.

Article 11

1. Contracting States shall afford one another the greatest measure of assistance in connection with criminal proceedings brought in respect of the offences. The law of the State requested shall apply in all cases.

2. The provisions of paragraph 1 of this Article shall not affect obligations under any other treaty, bilateral or multilateral, which governs or will govern, in whole or in part, mutual assistance in criminal matters.

Article 12

Any Contracting State having reason to believe that one of the offences mentioned in Article 1 will be committed shall, in accordance with its national law, furnish any relevant information in its possession to those States which it believes would be the States mentioned in Article 5, paragraph 1.

Article 13

Each Contracting State shall in accordance with its national law report to the Council of the International Civil Aviation Organization as promptly as possible any relevant information in its possession concerning:

(a) the circumstances of the offence;

(b) the action taken pursuant to Article 10, paragraph 2;

(c) the measures taken in relation to the offender or the allege offender and, in particular, the results of any extradition proceedings or other legal proceedings.

Article 14

1. Any dispute between two or more Contracting States concerning the interpretation or application of this Convention which cannot be settled through negotiation, shall, at the request of one of them, be submitted to arbitration. If within six months from the date of the request for arbitration the Parties are unable to agree on the organization of the arbitration, any one of those Parties may refer the dispute to the International Court of Justice by request in conformity with the Statute of the Court.

2. Each State may at the time of signature or ratification of this Convention or accession thereto, declare that it does not consider itself bound by the preceding paragraph. The other Contracting States shall not be bound by the preceding paragraph with respect to any Contracting State having made such a reservation.

3. Any Contracting State having made a reservation in accordance with the preced-

ing paragraph may at any time withdraw this reservation by notification to the Depositary Governments.

Article 15

1. This Convention shall be open for signature at Montreal on 23 September 1971, by States participating in the International Conference on Air Law held at Montreal from 8 to 23 September 1971 (hereinafter referred to as the Montreal Conference). After 10 October 1971, the Convention shall be open to all States for signature in Moscow, London and Washington.. Any State which does not sign this Convention before its entry into force in accordance with paragraph 3 of this Article may accede to it at any time.

2. This Convention shall be subject to ratification by the signatory States. Instruments of ratification and instruments of accession shall be deposited with the Governments of the Union of Soviet Socialist Republics, the United Kingdom of Great Britain and Northern Ireland, and the United States of America, which are hereby designated the Depositary Governments.

3. This Convention shall enter into force thirty days following the date of the deposit of instruments of ratification by ten States signatory to this Convention which participated in the Montreal Conference.

4. For other States, this Convention shall enter into force on the date of entry into force of this Convention in accordance with paragraph 3 of this Article, or thirty days following the date of deposit of their instruments of ratification or accession, whichever is later.

5. The Depositary Governments shall promptly inform all signatory and acceding States of the date of each signature, the date of deposit of each instrument of ratification or accession, the date of entry into force of this Convention, and other notices.

6. As soon as this Convention comes into force, it shall be registered by the Depositary Governments pursuant to Article 102 of the Charter of the United Nations and pursuant to Article 83 of the Convention on International Civil Aviation (Chicago, 1944).

Article 16

1. Any Contracting State may denounce this Convention by written notification to the Depositary Governments.

2. Denunciation shall take effect six months following the date on which notification is received by the Depositary Governments.

IN WITNESS WHEREOF the undersigned Plenipotentiaries, being duly authorized thereto by their Governments, have signed this Convention.

DONE at Montreal, this twenty-third day of September, one thousand nine hundred and seventy-one, in three originals, each being drawn up in four authentic texts in the English, French, Russian and Spanish languages.

Ratifications Deposited

Brazil
Canada
Chad
China
Denmark
German Dem. Rep.
Hungary
Israel
Mongolia
Niger
Panama
South Africa
Spain
Trinidad and Tobago
U. S. S. R.
United States
Yugoslavia

Glossary of Air Transport Terms

It is important to note that, of necessity, the definitions of air transport terms given in this Glossary have no legal force or official status. They have not been approved by the members of the Civil Aeronautics Board, nor would it be feasible or practical to attempt to obtain such approval, since meanings could vary significantly in different applications, and in any case would have to be stated in great detail, including a host of complex technical and precise limitations.

The definitions given here are meant to be brief and generally helpful, rather than technically precise and exhaustive. Wherever feasible, explanations have been couched in simple, straightforward language, as nontechnically as possible.

Numbers in parentheses following financial terms identify the accounts or items encompassed by each such term in CAB Form 41.

The definitions in this Glossary are presented as they appear in the Civil Aeronautics Board Handbook of Airline Statistics.

A

Accounts payable. The unpaid balance of amounts collected for transportation furnished by others and other collections as agent, and other open accounts payable. (2020, 2030, 2040, 2050)

Accrued Federal income taxes. Accruals for currently payable Federal income taxes. (2131)

Accrued personnel compensation. Accruals for unpaid compensation to personnel. (2110)

Adjusted U.S. mail and subsidy revenues. U.S. service mail pay and Federal subsidy adjusted from the period in which reported to the period in which earned, based on the rates, whether temporary or final, established by the Civil Aeronautics Board in orders issued through July 25, 1967.

Advances from associated companies. Net amounts due associated companies for notes, loans, and advances that are not settled currently. (2240)

Airborne speed. Often called "wheels-off wheels-on speed." The average speed of an aircraft while airborne, in terms of great-circle airport-to-airport distance. In the Handbook, it is calculated by dividing the sum of the airport-to-airport distances, in statute miles, by the number of actual airborne hours.

Aircraft and traffic servicing expenses. Compensation of ground personnel and other expenses incurred on the ground to protect and control the in-flight movement of aircraft, schedule and prepare aircraft operational crews for flight assignment, handle and service aircraft while in line operation, and service and handle traffic on the ground after issuance of documents establishing the air carrier's responsibility to provide air transportation, and in-flight expenses of handling and protecting all nonpassenger traffic including passenger baggage. (6400)

Aircraft miles or plane miles. The miles (computed in airport-to-airport distances) for each inter-airport hop actually completed, whether or not performed in accordance with the scheduled pattern. For this purpose, operation to a flag stop is a hop completed even though a landing is not actually made.

Aircraft revenue hours. The airborne hours in revenue service, computed from the moment an aircraft leaves the ground until it touches the ground again.

Air travel plan liability. The liability for deposits received under air travel plan contracts. (2150)

All-cargo carrier. One of a class of air carriers holding certificates of public convenience and necessity, issued by the CAB authorizing the performance of scheduled air freight, express, and mail transportation over specified routes, as well as the conduct of nonscheduled operations, which may include passengers. (All-purpose—or passenger/cargo—carriers often conduct part of their cargo operations with cargo aircraft, but such operations are never included in a statistical table on "all-cargo carriers.")

All-cargo service. Transport service established primarily for the transportation of freight and express. Could include mail.

All services. The sum total of scheduled plus nonscheduled services.

Amortization of developmental and preoperating expenses, etc. Charges to expense for the amortization of capitalized developmental and preoperating costs and other intangible assets applicable to the performance of air transportation and for obsolescence and deterioration of flight equipment expendable.

Assets. The items on the balance sheet of a business showing the book value of its resources.

Available seat-miles. The aggregate of the products of the aircraft miles flown on each inter-airport hop multiplied by the number of seats available on that hop, representing the total passenger-carrying capacity offered.

Available seats. The number of seats installed in an aircraft (including seats in lounges) exclusive of any seats not offered for sale to the public by the carrier, and inclusive of any seat sold.

Available seats per aircraft. The average number of seats available for sale to passengers, derived by dividing the total available seat-miles by the total aircraft revenue miles in passenger services.

Available ton-miles. The aggregate of the products of the aircraft miles flown on each inter-airport hop multiplied by the available aircraft capacity (tons) for that hop, representing the traffic-carrying capacity offered.

Average number of available seats per aircraft. Available seat-miles divided by the number of aircraft revenue miles in passenger service.

Average passenger trip length (Part III, line 50). Calculated by dividing the number of revenue passenger-miles in nonscheduled service by the number of revenue passenger originations in nonscheduled service. Hence, it gives one-way trip length. Trips in nonscheduled service almost never involve more than one airline, hence this is an "on-line" trip length. (Also see "on-line passenger trip length.")

Aviation gasoline. All piston-engine aircraft use a high-grade (high-octane) gasoline as a fuel, in contrast to the jet fuel (generally kerosene) used in turbine-powered aircraft. This piston-engine fuel is called "aviation gasoline"—or "avgas," for short. (Also see "jet fuel.")

B

Balance sheet. A statement of assets, liabilities, and stockholder equity (or equivalent interest of individual proprietors or partners) as at a particular date, as reported to the CAB by certificated route and supplemental air carriers on CAB Form 41.

Big Four. The four largest domestic trunk carriers (American, Eastern, TWA, and United). These carriers were first officially termed the "Big Four" in the 1949 edition of the Annual Report of the *Civil Aeronautics Board.* In this *Handbook,* a separation of operational statistics between the "Big Four" and "Other trunks" has been made retroactively to 1938.

C

Capital gains or losses, operating property. Gains or losses on retirements of operating property and equipment, flight equipment expendable parts or miscellaneous materials and supplies when sold or otherwise retired in connection with a general retirement program and not as incidental sales performed as a service to others. (8181.1)

Cargo aircraft. An aircraft expressly designed or converted to carry freight, express, etc., rather than passengers.

Cargo revenue ton-miles. The ton-miles of revenue freight, express and excess baggage.

Cash and special deposits. General and working funds available on demand which are not formally restricted or earmarked for specific objectives, and special deposits for payment of current obligations. (1010, 1030)

Certificated route air carrier. One of a class of air carriers holding certificates of public convenience and necessity, issued by the CAB, authorizing the performance of scheduled air transportation over specified routes and a limited amount of nonscheduled operations. This general carrier grouping includes the all-purpose carriers (i.e., the so-called passenger/cargo carriers) and the all-cargo carriers, and comprises all of the airlines certificated by the Board, except the supplemental air carriers. Certificated route air carriers are often referred to as "scheduled airlines," although they also perform nonscheduled service.

Charter revenues. Revenues from nonscheduled air transport services in which the party receiving the transportation obtains exclusive use of an aircraft and the remuneration paid by such party accrues directly to, and the responsibility for providing transportation is that of, the accounting air carrier.
Passenger charter revenues are from charter flights carrying only passengers and their personal baggage.
Freight charter revenues are from charter flights carrying either (1) freight only or (2) passengers and freight simultaneously. (3907.1, 3907.2)

Cities (Part VII, Tables 5a and 5b). Communities that are terminal points on an origin-destination trip.

Cities served (Part I, Table 1s). Communities receiving scheduled air service as of a specified date.

City pair (Part VII, Tables 6a, 6b, 6c, and 6d). The terminal communities in an air trip, i.e., the origin and destination on a one-way basis.

Coach passenger revenues. Revenues from the air transportation of passengers at fares and quality of service below first-class service but higher than or superior to economy service. (3901.2)

Coach service. Transport service established for the carriage of passengers at fares and quality of service below that of first-class service, but higher than or superior to the level of economy service.

Common stock. The par or stated value of common stock outstanding. In case of no-par stock without stated value, the full consideration received. (2840)

Construction work in progress. Accumulated direct and indirect costs for constructing and readying property and equipment for installation in operations. May include accumulated costs for uncompleted overhauls. (1689)

Current assets. Cash and other resources expected to be realized in cash, or sold, or consumed within one year. (1010-1420)

Current liabilities. Obligations the liquidation of which is expected to require the use, within one year, of current assets or the creation of other current liabilities. (2010-2190)

Current notes payable. Face value of notes, drafts, acceptances, or other similar evidences of indebtedness payable on demand or within one year to other than associated companies, including the portion of long-term debt due within one year of the balance sheet date (unless expected to require the use of resources other than current assets). (2010)

D

Dash (−). Indicates that an air carrier or carriers did not carry traffic or perform operations covered by the particular statistics except as footnoted for supplementals in tables III, IV and V.

d/b/a. Doing business as. For example, "The Slick Corporation, d/b/a Slick Airways" means that the firm whose official name is "The Slick Corporation" calls itself "Slick Airways" in its dealings with shippers. Thus, its aircraft are painted with the name "Slick Airways," its advertisements use the same name, etc.

Deferred charges. Debit balances in general clearing accounts including prepayments chargeable against operations over a period of years, capitalized expenditures of an organizational or developmental character, and property acquisition adjustments. (1820-1890)

Deferred credits. Credit balances in general clearing accounts including premiums on long-term debt securities of the air carrier. (2330-2390)

Deferred Federal income taxes. Credit balance of deferred income tax credits and debits arising from different treatment for tax and book accounting purposes of airworthiness reserve or self-insurance reserve provisions, depreciation allowances under provisions of sections 167 and 168 of the Internal Revenue Code, and preoperating, aircraft integration, route extension, or other developmental expenses. (2340)

Departures performed. Number of aircraft take-offs made.

Depreciation, flight equipment. Charges to expense for depreciation of airframes, aircraft engines, airframe and engine parts, and other flight equipment. (7075.1-7075.5)

Developmental and preoperating costs. Costs accumulated and deferred in connection with alterations in operational characteristics such as the development and preparation for operation of new routes and the integration of new types of aircraft or services. (1830)

Dividends. Includes dividends payable, in cash or in stock, to preferred and common stockholders, declared but not necessarily paid during the accounting period. The current liability is created by the declaration, the amount ordinarily being charged to retained earnings. (9830 and 9840)

Domestic operations. In general, operations within territory of the United States.

Domestic trunks (domestic trunk operations). Domestic operations of the domestic trunk carriers. This group of carriers operates primarily within the geographical limits of the 48 contiguous States of the United States (and the District of Columbia) over routes serving primarily the larger communities. International and territorial operations of these carriers are shown under "international and territorial operations," and not under "domestic trunk operations." Designation of the domestic "grandfather" carriers as "trunk carriers" was not pertinent until 1945-6, when "feeder" carriers (now called local service carriers) were granted certificates by the Board to perform local feeder air service.

E

Economy passenger revenues. Revenues from the air transportation of passengers at fares and quality of service below coach service. (3901.2)

Economy service. In domestic operations, transport service established for the carriage of passengers at fares and quality of service below coach service. In international operations, economy is the generally used term for coach service having taken the place of the term "tourist service."

Employees. See "total number of employees."

Excess baggage. Passenger baggage in excess of a free allowance based on volume or weight. This excess is subject to a charge for its transportation.

Excess baggage revenues. Revenues from the transportation by air of passenger baggage in excess of the free allowance. (3906.3)

Express. Property transported by air under published air express tariffs filed with the Civil Aeronautics Board. The transportation by air of express is conducted on the basis of agreements between the Railway Express Agency and the air carriers. (Data on express contained in Part II differ somewhat from the data contained in related tables of the other parts of the Handbook. Airlift International which inaugurated certificated scheduled domestic operations in January 1956, did not report domestic and international operations separately for 1956. In Part II, Airlift's express operations are included with the domestic all-cargo group. In the other parts of the Handbook, such operations are included with the international and territorial group.)

Express revenues. Revenues from the transportation by air of express as defined in tariffs filed with the Civil Aeronautics Board. (3906.1)

F

First-class passenger revenues. Revenues from the air transportation of passengers at standard fares, premium fares, or at reduced fares such as family plan and first-class excursion for whom standard or premium quality services are provided. (3901.1)

First-class service. Transport service established for the carriage of passengers at standard fares, premium fares, or at reduced fares such as family plan and first-class excursion for whom standard or premium quality services are provided.

Fixed-wing aircraft. Aircraft having wings fixed to the airplane fuselage and outspread in flight, i.e., nonrotating wings.

Flight equipment. Airframes, aircraft engines, and other flight equipment used in the in-flight operations of aircraft. (See "flight equipment—cost.")

Flight equipment—cost. Total cost to the air carrier of complete airframes, fully assembled engines, installed aircraft propellers and rotary wing aircraft rotors and similar assemblies, installed airborne communications and electronic navigational equipment and other similar assemblies, complete units of miscellaneous airborne flight equipment and costs of modification, conversion or other improvements to leased flight equipment. (1601-1607)

Flight-equipment expendable parts. Flight equipment replacement parts of a type recurrently expended and replaced rather than repaired or reused. (1310)

Flight-equipment interchange. An arrangement that provides single-plane service over a long route, without involving additional competitive carriers over one or more segments of the route. On a given interchange flight, a plane of one of the interchange partners flies the entire trip, but the crew is changed so that each carrier flies only over its own route segment. Most interchanges involve only two carriers, although occasionally there are three. Interchanges must be approved by the CAB.

Flight-equipment spare parts and assemblies. Parts and assemblies of material value which are rotable in nature, are generally reserviced or repaired and used repeatedly, and possess a service life approximating that of the property type to which they relate. (1608)

Flight stage. The operation of an aircraft from take-off to landing. (See "over-all flight stage length.")

Flying operations expenses. Expenses incurred directly in the in-flight operation of aircraft and expenses attaching to the holding of aircraft and aircraft operational personnel in readiness for assignment to an in-flight status. (5100)

Foreign air-carrier permit. A permit issued by the CAB to a foreign air carrier authorizing it to conduct air-transport operations between foreign countries and cities in the United States, usually in accordance with the terms of a bilateral air-transport agreement. (Also see "foreign-flag air carrier.")

Foreign-flag air carrier. An air carrier other than a U.S.-flag air carrier engaged in international air transportation. (Also see U.S.-flag carrier.) "Foreign air carrier" is a more all-inclusive term than "foreign-flag air carrier," presumably including those non-U.S. air carriers operating solely within their own domestic boundaries, but in practice the two terms are used interchangeably.

Foreign mail revenues. Revenues from the transportation by air of mail outside the United States by U.S.-flag carriers for a foreign government. (3903)

Freight. Property other than express and passenger baggage transported by air. (Only in comparisons with surface transportation—as in Part IX, Table 1—does "freight" include express and mail.)

Freight revenues. Revenues from the transporation by air of property other than express or passenger baggage. These revenues are predominantly from individually-waybilled shipments carried in scheduled service. (3906.2)

Fuel taxes. Excise taxes paid by the airlines on the aviation gasoline and jet fuel they purchase. Currently, there is a 2-cent-a-gallon Federal tax on aviation gasoline, but none on jet fuel. In addition, a number of the States levy State fuel taxes, some on aviation gasoline, some on both avgas and jet fuel. (See Part VIII, Item 2, for detailed data by year and by State.)

G

General and administrative expenses. Expenses of a general corporate nature and expenses incurred in performing activities which contribute to more than a single operating function such as general financial accounting activities, purchasing activities, representation at law, and other general operational administration not directly applicable to a particular function. (6800)

Grounding. A voluntary determination by a carrier or carriers or an order from the Federal Aviation Administration to refrain from flying a particular type of aircraft as a result of suspected or actual malfunction of such aircraft, until the cause can be determined and appropriate corrective action taken.

Ground property and equipment. Property and equipment other than flight equipment, land, and construction work in progress. (1630-1640.9)

H

Helicopter. A type of aircraft that derives lift from revolving "wings" or blades engine-driven about an approximately vertical axis. A helicopter does not have conventional fixed wings, nor in any but some earlier models is it provided with a conventional propeller, forward thrust and lift being furnished by the rotor. The powered rotor blades also enable the machine to hover, and to land and take off vertically.

Helicopter carriers. Domestic certificated route air carriers employing helicopter aircraft for their primary operations.

I

Incidental revenues, net. Revenues less related expenses from services incidental to air transportation, such as sales of service, supplies, and parts, and rental of operating property and equipment. (4600)

Income statement. A statement of revenues and expenses and resulting net income or loss covering a stated period of time, as reported to the CAB by certificated route and supplemental air carriers on CAB Form 41.

Income taxes for the period. Provisions for Federal, State, local, and foreign taxes, which are based upon net income. (9100)

Intangibles. Unamortized property acquisition adjustment; the cost less amounts amortized of leaseholds, patents and copyrights; and other intangible assets. (1870, 1880)

Interest expense. Interest on all classes of debt, including premium, capitalized interest, and expenses on short-term obligations; and amortization of premium, discount, and expense on short-term and long-term obligations. (8187)

International and territorial operations. In general, operations outside territory of the United States, including operations between United States points separated by foreign territory or major expanses of international waters. (See domestic operations)

Intra-Alaska operations. The granting of statehood to Alaska and Hawaii requires the inclusion of their intra-state operations with the domestic group even for the years prior to 1959. In early CAB publications, intra-Hawaii operations were included with domestic, and later treated separately as a territorial group. When intra-Alaska data became available, both intra-Hawaii and intra-Alaska were grouped, and continued to be treated, separately, as territorial operations until 1959, when they were included with domestic.

Intra-Hawaii operations. The granting of statehood to Alaska and Hawaii requires the inclusion of their intrastate operations with the domestic group. However, this *Handbook* includes such operations with the domestic group even for the years prior to 1959. In early CAB publications, intra-Hawaii operations were included with domestic, and later treated separately as a territorial group. When intra-Alaska data became available, both intra-Hawaii and intra-Alaska were grouped, and continued to be treated, separately, as territorial operations until 1959, when they were included with domestic.

Investment, total and total adjusted. See Total Investment and Total Adjusted Investment.

Investments and special funds. Long-term investments in securities of others exclusive of United States Government securities; funds set aside for specific purposes; and other securities, receivable equipment purchase deposits and applicable capitalized interest or funds not available for current operations. (1510-1550)

Investments in subsidiary and associated companies. Not investments in subsidiary companies, accounted for on the equity basis, and associated companies, accounted for on the cost basis, together with advances, loans and other amounts not settled currently. (1510)

J

Jet fuel. Practically all U.S. airlines use kerosene as the fuel in their turbine-powered aircraft. This kerosene is commonly referred to as "jet fuel," in contrast to the "aviation gasoline" used in piston-engine aircraft. Occasionally, a U.S.-flag carrier uses JP-4 instead of straight kerosene.

L

Land. The initial cost and the cost of improving land owned or held in perpetuity by the air carrier. (1679)

Loans guaranteed. Aircraft-purchase loans, guaranteed by the Federal Government, administered by the Department of Transportation, to assist local service, helicopter, intra-Alaska, intra-Hawaii, and certain other carriers in obtaining suitable flight equipment.

Local service carriers. Certificated domestic route air carriers operating routes of lesser density between the smaller traffic centers and between those centers and principal centers.

Local service carrier class mail rate. A plan adopted by the CAB in 1961 designed to provide local service carriers with strong incentives for greater operating efficiency by setting specific subsidy rates on the basis of average operating performance. Class rate I, II, III and IIIa incorporated a "profit sharing" devise by which carriers refunded any profit that was in excess of a previously determined rate of return on investment. Class rate IV, effective January 1, 1967 established a new concept of subsidy payments, based on a "revenue-growth sharing" feature whereby reductions in subsidy are tied to revenue growth.

Long-term debt. The face value or principal amount of debt securities issued or assumed by the air carrier and held by other than associated companies or nontransport divisions, which has not been retired or cancelled and is not payable within 12 months of the balance sheet date. (2210)

Long-term prepayments. Prepayments of obligations, applicable to periods extending beyond one year. (1820)

M

Maintenance, direct (expense). The costs of labor, materials, and outside services consumed directly in periodic maintenance operations and the maintenance, repair, or upkeep of airframes, aircraft engines, other flight equipment, and ground property and equipment. (5200)

Maintenance, indirect (expense). Overhead or general expenses of activities involved in the repair and upkeep of property and equipment, including inspections of equipment in accordance with prescribed operational standards. Includes expenses related to the administration of maintenance stocks and stores, the keeping of maintenance operations records, and the scheduling, controlling, planning, and supervision of maintenance operations. (5300)

Merger. The acquisition of one airline by another, either through purchase of stock or direct purchase of assets, and the merging of operations. As used in Part VIII, Item 11, "Mergers and acquisitions" also include changes in form of organization of an airline such as a change from individual proprietorship to the corporate form.

Mile. A statute mile (5,280 feet). Throughout the *Handbook,* only *statute* miles are used.

Military. Activities under charter or other contract with the Department of Defense.

Miscellaneous materials and supplies. Materials and supplies held in stock including motor fuels and lubricating oils, shop materials, expendable tools, stationery and office supplies, passenger service supplies, and restaurant and food service supplies. (1330)

Mixed-class service. Transport service for the carriage in any combination of first-class, coach (tourist), and/or economy (thrift) passengers on the same aircraft. The aircraft would also carry freight, express, and/or mail. Excludes all-first-class, all-coach, and all-economy services.

N

NA (not available). Indicates that the particular data were not required to be reported by air carriers even though operations were performed, or that the data are unavailable for inclusion in the *Handbook* for other reasons. For the years 1926 through 1937 some data either are not readily available from records of predecessor agencies or cannot be readily compiled from carrier reports filed with such agencies. (For the years subsequent to 1937, certain data have not been compiled, although they were reported. Such situations are generally footnoted rather than indicated as "NA.")

Net income after special items. The net gain of the business, i.e., the net of operating profit or loss, nonoperating income and expenses, income taxes, and special items. (9799)

Net income before income taxes. Operating profit or loss plus or minus nonoperating income and expenses, net. This is the net income before income taxes and special items. (8999)

Noncurrent liabilities. Obligations the liquidation of which is not expected to require the use, within one year, of current assets or the creation of current liabilities. (2210-2290)

Nonoperating income and expenses. Income and loss of commercial ventures not part of the common carrier air transport services of the accounting entity; other revenues and expenses attributable to financing or other activities that are extraneous to and not an integral part of air transportation or its incidental services. (8180-8189)

Nonoperating property and equipment—net. Cost, less related reserves for depreciation, of property and equipment (1) assigned to other than air transportation and its incidental services but not accounted for within a nontransport division and (2) property and equipment held for future use. (1799)

Nonpriority mail. Mail bearing postage for surface transportation that goes by air on a space-available basis at rates lower than those fixed for priority (i.e., air) mail.

Non-revenue flights. Flights and flights stages involving training, test, technical, positioning for scheduled flights, ferry, company business, publicity and forced returns for which no remuneration is received.

Nonscheduled freight. Data on nonscheduled freight operations for all-cargo carriers may not include total operations for certain carriers for a few years due to uncertainty regarding the inclusion or exclusion of operations under Department of Defense contracts.

Nonscheduled service. Revenue flights that are not operated in regular scheduled service, such as charter flights and all nonrevenue flights incident to such flights.

Nontransport revenues. Federal subsidy (where applicable) and incidental revenues, net (revenues less related expenses from services incidental to air transportation). (4100, 4600)

Notes and accounts receivable. Notes receivable and amounts due on open accounts. (1220-1280)

O

On-line passenger trip length. Average length of a passenger trip, calculated by dividing the number of revenue passenger-miles in scheduled service by the number of revenue passenger originations in scheduled service. Hence, it gives one-way trip length *in terms of only one carrier* or of a domestic or an international operation of a carrier, where these are reported separately to the CAB. Thus, "on-line passenger trip length" will be somewhat smaller than "passenger trip length" obtained from origin-destination surveys, since the latter figure gives one-way journey length regardless of the number of airlines involved in a specific one-way trip. This term pertains solely to scheduled service.

Operating expenses. Expenses incurred in the performance of air transportation. Includes direct aircraft operating expenses and ground and indirect operating expenses. (5100-7000)

Operating profit or loss. The profit or loss from performance of air transportation, based on over-all operating revenues and over-all operating expenses. Does not include nonoperating income and expenses or special items and is before income taxes. (7999)

Operating property and equipment. Land and units of tangible property and equipment that are used in air transportation services and services incidental thereto. (1600)

Operating property and equipment, net, as a per cent of cost. The cost of operating property and equipment less related depreciation and overhaul reserves as a per cent of the total cost of operating property and equipment before deducting such reserves.

Operating revenues. Revenues from the performance of air transportation and related incidental services. Includes (1) transport revenues from the carriage of all classes of traffic in scheduled and nonscheduled services including the performance of aircraft charters and (2) nontransport revenues consisting of Federal subsidy (where applicable) and the net amount of revenues less related expenses from services incidental to air transportation. (3900, 4100, 4600)

Other accrued taxes. Accruals for taxes, exclusive of Federal income taxes, constituting a charge borne by the air carrier. (2139)

Other current and accrued liabilities. Accruals for liabilities against the air carrier for personnel vacations, dividends declared but unpaid on capital stock, and other miscellaneous current and accrued liabilities. (2120, 2140, 2190)

Other current assets. Prepayments of rent, insurance, taxes, etc., which if not paid in advance would require the expenditure of working capital within one year, and other current assets not provided for in specific objective accounts. (1410, 1420)

Other deferred charges. Unamortized discount and expense on debt; unamortized capital stock expense; and debits, not provided for elsewhere, the final disposition of which must await receipt of additional information. (1840, 1850, 1890)

Other deferred credits. Unamortized premium on debt and credits, not provided for elsewhere, the final disposition of which must await receipt of additional information. (2330, 2390)

Other investments and receivables. Notes and accounts receivable not due within one year and investments in securities issued by others excepting associated companies. (1530)

Other noncurrent liabilities. Liabilities under company-administrated employee pension plans and for installments received from company personnel under company stock purchase plans, advances from associated companies and noncurrent liabilities. (2245, 2250, 2260, 2290)

Other nonoperating income and expenses, net. Capital gains or losses on retirement of nonoperating property and equipment and investments in securities of others, interest and dividend income, and other nonoperating items except capital gains or losses on operating property and interest expense. (8100, excluding 8181.1 and 8187)

Other paid-in capital. Premium and discount on captial stock, gains or losses arising from the reacquisition and the resale or retirement of capital stock, and other paid-in capital. (2890)

Other temporary cash investments. Securities and other collectible obligations acquired for the purpose of temporarily investing cash, other than those issued by the United States Government or associated companies. (1120)

Other transport revenues. Miscellaneous revenues associated with the air transportation performed by the air carrier, such as reservations cancellation fees, not covered under other revenue classifications. (3919)

Other trunks. Domestic trunk carriers other than the Big Four.

Over-all (ton-miles, load factor, available capacity, etc.). This term applies to the sum total of *passenger plus nonpassenger* traffic, i.e., to the sum of passenger, free baggage, excess baggage, freight, express, U.S. mail, and foreign mail.

Over-all aircraft revenue hours, scheduled service. Aircraft hours are the airborne hours computed from the moment an aircraft leaves the ground until it touches the ground at the end of the flight.

Over-all capacity per aircraft. The average over-all carrying capacity (tons) offered for sale per aircraft in revenue services, derived by dividing the over-all available ton-miles by the over-all aircraft miles flown in revenue services.

Over-all flight stage length. The average distance covered per aircraft hop in revenue service, from take-off to landing, including both passenger/cargo and all-cargo aircraft. Derived by dividing the over-all aircraft miles flown in revenue services by the number of over-all aircraft revenue departures performed.

Over-all operating expenses. See "operating expenses."

Over-all operating revenues. See "operating revenues."

Over-all revenue load factor. The per cent that total revenue ton-miles (passenger plus nonpassenger) are of available ton-miles in revenue services, representing the proportion of the over-all capacity that is actually sold and utilized.

Over-all revenue load per aircraft. The average over-all tonnage carried per aircraft in revenue services derived by dividing the over-all revenue ton-miles by the over-all aircraft miles flown in revenue services.

Over-all transport revenues. See "transport revenues."

P

Passenger-mile. One passenger transported one mile. Passenger-miles are computed by summation of the products of the aircraft miles flown on each inter-airport hop multiplied by the number of passengers carried on that hop.

Passenger enplanements. The total number of revenue passenger boarding aircraft, including originating and stopover or on line transfer passengers.

Passenger originations. The number of revenue passengers boarding aircraft in scheduled service at the points of initial enplanement on the reporting carrier's system, with the return portion of a round trip counted separately as an initial origination. Passengers traveling on an interline ticket are counted as an initial origination on each of the carriers in the journey.

Passenger revenues. Revenues from the transportation of passengers by air. These revenues are predominantly from individually ticketed passengers carried in scheduled service. (3901)

Passenger service expenses. Costs of activities contributing to the comfort, safety, and convenience of passengers while in flight and when flights are interrupted. Includes salaries and expenses of cabin attendants and passenger food expense. (5500)

Passenger ton-mile. One tone of passenger weight (including free baggage) transported one mile. (See also "passenger weight.")

Passenger weight. In general, for reporting purposes, a standard weight of 190 pounds per passenger (including free baggage) is used for domestic operations, and 215 and 200 pounds for first-class and coach passengers, respectively, in territorial and international operations.

Per cent scheduled aircraft miles completed. Scheduled aircraft miles completed as a per cent of scheduled aircraft miles.

Piston planes. An aircraft operated by engines in which pistons moving back and forth work upon a crankshaft or other device to create rotational movement.

Preferred stock outstanding. The par or stated value of preferred capital stock outstanding. In the case of no-par stock without stated value, the full consideration received. (2820)

Priority mail. Mail bearing postage for air transportation that goes by air on a priority basis at airmail service rates.

Productivity. Average total number of employees divided into the indicated traffic and financial measures for the year. (See "total number of employees.")

Promotion and sales expenses. Costs incurred in promoting the use of air transportation generally and creating a public preference for the services of particular air carriers. Includes the functions of selling, advertising and publicity, space reservations, and developing tariffs and flight schedules for publication. (6700)

R

Railway Express Agency. In November 1960, this organization adopted the trade name "REA Express." Its legal name remains "Railway Express Agency, Inc."

Rate of return on stockholder equity. The ratio (expressed as a percentage) of (a) net income after special items to (b) stockholder equity. A measure of the return upon the capital invested in the business by the stockholder. These rates of return are calculated on net income after special items inclusive of investment tax credits not allocated to cost of service and exclusive of such investment tax credits.

Rate of return on total investment. The ratio (expressed as percentage) of (a) net income after special items but before interest expense to (b) total investment, long-term debt, advances from associated companies, advances from nontransport divisions, stockholder equity-net less (beginning 1961) unamortized discount and expense on debt (debit).

Rate of return on adjusted investment. The ratio (expressed as a percentage) of (a) net income after special items but before interest expense allocated to long-term debt and including investment tax credits not allocated to cost of service in the case of computation: including investment tax credits, and exclusive of the above in case of computation: excluding investment tax credits, to adjusted investment (total investment as defined in previous term, less equipment purchase deposits and applicable capitalized interest).

REA Express. See "Railway Express Agency."

Reserves for depreciation. Accruals for depreciation of property and equipment.

Reserves for obsolescence and deterioration—expendable parts. Accruals for losses in the value of expendable parts. (1311)

Reserves for overhaul. Accumulated provisions for overhauls of flight equipment. (1629)

Reserves for uncollectible accounts. Accruals for estimated losses from uncollectible accounts. (1290)

Retained earnings adjustments. Charges or credits to unappropriated retained earnings, other than dividends, that reflect transfers to paid-in capital accounts or appropriations. (9840)

Retained earnings appropriated. Retained earnings segregated for contingencies and other special purposes, including retained earnings segregated in connection with self-insurance plans. (2930)

Retained earnings unappropriated. The cumulative net income or loss from operations of the air carrier less dividends declared on capital stock and amounts appropriated for special purposes. (2940, 2941)

Revenue aircraft departures performed. The number of aircraft take-offs actually performed in scheduled passenger/cargo and all-cargo services.

Revenue aircraft miles. The total aircraft miles flown in revenue service.

Revenue hours per aircraft per day-carrier's equipment. Average hours of productive use per day in revenue service of reporting carrier's equipment determined by dividing (1) *Aircraft days assigned to service-carrier's equipment* into (2) *Revenue aircraft hours* minus *Revenue hours on other carrier's interchange equipment* plus *Total hours by others on the carrier's interchange equipment.*

Revenue passenger. A person receiving air transportation from an air carrier for which remuneration is received by the air carrier. Air carrier employees or others receiving air transportation against whom token service charges are levied are considered nonrevenue passengers. Infants for whom a token fare is charged are not counted as passengers.

Revenue passenger enplanements. The count of the total number of revenue passengers boarding aircraft, including originating, stopover, and transfer passengers. This count may be measured on the basis of a standard number of passenger enplanements per on-line originating passenger.

Revenue passenger load factor. The per cent that revenue passenger-miles are of available seat-miles in revenue passenger services, representing the proportion of aircraft seating capacity that is actually sold and utilized.

Revenue passenger-mile. One revenue passenger transported one mile in revenue service. Revenue passenger-miles are computed by summation of the products of the revenue aircraft miles flown on each inter-airport hop multiplied by the number of revenue passengers carried on that hop.

Revenue passenger originations. The number of revenue passengers boarding aircraft at the points of initial enplanement on the reporting carrier's operation, with the return portion of a round trip counted separately as an initial origination. Passengers traveling on an interline ticket are counted as an initial origination on each of the carriers in the journey. In addition, a passenger traveling on a carrier that has two or more reporting entities, for which separate reports are filed with the CAB, is counted as an initial origination on each reporting entity. The above definition applies to Form 41 data (found in Parts I, II, and III), not to origin-destination data (in Part VII).

Revenue passengers per aircraft. The average number of passengers carried per aircraft in revenue passenger services derived by dividing the total revenue passenger-miles by the total aircraft miles flown in revenue passenger services.

Revenue ton-mile. One ton of revenue traffic transported one mile.

Revenue yields for scheduled freight and express services. The yields derived by relating ton-mile volumes to revenues reported for freight service and for express service, in some instances, indicate inconsistency in reporting traffic and revenue data for these services.

S

Scheduled aircraft miles. The sum of the airport-to-airport distances of all flights scheduled, excluding those operated only as extra sections to accomodate traffic overflow.

Scheduled aircraft miles completed. The aircraft miles performed on shceduled flights, computed solely between those scheduled points actually served.

Scheduled service. Transport service operated over an air carrier's certificated routes, based on published flight schedules, including extra sections and related nonrevenue flights.

Self-insurance reserves. Accruals through charges against income for uninsured losses. (2350)

Special funds. Special funds not of a current nature and restricted as to general availability. Includes items such as sinking funds, pension funds under the control of the air carrier, equipment purchase funds, and funds segregated as part of a plan for self-insurance. (1540, 1550)

Special income credits and debits, net (special items). Extraordinary credits and debits that are of sufficient magnitude that inclusion in the accounts for a single year would materially distort the total operating revenues or total operating expenses if included therein. (9796)

Special income tax credits and debits, net. Income taxes applicable to special income credits or debits and other extraordinary income tax items not allocable to income of the current accounting year. (9797)

Speed. All figures on speed that are presented in the *Handbook* are in *statute* miles per hour, unless otherwise indicated. (See "airborne speed.")

Stockholder equity. The aggregate book value of holders of the air carrier's stock in assets owned by the air carrier. (2995)

Subsidy. Revenues from the United States Government as direct grants for providing air transportation facilities, pursuant to section 406 (b) of the Federal Aviation Act. Does not include revenues from the carriage of mail at service rates or the performance of other contractual service for the Government. (4100)

Supplemental air carrier. One of a class of air carriers now holding certificates, issued by the CAB, authorizing them to perform passenger and cargo charter services supplementing the scheduled service of the certificated route air carriers. Supplemental air carriers are often referred to as "nonskeds," i.e., nonscheduled carriers. In Part II of this *Handbook,* all the operations of the supplemental air carriers are considered as nonscheduled, including individually-ticketed and individually-waybilled cargo. Even if the latter operations were to be considered as scheduled, the data are not available for years prior to 1961, since the carriers were not required to separate these types of traffic from total operations.

System. The sum total of all operations (domestic, international, or territorial) performed by an air carrier.

T

Ton. A short ton (2,000 pounds).

Ton-mile. One short ton transported one statute mile. Ton-miles are computed by summation of the products of the aircraft miles flown on each inter-airport hop multiplied by the number of tons carried on that hop.

Total general services and administration expenses. Passenger service, aircraft and traffic servicing, promotion and sales, and general and administrative expenses. (5500-6900)

Total Investment. Total investment; a sum of average (arithmetic mean) of five quarterly balances of stockholder equity, long-term debt less unamoritized discount and expense on debt and advances from associated companies and nontransport divisions; less equipment deposits and capitalized interest thereon. The five quarterly balance sheets used are as at the beginning date for the 12 month period plus the four quarterly reports representing the given 12 month period. All elements of investment are prorated between domestic and international territorial operations and distributed among operating divisions for carriers with more than, one reporting entity or division on the basis of reported operating expenses.

Total adjusted investment. Total investment (above) less average (arithmetic mean) of five quarterly balances of equipment purchase deposits and applicable capitalized interest.

Total number of employees. The number of full- and part-time employees, both permanent and temporary, during the pay period ended nearest December 15. Air carriers with more than one operation (domestic or international and territorial) generally do not report a breakdown of total employees corresponding to these operations so that the employee counts do not provide a reliable basis for measuring average productivity per employee in such separate operations.

Total transport revenues. See "transport revenues."

Tourist service. In international operations, this term once designated that service equivalent to domestic coach service. The term economy now designates such service.

Transport revenues. Revenues from the transportation by air of all classes of traffic in schedules and nonscheduled services, including the performance of charters. (3900)

Treasury stock. The cost of capital stock issued by the air carrier which has been reacquired by it and not retired or cancelled. (2990)

Turbine-powered aircraft. Includes aircraft with either turbojet, turbofan, turboprop, or turboshaft engines.

Turbofan planes. Aircraft operated by a turbojet engine whose thrust has been increased by the addition of a low pressure compressor (fan). The turbofan engine can have an over sized low-pressure compressor at the front with part of the flow by-passing the rest of the engine (front-fan or forward-fan) or it can have a separate fan driven by a turbine stage (aft-fan).

Turbojet planes. Aircraft operated by jet engines incorporating a turbine-driven air compressor to take in and compress the air for the combustion of fuel, the gases of combustion (or the heated air) being used both to rotate the turbine and to create a thrust-producing jet.

Turboprop planes. Aircraft in which the main propulsive force is supplied by a gas turbine driven conventional propeller. Additional propulsive force may be supplied from the discharged turbine exhaust gas.

Turboshaft helicopter. A helicopter powered by one or more gas turbine engines.

U

Unappropriated retained earnings. See "retained earnings unappropriated."

Unearned transportation revenue. The value of transportation sold, but not used or refunded, for travel over the air carrier's own lines. (2160)

United States Government securities. Investment in transferable obligations of the United States Government. (1110)

U.S.-flag carrier or **American-flag carrier.** One of a class of air carriers holding a certificate of public convenience and necessity issued by the CAB, approved by the President, authorizing scheduled operations over specified routes between the United States (and/or its territories) and one or more foreign countries. (Also see "foreign-flag carrier.")

U.S. mail revenues. Revenues from the transportation by air of United States mail at service mail rates established by the Civil Aeronautics Board. Includes priority and nonpriority mail revenues. (3902)

W

Weighted average route miles operated. The shortest distance connecting all of the points served by a carrier on all of its routes along flight paths authorized in its certificates of public convenience and necessity, computed separately for each reporting entity. These data are weighted for the time element involved in route changes and differ from certificated route miles which contain varying amounts of duplication in route segments. (Sometimes referred to as "unduplicated route miles.")

Work stoppage. An incident of labor-management strife arising from disputes over wages, hours, rules, and/or conditions of work, as well as from jurisdictional problems of craft representation of airline employees. A strike or lockout. Such incidents may or may not affect normally scheduled airline services.

Index